New Directions in the History of the Jews in the Polish Lands

Jews of Poland

Series Editor
ANTONY POLONSKY (Brandeis University)

 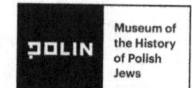

New Directions in the History of the Jews in the Polish Lands

Edited by **Antony Polonsky, Hanna Węgrzynek,**
and **Andrzej Żbikowski**

Boston
2018

The book was published within the framework of the Global Education Outreach Program, POLIN Museum of the History of Polish Jews.

This publication was made possible through the support of the Taube Foundation for Jewish Life & Culture, the William K. Bowes, Jr. Foundation, and the Association of the Jewish Historical Institute of Poland.

Library of Congress Cataloging-in-Publication Data

Names: Polonsky, Antony, editor. | Węgrzynek, Hanna, editor. | Żbikowski, Andrzej, editor.

Title: New directions in the history of the Jews in the Polish lands / edited by Antony Polonsky, Hanna Węgrzynek and Andrzej Żbikowski.

Description: Boston, MA: Academic Studies Press; Warsaw, Poland: POLIN Museum of the History of Polish Jews, [2017] |

Series: Jews of Poland | Includes bibliographical references and index.

Identifiers: LCCN 2017044794 (print) | LCCN 2017047212 (ebook) | ISBN 9788394914905 (e-book) | ISBN 9788394914912 (Open Access) | ISBN 9788394426293 (hardback)

Subjects: LCSH: Jews—Poland—History—Congresses. | Poland—Ethnic relations—Congresses. | Museums—Educational aspects—Poland—Congresses.

Classification: LCC DS135.P6 (ebook) | LCC DS135.P6 N475 2017 (print) | DDC 943.8/004924—dc23

LC record available at https://lccn.loc.gov/2017044794

Published by Academic Studies Press and by
POLIN Museum of the History of Polish Jews, 2018
ISBN 978-8-394914-90-5 (electronic)
ISBN 978-8-394914-91-2 (Open Access)
ISBN 978-8-395237-85-0

Book design by Kryon Publishing Services (P) Ltd.
www.kryonpublishing.com

Cover design by Ivan Grave
On the cover: The Monument to the Ghetto Heroes in Warsaw, in front of POLIN Museum building. Photo by www.pzstudio.pl

Academic Studies Press
28 Montfern Avenue
Brighton, MA 02135, USA
press@academicstudiespress.com
www.academicstudiespress.com

Contents

Foreword	ix
Introduction *Antony Polonsky, Hanna Węgrzynek, and Andrzej Żbikowski*	x
List of Contributors	lvi

PART ONE: Museological Questions

The Voice of the Curators

Something Old, Something New: Creating the Narrative for the Early Modern Galleries *Adam Teller*	1
The Nineteenth-Century Gallery *Sam Kassow*	13
The Interwar Gallery *Sam Kassow*	20
Curatorial and Educational Challenges in Creating the Holocaust Gallery *Maria Ferenc-Piotrowska, Kamila Radecka-Mikulicz, and Justyna Majewska*	29
Assumptions behind the Postwar Gallery of the Core Exhibition at POLIN *Stanisław Krajewski*	40

Comments on the Museum

Polish-Jewish Historiography 1970–2015: Construction, Consensus, Controversy *Moshe Rosman*	60
POLIN, the Medieval and Early Modern Galleries: A Comment *Kenneth Stow*	78

Modernism and Identity: Polish Jews Facing Change
in the Nineteenth Century   85
Tomasz Kizwalter

Hasidism in the Museum: The Social History Perspective   93
David Assaf

What's In, What's Out: A Critique of the Interwar Gallery   105
Michael Steinlauf

The Truth and Nothing But: The Holocaust Gallery
of the Warsaw POLIN Museum in Context   111
Omer Bartov

Perspectives: A Lithuanian Visit to the POLIN Museum
Holocaust Gallery   119
Saulius Sužiedėlis

Polin: A Bildungsroman   130
Marci Shore

A Historian's Response. Comments on the Postwar Gallery   134
Andrzej Paczkowski

Museums and Education

Jewish Tourism to Poland: The Opportunities for New Museum
Narratives to Recontextualize Jewish Histories   139
Jonathan Webber

Jewish Museums in Moscow   150
Victoria Mochalova

The Challenges of New Work in History and Education
about the Holocaust in Poland   170
Jolanta Ambrosewicz-Jacobs

PART TWO: Historiographic Questions

Premodern Poland–Lithuania

Did the Polish Nobility Take Seriously the Teaching
of the Catholic Church? Reflections on the Relations
between the Nobility, the Church, and the Jews   183
Adam Kaźmierczyk

Relations between Jews and Non-Jews in the Polish–Lithuanian
Commonwealth: Perceptions and Practices   198
Jürgen Heyde

Agreements between Towns and Kahals and their Impact on the Legal Status of Polish Jews   219
Hanna Węgrzynek

The Role and Significance of the Jews in the Economy of the Polish-Lithuanian Commonwealth: The State of Research and Research Directions   231
Jacek Wijaczka

Reassessment of the Jewish Poll-Tax Assessment Lists from Eighteenth-Century Crown of Poland   255
Judith Kalik

Frankism: The History of Jacob Frank or of the Frankists   261
Jan Doktór

The Nineteenth Century

Modern Times Polish Style? Orthodoxy, Enlightenment, and Patriotism   280
Israel Bartal

Jew-Hatred and Anti-Jewish Violence in the Former Lands of the Polish–Lithuanian Commonwealth during the Long Nineteenth Century   285
Darius Staliūnas

Those Who Stayed: Women and Jewish Traditionalism in East Central Europe   295
Glenn Dynner

Pauline Wengeroff: Between Tradition and Modernity, East and West   313
Shulamit Magnus

The Interwar Years

One Jewish Street? Reflections on Unity and Disunity in Interwar Polish Jewry   324
Gershon Bacon

Not Just *Mały Przegląd*: The Ideals and Educational Values Expressed in Jewish Polish-Language Journals for Children and Young Adults   338
Anna Landau-Czajka

Legitimizing the Revolution: Sarah Schenirer and the Rhetoric of Torah Study for Girls   356
Naomi Seidman

Contested Jewish Polishness: Language and Health
as Markers for the Position of Jews in Polish Culture
and Society in the Interwar Period 366
  Katrin Steffen

The Holocaust

Historiography on the Holocaust in Poland: An Outsider's
View of its Place within Recent General Developments
in Holocaust Historiography 386
  Dan Michman

The Dispute over the Status of a Witness to the Holocaust: Some
Observations on How Research into the Destruction
of the Polish Jews and into Polish–Jewish Relations
during the Years of Nazi Occupation Has Changed since 1989 402
  Andrzej Żbikowski

Beyond National Identities: New Challenges in Writing
the History of the Holocaust in Poland and Israel 423
  Daniel Blatman

The Postwar Period

Violence against Jews in Poland, 1944–47: The State
of Research and its Presentation 442
  Grzegorz Berendt

The Jews and the "Disavowed Soldiers" 452
  August Grabski

In or Out? Identities and Images of Poland among Polish Jews
in the Postwar Years 472
  Audrey Kichelewski

Index 485

Foreword

We are very happy to introduce this collection of scholarly papers which were first delivered at the International Conference "From Ibrahim ibn Jakub to 6 Anielewicz Street", organized to mark the opening of the core exhibition of POLIN Museum of the History of Polish Jews in Warsaw. The Conference was jointly organized by POLIN Museum and the Jewish Historical Institute in Warsaw and it took place within the framework of the Museum's Global Education Outreach Program. Financial support was provided by the Taube Foundation for Jewish Life & Culture, the William K. Bowes, Jr. Foundation, and the Association of the Jewish Historical Institute of Poland.

The conference showed how much progress has been made in the last thirty years in illuminating the multi-faceted history of the Jews in the Polish lands. It demonstrated that there is now an international community spanning Poland, Israel, Eastern and Western Europe, and North America devoted to examining this important topic. This community and the development of Polish-Jewish studies provided solid historiographic basis for the creation of the narrative core exhibition of POLIN Museum.

We are confident that this volume will have the widest possible circulation and will contribute to making better known the achievements of the Jews of the Polish lands and their complex and often fruitful co-existence with their neighbors.

Dariusz Stola,
Director of POLIN Museum of the History of Polish Jews
Paweł Śpiewak,
Director of the Jewish Historical Institute

Introduction

ANTONY POLONSKY, HANNA WĘGRZYNEK, and ANDRZEJ ŻBIKOWSKI

The essays in this volume are expanded versions of papers presented at the conference held in May 2015 to introduce the scholarly community to the permanent exhibition at POLIN Museum of the History of Polish Jews. As Moshe Rosman shows in his chapter in this book, "Polish-Jewish Historiography 1970–2015: Construction, Consensus, Controversy," in the last forty-five years tremendous progress has been made in the study of the Polish-Jewish past. The enormously disruptive impact of the Holocaust, Stalinism, and the imposition of Marxist-Leninist norms of historical writing in People's Poland meant that a new cadre of scholars had to be created from the 1980s and that many topics had to be investigated anew. At the scholarly conference at Oxford in September 1984 on Polish–Jewish relations (one of the turning points in the revival of interest in the history and culture of Polish Jews), Stefan Kieniewicz, the doyen of nineteenth-century Polish historians, observed:

> After the Holocaust and the post-war exodus, research in this field was mostly conducted outside Poland; these findings and publications are hardly available and, in any case, their language is unfamiliar to my countrymen. The researchers are hindered, too, I fear, because of an inadequate knowledge of purely Polish affairs. It is indeed unfortunate that there is now in Poland no one who is able to study and revive the history of Polish Jews—a history that is most important to the Polish people, for its own sake and because of the Jewish participation in or contribution to our national past.[1]

---

1 Stefan Kieniewicz, "Polish Society and the Jewish Problem in the Nineteenth Century," in *The Jews in Poland*, ed. Chimen Abramsky, Maciej Jachimczyk, and Antony Polonsky (Oxford: Basil Blackwell, 1986), 71.

Kieniewicz was concerned with the neglect of Jewish topics in mainline Poland historiography, and he was largely correct that these were for the most part omitted from the principal scholarly works on the history of Poland. He failed to mention and was probably not aware of the large body of research produced by the Jewish Historical Institute (Żydowski Instytut Historyczny) throughout the postwar years.

In addition, after 1945 Poles and Jews (insofar as these are mutually exclusive categories, which is not always the case) were divided, above all, by their diametrically opposed and incompatible views of a shared but divisive past which made its investigation both difficult and controversial. The experiences of the war and the imposition on Poland of an unpopular and unrepresentative communist dictatorship gave a new lease on life to the "romantic" view of Polish history that saw Poland as the "Christ of nations," a country of heroes and martyrs that had unstintingly sacrificed itself for Western values and whose efforts had never been appreciated or understood by the materialistic West. In this history, Jews figured in a largely negative way. Pre-partition Poland–Lithuania had been a "land without stakes," a country committed to religious toleration that had given the Jews shelter when they had been persecuted elsewhere. In this view, the Jews had not appreciated this hospitality—they had always remained a people apart, with their own language and culture and little sense of loyalty to Poland. For the most part, they had been better off than most Poles and had always been ready to profit at the expense of the latter. In the modern period this was exemplified by the way they had prevented the formation of a "native" middle class and by their refusal to support Polish aspirations in the East at the end of the First World War. They had sought foreign territorial intervention to guarantee themselves special protection in the interwar period and had been a key element in the antinational communist movement.

According to this stereotypical view, at the outbreak of the Second World War, Jews had welcomed the Red Army when it treacherously invaded eastern Poland and had collaborated on a large scale with the Soviet occupiers. Under Nazi occupation, Poles had suffered more than any other nation. They had refused to collaborate and their large-scale resistance had led to tremendous suffering, culminating in the German destruction of Warsaw. They were not implicated in the mass murder of Jews on Polish soil—on the contrary, many Poles lost their lives trying to save Jews. Jews nevertheless played a prominent role in the communist regime after 1944 and in its security apparatus. In the West, Jews have shown little awareness of the complexities of the Polish situation and have constantly blackened the name of Poland.

Not surprisingly, this interpretation of the Polish past was not shared by most Jews. Their image of Poland was shaped partly by their memories of Polish behavior before, during, and after the war and, more particularly, by the views expressed by Polish Jewish survivors of the Holocaust. Nearly 90 percent of Poland's three-and-a-half million Jews perished during the Second World War, and those who survived had, for the most part, bitter memories. They remembered the anti-Jewish violence that had accompanied the establishment of Polish independence and the intensification of anti-Semitism after the death of Józef Piłsudski in 1935. They believed that most of their Polish fellow citizens had been indifferent to the fate of the Jews under Nazi rule and that a significant minority had denounced Jews to the Nazis or participated in anti-Jewish violence, those who fell into these categories far outnumbering the small number of rescuers. They were shocked by the persistence of anti-Semitism as exemplified in the anti-Jewish violence after 1944 and the "anti-Zionist" purge of 1968, and regarded the attempt to stigmatize Jews for the behavior of a small number of communists of Jewish origin as an anti-Semitic reflex and an attempt at imposing collective responsibility on the Jews.

In the late 1970s and 1980s, the situation began to change. In Poland, a new willingness to examine the thorny problem of Polish–Jewish relations grew out of the rise in interest in the Polish–Jewish past that was a feature of those years. There was increasing awareness in Polish oppositional circles that Poland had been for nearly seven hundred years one of the main centers of the Jewish Diaspora, and from the early 1980s onward the importance of the development of this community for Polish life was widely recognized. Departments of Jewish history were created at the Jagiellonian University in Kraków, the University of Warsaw, the University of Lublin, and a number of other academic centers. Books on Jewish subjects disappeared rapidly from shops, plays on Jewish themes were sold out, and performances of visiting Israeli dance companies or orchestras were greeted with rapturous applause. Jewish history and culture were also among the subjects studied by the underground "flying university" (Żydowski Uniwersytet Latający, abbreviated as ŻUL, which in Polish means "bum") in the late 1970s. Similarly, at that time the Roman Catholic Church and the opposition began to sponsor "Weeks of Jewish Culture" in a number of cities, during which schoolchildren and university students attended lectures on Jewish topics and participated in the restoration of Jewish cemeteries. Catholic monthlies such as *Znak* and *Więź* devoted entire issues to Jewish topics, a phenomenon that has continued since the end of communism in 1989.

This interest was partly nostalgic in character. Poland had become practically mono-ethnic and mono-religious (although this homogeneity should not be exaggerated, given the significant presence minorities in the country, such as Ukrainians, Belarusians and Silesians, who together made up 10 percent of the country's population), and there was a genuine sense of loss at the disappearance of the more colorful Poland of the past, with its mixture of religions and nationalities. It did, however, have a deeper character. The experiences of the Solidarity movement in 1980–1981 gave Poles a greater sense of self-esteem. In sharp contrast with the traditional stereotype of Poles as quixotic and impractical political dreamers, in these years Poland astonished the world with its political maturity. A nonviolent movement challenged the might of the Soviet empire for nearly a year and a half, and though it was finally crushed, it paved the way for the negotiated end of communism less than ten years later. Under these conditions, there was a greater willingness to look at the more controversial aspects of the Polish past and to consider again more critically how Poles had treated the other peoples alongside whom they had lived, above all Jews and Ukrainians.

Increasingly, too, particularly among the younger generation, there was a growing awareness of the problematic character of the anti-Zionist campaign of 1968. At the time, the prevailing mood was that this was merely a settling of accounts among the communist elite and that all the party factions fighting for power were equally tainted. By the late 1970s, however, the realization that one of the consequences of those years had been to deprive Poland of most of what remained of its Jewish intelligentsia, and that society had allowed itself to be manipulated by the crude use of anti-Semitic slogans, led to an increasing feeling of anger. The role of the 1968 crisis in depriving the communist regime of political legitimacy has, in general, been greatly underestimated.

In Israel, North America, and Europe there was also a growing awareness of the importance of the Polish Jewish past. A number of Polish-born historians had settled in Israel and played a crucial role in the development of the academic activities of Yad Vashem and the Hebrew University, above all Yisrael Gutman and Chone Shmeruk. Gutman, who was born in Warsaw and had participated in the Warsaw ghetto revolt and survived Auschwitz, wrote seminal accounts of both the Warsaw ghetto uprising and the experience of the Jews in Warsaw under Nazi occupation while Shmeruk, also born in Warsaw, who emigrated to Israel in 1949, investigated all aspects of the Polish Jewish past from the development of modern Yiddish canonical and noncanonical literature to Hasidism and the Haskalah (Jewish Enlightenment).

In the United States the atmosphere was also changing. In September 1979, representatives of the American Jewish Committee and Polish-American cultural, religious, and academic organizations met at Saint Mary's College, Orchard Lake, Michigan, and established the Polish-American Jewish-American Task Force "to overcome misunderstanding and to promote mutual respect" by exploring shared historical experiences and contemporary common concerns. By 1988 the organization was so well established that it transformed itself into the National Polish-American Jewish-American Council (NPAJAC) with the backing of the Polish American Congress (PAC) and the American Jewish Committee. The PAC withdrew in 1996 after objections to the anti-Semitic utterances of its president, Edward Moskal, but the key Polish figures on the council remained associated with it.

In 1981, the task force had proposed a national conference on Polish-Jewish relations, and this took place at Columbia University in March 1983 on the theme "Poles and Jews: Myth and Reality in the Historical Context." It was preceded by a pre-conference symposium, "Poles and Jews in the New World," which showed how far apart the two sides still were and how much needed to be done to overcome mutual acrimony. This conference was followed by similar gatherings at Oxford in September 1984, at Brandeis University in the spring of 1986, at the Jagiellonian University in September 1986, and in Jerusalem at the Hebrew University between January 31 and February 5, 1988.

This sequence of conferences created a new situation. In the first place, it created an international cadre of scholars involved in Polish–Jewish history and provided them with a forum in which they could express their views. Before 1980 the number of publications in this field, particularly in English, was very small. Volumes were produced of the conference papers given at Oxford, Brandeis, and Kraków. More importantly, in Oxford the decision was taken to establish a scholarly annual, first entitled *Polin: A Journal of Polish-Jewish Studies* and later renamed *Polin: Studies in Polish Jewry*. From its inception, its international editorial board transcended ideological and ethnic frontiers. It attempted to encourage research on an interdisciplinary basis and sought contributions from many disciplines—history, sociology, politics, anthropology, linguistics, literature, and folklore—and from a wide variety of viewpoints.

The revival of interest in the Polish Jewish past accelerated with the end of communism in Poland and the Soviet Union in 1989–1991, and in the last three decades an enormous amount of research has been undertaken on all aspects of the history and culture of Polish Jews. Historical study seems to oscillate between detailed investigation and attempts at providing a synthesis of existing knowledge. Attempts to synthesize this vast amount of new research began in the 1990s, reflecting also a new maturity in this field of study. Among them one could mention *Żydzi w Polsce. Leksykon, dzieje i kultura* (The Jews in Poland. A lexicon on their history and culture), edited by Jerzy Tomaszewski and Andrzej Żbikowski (Warsaw, 2001) and *The YIVO Encyclopedia of Jews in Eastern Europe*, published in 2008; the two historical dictionaries, *Historia i kultura Żydów Polskich. Słownik* (The history and culture of Polish Jews. A dictionary) by Alina Cała, Hanna Węgrzynek, and Garbriela Zalewska (Warsaw, 2000) and *Polski Słownik Judaistyczny* (The Polish Judaic dictionary, 2 volumes), edited by Zofia Borzymińska and Rafał Żebrowski (Warsaw, 2003); Gershon D. Hundert's *Jews in Poland–Lithuania in the Eighteenth Century: A Genealogy of Modernity* (Berkeley and Los Angeles, 2004); Israel Bartal's *The Jews of Eastern Europe, 1772–1881*, translated by Chaya Naor (Philadelphia, 2005), which is part of the two-volume *Kiyum veshever: yehudei polin ledoroteihem* (Broken chain: Polish Jewry through the ages), edited by Israel Bartal and Israel Gutman (Jerusalem, 1997); and Antony Polonsky's three-volume *The Jews in Poland and Russia* (Oxford and Portland, Oregon, 2010, 2012). The narrative presented in POLIN Museum of the History of Polish Jews in Warsaw can also be considered to be a metahistorical account of the thousand-year history of Jews in the Polish lands.

How far has this new research modified our picture of the Polish Jewish past? In this introduction, we will not provide a detailed account of the changes that have taken place—this has been done by Moshe Rosman in his article—but rather sketch out the new directions that research has taken and the way this was reflected in the papers presented at the conference, which was divided into five sections, dealing with the years down to 1795, the long nineteenth century, the interwar period, the Holocaust, and the postwar years.

Certainly, in the last forty-five years our understanding of Jewish life down to the partitions of Poland–Lithuania in the late eighteenth century has been broadened, deepened, and, in some important areas, modified. Recent research has clarified the situation of the Jews there, demonstrating that they had a strong sense of rootedness, which created a situation in which the Jewish population of the Polish–Jewish Commonwealth grew from between 6,000 and 30,000 in 1500 to 750,000 in the middle of the eighteenth century, making it the largest Jewish community in the world. Their security was not absolute, and there was a strong awareness of its fragility. As in early medieval Europe, whose conditions were in many ways recreated in Poland–Lithuania, the Jewish elite took the view that toleration of the Jewish community was granted in exchange for the economic services it performed and the taxes it paid. Judith Kalik in her article examines the problems raised in describing how the main tax levied on Jews, the poll tax, was assessed in Crown Poland in the eighteenth century.

The Jewish sense of relative security and rootedness had a number of sources. In the first place the Polish–Lithuanian state was, to use modern and in some ways anachronistic terms, multiethnic and multireligious. In spite of the differences from modern conditions, it is certainly the case that the Jews were not the only religious or social outsiders, or indeed the most numerous. In addition, the state and even more so the "political nation" of the nobility was committed to the principle of toleration among different Christian denominations, however much this was attenuated, particularly after the growing strength of the Counter-Reformation in Poland–Lithuania.

The Jews also occupied a defined niche in Polish society. They had been invited into Poland by the rulers from the eleventh century and were, by and large, protected by the kings and princes and by the charters which had been granted to them, starting with that issued by Bolesław of Kalisz in 1264 and then by those issued by all Polish kings starting with Kazimierz the Great (r. 1333–70). In the royal towns, such as Kraków, Brześć, Poznań, and Lwów, which were ultimately under the jurisdiction of the king or his governor (*wojewoda*), Jews were able to establish flourishing communities. In such towns, Jews frequently lived outside the main town as in Lublin or in neighbouring towns, as was the case with Kazimierz near Kraków.

From 1539, the crown relinquished its jurisdiction over the Jews who lived on noble estates, and Jews now established themselves in increasing numbers in the small towns established on these estates. In particular, they began to move to Ukraine, which in 1569 had been transferred from the Grand Duchy of Lithuania to the Korona (the Crown of Poland), where they settled in the towns established by the great Polish magnates. By the mid-seventeenth century, a large proportion of the Jewish population lived in towns and villages owned by nobles. Of the sixteen towns in eighteenth-century Poland–Lithuania in which there were more than two thousand Jews, ten belonged to nobles.

This "marriage of convenience" between the nobility and the Jews did not involve much mutual respect. The former looked on the Jews with contempt. Since they believed that "only agriculture deserves to be called work" and that "it is a sin and a shame to engage in trade," they regarded Jewish merchants, like those from Italy and Germany who also settled in Poland, as swindlers, deceivers, and criminals. The nobles valued above all physical strength, courage, and skill in battle, and despised the Jews as weak, cowardly, harmful, and parasitic. The diaries of noblemen are marked by xenophobia, and particularly by a dislike of Jews. The Jews for their part regarded their noble patrons as spendthrift and immoral. Yet, for a long period both needed the other, and this formed the basis for their relations. Since the nobles needed their Jewish agents, they granted many privileges to Jewish communities in the towns on their estates. The nobles had the upper hand in relation to their leaseholders (*arendators*), but the typical leaseholder was conscious of his own power and willing to defend his interests against his noble patron.

Although Jewish life was devastated by the violence of the mid-seventeenth century, sparked off by the revolt of Bohdan Khmelnytsky, it soon recovered. In restoring their devastated estates, the nobility, especially the magnates, relied to an even greater extent than previously on the use of Jews. The way the specific situation of the Jews developed in the Polish–Lithuanian Commonwealth is described in the article of Adam Teller, one of the creators of the galleries dealing with the premodern period. Jürgen Heyde examines the way the Jews were perceived and how this affected their treatment, while Hanna Węgrzynek investigates the agreements between towns and *kehillot* and their influence on Jewish legal status.

In addition, the more difficult economic conditions of the early eighteenth century led to an exodus of German and Italian burghers, whose role in Polish trade was often filled by Jews. In an article published in 1991 (but written in 1986), Jan Małecki observed in the context of Jewish trade in Kraków that "post-war literature on the subject of Jewish trade in pre-partition Poland is very scanty."[2] There is still much research to be done but recent studies, above all the publication of sources,[3] have given us a fuller picture. They have shown

---

2 Jan M. Małecki, "Handel żydowski u schyłku XVI i w 1 połowie XVII w. w świetle krakowskich rejestrów celnych [Jewish trade at the end of the sixteenth and in the first half of the seventeenth centuries in the light of the tax records of Kraków]," in *Żydzi w dawnej Rzeczypospolitej. Materiały z konferencji "Autonomia Żydów w Rzeczypospolitej szlacheckiej". Międzywydziałowy Zakład Historii i Kultury Żydów w Polsce, Uniwersytet Jagielloński, 22–26 IX 1986*, [Jews in the Polish-Lithuanian Commonwealth. Articles from the conference "Jewish Autonomy in the Noble Republic"], ed. Andrzej Link-Lenczowski and Tomasz Polański (Wrocław–Warsaw–Kraków: Zakład Narodowy im. Ossolińskich, 1991), 214.

3 *Żydzi polscy 1648–1772. Źródła* [Polish Jews 1648-1772. Sources], ed. Adam Kaźmierczyk (Kraków: Uniw. Jagielloński, Katedra Judaistyki, 2001); *Gminy żydowskie w dawnej Rzeczypospolitej. Wybór tekstów źródłowych* [Jewish Communities in the former Polish-Lithuanian Commonwealth. A Selection of Sources], ed. Anna Michałowska (Warsaw: Dialog, 2003); *Sejmy i sejmiki koronne wobec Żydów. Wybór tekstów źródłowych* [Sejms and sejmiki on Jews. A selection of sources], ed. Anna Michałowska-Mycielska

that while the Jewish participation in Polish trade was relatively limited in the sixteenth century, by the end of the seventeenth and during the eighteenth century they played a dominant role in both the local and international trade of the commonwealth. This topic forms the subject of the article by Jacek Wijaczka.

At the same time as they occupied a clearly defined niche in Polish society, the Jews were also a pariah group, espousing a religion that was rejected as both false and harmful by the dominant Roman Catholic Church. The supersessionist claims of Christianity had been set out by St. Paul, and the essence of the position of the church was formulated by St. Augustine in the fifth century. It held that the Jews were to be tolerated in an inferior position in order to demonstrate the truth of Christianity.

This position was codified as part of canon law at the Third and Fourth Lateran Councils in Rome in 1179 and 1215. The Catholic church in Poland consistently tried to implement the directives of the Vatican on Jewish matters. At the Provincial Church Council of Wrocław in 1267 (which had jurisdiction over Gniezno, the seat of the primate of the Polish Church), it was laid down that Christians were forbidden to invite Jews to weddings and other feasts, to share meals with them, to dance with them, to buy their food, or to go to the baths with them. There were limitations on the rights of Jews to lend money,

---

(Warsaw: Wydawnictwa Uniwersytetu Warszawskiego, 2006); *Sejm Czterech Ziem. Źródła* [The Council of the Four Lands. Sources], ed. Jakub Goldberg and Adam Kaźmierczyk (Warsaw: Wydawnictwo Sejmowe, 2011); *Materiały źródłowe do dziejów Żydów w księgach grodzkich lubelskich z doby panowania Augusta II Sasa 1697–1733* [Documents on the history of the Jews in the Lublin Castle Court Records during the reign of Augustus II of Saxony 1697–1733], ed. Henryk Gmiterek with an introduction by Adam Teller (Lublin: Archiwum Państwowe w Lublinie, 2001); *Materiały źródłowe do dziejów Żydów w księgach grodzkich lubelskich z doby panowania Michała Korybuta Wiśniowieckiego i Jana III Sobieskiego 1669–1697* [Documents on the history of the Jews in the Lublin Castle Court Records during the reigns of Michał Korybut Wiśniowiecki and Jan III Sobieski 1669–1697], ed. Henryk Gmiterek (Lublin: Wydawnictwo Uniwersytetu Marii Curie-Skłodowskiej, 2003); *Materiały źródłowe do dziejów Żydów w księgach grodzkich lubelskich z doby panowania Władysława IV i Jana Kazimierza Wazów 1633–1669* [Documents on the history of the Jews in the Lublin Castle Court Records during the reigns of Władysław IV and Jan Kazimierz Vasa 1633–1669], ed. Henryk Gmiterek (Lublin: Wydawnictwo Uniwersytetu Marii Curie-Skłodowskiej, 2006); *Materiały źródłowe do dziejów Żydów w księgach grodzkich lubelskich z doby panowania Zygmunta III Wazy 1587–1632* [Documents on the history of the Jews in the Lublin Castle Court Records during the reign of Zygmunt III Vasa 1587–1632], ed. Henryk Gmiterek (Lublin: Archiwum Państwowe w Lublinie, 2014). See also the pioneering work of Moshe Rosman, "Polish Jews in the Gdańsk Trade in the Late 17th and Early 18th Centuries," in *Danzig between East and West: Aspects of Modern Jewish History*, ed. Isidore Twersky (Cambridge, MA: Harvard University Press, 1985), 111–20.

and separate Jewish residential quarters had to be established. It was also decreed that there should be only one synagogue in any town. Jews should be compelled to wear horned hats, were forbidden to employ Christian servants, and were to stay indoors with their windows closed when the Holy Sacrament was carried past. Finally, they were prohibited from holding public office, particularly the office of customs or toll collector.

These regulations appear to have been ineffective since Jews lived in Kraków and elsewhere in close proximity to Christians. There is also no record of their actually wearing special markers on their clothes. The *ad limina* reports sent by the Polish bishops to the Holy See in the seventeenth and eighteenth centuries, particularly those from the latter part of this period, reflect the dissatisfaction of the Catholic hierarchy at its inability to impose the norms of behavior called on by canon law. The Church hierarchy recognized that it was difficult to attack the position of the Jews since, in addition to their "cunning," they enjoyed the protection and support of the nobility and of some monastic orders, with whom they had strong economic ties. In addition, the fact that church bodies invested literally millions of zlotys with Jewish kehillot was a crucial factor creating relations between the Jews and local Catholic hierarchy.[4]

---

4 Judith Kalik, "Jews in Catholic Ecclesiastic Legislation in the Polish–Lithuanian Commonwealth," *Kwartalnik Historii Żydów* 209 (2004): 26–39; "Patterns of Contact between the Catholic Church and the Jews in the Polish–Lithuanian Commonwealth: The Jewish Debts," in *Scripta Hierosolymitana* 38: *Studies in the History of the Jews in Old Poland in Honor of Jacob Goldberg*, ed. Adam Teller (Jerusalem: Magnes Press, 1998), 102–22; "'Zastaw' (Deposit) and 'Wiederkauf' in the Economic Activity of the Jews in the Polish–Lithuanian Commonwealth," in *Jewish Entrepreneurship in Modern Times: East Europe and Eretz Israel*, ed. Ran Aharonsohn and Shaul Stampfer (Jerusalem: Magnes Press, 2000), 25–47; Adam Teller, "General Arenda and the General Arendarz in Eighteenth Century Lithuania," in *Jewish Entrepreneurship in Modern Times: Eastern Europe and Erets Yisra'el*, ed. Ran Aharonsohn and Shaul Stampfer (Jerusalem: Magnes Press, 2000), 48–78; Adam Kaźmierczyk, "Polscy biskupi wobec Żydów w XVIII wieku" [Polish Bishops on the Jews in the eighteenth century], in *Rzeczpospolita wielu wyznań; materiały z międzynarodowej konferencji Kraków 18 listopada 2002* [A Multi-confessional Republic; proceedings of an international conference in Kraków, 18 November 2002], ed. Adam Kaźmierczak et al. (Kraków: Księgarnia Akademicka, 2004), 349–56; Hanna Węgrzynek, "The attitude of the Catholic Church towards Jews in Poland at the Beginning of the 18th Century," *Kwartalnik Historii Żydów* 4 (2006): 662–68; "Was the Catholic Church in Poland Afraid of Conversion to Judaism in the Early Sixteenth Century?" *Kwartalnik Historii Żydów* 1 (2005): 5–10; "The Catholic Church and Jewish Books in the Polish–Lithuanian Commonwealth from the Sixteenth to Eighteenth Century," in *The Roman Inquisition, the Index and the Jews. Contexts, Sources and Perspectives*, ed. S. Wendehorst (Leiden: Brill, 2004), 59–70; "The Legislation of the Catholic Church in Poland relating to Jews," *Kwartalnik Historii Żydów* 212 (2004), 502–10; "The Catholic Church and the Jews in the

The Black Death appears to have had relatively little impact in Poland; indeed, this may be one of the reasons why the Jews who were being expelled from elsewhere in Central Europe were able to settle there. But accusations of child murder and host desecration became well established in early modern Poland. The last known ritual murder trial in eighteenth-century Poland took place in Olkusz, near Kraków, and did not result in a conviction. The ending of these trials was the result first of the growing influence of the Enlightenment. The great Dutch jurist Hugo Grotius had as early as 1636 declared in response to a letter from a Polish Protestant, Jerzy Słupecki, that accusations that Jews used Christian blood were false and that testimony obtained under torture was worthless. Also important was the influence of the eighteenth-century papacy. Both Benedict XIV (1740–58) and Clement XIII (1758–69) condemned these trials, the latter on the basis of a report by Cardinal Lorenzo Ganganelli, who was to succeed him as Clement XIV (1769–74). According to them, "there was no evidence that Jews need to add human blood to their unleavened bread [called] matzah."[5] In June 1775, in the course of a ritual murder trial in Warsaw in which all the accused were acquitted, the use of torture as a means of obtaining evidence was widely criticized. The following year it was abolished by the Sejm, and no further trials were mounted before the final partition of Poland–Lithuania. Nevertheless, the bishops, such as Kajetan Sołtyk, bishop of Kraków from 1759 to 1788, continued their attempts to reduce what they regarded as the harmful influence of the Jews.

In addition to the problems they faced as the exponents of a despised and scorned religion, the Jews were also subject to periodic outbreaks of popular violence. In towns, Jews were sometimes harassed by Jesuit students or local residents. Such incidents took place in Lublin, Lwów, Kraków, Płock, and Poznań. The worst eruptions of anti-Jewish violence occurred in the eastern provinces of the commonwealth, where the role of the Jews as the agents of Polish or Polonized magnates, mainly Catholics, aroused the hatred of the local Orthodox peasantry and Cossacks. Thus, during the Khmelnytsky uprising and the wars which followed, Jews were massacred not only by the Cossacks but

---

Kraków Diocese during the Sixteenth Century," History.Pth.Net.Pl, www.history.pth.net.pl, originally in Polish: "Kościół katolicki a Żydzi w Małopolsce w XVI wieku," in *Kościół katolicki w Małopolsce w średniowieczu i we wczesnym okresie nowożytnym* [Catholic Church in Małopolska in the Middle Ages and in the Early Modern Period], ed. Waldemar Kowalski and Jadwiga Muszyńska (Kielce: Kieleckie Towarzystwo Naukowe, 2001), 225–36.

5 See Cecil Roth, ed., *The Ritual Murder Libel and the Jew: The Report by Cardinal Lorenzo Ganganelli (Pope Clement XIV)* (London: The Woburn Press, 1935).

also by Swedes and Muscovites. Violence remained endemic in the Polish part of Ukraine in the late seventeenth and eighteenth centuries, much of it perpetrated by Haydamaks (*haydamaky*; outlaws), who went from banditry to opposition to Polish rule. In his article, Kenneth Stow examines the way the policy of the Catholic Church toward the Jews changed in the early modern period, while Adam Kaźmierczyk investigates the complex relationship between the church, the nobility, and its Jewish clients.

One area where considerable new research has been done in recent years has been in the investigation of Jewish religious and spiritual life, particularly after 1648. Although the community quickly overcame the crisis, the scars it left created a new religious climate. Traditional society continued and developed new themes in rabbinic thought, but the real historical development of the age was now more in the direction of mysticism and messianism. Given their theological universe, inevitably some Polish Jews claimed that their community was being punished for the iniquities of their generation. Calls for repentance were widespread. This climate of penitence created a mood favorable to messianic expectations, and many Jews saw in the suffering and martyrdom the community experienced in the mid-seventeenth century the "birth pangs of the Messiah." There is some dispute as to how widespread was the support in Poland for the messianic pretender in Turkey, Shabbetai Zevi. However, there are indications that the messianic expectations aroused by him in Poland–Lithuania led some Jews to believe that they would soon be able to take revenge for their sufferings and that this seems to have provoked anti-Jewish violence in a number of places, including Pińsk and Vilna in 1666, which was also a year that in the Christian calendar aroused messianic expectations. Certainly, a number of Polish Jews traveled to meet Shabbetai in Gallipoli, both as individuals and as community representatives. There was clearly not widespread uncritical messianic fervor in Poland–Lithuania, but the Sabbatean crisis made its impact there, as it did in the entire Jewish world.

The late seventeenth and eighteenth centuries were characterized by a number of new phenomena on the religious landscape of Polish Jewry: the persistence of Sabbateanism; the activities of a new and more sinister messianic pretender in the form of Jacob Frank, a Sephardi Jew from Salonika; and the emergence of a major religious revival linked with the Baal Shem Tov and his adherents. There now occurred a major shift in religious values. This was above all the result of the popularization of kabbalistic and mystical religious concepts, which had previously been confined to a small and esoteric circle, but which now gained a much greater following with the growth in printing and distribution of popular and often inexpensive kabbalistic tracts. Written in easily understood language, they guided the reader through prayer services and rituals associated with the life cycle, to which were attributed a cosmic and mystical significance. One important aspect of Polish Kabbalah was the degree to which its adherents were preoccupied with the theory of evil and the world of devils and spirits.

The increasing influence of Kabbalah and the widespread distribution of kabbalistic texts had a number of important consequences for the character of religious observance. Carrying out the commandments of the law now had a cosmic meaning, affecting the hidden divine realm, and advancing or retarding progress toward redemption. Careful and proper observance became, therefore, a matter of fateful significance. This system of understanding erased the differences in degree and weight between the fulfillment of one Commandment and another. Moreover, one had to be conscious of this while performing the Commandment or reciting the prayer. This consciousness was ritualized by the kabbalists in the form of *kavanot* (mystical devotions), which are intentional formulas preceding observance or recitation and intended to focus the mind of the devotee on the symbolic connotation of the act about to be performed or the prayer about to be recited.

A new significance attached to the kabbalistic elite so that traditional Jewish society now had a second religious elite. The rabbinic elite did retain some of its traditional prestige, and rabbinic positions were eagerly sought after, sometimes leading to bitter and protracted disputes. Alongside the rabbinic scholar there now emerged a new type of kabbalist, distinct from those who had wandered from place to place, looking (often unsuccessfully) for support from rich Jews. This new group was felt to be as worthy of respect as the rabbinate and equally entitled to public support. Individual mystics and small groups of kabbalists appeared in numerous communities. They devoted themselves to the study of esoteric doctrine, prayed separately in their own *kloyzn* (prayer rooms), and were thought to benefit the community that supported them by their special access to heaven. They not only prayed separately but also made use of the Lurianic prayer book (*nusaḥ ha'ari*) and, following a custom established in Safed, met for the third meal on the afternoon of the Sabbath, wearing white robes. These circles also maintained the prevalent penitential tone. They called for the avoidance of "frivolity," advocating instead constant mourning over the exile and a continuous flight from sin.

While the rabbinic elite saw itself as set above the masses because of its learning, it also saw its role as a public one through teaching, judging, and preaching. The situation of the kabbalists was different. In the words of Jacob Katz, "the kabbalist elite saw itself as divided from the masses by a wide chasm even in the practical sphere. The only relationship possible between them and the masses was one of *shlihut* (agency or proxy). The few were transformed into exacting performers of the precepts on behalf of the many."[6] Because of this, they were supported by the communities directly or through exemption from taxation. In the eyes of the community, they were precious, exceptional individuals (*yeḥidei segulah*) and "servants of God."

Connected with this kabbalistic elite but also separate from it were the many faith healers—*ba'alei shem* (masters of the Name, i.e., people able to cast spells using the name of God). These *ba'alei shem* cured disease, physical and spiritual, through the use of the secret names of God, the employment of amulets and charms, as well as numerology. They were familiar with the "other side" of creation (that controlled by evil forces), and since it was widely believed that illness was caused by demons, exorcism played a large part in their cures.

This new spiritual climate constitutes the background to the two major developments in the religious life of Polish Jewry in the eighteenth century: the messianic movement associated with the enigmatic figure of Jacob Frank and the emergence and development of Hasidism. Frankism was an even more disturbing and disruptive phenomenon than Shabateanism and did not hesitate to adopt openly anti-Jewish positions, including accusing Jews of the blood libel. In recent years, it has been the subject of a number of major studies.[7] This issue is reviewed in the article of Jan Doktór.

The emergence and development of Frankism forms an important element in the background to the rise of Hasidism, a movement for Jewish religious revival that came to be marked by charismatic leadership and a stress

---

6 Jacob Katz, *Tradition and Crisis: Jewish Society at the End of the Middle Ages* (New York: New York University Press, 1993), 194.
7 Paweł Maciejko, *The Mixed Multitude: Jacob Frank and the Frankist Movement, 1755–1816* (Philadelphia: University of Pennsylvania Press, 2011) and Jan Doktór, *Jakub Frank i jego nauka na tle kryzysu religijnej tradycji osiemnastowiecznego żydostwa polskiego* [Jakub Frank and his teaching against the background of the crisis of religious tradition of eighteenth-century Polish Jewry] (Warsaw: Instytut Filozofii i Socjologii PAN, 1991), *Śladami mesjasza-apostaty. Żydowskie ruchy mesjańskie w XVII i XVIII wieku a problem konwersji* [In the footsteps of the Messiah-Apostate. Jewish messianic movements in the seventeenth and eighteenth centuries and the problem of conversion] (Wrocław: FNP, 1998), and *Misjonarze i żydzi w czasach mesjańskiej zawieruchy 1648–1792* [Missionaries and Jews during the period of messianic upheavals 1648–1792] (Warsaw: Żydowski Instytut Historyczny im. Emanuela Ringelbluma, 2012).

on mystical communion with God. Our understanding of the emergence and development of Hasidism has developed rapidly in recent years as scholars have adopted a much more critical approach to the sources.[8] It has become apparent that the earliest sources, in particular some of the authenticated sayings and early letters of the Baal Shem Tov (or Besht), the initiator of the movement, raise relatively few problems of interpretation. This is also true of the material found in Polish archives, primarily those of the Sieniawski-Czartoryski estate, which owned the town of Międzyboż (Medzhybizh), where the Besht spent the last twenty years of his life. This is not the case with the hagiographic material, whether in the form of the sayings of the Besht that were recorded later or the account of his activities, as recounted in *Shivḥei habesht* (In Praise of the Baal Shem Tov), and those of his successors. This material, among the most characteristic and attractive produced by the movement, is clearly hagiographic, teaching a moral lesson, and it cannot be seen as historical in the modern sense. Legends about the Besht arose from the very start of his preaching. Care and skill is needed to extract the kernels of historical evidence that are to be found in it. In addition, the role of editors and the way the material was modified in subsequent editions needs to be carefully analyzed.

As a result of recent research, we know a great deal more about the Besht and his activities in Międzyboż. The town was no rural backwater. It had a population of 5,000, of which 2,000 were Jews, and was one of the largest Jewish communities in Poland. The Besht was invited to come to Międzyboż as the resident kabbalist, healer, and leader of the *beit midrash*, which made him a man of substance with a reputation. There was already a circle of kabbalists and mystics in the town, of which he became the most prominent. He lived in a house belonging to this community and was exempt from tax. Some of his associates received a weekly stipend from the kahal budget, and he is described in the documents as a *kabbalista* and a *doktor*, i.e. scholar. The same documents show that he employed a number of men, including the *pisarz balszema* (the Baal Shem's scribe). In addition, two members of the *beit midrash* were sponsored by the Międzyboż community with one or two zlotys per week.

The Besht was thus a respected member of the Jewish community; he did not see himself as a radical or as called upon to support the lower orders against the communal oligarchy. He was also not interested in creating anything more

---

8 On this see, Moshe Rosman, *Founder of Hasidism: A Quest for the Historical Ba'al Shem Tov* (Berkeley: University of California Press, 1996) and Immanuel Etkes, *The Besht: Magician, Mystic and Leader* (Waltham, MA: Brandeis University Press; Hanover, NH: University Press of New England, 2005).

than a small circle of like-minded mystics and in this respect resembled the many other circles of mystics in eighteenth-century Poland–Lithuania, led by charismatic figures. What was different about the Besht? In the first place, he seems to have modified in a significant manner the concept of the tzaddik, who was transformed in hasidic thought from a righteous person approved by the celestial court in the days between New Year and the Day of Atonement into a mediator between the divine and the human realms, a development linked with the kabbalistic concept of the ninth manifestation of the Divine Presence (known as *yesod*) in the system of divine emanations, which brought divine power to the earth.

Another new element in the teaching of the Besht was its anti-asceticism, very different from the pessimistic and sin-laden atmosphere that had become a feature of the religious culture of Polish Jewry. In the Besht's view, evil differs from good only by degree in the hierarchy of holiness. As a result, the sinner is not completely rejected by the compassionate God, but always has the potential for self-improvement. Indeed, an evil impulse is not wholly evil. It carries within it the possibility of redemption if it can be redirected to become a force for good.

The Besht also stressed the importance of prayer, which would enable the individual to achieve union (*devekut*) with God. For this union, intensity of feeling rather than learning was what was crucial. Ecstatic enthusiasm (*hitlahavut*) was the goal—the experience of spiritual exultation as the soul is elevated toward God. This later became central to Hasidism and clearly owes a great deal to the personal faith and religious practice of the Besht.

However, in spite of this stress on prayer rather than study, the Besht's teachings should not be seen as an anti-intellectual revolt against the excessive legalism of rabbinic Judaism led by charismatic, populist, and barely educated figures—a view most strongly advanced by Simon Dubnow. It attracted men with great scholarly gifts, such as Jacob Joseph of Połonne (Polonne) and Shneur Zalman b. Barukh of Łady (Liady) (1745–1813). Among many of its early adherents were yeshiva students and members of the scholarly elite. To them one of the attractions of the movement was its rejection of the characteristic forms of Talmudic argument in Poland. The Besht's charge in *Shivḥei habesht* that the rabbis were inventing "false premises" was probably also intended to refer to casuistry.

Two other features of the Besht's teaching and practice also seem to stand out. Unlike other mystics, he was concerned with the salvation not only of himself and his small circle, but also of all Israel, as in his interventions over such matters as Haydamak attacks on Jews, religious persecution including ritual murder accusations, and epidemics. Finally, in the proto-court created around his extended family we can see the beginnings of the court of the individual tzaddik, which was such a characteristic feature of Hasidism.

On his death in 1760, the Besht left behind only a small circle of followers. It was they, and above all Jacob Joseph of Połonne and Dov Baer, the Magid of Międzyrzecz, who were responsible for the emergence of the hasidic movement and for its rapid expansion. The way the emergence and spread of the hasidic movement has been depicted in museums, and, in particular in POLIN Museum, is the subject of the article by David Assaf.

The main theme in the discussion of the history of Jews in the Polish lands in the "long nineteenth century" has long been why the west European pattern of integration, whereby Jews were transformed from a religious and cultural community transcending state boundaries into citizens of their respective countries, was not followed in this area. How this issue is described in POLIN Museum is discussed in the article by Tomasz Kizwalter. This integrationist narrative, which, in different forms, attributes the failure of Jewish integration to the resistance of Polish society, to the size and conservatism of the Jewish community, and to the negative effects of foreign rule, has shown great durability. One of the main reasons for this has been the continuing influence of what Marcin Wodziński has described as "the emancipation-oriented narrative imposed on us by Artur Eisenbach"[9] and set out in the latter's books such as *Kwestia równouprawnienia Żydów w Królestwie Polskim* (The Question of the Equality of the Jews in the Kingdom of Poland, Warsaw, 1972); *Wielka Emigracja wobec kwestii żydowskiej* (The Great Emigration and the Jewish Question, Warsaw, 1976); *Z dziejów ludności żydowskiej w Polsce w XVIII i XIX wieku* (On the history of the Jewish population in Poland in the eighteenth and nineteenth centuries, Warsaw, 1983); and *Emancypacja Żydów na ziemach polskich* (Warsaw, 1987), translated into English as *The Emancipation of the Jews in Poland, 1780–1870* (Oxford, 1991).

Eisenbach, whose first wife (who died in the Holocaust) was the sister of Emanuel Ringelblum, was a compelling advocate of this position. He was very strongly attracted to the integrationist vision of a society, which would transcend ethnic and religious divisions, inspired in his case by his Marxist beliefs.

---

9 Paper presented at the conference "Recovering Forgotten History: The Image of East-Central Europe in Anglo-Saxon Textbooks," Kraków, June 2013, unpublished in the possession of Antony Polonsky.

Describing *Emancypacja Żydów na ziemiach polskich,* he summed up his life's work in the following way:

> In writing this book, I had a sense of participating in the dramatic decades long striving of the Jewish community to abolish entrenched barriers, which were not only political, but also psycho social. I must confess that it required a major effort of will to prevent my emotional involvement from affecting an objective presentation of the events. I leave it to my readers to determine whether I have succeeded in attaining such an objectivity.[10]

This was a point of view shared by Stefan Kieniewicz. He concluded his article titled "Assimilated Jews in Warsaw in the Nineteenth Century" in the volume *The Jews of Warsaw* with the following words:

> One last reflection: in our century of rampant national egoism and intensified scorn for "alien" elements, it is worth showing more understanding for such a distant, fleeting attempt at Polish–Jewish rapprochement, an attempt to overcome old antagonisms—an attempt which could indeed have proved more fruitful, but which did not disappear completely, leaving no echoes.[11]

It long seemed as if the authoritative works of Eisenbach produced the last words on the subject of Jewish integration in the nineteenth century. Nevertheless, it has become apparent from recent research that the Eisenbach narrative has serious flaws. It has resulted in a failure to recognize other, often more important, trends—legislation not connected with emancipation, the history of the Haskalah, everyday life, demography, and Jewish religious reform. It overemphasized the importance of the *maskilim* and the integrationists and largely ignored more conservative and religious elements within Jewish society.[12]

---

10 Artur Eisenbach, *The Emancipation of the Jews in Poland, 1780–1870* (Oxford: Basil Blackwell, 1991), 5.
11 Władysław T. Bartoszewski and Antony Polonsky, eds., *The Jews in Warsaw* (Oxford: Basil Blackwell, 1991), 168.
12 Among the important recent works on acculturation and assimilation one could mention François Guesnet, *Polnische Juden im 19. Jahrhundert: Lebensbedingungen, Rechtsnormen und Organisation im Wandel* [Polish Jews in the nineteenth century: Conditions of life, legal norms and changing organizational structure] (Cologne: Böhlau, 1998); Stanislaus Blejwas, "Polish Positivism and the Jews," *Jewish Social Studies* NS 46, 1 (1984): 21–36 and *Realism in Polish Politics: Warsaw Positivism and National Survival in Nineteenth-Century*

These form the subject of the article by Glenn Dynner, in which he examines in the context of the position of women in traditional Jewish society. In addition, the accepted interpretation has tended to blur the differences between the very different policies pursued by the partitioning powers in the different areas of Poland, Prussian Poland, Galicia, the Kingdom of Poland, and the autonomous, semi-constitutional state in dynastic union with the Romanovs, created at the Congress of Vienna to satisfy, at least in part, the national aspirations of the Poles and the areas directly incorporated into the tsarist empire.

One of the main themes in nineteenth-century Polish social history is the gradual ending of the social, economic, and political dominance of the *szlachta* in Polish society, which took place at a different pace in the various partitions, with implications for the Jews. The undermining of noble hegemony was followed by the emergence in the late nineteenth century of the modern Polish nation and also of the spread of the national idea to Ukraine, Lithuania, and, more slowly, to Belarus. The development of a political consciousness within the peasantry and its link to the growth of anti-Semitism is discussed in the articles by Tomasz Kizwalter and Darius Staliūnas. These developments stimulated the emergence of the new Jewish politics that stressed ethnicity rather than religion as the marker of Jewish identity. Certainly, in the Kingdom of Poland, the period between 1890 and 1914 saw a fundamental transformation of Polish political life and the emergence of new political movements that challenged the dominance of the Positivists, the exponents on Polish soil of a variant of Western liberalism, and the Jews who were associated with them. Of these

---

Poland (New Haven, CT: Yale Concilium on International and Area Studies, 1984); Alina Cała, *Asymilacja Żydów w Królestwie Polskim (1864–1897)* [The Assimilation of the Jews in the Kingdom of Poland, 1864–1897] (Warsaw: Państwowy Instytut Wydawniczy, 1989); Shmuel Feiner, *Haskalah and History*, trans. Chaya Naor and Sondra Silverston (Oxford: Littman Library of Jewish Civilization, 2002); Jerzy Jedlicki, *Nieudana próba kapitalistycznej industrializacji. Analiza państwowego gospodarstwa przemysłowego w Królestwie Polskim XIX w.* [An unsuccessful attempt at capitalist industrialization: An analysis of state-owned economic enterprises in the Kingdom of Poland in the nineteenth century] (Warsaw: Książka i Wiedza, 1964) and *A Suburb of Europe: Polish Nineteenth-Century Approaches to Western Civilization* (Budapest: Central European University Press, 1999), English translation of *Jakiej cywilizacji Polacy potrzebują. Studia z dziejów, idei i wyobraźni XIX wieku* (Warsaw: W. A. B., 1998); Agnieszka Jagodzińska, *Pomiędzy. Akulturacja Żydów Warszawy w drugiej połowie XIX wieku* [Between. The Acculturation of the Jews of Warsaw in the second half of the nineteenth century] (Wrocław: Wydawnictwo Uniwersytetu Wrocławskiego, 2008); Theodore Weeks, *From Assimilation to Antisemitism: The "Jewish Question" in Poland, 1850–1914* (DeKalb, IL: Northern Illinois University Press, 2006); and Joshua Zimmerman *Poles, Jews and the Politics of Nationality: The Bund and the Polish Socialist Party in Late Tsarist Russia* (Madison: University of Wisconsin Press, 2004).

new movements, the most important were integral nationalism, in the form of the National Democratic movement led by Roman Dmowski, and socialism, both in national and revolutionary forms. Within the Jewish world, the dominance of the integrationists was challenged by the adherents of Zionism and of socialism.

In recent years, there has developed a renewed interest in the religious history of Jews in the nineteenth century. Simon Dubnow, one of the founders of the school of Eastern European Jewish history, ended his history of Hasidism in 1815. According to him, this was the end of "the period of growth and expansion" and the beginning of "the period of the predominance of tsadikim and the struggle against the Haskalah movement," during which "the cult of tsaddikim obscur[ed] the light of Jewish rationalism and arous[ed] fanatical hatred of freedom of thought."[13] Similarly neither Ben-Zion Dinur nor Shmul Horodetsky devoted much attention to the nineteenth-century evolution of Hasidism.[14]

New research has fundamentally altered our understanding of the spread of Hasidism. This research took as its starting point the volume *Hasidism Reappraised* (London, 1996), edited by Ada Rapoport-Albert. This was followed by the organization under the auspices of Arthur Green, David Assaf, Ada Rapoport-Albert, and Marcin Wodziński of a conference in 2004 at the University of Wrocław on the theme of "Hasidism in Poland: New Perspectives." It led to the creation in the academic year 2007–2008 of a research group "Towards a New History of Hasidism," organized by David Assaf at the Institute of Advanced Studies (IAS) of the Hebrew University and, in 2009, to a new conference at University College London on the same theme.

---

13 Simon Dubnow, *Toldot hahasidut* (Tel Aviv: Dvir, 1930–31), 37.
14 For Horodetsky, see Shmul A. Horodetsky, *Haḥasidut veḥasidim*, 4 vols. (Tel Aviv: Dvir, 1928–43). A number of scholars have examined this question in recent years, in particular David Assaf, *Derekh ha-malkhut: R. Yisrael me-Ruz'in u-mekomo be-toldot ha-ḥasidut* (Jerusalem: Merkaz Zalman Shazar le-toldot Yiśra'el, 1997), translated into English as *The Regal Way: The Life and Times of Rabbi Israel of Ruzhin* (Stanford, CA: Stanford University Press, 2002); Paul I. Radensky, "Hasidism in the Age of Reform: A Biography of Rabbi Duvid ben Mordkhe Twersky of Tal'noye" (PhD diss., Jewish Theological Seminary of America, 2001); Glenn Dyner, *"Men of Silk": The Hasidic Conquest of Polish Jewry, 1754–1830* (Oxford: Oxford University Press, 2006); and Marcin Wodziński, *Oświecenie żydowskie w Królestwie Polskim wobec chasydyzmu: dzieje pewnej idei* (Warsaw: Wydawnictwo Cyklady, 2003), translated into English as *Haskalah and Hasidism in the Kingdom of Poland: A History of Conflict* (Oxford: Littman Library of Jewish Civilization, 2005).

Much of the research produced in this way was published in a special edition of the journal *Jewish History* in 2013.

The new research demonstrates clearly that the development of Hasidism as a movement was a phenomenon of the late eighteenth and early nineteenth century. As stated above, on his death in 1760 the Besht left behind only a small circle of followers. It was these followers who developed still further aspects of his theology, above all the distinction between the tzaddik and his followers. The older historiography of Hasidism argued that the Besht designated Dov Baer, the Magid of Międzyrzecz, as his chosen successor and that it was he who gave organizational structure to the movement and sent his followers to different areas of the Polish–Lithuanian Commnonwealth and its successor states to spread the message. This view is clearly untenable. It was only when confronted with the opposition of Elijah ben Eliezer, the Vilna Gaon, in spring 1772 that the Magid attempted, through his followers Menaḥem Mendel of Vitebsk and Shneur Zalman of Liady, to demonstrate the impeccable orthodoxy of the new movement and to use his established reputation both as a Talmudist and as an ascetic kabbalist to dispel fears about its allegedly messianic and even Shabatean character. It is to the disciples of the Magid that, in the next two generations, the emergence of something like an organized hasidic movement should be attributed. This movement was decentralized from the outset. The leading role of the Magid was not universally recognized within the circle linked with the Besht and, in addition, the Besht's son Zevi was clearly unable or unwilling to take up his role.

Hasidism now expanded rapidly into the rest of Ukraine and, more slowly and with less success, into Galicia, the Kingdom of Poland, and the former Grand Duchy of Lithuania. It was unable to find a foothold in Wielkopolska. Outside the historic borders of Poland–Lithuania, it also established itself in present-day Romania, Moldova, Slovakia, and Hungary. In an important article, Shaul Stampfer has examined the reasons for the rapid spread of Hasidism in the late eighteenth and first half of the nineteenth century, which he describes as "the period of its greatest growth."[15] Above all, what made possible the spread of the movement to individual communities was the institution of the *shtibl* that "by combining synagogue with social framework, created an attractive venue for *Hasidim* to gather, to spend time, and to attract new adherents."[16] *Shtiblekh* appeared relatively early in the development of Hasidism.

---

15 Shaul Stampfer, "How and Why Did Hasidism Spread," *Jewish History* 27 (2013): 201–19.
16 Ibid., 201.

Such a type of prayer house was not used by the Besht, although he prayed regularly in a special synagogue. By 1772, *shtiblekh* figure in the criticisms voiced by the opponents of Hasidism in Vilna. By 1818, the Polish *maskil* Abraham Stern could write:

> in the towns and the hamlets these sect members, the Hasidim ... try to have a private building or a separate school' in which to conduct services, pretending that they have differently established forms of prayers ... however, social assignations of a shady nature are their main aim.[17]

The *shtibl* differed from the synagogue or prayer hall (*beit midrash*), in both of which "eating, sleeping, and levity were prohibited." It was, in Stampfer's words,

> not only a place for prayer and study but also for festive meals and for activities that appeared to be social and recreational. There was also much more toleration of levity and of the telling of stories (hasidic and otherwise) than in the synagogue. In many respects, the atmosphere in a *shtibl* resembled that of a club or a pub more than it resembled the atmosphere traditionally regarded as appropriate for a place of worship, where one was expected to commune with the Creator.[18]

The *shtibl* was thus the key to the diffusion of the movement. Where *shtiblekh* could not be established, Hasidism usually failed to spread. *Minyanim* separate from the main communal synagogue were not new in Jewish life, and private *kloyzn* had existed for some time. What made the *shtibl* different was that while the membership of a *kloyz* was limited to a select group of scholars, the *shtibl* was open to all. *Shtiblekh* seem to have been established for the most part not by *tzaddikim* sending out missionaries to gain converts but were "entirely the product of local grassroots initiative by individuals who had been exposed to Hasidism at one of the early hasidic courts."[19]

Hasidism spread first in Ukraine. This area was adjacent to the original core of the movement and it expanded rapidly in the first decades of the nineteenth century, so that by 1825 the power of the different hasidic dynasties, courts, and

---

17 Marcin Wodziński, *Źródła do dziejów chasydyzmu w Królestwie Polskim, 1815–1867, w zasobach polskich archiwów państwowych* [Sources on the history of Hasidism in the Kingdom of Poland in the collections of Polish state archives] (Kraków: Austeria, 2011).
18 Stampfer, "How and Why Did Hasidism Spread," 206.
19 Ibid., 209.

leaders (*admorim*)²⁰ in the provinces of Kiev, Podolia, Minsk, and Mogilev had become so entrenched that spheres of influence had to be agreed upon among them.²¹ It proved more difficult to establish Hasidism in Lithuania, where resistance to the movement was more effective than in Ukraine above all because of the opposition of the local rabbinate and its spiritual head, Elijah ben Solomon Zalman (the Vilna Gaon), who were supported by local Jewish communal institutions. Nevertheless, there were, from the first days of the emergence of Hasidism, adherents of the movement in the Grand Duchy. A major hasidic center was established in the town of Karlin near Pińsk.²² Even more important was that led by Shneur Zalman of Liady, who established his court in Łoźno (Liozno). In the first decades of the nineteenth century, Hasidism also came to play a significant role in the religious life of Galicia and the Kingdom of Poland.²³

The one area of former Poland–Lithuania where Hasidism was unable to establish itself was Wielkopolska. There were a number of reasons for this. It was a region where rabbinic Judaism was well established; the major rabbinic figure in the area at the end of the eighteenth and beginning of the nineteenth century, Akiva ("the Younger") b. Moses Guens Eger, was an effective opponent of Hasidism. In addition, the successful modernization of the communal structure created an effective barrier to the spread of Hasidism.

One final area that has aroused much interest in the last thirty years has been the history of Jewish women and of gender in Jewish life. David Biale's pioneering work, *Eros and the Jews: From Biblical Israel to Contemporary America*

---

20 Admor, from *adoneinu vemoreinu*, "Our Master and Teacher."
21 On the geographical patterns of the spread of the movement, see Assaf, "Hasidism and its Expansion: The Effectiveness of the Rabbi Nehemiah Yehiel of Bychow, the Son of the Holy Jew," in *Studies of Jewish Culture in Honor of Chone Shmeruk* [in Hebrew], ed. Israel Bartal, Ezra Mendelsohn, and Chava Turniansky (Jerusalem: The Zalman Shazar Center for Jewish History, 1993), 269–98 and "'Polish Hasidism or 'Hasidism in Poland'": On the Problem of Hasidic Geography" [in Hebrew], *Gal-Ed On the History of the Jews in Poland* 14 (1995), 197–206.
22 Wolf Rabinovich, "Karlin Hasidism," *YIVO Annual of Jewish Social Science* 5 (1950): 125–26. For the problem of the spread of Hasidism to Lithuania, see also Zalkin, "Where Was Hasidism Not Able to Win Over the Majority?" in *Within Hasidic Circles: Studies in Memory of Mordecai Wilensky* [in Hebrew], ed. Emanuel Etkes, David Assaf, Israel Bartal, and Elhanan Reiner (Jerusalem: The Bialik Institute: 1999), 21–50.
23 On this see Assaf, *The Regal Way*; Dynner, "*Men of Silk*"; Marcin Wodziński, *Oświecienie żydowskie w Królestwie Polskim wobec chasydyzmu. Dzieje pewnej idei* [The Jewish Enlightenment in the Kingdom of Poland and its attitude to Hasidism. The history of a certain idea] (Warsaw, 2003); *Władze Królestwa Polskiego wobec chasydyzmu: Z dziejów stosunków politycznych* [The Authorities of the Kingdom of Poland and their handling of Hasidism: on the history of a political relationship] (Wrocław: Wydawnictwo Uniwersytetu Wrocławskiego, 2008).

(New York, 1992) with its discussion of the way gender issues operated both in the pre-modern period and in the period of the Haskalah has been followed by a spate of new research on this topic, stressing this issue throughout the long history of Polish Jewry. It has also been the topic of a special volume of *Polin: Studies in Polish Jewry* (volume 18), edited by Paula Hyman and Chae-Ran Freeze.[24] This topic forms the subject of Shulamit Magnus's article on Pauline Wengeroff, who also figures prominently in the nineteenth-century gallery of the permanent exhibition.

At the Oxford conference, the late Ezra Mendelsohn, then one of the younger scholars of the Polish–Jewish past, delivered a brilliant tour de force. It had the provocative title "Interwar Poland: Good for the Jews or Bad for the Jews?" In it he observed that two opposing groups, one "optimistic" and the other "pessimistic," can be observed in the historiography of interwar Polish Jewry. In his words:

> The attitude of most Jewish scholars has been, and continues to be, that interwar Poland was an extremely anti-semitic country, perhaps even uniquely anti-semitic. They claim that Polish Jewry during the 1920s and

---

24 That volume contains an important bibliography by compiled by Karen Auerbach. As a result, we list here only a small number of the many works on this topic. Edward Fram, *My Dear Daughter: Rabbi Benjamin Slonik and the Education of Jewish Women in Sixteenth-Century Poland* (Cincinnati, OH: Hebrew Union College Press, 2007); Ada Rapoport-Albert "On Women in Hasidism, S. A. Horodecky and the Maid of Ludmir Tradition," in *Jewish History: Essays in Honor of Chimen Abramsky*, ed. Ada Rapoport-Albert and Steven J. Zipperstein (London: Peter Halban, 1988), 498–525; Saul Stampfer, "Gender Differentiation and Education of the Jewish Woman in Nineteenth-Century Eastern Europe," *Polin* 7 (Oxford, 1992), 63–87; Eliyana Adler, *In Her Hands: The Education of Jewish Girls in Tsarist Russia* (Detroit: Wayne State University Press, 2011); Tova Cohen, *One Beloved and the Other Hated: Between Reality and Fiction in the Depiction of Women in Haskalah Literature* [in Hebrew] (Jerusalem: Magnes Press, 2002); Iris Parush, *Reading Jewish Women: Marginality and Modernization in Nineteenth-Century Eastern European Jewish Society* (Hanover, NH: University of New England Press for Brandeis University Press, 2004); Pauline Wengeroff, *Memoirs of a Grandmother: Scenes from the Cultural History of the Jews of Russia in the Nineteenth Century*, 2 vols. (Stanford, CA: Stanford University Press, 2010, 2015); Magnus, *A Woman's Life: Pauline Wengeroff and Memoirs of a Grandmother* (Oxford: Littman Library of Jewish Civilization, 2015); Puah Rakovsky, *My Life as a Radical Jewish Woman: Memoirs of a Zionist Feminist in Poland*, ed. Paula E. Hyman, trans. Benjamin Harshav with Paula E. Hyman (Bloomington, IN: Indiana University Press, 2002); ChaeRan Freeze, *Jewish Marriage and Divorce in Imperial Russia* (Hanover, NH: University Press of New England for Brandeis University Press, 2002); Laura Engelstein, *The Keys to Happiness: Sex and the Search for Modernity in Fin-de-Siècle Russia* (Ithaca, NY: Cornell University Press, 1992); Edward Bristow, *Prostitution and Prejudice: The Jewish Fight against White Slavery, 1870–1939* (New York: Clarendon Press, 1983); and Keely Stauter-Halstead, *The Devil's Chain: Prostitution and Social Control in Partitioned Poland* (Ithaca, NY: Cornell University Press, 2015).

1930s was in a state of constant and alarming decline, and that by the 1930s both the Polish regime and Polish society were waging a bitter and increasingly successful war against the Jewish population.[25]

This was the point of view of surviving prewar Polish Jewish scholars such as Raphael Mahler, Jacob Lestchinsky, and Isaiah Trunk.[26] Similar views were also expressed by the postwar Polish Jewish historian Paweł Korzec and by a number of Israeli historians, including Moshe Landau, Shlomo Netzer, and Emanuel Melzer.[27] This point of view is most clearly expressed by Celia Heller in her book *On the Edge of Destruction* (New York, 1977). Her thesis is clearly encapsulated in the title. In her view, the period between the two World Wars was a rehearsal for the Holocaust. Polish actions had by 1939 pushed the Jews to "the edge of destruction," and it only remained for the Nazis to complete what the Poles had begun.

This pessimistic view of the situation of Jews in interwar Poland has not gone unchallenged, by both Jewish and non-Jewish historians. The most eloquent of the Jewish "optimists" is Joseph Marcus. Marcus, who is sympathetic to the Orthodox party Agudas Yisroel, reserves his greatest condemnation for what he refers to as the "reformers" of Jewish life in Poland. Blinded by their Zionist and socialist obsessions, they had a great deal to do with the economic

---

25 Ezra Mendelsohn, "Interwar Poland: Good for the Jews or Bad for the Jews," in *The Jews in Poland,* ed. Chimen Abramsky, Maciej Jachimczyk, and Antony Polonsky (Oxford: Basil Blackwell, 1986), 130.

26 For Mahler's views see *The Jews of Poland between Two World Wars* [in Hebrew] (Tel Aviv: Dvir, 1968); for Lestchinsky's, see "The Anti-Jewish Program: Tsarist Russia, the Third Reich, and Independent Poland," *Jewish Social Studies* 3, no. 2 (April 1941): 141–58; for Trunk, "Der ekonomisher antisemitizm in Poyln" [Economic Anti-Semitism in Poland], in *Studies on Polish Jewry 1919–1939*, ed. Joshua A. Fishman (New York: YIVO, 1974), 3–98.

27 Paweł Korzec, *Juifs en Pologne: La question juive pendant l'entre-deux-guerres* [Jews in Poland: The Jewish Question between the Two World Wars] (Paris: Presses de la Fondation nationale des sciences politiques, 1980) and "Antisemitism in Poland as an Intellectual, Social and Political Movement," *Studies on Polish Jewry* (New York: YIVO, 1974), 12–104; Moshe Landau, *Miut leumi lohem: ma'avak yehudey polin 1918–1928* [A Militant National Minority: The Struggle of Polish Jews 1918–1928] (Jerusalem: Merkaz Zalman Shazar le-toldot Yisra'el, 1986); Shlomo Netzer, *Ma'avak yehudey polin al zehuyoteyhem haezrahiyot vehaleumuyot (1918–1922)* [The Struggle of Polish Jews for their Civil and National Rights (1918–1922)] (Tel Aviv: Universiṭat Tel Aviv, 1982); Emanuel Melzer, *Ma'avak medini bemalkodet: yehudei polin 1935–1939* [Political Struggle in a Blind Alley: Polish Jews 1935–1939] (Tel Aviv: ha-Makhon le-ḥeker ha-tefutsot, 1982), with the English translation, *No Way Out: The Politics of Polish Jewry 1935–1939* (Cincinnati: Hebrew Union College Press, 1997).

decline of Polish Jewry. According to Marcus, Jews in Poland were able to hold their own economically and were, in fact, better off than the majority of the population. They were more than capable of withstanding the assaults to which they were subjected in the 1930s. The real problem, in Marcus's view, was Polish poverty and Jewish overpopulation: "The Jews in Poland were poor because they lived in a poor, undeveloped country. Discrimination added only marginally to their poverty."[28]

These views have been echoed by many Polish scholars. Their position has been best articulated by the British historian of Poland, Norman Davies. In his history of Poland, *God's Playground*, he claims that "the condition of Polish Jewry in the interwar period is often described out of context." This, he states, was the responsibility of Zionists, who needed to paint the situation in Poland in the blackest of colors in order to justify their own political position. Like Marcus, he argues that the intractable nature of the Jewish question was the result of the poverty of the reborn Polish state and "an unprecedented demographic explosion" that "countermanded all attempts to alleviate social conditions." The Jews were only one of many ethnic groups in conflict with the Polish government, and they were not singled out for special treatment by Polish chauvinists, who were equally hostile to Germans and Ukrainians. They also had important allies in Polish political circles. Referring to the "so-called pogroms" of 1918 and 1919, Davies also claims that the scale of anti-Jewish violence in Poland has been exaggerated. He cites the cultural creativity of the Polish Jewish community as evidence that its situation was not as desperate as is sometimes believed, referring to the "essential dynamism of Polish Jewry at this juncture. All was not well: but neither was it unrelieved gloom."[29]

Mendelsohn concluded his article as follows:

> Interwar Poland was therefore bad for the Jews, in the sense that it excluded them from first-class citizenship in the state. This had led, by the late 1930s, to a widespread feeling among Polish Jews, and especially among the youth, that they had no future in Poland, and that they were trapped. Interwar Poland was good for the Jews because, among other things, it provided an environment in which forces were unleashed in the

---

28 Joseph Marcus, *Social and Political History of the Jews in Poland, 1919–1939* (Berlin: Mouton Publishers, 1983).
29 Norman Davies, "Żydzi: The Jewish Community," chapter 9, in *God's Playground: A History of Poland in Two Volumes. Volume II: 1795 to the Present* (Oxford: Oxford University Press, 1981), 240–66.

Jewish world which many Jews regarded then, and today, as extremely positive. This is not to give an ambiguous answer to the question posed at the outset, but to show that more than one answer is possible. Indeed, more than one answer is necessary. I think we can say that of Jewish history in interwar Poland that it was "the best of times and the worst of times." The best of times in the sense of the extraordinary creativity of Polish Jewry, the worst of times in the sense of the fulfilment of the bleakest prophecies, made mostly by Zionists, concerning the imminent fate of the East European diaspora.[30]

In the last three decades, considerable research has been conducted both in Poland and elsewhere on the situation of the Jews in interwar Poland, much of it stimulated by Mendelsohn's suggestions. It has also been increasingly recognized how important it is to try to free ourselves from the distorting lens imposed upon us by the events of the Second World War. Polish Jewry was almost entirely destroyed in the brief years of the Nazi Holocaust. However, this destruction did not follow logically from earlier developments. For the historian, the dilemma is that while it is impossible to cast out of one's mind the tragic fate of Polish Jewry, one cannot see clearly how Polish Jewry might have evolved had different conditions prevailed. A number of contradictory processes may be observed in the evolution of Jewish life in interwar Poland. In his article, Michael Steinlauf reflects on how these are depicted in the interwar gallery. On the one hand, these years saw increasing acculturation and Polonization, which is discussed in Katrin Steffen's article. This led to the emergence of Polish-language dailies intended for a Jewish reading public. Several of them produced supplements for young Jews—these form the subject of Anna Landau-Czajka's article on *Mały Przegląd* and *Dzienniczek*. Those years also saw the emergence of a group of major Polish Jewish writers, who wrote both in the Jewish languages and in those of the larger society. Polish literature in the twentieth century cannot be understood without taking into account the works of writers such as Bolesław Leśmian, Julian Tuwim, Antoni Słonimski, and Bruno Schulz. The importance of these writers is stressed in the museum.

Yet the Polish–Jewish symbiosis, comparable to similar phenomena in the German-speaking lands and the United States, was limited by the failure of Jewish integration, which provoked a range of different Jewish responses that form the subject of Gershon Bacon's article "One Jewish Street? On

---

30 Ezra Mendelsohn, "Interwar Poland," 139.

Unity and Disunity in Interwar Polish Jewry." In spite of the strength of Zionism and of Jewish socialism (Bundism), a large proportion of Polish Jews remained Orthodox. How modern developments led to innovative attempts to keep young women in the Orthodox fold is the subject of Naomi Seidman's article "Legitimizing the Revolution: Sarah Schenirer and the Rhetoric of Torah Study for Girls." The hope that independent Poland and Lithuania would prove democratic and pluralistic and would find an appropriate place for its Jewish minority was dashed. By the 1930s, these countries had become increasingly authoritarian, while the attraction of fascist ideas and of radical solutions to the "Jewish problem" grew, particularly among young zealots. By the outbreak of war in 1939, the situation of the Jews in Poland had become desperate. In recent historiography, all of these themes have been extensively examined, above all the role of Jews in Polish political life; Jewish acculturation; and the growth of anti-Semitism, particularly after the death of the charismatic leader Józef Piłsudski in 1935; the result of the contagious effect of the Nazi regimes' successful disenfranchisement and expropriation of one of the best integrated Jewish communities in Europe; the persistence of the Great Depression; and the attempts of a section of the government camp to win support from anti-Semitic right-wing youth.[31]

---

31 The following are only a few of the products of recent research: Jerzy Tomaszewski, *Rzeczpospolita wielu narodów* [A republic of many nations] (Warsaw: Czytelnik, 1985); *Ojczyzna nie tylko Polaków: Mniejszości narodowe w Polsce w latach 1918–1939* [A Fatherland not only for Poles: National minorities in Poland in the years 1918–1939] (Warsaw: Młodzieżowa Agencja Wydawnicza, 1985); Gershon Bacon, *The Politics of Tradition: Agudat Israel in Poland, 1916–1939* (Jerusalem: Magnes Press, 1996); Robert Blobaum, ed., *Antisemitism and Its Opponents in Modern Poland* (Ithaca, NY: Cornell University Press, 2005); Melzer, *Ma'avak medini bemalkodet*; Jolanta Żyndul, *Zajścia antyżydowskie w Polsce w latach 1935–1937* [Anti-Semitic incidents in Poland in the years 1935–1937] (Warsaw: Fundacja im. K. Kelles-Krauza, 1994); Ronald Modras, *The Catholic Church and Antisemitism: Poland, 1933–1939* (Chur, CH: Published for the Vidal Sassoon International Center for the Study of Antisemitism (SICSA), the Hebrew University of Jerusalem by Harwood Academic Publishers, 1994); Ezra Mendelsohn, *Zionism in Poland: The Formative Years, 1915–1926* (New Haven, CT: Yale University Press, 1981); Joanna Michlic, *Poland's Threatening Other: The Image of the Jew from 1880 to the Present* (Lincoln, NE: University of Nebraska Press, 2006); Szymon Rudnicki, *Żydzi w parlamencie II Rzeczypospolitej* [Jews in the Parliament of the Second Polish Republic] (Warsaw: Wydawnictwo Sejmowe, 2004, second edition 2015); Laurence Weinbaum, *A Marriage of Convenience: The New Zionist Organization and the Polish Government* (Boulder, CO: East European Monographs, 1993); Artur Sandauer, *On the Situation of the Polish Writer of Jewish Descent in the Twentieth Century* (Jerusalem: Magnes Press, 2005); Eugenia Prokop-Janiec, *Międzywojenna literatura polsko-żydowska jako zjawisko kulturowe i artystyczne* [Interwar Polish-Jewish literature as a cultural and artistic phenomenon] (Kraków: Universitas, 1992); Nathan Cohen, *Book, Writer, and Newspaper: The Jewish Cultural Centre in Warsaw*

It is in the area of the vexed and controversial question of Polish–Jewish relations during the Second World War that the greatest progress has been made. At the Oxford conference, the London-based Rafael Scharf, one of the main organizers of the conference and a key figure in Polish–Jewish dialogue, gave a speech with the telling title *Cum ira et studio* ("with anger and partisanship"), a play on the well-known statement by the Roman historian Tacitus, that history should be written *sine ira et studio*—without anger and partisanship. In it he expressed his pain at the fact that the "fabric of Polish-Jewish cohabitation on Polish soil has been irreversibly destroyed." He referred to the "trauma of unreciprocated love" of the Jews of "this last generation, nearing its close," who "cannot erase from their hearts this country where 'they were born and grew up,' where ... they loved the landscape, the language, the poetry; where they were ready to shed their blood for Poland and to be her true sons. That this was evidently not enough leaves them broken-hearted."

This speech seems to have been a key factor in leading the Kraków-based literary critic Jan Błoński to write his article "Biedni Polacy patrzą na getto" (The poor Poles look at the ghetto) in *Tygodnik Powszechny* on January 11, 1987,[32] a major turning-point in the discussion of Polish–Jewish issues in postwar Poland. In it he called on Poles to accept some degree of responsibility for the fate of their Jewish fellow citizens under Nazi occupation. He explicitly referred to Scharf's speech as the spur that led him to take up his pen:

> I recall one moving speech at the Oxford conference, in which the speaker started by comparing the Jewish attitude to Poland to unrequited love. Despite the suffering and all the problems which beset our mutual relations, he continued, the Jewish community had a genuine attachment to their adopted country. Here they found a home, a sense

---

1918–1942 [Sefer, sofer, ve'iton: merkaz hatarbut hayehudit bevarshah 1918–1942] (Jerusalem: Magnes Press, 2003); Marci Shore, *Caviar and Ashes: A Warsaw Generation's Life and Death in Marxism, 1918–1968* (New Haven, CT: Yale University Press, 2006); Katrin Steffen, *Jüdische Polonität. Ethnizität und Nation im Spiegel der polnischsprachigen jüdischen Presse 1918–1939* (Göttingen: Vandenhoeck und Ruprecht, 2004); Anna Landau-Czajka, *Syn będzie Lech ... Asymilacja Żydów w Polsce międzywojennej* [Your son will be named Lech ... The assimilation of Jews in interwar Poland] (Warsaw: Wydawnictwo "Neriton," 2006); and Joanna Nalewajko-Kulikov, *Obywatel Jidyszlandu: Rzecz o żydowskich komunistach w Polsce* [A citizen of Yiddishland: On Jewish communists in Poland] (Warsaw: Wydawnictwo "Neriton," 2009).

32 Jan Błoński, "Biedni Polacy patrzą na getto" [The poor Poles look at the ghetto], *Tygodnik Powszechny*, January 11, 1987. For an English translation, see Antony Polonsky, ed., *"My Brother's Keeper?" Recent Polish Debates on the Holocaust* (London: Routledge, 1990), 34–52.

of security. There was, conscious or unconscious, an expectation that their fate would improve, the burden of humiliation would lighten, that the future would gradually become brighter. What actually happened was exactly the opposite. "Nothing can ever change now," he concluded. Jews do not have and cannot have any future in Poland. "Do tell us, though," he finally demanded, "that what has happened to us was not our fault. We do not ask for anything else. But we do hope for such an acknowledgment?"

The controversy over Błoński's article revealed that the desire to come to terms with the more problematic aspects of the Polish–Jewish past was still to be found only within a minority of the Polish intelligentsia and was certainly not shared by society as a whole. Indeed, the article caused widespread shock in Poland, and Błoński's position was rejected by most of the two hundred individuals who participated in the debate. Characteristically, similar criticism was voiced by people with very different ideological backgrounds, ranging from communist official circles to the right wing of Solidarity. Many accused Błoński and the editors of *Tygodnik Powszechny* of playing into the hands of Poland's enemies and of endorsing anti-Polish propaganda, and some even called for Błoński to be prosecuted under the Polish criminal code for "slandering the Polish nation."

Yet in spite of views of this sort, the Błoński article did signal a new attitude in Poland and was understood in this sense by Jews involved in Polish–Jewish interaction. The parameters of the debate in Poland in the 1990s seemed to have been set by Błoński and his critics. Indeed, the decade of the 1990s saw a series of set-piece debates similar to that ignited by Błoński's article, among them one initiated by the publication in the main Polish daily newspaper, *Gazeta Wyborcza*, on January 29/30, 1994, of an article by a young (non-Jewish) historian, Michał Cichy, discussing anti-Jewish attitudes and actions by Polish military organizations and the civilian population during the sixty-three-day Warsaw uprising. A second was provoked by the exchange in the Roman Catholic *Tygodnik Powszechny* in late 1997 between Fr. Stanisław Musiał and Fr. Waldemar Chrostowski on the reaction of the Polish hierarchy to the anti-Semitic utterances of Solidarity hero Lech Wałęsa's Gdańsk confessor, priest Henryk Jankowski, and a third stimulated by sociologist Hanna Świda-Ziemba's article, "The Disgrace of Indifference," in *Gazeta Wyborcza* on August 17, 1998, which repeated in sharper form the arguments set out by Błoński.

What is striking about these debates is their moral character. It is no accident that several of them took place in a Catholic periodical. They are mostly conducted by theologians, philosophers, and literary critics. This is why Jerzy Turowicz, the veteran editor of *Tygodnik Powszechny*, who died in 1998, found it necessary to point out that the argument between the two sides was "conducted on totally different planes."[33]

At the same time, two new developments stimulated a more fundamental rethinking of attitudes toward Jews and the "Jewish question." The first was the large mass of new historical material produced in the years since 1989. This provided a much fuller picture of Polish–Jewish relations in the twentieth century, showing clearly how desperate the situation of the Jews had become by 1939, with the majority in Polish society and in Polish political parties now adopting the position that the "solution" to the "Jewish problem" was the voluntary or compulsory removal of most Jews from Poland.

The second important development was the emergence of some new Polish Jewish writers and the more widespread distribution in Poland of works of already established such authors. The 1990s were marked by an outburst of creativity by Hanna Krall and Henryk Grynberg, publication of important new writers including Wilhelm Dichter, and works by authors such as Michał Głowiński, who dealt extensively with their previously concealed Jewish backgrounds. All had in common their experience in the war as children hidden on the "Aryan" side and their maturing into adults in the complex postwar years. Their work gave a graphic and largely negative picture of what it was like to be a Jew in a hostile environment both during the war and under communism.

This was the context for the debate provoked by the publication of Jan T. Gross's *Neighbors* (Princeton, 2001), first published as *Sąsiedzi: Historia zagłady żydowskiego miasteczka* (Neighbors: The history of the destruction of a Jewish shtetl; Sejny, 2000). On the basis of evidence produced for a trial in 1949, the book describes in detail an incident in the summer 1941 in the town of Jedwabne in the northeast of today's Poland in which, with some German incitement but little actual assistance, the local population brutally murdered the overwhelming majority of its Jewish neighbors. Almost the entire Jewish population, along with many Jewish refugees from other localities, were driven out of their homes and herded to the market place. Many were beaten to death with poles, brooms, or axes. Some were murdered at the Jewish cemetery. The

---

33 Jerzy Turowicz, "Polish Reasons and Jewish Reasons," in Polonsky, *"My Brother's Keeper?"* 138.

vast majority (perhaps as many as 700) was forced to enter a barn near the cemetery, which was then set on fire, burning alive those inside.

The debate on Jedwabne was the most serious, protracted, and profound on the issue of Polish–Jewish relations since the end of the war. Gross's work has stimulated a new school of Holocaust historians in Poland at the Centrum Badań nad Zagładą Żydów (Polish Center for Holocaust Research) in Warsaw, who have concentrated on the final stage of the Holocaust in Poland that took place after the liquidation of the ghettos in the large towns. In the smaller towns of Poland, the ghettos were more porous and many Jews were able to escape—one of these historians, Andrzej Żbikowski, estimates the numbers to be more than 300,000. However, Polish–Jewish relations in these towns had been more distant before the war. The Jews who sought shelter among the local population often did not find it, and fewer than 50,000, according to his estimate, survived to the end of the war, as they were hunted down by the German occupying authorities and, in some well-documented cases, murdered by underground units or betrayed by the local population.[34] Such was the fate of the Trinczer family in Gniewczyna in southeastern Poland, described in the Catholic monthly *Znak* in 2008 in articles by Dariusz Libionka and Tadeusz Markiel, an eyewitness. It has now been the subject of a book-length study by Alina Skibińska and Tadeusz Markiel.[35] Different aspects of the problems aroused by the study of the Holocaust in Poland are discussed in the articles by Dan Michman, Andrzej Żbikowski, Daniel Blatman, Omer Bartov, and Saulius Sužiedėlis, while Jolanta Ambrosewicz-Jacobs examines the challenges new historiography poses for education about the Holocaust in Poland.

There has also been considerable debate between the more apologetic and more self-critical historians in Poland on the evaluation of the number and motivation of those Poles who risked their lives to rescue Jews.[36] Although some valuable work had been done on this problem before 1989, most notably by Teresa Prekerowa, the official line, particularly after 1968, stressed the high

---

34 Andrzej Żbikowski, "'Night Guard': Holocaust Mechanisms in the Polish Rural Areas, 1942–1945," *East European Politics and Societies* 3 (2011): 512–29.

35 *Jakie to ma znaczenie, czy zrobili to z chciwości? Zagłada domu Trynczerów* [What does it matter if they did it out of greed? The murder of the Trynczer family] (Warsaw: Stowarzyszenie Centrum Badań nad Zagładą Żydów, 2011).

36 This issue is discussed in a nuanced and balanced manner by Joanna Michlic in her article "'The Many Faces of Memories': How Do Jews and the Holocaust Matter in Postcommunist Poland," in *Lessons and Legacies*, ed. and with an introduction by Hilary Earl and Karl A. Schleunes, vol. 11 of *Expanding Perspectives on the Holocaust in a Changing World* (Evanston, IL: Northwestern University Press, 2014), 156–62.

number of rescuers, downplayed the fact that their actions were often disapproved of by society, and failed to differentiate the different categories of rescuers, protectors, and helpers or to examine their motivations. This approach was continued by Gross's critics in the controversy aroused by his *Sąsiedzi* and gained the support of the right-wing government of the Kaczyński brothers after 2005. It played an important role in the politics of memory (*polityka historyczna*) initiated by that government, whose goals were made explicit by Jarosław Kaczyński, who argued that:

> we are faced with a situation where in the next few decades or less World War II will be understood as two great crimes: the Holocaust, in which Poles allegedly took part, and the expulsion of the Germans [from Eastern Europe in 1945], also in part the outcome of Polish actions.[37]

In the debate over Gross's book, his critics frequently alluded to the more than 6,300 Christian Polish rescuers of Jews who have so far been honored by the Yad Vashem Memorial Institute in Jerusalem. They often claimed that this figure was only a fraction of the total number. Thus, Marcin Urynowicz, basing himself on the numerical estimates made by Gunnar Paulsson of Jews who survived in wartime Warsaw, which many scholars have argued are exaggerated, asserted that there were 400,000 Christian Polish rescuers of Jews.[38] They also frequently alluded to the heroic actions of people like Irena Sendler in Warsaw, whose organization saved at least 700 Jewish children from the Warsaw Ghetto, and the Ulma family in Markowa in the Rzeszów district of Poland, who were murdered by the Germans along with the Jews they were sheltering.

The apologetic character of much of this research led to attempts to place the situation of rescuers in a larger historical context, stressing how they were frequently regarded with hostility by the surrounding population and pointing out the often complex character of their motivation in providing assistance. The figures given by Urynowicz were subjected to a devastating critique by Jacek Leociak and Dariusz Libionka,[39] while research has also elucidated the complex situation in the Rzeszów district, where, after the murder of the

---

37 "Antypolski paszkwil" [An Anti-Polish Slander], *Gazeta Wyborcza* [Electoral Journal], February 9–10, 2008.
38 Marcin Urynowicz, "Liczenie z pamięci" [Dealing with memory], *Tygodnik Powszechny* [The Universal Weekly], October 30, 2007. Paulsson's estimate is found in *Secret City: The Hidden Jews of Warsaw, 1940–1945* (New Haven, CT: Yale University Press, 2002).
39 "Żonglerka liczbami" [A juggler with numbers], *Tygodnik Powszechny*, November 27, 2007.

Ulmas, a large number of families who were hiding Jews handed them over to the Nazis or the Polish police, or, in some cases, murdered them.[40] A whole issue of the yearbook *Zagłada Żydów. Studia i Materiały* was devoted to this subject. It included several articles examining paid rescuers, some of whom later denounced those they rescued or murdered their Jewish charges. There have also been other important works on this topic.[41] The last word has clearly not been said on this important matter, and the need for a comprehensive and nuanced history of the rescue of Jews in Poland is one of the tasks still awaiting the investigation of the Holocaust in Poland.

What has become clear in these debates is that adoption, planning, and implementation of a policy of the mass murder of the Jews here was the work of the Nazi leadership and the German people who for the most part willingly and unwillingly followed their lead. At the same time, the Nazis gave considerable incentives, both political and material, to those who participated in this genocide and brutally punished, sometimes by death, those who attempted to assist their Jewish neighbors. One important way forward in the treatment of this issue is to compare the responses of the different national groups of the area to the anti-Jewish genocide—Poles, Lithuanians, Ukrainians, and Belarusians. In addition, these groups—unlike the Jews—for most part saw themselves as fighting two occupying forces during the Second World War: the Nazis and the Soviets. In spite of the reservations many Jews had about Soviet policy, the Soviets gave them the opportunity to survive, and they therefore had no choice but to support them.

---

40 Elżbieta Rączy, *Pomoc Polaków dla ludnosci żydowskiej na Rzeszowszczyźnie, 1939–1945* [The assistance of Poles to the Jewish population in the Rzeszów area] (Rzeszów: Instytut Pamięci Narodowej—Komisja Ścigania Zbrodni przeciwko Narodowi Polskiemu, 2008).

41 Among them one could mention Jan Grabowski, "Rescue for Money: Paid Helpers in Poland, 1939–1945," *Search and Research: Lectures and Papers* 13 (Jerusalem, 2008); Witold Mędykowski, "Sprawiedliwi, niesprawiedliwi? O złożoności stosunków pomiędzy ratującymi a ocalonymi w okresie Zagłady [Righteous, unrighteous? On the complicated relations between rescuers and rescued during the Holocaust]," in *Z dziejów polsko-żydowskich w XX wieku* [On Polish-Jewish history in the twentieth century], ed. Edyta Czop and Elżbieta Rączy (Rzeszów: Instytut Pamięci Narodowej—Komisja Ścigania Zbrodni Przeciwko Narodowi Polskiemu, Oddział w Rzeszowie, 2009), 27–37; Andrzej Żbikowski, ed., *Polacy i Żydzi pod okupacją niemiecką 1939–1945: Studia i materiały* [Poles and Jews under German occupation 1939-1945: Studies and documents] (Warsaw: Instytut Pamięci Narodowej—Komisja Ścigania Zbrodni przeciwko Narodowi Polskiemu, 2006), chapters 9 and 10, by Elżbieta Rączy and Anna Pyżewska, respectively; Jacek Leociak, *Ratowanie: Opowieści Polaków i Żydów* [Rescue: Stories of Poles and Jews] (Kraków: Wydawnictwo Literackie, 2010); and Małgorzata Melchior, *Zagłada i tożsamość: Polscy Żydzi ocaleni "na aryjskich papierach"* [The Holocaust and identity: Polish Jews saved on "aryan papers"] (Warsaw: Wydawnictwo IFiS PAN, 2004).

Great progress has also been made in the study of the postwar years, both in the period down to the negotiated end of communism in 1989 and in the more than a quarter of a century of democratic rule.[42] A number of themes can be observed in the history of the Jews in Poland which extend over the whole period. The underlying assumptions of the presentation of the postwar years in POLIN Museum form the subject of the article by one of its curators, Stanisław Krajewski, and are discussed in the articles by Andrzej Paczkowski and Marci Shore. The first was the failure to establish a viable Jewish community in the period of communist rule between 1944 and 1989. Only 350,000 of the estimated prewar Jewish population in 1939 of 3,330,000 were still alive at the end of the war, of whom perhaps 50,000 had survived in Poland. Not all of them returned to Poland from the Soviet Union, where the largest proportion had survived. As a result, in the immediate postwar period, the Jewish population of the country numbered nearly 300,000. They were, for the most part, resettled in the western territories acquired from Germany. Łódź, the largest undestroyed city in the country, also became a major Jewish center. Many of the Jews who had survived were unwilling to remain in a country where most of their relatives and friends had perished, while their experience of the Soviet Union made them unwilling to live under a communist dictatorship. They were, moreover, threatened by a wave of anti-Jewish violence. Andrzej Żbikowski points out that "there is no way of establishing accurately the number of Jews murdered directly after the war." In his view, the present state of research indicates that at least 650–750 Jews perished in this way and that "there were probably many

---

42 *Jewish Presence in Absence: Aftermath of the Holocaust in Poland, 1945–2010*, ed. Feliks Tych and Monika Adamczyk-Garbowska (Jerusalem: Yad Vashem, International Institute for Holocaust Research, 2014), an English translation of *Następstwa zagłady Żydów: Polska 1944–2010* (Lublin: Wydawnictwo Uniwersytetu Marii Curie-Skłodowskiej; Warszawa: Żydowski Instytut Historyczny im. Emanuela Ringelbluma, 2012); Alina Cała, *Ochrona bezpieczeństwa fizycznego Żydów w Polsce powojennej. Komisje specjalne przy Centralnym Komitecie Żydów w Polsce* [The personal protection of Jews in postwar Poland. The Special Commissions of the Central Committee of Jews in Poland] (Warsaw: Żydowski Instytut Historyczny im. Emanuela Ringelbluma, 2014); Andrzej Żbikowski, *Sąd społeczny przy CKŻP. Wojenne rozliczenia społeczności żydowskiej w Polsce* [The Social Court of the CKŻP. Coming to terms with the legacy of the war in the Jewish community in Poland] (Warsaw: Żydowski Instytut Historyczny im. Emanuela Ringelbluma, 2014); August Grabski, *Centralny Komitet Żydów w Polsce (1944–1950). Historia polityczna* [The Central Committee of Jews in Poland 1944–1950. Politic history] (Warsaw: Żydowski Instytut Historyczny im. Emanuela Ringelbluma, 2015); Piotr Kendziorek, *Program i praktyka produktywizacji Żydów polskich w działalności CKŻP* [The program and practice of the productivization of the Jews in the activity of the CKŻP] (Warsaw: Żydowski Instytut Historyczny im. Emanuela Ringelbluma, 2016).

more tragic incidents of which no written evidence has survived."⁴³ Feliks Tych estimates the number killed as around 2,000.⁴⁴

The violence was the result of a number of factors. The war had not brought an end to anti-Semitism or seriously compromised the anti-Semitic ideology, since the Nazis had persecuted the Polish radical Right, the main supporters of anti-Semitism in Poland, as fiercely as they did all other manifestations of Polish resistance to their rule. In addition, anti-Semitism had been deliberately encouraged by the Nazis and intensified by the long-standing identification of Jews with communism. This was reinforced by the belief in extensive Jewish collaboration with the Soviet occupying authorities in eastern Poland between 1939 and 1941 and by the presence of a number of people of Jewish origin in prominent positions in the postwar government. In these circumstances, old superstitions could take on a new incarnation. The worst outbreak of anti-Jewish violence took place in Kielce in July 1946, when the 200 Jewish survivors of the prewar community of around 18,000 were attacked by an angry mob, incited by rumors that a Christian boy had been abducted by the Jews, who needed his blood because their wartime experiences had left them anemic. In the ensuing mayhem, forty-two Jews were murdered and another thirty were murdered in the vicinity of the town.

One important factor in the violence was the failure of the Catholic church to condemn it unequivocally. Anti-Semitism in the immediate postwar period was also intensified by the fear of those who had benefited from the expropriation of Jewish property that they would be forced to return it to its former owners and by the breakdown of law and order, which had begun during the Nazi occupation and led to a general barbarization of society and an increase in crime. The massive postwar expulsions of Germans, Poles, and Ukrainians encouraged those who thought that Poland's few remaining Jews could also be expelled. Anti-Jewish violence was also a product of the near civil war conditions. This violence is discussed in the articles by Grzegorz Berendt and August Grabski.

In all, by 1950, some 180,000 Jews had left the country, most of them going to Israel, leaving an estimated number in Poland in 1955 of between 72,000

---

43 Andrzej Żbikowski, "The Post-War Wave of Pogroms and Killings," in *Jewish Presence in Absence: Aftermath of the Holocaust in Poland, 1945–2010*, 94.
44 Discussion at the conference "The Aftermath of the Holocaust: Poland 1944–2010," The inaugural conference of the Diana Zborowski Center for the Study of the Aftermath of the Holocaust, a part of the International Institute for Holocaust Research at Yad Vashem, October 3–6, 2010.

and 80,000. Some have questioned whether this remnant could be described as a functioning community. Certainly, only a small proportion declared themselves Jewish in their personal documents, or belonged to one of the two Jewish communal organizations. In effect, what made them Jewish was that they were so regarded by the surrounding society and the authorities.

The years 1956–1958 saw a further exodus of Jews from Poland, which continued into the early 1960s. This was caused, at least in part, by a sense of insecurity arising out of the open expression of anti-Jewish sentiments, which accompanied the crisis that brought Władysław Gomułka to power. Anti-Jewish hostility had a number of sources. In part, it was the product of the interparty struggle in which the hardline Natolin group within the Polish United Workers' Party (Polska Zjenoczona Partia Robotnicza—PZPR) used anti-Jewish slogans to strengthen their position and discredit their opponents. In addition, hostility to Jews seems to have been fairly widespread in the party, in part among those who felt that political liberalization would threaten the social advances they had made in the previous decade. As was the case later with the partisans, anti-Semitism was also a tool with which to purge one's opponents. There was, in addition, a grassroots anti-Semitism, which drew on the well-established stereotype of Judaeo-communism and on the belief that Jews had played a key role in the Stalinist system. It is not clear how widespread such sentiments were.

There were other factors in the Jewish exodus. Emigration had been halted in 1951, and many of those who had wanted to leave then now took the opportunity to do so. So too did many of the 18,000 Jews who were able to return to Poland (along with another 249,000 Poles) under the new repatriation agreement with the Soviet Union signed in November 1956. In all, between 1956 and 1960 more than 51,000 Jews along with non-Jewish members of their families left Poland, including 13,000 repatriates. By the early 1960s, the Jewish population had stabilized at somewhere between 22,000 and 35,000, most of whom had no affiliation with the organized Jewish institutions.

A further exodus took place as a consequence of the "anti-Zionist" campaign of 1968, in which some 9,000 people lost their jobs, the great majority of them Jews. At this time, more than 15,000 Jews and non-Jewish family members left Poland for Israel, Western Europe, and North America. Those who left were given a travel document stating that the bearer was "not a Polish citizen" and were required to declare that their destination was Israel, where only approximately a quarter of them settled. Those who emigrated in these different periods retained some links with Poland and also influenced how

Poland was understood in the outside world. This topic is the theme of Audrey Kichelewski's article, "In or Out? Identities and Images of Poland among Polish Jews in the Postwar Years."

Jan T. Gross has characterized fear as the main emotion felt by those Jews in Poland in the immediate postwar years who had survived the Holocaust. It is certainly true that the anti-Jewish violence and the problems inherent in regaining property taken during the war created serious difficulties for Jewish survivors. At the same time, there was also hope, shared by many Poles, that the new Poland would prove democratic and pluralistic and that it would be possible to find a place in it for the surviving Jews. This is a second theme in the postwar history of the Jews in Poland. The key factor in the revival of Jewish life was the Central Committee of Jews in Poland (Centralny Komitet Żydów w Polsce; CKŻP), which had the support of a number of international Jewish organizations, above all the American Joint Jewish Distribution Committee. One of the main preoccupations of the Jewish leadership in Poland and its foreign supporters was to create a stable economic base for the surviving Jews. A significant proportion of the funds from outside also went to support the Jewish school system. A major concern of the Jewish organizations in postwar Poland was to provide for those children who had survived and also to reclaim children who had been adopted by non-Jewish families or were being sheltered in convents. An umbrella Zionist organization, *Koordynacja*, was established to find such children, and until April 1948 more than 1,000 lived at some stage in its homes. There was also strong competition between the Zionists and the communists for control of orphaned children.

Apart from the Orthodox, all the main Jewish political groupings were represented on the CKŻP, the Zionists, the Bundists, and the communists, and this became the main arena for the political conflicts on the Jewish street. When it was formed in Lublin late in 1944, it had a clear Zionist majority. In 1946, as a result of negotiations between the various Jewish groupings, its presidium was made up of thirteen Zionists, four Bundists, six communists, and two representatives of the Union of Jewish Partisans (Związek Partyzantów Żydowskich). The Orthodox Agudah and Mizrahi parties refused to participate because of the failure of the CKŻP to observe the Sabbath. In addition, the needs of religious Jews were catered for by the Organizational Committee of Jewish Religious Associations (Komitet Organizacyjny Żydowskich Zrzeszeń Religijnych), which was soon renamed the Jewish Religious Congregation (Kongregacja Wyznania Mojżeszowego) and which, in August 1949, became the Religious Union of the Jewish Faith (Związek Religijny Wyznania Mojżeszowego).

Attempts were also made to revive Jewish culture. The most successful was the project to document the tragic fate of the Jews during the war. On August 29, 1944, barely a month after the liberation of Lublin, a group of five Polish Jews established the Historical Commission (Komisja Historyczna), affiliated to the Jewish Committee, which four months later was reorganized as the Central Jewish Historical Commission in Poland. It sought to collect testimonies from the survivors, calling on them to assist by "immediately delivering [to the members of the Commission] any materials at present in private hands" and providing accounts of their wartime experiences, since "each and every Jew that has remained alive is a part of history."[45] The importance of these testimonies is highlighted by a number of the contributions to this volume. Subsequently, many memorial books (*yizker-bikher*) were produced, almost all outside Poland, which both allowed the expression of collective trauma and provided valuable information to historians.

The history of Polish Jewry, like the history of Poland itself, took a radical new turn with the communist establishment of a monopoly of power in 1947. The authorities now proceeded, under the close supervision of the Kremlin, to impose their own "solution" to the "Jewish question," which involved the suppression of all groups not under direct communist control. In February 1949, the CKŻP was taken over by the communists, and its chairman, Emil Sommerstein, and a number of other noncommunist members, including Adolf Berman, the brother of Jakub Berman, the éminence grise of the regime, responsible for propaganda, ideology, and the security services. Like the Polish Socialist Party, the Bund was forced to unite with the Polish Workers' Party (Polska Partia Robotnicza; PPR), and all independent Jewish newspapers were suppressed. From the second half of 1948, the Jewish section of the PZPR, like the party as a whole, began to attack Zionism much more aggressively, and, in July 1949, the Ministry of Public Administration prohibited the organization of Zionist summer camps. In the autumn, all Zionist parties were banned. In April 1949, the various Jewish school networks, which now had around 3,000 Jewish pupils (60 percent of the Jewish age cohort) in eighteen schools, were taken over by the government. In October 1950, the CKŻP merged with the Jewish Cultural Society (Żydowskie Towarzystwo Kultury; ŻTK), which

---

45 "Tzu Ale Yidn in Poyln/Do Wszystkich Żydów w Polsce" [To All Jews in Poland: Appeal in Yiddish and in Polish], Towarzystwo Przyjaciół Centralnej Żydowskiej Komisji Historycznej przy CKŻ w Polsce, Łódź, ul. Narutowicza, 25. YIVO, RG 1258, box 11, file 474. Signed by the President Dr. Szykier, the vice president Dr. Mandelbaum, and the secretary Dr. Balberyszski.

had been set up in autumn 1947 to form the Social-Cultural Association of Jews in Poland (Towarzystwo Społeczno-Kulturalne Żydów; TSKŻ), firmly under communist control and with no political role. Already in the previous year the Joint Distribution Committee had been compelled to halt its activities in Poland.

One of the most disputed issues in the historiography of this period is the role played by communists of Jewish origin in the new regime. The war had certainly strengthened the perceived identification of Jews with communism. In their hope that the new regime would remedy the defects of the Second Republic, Jewish supporters of the new order were at one with a significant part of the Polish intelligentsia. In addition, in the near civil war conditions of postwar Poland the Jewish community could expect protection only from the new communist-dominated authorities.

Communists of Jewish origin played a significant, though not dominant, role in the new regime. In the political apparatus, they included Jakub Berman; Roman Zambrowski, who had been one of the principal creators of the communist-dominated Polish army in the USSR; and Hilary Minc, a key economic planner. Jews also played a key role in the cultural policy of the new regime, among them Jerzy Borejsza, the founder of the journal *Odrodzenie* and chief executive of the Czytelnik publishing house, until he was dismissed from all his positions in 1949.

However, anti-Semitism was also not absent from the PPR itself. Official government policy was to defend the Jews and foster their economic rehabilitation, but within the party some factions were much less sympathetic to the difficult plight of the Jews. This was also the case in the local administration. In the country as a whole, Jews were widely viewed as playing a key role in the security apparatus of the new regime. Certainly, there were a number of Jews in leading positions in the security apparatus, including Anatol Fejgin, the head of the notorious Tenth Department of the Ministry of Public Security (Ministerstwo Bezpieczeństwa Publicznego; MBP), which was responsible for the surveillance of all members of the PZPR, and his deputy Józef Światło. At the same time, there was a strong tendency to categorize as Jews anyone of whom one disapproved. Thus, in his account of his tenure as American ambassador in Poland, Arthur Bliss Lane, writing presumably under the influence of his Polish contacts, described Stanisław Radkiewicz, the non-Jewish minister of public security, as "a good-looking man, apparently of Russian Semitic origin, with carefully combed oily black hair, a keen mobile aesthetic face."[46]

---

46 Arthur Bliss Lane, *I Saw Poland Betrayed* (Indianapolis: Bobbs-Merrill Co., 1948), 165.

Introduction

Our understanding of the situation in Poland, as of that in the Soviet Union, has been transformed by the opening of archives, which give a much fuller picture both of the role of Jews in the Polish security apparatus in the immediate postwar years and of the process by which they were purged from it after the death of Stalin. They have revealed that Jews made up a significant proportion of the workforce of the Ministry of Public Security, though never a majority, and that Soviet "advisors" played a key role. The percentage of Jews in the head office fluctuated between 30 and 40 percent, with the exception of the years 1944 and 1945, when it was somewhat lower. In the local administration, the percentage of people of Jewish origin was much smaller. Of course, these were communists and internationalists far from any involvement in Jewish life. They entered the security service at a time in which the struggle to impose communism was particularly intense and when loyalty to the system was the overriding criterion both of the Polish communist leadership and their Soviet overlords.

After 1956, Jews were to be largely purged from the security apparatus. Even in the period between 1944 and 1955 their role had aroused opposition among "native" communists, who felt that the significant number of people of Jewish origin in important governmental positions increased their own unpopularity in Polish society and barred their path to high office. Why was it that Jews were allowed to hold a considerable number of important posts in the security apparatus in Poland when they had already been removed from such positions in the Soviet Union, at a time when Stalin was engaged in the destruction of the Soviet Yiddish cultural establishment and in a full-scale purge of "Jewish cosmopolitans"?

At its root, the presence of communists of Jewish origin in significant positions in the security apparatus must be seen as a consequence of Stalin's deep distrust of the Poles. It took place at the same time as the purge of Yiddish cultural activists in the Soviet Union and the wider campaign against "cosmopolitanism," which was essentially an attack on Russified Jews within the new Soviet intelligentsia. The retention of Jews in these positions in Poland was clearly intended by Stalin to be a temporary expedient until a larger group of reliable local communists could be trained. Indeed, the history of Polish communism can be seen as the unsuccessful attempt to create such a group.

The thaw period from 1954 to the early 1960s saw the final removal of Jews from the security apparatus. A series of defections by intelligence officers of Jewish origin in the Polish Military Intelligence Service, which started with that of Paweł Monat in September 1959, had already set in motion a succession of countermeasures that aroused intense suspicion and paranoia, as well as anti-Semitism, throughout the military and in the state security organs. Investigations accused Jews collectively of disloyalty and undermined the position of those among them who remained inside the party state apparatus. One result was that the most senior Polish Jew in the party, Politburo member Roman Zambrowski, was forced to resign in 1963.

At the same time, among those who remained in Poland, the processes of acculturation and Polonization proceeded rapidly—another major theme in postwar Jewish history in Poland. This made the revival of Yiddish cultural life difficult to achieve. A number of major Yiddish writers, including Chaim Grade and Avrom Sutzkever, spent short periods in Poland after the war, but soon moved on to the United States and Israel. Some other surviving Yiddish writers, like Itsik Manger, Sholem Asch, and Isaac Bashevis Singer, remained in the West. A small number did reestablish themselves in Poland, including Binem Heller, Leib Olitski, Hadasah Rubin, Lili Berger, Moshe Szkliar, Shlomo Beilis-Legis, and Daniel Kac, but most subsequently emigrated in 1956 and 1968.

One index of Jewish acculturation was the large role played in Polish literary life by people of Jewish origin and the emergence of what has been called "the Jewish School of Polish Literature"—a group of writers including Julian Stryjkowski, Stanisław Wygodzki, Henryk Grynberg, Bohdan Wojdowski, and Hanna Krall—who have explored the main dilemmas faced by Polish Jewry, above all, how to record and memorialize the Holocaust and how to go on living in the country where it took place and where the attitude of the majority of the population left a great deal to be desired.

A third theme is the slow and incomplete revival of Jewish life since 1989. The events of 1968 dealt a devastating blow to organized Jewish life in Poland. In 1971, a publication of the New York–based Committee for Jews in Poland described the "recent exodus of the Jews from Poland" as "the end of a thousand years." Yet, from the late 1970s, Jewish life began to revive. People of Jewish origin, including Stanisław Krajewski, Konstanty Gebert, and Adam Michnik, who came from the Polonized Warsaw Jewish milieu, played a large role in the political unrest that ultimately gave rise to Solidarity in the summer of 1980. In the summer of 1979, the American sociologist Carl Rogers had conducted a workshop in Poland. Approximately ten of those attending discovered that they shared a similar Jewish background, which became apparent during a special smaller session devoted to the subject of Jews in Poland. Discussion of their Jewish background continued in Warsaw and involved members of the liberal Club of the Catholic Intelligentsia (Klub Inteligencji Katolickiej). As early as

1971, members of the club organized the first annual Week of Jewish Culture, intended to provide a better "understanding of the rich and yet poorly known culture" of a people that "lived among us for centuries" and whose "gigantic tragedy in the last war we witnessed." The discussions took place in different private apartments in order to circumvent restrictions on meeting. The group called itself the Jewish Flying University (Żydowski Uniwersytet Latający; ŻUL), modeling itself on the Flying University organized by the democratic opposition, itself drawing on experiences of the similar movement that had functioned under Russian rule before 1914.

The group, which numbered nearly one hundred, met periodically until the imposition of martial law in December 1981. According to one of its founders, Konstanty Gebert, they regarded themselves as the "last Jews" of Poland, although the nature of their Jewish identity was still undefined. Essentially, their interest in their Jewish background was driven not so much by a desire for Jewish continuity or religious belief as by their opposition to the communist regime and the desire to shape a Polish identity with which they could identify.

As martial law was relaxed, the group resumed its activities and, in April 1983, it took part in an alternative, oppositional celebration of the fortieth anniversary of the Warsaw Ghetto Uprising. Their activities continued on a larger scale after the negotiated end of communism in 1989. It is difficult to give an accurate estimate of the number of Jews who remained in Poland. According to the Polish census of 2002, some 1,100 people gave their ethnicity as Jewish. The 2005 survey of the Jewish population estimates the core Jewish population as 3,300. These figures clearly underestimate the number of people with some connection to Jewish life; according to Michael Schudrich, chief rabbi of Poland, there are at least 30,000–40,000 Jews in Poland. The number of people with some connection to the Jewish world is considerably larger.

With the end of communism and the decline in hostility to Jews, more people have been willing to acknowledge their Jewish identity, while significant numbers of "hidden children" were told of their Jewish roots by their Christian foster parents. Although the community is small, it has shown remarkable dynamism since 1989, partly as a result of a new generation of leaders, above all the journalist Konstanty Gebert and the philosopher Stanisław Krajewski. The two principal Jewish organizations remain the Union of Jewish Religious Communities, which was reorganized in 1993, and the Social and Cultural Association of Jews, which existed throughout the communist period but which has been transformed since 1989. Each has around 2,000 members.

Other smaller Jewish organizations are the Polish Union of Jewish Students, reorganized in March 2007 as the All-Poland Jewish Youth Organization (Żydowska Ogólnopolska Organizacja Młodzieżowa) and the Association of Children of the Holocaust (Stowarzyszenie Dzieci Holokaustu), which is made up of child survivors. The Ronald S. Lauder Foundation funds the Lauder-Morasha School, the only Jewish school in Warsaw, as well as summer and winter camps. Additional funding for the community is provided by the Ted Taube Foundation and from proceeds of the restitution of communal property under a law passed in 1997. The Lauder Foundation has also sponsored the publication of a high-quality monthly, *Midrasz*, originally edited by Konstanty Gebert and now by Piotr Paziński, which is devoted to past and present Polish Jewry. The Joint Distribution Committee and the Jewish Agency both have offices in Poland. In 2004, the late Chris Schwarz, a British photographer, and Professor Jonathan Webber of the University of Birmingham founded the Galicia Jewish Museum in Kazimierz, dedicated to the celebration of Jewish culture in Galicia and the commemoration of victims of the Holocaust. In June 2007, the cornerstone was laid of the ambitious museum of the history of Polish Jews in Warsaw, with a remarkable design by two Finnish architects, Rainer Mahlamäki and Ilmari Lahdelma. In Oświęcim, under the influence of the New York–based philanthropist Fred Schwarz, the Auschwitz Jewish Center has been established with a prayer hall and museum, located in the premises of a prewar *beit midrash*.

Some aspects of the revival of Jewish life in Poland have only been possible because of the participation of non-Jewish enthusiasts. The Kraków Festival of Jewish Culture, first held in 1988 and organized by Janusz Makuch, has become an annual event, drawing more than 20,000 people for eight days of music, theater, art exhibitions, and workshops, led mostly by Jewish performers and educators from Europe, Israel, and North America. The Center for Jewish Culture, established in 1993 by the Judaica Foundation and headed by Joachim Russek, runs programs of Jewish and civic interest in a restored *beit midrash* in Kazimierz. Finally, the Pogranicze (Borderland) Foundation was established in 1990 by Krzysztof Czyżewski in Sejny, near the Polish border with Lithuania, Belarus, and the Kaliningradskaya oblast. Its goal is to examine and commemorate the multicultural and multiethnic heritage of this region.

Jewish studies have also thrived. The Jewish Historical Institute, established in 1947, has had a new lease of life since 1989 and has reorganized its archives and undertaken an extensive program of publication under its former director Feliks Tych, which was extended by his successors, Eleonora Bergman and Paweł

Śpiewak. Its journal, *Kwartalnik Historii Żydów* (formerly *Biuletyn Żydowskiego Instytutu Historycznego*), is one of the best in the field. Impressive Jewish studies programs have also been established at the universities of Warsaw, Lublin, Poznań, Wrocław, Gdańsk, and Łódź and at the Jagiellonian University in Kraków. In 1995, the Polskie Towarzystwo Studiów Żydowskich (Polish Association for Jewish Studies) was formed with its headquarters in the department of Jewish studies at the Jagiellonian University. Today it has around ninety members.

One of the most difficult tasks facing the community is the preservation of Jewish heritage in Poland. Poland has more than 400 synagogues still standing, which are used for various purposes, some appropriate and others not. In addition, there are at least 1,400 Jewish cemeteries, a few well preserved, many in a perilous state. Some of the synagogues have been returned to the community under the communal restitution law, but resources for large-scale preservation are not available.

Certainly, the efforts of all those involved in the recreation of Jewish life in Poland have been little short of Herculean. Yet, at the same time, a note of caution should be added. It may be possible for a Jewish community as small as that in Poland to survive on the basis of pride in its past, rather than upon the existence of a critical mass of Jews prepared to commit themselves to sustaining the collective Jewish existence. It remains an open question as to whether this community can again become self-sustaining and a significant cultural center, even on a much smaller scale than in its heyday.

A final theme is the slow posthumous integration of the Jews into Polish history and the attempts to come to terms with the painful legacy of the past. We have already discussed this process in the context of the debates about the Holocaust. A major factor in this is the opening of POLIN Museum of the History of Polish Jews. It is located on a highly symbolic square, site of the imposing monument of Natan Rapoport to the "Jewish People, Its Martyrs and Fighters" and also of monuments to Jan Karski and Willy Brandt and a passageway named after Irena Sendler, who was responsible for rescuing a large number of Jewish children from the Warsaw Ghetto. It is a stone's throw away from 18 Miła Street, the site of the bunker where, at the end of the Warsaw Ghetto uprising, its leaders, including Mordecai Anielewicz, died rather than be taken prisoner by the Germans. We believe that its permanent exhibition, which offers a vivid picture of the complex past of what was once the largest Jewish community in the world, will transform the way the history of Polish Jews is understood and appreciated in Poland and the world, for Poles, Jews, and the international public. We believe that the essays in this volume will not only give a clear picture of the present state of the historiography of the long history of the Jews in the Polish lands but will also show how the permanent exhibition of the museum was put together and how it has attempted to portray this history. It is our hope that in the discussion of problems in Polish–Jewish relations, we are now beginning to enter a new stage, in which apologies and apologetics will increasingly be replaced by careful and detailed research and reliable firsthand testimony. The goal should be to move beyond strongly held, competing, and incompatible narratives of the past and reach some consensus that will be acceptable to all people of goodwill and will bring about a degree of normalization both in Poles' attitudes to the past and in Polish–Jewish relations. We strongly believe this book will contribute to this process.

* * *

We are extremely grateful to all those scholars who have contributed to this important volume. We should also like to thank Magdalena Prokopowicz, Publications Officer at POLIN Museum of the History of Polish Jews, Joyce Rappoport, Academic Studies Press and especially Kira Nemirovsky, its production manager, and editors at POLIN Museum of the History of Polish Jews, Tamara Łozińska and Zofia Sochańska, for their help in editing and producing it. Financial support has been provided by the Museum's Global Education Outreach Program, the Taube Foundation for Jewish Life & Culture, the William K. Bowes, Jr. Foundation and the Association of the Jewish Historical Institute of Poland.

List of Contributors

Jolanta Ambrosewicz-Jacobs is director of the Center for Holocaust Studies at the Jagiellonian University in Kraków and teaches courses on the Holocaust at the Institute for European Studies. She has been a Pew Fellow at the Center for the Study of Human Rights at Columbia University and the 2011–12 Ina Levine Scholar at the United States Holocaust Memorial Museum. Among her publications are *Me—Us—Them: Ethnic Prejudices and Alternative Methods of Education: The Case of Poland* (Kraków, 2003) and *Tolerancja. Jak uczyć siebie i innych* (Tolerance. How to teach ourselves and others; Kraków, 2003, 2004). She edited *The Holocaust. Voices of Scholars* (Kraków, 2009); coedited, with Krystyna Oleksy, *Pamięć. Świadomość. Odpowiedzialność* (Remembrance, awareness, responsibility; Oświęcim, 2008); and coedited, with Leszek Hońdo, *Why Should We Teach about the Holocaust?* (Kraków, 2003, 2004, 2005).

David Assaf is professor of modern Jewish history and head of the department of Jewish history at Tel Aviv University. He holds the Sir Isaac Wolfson Chair of Jewish Studies and is director of the Institute for the History of Polish Jewry. His field of expertise is the history and culture of the Jewish traditional society in Eastern Europe, especially the history of Hasidism during the nineteenth century. He has published numerous books and articles in his field, including *The Regal Way: The Life and Times of Rabbi Israel of Ruzhin* (Stanford, CA, 2002); *Bratslav: An Annotated Bibliography* (Jerusalem, 2000); *Untold Tales of the Hasidim: Crisis and Discontent in the History of Hasidism* (Waltham, MA, 2010); and, most recently, *Beguiled by Knowledge: Anatomy of a Hasidic Controversy* (Haifa, 2012), which won the Bahat prize for the best scholarly book of 2010.

Gershon Bacon is associate professor of Jewish history at Bar-Ilan University, where he holds the Marcell and Maria Roth Chair in the History and Culture of Polish Jewry. Among his publications are *The Jews of Poland and Russia: Bibliographical Essays* (Bloomington, IN, 1984), *The Politics of Tradition: Agudat Yisrael in Poland, 1916–1939* (Jerusalem, 1996; expanded Hebrew edition, 2005), *From "Poland" to "Eastern Europe": East European Jewry, 1772–1914* (in Hebrew; Jerusalem, 1998), and numerous articles and reviews.

Israel Bartal is professor emeritus of Jewish History, and the former dean of the faculty of humanities at the Hebrew University of Jerusalem (2006–10). Since 2006, he has been the chair of the Historical Society of Israel. Professor Bartal has taught at Harvard, McGill, University of Pennsylvania, and Rutgers, as well as at Moscow State University. He is the author of *The Jews of Eastern Europe, 1772–1881* (Philadelphia, 2005, 2006; published also in Hebrew, Russian, and German).

Omer Bartov is the John P. Birkelund Distinguished Professor of European History at Brown University. He is the author of numerous books, including *Hitler's Army* (1991), *Murder in Our Midst* (1996), *Mirrors of Destruction* (2000), *Germany's War and the Holocaust* (2003), *The "Jew" in Cinema* (2005), and *Erased: Vanishing Traces of Jewish Galicia in Present-Day Ukraine* (2007). He is also the editor of several volumes, including (with Eric Weitz) *Shatterzone of Empires* (2013). Bartov's latest book, *The Voice of Your Brother's Blood: Buczacz, Biography of a Town*, will be published with Simon and Schuster.

Grzegorz Berendt is associate professor in the department of history at Gdańsk University and head of the Regional Public Education Office of the Institute of National Remembrance in Gdańsk. His research interests include the history of Polish Jews, Polish–Jewish relations during the Holocaust, and the policy of the authorities in the People's Republic of Poland toward the Jewish population in the years 1970–89. His books include *Żydzi na terenie Wolnego Miasta Gdańska w latach 1920–1945 (Działalność kulturalna, polityczna i socjalna)* (Jews in the Free City of Danzig in the Years 1920–1945 [Cultural, Political, and Social Activities]; Gdańsk, 1997); *Żydzi na gdańskim rozdrożu (1945–1950)* (Jews at the Crossroads in Gdańsk [1945–1950]; Gdańsk, 2000); and *Życie żydowskie w Polsce w latach 1950–1956. Z dziejów*

Towarzystwa Społeczno-Kulturalnego Żydów w Polsce [Jewish Life in Poland in the Years 1950–1956: From the History of Social-Cultural Association of Jews in Poland] (Gdańsk, 2006).

Daniel Blatman is Max and Rita Haber Professor in Contemporary Jewry and Holocaust Studies at the Hebrew University of Jerusalem. He is the former director of the Center for the Study on the History and Culture of Polish Jewry and the Institute of Contemporary Jewry. He has published various articles and books on the history of Polish Jewry in the twentieth century, the Jewish labor movement in Eastern Europe, the Jews in the Warsaw Ghetto, Polish–Jewish relations during the Holocaust and its aftermath, and on Nazi extermination policy. Among his books are *For Our Freedom and Yours: The Jewish Labor Bund in Poland 1939–1945* (London, 2003, translated into Hebrew and French), *Reportage from the Ghetto: The Jewish Underground Press in the Warsaw Ghetto* (Jerusalem, 2005, Hebrew, French), and *The Death Marches, The Final Phase of Nazi Genocide* (Cambridge, MA, 2011; translated into Hebrew, French, German, and Italian). He has been awarded the Jacob Buchman Memorial Prize, the Yad Vashem International Prize in Holocaust Studies, and was a finalist at the National Jewish Book Awards in 2011.

Jan Doktór defended his doctoral dissertation "Mesjańskie nauczanie Jakuba Franka jako reakcja na kryzys religijnej tradycji osiemnastowiecznego żydostwa polskiego" (The messianic teaching of Jakub Frank as a reaction to the crisis in religious tradition within eighteenth-century Polish Jewry) in 1990 at the Institute for Philosophy and Sociology of the Polish Academy of Sciences in Warsaw. It was published the following year as *Jakub Frank i jego nauka* (Jakub Frank and his teaching). He received his habilitation at the University of Warsaw for his monograph *Śladami mesjasza-apostaty. Żydowskie ruchy mesjańskie w XVII i XVIII wieku a problem konwersji* (In the footsteps of the apostate Messiah: Jewish messianic movements in the seventeenth and eighteenth centuries and the problem of conversion; Wrocław, 1998). He is at present a researcher at the Jewish Historical Institute in Warsaw and chief editor of *Kwartalnik Historii Żydów*. He is the author of *W poszukiwaniu żydowskich kryptochrześcijan; Dzienniki ewangelickich misjonarzy z ich wędrówek po Rzeczypospolitej w latach 1730–1747* (In search of Jewish crypto-Christians; The diaries of Protestant missionaries and their travels in the Polish–Lithuanian Commonwealth, 1730–1747; Warsaw, 1999); *Początki chasydyzmu polskiego* (The beginnings of

Polish Hasidism; Warsaw, 2004, with Magdalena Bendowska); *A World Hidden in Books* (Warsaw, 2011); and *Misjonarze i żydzi w czasach mesjańskiej zawieruchy 1648–1792* (Missionaries and Jews in the time of messianic turmoil, 1648–1792; Warsaw, 2012). He has also edited the Frankist manuscripts *Rozmaite adnotacje, przypadki, czynności i anegdoty Pańskie* (The various annotations, fortunes, acts and anecdotes of the Lord; Warsaw, 1996) and *Księga słów Pańskich; Ezoteryczne wykłady Jakuba Franka* (The book of the words of the Lord: The esoteric lectures of Jakub Frank; Warsaw, 1997, 2 volumes), as well as *Sefer shivkhey Habesht* (The book in praise of the Besht).

Glenn Dynner is professor of Judaic Studies and Chair of Humanities at Sarah Lawrence College. He is author of *"Men of Silk": The Hasidic Conquest of Polish Jewish Society* (Oxford, 2006) and *Yankel's Tavern: Jews, Liquor and Life in the Kingdom of Poland* (Oxford, 2013). He is editor of *Holy Dissent: Jewish and Christian Mystics in Eastern Europe* (Detroit, 2011) and co-editor of *Polin*, volume 27, and of *Warsaw: The Jewish Metropolis: Essays in Honor of the 75th Birthday of Professor Antony Polonsky* (Leiden, 2015).

August Grabski is a research worker at the Jewish Historical Institute in Warsaw and a lecturer at SWPS University of Social Sciences and Humanities. He has written widely on many aspects of Jewish life in Poland since 1918, and in particular on Jewish communists and on the antifascist armed struggle. He is the author of *Centralny Komitet Żydów w Polsce (1944–1950): historia polityczna* (The Central Committee of *Jews* in Poland [1944–1950]: A political history; Warsaw, 2015) and editor of *Rebels against Zion: Studies on the Jewish Left anti-Zionism* (Warsaw, 2010).

Jürgen Heyde has been a research associate at the Centre for the History and Culture of East Central Europe (Geisteswissenschaftliches Zentrum Geschichte und Kultur Ostmitteleuropas; GWZO) at the University of Leipzig since 2014, and teaches east European history and Jewish history at Martin Luther Universität Halle-Wittenberg, where he was awarded his habilitation in 2009. Before coming to Halle in 2003, he was a research associate at the German Historical Institute in Warsaw (1998–2003). His most recent book is *Transkulturelle Kommunikation und Verflechtung: die jüdischen Wirtschaftseliten in Polen vom 14. bis zum 16. Jahrhundert* (Intercultural Communication and Interconnection: the Jewish Economic Elites in Poland from the Fourteenth to the Sixteenth Centuries, Wiesbaden, 2014).

Judith Kalik teaches East European history at the Hebrew University of Jerusalem and specializes in the early modern period of Eastern European Jewish history. She is the author of *The Polish Nobility and the Jews in the Dietine Legislation of the Polish–Lithuanian Commonwealth* (Jerusalem, 1997, in Hebrew) and *Scepter of Judah: The Jewish Autonomy in the Eighteenth-Century Crown Poland* (Leiden, 2009).

Samuel Kassow is Charles Northam Professor of History at Trinity College and curator of the galleries on the nineteenth century and the interwar period at POLIN Museum of the History of Polish Jews in Warsaw. He is the author of *Students, Professors and the State in Tsarist Russia* (Berkeley, 1989), *Between Tsar and People* (Princeton, 1991), and *Who Will Write Our History: Emanuel Ringelblum, the Warsaw Ghetto and the Oyneg Shabes Archive* (Bloomington, IN, 2007); and editor of *The Clandestine History of the Kovno Jewish Ghetto Police* (Bloomington, IN, 2014).

Adam Kaźmierczyk is associate professor in the Institute of Jewish Studies, Jagiellonian University, Kraków. His research focuses on early modern Poland, Polish–Jewish relations in the early modern period, and the legal status of Jews in the seventeenth and eighteenth centuries. He is the author of several books, including *Żydzi polscy 1648–1772. Źródła* (Polish Jews, 1648–1772: Sources; Kraków, 2001); has worked on the documents on *Va'ad Arba Aratzot* (Council of the Four Lands); and published *Sejm Czterech Ziem. Źródła* (The Council of the Four Lands: Sources; Kraków, 2011). Most recently he has been researching conversions to Christianity from the seventeenth to the eighteenth century and Jewish territorial self-government.

Audrey Kichelewski completed her doctorate at the Sorbonne, with a dissertation on "*Les Survivants. La place des Juifs dans la société polonaise (1944–1949)*" (The Survivors. The Place of Jews in Polish Society [1944–1949]). She is a teaching assistant at the University of Strasburg and at the Historical Institute of Warsaw University.

Tomasz Kizwalter is professor of history in the Institute of History at the University of Warsaw. His main field is the history of ideas of collective consciousness in the nineteenth and twentieth centuries, in particular the problems of modernization and of the formation of nations. Among his books are *Kryzys Oświecenia a początki konserwatyzmu polskiego* (The Enlightenment and the beginnings of Polish conservatism; Warsaw, 1987), *"Nowatorstwo i rutyny." Społeczeństwo Królestwa Polskiego wobec procesów modernizacji (1840–1863)* ("Innovation and routine": The Society of the Kingdom of Poland confronted with modernization; Warsaw, 1991), *O nowoczesności narodu. Przypadek Polski* (On the modern character of the nation: The case of Poland; Warsaw, 1999), and *W stronę równości* (Towards equality; Kraków, 2014).

Stanisław Krajewski is professor of philosophy at the University of Warsaw. He has been the Jewish cochair of the Polish Council of Christians and Jews since 1991 and cocreator of the postwar section of the exhibition in the Warsaw POLIN Museum of the History of Polish Jews. He has published papers and books in the field of logic and the philosophy of mathematics, as well as articles and books on Judaism, Jewish experience and Christian–Jewish dialogue, including *Poland and the Jews: Reflections of a Polish Polish Jew* (Kraków, 2005) and, as coeditor, *Abraham Joshua Heschel: Philosophy, Theology and Interreligious Dialogue* (Kraków, 2009).

Anna Landau-Czajka is professor in the Institute of History of the Polish Academy of Sciences and of the department of social sciences of the Warsaw University of Life Sciences. She is the chair of the Programmatic Council of the Jewish Historical Institute. Her main interests are Polish–Jewish relations, the history of women, and the social history of the twentieth century. Among her books are *W jednym stali domu . . . Koncepcje rozwiązania kwestii żydowskiej w publicystyce polskiej lat 1933–1939* (They live in the same house: Conceptions of how to "solve" the "Jewish Question" between 1933 and 1939; Warsaw, 1998), *Co Alicja odkrywa po własnej stronie lustra. Życie codzienne, społeczeństwo, władza w podręcznikach dla dzieci najmłodszych 1785–2000* (What Alice found on her side of the mirror: Everyday life, society and government in textbooks for elementary schoolchildren, 1785–2000; Warsaw, 2002), and *Syn będzie Lech . . . Asymilacja Żydów w Polsce międzywojennej* (Your son will be called Lech . . . Assimilation of Jews in interwar Poland; Warsaw, 2006). She has published a series of articles in the collective work edited by Anna Żarnowska and Andrzej Szwarc, *Kobieta i małżeństwo: społeczno-kulturowe aspekty seksualności. Wiek XIX i XX* (Woman and marriage: Socio-cultural aspects of sexuality in the nineteenth and twentieth centuries; Warsaw, 2004). Her most recent book is *Polska to nie oni. Wizerunek Polski i Polaków w polskojęzycznej prasie żydowskiej okresu międzywojennego* (Poland is not only them: The image of Poland and Poles in the Polish-language Jewish press in the interwar period; Warsaw, 2015).

Shulamit Magnus is professor of Jewish studies and history at Oberlin College, where she teaches a wide range of courses in Jewish history. A social and cultural historian, she specializes in the modern period in Europe and is particularly interested in questions of identity, the workings of gender in Jewish society, and Jewish women's history. She is author of *Jewish Emancipation in a German City: Cologne, 1798–1871* (Stanford, CA, 1997); an unabridged translation of and commentary on Pauline Wengeroff, *Memoirs of a Grandmother* (Stanford, CA, 2010, 2014), volume one of which won the National Jewish Book Award and volume two of which won the Hadassah-Brandeis Institute Translation Prize; and a biography entitled *A Woman's Life: Pauline Wengeroff and Memoirs of a Grandmother* (Oxford, 2015).

Justyna Majewska graduated in cultural studies and museum studies and is a doctoral candidate at the Polish Academy of Sciences, where she is working on a doctoral dissertation on various visions of social changes in the Warsaw Ghetto. She is a fellow of the European Holocaust Research Infrastructure and curator of the Holocaust Gallery at POLIN Museum of the History of Polish Jews. She runs the office of the journal *Zagłada Żydów. Studia i Materiały* and is a member of the editorial team publishing the Ringelblum Archive, which was awarded the prize of the Polish Pen Club in 2016. She works at the Emanuel Ringelblum Jewish Historical Institute.

Dan Michman is professor of modern Jewish history and chair of the Finkler Institute of Holocaust Research at Bar-Ilan University, and serves also as head of the International Institute of Holocaust Research and incumbent of the John Najmann Chair in Holocaust Studies at Yad Vashem. He is member of the editorial boards of several scholarly periodicals and of many academic committees and boards of institutions in Israel and abroad. His publications cover a broad variety of topics regarding the Holocaust and its impact and memory. Among his books are *Days of Holocaust and Reckoning*, 1–12 (published in Hebrew, Spanish, Russian, and Ukrainian); *Holocaust Historiography: A Jewish Perspective: Conceptualizations, Terminology, Approaches and Fundamental Issues* (published in six languages); and *The Emergence of Jewish Ghettos during the Holocaust* (published in English, German, and Hebrew). Among volumes he edited or coedited are *Post-Zionism and the Holocaust: The Role of the Holocaust in the Public Debate on Post-Zionism in Israel*, volumes 1–2 (Hebrew); *Holocaust Historiography in Context: Emergence, Challenges, Polemics and Achievements*; and *Pius XII and the Holocaust. Current State of Research.*

Victoria Mochalova received her doctorate at the Institute for Slavic and Balkanic Studies (ISBS), Academy of Sciences USSR (now the Russian Academy of Sciences, or RAS), Moscow, with a thesis on Polish popular literature in the sixteenth and seventeenth centuries. This was published as *Mir naiznanku: narodno-gorodskaia literatura Pol'shi XVI–XVII vv.* (The world inside out: the folk and urban literature of Poland in the sixteenth and seventeenth centuries; Moscow, 1985). Since 1997 she has been director of the Moscow "Sefer" Center for the University Teaching of Jewish Civilization and head of the Center for Slavic Jewish Studies, Institute for Slavic Studies, RAS, Moscow.

Andrzej Paczkowski is professor of history in the Institute of Political Studies of the Polish Academy of Sciences. He is a specialist in postwar Polish history, especially the history of the Communist Party and the security apparatus. Among his books are *Prasa polska w latach 1918–1939* (The Polish Press in the years 1918-1939; Warsaw, 1980), *Pół wieku dziejów Polski 1939–1989* (Warsaw, 1995; translated into English as *The Spring Will Be Ours: Poland and the Poles from Occupation to the Freedom, 1939–1989*; University Park, PA, 2003), *Droga do "mniejszego zła": Strategia i taktyka obozy władzy, lipiec 1980-styczeń 1982* (The road to the "lesser evil": The tactics of the ruling group, July 1980 to January 1982; Warsaw, 2002), and *Trzy twarze Józefa Światły: przyczynek do dziejow komunizmu w Polsce* (The three faces of Józef Światło: A contribution to the history of Communism in Poland; Warsaw, 2009). He is a member of the board of the Institute of National Memory. He is a member of the Council of the Institute of National Remembrance.

Maria Ferenc-Piotrowska holds a BA in philosophy and an MA in sociology. She is a fellow of European Holocaust Research Infrastructure and is currently working on her PhD at Warsaw University on sources and meanings of information in the Warsaw Ghetto. She is a curator of the Holocaust Gallery at POLIN Museum of the History of Polish Jews and a Fellow of the European Holocaust Research Infrastructure and the Polish National Science Centre. She is the editor of three volumes of the Ringeblum archive publication project and works at the Emanuel Ringelblum Jewish Historical Institute.

Antony Polonsky is emeritus professor of Holocaust studies at Brandeis University and chief historian of POLIN Museum of the History of Polish Jews, Warsaw. Until 1991, he was professor of international history at the London School of Economics and Political Science. He is chair of the editorial board of *Polin: Studies in Polish Jewry*; author of *Politics in Independent Poland* (Oxford, 1972), *The Little Dictators* (London, 1975), and *The Great Powers and the Polish Question* (London, 1976); coauthor of *A History of Modern Poland* (Cambridge, 1980) and *The Beginnings of Communist Rule in Poland* (London, 1981); and coeditor of *Contemporary Jewish Writing in Poland: An Anthology* (Lincoln, NE, 2001) and *The Neighbors Respond: The Controversy over the Jedwabne Massacre in Poland* (Princeton, 2004). His most recent work is *The Jews in Poland and Russia*, volume 1, 1350 to 1881; volume 2, 1881 to 1914; volume 3, 1914 to 2008 (Oxford, 2010, 2012), published in 2013 in an abridged version, *The Jews in Poland and Russia: A Short History*.

Kamila Radecka-Mikulicz is curator of the Holocaust Gallery at POLIN Museum of the History of Polish Jews, senior specialist at POLIN Exhibition Department. She is a museologist and narrative exhibitions designer; she currently works in POLIN Museum Exhibitions Department. She was a participant of the Exhibiting Contemporary History Programme at the Europäisches Kolleg Jena. She has an MA in philosophy from Warsaw University and was a graduate of the first class of the Polin Academy. At present she is working on her PhD devoted to interwar society of Jews living in Chełm in the Tadeusz Manteuffel Institute of History, Polish Academy of Sciences.

Moshe Rosman is professor in the Koschitzky Department of Jewish History and Contemporary Jewry of Bar-Ilan University in Israel. He specializes in early modern Polish Jewish history. Among his books are *The Lords' Jews: Magnate–Jewish Relations in the Polish–Lithuanian Commonwealth during the Eighteenth Century* (Cambridge, MA, 1990); *Founder of Hasidism: A Quest for the Historical Ba'al Shem Tov* (Berkeley, 1996), and *How Jewish Is Jewish History?* (Oxford, 2007).

Naomi Seidman is Koret Professor of Jewish Culture and director of the Richard S. Dinner Center for Jewish Studies at the Graduate Theological Union. She is the author of *A Marriage Made in Heaven: The Sexual Politics of Hebrew and Yiddish* (Berkeley, 1997) and *Faithful Renderings: Jewish–Christian Difference and the Politics of Translation* (Chicago, 2006). Her third monograph, *The Marriage Plot, or, How Jews Fell in Love with Love, and with Literature* (Stanford, CA, 2016). She is presently working on a translation of Sarah Schenirer's collected writings, and a study of the emergence of Orthodox Jewish girls' education in interwar Poland, the latter for Littman Library.

Marci Shore is associate professor of History at Yale University. She is the translator of Michał Głowiński's *The Black Seasons* and the author of *Caviar and Ashes: A Warsaw Generation's Life and Death in Marxism, 1918–1968* (New Haven, CT, 2006), and *The Taste of Ashes: The Afterlife of Totalitarianism in Eastern Europe* (New York, 2013).

Darius Staliūnas received his PhD from Kaunas Vytautas Magnus University in 1997. He joined the Lithuanian Institute of History in 1992, where since 2000 he has been a deputy director. He is the author of *Making Russians: Meaning and Practice of Russification in Lithuania and Belarus after 1863* (Amsterdam, 2007) and coeditor of *Pragmatic Alliance: Jewish–Lithuanian Political Cooperation at the Beginning of the 20th Century* (Budapest, 2011). His research interests include issues of Russian nationality policy in the so-called northwestern region (Lithuania and Belorussia), ethnic conflicts, and problems of historiography and places of memory in Lithuania.

Katrin Steffen is a research associate of the Nordost-Institut of the Universität Hamburg. Her main research interest is the acculturation and Polonization of Polish Jews. She is the author of *Jüdische Polonität: Ethnizität und Nation im Spiegel der polnischsprachigen jüdischen Presse 1918–1939* (Jewish Polishness: Ethnicity and Nation in the Light of the Polish-language Jewish Press 1918–1939; Göttingen, 2004) and editor (with Imke Hansen und Joachim Tauber) of *Lebenswelt Ghetto: Alltag und soziales Umfeld während der nationalsozialistischen Verfolgung* (The Lifeworld of the Ghetto: Everyday Life and Social Environment during the National Socialist Persecution; Wiesbaden, 2013).

Michael Steinlauf is professor of history and director of the Holocaust and genocide studies program at Gratz College in Philadelphia. He is the author of *Bondage to the Dead: Poland and the Memory of the Holocaust* (Syracuse, NY, 1997), which examines how Poles have reacted to the Holocaust in the decades since the end of the Second World War. He is also a contributing editor to *The YIVO Encyclopedia of Jews in Eastern Europe*. His writings, including studies of Polish–Jewish relations, Yiddish theater, and the Jewish press in Eastern Europe, have been translated into Hebrew, Polish, German, and Italian. Professor Steinlauf has also been active in Jewish memory work in Poland, including serving as chief historical advisor (1998–2007) for POLIN Museum of the History of Polish Jews. He is currently at work on a study of the Yiddish writer and activist Y. L. Peretz.

Kenneth Stow is professor emeritus of Jewish history at the University of Haifa, and has been a visiting professor at Yale, the University of Michigan, the University of Washington, Smith College, the University of Toronto, and the Pontifical Gregorian University. He has twice been a fellow at the Israel Institute of Advanced Studies at the Hebrew University of Jerusalem, and has also been a Bodini Fellow at the Italian Academy for Advanced Studies at Columbia University. He received his PhD in 1971 from Columbia University. He founded the journal *Jewish History* and served as its editor for twenty-five years, until 2012. He is the author of *The Jews: A Mediterranean Culture* (Bari, 1994); *Alienated Minority: The Jews of Medieval Latin Europe* (Cambridge, MA, 1992; Hebrew translation, Jerusalem, 1997; Russian translation, Moscow, 2008); *The Jews in Rome*, volumes 1 and 2 (Leiden, 1995, 1997); *Theater of Acculturation: The Roman Ghetto in the Sixteenth Century* (Seattle, 2001; Italian translation, Rome, 2014); *Jewish Dogs, An Image and Its Interpreters: Continuity in the Jewish–Catholic Encounter* (Stanford, CA, 2006); *Popes, Church, and Jews in the Middle Ages* (Aldershot, 2007); and *Jewish Life in Early Modern Rome: Challenge, Conversion, and Private Life* (Aldershot, 2007). His current research is on the effects of legal change on deconfessionalization and Jewish emancipation in the early modern and modern periods.

Saulius Sužiedėlis is professor emeritus of history at Millersville University of Pennsylvania. He was born in Gotha, Germany, in 1945 and grew up in the Lithuanian community of Brockton, Massachusetts. He served with the US Peace Corps in Ethiopia from 1967 to 1969. Professor Sužiedėlis received his PhD in Russian and Eastern European history from the University of Kansas in 1977. From 1982 to 1987, he was a research historian specializing in Nazi war crimes for the US Department of Justice, and during 1989 to 1990 he worked as a radio journalist and commentator for the Voice of America. Among his works are the introduction to the Lithuanian edition of Avraham Tory's *Surviving the Holocaust* (Vilnius, 2000); with Christoph Dieckman, *The Persecution and Mass Murder of Lithuanian Jews during Summer and Fall of 1941: Sources and Analysis* (Vilnius, 2006); and *Historical Dictionary of Lithuania* (2nd ed., Lanham, MD, 2011. Since 1998, he has been a member of the International Commission for the Evaluation of the Crimes of the Nazi and Soviet Occupation Regimes in Lithuania. Between 2007 and 2010 he served as director of Millersville University's Annual Conference on the Holocaust and Genocide. In 2013, he was awarded an honorary doctorate from Vytautas Magnus University in Kaunas in recognition of his work in furthering the study of humanities there and for his contributions to Holocaust research.

Adam Teller is associate professor in the departments of history and Judaic studies at Brown University. He studied at Oxford University and the Hebrew University of Jerusalem. He has written extensively on the economic, social, and cultural history of the Jews in the Polish–Lithuanian Commonwealth. His two monographs, both published in Hebrew, are *Living Together: The Jewish Quarter of Poznań and its Population in the Seventeenth Century* (Jerusalem, 2003) and *Money, Power and Influence: The Jews on the Radziwiłł Estates in Eighteenth Century Lithuania* (Jerusalem, 2006). He has held a National Endowment for the Humanities Fellowship at the Center for Jewish History in New York and been a visiting professor at Columbia University, Johns Hopkins University, the University of Pennsylvania, and Yeshiva University. His current project deals with Polish Jewish refugees during the seventeenth century.

Jonathan Webber is a British anthropologist. He taught Jewish studies for twenty years at Oxford University, then spent eight years as UNESCO Professor in Jewish and Interfaith Studies at the University of Birmingham (UK), and then five years as a professor at the Jagiellonian University, Kraków. Among several long-term projects he has undertaken in Poland, he was a founding member of the International Council of the Auschwitz Museum, on which he served for twenty years; and he was the founding chair of the Galicia Jewish Museum in Kraków.

Hanna Węgrzynek is a historian, the chief specialist for research and historical projects at POLIN Museum of the History of Polish Jews in Warsaw, and a lecturer in postgraduate Polish-Jewish Studies at the Institute of Literary Research of the Polish Academy of Sciences. In her research she focuses on Jewish-Christian relations from the fifteenth to the eighteenth century and Jewish presence in Warsaw in the same period. She is also engaged in popularization of Jewish history and especially the Holocaust in Polish school curricula. She is the author of books and articles devoted to the history of Jews in Poland including *"Czarna legenda" Żydów. Procesy o mordy rytualne w dawnej Polsce* (The "black legend" of the Jews: Trials for alleged ritual murder in old Poland; Warsaw, 1995); *The Treatment of Jewish Themes in Polish Schools: The Central and East European Curriculum Project* (New York, 1998); *Historia i kultura Żydów polskich. Słownik* (The history and culture of Polish Jews. A dictionary; Warsaw, 2000–in cooperation with Alina Cała and Gabriela Zalewska); *Milles ans des Juifs en Pologne* (Warsaw, 2004); *Żydzi i Polacy w okresie walk o niepodległość*

1914–1920 (Jews and Poles during the fights for independence 1914–1920, ed.; Warsaw, 2015); *Regestr osób żydowskich spisany w miesiącu styczniu roku 1778 w Warszawie* (Register of the Jews set up in Warsaw in January 1778; Warsaw 2016–Klio Prize 2016).

Jacek Wijaczka is a professor in the Institute of History and Archivistics at the Mikołaj Kopernik University in Toruń. His research interests include the history of Ducal and Royal Prussia from the sixteenth to the eighteenth centuries, Polish–German relations in the early modern period, and witchcraft trials as well as the history of the Jews in the Polish–Lithuanian Commonwealth down to the partitions. Among his publications are *Procesy o mordy rytualne w Polsce w XV–XVIII wieku* (Ritual murder trials in poland from the fifteenth to the eighteenth centuries; with Zenon Guldon; Kielce, 1995), *Stosunki dyplomatyczne Polski z Rzeszą Niemiecką w czasach panowania cesarza Karola V (1519–1556)* (Diplomatic relations between Poland and the German Reich during the Reign of Charles V; Kielce, 1998); *Procesy o czary w Prusach Książęcych (Brandenburskich) w XVI–XVIII wieku* (Witchcraft trials in Royal Prussia [Brandenburg] from the sixteenth to the eighteenth centuries; Toruń, 2007); and *Albrecht von Brandenburg-Ansbach (1490–1568). Ostatni mistrz zakonu krzyżackiego i pierwszy książę "w Prusiech"* (Albrecht of Brandenburg-Ansbach [1490–1568]. The last master of the Teutonic Knights and the first prince "in Prussia"; Olsztyn, 2010).

Andrzej Żbikowski was born in Warsaw in 1953 and since 1985 has worked at the Jewish Historical Institute. He defended his doctoral dissertation in the department of history at the University of Warsaw, and it was published in 1994 under the title *Żydzi krakowscy i ich gmina. 1869–1919* (The Jews of Kraków and their communal organization). In 1996 he published an illustrated history entitled *Żydzi* (Jews) in the series *A to Polska właśnie* (And this is indeed Poland) and is also the author of *U genezy Jedwabnego: Żydzi na Kresach Północno-Wschodnich II Rzeczypospolitej: wrzesień 1939-lipiec 1941* (On the origins of Jedwabne: Jews in the north-eastern borderlands of the Second Republic; Warsaw, 2006). His most recent book is *Karski* (Świat Książki, Warsaw, 2011).

MUSEOLOGICAL QUESTIONS

The Voice of the Curators

Something Old, Something New: Creating the Narrative for the Early Modern Galleries

ADAM TELLER

In this essay, I shall present the two early modern galleries not as I would in a normal academic setting. This would usually involve addressing some research question, garnering the necessary sources, discussing them, and then giving my answer in the conclusion. However, though as the academic team leader of these two galleries I did do (and commission) a huge amount of source work, much of which cannot even be seen in the exhibit, the truly interesting and challenging aspects of the job were somewhat different.

My role as academic team leader was first and foremost to determine the narrative line of the exhibit, then to direct the collection and collation of all the material to support it, and finally to help construct that narrative using the language of a museum. This meant learning new ways of creating narratives and addressing historical issues. Learning just the basics of this museological language, with the help of the museum designers, Event Communications from London and Nizio Design International of Warsaw,[1] was a slow and painful process. Nonetheless, it enriched my thinking

---

1 http://www.eventcomm.com/ and http://nizio.com.pl/en/.

about history in some very interesting ways. It is that which I would like to discuss here.

I found that working on a so-called "narrative museum" presented me with a range of problems, many of which are not apparent in the written presentation of research. My comments will focus on what seemed to me the two most significant of these when I originally joined the museum team. The first was connected with the very nature of the project itself: How was I to acknowledge that I was not writing a book to be read anywhere, but making a concrete exhibit that would exist in a certain place and a certain setting? Such considerations are alien when writing, but in all honesty could not be ignored here. The second concerned the very means by which the narrative and the galleries' messages were to be conveyed. The museological genre presents historical narratives in ways that are quite different from the kind of monographic writing historians usually do.

In practical terms, these concerns soon translated themselves into a question to be posed in the galleries and a choice to be made in the way the narrative would be constructed. The overarching question that I wanted the galleries to ask (and which I believed that the museum as a whole should be concerned with) was this: What was Polish about Polish Jews? Clearly, Polish Jewry belonged to a much broader Jewish collective. However, at the same time they also created, in the place where they lived, a highly distinctive civilization that was identifiably Polish.[2] This issue surely had to be at the heart of a Jewish museum that would physically stand in the center of Warsaw and be a place visited by two major audiences—Poles and Jews (though of course it was clear that myriad others would visit, too). The question being asked, "What was Polish about Polish Jews?" was by no means as simple as it seemed, for it required visitors to rethink not one, but two concepts: What might Polishness mean in a Jewish context, and how could the concept of "Polishness" in its Polish context be expanded to include Jews?[3]

The choice to be made concerned the exposition of the narrative. From the outset, the policy was to reduce—if not eliminate—the so-called *Museum*

---

2   This concept was first developed by Gershon D. Hundert. See Gershon D. Hundert, *The Jews in a Polish Private Town: The Case of Opatów in the Eighteenth Century* (Baltimore, MD: Johns Hopkins University Press, 1992); ibid., *Jews in Poland–Lithuania in the Eighteenth Century: A Genealogy of Modernity* (Berkeley: University of California Press, 2004).

3   I have examined this idea in a little more depth in Adam Teller, "Polish–Jewish Relations: Historical Research and Social Significance. On the Legacy of Jacob Goldberg," *Studia Judaica* 15, nos. 1–2 (Kraków, 2012): 27–47.

Voice (i.e., the historian's voice). Instead, we were to allow the voices from the past to "speak for themselves." What this really meant was that we could not say what we wanted to in a direct way. In the end, there were two main tools available to get the message across: the first was the choice of materials and voices to be presented; the second was what one might term the *Museum Path*. In a narrative museum like this one, the way visitors are led from exhibit to exhibit is a very powerful, physical way of determining the narrative that is being told. In fact, it is its own kind of *Museum Voice*, but one that cannot be seen or heard. It seemed to me, however, that the answer to the question I wanted to pose would not be found in a classic historical narrative. The Polishness of Polish Jews can really only be discovered by a process of exploring different aspects of their society and culture.

This presented a problem. Constructing a single narrative line for the galleries would get in the way of the kind of exploration that needed to be done. However, you cannot make a narrative museum without a narrative. So, with the help of the designers, the place of the narrative in the galleries was changed—it moved away from the center of the story being told. In the Paradisus Judaeorum gallery, the narrative is pushed to the right-hand wall. There it is possible to explore the development of the Jews' legal status in the context of the Polish–Lithuanian Commonwealth, as well as their rapid demographic expansion across its huge territory, and their penetration of its economy. This is because the issues of demography, economy, and evolving legal status are here understood as the "motors" that drove early modern Polish Jewish history. However, by concentrating them on the right-hand wall, we could free up the rest of the gallery as a kind of open space in which visitors could explore the Polish Jewish civilization of the period.

This was, however, to be a structured exploration with delineated themes: when visitors enter the Paradisus Judaeorum gallery, they are confronted with three lines of sight. On the right is what we have called the narrative wall; straight ahead are exhibits dealing with the Jews' social and political structures—the model of Kraków and Kazimierz and beyond it the exhibits concerning the community and the Council of Four Lands. To the left are exhibits exploring, in various ways, the role of religion (Judaism and Christianity) in forming Polish Jewish culture. These touch on matters of religious tolerance and intolerance, the work of the great Rabbi Moshe Isserles in giving Jewish law a Polish coloring, and the development of Hebrew publishing in Poland in both its local, Polish, and transregional, Jewish contexts.

The second gallery—Miasteczko (The Jewish Town)—structures the narrative in a different way. It is presented as visitors first enter the gallery, where it places the development of the Jewish small town in the context of Poland–Lithuania's reconstruction following the Khmelnytsky uprising and the Swedish and Muscovite wars. The body of the gallery is meant to allow visitors to explore small-town civilization for themselves, so narrative issues are not much in evidence. The narrative is picked up again toward the end of the gallery, when visitors are invited to consider the ways in which Polish–Lithuanian Jewry attempted to reorganize its religious and social life from about the 1740s on. Since these ideas would play out much more clearly in the nineteenth century, this concluding section of Miasteczko gets the visitors back onto a central *Museum Path* leading to the nineteenth-century gallery.

The Miasteczko gallery itself is organized with two major focuses representing its two main themes—daily life (social, economic, and cultural) in the central market square and the buildings around it (tavern, home, church) and Jewish religiosity and spirituality in the small-town setting, represented by the synagogue. True to the structure of the small towns, the synagogue is set back from the square and so is not immediately apparent.[4] There is an element of path-building here. The idea is for visitors to explore the small town itself before seeing the overwhelming synagogue exhibit. There is no effort, however, to force this path on them.

In fact, there is only one place where a *Museum Path* is imposed, and that is in the presentation of the anti-Jewish violence of the mid-seventeenth century. I felt it important that every visitor face—and as far as possible experience—violence as an integral part of how Polish–Lithuanian Jews lived. It is therefore impossible to move from Paradisus Judaeorum to Miasteczko without walking through what we called the "Corridor of Fire," which was designed to be as threatening and frightening as the designers could make it.[5]

Once the narrative line had been structured in order to create space for visitors to explore the Polish Jewish civilizations of the sixteenth and early

---

4 Maria i Kazimierz Piechotkowie, *Bramy Nieba: Bóżnice murowane na ziemiach dawnej Rzeczypospolitej* [Gates of Heaven: Masonry synagogues on the territory of the former Polish-Lithuanian Commonwealth], 2nd ed. (Warsaw: Polish Institute of World Art Studies, POLIN Museum of the History of Polish Jews, 2017).

5 This exhibit, together with the immediately preceding one—on the Jews' role in the *arenda* system—also enabled me to examine in at least some detail the difficult relations between the Polish Crown and the Roman Catholic Church and the population of Ukraine in this period and the part played by Jews in these developments. It was illustrated by a huge reproduction of the map of seventeenth century Ukraine drawn by Guillaume de Beauplan. See Guillaume Le Vasseur, Sieur de Beauplan, *A Description of Ukraine*, ed. Andrew Pernal and Dennis Essar (Cambridge, MA: Harvard University Press, 1993).

seventeenth centuries and then the later seventeenth and eighteenth centuries, those civilizations had to be presented in all their Jewishness and their Polishness. Fortunately, in doing this, it was possible to use the results of a generation or two of academic research, which had very much emphasized this issue. However, though the scholarship would be well known to those of my colleagues who would come to the exhibit, for most visitors the message would be quite new. Many of the materials that made up the exhibits were also previously unknown—the result of intensive work undertaken by a small and extremely dedicated group of curators, who spent long hours chasing up possible exhibits and generally doing the hard work without which such a museum simply could not come into being.[6]

Presenting the Polishness of Polish Jews involved, in some cases, the reworking of accepted and popular views of Polish Jewish history. In the first gallery, I had the enormous pleasure of doing this together with Igor Kąkolewski of the Center for Historical Research of the Polish Academy of Sciences in Berlin, who demonstrated truly astonishing expertise not only in his grasp of the historical materials themselves, but also in their presentation in new and unexpected ways.

One of the most important examples of destabilizing a popularly accepted view of history is in the exhibit of religious tolerance in sixteenth-century Poland. While the phenomenon is emphasized in the gallery, it is separated from the idea generally accepted in Poland that it was religious tolerance that encouraged Jews to settle there. This was clearly not the case—Jewish immigration to Poland was largely over when Polish culture adopted its principles of toleration, most notably during the Confederation of Warsaw in 1573.[7] Visitors will thus look in vain for signs of Jewish immigration in the tolerance exhibit. Instead they will find voices questioning the degree of tolerance extended to the Jews by the Roman Catholic Church, with a panel on the spread of blood libel accusations.[8] In terms of genuine religious interactions, the exhibit

---

6 These included Maciej Gugała, Ewa Małkowska-Bieniek, Dr. Małgorzata Stolarska-Fronia, and Kalina Gawlas. I owe them all my thanks.

7 The classic, though now somewhat outdated, study of tolerance in early modern Poland is Janusz Tazbir, *State without Stakes: Polish Religious Toleration in the Sixteenth and Seventeenth Centuries* (Warsaw: Kościuszko Foundation, 1973).

8 On this, see Hanna Węgrzynek, "Czarna legenda" Żydów: Procesy o rzekome mordy rytualne w dawnej Polsce [The "Black legend" of the Jews: Trials for alleged ritual murder in old Poland] (Warsaw: Wydawnictwo Bellona: Wydawnictwo Fundacji Historia pro Futuro, 1995); Magda Teter, *Sinners on Trial: Jews and Sacrilege after the Reformation* (Cambridge, MA: Harvard University Press, 2011).

explores the connections between the Jews, represented by the Karaite Isaac of Troki and the radical Protestant Socinians, represented by Szymon Budny and Marcin Czechowic. Even this is not a one-sided presentation, however. The existence of religious discussion—and even admiration—between the groups is shown, alongside the religious hostility that developed between them.[9]

In short, what can be seen is a form of religious tolerance full of internal tensions. Perhaps the most graphic example of this may be found in the prominent exhibit of the Dance of Death. In this baroque picture, found in the Church of St. Bernardine of Siena in Kraków, the Jews form one of the groups in Polish society invited to participate together in the Dance of Death, while at the same time being described in the most vituperative terms of ugliness and stench.[10] At least one visitor commented that this form of "hated inclusion" really sums up the message of the gallery—if not of the museum as a whole.

It is not only conceptions of history popular in Poland that are reexamined in Paradisus Judaeorum. Jewish popular memory—particularly of its religious tradition—also comes under the spotlight. This is done in the exhibit on Moshe Isserles, rabbi of Kraków, best known for his glosses to the Jewish Law Code, the *Shulḥhan arukh*. Isserles's comments transformed that text from a parochial volume meant just for Sephardic Jews into an authoritative codex serving the Jewish people as a whole.[11] In Jewish religious culture, Isserles is revered as one of the greatest rabbis and a thinker of enormous originality and independence.[12] He is also accepted as the foremost representative of Ashkenazic Jewry broadly understood. All of this appears in the exhibit. However, alongside it, the visitor can see the letter, in Latin, by the Wojewoda (royal governor) of Kraków appointing him to the rabbinate—presumably after a suitable payment was made by his father.[13] We also learn that the customs Isserles introduced into the *Shulḥan arukh* as pan-Ashkenazic were in fact much more locally Polish. What he termed "Ashkenazic Custom" was very often what he

---

9 Wiktor Weintraub, "Tolerance and Intolerance in Old Poland," *Canadian Slavonic Papers* 13, no. 1 (1971): 21–44; Judah Rosenthal, "Marcin Czechowic and Jacob of Bełżyce: Arian–Jewish Encounters in 16th-Century Poland," *Proceedings of the American Academy for Jewish Research* 34 (1966): 77–97.

10 "Lewd Turks, Hideous Jews, / Why does Death not abhor you? / It ignores the Jews' stench, / And prances with these savage peoples."

11 Elchanan Reiner, "The Ashkenazi Elite at the Beginning of the Modern Era: Manuscript versus Printed Book," *Polin* 10 (Oxford, 1997): 85–98.

12 Asher Siev, *Rabbeinu Moshe Isserles* (New York: Yeshiva University Press, 1972).

13 Copied from Archiwum Główne Akt Dawnych w Warszawie (Central Archive of Historical Records in Warsaw), Metryka Koronna, vol. 73, fol. 382.

was used to seeing around him.[14] Here, then, it seems quite clear what was "Polish" about this, the most famous "Polish Jewish" rabbi.

Perhaps the easiest place to demonstrate this kind of Jewish Polishness (or Polish Jewishness) was in the exhibit on the Jewish kahal (community)—often described as an organ of Jewish autonomy. Its basis was a passage from the Kraków communal constitution of 1595 (originally in Yiddish), which reads

> The President of the Community Council must keep the key of the chest containing the community's privileges [and other records]. The chest itself should be in the possession of the official voted to this position every year.[15]

This is a museum designer's dream! What could be simpler than to make an exhibit of a chest in which, alongside the community's *pinkas* (record book) kept in Hebrew and Yiddish, the visitor can see copies of the Latin and Polish privileges and legal documents on which the community, as an institution, was founded. This is a very simple, but very graphic, way of expressing both the Jewishness and the Polishness of the kahal: it was at one and the same time the body through which the Jews organized their own social, economic, and cultural lives, and also a legally constituted institution that formed an integral part of the Polish–Lithuanian polity.[16] It is not the content of the documents that tells the story, simply their juxtaposition.

The second of the two galleries—Miasteczko—presented quite a different challenge. Paradisus Judaeorum tells a story with large themes, such as religious tolerance, the Jewish community, and the history of the Hebrew book. Here, however, visitors explore the Jewish civilization that grew and developed in the small towns in the east of the commonwealth during the eighteenth century. Thus, the treatment needs to be more or less local in nature, with one problem being to preserve a sense of the connection with the broader developments of the period.

---

14 Joseph Davis, "The Reception of the Shulhan 'Arukh and the Formation of Ashkenazic Jewish Identity," *AJS Review* 26, no. 2 (2002): 251–76.
15 *Statut krakowskiej gminy żydowskiej z roku 1595 i jego uzupełnienia* [The statute of the Kraków Jewish community of 1595 and its addenda], ed. Majer Bałaban (reworked by Anna Jakimyszyn) (Kraków: Księgarnia Akademicka, 2005), XII no. 15.
16 Jacob Goldberg, "The Role of the Jewish Community in the Socio-Political Structure of the Polish–Lithuanian Commonwealth," *Polin* 22 (Oxford, 2010): 142–55.

The effect sought after is again one of destabilization. This kind of small town as a physical phenomenon is well known to Poles (and to Europeans generally), while in Jewish culture, the small town, known as a shtetl, is an imaginary construct of a mythical Jewish place.[17] So, the idea is that Polish visitors to this exhibit will come expecting to see something familiar, but find something they did not know, while Jews will come expecting to have their preconceptions confirmed, but find something quite alien.

Normal scholarly practice would discuss the mixed nature of these small towns on the basis of detailed examination of the documentary sources. This was clearly impossible here. Different tools were needed. The first of these was the use of facades. When standing in the central square of the gallery—a representation of the town's market square—the visitor cannot see inside the different exhibits. They are within different buildings, only whose front is visible. This creates a sense of familiarity in anyone who knows what such towns look like. However, once you go behind the facade, a whole world of Jewish experience is revealed, quite strange and alien to the non-Jewish visitor: Jewish tavern keepers, the women's world of the Jewish home, and, finally, the synagogue itself. What is familiar in the Polish landscape on the outside in fact hides behind it a vibrantly Jewish culture, quite unknown to non-Jews who do not bother to look there. The *miasteczko* is not what you expected.

For the Jewish visitor, expecting to come to a quintessentially Jewish shtetl, the very central square signals something different. The market square itself is presented as a place of economic and social interaction between Jews and non-Jews.[18] The facade of the tavern has non-Jewish figures lounging outside. Inside the tavern, the visitor learns not only that Jews and non-Jews interacted there socially on a daily basis, but also that the alcohol business tied them into a much broader economic web, at whose head stood the Polish magnates, and in which non-Jews played various significant roles.[19]

The tavern dialogues between Jews and non-Jews, found on its back wall, are local in nature, drawn from a range of sources, including the memoirs

---

17 On this issue see the collected studies in Antony Polonsky, ed., *The Shtetl: Myth and Reality*, Polin 17 (Oxford, 2004): 3–275.
18 Adam Teller, "The Shtetl as an Arena for Polish–Jewish Integration in the Eighteenth Century," *Polin* 17 (Oxford, 2004): 25–40.
19 On this, see Moshe Rosman, *The Lords' Jews: Magnate–Jewish Relations in the Polish–Lithuanian Commonwealth during the Eighteenth Century* (Cambridge, MA: Harvard University Press for the Center for Jewish Studies, Harvard University, and the Harvard Ukrainian Research Institute, 1990), 106–42.

of Solomon Maimon and court records from Rzeszów.[20] The documents screened in its front tell of the tavern's wider connections in the *szlachta*, particularly the magnate, economy. Thus, Jewish visitors will, it is hoped, be forced to move away from the idea that the shtetl was a kind of "bubble" of Jewish life isolated from its non-Jewish surroundings. Instead, they should see a small town, full of Jewish life, culture, and religion, that actually formed an integral part of a broader non-Jewish society and was a place of constant interaction between Jews and non-Jews.

Another important place in which to reconsider accepted narratives was the church exhibit. Just having such a space is a challenge to the traditional Jewish vision of the shtetl, in which, if a church even appears, it is a shadowy and unknown place. However, once the museum visitors go into the church, they find yet another space filled with Jews—and in some quite unexpected situations. Of course, the elements that everyone expects to see in an exhibit on Roman Catholic Church–Jewish relations in eighteenth-century Poland–Lithuania can be found there: anti-Jewish preaching, forced conversion, the blood libel, and so on.[21] Yet there are other, much-less expected stories in evidence: prominent among them is that of the false messiah, Jacob Frank, who led thousands of his followers into converting to Catholicism (though that was by no means as simple a process as it might sound).[22] Also to be found is evidence of some internal struggles within the Catholic hierarchy concerning the treatment of Jews, arguing against forced conversions and blood libel accusations.

Prominent in that regard is the Papal Bull *A quo primum* of 1751, which was highly critical of the Roman Catholic Church in Poland. The issue causing all the anger was the remarkable phenomenon of Roman Catholic Church institutions in the Polish–Lithuanian Commonwealth lending money to Jewish bodies. This phenomenon was unique to Poland, where Jewish communities and councils had presumably come to be seen as a blue-chip investment for church money. Of course, the outcome was a complete reversal of the medieval

---

20 Solomon Maimon, *An Autobiography*, trans. J. Clark Murray (Urbana: University of Illinois Press 2001), 25–26; Adam Kaźmierczyk, ed., *Żydzi polscy 1648–1772: Źródła* [Polish Jews 1648–1772: Sources] (Kraków: Uniw. Jagielloński, Katedra Judaistyki, 2001), 169–71.
21 For a survey of these developments, see Magda Teter, *Jews and Heretics in Catholic Poland: A Beleaguered Church in the Post-Reformation Era* (Cambridge: Cambridge University Press, 2006).
22 Paweł Maciejko, *The Mixed Multitude: Jacob Frank and the Frankist Movement 1755–1816* (Philadelphia: University of Pennsylvania Press, 2011).

anti-Jewish stereotype of the Jew as usurer. Here, it was the church that was lending money to Jews—and it was that that raised the Pope's ire.[23]

In this exhibit too, because it was impossible to say openly that Catholic–Jewish relations were much more complex than is generally thought, another way had to be found to do so. In this case, it involved using the space designed to represent a church (as well as some of the panels) to evoke commonly held views of hostile and violent Catholic–Jewish interactions, while placing within that space a number of other panels that would tell a different story in order to destabilize old conceptions. The problem here, however, is that, without a *Museum Voice*, one can only hope that visitors get this complex message from just the structure of the exhibit.

Of course, it is impossible to think of the eighteenth-century gallery without considering the synagogue roof. This vibrant reconstruction of the riotously colorful painted synagogue from the small town of Gwoździec was based on the meticulous research into that now destroyed building by Thomas Hubka.[24] While stunningly beautiful in its own right, the synagogue roof served the purposes of the gallery in many different ways. First of all, set back—and so invisible—from the market square, it not only mirrors the common placing of such buildings in the small towns, but also fits the gallery's vision of a vibrant Polish Jewish culture largely hidden behind the physical facades of the small town. It destabilizes common preconceptions—held by Jews and non-Jews—of Eastern European synagogues as dark, dank, and musty places. It also puts in question the idea that Polish Jews, piously following halakha (Jewish Law), strenuously avoided artistic activity.[25] Finally—and most visibly—it tells the visitors that the small town was home to a pervasive and colorful Jewish folk culture.

It serves the gallery's purposes in other ways, too. As Hubka's research showed, while the interior of the synagogue was an expression of Jewish religious and cultural values, the way it was built and its external features fitted very

---

23 Judith Kalik, "Patterns of Contact between the Catholic Church and the Jews in the Polish–Lithuanian Commonwealth: The Jewish Debts," in *Studies on the History of the Jews in Old Poland: Scripta Hierosolymitana*, vol. 38, ed. Adam Teller (Jerusalem: Magnes Press, 1998), 102–22.

24 Thomas C. Hubka, *Resplendent Synagogue: Architecture and Worship in an Eighteenth-Century Polish Community* (Hanover, NH: Brandeis University Press, published by University Press of New England, 2003).

25 On the complex connections between law and praxis in early modern Polish Jewish society, see Edward Fram, *Ideals Face Reality: Jewish Law and Life in Poland, 1550–1655* (Cincinnati, OH: Hebrew Union College Press, 1997).

much into what he called "the architectural vernacular" of the small town.[26] Thus, by reconstructing not just the ceiling but also the intricate system of wooden beams that supported it, we demonstrate in a most graphic way the architectural "Polishness"—perhaps, better, "localness"—of this most Jewish of buildings.

The genius of the exhibit lies in its construction. This was wholly a result of Barbara Kirshenblatt-Gimblett's astonishing vision for the museum and deep understanding of museum language. On the basis of the materials collected by Hubka, Kirshenblatt-Gimblett, who was the head of the Core Exhibit's Academic Team (and is now program director of the Core Exhibit), worked with a company called Handshouse Studio to have the ceiling reconstructed (at slightly less than original scale) by using original building and decorative techniques.[27] This was done by groups of students in a number of closely supervised workshops.

What was created was something that was on the one hand authentic to history, but on the other entirely new. The twenty-first century visitor is able to stand under, and marvel at, an actual painted roof of a building that was destroyed more than seventy years ago. In a strange way, the past actually becomes the present. What Kirshenblatt-Gimblett seems to have understood at the outset is that this is the imperative of the museum as a whole. It is trying to evoke, in the most authentic way possible, the historical experience of generation after generation of Polish Jews, in a form that would be immediately accessible to a twenty-first-century audience. In metaphorical terms, it might be called "the past bursting into the present." This, by the way, is the reason that the timbers of the synagogue roof exhibit break through the ceiling of the museum as a whole and are visible in the entrance hall.

Therefore, as one of the historians charged with supervising this process of letting the early modern past break into our present, I found myself stripped of many of the tools of my trade. I was forced to learn a new language of historical presentation and to rethink the way I understood the construction of narrative and historical argumentation in order to do so. This could be, as I hope this paper has shown, extremely enlightening and enriching. It was very often, however, an extremely uncomfortable process, which involved a lot of pushing and prodding by the designers from Event Communications, whose input into the development of the galleries was enormous.

---

26 Hubka, *Resplendent Synagogue*, 23, 47–48.
27 http://www.handshouse.org/.

Today, I am also painfully aware that when my historian colleagues look at the galleries, they (each in her or his own way) are likely to find some of the choices made in them strange or even misguided. This is natural for every piece of academic work, but the exigencies of museum design have rather prevented me from presenting the documentary basis with which to justify what I chose to do. Though a huge amount of detailed research was undertaken before the design process got underway, it cannot be seen, and so some of what was done may look arbitrary and questionable. On the other hand, it is my hope and belief that when they come to look at the galleries as a whole, my colleagues will find this museological presentation of early modern Polish Jewish history and culture in all its Jewishness and all its Polishness true to a vision of the past that we all, to one degree or another, share.

The Nineteenth-Century Gallery[1]

SAM KASSOW

The nineteenth-century gallery presented special problems that made the development of coherent narratives especially difficult. The gallery begins with the Partitions of Poland and ends with the First World War. In other words, it is the only gallery in the museum where Poland does not exist as a defined political entity. How, then, could one decide which territories were Polish and which Jews were Polish Jews? While the case of Warsaw or Kraków was fairly straightforward, others were not. Over the course of the long nineteenth century, educated Jews in Vilna gravitated towards Russian culture, while in Poznań they opted for German. In Lwów, by contrast, acculturating Jews shifted from German to Polish culture in the last quarter of the nineteenth century.

In addition to problems of definition, we had to find narrative strategies that could make sense out of a long nineteenth century often perceived all over Europe as an accelerating cycle of disruption and uncertainty. For Charles Dickens's Stephen Blackpool in the 1854 novel *Hard Times*, caught in the miseries of the industrial revolution, "it was all a muddle." Six years earlier, Karl Marx had written in the *Communist Manifesto* that "all that is solid melts into air, all that is sacred in profaned."

---

1 As one of the two lead scholars of the "Encounters with Modernity" gallery, and the lead scholar of the interwar gallery "On the Jewish Street" I would like to begin this essay with some well-deserved thank yous: to Barbara Kirshenblatt-Gimblett, whose insights were worth a dozen graduate seminars; to Marcin Wodziński and his unrivaled knowledge of Polish–Jewish history; to Renata Piątkowska and Anna Mizera, the wonderful curators of the "Encounters with Modernity" gallery; and last but not least to Tamara Sztyma and Michał Majewski, the talented and resourceful curators of the interwar gallery.

Did our ordinary shtetl Jew in 1870, let's call him Khaim Yankel, read Marx? Probably not. But if his shtetl was in decline because of the ruin of the Polish landowner or because a new railroad passed it by, he might well have decided to seek his fortune in Łódź, the "Polish Manchester," where his sons and even his daughters could then have read the *Communist Manifesto* in Yiddish translation. And there is no denying that for all his verbal fireworks, Sholem Aleichem's Tevye the Dairyman was struggling to understand a world that was falling apart in front of his eyes: daughters whom he could no longer control as they married revolutionaries, ran off with gentiles, and sadly even committed suicide. Sholem Aleichem's other stories also revealed the disquieting disparity between powerless Jews, armed only with moral faith and language, and new forces only half-understood. The little Jews of Kasrilevke tried to make sense of the Dreyfus Affair and that new-fangled invention, the newspaper, as they pondered modern anti-Semitism and the ominous collision of their half-real, half-imagined shtetl with a dangerous outside world. Motl Peisi, the cantor's son, joined the millions of Jews seeking a new life in America, while Tevye's hapless cousin Menakhem Mendl charged off to Odessa to embrace speculative capitalism with pathetic gusto. The gallery tried to highlight some of the major challenges of the long nineteenth century—anti-Semitism, capitalism, industrialization, urbanization—on many intersecting levels: on Jewish individuals, on the Jewish collective, and on Polish–Jewish relations.

The example of Sholem Aleichem also serves as a reminder of another issue that complicated the planning of the gallery: the important differences between "Jewish space" and "Polish space." No Museum of Polish Jewish History should ignore the impact of writers like Sholem Aleichem and their key role in the creation of a new Yiddish culture. Yet one noted Polish historian, whose work I respect greatly, adamantly opposed the inclusion of Sholem Aleichem in the gallery. After all, she said, how could you call him a Polish Jew? He was from Ukraine and spoke Russian at home! And while we're at it, she continued, what's this nonsense about bringing in Bialik? What did his seminal poem on the 1903 Kishinev pogrom, *City of Slaughter*, have to do with Poland?

At the beginning of our gallery, about one million Jews were living on the Polish lands. There were few factories, no railroads, and no mass press. Łódź was just a tiny village. By the end of our long nineteenth century—1914 actually—around six million Jews were living in the lands of the old commonwealth. Łódź had expanded from a small village to a city with almost 200,000 Jews. The Jewish workers of the socialist Bund had fought pitched battles with Cossacks on urban barricades. A young man named David Green had left Poland for

Palestine and had changed his name to David Ben-Gurion. New Yiddish daily newspapers like *Haynt* and *Moment*, with circulations of 100,000, had replaced the Hebrew weeklies. Two million Jews had left for new continents. Yiddish writers and playwrights on both sides of the ocean composed novels and plays that offered new models of individual and collective behavior. Not only young men but also tens of thousands of women were working in small factories and workshops.

And, by 1914, little remained of the great Polish Jewish brotherhood, of the *zbratanie* of 1861 and 1863, but poignant memories. The historian and poet Aleksander Kraushar had already found his way to the baptismal font. And while Rabbi Izaak Cylkow's successor at the Tłomackie synagogue, Samuel Poznański, gave eloquent sermons in Polish, he did so as a Zionist, not as a "Pole of the Mosaic persuasion." *Izraelita*, the venerable tribune of Polish Jewish integrationism, was all but moribund, while a major leader of Polish liberal progressivism, Aleksander Świętochowski, now had bitter things to say about the very Jews whose cause he had long championed. As long as they wanted to be Poles, Świętochowski declared, he defended them. But Yiddish? The Bund? Zionism? This was rank betrayal. His anger also helps to answer the question why modern Poland failed to develop a vibrant liberal democratic party committed to a civic definition of Polishness and to ethnic toleration.

This long nineteenth century saw the transformation not only of Jewish national narratives but also of those of their gentile neighbors; it saw a new Polish nationalism, no longer the domain of the *szlachta* but aiming to include wider strata of the Polish nation, a new Ukrainian nationalism that honed and sharpened traditional mistrust of Poles and Jews.

The challenges the lead scholars faced were obvious. How could we develop a cogent narrative that eschewed simplistic dichotomies, false teleologies, and misleading perceptions of historical change as a zero-sum game? For example, modernization and secularization did not automatically mean a corresponding eclipse of religion but indeed encouraged traditional Jews to pursue new strategies of adaptation. The erosion of the short-lived period of Polish positivism and Polish Jewish rapprochement, followed by a marked growth in Polish anti-Semitism, did not necessarily mean that young middle-class Jews turned away from Polish culture or Polish education. And as many scholars have shown, most recently Scott Ury, what is loosely called modernization—the growth of cities, elections, new forms of mass communication and mass culture—more often than not inflamed ethnic tensions in mixed areas rather than assuaged them. Nuance is an important aspect of the historian's craft, but it lends itself much more easily to the printed page rather than to museum space.

Another problem, often pointed out by Marcin Wodziński, was the pitfall of "Warsaw-centrism." So much happened in that city that it became all too easy to overemphasize Warsaw at the risk of neglecting other cities and regions.

As I struggled with finding a workable narrative strategy for my part of the gallery, 1860–1914, I decided on a railroad station as a major spatial anchor. What better space was there to present larger themes and individual stories: macroeconomic transformation and how different people responded to it? The exhibit shows the station as a place where different individuals began life-changing journeys. Puah Rakovsky leaves a loveless marriage and a stultifying religious world to move to Warsaw and fight for women's rights. Avrom Zak says goodbye to his little shtetl and travels to Warsaw to realize his dream of becoming a writer. David Green starts his journey to Palestine and to greatness. The layout of the station, the background noise, the timetables, and the ticket windows all suggest new perceptions of space and time. I only regret that we couldn't include that wonderful Yiddish folk song about the frightened religious Jew who sees a train for the first time: "tsi hot men azoy gezen, tsi hot men azoy gehert, az fayer un vaser zol gisn fun a ferd, oy a ferd a groyser, mit an eyzernem koyekh, fun untn gist men vaser, fun oybn geyt a royekh": Can you believe such a thing: a huge horse who eats up burning coals and boiling water! God, kill this thing so religious Jews would not, God forbid, violate the Sabbath.

The train station opens up many suggestive themes: the role of tycoons like Jan Bloch and Leopold Kronenberg in the development of the Polish economy; the sheer transformation of the built landscape through the erection of new wrought-iron bridges and palatial railroad stations; crowded compartments where Jews and gentiles mix. It leads the visitor to look at the world of work and the impact of industrialization. While the industrialization story focuses on Congress Poland and the Pale we do not neglect Galicia, and especially the oil workers of Borysław. We also tried in the industrialization story and elsewhere to deal with issues of gender. While Jewish women labored for wages even worse than those paid to men, the visitor can ponder Shmarye Levin's assertion that, given a choice, Jewish women in Grodno still preferred the factory to work as domestic servants.

The railroads linked the textile, clothing, and tobacco factories of Łódź, Warsaw, and Białystok with the huge Russian markets and thus transformed the economy of Congress Poland and the Pale of Settlement. But new markets required not only technology and entrepreneurs but also skilled agents. The visitor can learn the story of the colorful and resourceful *kommivoyagers*, the hustlers who shopped Łódź textiles to merchants in distant Russian and Siberian towns and thus assured indispensable customers.

The station space also leads the visitor to ponder how industrialization exacerbated the social and economic polarization of Jewish society. One exhibit features fabulously wealthy Jewish millionaires, represented by the Łódź textile tycoon Israel Poznański and his imposing palace. Facing Poznański's palace is a depiction of the squalid slum of Bałuty, where the Jewish workers of Łódź labored in small dank workshops. We also show the powerful role of religious imagery in the rise of a Jewish labor movement. Labor organizers and radicals quickly learned that the best way to reach the Jewish worker, at least at first, was to use the language of the Bible, not the slogans of Marx (those came later). They spoke the workers' language—simple, direct, and full of religious references. Shouldn't Jews fight for justice and confront evil? Does the Bible not tell employers to give honest wages for a day's work? One early socialist newspaper declared that it would "write about the workers' fate, their suffering and struggle. The newspaper will be like a shofar. It will wake them up and urged them to action."

The theme of industrialization and modernization conveyed in the railway station was closely linked to the rise of new professional and business strata and a generation of young Jewish men and women attracted to the Polish language and culture. In this way, the railway station opens out to spaces and visuals that convey the hope of Jewish integration into Polish culture and society: Aleksander Lesser's painting of the Funeral of Polish patriots, the model of the Tłomackie synagogue, vignettes of the assimilated philanthropists Ludwik Natanson and Hipolit Wawelberg, the story of Izaak Cylkow, the Polish patriot who became the first rabbi of the Tłomackie synagogue. To avoid excessive Warsaw-centrism, we also highlighted the story of the Galician Jewish painter Maurycy Gottlieb, his love of Poland, his encounters with anti-Semitism, his use of Jewish and Polish themes, and his premature death. We also introduce Heinrich Graetz, Sh. Ansky, and Simon Dubnow to show other forms and gradations of acculturation and integration to Russian and German culture.

The themes of violence, autoemancipation, Yiddish or Hebrew, and revolution offer a stark counterpoint to the story of integration. Historians may debate long-held assertions, argued by Jonathan Frankel and others, that 1881 was an important turning point in modern Jewish history. Such scholars like Frankel argued that 1881, which saw an unexpected wave of pogroms that followed the assassination of Russian Tsar Alexander II, sparked many key changes: the beginning of mass Jewish emigration from Eastern Europe; a reevaluation of the Haskalah and its optimistic hopes for Jewish integration into European culture; a new search for national self-definition exemplified by Lev Pinsker's 1882 pamphlet titled *Autoemancipation*; the rise of new political ideologies such as Zionism and Jewish socialism; the rise of new secular literature in Yiddish and Hebrew; the impact of a new Yiddish theater.

Whatever the strengths or shortcomings of Frankel's thesis, it does provide a framework that allows the visitor to ponder questions about the many important choices that Jews had to make by the end of the nineteenth century. What the exhibit tries to do is to engage the visitor by posing questions about language, territory, and political tactics that underscore the wide array of choices that Jews had to make. One narrative strategy underscores the role of the major Yiddish writer Y. L. Peretz who, influenced by the impact of the great Romantic poets on Polish culture, regarded the Jewish writer and artist as a modern-day prophet who could provide leadership for the Jewish people and forge a new national consciousness.

What concerns do I have about the gallery? It proved difficult to present what I would call "the third dimension," Jewish exposure to competing nationalisms. In eastern Galicia, Jews, especially professionals and intellectuals, found themselves in the crossfire of competing Polish and Ukrainian nationalisms. In Lithuania and Belarus, the same Jews found themselves caught between their attraction to Russian culture and Polish accusations that they were abetting Russian colonizers. In both East Galicia and in the Russian Empire, one Jewish response to this dilemma was to choose Zionism or Bundism, a Jewish option that would have a major impact on the development of modern Jewish politics. Piłsudski had accused Jewish revolutionaries of favoring Russification. This "third dimension" was certainly considered but telling this story within the constraints of museum space proved to be unexpectedly difficult.

I also have second thoughts about how we portray anti-Semitism. The story of the December 1881 pogrom is not as sharp as it could be. To be sure, we show Aleksander Kraushar's haunting poem of disappointment and even betrayal. But will the average visitor, especially the non-Polish visitor, understand what Kraushar meant when he saw his dreams of Polish Jewish integration collapsing in an outbreak of violence and hatred? The exhibit certainly shows how a new, more pernicious kind of anti-Semitism developed in the late nineteenth century, one key example being Jeleński's newspaper *Rola*, which began publication in 1883. Visitors can ponder Aleksander Świętochowski's statement about the widespread and growing antipathy in Polish society toward Jews. The exhibit shows the blood libel in Chojnice and the 1912 economic boycott that marked a fateful turning point in Polish–Jewish relations. The story of anti-Semitism in the gallery is presented as part of a larger narrative, rather than as a distinct theme with its own space. Therefore, reasonable people might well object that the average visitor might easily miss the point. One might also object that not enough is said about Roman Dmowski and the role he played in the development of modern Polish anti-Semitism. Of course, the many and exhaustive discussions about the planning of the exhibit included these issues. But considerations of space forced many difficult decisions. It is to be hoped that some of these shortcomings, for which I take some responsibility as a lead historian, can be corrected in the future.

The Interwar Gallery

SAM KASSOW

Compared to the "Encounters with Modernity" gallery, the interwar gallery, "On the Jewish Street," was in some ways much easier to design. Instead of the partitions, there was a Polish state, although the tumultuous and confused transition period from 1918 to 1921 presented designers with some interesting challenges. There was also a wealth of visual and textual sources.

Yet the gallery also presented challenges of its own. It ends on September 1, 1939, as surprised citizens look up to the sky. Can one—should one—depict interwar Polish Jewry without referring to the looming disaster?

Not so long ago people who looked for books on prewar Polish Jews could choose from such titles as *On the Edge of Destruction* by Celia Stopnicka Heller, *No Way Out* (the title of the English translation from the Hebrew original) by Emanuel Melzer, or *Oyfn rand fun opgrunt* (On the edge of the abyss) by Jacob Leshchinsky. There was also the 1966 film titled *The Last Chapter*, directed by Benjamin and Lawrence Rothman. It is not my intention to denigrate these valuable projects, but there is no denying the message that these titles convey.

At a conference on the museum held at Princeton University in April 2015, some first-rate scholars criticized the exhibit because it avoided any hint of foreshadowing: the prism of the Holocaust was notably absent from the many lenses through which visitors viewed this gallery. The catastrophe, they emphasized, was too important to be put "into brackets." As a child of Holocaust survivors born in a displaced persons camp in Germany in 1946, just one month after my parents left Poland with the Bricha (the underground Zionist organized effort that helped Jewish Holocaust survivors to emigrate to Palestine), I understand this view quite well. I well remember their story about how, in 1946, they felt much safer in Germany than in Poland. I am also quite aware that the escalating anti-Semitism of the late 1930s, as well as the largely hostile attitude of the Roman Catholic Church, played no small role in what was at best the indifference of large parts of the Polish population during the war, as well as in the widespread violence and murder of Jews by Poles analyzed by Jan Tomasz Gross, Jan Grabowski, Barbara Engelking, and others. Reasonable people can disagree about how to show this anti-Semitism in museum space, and, frankly, there is some room for improvement on our part, both in the transition space and in the interwar gallery.

But, as a historian, I totally supported and continue to support a basic principle outlined by Barbara Kirshenblatt-Gimblett: this is a museum about Polish Jewish life, not a museum about Polish anti-Semitism or about Polish–Jewish relations. Another key principle was that there be no back shadowing, that we would use no texts written after 1939. Therefore, the exhibit is titled "On the Jewish Street," not "On the Edge of Destruction." There were indeed many Jews who felt trapped in Poland and frantically tried to leave. But there were others, like Senator Ozjasz Thon, who reminded his brothers and sisters in 1932 that, for all its serious problems, it was only Polish Jewry—not US Jewry, not Soviet Jewry—that had the intellectual resources and national vitality to lead the Jewish people. The Yiddish poet Melekh Ravich recalled that, in 1934, he ran into the young historian Emanuel Ringelblum on a Warsaw street. Ravich was about to migrate to Australia, and he told Ringelblum to get out of Poland as fast as he could. But Ringelblum replied that he believed that Polish Jewry had a future. By the same token, Lucy Dawidowicz recalled how, in the summer of 1939, YIVO director Max Weinreich was preparing for the third world conference of the YIVO scheduled to take place in 1940. Weinreich wanted Dawidowicz to remain in Vilna as a graduate student. He too was optimistic about the future. Foolishness? False optimism? Whistling past the graveyard? Perhaps. We can even safely assume that most Polish Jews were not as sanguine as Weinreich. But we have to tell their story based on what they knew then, not on what we know now.

One major theme in the galley is the sheer diversity of interwar Polish Jewry. It included Jews in big cities and small towns, Polish speakers and Yiddish speakers, yeshiva students and Bundists. Interwar Polish Jewry was also a work in progress, as Jews from the different partitions slowly overcame their cultural differences to find a common identity as "Polish Jews." Just as Warsaw brought together long-divided Poles, so too did it bring together Jews thanks to its growing role as the center of political parties, the mass press, and welfare organizations. On the eve of the war, one in four Jews lived in one of the five largest cities, but half still lived in small towns. But at the same time, the most remote Jewish shtetl was linked to and influenced by the big city: Yiddish newspapers, lectures by visiting writers, hard-fought political campaigns, and even dance competitions and beauty contests. There was a powerful tide of secularization, but the exhibit does not forget the many Polish Jews who journeyed to their rebbe, or studied a page of Mishna or *Eyn Yankev* after work.

Although Polish Jewry constituted an enormous reservoir of Jewish national energy, we tell the story not just of a collective but also of individuals who hiked, danced, loved jazz, who lived their own lives, worried about their personal problems, and, like everybody else, played their childhood games, skipped school, struggled through adolescence, fell in love, married, and raised children. One of Jewish Poland's most beloved songwriters, Mordkhe Gebirtig, penned a song about a Jewish girl who insisted that her religious boyfriend Leibke learn how to dance:

> You can be what you want,
> a Zionist, a Bundist—who cares?
> But Leibke, the time will come
> when even the most religious Jews
> will have to learn the Tango and the Charleston!

The literal translation of the Yiddish expression *di yidishe gas* is "the Jewish street," but the wider meaning is "the Jewish world"—referring to the creation of a modern Jewish world that was at once diverse and nationally conscious, rooted in Poland and yet distinctively Jewish. During the interwar years, Poland became a living laboratory for experiments in modern Jewish life. These adventures produced new models of politics, self-help, and culture. Polish Jews saw themselves—and were often seen by others—as the most culturally vibrant Jewish community in the world. Because the war cut these developments short, a stroll down the "Jewish Street" of the interwar gallery highlights beginnings, rather than final results, and journeys, rather than final destinations.

The gallery is divided into four parts: politics, culture, daily life, and growing up. It is preceded by a very important transitional gallery that shows the tumultuous events of the First World War, the sheer scale of destruction and economic dislocation, the paradoxical interplay of violence, and the consciousness of a plastic moment rife with possibilities for the future: the collapse of empires, the rebirth of Poland, the Balfour Declaration, the Bolshevik revolution. We remind the visitor that the new Poland had been ravaged by years of war, that the violence continued until 1921 and that the new state had to fight all its neighbors on all its borders. Polish–Jewish relations had deteriorated on the eve of the war and did not improve once the fighting had started.

The violence and chaos of war provided fertile ground for rumors, innuendo, and paranoia, which helped spark the many Polish pogroms and acts of violence against Jews between 1918 and 1920. Among the worst examples were the Lwów pogrom of November 1918, the shooting of thirty-five participants at a Jewish meeting in Pińsk in April 1919, and the murder of fifty-five Jews when the Polish army took Vilna in April 1919. We show all of this, but, frankly, I think these events could be portrayed more clearly and forcefully. For example, the visual in the transition gallery might give the visitor the mistaken impression that Jews actually collaborated with Ukrainians in Lwów, which was not true. And the picture of Jewish children hiding in Lwów does not convey the sheer brutality and violence of that pogrom.

Anti-Jewish violence abated once the fighting died down, and the Polish constitution of March 1921 did guarantee all citizens equal rights. Like other citizens, Polish Jews could vote, and they certainly enjoyed much more liberty than their brethren across the border in the Soviet Union. In practice, however, Polish Jews felt that they were second-class citizens, and there persisted an inherent tension between the idea of Poland as a nation-state of Poles and Poland as a multiethnic democracy with equal rights for all its citizens. Historians have long argued about the position of Jews in the interwar years. Ezra Mendelsohn reminded us that before we blithely describe Polish anti-Semitism and discrimination, we should try to remember the real problems that Poland faced and that Jews were not the only minority. Jerzy Tomaszewski remonstrated with Shie Trunk over the latter's assessment of state anti-Semitism aimed at destroying the economic bases of Jewish life. Tomaszewski asserted that the issue of economic anti-Semitism had to be put into the context of the serious economic problems of the Second Republic and the efforts of the state, often misguided, to solve them. In an important 1984 study, Joseph Marcus argued that while Polish Jewry was undergoing a serious crisis of pauperization, on a per-capita basis Polish Jews were still better off than their Polish neighbors.

I am not citing this to whitewash the very real discrimination that Jews faced in interwar Poland but only to show that there are serious scholarly debates that are not easy to present in museum space. In our timeline, we show the terrible effects of Władysław Grabski's tax policies, the *numerus clausus* in university admissions, the ghetto benches, the violence in the universities, an attack on Professor Marceli Handelsman, a letter from a Jewish student beaten up in Lwów, the Przytyk pogrom, a burning house during the Minsk pogrom, the restrictions on ritual slaughter, and Julian Tuwim's cry of anguish against Polish anti-Semitism. We explain why the surging popularity of the Bund on the eve of the war was linked to its battle against escalating anti-Jewish violence.

Is this enough? Could we have done more? Certainly, I think we should have paid more attention to the role of the Roman Catholic Church. As for the rest, there is room for an honest and frank discussion. As part of this discussion, we should remember that although Józef Piłsudski did far less than many Jews hoped, he commanded the respect of the vast majority of the community who understood that he did not regard them as harmful aliens and who did his best to clamp down on anti-Semitic violence. The case of Piłsudski underscores the sad fact that Polish Jews were better off under an authoritarian strongman than they were under parliamentary democracy. A more robust Polish economy and more available resources might have improved Polish–Jewish relations. But that is hypothetical.

Polish Jews waged a tough battle in parliament, in city councils, in the press, and even in the streets to defend their rights. We concentrate three major Jewish political currents: Zionism, the religious Aguda, and the socialist Bund. If Jewish political parties won few victories in the Polish parliament, they nonetheless accomplished a great deal "on the Jewish street" itself. Their greatest success was in the total way of life they offered their followers: providing schools, summer camps, sports, clubs, health care, and a wide range of social and cultural activities. We show the strengths of the various movements: Zionism as the one political trend that had across-the-board appeal, that bridged Polish and Jewish cultures through its emphasis on nationalism, romantic pathos, heroism, individual sacrifice, and the historical challenge of reviving a great state, that built the Tarbut schools and the youth movements from whose ranks came Abba Kovner, Mordecai Anielewicz, and Menachem Begin. Without the 140,000 Polish Jews who immigrated to Palestine before the war, there would have been no State of Israel.

We show the Aguda, whose fortunes rose under Piłsudski and fell after his death, and we stress its remarkable ability to adapt to new challenges in Jewish life: the Bais Yaakov schools, modernized heders, a robust press, the Lublin yeshiva, cooperation of hasidic rebbes (Ger) and Lithuanian sages (Khayim Oyzer). We have a good exhibit on the Bund and explain why on the eve of the war it became the most popular Jewish party, especially in the big cities. In the 1938 municipal elections, the Bund won seventeen out of twenty Jewish seats.

Our culture gallery—based on the exhibits of Vilna, Tłomackie 13, the Café Ziemiańska, an art salon, and popular culture—recognizes certain paradoxes. Yiddish literature and Yiddish theater remained very creative, even though Yiddish was on the defensive on the Jewish street. Despite growing anti-Semitism and the collapse of traditional assimilationism, more Jews than ever spoke Polish as their first language—while remaining proudly Jewish. Meanwhile, Palestine displaced Poland as the center of Hebrew culture.

But the story of Jewish culture in interwar Poland was hardly a simple zero-sum game, where one language triumphed at the expense of another. Instead, as the late Chone Shmeruk pointed out, Polish Jewry between the wars developed a culture that was polylingual, marked by a rich interplay of Yiddish, Polish, and Hebrew. Even as more and more Jews spoke Polish as their first language, they still flocked to the Yiddish theater and learned Hebrew. Yiddish speakers avidly devoured Polish literature, whether in the original or in Yiddish translation. In addition, the best-selling Yiddish books were often translations from other literatures. The last thing Polish Jews wanted was to live in a cultural ghetto.

The "newspaper wall" shows the front pages of dozens of Jewish newspapers in Yiddish, Hebrew, and Polish. Visitors can explore two of them in depth at interactive stations devoted to the Yiddish daily *Haynt* and to *Nasz Przegląd*, a Zionist-leaning daily in Polish. We encourage the visitor to ask why Polish-speaking Jews felt that they needed their own daily newspapers, rather than read the mainstream Polish press with perhaps a Jewish weekly or monthly. We raise the whole issue of what Katrin Steffen called "Jewish Polishness," the self-affirming Jewish culture in the Polish language that was becoming more and more salient.

An essential component of the culture section of the gallery is the Vilna exhibit, which shows Vilna as the imaginary capital of a world state called Yiddishland. Its claim to this status rested on its famed Yiddish schools, on the writers' group Yung Vilna, on the YIVO (Yiddish Scientific Institute), and on the fact that it was in Vilna that even the Jewish middle and professional classes used Yiddish, at least in public. As the Yiddish cultural critic Nokhem Shtif once wrote, "Peretz may have written in Warsaw. But he was read in Vilna." More Jewish children attended Yiddish-language schools in Vilna than in Warsaw. In the 1930s, Vilna was the only city in Poland that supported a first-rate Yiddish high school, the Realgymnasium.

The culture exhibit then moves to Warsaw and the legendary writers' club at Tłomackie 13, which its members affectionately called *di bude* (the Shack). Tłomackie 13 had a buffet, a record player to which Yiddish writers would practice the tango, and a main hall where debates and talks would happen several times a week. Tłomackie served as a key cultural link between the center and the provinces; each weekend its writers fanned out all over Poland to give lectures. But the exhibit, with its large portrait of Y. L. Peretz, also reminds the visitor that Tłomackie never overcame the loss of that great writer. Peretz, the one person who might have united the fractious Yiddish writers and artists, was gone.

The culture exhibit also reminds the visitor of the growing role of Polish-speaking Jews through the evocation of the legendary Café Ziemiańska. This was where Warsaw's literary intelligentsia and artistic elite gathered—jazz musicians, cabaret wits, playwrights and artists, well-known singers and Jewish composers and bandleaders, among them Artur Gold and Jerzy Petersburski.

The second level of the gallery depicts daily life and growing up. The exhibit shows the variety of daily life by taking the visitor on tours of different cities and towns. In interwar Poland, *krajoznawstwo*—literally, knowing the land—promoted educational tourism and fostered a shared identity among Poles. But Jews were, for the most part, not welcome in the *krajoznawstwo* movement, and Polish guidebooks tended to ignore Jews or to slight them.

In 1931, Jews founded their own *krajoznawstwo* movement called *landkentenish*, a direct translation. The *landkentenish* movement considered self-knowledge central to the struggle of Polish Jewry for its political rights and economic survival. It stressed emphasizing their rootedness in the country. Organized kayaking, mountain climbing, cross country skiing, and photography all served to demonstrate that Jews were natives rather than unwanted guests. In the words of Mikhl Burshtin, a *landkentenish* activist, "All along the Polish rivers lie towns and settlements with a rooted and diverse Jewish life that stretches back hundreds of years."

Landkentenish is the inspiration for the presentation of daily life in the Second Polish Republic. Through travel to thirteen towns the visitors can see a broad panorama of everyday Jewish life. The exhibit intended to use certain towns to highlight specific issues: Kolbuszowa for economics and the marketplace, or Nowogródek for self-help and relations with emigrant societies. Szczuczyn is presented through the lens of the photography studio of Zalman Kaplan, and Drohobycz from the perspective of the writer and artist Bruno Schulz. Kazimierz Dolny (Kuzmir in Yiddish), an iconic Jewish town and artists' colony on the Vistula, is shown through the eyes of painters, photographers, and filmmakers. Bobowa, a hasidic center, is shown through the photo reportage of the wedding of the daughter of the Bobover rebbe, a spectacular event in 1931 that attracted thousands of guests. Gdynia, the newest and smallest Jewish community in the Second Polish Republic, appears as the place to which Jewish visitors from abroad arrived and from which Polish Jews emigrated. Działoszyn is described as a sleepy place in the autobiography of a young man in despair about his future.

The last part of the gallery deals with growing up: childhood, family life, self-help, education, and youth movements. Young people speak in their own voices, which the exhibit evokes through the many youth autobiographies sent to the YIVO. These quotations reflect their struggles, hopes, and dreams. The visitor can also peruse a "family album" in the form of an interactive table on which are scattered photographs of various kinds of families and quotations that reveal their generational conflicts. There is also a courtyard where visitors can craft the toys that children made for themselves. In the background one can hear the voices of children, counting in Yiddish, playing a game of hopscotch.

For Jewish parents, nothing was more important than education. Jewish parents had to choose whether to send their children to Polish primary schools, which were free, or to Jewish schools, where, it was argued, Jewish children could develop self-assurance in an atmosphere free of anti-Semitism. Sixty percent of Jewish children attended Polish public schools, and about 180,000 children were attending Jewish schools by the mid-1930s. Many of those who went to Polish public schools also went to Jewish after-school lessons. Through an evocative classroom furnished with a blackboard and desks, the visitor can see the entire range of schools open to Jews: the Yiddish secular schools of CYSHO, the Hebrew Zionist Schools of Tarbut, the religious schools and vocational schools. The visitor can also see that as a child grew older, educational opportunities steadily narrowed. Few made it to secondary school and only a tiny handful to the universities.

In the face of growing generation tensions, economic difficulties, and shrinking educational opportunities, Jewish adolescents in interwar Poland turned to each other and developed a strong peer culture based on youth movements. Youth movements gave their members a home away from home, an alternative family, and a nurturing counterculture. Ideology played a major role, but so did literature and theater. Most youth groups had a room, *lokal*, and a library, the setting for presenting Jewish youth as they approached adulthood. No generation in Jewish history read as intensely and voraciously as the young Jews of interwar Poland, as shown in the "card catalogue" of the books they were reading. Literature raised questions that were often debated in a *kestl ovnt*, during which young people would reach into a box and pull out a topic to be discussed. The subjects that most concerned them—love, sex, conflicts with parents, their future—are captured in quotations from their autobiographies projected on a wall in a setting evocative of a *kestl ovnt*. The youth movements also sponsored amateur plays and mandolin orchestras, long hikes and sporting events, as illustrated in the photographs and posters that cover the walls. On a table are notebooks introducing the young Jews whose autobiographies were quoted throughout the presentation of growing up. Jewish youth looked to the future with a mixture of hope and uncertainty.

As economic conditions worsened, Polish Jews developed an impressive array of organizations. Featured here are promotional films made by TOZ, CENTOS, and the Medem Sanatorium. TOZ, the Society for Safeguarding the Health of the Jewish Population, established clinics in many cities and towns. CENTOS, the Organization for Child and Orphan Care, promoted modern approaches to childrearing and childcare. The Medem Sanatorium, which was supported by Jewish socialists, cared for children and youth from working-class families at risk for tuberculosis, while also taking a progressive approach to their emotional and intellectual development.

Polish Jewry was a community beset by challenges and difficulties. But few communities in the history of the Jewish people showed more resilience, vitality, and national consciousness than did the Jews of interwar Poland. In the last months of peace, they joined their fellow citizens in an effort to bolster Poland's defenses. Meanwhile, they educated their children, helped each other, and continued to fight for their rights and national dignity. Even as they saw dark clouds on the horizon, they continued to hope for a better tomorrow.

Curatorial and Educational Challenges in Creating the Holocaust Gallery[1]

MARIA FERENC-PIOTROWSKA,
KAMILA RADECKA-MIKULICZ,
AND JUSTYNA MAJEWSKA

ASSUMPTIONS

One of the basic assumptions upon which the narrative of the core exhibition has been constructed is that Jewish history is an inseparable part of Polish history. This axiom applies also to the Holocaust Gallery: the Shoah is portrayed as an integral element of Polish history. A second assumption employed in all the galleries is immersion in the visual language of the historical period and in the perspective of "there and then." Thus, the narrative of the Holocaust Gallery is based, in part, on documents assembled by the Oyneg Shabes group (the Ringelblum Archive). At the same time, the voices from the past are accompanied by a contemporary museum voice which provides context. This leads to the third assumption: the core exhibition is a space for a recreated "theater of history" which emerges in front of the eyes of visitors, bringing history back to life. This does not, however, imply staging but rather

---

1 An early version of this article was published as "Wyzwania kuratorskie i edukacyjne związane z tworzeniem galerii Zagłada Wystawy Głównej Muzeum Historii Żydów Polskich" [Curatorial and educational challenges in creating the Holocaust Gallery in the core exhibition of the Museum of the History of Polish Jews] in *Auschwitz i Holokaust. Edukacja w szkole i w miejscu pamięci* [Auschwitz and the Holocaust. Education in the school and the place of memory], ed. Piotr Trojański (Oświęcim: Państwowe Muzeum Auschwitz-Birkenau, 2014), 377–89.

creating dramatic effects which reconstruct iconic places and images of the period represented.²

Within these defined parameters, the curatorial team of the Holocaust Gallery set itself the goal of creating a display that was not "merely" historical, but which, above all, stressed loneliness as the fundamental Jewish experience during those years. This loneliness had various dimensions, both physical, resulting from isolation in ghettos, but also existential, linked to the indifference of the surrounding world to placing the Jews beyond the moral universe of the non-Jewish witnesses.³

In addition to these principles common to all the galleries, the team of the Holocaust Gallery has relied also on specific assumptions relating exclusively to this part of the exhibition. The museum is located in the Muranów district in Warsaw, in the heart of the former Warsaw ghetto, opposite Natan Rapoport's famous Monument to the Ghetto Heroes. The Holocaust Gallery is actually situated on a part of what was formerly Zamenhof Street, along which Jews were driven toward the Umschlagplatz, from where they were transported to the Treblinka death camp. Thus, the building's location creates a link between a real site and historical accounts. In order to underscore this *genius loci*, special emphasis is placed on the history of the Warsaw Ghetto, the largest ghetto in occupied Europe. While recognizing its uniqueness and specific character, it can be seen as a *pars pro toto* for other ghettos.

EXHIBITION SPACE

The gallery devoted to the Holocaust begins as a continuation of the display on the interwar period. Walking past the facades of apartment blocks, the visitor approaches a photograph of a group of people looking up at the sky. This scene depicts the outbreak of the Second World War: the people are watching a German airplane over Warsaw; the buildings crumble into ruins under the impact of German bombing, and so does the prewar world.

The September campaign is presented through the eyes of a sixteen-year-old eyewitness, Stanisław Kramsztyk from Warsaw. Raised in an assimilated

---

2 For more on the premises of "retelling history," see Barbara Kirshenblatt-Gimblett, "Theater of History," in *Polin. 1000 Year History of Polish Jews*, ed. Barbara Kirshenblatt-Gimblett and Antony Polonsky, Museum of the History of Polish Jews (Warsaw: Museum of the History of the Polish Jews, 2014), 30–35.

3 Barbara Engelking and Jacek Leociak, "Holocaust, 1939–1945," in *Polin. 1000 Year History of Polish Jews*, 289–290.

Jewish family, Stanisław cut out of newspapers communiqués about the Polish army's operations. The communiqués, initially full of élan and optimism, gradually became a chronicle of the Polish army's defeat. Moving further into the gallery, visitors learn in detail about the Soviet and German occupations, as well as about the dynamic process of separating and isolating Jews from the rest of the society in occupied Poland. This followed a sequence of humiliation, visible identification, directives to provide forced labor, confiscation of property, and ghettoization.

The next part of the gallery is devoted to the Warsaw Ghetto. The sealed Jewish district is depicted at two stages of its existence, focusing first on life in the shadow of death and then on the period from the great deportation in summer 1942 to the uprising in the ghetto in April 1943. The narrators leading visitors through the complex and dramatic reality of life in the ghetto are Adam Czerniaków, chairman of the Jewish Council (Judenrat), and Emanuel Ringelblum, the founder of the Oyneg Shabes group—the clandestine archive of the Warsaw Ghetto. Czerniaków represents the official, administrative side of the ghetto's life; Ringelblum exemplifies the illegal and unofficial one. The narrative is structured around a collision between two conflicting strategies: the German-imposed ruthless regulation of life in the ghetto and Jewish reactions to this imposed reality.

The next gallery space is devoted to the "Aryan Side." Visitors see it for the first time when standing on the bridge tying together the two narratives of the Warsaw ghetto. It plays the role of a link between the story of life in the shadow of death and that of the great deportation in the summer of 1942 and its consequences, but the bridge is also a recreation of the footbridge over Chłodna Street in Warsaw linking the small and the large ghettos. In the actual space devoted to the "Aryan Side," the chronology line takes a detour: the narration begins again in 1940 and culminates in the collapse of the Warsaw uprising in 1944. Here visitors learn about the reality of life in occupied Poland from Polish perspective, molded by the German reign of terror which the Polish Underground State tried to resist. Both these factors deeply affected Polish–Jewish relations during the war. The "Aryan Side" leads to the exhibit devoted to Jews in hiding and the complexity of relations between those in need of help and those who helped. By depicting many different stories of such Jews, we attempt to show the whole spectrum of attitudes, from help to betrayal and murder.

The next space moves visitors back in time to June 1941 when the Third Reich attacked the Soviet Union and a new stage in the war began. The activities of the Einsatzgruppen are covered here, as are the examples of pogroms carried out by the local population (Lwów and Jedwabne), the operations of the first death camp—Kulmhof (Chełmno on Ner)—as well as the decisions taken at the 1942 Wannsee Conference, which was followed by Aktion Reinhardt—the murder of Polish Jewry and the transportation of European Jews to death camps located on the territory of the occupied Poland. Only now is the visitor confronted with the German plan for the systematic destruction of the Jews. The next space, the Shoah Corridor, presents the history of two death camps: Auschwitz II–Birkenau and Treblinka II. A dramatic effect forms a coda to the gallery: an empty space, devoid of information, a place for reflection where the visitor can absorb and internalize the losses.

Then comes the postwar gallery which opens with the information of what the free world knew about the Holocaust during the war. The narration then focuses on the liberation of the camps and the formation of the so-called Lublin government in July 1944. The narrative in this final gallery continues right down to the present.

CURATORIAL DECISIONS

The curatorial challenges we faced were to a great extent linked to the decisions that a curator must take when working on an historical exhibit in a narrative museum. The message the exhibition wants to deliver and hence the visitor's reactions and conclusions depend on these decisions. We formulated a number of questions while shaping and organizing our narrative:

> What is important in our story?
> What should a visitor take away from the exhibit?
> Who is the subject of the exhibit's narrative?
> Whose perspectives do we want to present in the narrative? Why?
> How can we use the language of a museum to talk about the Holocaust?
> How do we define the Holocaust?

This final issue is particularly important, since the definition of the Holocaust influences how it is depicted in the exhibit. The emphasis in the story depends on which school of historiography the curators follow. To some, the Holocaust is synonymous with the "final solution"; others acknowledge that the Holocaust is, above all, the process of physical annihilation.[4] In our exhibit, the emphasis

---

4 Avner Shalev, Dan Michman, David Silberklang, "Ścisła pamięć o Zagładzie w Muzeum Historii Holokaustu w Yad Vashem. Odpowiedź na artykuł Amosa Goldberga" [An accurate

has been placed on "life in the shadow of death"—in other words, on the totality of the Jewish experience in German-occupied Poland: from ghettoization to death. We were especially concerned to show the differences in Jewish attitudes toward persecution.

A key component of the authorial concept in the Holocaust Gallery has been to build a narrative based on testimony from the period of the events depicted, from the perspective of "there and then," not retrospectively. Together with the narrators who describe events, visitors go back to the beginning of the war. They see events through the eyes of individuals who do not yet know what is going to happen. This approach allows the visitor to understand that "life in the shadow of death" had the appearance of normality as well as a number of other specific attributes. Of course, visitors are fully aware of what happens later, but the aim of this stratagem is to show the gulf between the contemporary perception of reality, which views events as they develop, and historical knowledge that always examines the past with an awareness of what happened later. Thus, the process of defining the Holocaust is a subconscious theme of our story.

Using only contemporaneous texts, we operate in a manner different to many other exhibitions on the Holocaust, which adopt an historical perspective based on the testimony of a small number of survivors. Seen thus, the Shoah becomes inevitable, and the story of any wartime experience is filtered through knowledge of what subsequently happened.

STRATEGY ON TEXTS

The basic message is aimed at a typical student in a Polish secondary school and the information is divided into three layers. The first layer usually consists of a photograph or an original quotation (together with a translation) of not more than twenty words. In the Holocaust Gallery, in addition to Polish, visitors encounter Yiddish, Hebrew, and German. It is made very clear what kind of source the visitor is experiencing; who is the author, in what language it was originally written, and in what circumstances.

The second layer is usually a commentary expanding on the context of the source. This is no arbitrary text and it is not written from the point of view of an omniscient historian: its aim is more to inquire, inspire, and encourage

---

memory of the Holocaust in the Yad Vashem Museum of the History of the Holocaust. A response to the article by Amos Goldberg], *Zagłada Żydów. Studia i Materiały* 7 (2011): 364.

reflection. We convey the third layer of information (in-depth knowledge) using multimedia devices or in narrative captions to the photographs.

TOPOGRAPHY OF THE GALLERY

The topography of the Holocaust Gallery reflects its thematic structure. It also creates a symbolic geography of the places we are describing.[5] The Warsaw Ghetto section is the most firmly embedded in the topography.

We also understand topography metaphorically, as a way of looking at things. We indicate this especially in the case of the bridge over Chłodna street and the "Aryan Side." From the bridge, joining the two parts of the story of the Warsaw Ghetto, we look down on the street below. From the perspective of the Jews imprisoned in the ghetto, the street appears idyllic, and becomes the object of longing and nostalgia. When visitors later find themselves on the "Aryan Side," they encounter more closely the Polish experience of the occupation and they realize that the idyll was only illusory.

Our aim is to show visitors that the Holocaust occurred in a specific place, and that acceptance of this fact is essential when reflecting on what has happened. On the one hand, occupied Poland was a peripheral country terrorized by the Germans, deprived of its sovereignty and situated far from the eyes of world public opinion, while, on the other hand, it possessed an adequate infrastructure whose scope allowed the Germans to carry out the mass annihilation of Polish and European Jews. The Germans surveyed the sites of future death camps and selected remote and inaccessible spots that made escape difficult.

An example of place where the topography plays a specific role is the exhibit on the Umschlagplatz in Warsaw, where Jews destined for deportation to Treblinka were held. To get to the Umschlagplatz space, visitors go down stairs from the mezzanine. On each step, there is a name of a street in the Warsaw ghetto from which Jews were successively evicted. Opposite the stairs there is an enlarged photograph of the Umschlagplatz—a fenced-off stretch of Stawki Street and a view of the street heading east. Visitors see a crowd of people awaiting deportation and German guards. On the floor, there is a

---

5 In her article "Kicz i Holokaust, czyli pedagogiczny wymiar ekspozycji muzealnych" [Kitsch and the Holocaust, or the pedagogical dimension of museum exhibitions], *Zagłada Żydów. Studia i Materiały* 6 (2010): 74–86, Anna Ziębińska-Witek describes the meaning of the exhibition's topography; see also *Historia w muzeach. Studium ekspozycji Holokaustu* [History in museums. A study of the representation of the Holocaust] (Lublin: Wydawnictwo Uniwersytetu Marii Curie-Skłodowskiej, 2011), 71–73.

copy of a map of the Umschlagplatz by Henryk Rudnicki, who was there in the summer of 1942, but managed to avoid deportation.

PERSPECTIVES

The issue of perspectives is the key concept of the Holocaust Gallery. We use the classic distinction between perpetrators, victims, and bystanders formulated by Raul Hilberg.

The victims' perspective dominates the exhibition. Because of its inner variety and complexity, it would be better to speak of victims' perspectives. We weave our story from the voices of a great many narrators, who present different, sometimes contradictory attitudes and survival strategies (an example would be the quotation of different opinions after Adam Czerniaków's suicide). It is important for us to give a voice to as many testimonies as possible, thereby returning to victims their subjectivity and identity, which is not possible in more linear narrations.

In the story of the Warsaw Ghetto, the strategies of the victims are delineated, above all, by the character of the narrators. Adam Czerniaków, who was the chairman of the Warsaw Jewish Council responsible to the Germans, represents the strategy of surviving by seeking a *modus vivendi* with the Germans. Emanuel Ringelblum, historian, community organizer, and creator of the underground archive of the ghetto, by contrast, exemplifies the sphere of underground organizations' activities. In each thematic space in the exhibit devoted to life in the ghetto before the great deportation, the visitor is confronted with these two perspectives, expressed in quotations from Czerniaków's and Ringelblum's diaries. The visitor will find in each traces of the same ghetto reality, but different approaches to and attempts at solving the ghetto inhabitants' problems.

In the Holocaust Gallery, the perspective of bystanders is the Poles' perspective, firmly embedded in relations between Poles and Jews. Hence the Bridge over the "Aryan Side" is one of the key points in our narrative—in it, victims gaze at witnesses and witnesses gaze at victims, passing and exchanging glances. We feel that the relationship between these two groups must be analyzed in relation to the geographical and cultural contexts in which the Holocaust took place. Focusing on Polish–Jewish relations encourages the visitor to reflect on how these relations developed at the time of the Holocaust in occupied Poland, not what they were like during the Holocaust in general. We have tried to show the difference in the attitudes of Hilberg's bystanders and underscore that they were active, functioning individuals sometimes having influence—at times positive, at times negative—on the course of events and on the victims' fate.

The perspective of bystanders to the Holocaust is shown to the visitor in all its complexity. In September 1939, Jews and Poles experienced the opening phases of the war similarly. It was only during the early stages of the occupation when the Germans introduced segregation, discriminatory regulations, and then confined Jews in ghettos that these perspectives diverged. In the section of the gallery called "Aryan Side," we focus on the Polish experience of the occupation, which formed the Poles' attitude toward the Holocaust. In three color photographs of the burning Warsaw Ghetto taken during the uprising, we discover the perspective of Poles looking at the ghetto. The pictures were taken from the roof of a building on the "Aryan" side of Warsaw, some distance from the ghetto and from the fire raging there. This is a metaphor for the gulf between the situation of bystanders and victims, as well as for the sharp division of the city into Jewish and non-Jewish sections.

The perpetrators are continuously present throughout the exhibit's narrative, above all in the visual layer. One of the attributes of their power is the camera which furnished them with the ability to capture in photographs what they saw and how they saw it. Photographs show how German soldiers saw Jews. Soldiers carrying out mass shootings in the East after the invasion of the USSR and those working in death camps took pictures. The Germans treated photographs as trophies, curiosities, personal souvenirs of war—we, however, treat them not as objective documents, but rather as a condensation of the photographer's impression, which is never objective about its subject.[6]

This is the case with the report of General Jürgen Stroop, who suppressed the Warsaw Ghetto Uprising in 1943. Stroop prepared a report for Reichsführer-SS Heinrich Himmler titled "The Jewish residential district of Warsaw no longer exists!" To specific daily reports, he attached fifty-three photographs, showing the uprising from the German perspective. Copies of selected pages with photographs in their original dimensions are displayed on one side of a free-standing panel placed in the center of the exhibit presenting

---

6 See Ziębińska-Witek, "Kicz i Holokaust, czyli pedagogiczny wymiar ekspozycji muzealnych," 216–26; Janina Struk, *Holokaust w fotografiach. Interpretacja dowodów* [The Holocaust in photographs. Interpretation of the evidence], trans. Maciej Antosiewicz (Warsaw: Prószyński i S-ka, 2007) and Amos Goldberg, "Czy w Nowym Muzeum Historii Zagłady Yad Vashem znajdziemy 'Innego'?" [Can we find the "Other" in the new Yad Vashem Museum of the History of the Holocaust], *Zagłada Żydów. Studia i Materiały* 7 (2011): 350–51.

the Jewish narrative of the uprising. In this way, we deconstruct Stroop's report and show the perspective from which it was written.

Aware of their ambiguous character, we approach photographs taken by the perpetrators with care. They are a trace, a depiction of a certain slice of vanished reality and sometimes its sole visual record. We intend that the filter through which visitors view them should be the testimony of the victims. A more general concept of using visual material connected to the Holocaust, which is discussed below, has defined the way in which we approach these photographs.

Similarly, in the Shoah Corridor the perpetrators' perspective is confronted with that of the victims. Here the narrative leads to the death camps in Auschwitz II-Birkenau and Treblinka II, and the visitor is faced with information about what took place there. We narrate the story of Treblinka in the words of escapees, presenting fragments of their manuscripts and their sketch-maps of the camp. On the opposite wall, the story of Auschwitz II-Birkenau is narrated from the perpetrators' perspective, using photographs taken by the Germans of the arrival of a transport of Hungarian Jews at the camp and their path to the gas chambers, with quotations from Rudolf Höss's autobiography. However, the narrative conclusion to this space, as well as to the whole exhibit on the Holocaust, is depicted through the testimony of the victims: on the final wall of the Shoah Corridor are displayed copies of four illicit photographs taken secretly by members of the Auschwitz II-Birkenau Sonderkommando, as well as an extract of Lejb Langfus's testimony, which described the murders in the gas chambers.

PHOTOGRAPHS

As mentioned above, perpetrators are the authors of most of the photographs displayed in the galleries. Wishing to avoid suggesting to visitors that this German perspective is objective, we consistently emphasize the context in which a photograph was taken.

Another problem was whether, in describing the Holocaust, one was glamorizing horror. Using pictures of dead bodies without careful consideration and removing photographs from the context, place, and situation in which they were taken can mean that they become those thoughtlessly repeated "icons of the Holocaust" that mass culture grinds up and incorporates into its armory. We feared that at a time when "watching the pain of others" has become merely entertainment experienced without great emotion when watching the news, visitors can respond with simple indifference, shutting themselves off from the content or manifesting an excessively emotional response, which results only in superficial feelings of empathy for the victims.[7] Our view is that such photographs have greater impact when they are used sparingly.

We have considered carefully every case where we used photographs. For instance, to support the narrative about religious life in the Warsaw Ghetto, we use an enlarged photograph of a corpse clothed in rags with the face covered with a newspaper. The photograph is accompanied by a text on the collapse of the traditions associated with death and funeral rituals. In the Warsaw Ghetto, most Jews were unable to afford the luxury of burying a family member—in the shadow of the extreme destitution that was rife in the ghetto, it was common to leave corpses on the street. We interpret the gesture of covering a dead person's face with a newspaper as an attempt to preserve cultural norms in extreme circumstances.

BETWEEN AESTHETICS AND THE ETHICS OF REPRESENTATION

The meta-rule of the Holocaust Gallery is minimalism. The use of each text, photograph, or item is justified by the constructed narrative. In this way, we wanted to enter into a dialogue with the visitor, to encourage him or her to make the effort to create meanings for the exhibit's constituent elements. It was important for us that the Holocaust Gallery not rely on facile emotions that the visitor would quickly shake off. This premise defined the character of the gallery's conclusion. The Holocaust is not part of a logical historical continuum, a continuation or natural outcome of earlier developments. Hence, in the POLIN core exhibition, the Holocaust Gallery has not been made part of any larger structure; no message is drawn from it and no final interpretation of it has been made. We agree with Anna Ziębińska-Witek that exhibitions that provide visitors an opportunity for individual interpretation should be made difficult for them. In her words: "Unfinished and ambiguous stories require engagement of the visitor, forcing a confrontation with his or her expectations which are linked with a specific way of 'telling history.'"[8]

Our goal has been to find a form for this story that will discourage visitors either from slipping into facile sentimentalism or retreating into indifference. Hence, the principal narrative method is the written word—a medium to which the victims had access (as distinct from photography, which was a

---

7 Ziębińska-Witek, "Kicz i Holokaust, czyli pedagogiczny wymiar ekspozycji muzealnych."
8 Ibid.

medium to which mainly the perpetrators had access). Hence a certain amount of effort is required from the visitor to access the gallery's message; the more detailed the information desired, the greater the effort.

We have indicated a clear boundary between seeing events from a Jewish perspective, which we invite our visitors to do, and building a sense of false identification between visitors and victims. This identification can be a strategy for visitors to help block out feelings of unease and depression.[9] This, in our view, is an aesthetic which is melodramatic in character since it expresses crisis and menace, but also immediately restores the moral order. It also means that the nightmare of the Holocaust becomes easier to assimilate[10] and can even become somewhat uplifting.[11]

We have wanted contact with the various perspectives of bystanders, victims, and perpetrators, which we present in the exhibit, to block such processes. We hope that visitors will understand that experiencing the Shoah as such is not possible for them and that the goal of the exhibit is not to create a simulation of this experience.

INTERPRETATION

The exhibit is not a finished text, but like every text it possesses its own autonomy. We do not have the tools which would give us full control over the visitors' experience. Experiencing the exhibit is a far more complete experience than reading about it: the dramatic effect, the exhibit's aural and visual layers, and the presence of other visitors are also significant. Visitors' convictions, their emotional readiness to engage with the content presented, the knowledge with which they start their visit, also play a key role. It should be emphasized that the interpretation presented here is only one of many possible. From the moment of the opening of the core exhibition, the Holocaust Gallery began its own life, independent of our control. It is for visitors to decide whether the curators' and scholars' vision is comprehensible, and whether our goals have been at least partially achieved.

Translated by Jarosław Garliński

---

9 Goldberg, "Czy w Nowym Muzeum," 353.
10 Amos Goldberg, "Głos ofiary i estetyka melodramatu w historii" [The voice of a victim and the aesthetics of melodrama in history], *Zagłada Żydów. Studia i Materiały* 5 (2009): 231.
11 Goldberg, "Czy w Nowym Muzeum," 356–57.

Assumptions behind the Postwar Gallery of the Core Exhibition at POLIN

STANISŁAW KRAJEWSKI

INTRODUCTION

Devising the post–Second World War section of the core exhibition—the work of Helena Datner and myself—took several years. In the final, most intense years we worked with a team of curators, including Justyna Koszarska-Szulc, Judyta Pawlak, Artur Tanikowski, and Franciszek Zakrzewski. We always were under the guidance of Barbara Kirshenblatt-Gimblett. It was a rewarding experience, although at times serious tensions emerged.

We never tried to articulate fully the assumptions behind our work. For some time, we worked as if we had no assumptions other than those explicitly introduced by Barbara Kirshenblatt-Gimblett. Among them were, for example, the hardly controversial (for us) principle that the story of Polish Jews is to be told in relation to the history of Poland, and the much less obvious requirement to use only quotations from the period and not from later sources. Some other assumptions became clearer when we discussed problematic issues with the authors responsible for the other periods of the core exhibition. For example, we agreed to define Polish Jews as the Jews living in the territory of Poland of the given period. Thus, the postwar section was to be basically about Jews in postwar Poland, and not those in prewar Polish lands or living in America. More assumptions emerged when we were met with criticism, especially by those who had different visions of the exhibition. For instance, we were rejecting the idea that all "famous" Polish Jews must be shown in the exhibition. Actually, the very problem of who was a Jew became exceptionally acute in relation to our period. Particularly strong were the controversies regarding the manner of presenting "Jewish communists."

In this chapter, I present a list of the assumptions that—it seems to me—were guiding our work. It is highly probable that I have not realized all of them. Nevertheless, I hope that a more comprehensive picture could arise from my remarks than that which appears in discussions of the separate topics covered in our gallery.

In addition to reflection on our work and discussions I had with other creators of the museum, two printed articles have proved very helpful. First, I call attention to Barbara Kirshenblatt-Gimblett's essay (2014) in the museum's catalogue on principles behind the core exhibition.[1] Second, I have been influenced by the first chapter of Moshe Rosman's *How Jewish Is Jewish History*[2] and his essay on decisions about the selections in POLIN Museum (2012).[3] Many assumptions that come to mind could apply to all of the exhibits, but applying them to the postwar period created specific problems that are discussed below.

JEWS OF POLAND

Among the necessary decisions were not only rather obvious ones such as determining "Who was a Jew?" (see below), but also much less obvious questions, including, "What is our metahistorical narrative?" One could try to avoid such issues, but I believe with Moshe Rosman that "there is no escaping connecting one's impeccably researched and source-grounded historiographical small story to some extrapolated, contingent, refutable, metahistorical Big Story."[4] According to him, the lack of a master narrative in a museum produces confusion. What, then, is the master narrative of the Warsaw Museum? Is it "the larger renewed Polish-Jewish history that has

---

I am grateful to Barbara Kirshenblatt-Gimblett for her useful comments and help in editing this paper.

1 Barbara Kirshenblatt-Gimblett, "Theater of History," in *Polin. 1000 Year History of Polish Jews*, ed. Barbara Kirshenblatt-Gimblett and Antony Polonsky, Museum of the History of Polish Jews (Warsaw: Museum of the History of the Polish Jews, 2014), 30–35.
2 Moshe Rosman, *How Jewish Is Jewish History?* (Oxford: Littman Library of Jewish Civilization, 2007).
3 Moshe Rosman, "Categorically Jewish, Distinctly Polish: The Museum of The History of Polish Jews and the New Polish-Jewish Metahistory," *Jewish Studies: An Internet Journal* 10 (2012): 361–87, http://www.biu.ac.il/JS/JSIJ/10-2012/Rosman.pdf.
4 Ibid., 362.

developed over the past thirty or forty years," as mentioned in *The YIVO Encyclopedia*[5] and in Antony Polonsky's volumes on the Jews of Poland and Russia.[6] This new approach is characterized by a stress on the multinational commonwealth (Rzeczpospolita Wielu Narodów), the awareness that Jews lived in Poland rather than in an insulated "Yiddishland," and, even more strongly, that they were part of Poland.

I certainly agree that in the postwar section it is assumed that Jews are in Poland and of Poland. In this period, however, one of the defining elements is the absence of the commonwealth. The wartime murders and postwar changes of borders and transfers of millions have led to the present-day Poland, ethnically and religiously homogeneous as never before. At the same time, a segment of intelligentsia, including some historians and, for instance, Pope John Paul II, have referred to the multiethnic "Jagiellonian" Poland as the ideal, the source of cultural richness and a reason for pride, almost a lost paradise. This picture reflects, however, a way of thinking, not realities on the ground.

I became aware at some point that we had implicitly assumed some answer to the question "Is the Diaspora good or bad?" Our answer was not a simple *yes* or a simple *no* answer, but did take the view that it was more good than bad. We assumed that the story of Jews in Poland was naturally to be told about their life *in* Poland. It reflected the life of many generations for which the Diaspora, in our case Poland, was their element. Many could have dreamt about Eretz Israel or about the *goldene medine* across the ocean, but everyone was immersed in their own lives and environments. Even in bad times, and there was no shortage of bad times in post-Shoah Poland, everyday life has rarely been a nightmare. To be sure, most Jews emigrated from postwar Poland, but those who did not were definitely part of Poland. Those who left felt disenchantment and resentment against Poland, typical for emigrants.

The general aim of the postwar section is to reflect all varieties of experience of Jews in Poland and also to show Poland, the environment of those Jews, stressing the aspects that are important from their perspective.

---

5   *The YIVO Encyclopedia of Jews in Eastern Europe*, ed. Gershon D. Hundert (New Haven, CT: Yale University Press, 2008); see http://www.yivoencyclopedia.org.
6   Antony Polonsky, *The Jews in Poland and Russia*, vol. 1: *1350–1881*, vol. 2: *1881–1914*, vol. 3: *1914–2008* (Oxford: Littman Library of Jewish Civilization, 2010, 2012).

A NEW CHAPTER

Some issues are specific to the postwar period. Above all, there is the assumption that the museum should contain a postwar chapter. The very idea that the Shoah does not end the story may be surprising and disconcerting to many foreign Jewish visitors for whom the Holocaust is the most important "emblematic" point of Polish Jewish history. Yet the authors' experience is clear: there have been and still are Jews in postwar Poland. Of course, no comparison with prewar Jewish communities makes sense. Nevertheless, the postwar history is not only a footnote to the Shoah, but constitutes a separate chapter. Though the chapter is small and modest, it is still interesting as it involves events and topics that did not occur in earlier chapters of Jewish history in Poland. Among the new phenomena are, for example, the presence of Jews in top positions of power, the extent of assimilation, and, of course, the legacy of the Shoah—from devastation to mass graves to the uneasy and fading Polish memory of the former Jewish presence.

Everyone working on the last decades is inevitably vulnerable to criticism from virtually everyone else. Each visitor remembers her lifetime, so she feels she is an expert and best knows what should be shown and what should not. Therefore, each decision is bound to be contested; for some there will be too much and for others too little about anti-Semitism, communism, Orthodox Jews, assimilated Jews, Jewish organizations, events of general Polish life, emigration, fear, achievements, and so on.

One question appears naturally, and often results in frustration: "Am I there?" A visitor with a personal connection to the story told in the museum asks: Can I meet someone like myself, my grandfather, my friends, my town? Disappointment is almost inevitable. There is no way to show everyone, every place and event. However, our ambition was to represent all patterns of surviving the war, all important types of identity, attitudes, and behavior among Jews, and all social trends—from Zionist emigration to communist assimilation.

The most unusual aspect of the postwar section results from the fact that Helena Datner and myself, and also her father, actively participated in the story we tell. Indeed, nearly all the topics presented in the exhibition are known to us or our family members from personal experience. We have tried to avoid the presentation of ourselves or our own items, but sometimes they were superior to anything else available to us. The decision to show them was made by the rest of the team. Thus, we included Szymon Datner's speech at the trial after the pogrom in Sokoły, and his notes and photographs from his 1947 journey to Palestine (he later returned to Poland); then a picture of a group of friends, including myself, in the synagogue in Warsaw in 1987, and the photographs of Jewish cemeteries taken in the 1970s and 1980s by my wife, Monika Krajewska. Actually, I observed that we could have shown the whole postwar period, nearly all of its themes, events and subtleties, if we had told in detail the story of our two families.

JEWS IN POLAND RATHER THAN POLISH JEWS

We describe Jews who lived in Poland. This excludes many Polish Jews, from prewar emigrants to those who remained in the Soviet Union (where the majority of Jews who had lived in Poland in 1939 survived) to the postwar emigrants, who became important only after having left Poland, in Israel or in other countries. If we wanted to include them and their children, the story would be different. It would be very interesting but fragmented, located mostly far away from Poland.

In the exhibition, there are some exceptions to the rule that we show only Jews in Poland. Sometimes those who left remained part of the story not only during the period they were living in Poland and while they were in the process of leaving, but also during the short period after their emigration. We devoted a lot of space to postwar emigration in the 1940s: the displaced persons' camps in Germany are presented in considerable detail because most of the people there were Polish Jews who had just left. One can listen to several interviews, in various languages, recorded in those camps by an American researcher, David Boder, who used a new invention, the tape recorder, to capture their experiences, attitudes, fears, and hopes. Another example: interviews with young emigrants in 1968, living on a ship in Denmark, are presented in a very interesting film by Marian Marzyński. They talk about Poland, their identity, and their reasons for emigration. It is immediately clear how Polish they are and how much they reveal about Poland from their angle, that is, the position of young assimilated Jews, happy to sing in Yiddish, who would not have emigrated had the anti-Semitic campaign not taken place.

Even when after deciding to mainly show only Jews in Poland, another presentation difficulty remained: it is unclear how many Jews lived in Poland after the war. In the immediate postwar years, more than 250,000 Jews passed through Poland, perhaps as many as 300,000. All estimates are approximate. Scholars of the subject present divergent data. (For example, see the chapter by Albert Stankowski in Tych and Adamczyk-Garbowska's book.)⁷ We decided to refer to *The YIVO Encyclopedia* as the authoritative source; David Engel writes there that from 1944 to 1946 some 266,000–281,000 Jews passed through the country. Hence the number given in a large inscription on the wall: more than 250,000. For later periods, it is possible to say how many Jews officially emigrated or were repatriated (from Russia), but to say how many were living in Poland is very difficult. Too many among them were fully assimilated, hidden, or just so marginally Jewish that it would not make much sense to count them. We did not try to present a definite number for the years 1968, 1980, 1989, or 2014.

The entire postwar period is marked by successive waves of Jewish emigration from Poland: in 1945–46, 1949–51, 1957–59, and 1968–69. Emigration by individuals has also occurred, often with great difficulties, virtually every year, but the numbers of such emigrants is small. It is only in the last two decades that some Jews have returned to Poland, including a few emigrants who left in 1968. Is this a phenomenon significant enough to deserve a mention in the exhibition? I tended to believe that yes, and my favorite example is Adam Ringer, about whom his Swedish wife said that real life was for him only in Poland before emigration and in Poland after his return, and that the quarter of a century in Sweden was like a break. Helena Datner believed, however, that the returns were too rare to be included in our story.

ONE NARRATIVE

The exhibition is organized as one continuous narration. It is multimedia and multilayered, but it still remains one continuous narration. This does not mean that one dimension of history is chosen and others are ignored. Rather, the situation of choice is staged and the major options are presented so that the exhibition evokes the need to make a choice that was facing Jews in a given historical moment. In the postwar story of the 1940s one encounters the fundamental question of whether "to stay or to leave." Most Jews left Poland, but we present the reasons, arguments, and historical circumstances for both those who left and those who stayed. Side by side, we show different newspaper articles, Zionist activities, communist and other non-Zionist activities, and diverging opinions expressed in interviews gathered by Irena Hurwic-Nowakowska.

---

7 Albert Stankowski, "How Many Polish Jews Survived the Holocaust?" in *Jewish Presence in Absence: Aftermath of the Holocaust in Poland, 1945–2010*, ed. Feliks Tych and Monika Adamczyk-Garbowska (Jerusalem: Yad Vashem, International Institute for Holocaust Research, 2012), 205–16.

One narrative also means that no separate display can produce an ahistorical answer to such basic questions as: who is a Jew, what is anti-Semitism, what is Judaism, and so on: "There are no trans-historical thematic galleries, as proposed in the master plan" that served as the basis for the work on the exhibition.[8] There is therefore no compact synthetic treatment of communism or anti-Semitism in the postwar period, but in many places a wealth of material is presented to explain these phenomena. For example, there is a display on anti-Jewish violence in Poland in 1945–46, and we show the importance of that violence for the emigration—indeed, the Kielce pogrom induced an "emigration panic"—but we refrain from the conclusion that those acts of violence define the postwar period. However, we also do not claim they do not. The issue remains open, opinions from the period are quoted, and each visitor can decide for himself or herself.

It must be admitted that the post-1989 section of the gallery has not been properly developed, even though there had been various plans on how to do this. The lack of space and constraints imposed by the architect allowed only a video presentation and monitors with interviews of contemporary Jews. They show how Polish (and Jewish) these Polish Jews are, and how important Jewish history remains for both Poles and Jews abroad. This importance constitutes the unifying element of the Polish Jewish story in the present period. In an extended sense, it is also a common component of the whole core exhibition.

JEWISH EXPERIENCE IN RELATION TO POLISH CONTEXT

While the idea that the history of Jews in Poland is an integral part of the history of Poland has not been controversial among the creators of the museum, it took effort to assimilate the idea that the Jewish story is not to be presented as an addition, or a footnote, to the history of Poland. It is "an integral rather than contextual history of Polish Jews,"[9] so we tried to present events through relating Jews to Polish realities—where this was possible and would not introduce distortions.

In the postwar section this means, for example, that Stalinization and the Solidarność (Solidarity) movement are presented to a considerable extent through the eyes of Jews or Jewish institutions of the given period. The more the Polish Jews assimilated and participated in general Polish life—which is

---

8 Kirshenblatt-Gimblett, "Theater of History," 33.
9 Ibid., 32.

the increasingly present pattern in the postwar period—the more the general events should be shown.

The beginning of Stalinization in 1948 is shown by both a photograph of the congress of the new "united" Communist Party and by an enlarged copy of the stamps of the Jewish communities formally dissolved at that time. In the museum's comment, it is made clear that the dissolution was an example of a larger policy, the removal of independent institutions from public life. In Jewish life, that was initiated by communist leaders active within the Jewish community.

Solidarność of 1980–81 is presented as a movement with a strong Catholic component (a large photograph of kneeling people communicates this immediately), an aspect that could not be ignored by Jews. We also say that censorship was much milder, which made possible the lifting of the taboo on Jewish topics. In addition, we mention the government's anti-Semitic attacks on the opposition connected to Solidarność for being too "Jewish," as well as anti-Semitic tendencies inside Solidarność, epitomized by the statement by Marian Jurczyk about the composition of the government: "three-quarters are Jews who betrayed our nation."

A unique look at the Solidarność movement is possible through the use of a film made by Marian Marzyński. A Jewish emigrant in 1968, he returned to Poland in 1981 in search of the traces of his former life, including the convent in which he had been hidden as child, and found the fascinating grassroots movement. He filmed a group of young activists who gathered in a park and then met with government representatives. Sizeable fragments of the movie are shown.

The methodology of "integral" as opposed to contextual Jewish history related to Poland is best visible in our attempts to deal with one episode that had nothing to do with Jews. We were supposed to show the admittance of Poland to NATO in 1999. A normal way would be to display a picture or newspaper headline or just give a short description. Was it possible to refer to some "Jewish connection"? One idea came to mind: the accession was signed on behalf of Poland by its foreign minister, Bronisław Geremek, who was born Jewish. Yet his Jewishness was totally irrelevant to the event so I (and Helena) rejected in advance the idea that he could be shown in this situation as a Jew. Instead, I tried to use the statement by the board of the Union of Jewish Religious Communities in Poland supporting Poland's joining the alliance. This was a minor fact for general Polish history, but a good illustration of the attitudes of Polish Jews. I remembered the statement, which was of some political importance at that time, but, unfortunately, I was unable to find its text, and in fact the episode could not be included in the final exhibition.

WE SHOW AVERAGE JEWS, NOT JUST FAMOUS ONES

Many quotations in the exhibits come from average, unknown people, as, for example, from the survey from the late 1940s by Irena Hurwic-Nowakowska. Photo albums showing the activities of children in Lower Silesia shortly after the war, and photographs of Jewish youth camps in the 1960s, give a taste of the lives of average Jews. The individual stories of eight emigrants from 1968 tell both of people who were important in Polish culture, like Józef Hurwic, professor of chemistry who edited an excellent popular science monthly, and people unknown to the general public.

It might seem uncontroversial to consider as heroes the average people who have carried on the story of Polish Jews. Yet we have been criticized for showing individual Jews to exemplify or illustrate a point rather than to show their achievements. Although many notable writers, artists, scientists, Zionist leaders, rabbis, and also communist leaders are included, many others are not. Had we wanted to mention all, we would have produced an encyclopedia. It would have been a different endeavor, one not appropriate for a responsible history exhibition. Lists of famous Jews are already found in encyclopedias and books, offline and online. At the urging of its stakeholders and donors, the museum is preparing a separate space, "In Good Company," where visitors can explore the lives and achievements of distinguished Polish Jews. In contrast, our aim in the core exhibition was to present a comprehensive history of Polish Jews, a story of average Jews, not just those who were famous or infamous.

Our quotations and photographs are there to illustrate general points, trends present among Jews, or attitudes toward Jews. Some persons are average, some notable. For example, three presidents of the Central Committee of Jews in Poland (CKŻP) in the 1940s—Emil Sommerstein, Adolf Berman, and Hersz Smolar—appear in succession, in a sequence that reveals how each one was progressively more communist than his predecessor.

Monitors on the wall of registration cards that opens the postwar gallery present three categories of survivors who filled out registration cards: those who returned from concentration camps, those who came out of hiding, and those who were repatriated from Russia. A fourth blank screen represents those who did not register. Individuals were chosen to show the variety of experiences and, in some cases, because those individuals would reappear later in the gallery. However, the short biographies provided there summarize their lives only up to the late 1940s, in accordance with the general methodology of not anticipating later events, a guiding principle of the exhibition's mode of narration. Jews participated in various events not necessarily *as* Jews. We had to grapple with the problem of some individuals, either well known or not, who participated in events that had no direct Jewish content. Should we identify these individuals as Jews? As mentioned above with respect to the purported mention of Bronisław Geremek, we decided against doing so. This was our principle, based on our strong wish to avoid unmasking or calling attention to someone's Jewish identity (a popular technique of anti-Semites) for no good (or for a suspect) reason. Thus, we avoided mentioning people's former Jewish-sounding names. There are exceptions, especially cases where former and later names are mentioned in order to tell a story of assimilation, for example, in the cases of Sara Hurwic, who changed her name to Irena Nowakowska, and Artur Nacht-Samborski, the painter, who combined his prewar Jewish name and his wartime "Aryan" name.

Generally, as it turns out, it was not possible to be consistent in this regard. There were times when we wanted to indicate that Jews were among participants, even though Jewishness had nothing to do (at least on the surface) with their motives. For example, in 1977, there was a hunger strike at a church in Warsaw, by opposition activists in defense of workers arrested in the wake of the 1976 protests. It was a notable event in the history of that period. We wanted to indicate that there were Jews among them; four names are mentioned in the caption, two which sound Jewish and two not (one of these a monk). We do not identify anyone in the photograph as Jewish, in accordance with our general principle and in the hope that the sound of the Jewish-sounding name will render the matter as self-evident. Some critics have claimed, however, that without specifying who is Jewish and who is not, visitors will assume from the two Jewish-sounding names that all four are Jews.

Maneuvering between the Scylla of unmasking and the Charybdis of hiding or not noting Jewishness proved very difficult. And this problem indicates an even more fundamental matter, that of Jewish identity, not only by ascription, but also by identification.

WHO IS JEWISH?

Jewish identities can range from complete to marginal, and we did not want to miss this variety in our exhibition. There is no simple answer to the question about whether a person is Jewish or not. We wanted to demonstrate the existence of degrees of Jewishness, the different depth of Jewish roots, diverging levels of Jewish identification, and the possible differences between self-perception and perception by others, both by other Jews and in the non-Jewish environment. The issue of "Jewish origins" as opposed to being Jewish becomes increasingly important in each subsequent decade of postwar Poland. In contemporary Polish synagogues, the overwhelming majority of the participants have only partial Jewish roots, and many have therefore gone through a formal conversion process to Judaism. There exist also those who have converted without having Jewish ancestors. (Let me add that the story of converts after 1989 is not shown, not only due to the limited space and scope of the post-1989 section, but also because of the delicacy of the matter—according to Jewish law, converts must not be reminded of their conversion.)

It is not easy to show the shades of identity in an exhibition where visitors seem to expect that each character in the story is clearly Jewish or not at all Jewish. This simplification is corrected in Marzyński's interviews with young emigrants in 1968 and, more directly, in interviews presented at the end of the core exhibition in which several individuals living in present-day Poland answer questions pertaining, among other things, to their Jewish identity.

The ultimate problem, most relevant to the postwar section, is how to illustrate assimilation. Successful assimilation is, almost by definition, impossible to present, because those who have undergone this process identify as Polish and are Jewish only by origin. At the same time, the issue of assimilation is so fundamental for the postwar period that it cannot be omitted. We have found some ways to deal with this issue. First, on the registration wall at the opening of the gallery stands an empty monitor, with a caption mentioning those "who decided not to register," located alongside monitors with the names of those who did so. While assimilated Jews were among those who registered and not all those who did not register were assimilated, the blank screen at the very least raises the question of why some Jews did not add their names. Second, we show general trends such as the gradual dominance of the Polish language. In the presentation of Jewish clubs of the 1950s and 1960s, we show how the Yiddish-speaking leadership responded to the increasing use of Polish among Jewish youth by sponsoring Jewish rock bands that performed songs in Polish.

This is, a critic would say, acculturation rather than assimilation. These young members of the clubs remained Jewish. In order to show real assimilation, one can take advantage of the moments when it gets questioned. This is the third method: a crisis of assimilation provides the best occasion to talk about it. We show this through noting writers and artists who reflected on their lives before, during, and after the war—and who expressed their personal dilemmas. Perhaps the clearest expression of the crisis of assimilation occurred in the period beginning in 1968. For example, the exhibition presents a young 1968 emigrant who had not even known his mother was Jewish before his parents decided to emigrate—incidentally, he is now a well-known Swedish journalist.

An interesting phenomenon has been taking place since the 1980s and has grown significantly in the last twenty years: some Poles from assimilated families with Jewish ancestry began the journey of de-assimilation. They do not lose their Polishness, but they acquire an active Jewish identity.[10] This current belongs principally to the post-1989 section of the exhibition. What, however, about those who have never entered Jewish life? Must they remain outside the exhibition's purview?

To include in the exhibition individuals who have no connection to Jewishness other than their ancestors seemed to us unacceptable, because it would probably mean imputing Jewish identity against the will of the depicted person—that is, making them Jews by ascription, rather than through self-identification. If, however, the Jewishness of this person becomes a matter of personal identification or public ascription, his or her story falls within our scope. Such is the case of those who emigrated because they were (or were called) Jews. Similarly, individuals active in Polish public life who were attacked for being Jews, on whatever grounds, have been "unmasked" and that alone may be reason for inclusion in the story. These are among the ways that even assimilated and invisible Jews can enter the Jewish story.

Again, it is hard to be completely consistent. Clearly, some moral constraints have been applied. I would assume that the right to privacy involves the right not to be shown as a Jew in a museum of Jewish history. This is particularly relevant in the Polish context when we think about active Catholics, among them former Jews. On the other hand, the public has the right to information and expects the complete story of public persons as presented by their biographers. Whom, then, could we show without feeling we have done something wrong? We have effectively reached the following solution so that self-definition is not ignored. In each case, we try to imagine what the person's reaction would

---

10 For more on this, see Stanisław Krajewski, *Poland and the Jews: Reflections of a Polish Jew* (Kraków: Wydawnictwo Austeria, 2005) and Katka Reszke, *Return of the Jew: Identity Narratives of the Third Post-Holocaust Generation of Jews in Poland* (Brighton, MA: Academic Studies Press, 2013).

be to being described as a Jew. We include those who, according to our best knowledge, can be included in Jewish history, and at the same time, would like to be included (following a moral criterion).[11]

STEREOTYPES ARE NOT OUR POINT OF DEPARTURE

Although I never consciously formulated this thought, it has always been clear to us that Jews were not a "problem" that required a solution. We just wanted to describe Jewish life and Jewish presence in Poland. Jews were and *are* part of Poland, even though the number of Jews is very small. This subject occurred early on and was often repeated by Barbara Kirshenblatt-Gimblett: "Small number, big presence." This presence in Polish consciousness, memory, and imagination contributes to the persisting image of Jews as, still, a problem to solve. Paradoxically, although the actual number of Jews in Poland is small, by any measure, a recurring theme in Polish consciousness is "too many"—too many Jews among communists, among the secret police before 1956, among dissidents after 1956, among anticommunists after 1968, among filmmakers and writers (always), among government ministers after 1989, and so on. We do not share this opinion and we never wanted to make it the starting point for our historical narrative—in other words, to construct a story whose goal would be to disprove it, as that would mean treating it as a serious option that we would be inadvertently confirming.

One point adopted by the museum team was: let us not begin with misperceptions. This means that we never tried to construct our story with the aim of answering the expectations of the public, whether to deny or confirm them. Beginning with them even only to dismantle them would be an indirect confirmation to many a visitor. In the postwar context this meant, in particular, the rejection of two strong expectations: to present, on the one hand, leading Jewish communists, and, on the other, to show Jews who contributed greatly to Polish culture.

First, it seems that a large segment of Polish opinion expected us to present a list of Jewish communist leaders and especially the leadership and rank-and-file members of the security apparatus from the early 1950s. Had we done so, even if we explained that their Jewishness was irrelevant to their policies because Jewish and non-Jewish communists were doing exactly the same things, we would still have confirmed the image of the ruling Jews. On the other

---

11 Stanisław Krajewski, *Żydzi i...* [Jews and...] (Kraków: Austeria, 2014), chapter 7.

hand, we did want to show the presence of Jews in the communist power elite and security apparatus, and I believe we succeeded. There is another reason why compiling a list of Jewish communists, a favorite pastime of anti-Semites, or dedicating a separate section to them would be problematic: if we compiled such a list, we should also do one for Jews in, say, KOR (Workers' Defense Committee), the main organized anticommunist opposition group from the 1970s. This unacceptable method was used at that time by the government to discredit KOR. There is no reason to emphasize the ethnic origin of some of those leaders if their origin had no direct influence on their activities. Indirectly, their origin might have played a role, but this is too unclear and subtle to make it part of the exhibition. The same arguments can be given about communists: Why single out Jewish origins and not noble or peasant origins of other communists (or members of KOR)? Those who want to indicate Jewishness assume—I believe—that communism (or KOR) is somehow "Jewish." And this is exactly the view we did not want to endorse.

Second, many well-wishing Poles, including some politicians involved in the museum project, and many Jews, including some donors, hoped that the museum would highlight famous Jews and show their contributions to Polish and world culture. There are several reasons why we did not do this, limitations of space aside. First is the question of relevance of ethnic origin to the achievement. Second is our principle of selecting individuals whose stories illustrate a general trend. Third, and even more fundamental, is our wish to avoid triumphalism and apologetics. One might also argue that if famous men and women are highlighted, then why not also infamous ones—outstanding fraudsters or detested officials?

No Jewish or Polish expectations were met with regard to lists of Jews. More generally, we avoided these and other popular visions of how the history of Polish Jews should be told. In particular, we accepted no teleology, that is, no assumption to the effect that this history was aimed at some specific end, or that a certain state of affairs was the logical conclusion of the historical process. The museum avoided a Shoah-oriented teleology, the idea that the Polish or European Diaspora ended with the Shoah. Nor did we subscribe to a Zionist teleology, to the idea that history was leading to the State of Israel. We do show how most Jews in Poland after the war supported the Zionist cause and were happy to witness the establishment of Israel, but we do not condemn those who did not. Assimilationists also have their say, and since it is they and their descendants who remained in Poland, they are increasingly the focus of the museum's narrative—until, that is, the emergence of de-assimilation. And yet we neither confirm nor denounce the assimilationist ideology, the view that it is better for Polish Jews to become Poles, or the related view that postwar history leads either to emigration or to complete Polonization. This is an example of a wider policy: we tried as much as we could to avoid judgments.

NONJUDGMENTAL APPROACH

Leaving the ideological disputes undecided is not the only way the constructors of the exhibition assumed a nonjudgmental attitude—something not to be confused with a refusal on our part to "take a stand." Rather, we showed side by side various interpretations of events from the period, even if we, in retrospect or in our involvement in the time of the event, had a clear preference. Our goal was rather to capture the dilemmas of the period and to create an opening for visitors to reflect on them. This is best illustrated by how we presented explanations of the Kielce pogrom and also the later Błoński debate.

The Kielce pogrom of July 4, 1946, is presented in the exhibition in considerable detail: the basic facts are given and the funeral, the trial of the killers, and the consequences (emigration panic) are presented. They are accompanied by four interpretations of the pogrom, presented side by side: for the communists, the pogrom was the work of reactionary anti-governmental forces; for the anti-communist underground, the communists were the ones who provoked the pogrom in order to discredit their opponents; for the church, killing is unacceptable, but Jews are responsible for the hatred against them since they hold so many positions of power; and for intellectual observers, the moral challenge is stressed, resulting from the large number of people who took part. All four explanations are given without comment, although we personally identified with the last one.

In 1987, a significant public debate took place following publication of the article "Biedni Polacy patrzą na getto" (The poor Poles look at the ghetto), in which Jan Błoński wrote about the Polish share of responsibility for the Shoah because Poles witnessed it. The exhibition presents the article, which appeared in a Catholic weekly, alongside the angry reaction by Władysław Siła-Nowicki, who rejected any mention of "allegedly unfulfilled moral obligations." Again, our preferences were very strongly on the side of Błoński, but this is no way reflected in the exhibition, which, as a matter of principle, tells the story in multiple voices.

Nonetheless, visitors, commentators, and critics may discern a different meta-narrative, one that was not intended by us, and having nothing to do with the treatment of Jews in and of Poland. It cannot be denied that the authors subconsciously issue messages in favor or against a case. One such suggestion was made by Konstanty Gebert, who wrote that the (entire) core exhibition reflects an approach proper to the Bund or the Folkist Party. The terms he used are rather unfortunate, but the point is interesting. Namely, the exhibition shows mostly Jews as a collective, a group, a people, rather than as individuals. There is something to this: the exhibition is about Jewish life in the widest sense of the term, but it is not about the life of all Jews in the widest sense of the term. Yet in the postwar section enough is said about assimilation to give a taste of the situation of even individual fully Polish Jews.

Another suggestion of bias was communicated to me by Hanno Levy. He noticed that in the entire exhibition dangers to Jews come from outside Poland. In this sense, it is a very Polish exposition. There is something to this, but it seems, again, that it does not apply to the postwar section where anti-Jewish violence and other attacks were committed by Poles.

JEWS AND COMMUNISM

It was important to us to show the relations of Jews to communism, especially in the years 1945–55, without apologetics and without lending credibility to the anti-Jewish stereotype of communism as a Jewish enterprise and of Jews as a ruling group. In several places, we present the positive attitude of Jewish institutions to the new regime and the high proportion of Jews among the power elite. We also show mass emigration from communist-dominated Poland and, in later years, Jewish presence in anticommunist activities.

At the very beginning of the postwar story, we show the gratitude of Jews in hiding to the Soviet army that liberated them. To those Jews, there was no doubt that the communists brought freedom. Then, when presenting the political changes right after the war, we underline the clause in the proclamation of the de facto government (the communist-dominated Polish Committee of National Liberation—Polski Komitet Wyzwolenia Natodowege; PKWN) of 1944 stating that "Jews, who were being exterminated by the occupier in a bestial fashion, will be able to rebuild their lives, and will have full equality, in law and in fact." For Jews, this declaration spoke the language of hope. We indicate that Jewish organizations, including the Zionists and Bundists, called on Jews to vote in the 1946 referendum in response to the communist appeal.

The Stalinist section contains the statement from the 1949 report by the Soviet ambassador to Poland; it says that at the Ministry of Public Security "from deputy ministers to department heads, there is not a single Pole. There are only Jews." We do not editorialize, but we do communicate the threat that this statement represented to those and other Jews by adding the sentence following the one just quoted: "It is not yet the moment for a comprehensive solution in the fight against Jewish nationalism in the Polish party."[12]

We are able to provide an even more direct account of Jewish Stalinists through the American Jewish Joint Distribution Committee's report, which we present in the post-1956 section. The report attributes anti-Semitism in 1956 in part to the fact that Jews were "proportionally more numerous and more conspicuous in the communist regime in Poland than in any other country."

During our final discussions, we confronted the dilemma of how to illustrate the Jews who were among the top leaders of Stalinist Poland. We wanted to avoid attaching such labels as *Jew* and *non-Jew* to individual figures. While we did not want to hide the presence of individuals of Jewish origin, we also did not want to create the impression that all the top leaders were Jews, which would have been the case had we shown only those leaders of Jewish origin. Our solution was to provide short biographies of all leaders on the dais in a photograph from the 1948 Communist Party congress. Those biographies clearly show that three of them were born Jews and abandoned Judaism, just as the three others were born Christian and abandoned Christianity.

Finally, in the display of the end of the Stalinist period, the life of Józef Światło is briefly described—his evolution from Zionism to communism, his position as a top-level political police officer (he arrested both the former chief of the Communist Party, Władysław Gomułka, and the head of the Polish Catholic Church, Cardinal Stefan Wyszyński), and his escape in 1953. We also present excerpts from his famous broadcasts on Radio Free Europe, the highly influential American-sponsored anticommunist radio station.

Is this presentation of the issue of communism sufficient? Two kinds of criticism seem reasonable to me. First, we offer no explanation for why relatively so many Jews were in the power elite of that time. A proper explanation, assuming one can be offered, would require an extended discussion more appropriate for a publication than this exhibition. While the remarks in the museum's catalogue[13] do address this question, visitors in the exhibition cannot be expected to consult the catalogue. In addition, leaving the questions open is one of the

---

12 Quoted in Aleksander Kochański, ed., *Polska w dokumentach z archiwów rosyjskich 1949–1953* [Poland in documents from the Russian archives, 1949–1953] (Warsaw: Instytut Studiów Politycznych PAN, 2000), 46.

13 Stanisław Krajewski, "Postwar Years, from 1944 till Now," in *Polin. 1000 Year History of Polish Jews*, 378–79.

principles stated by Barbara Kirshenblatt-Gimblett: the *how* takes precedence over the *why*. "If *how* is presented well, possible answers to the question of *why* will emerge."[14] The second criticism is more general and applies to many other issues. Visitors may be so tired by the time they get to the postwar section that they are hardly able to watch attentively the videos, notice short quotations, and compare biographies. A few will focus on the postwar section, but the average visitor is likely to miss the message so carefully incorporated into the story. I believe this is a problem. Yet I also think that each visitor is bound to feel that the story is complex and that no simple explanation is sufficient.

TO RETAIN INTEGRITY

The postwar section of the core exhibition is especially vulnerable because so many individuals and institutions would like to intervene with suggestions. Among the most attentive are politicians, especially those who are in power. For most of the time, the team working on the exhibition was insulated from political pressures. Jerzy Halbersztadt, who directed the project for fifteen years, fiercely defended the intellectual independence of the exhibition team. We could assume and never needed to express what was always clear to us: the story must be presented in an honest way, according to our best knowledge. This meant, among other things, that we wanted to present anti-Semitism properly.

We show several examples of postwar anti-Jewish feeling and activities. Venomous leaflets showing bloody "Jewish-Bolshevik beasts" appear in the video describing political changes, along with a quotation from the diary of a famous writer, Maria Dąbrowska, who wrote, "I suffer at the thought that Jews, protected by Russia, may once again take over the economic life of the country—what a dreadful wrong that would be." This statement clearly shows that anti-Semitism was not limited to the lower classes. Moreover, it shows how even highly sophisticated Poles could refer to Jews in prewar terms, as if the Shoah had not taken place.

We present postwar anti-Jewish violence extensively. There is not only a sizable display on the Kielce pogrom, but also presentations of several other horrible attacks that took place in various localities and that together convey the message that violence against Jews could happen anywhere, anytime.

---

14   Kirshenblatt-Gimblett, "Theater of History," 33.

A headline taken from the Jewish news agency of that time that reads "Murders of Jews Don't Stop" appears in large letters on the wall.

Included in a later section are displays about the anti-Semitic "Doctors' Plot" in Moscow and the Slánský trial in Prague, with its very strong "anti-Zionist" aspect. We also mention the harassment of Jews in 1956, and the anti-Semitic campaign of 1968 is presented in a dramatic way: denouncing leaders of student revolt as Jews or as manipulated by Jews, removing "Zionists" from jobs, or pushing Jews to emigrate. Finally, we present the virtual taboo on Jewish topics in the 1970s, and show how before 1989 the government tried to discredit the opposition by pointing to its Jewish or "Jewish" members (which incidentally discredited anti-Semitism among anticommunist activists at that time).

Whether the presentation of anti-Semitism is sufficient can of course be debated. I believe it is. Interestingly, since the opening, there has been strong criticism of the museum by some Polish scholars of a younger generation who want to fight anti-Semitism and detect its deep roots in the Polish (sub)consciousness. They would like our exhibition to place greater emphasis on anti-Semitism. I believe that they are angry that the museum is not part of their campaign to force Polish society to confront its own anti-Semitic attitudes and actions. I can sympathize with their agenda, but this is not a museum of anti-Semitism. It is a museum of Jewish life.

We were also urged to give greater prominence to Polish heroes: Jan Karski, who informed the Allied leaders about the mechanism of the Shoah, and Irena Sendler, who led a successful group effort to rescue Jewish children. I admire both of them immensely and they find their place in the story, first of all in the Holocaust Gallery, but this not a museum of Polish–Jewish relations, whether of its worst qualities (anti-Semitism) or the best (Polish Righteous). It is a museum of life.

Some Polish politicians have expressed their expectation that the museum should serve the Polish raison d'état. What they mean is quite clear: let us show how good it was for Jews in Poland in spite of the occasional hardships. This would be consistent with the idea that a state-sponsored and state-controlled museum should contribute to the creation of a narrative that would strengthen the nation. Declarations in this vein can feel quite threatening; they seem to demand a distorted presentation that would make Poles feel good. That is why Helena Datner left the project and was absent in the last months, when the final negotiations concerning the controversial topics took place. Fortunately, I had support from the other members of the team, of our chief curator, Barbara Kirshenblatt-Gimblett, and of the chief historian, Antony Polonsky.

It turned out that the politicians who could have a real influence on the shape of the exhibition had the good sense to realize that only a truthful presentation could make a really positive impact on Poland's image, namely, as a country prepared to confront the best and the worst of its history. Such a positive impact was a major outcome of the great national debate prompted by Jan Gross's book on the murder of Jews by their neighbors in Jedwabne in July 1941.[15] Poles have been divided on the issue, but the taboo against speaking openly about it is gone. It was also helpful that the politicians, who were concerned with how the postwar gallery dealt with difficult, painful, and sensitive issues, enlisted the best Polish historians of the postwar period to offer their expertise. Let me add that it is easy to imagine that another government could have, or can, try to force us to include direct propaganda.

I am glad to say that the result of the 2014 negotiations was generally satisfactory. We were able to arrive at solutions without compromising the historical integrity of the gallery. We have succeeded in introducing only such changes that do not alter the essential message. In a few cases, the message came to be expressed in a less emphatic way, but it was still not lost. To give an example, the comment on the events of 1968 by Zygmunt Hertz was replaced with one by Mieczysław Rakowski. Whereas Hertz had stated in a letter that the anti-Semitic campaign had worked, and that the idea that the Polish people would be against whatever was proposed by the government should be discarded, Rakowski wrote in his diary that "anti-Zionist propaganda brings effects … antisemitism is a real political, moral, ethical category." Similarly, the comment by Witold Kula on the Kielce pogrom was changed to one by Stanisław Ossowski, who represented a similar milieu of liberal intelligentsia. The main reason for the changes was that Kula had followed newspaper reports and wrote about the extreme right-wing NSZ organization as the organizer of the pogrom, which was not true. To take issue with this error in a caption would confuse the message. In contrast, Ossowski wrote about "pogrom enthusiasm," noting that the entire town "participated passively in the Kielce crime." The substitution of quotations in no way distorted the main message.

Ultimately, it is in the best interest of Poland's raison d'état to have an honest exhibition. I think we have one.

---

15 Jan T. Gross, *Neighbors: The Destruction of the Jewish Community in Jedwabne, Poland* (Princeton, NJ: Princeton University Press, 2001).

Comments on the Museum

Polish–Jewish Historiography 1970–2015: Construction, Consensus, Controversy

MOSHE ROSMAN

A NEW INFRASTRUCTURE

Beginning around 1970, a new infrastructure for the study of Polish Jewish history gradually came into being. The new *Encyclopaedia Judaica* appeared in 1972 with many articles on subjects related to the history of Polish Jewry. Yad Vashem began publishing its encyclopedia of Jewish communities, *Pinkas Ha-Kehillot*, 22 vols. (Jerusalem: Yad Vashem, 1969–2007). The late 1960s and early 1970s saw a flurry of reprints or translations of some classic works of historiography that were of great importance for this subject, for example, Israel Zinberg's *History of Jewish Literature*, 12 vols. (New York, 1972–78); Simon Dubnow's *History of the Jews in Russia and Poland*, 3 vols. (n.p.: Plain Label Books, 1975; it was also republished in 2012 by Forgotten Books); Salo W. Baron's *The Jewish Community*, 3 vols. (Westport, CT, 1973), Azriel Natan Frenk's *Burghers and Jews in Poland* [Hebrew] (Jerusalem: n.p., 1969); Bernard Dov Weinryb's *Neueste Wirtschaftsgeschichte der Juden in Russland und Polen* (Hildesheim, 1972).

In addition, key primary sources were also reprinted or translated; for example: *The Memoirs of Ber of Bolechów* (Jerusalem, 1972 [Hebrew]; New York, 1973 [English]); the 1595 by-laws of the Kraków community (Jerusalem, 1975; published later in a Polish edition, translated and edited by Anna

Jakimyszyn [Kraków, 2005]); *The Pinkas of Medinat Lita* (Jerusalem, 1969); *Shivhei Ha-Besht: In Praise of the Ba'al Shem Tov* (Bloomington, IN, 1971, followed by several later printings). A new scholarly journal, *Gal-Ed*, devoted to the study of Polish Jewry, was established at Tel Aviv University in 1973.

New bibliographical work also appeared. There were the bibliographical appendixes in encyclopedia articles, most notably in the *Encyclopaedia Judaica* (Jerusalem, 1972). There also appeared annual bibliographies in the first issues of *Gal-Ed* and various specialized bibliographies and bibliographical essays. Most significant was Gershon D. Hundert and Gershon Bacon's book of bibliographies and bibliographical essays: *The Jews in Poland and Russia* (Bloomington, IN, 1984).[1]

Some of the material in this article appeared in a Hebrew essay in Israel Bartal, Israel Gutman, eds., *The Broken Chain: Polish Jewry Through the Ages* (Jerusalem: Shazar, 2001), vol. 2, 697–724.

1 The bibliography of Gershon Hundert and Gershon Bacon, *The Jews in Poland and Russia: Bibliographical Essays* (Henceforth: H-B 1984) was published by Indiana University Press in Bloomington in 1984. In addition to the standard general bibliographic publications, *Bibliografia Historii Polski* [Bibliography of Polish history], *Index of Articles in Jewish Studies* (*RAMBI*), and the *American Bibliography of Slavic and East European Studies*, other bibliographies which can be consulted with relevance to postwar historiography are David Bass, "Bibliographical List of Memorial Books Published in the Years 1943–1972," *Yad Vashem Studies* 9 (Jerusalem, 1973): 273–321 [later superseded by Zachary Baker's bibliographic appendix included in Jack Kugelmass and Jonathan Boyarin, eds., *From A Ruined Garden*, 2nd expanded ed. (Bloomington: Indiana University Press, 1998), 273–340]; Zalman Kratko, "Bibliography: Articles on the Jews in Poland Published in Hebrew, Yiddish and Polish in the Year 1971" [in Hebrew], *Gal-Ed* 1 (Tel Aviv, 1973): 339–348; "Bibliography ... 1972, 1973," *Gal-Ed* 3 (Tel Aviv, 1976): 397–421; "Bibliography ... 1974, 1975," *Gal-Ed* 4–5 (1978): 677–710; Ezra Mendelsohn, *The Jews of East-Central Europe between The Two World Wars: A Selected Bibliography* (Jerusalem: Zalman Shazar Center, 1978); Jerzy J. Lerski and Halina T. Lerski, *Jewish-Polish Coexistence: A Topical Bibliography* (New York: Greenwood Press, 1986); Abraham G. Duker, "History of the Jews in East Central Europe: Bibliographical Guide" (Columbia University, Department of History, Stencil, n.d.); *YIVO Bibliyografye* (Bibliography of the publications of the Yidishe Visenshaftlikhe Institut) for publications of 1942–50 (New York: YIVO, 1955). See also the bibliographical essays by Andrzej Chojnowski, "The Jewish Community of the Second Republic in Polish Historiography of the 1980s," *Polin* 1 (Oxford, 1986): 288–99; David Engel, "Works in Hebrew on the History of the Jews in Inter-War Poland," *Polin* 4 (Oxford, 1989): 425–33; "Writing Polish-Jewish History in Hebrew," *Gal-Ed* 11 (Tel Aviv, 1989): 15–30; Gershon D. Hundert, "Recent Studies Related to the History of the Jews in Poland from Earliest Times to the Partition Period," *The Polish Review* 18 (1973): 84–99; "Polish Jewish History," *Modern Judaism* 10 (1990): 259–70; Gershon Bacon, "Rich Harvest: Recent Books on Polish Jewry," *Jewish Studies* 31 (1991): 51–61; Ezra Mendelsohn, "Jewish Historiography on Polish Jewry in the Interwar Period" [in Hebrew], *Jewish Studies* 31 (1991): 23–32, English version in: *Polin* 8 (1994): 3–13; *The Jews of East Central Europe between the World Wars*

Another important development was the first signs of weakening of the ostensibly monolithic communist regime and the availability of archival material from Eastern European countries which began trickling (mostly as microfilm) into the Central Archive for the History of the Jewish People in Jerusalem (some as early as the late 1950s) and other archival collections. This made it possible for scholars outside the Soviet bloc to begin to entertain the possibility of finding new archival sources. Finally, in the late 1970s, Western Jewish scholars began visiting Polish archives, making significant discoveries.

An additional component in the new research infrastructure was the publication of several anthologies and synthetic works that provided summaries and interpretations of basic material, thus helping to define a new research agenda. To give just a few examples: Raphael Mahler's *Jews in Poland between the Two World-Wars: A Socio-Economic History on a Statistical Basis* (Tel Aviv, 1969 [Hebrew]), while intended as a polemic to prove the untenability of Jewish existence in interwar Poland, provided a statistical foundation for future historiography of the Jews in Independent Poland,[2] which then, as Mahler noted in the preface, "still await[ed] its researcher and author." Bernard Johnpoll opened up the central topic of Jewish politics in interwar Poland with his *The Politics of Futility: The General Jewish Workers' Bund of Poland, 1917–1943* (Ithaca, NY, 1967). A collection of articles, *Studies on Polish Jewry*, ed. Joshua Fishman (New York, 1974 [Yiddish and English]), provided extensive analyses of

---

(Bloomington: Indiana University Press, 1983, 1987), 287–92 and his Hebrew bibliography of the same title, (Jerusalem: Zalman Shazar Center, 1978); in addition, Mendelsohn published a new edition of Bałaban's *Bibliography of the History of the Jews in Poland and Neighboring Countries, 1900–1930* (Jerusalem: Hotsa'at ha-Federatsyah ha-'olamit shel Yehude Polin, 1978); Moshe Rosman, "Reflections on the State of Polish-Jewish Historical Study," *Jewish History* 3 (1988): 115–30; Adam Teller, "Jews and Poles on Polish Jews: Recently Published Research on the History of the Jews in Poland," *Jewish Studies* 34 (1994): 77–84; Daniel Tollet, "Les Juifs dans la Republique nobiliaire polonaise (XVI–XVIII siècles) dans l'historiographie de la Pologne Populaire (1950–1985)" [The Jews in the Polish Noble Republic (XVI–XVIII centuries) in the historiography of People's Poland (1950–1980)], in *Między historią a teorią* [Between History and Theory], ed. Marian Drozdowski (Warsaw: Państwowe Wydawnictwo Naukowe, 1988), 322–37; Isaiah Trunk, "On the History of Polish-Jewish Historiography" [in Hebrew], *Gal-Ed* 3 (1976): 245–68; K. Pawel [Paweł Korzec], "Comments on the Subject of Jews in Recent Polish Historiography," ibid., 269–78. For a bibliography on Hasidism see the new synthetic history of Hasidism edited by David Biale, Princeton University Press, 2017.

2   This went beyond Szyja Bronsztejn's *Ludność żydowska w Polsce w okresie międzywojennym* [The Jewish Community of Poland in the interwar years] (Wrocław: Zakład Narodowy im. Ossolińskich, 1963).

a number of essential topics, such as anti-Semitism, economic history, assimilation, social welfare, youth movements, and periodical literature. It also contained a collection of documents.

Celia Heller's *On the Edge of Destruction* (New York, 1977), while controversial, was the first serious, full-length monographic treatment of the interwar period as a whole, at once summarizing old knowledge, developing the relatively new theme of assimilation, and clearly expressing the by then conventional viewpoint that the overall pattern for Jewish existence in interwar Poland was impressive cultural creativity in the face of official discrimination and unofficial hatred.

Lucjan Dobroszycki and Barbara Kirshenblatt-Gimblett's *Image before My Eyes: A Photographic History of Jewish Life in Poland, 1864–1939* (New York, 1977; republished 1994), presented a more varied, realistic, and representative view of Polish Jewry than had Roman Vishniac's *Polish Jews: A Pictorial Record*, thirty years earlier (New York, 1947).

In the same decade—the 1970s—the Jewry of the early modern Polish–Lithuanian Commonwealth received a thorough reconsideration in Bernard Dov Weinryb's *The Jews of Poland: A Social and Economic History of the Jewish Community in Poland from 1100 to 1800* (Philadelphia, 1972) and then in Salo W. Baron's sixteenth volume of his *Social and Religious History of the Jews: Poland–Lithuania, 1500–1650* (New York and Philadelphia, 1976). These two books, while differing in approach, emphasis, and interpretation, did share characteristics that signaled a departure in scholarship.

First, both insisted on viewing the history of the Jews in Poland as inextricably bound up with Polish history. Unlike earlier writing, the Polish context figured prominently in their books. Second, in comparison with works in Hebrew, these books barely touched on the topic of Jewish autonomy. Zionist and Israeli historians saw in Jewish autonomous institutions, especially as they were so comprehensively articulated in Poland, an iteration of a hoary Jewish political tradition that prepared for Jewish political independence and reached its apotheosis with Israel.[3] Baron and Weinryb, writing in the Diaspora, chose not to emphasize this aspect of the Polish Jewish experience. Third, the positive overall tone of Weinryb and Baron's narratives contrasted sharply with the conventional view of Polish Jewish history

---

3 For example, many of the articles gathered in Israel Halpern, *East European Jewry: Historical Studies* (Jerusalem: Magnes Press, 1968) [in Hebrew]; Haim Hillel Ben-Sasson, ed., *A History of the Jewish People* (Cambridge, MA: Harvard University Press, 1976).

as fundamentally a tragic story. Both presented this history as more light than shadow, a distinct counterproof to the lachrymose theory of Jewish history that Baron had criticized so consistently throughout his career.[4] This was to be a harbinger of things to come.

THE FORMER POLES

In addition to new tools and new interest, beginning in the 1970s there was finally a new cadre of scholars who could take up the mantle of those who had perished in the Holocaust. The first of these were Polish Jews who had received their early education in Poland and then, migrating, mainly to Israel, shortly before or just after the war, completed their doctoral dissertations there in the 1960s and 1970s. They were later joined by a number of their generational peers who had remained in Poland after the war, and received advanced education there, but left for Israel or the West in the wake of developments in the mid 1950s and late 1960s.

Shlomo Netzer, Emanuel Melzer, and Moshe Landau wrote detailed, tightly focused monographs on the politics of Jewish existence in Poland during the interwar years.[5] Where earlier works had generalized on the basis of examples and selected statistics, these new studies were based on exhaustive primary documentation and statistical analysis and presented a much more nuanced and penetrating portrayal of their subjects. Bina Garncarska-Kedari and Sabina Lewin opened up new topics, exploring economic and educational

---

4 This view was already expressed by Baron in an article in the *Menorah Journal* in 1928, "Ghetto and Emancipation," reprinted in ed. Leo W. Schwarz, *The Menorah Treasury* (Philadelphia: Jewish Publication Society, 1973), 50–63, esp. 63; cf. Salo W. Baron, "Newer Emphases in Jewish History," in *History and Jewish Historians* (Philadelphia, PA: Jewish Publication Society, 1964), 96; David Engel, "Salo Baron's View of the Middle Ages in Jewish History: Early Sources," in *Studies in Medieval Jewish Intellectual and Social History*, ed. David Engel et al. (Leiden: Brill, 2012), 299–315; "A Colleague Is Not a Sacred Authority: Reflections on Salo Baron's Scholarly Opus," *AJS Review* 38 (2014): 441–45; Adam Teller, "Revisiting Baron's 'Lachrymose Conception': The Meanings of Violence in Jewish History," ibid., 431–39.

5 Moshe Landau, *Miut Leumi Lohem* (Jerusalem: Zalman Shazar Center, 1986); Emanuel Melzer, *Ma'avak medini be-malkodet* (Tel Aviv: ha-Makhon le-ḥeker ha-tefutsot, 1982), English version: *No Way Out: The Politics of Polish Jewry, 1935–1939* (Cincinnati, OH: Hebrew Union College Press, 1997); Shlomo Netzer, *Ma'avak yehudei polin al zekhuyotaihem ha-ezrahiyot ve-ha-leumiyot* [The struggle of Polish Jews for their civil and national rights] (Tel Aviv: University of Tel Aviv Press, 1980). For bibliographic details on other works of these scholars and the others mentioned in the following paragraphs, consult the bibliographic works cited in note 1 above as well as the online catalogue of the National Library of Israel and the RAMBI Index of Articles on Jewish Studies.

factors, respectively, in the formation of the various Jewish class groupings and intelligentsia in the nineteenth century.[6]

A new research theme was the reestablishment of Polish Jewry in the postwar period; here Hannah Shlomi and Yisrael Gutman took the lead.[7] There were also new surveys of Poland's Jews in the interwar period. Paweł Korzec presented his thesis on the all-pervasiveness of anti-Semitism in determining the Jewish policy—and other policies—of the Polish state.[8] Joseph Marcus showed how the Jews' actual economic status was more a function of general economic conditions than specific discriminatory policies and asserted, to the consternation of most reviewers of his book, that Jewish political efforts—the *struggle* alluded to in the titles of each of the three books by Netzer, Landau, and Melzer and detailed by them—aimed at securing Jewish civil, political, and minority rights were misguided.[9]

Representatives of this group of historians also revisited the pre-partition period. Jacob Goldberg, Mordechai Nadav, and S. Artur Cygielman initiated a broad reinterpretation of the history of the Jews of the Nobles' Commonwealth by demonstrating the paramount relevance of Polish archival sources to Polish Jewish history, even in the period when Jews were at their most "traditional." On the basis of their analyses of Polish material, the paradigm of symbiosis began to challenge the traditional concept of parallel societies as the most appropriate trope for the Polish–Jewish relationship. Moreover, both Goldberg and Cygielman published source collections and Nadav prepared an edition of the communal record book of Tiktin (Tykocin), which all have great potential as teaching and research tools.[10]

---

6 Bina Garncarska-Kadari, *Helkam shel ha-yehudim be-hitpathut ha-ta'asiya shel varsha* [The role of the Jews in the development of industry in Warsaw] (Tel Aviv, 1985); Sabina Lewin, *Perakim be-toldot ha-hinuch ha-yehudi be-polin* [Chapters in the history of Jewish education in Poland] (Tel Aviv, 1997); for further bibliography see H-B and RAMBI.

7 Hannah Shlomi, ed., *Asufat ma'amarim le-toldot she'erit ha-pletah be-polin* [A collection of articles on the history of Jewish survivors in Poland] (Tel Aviv: ha-Merkaz le-ḥeker toldot ha-Yehudim be-Polin u-morashtam: ha-Makhon le-ḥeker ha-tefutsot, 2001); Israel Gutman and Avital Saf, eds., *She'erit ha-pletah 1944–1948: Rehabilitation and Political Struggle* (Jerusalem: Yad Vashem, 1990); cf. RAMBI Index.

8 Pavel Korzec, *Juifs en Pologne* [Jews in Poland] (Paris: Presses de la Fondation nationale des sciences politiques, 1980); cf. RAMBI.

9 Joseph Marcus, *Social and Political History of the Jews in Poland, 1919–1939* (Berlin: Mouton Publishers, 1983).

10 Jacob Goldberg, *Jewish Privileges in the Polish Commonwealth*, 3 vols. (Jerusalem: Israel Academy of Sciences and Humanities, 1985–2001); Shmuel Artur Cygielman, *The Jews of Poland and Lithuania until 1648: Prolegomena and Annotated Sources* [in Hebrew]

The leading figure in this period in the study of the cultural history of Polish Jewry was Chone Shmeruk. Based on his profound knowledge of Yiddish literature and complete conversance with Polish culture, he illuminated numerous aspects of Jewish customs, Jewish *mentalité*, and Jewish intellectual development in Poland from the sixteenth century until the Holocaust.[11]

THE "SABRAS"

Another group of scholars identifiable by its demographic and educational background were Jews born and educated in Israel. Younger than the previous group (and mainly students of theirs or of their older contemporaries, such as Shmuel Ettinger, Jacob Katz, and Israel Halpern), for people like Yishai Shahar, Yaakov Elbaum, Immanuel Etkes, Yaakov Hisdai, Elhanan Reiner, Zev Gries, Israel Bartal, and David Assaf, Polish Jewish history was a subset within broader interests. Their main focus was elsewhere on such subjects as Ashkenazic, or Eastern European, Jewish culture, Hasidism, Land of Israel studies, and Haskalah. They came to Polish Jewry primarily via Jewish texts and concentrated on intellectual and religious history and the history of cultural institutions.[12] There was also a somewhat younger and smaller group of Israeli scholars, trained primarily in Israel—among them Ido Basok, Ela Bauer, Daniel Blatman, Judith Kalik, Tamar Salmon-Mack, and Adam Teller—who actually specialized in Polish Jewish history.[13]

(Jerusalem: Zalman Shazar Center, 1991); *Jewish Autonomy in Poland and Lithuania until 1648* (Jerusalem: Self-published, 1997); Mordechai Nadav, *The Minutes Book of the Jewish Community Council of Tykocin, 1621–1806* [in Hebrew], 2 vols. (Jerusalem: Israel Academy of Sciences, 1996). For other works by these authors, see H-B and RAMBI.

11 For his bibliography, see *Ke-Minhag ashkenaz u-polin: Studies in Honor of Chone Shmeruk*, eds. Israel Bartal, Ezra Mendelsohn, Chava Turniansky (Jerusalem: Zalman Shazar Center, 1993), 413–28. Of particular interest in the present context is the collection of his articles entitled *Yiddish Literature in Poland: Historical Studies and Perspectives* [in Hebrew] (Jerusalem: Magnes Press, 1981).

12 For bibliography by these scholars see (cf. note 1): H-B 1984; Bacon, "Rich Harvest," 1991; Stephen D. Corrsin, "Works on Polish Jewry, 1990–1994: A Bibliography," *Gal-Ed* 14 (1995): 131–233; Gershon D. Hundert, "Polish Jewish History," *Modern Judaism* 10 (1990): 259–270; idem, "Bibliography of Polish-Jewish studies 1993," *Polin* 9 (1996): 305–318; Teller, "Jews and Poles," 1994; RAMBI Index.

13 For the purpose of this essay I am not including scholars whose main subject is the Holocaust, even though their work is connected to Polish–Jewish history.

THE WESTERNERS

A third group is composed of people raised or largely educated outside of both Poland and Israel, such as Karen Auerbach, Gershon Bacon, Glenn Dynner, David Engel, David Fishman, Edward Fram, Gershon D. Hundert, Samuel Kassow, Hillel Levine, Ezra Mendelsohn, Antony Polonsky, Moshe Rosman, Robert M. Shapiro, Shaul Stampfer, Michael Steinlauf, and Daniel Tollet. Most are distinguished by their ability to combine Polish and Jewish sources, their familiarity with trends in Western historiography and—in comparison to the survivors and émigrés—their lack of intense emotional attachment to Polish Jewry of the interwar and Holocaust periods. With some notable exceptions, most of their studies are heavily dependent on archival and/or quantifiable material. They have significantly furthered the process of articulating a broad new view of Polish Jewry. One feature of this is the attempt to clarify the degree to which the Jews indeed were *of* Poland and not merely *in* it; that is, inextricably linked to the social, cultural, economic, and even political processes of the country. Hundert, for example, titled one of the chapters of his book, *The Jews in a Polish Private Town* (Baltimore, 1992), "Jews and *Other* Poles." For these writers, there was no celebrating the heroic achievements of Polish Jewry and even candid admissions of shortcomings. Thus, Mendelsohn enumerated the "failures of Jewish nationalism,"[14] while others have written about Jewish criminality and belligerence, without apology. With regard to non-Jews and, more specifically, anti-Jewish behavior, these writers have exhibited a willingness to entertain "structural" factors of politics, economics, sociology, tradition, and so on, in the fomenting of persecution. However, they still typically maintain that non-Jews made a choice when they attacked or discriminated against Jews and that in the decision process the identity of the victim was not incidental.[15]

---

14 *The Jews of East Central Europe between the Wars* (Bloomington: Indiana University Press, 1983), 81.

15 See, for example, the studies in *Polin* 24 (Oxford, 2012): *Jews and Their Neighbors in Eastern Europe Since 1750*, eds. Israel Bartal, Antony Polonsky, Scott Ury. See also (cf. note 1) Engel "Works in Hebrew," 1989, Engel, "Writing Polish-Jewish History," 1989; Mendelsohn, "Jewish Historiography," 1991, 1994; Hundert, "Recent Studies," 1973, 1990; Gershon Bacon, "Unchanging View: Polish Jewry as Seen in Recent One Volume Histories of the Jews," *Polin* 4 (1989): 390–401; Teller, "Jews and Poles," 1994. Samuel Kassow, "Polish–Jewish relations in the writings of Emmanuel Ringelblum," in *Contested Memories*, ed. Joshua Zimmerman (New Brunswick, NJ: Rutgers University Press, 2003), 142–57.

THE POLES

A fourth group consisted of (mainly non-Jewish) scholars born and educated within Poland (and to a lesser extent non-Jews outside of Poland) who began to define within the broad subject of Polish history subjects that centered on the Jewish experience. The reasons for this are connected to the liberalization, new-style nationalism, and turn to the West experienced in Poland in the late 1970s and the 1980s. Polish historians searching for the historical roots of a noncommunist, liberal, independent, democratic, "Polish" Poland found them in the multinational Poland of the past. In the conventional Polish historiography on this "commonwealth of many nationalities," the subject of the Jews was the one that was treated the most superficially. Yet it was precisely this subject that seemed still to be an issue for Polish society, mostly because of a residual widespread image of Polish anti-Semitism in the world and lingering mutual recriminations with regard to the fate of the Jews in Poland in the twentieth century.[16]

Curiosity over this paradox became an opportunity for serious research when the political atmosphere of the 1980s led to the initiation of an unprecedented series of international conferences. Perhaps most significantly, the journal *Polin* was founded after the 1984 conference in Oxford. On its pages, for the first time since before the war, and in a sense for the first time ever, Jewish and Polish scholars were engaged in serious reciprocal academic discourse.[17]

---

16 See Moshe Rosman, "Categorically Jewish, Distinctly Polish: The Museum of the History of Polish Jews and the New Polish-Jewish Metahistory," *Jewish Studies: An Internet Journal* 10 (2012): 366–69.

17 For collected conference papers and other international general collected studies on the subject, see *Conference on Poles and Jews: Myth and Reality in the Historical Context*, ed. John Micgiel, Robert Scott, Harold B. Segel (New York: Columbia, 1983); *The Jews in Poland*, ed. Chimen Abramsky, Maciej Jachimczyk, and Antony Polonsky (Oxford: Blackwell, 1986); *Studies on Polish Jewry: Paul Glikson Memorial Volume*, ed. Ezra Mendelsohn and Chone Shmeruk (Jerusalem: Zalman Shazar Center, 1987); *The Jews of Poland Between Two World Wars*, ed. Yisrael Gutman et al. (Hanover, NH: Published for Brandeis University Press by University Press of New England, 1989); *Studies in the History and Culture of East European Jewry*, ed. Gershon Bacon and Moshe Rosman, *BarIlan* 24–25 (1989); *The Jews in Warsaw*, ed. Władysław T. Bartoszewski and Antony Polonsky (Oxford: Blackwells, 1991); *The Jews in Poland*, ed. Andrzej K. Paluch (Kraków: Jagiellonian University, Research Center on Jewish History and Culture in Poland, 1992); *The Jews in Old Poland*, ed. Antony Polonsky, Jakub Basista, Andrzej Link-Lenczowski (London: I. B. Tauris, 1993) [somewhat different Polish version: *Żydzi w dawnej Rzeczypospolitej*, ed. Andrzej Link-Lenczowski and Tomasz Polański (Wrocław: Zakład Narodowy im. Ossolińskich, 1991)]; *From Shtetl to Socialism: Studies from Polin*, ed. Antony Polonsky (Oxford: Littman Library of Jewish

As late as 1986 Andrzej Chojnowski could write, "The Jewish question is still examined in recent [Polish] historiography in a most fragmentary manner."[18] By 1994, however, more than one-third of the 867 items listed in Corrsin's bibliography were published in Polish or by Poles in other languages. As perusal of the contents of the various collected studies shows, both prominent and younger Polish historians have written individual studies relating to Jewish topics. Others, like Zenon Guldon, Jerzy Holzer, Piotr Wróbel, and, especially, Jerzy Tomaszewski, made the history of the Jews in Poland one of their specialties. Many scholars specializing in Jewish studies—such as Maurycy Horn, Alina Cała, Helena Datner, Paweł Fijałkowski, Daniel Grinberg, Marian Fuks, Eleonora Bergman, Hanna Węgrzynek, Rafał Żebrowski, and Jan Doktór—made their academic home in the Jewish Historical Institute (ŻIH) and many contributed to its publication, the *Biuletyn Żydowskiego Instytutu Historycznego* (BŻIH). In recent years, the Jagiellonian University in Kraków's Research Center on Jewish History and Culture in Poland, first under the leadership of Józef Andrzej Gierowski and currently headed by Michał Galas, has made significant strides in gathering bibliographic material and sponsoring research. The History Institute of Warsaw University also sponsors a Center for Jewish Studies where Jerzy Tomaszewski was a pioneer. Then there is the growing Jewish studies program at Wrocław University, founded by Marcin Wodziński. In addition, there are various Jewish studies options at many other Polish institutions of higher education. These university and academy settings have produced a raft of productive scholars—people like Monika Adamczyk-Garbowska, Michał Galas, Edyta Gawron, Stefan Gąsiorowski, Agnieszka Jagodzińska, Anna Jakimyszyn, Anna Michałowska, Adam Kaźmierczyk, Joanna Nalewajko-Kulikow, Eugenia Prokop-Janiec, Bożena Szaynok, Hanna Zaremska, Jolanta Żyndul, and many others—who have had a significant impact on Jewish studies worldwide.

Scholars outside of Poland, such as Norman Davies, Frank Golczewski, Edward Wynot, Theodore Weeks, and Karen Underhill have made important

---

Civilization, 1993); *Ke-Minhag ashkenaz u-polin: Studies in Honor of Chone Shmeruk*, ed. Israel Bartal, Ezra Mendelsohn, and Chava Turniansky (Jerusalem: Zalman Shazar Center, 1993); *Hasidism Reappraised*, ed. Ada Rapoport-Albert (Oxford: Littman Library of Jewish Civilization, 1996); *Studies in the History of the Jews in Old Poland in Honor of Jacob Goldberg*, ed. Adam Teller (Jerusalem: Magnes Press, 1998). In addition, most of the volumes of *Polin* have been devoted to specific subjects. There were a number of conferences at Polish universities that focused on the Jews of a particular region or city. For bibliographic details of these conferences' proceedings, see Teller, "Jews and Poles," 1994 and Corrsin 1995.

18 Andrzej Chojnowski, "The Jewish Community of the Second Republic in Polish Historiography of the 1980s," *Polin* 1 (1986): 298.

contributions to the new trend to include the history of the Jews in Poland as part of the history of Poland.[19]

NEW SCHOLARS, NEW SCHOLARSHIP

By now, I think it is fair to say that there are probably more scholars and certainly more students in Poland's centers of Jewish studies in Warsaw, Kraków, and Wrocław, as well as elsewhere in Poland, Lithuania, Ukraine, Russia, and Germany than in the United States, Israel, and the UK combined. There are also both old and new Polish journals devoted exclusively to Jewish Studies, such as *BŻIH*, *Studia Judaica*, and *Scripta Judaica Cracoviensia*.

However, it is becoming much more difficult to classify scholars in terms of geographical origin and training. Many scholars—Natalia Aleksiun, François Guesnet, Yvonne Kleinmann, Jürgen Heyde, Judith Kalik, Marci Shore, Katrin Steffen, Adam Teller, Magdalena Teter, Scott Ury, and Marcin Wodziński are examples—tend to be "hybrid," originating in one place and being trained in another, or several others, while participating in various international scholarly forums and projects throughout their careers. The biannual workshop for Polish and Israeli doctoral candidates in Polish Jewish studies and the POLIN Museum research fellowships for doctoral and postdoctoral candidates encourage such cross-fertilization.

The result of all of these new approaches, resources, and scholars is a plethora of scholarship, literally thousands of studies, large and small. Taken all together they have forged a new master narrative and new historiographical agenda. There is now broad agreement with Jakub Goldberg's famous observation that there is no history of Poland without the Jews and no history of the Jews without Poland.

Perhaps the most salient feature of the new, politically unfettered Polish historiography on Polish Jewry is what Adam Teller has termed the objective of "reinsertion" of Jews into Polish history.[20] Whereas, traditionally, Polish

---

19 For bibliography, see the sources in note 1. In my 1988 article in *Jewish History*, I discussed the significance of Davies's book, *God's Playground: A History of Poland* (Oxford: Oxford University Press, 1982). On trends in studying and publishing about Jews in Poland, see Zachary M. Baker, "The Chosen Book: Reinventing the Jew in Absentia: Recent Judaica Publishing Trends in Poland," *Judaica Librarianship* 5 (1989–90), 62–66; Grażyna Chłodnicka, *Literatura żydowska 1946–1992* (Koszalin: Wojewódzka Biblioteka Publiczna im. Joachima Lelewela, 1993); Natan Gross, "Requiem for the Jewish People: Polish Literary Judaica in the Years 1987–1989," *Polin* 6 (1991): 295–308; Tollet, "Les Juifs," 1988 (note 1 above); Marcin Wodziński, "Jewish Studies in Poland," *Journal of Modern Jewish Studies* 10 (2011): 101–18.

20 Teller, "Jews and Poles," 80.

scholars viewed Jews as marginal, even alien, to Polish history, they are now considered to be an essential element in the narrative of multiethnic Poland's historical development. The studies of contemporary Polish scholars exploit sources that were previously ignored—and are much less accessible to foreigners—and combine them with the perspective gained from an intimate knowledge of Polish history to explain the Jewish experience as part and parcel of the larger Polish one. Sometimes they imply (if only by omission) that Polish Jews' connection to Judaism, Jewish history, and Jewish people outside of Poland was analogous to Poles' connections to Christianity, Christian history, and Christians outside of Poland. In other words, Polish Jewry was first and foremost Polish. The larger Jewish context is more amorphous and less vital. POLIN Museum is an example of this perspective.

Another prominent characteristic of this new historiography is its tendency to present Polish–Jewish relations in, to borrow David Engel's term, "objectivist" as opposed to "subjectivist" terms.[21] Age-old anti-Jewish ideology and prejudice did not a priori condemn Jews to discrimination and persecution. Rather, material considerations of economics and sociology that conditioned the historical situation in Poland at any given time led to objective conflicts of interests between Jews and Poles, whether the subject is residency restrictions in the seventeenth century or boycotts of Jewish merchants in the twentieth. Furthermore, since Jews are now part of the Polish story, there is a marked proclivity on the part of Polish historians to engage in local and micro-level studies of Jews in a specific locality or of a particular Jewish institution. Methodologically, this minimizes—although it does not eliminate—the need to use Jewish sources. Substantively, it entails introducing many fine distinctions and nuances to generalizations found in the traditional Jewish historiography based on macro-level studies and representative examples, making it harder to speak about "the" Polish Jews.[22]

NEW AGENDAS

In the future, there may be a new emphasis, by Jewish scholars at least, on what tied Polish Jews to Jewish history outside of Poland. There certainly is room fully to document and analyze the cultural, economic, and social connections

---

21 Engel (note 1), "Writing Polish-Jewish History"; cf. sources cited in note 15 above.
22 On the tendencies in Polish historiography and for examples of the phenomena alluded to here, see especially Wodziński, "Jewish Studies," 2011 (note 19) and the other sources cited in notes 15 and 19 above.

among Jews in Poland and Jews in western Ashkenaz before the Haskalah. One obvious central theme is the relationship between Polish Jewry and German court Jews; another is patterns and institutions of Torah study in all Ashkenaz. For the interwar period, there is a need to realize Mendelsohn's call for much more comparative study of the circumstances of the Jews (and other minorities) throughout Eastern Europe.

With regard to the integrative trend, however, for both the pre-partition and later periods much more can be done on the question of cultural and social relations. The current literature is contradictory as to whether there was meaningful cultural contact between Jews and gentiles in Poland. When and to what extent did social relations move beyond the utilitarian?

Periodization has also been altered, especially with respect to pre-partition Jewish history. The pre- and post-1648 distinction is now much less emphasized. With the material effects of the mid seventeenth-century persecutions and dislocations shown to have dissipated, the eighteenth century viewed as much less "crisis"-filled than previously asserted, and the continuity of institutions established, the focus is on the early modern period of Polish Jewry as an integral unit, usually defined as the sixteenth century to the partitions.

This period has been heavily studied. In particular, the importance of the relationship between Jews and the landowning aristocratic nobility has been extensively explicated and emphasized. Lately, young researchers have begun turning toward renewed study of the relationship between royal or state institutions and the Jews, the long-overlooked subject of the various churches and the Jews, and deeper investigation of social relations between Jews and Christians. In particular, there is newfound curiosity about Jewish conversion and converts to Christianity. There is also a refreshing new interest in the history of Jews in the Grand Duchy of Lithuania as a subject in its own right, separate from the history of the Jews in Poland.[23]

In addition, there are also signs of new exploration of the pre-1500 period. Much more needs to be done on the history of early Jewish migration and settlement. There is also a need to explore economic and cultural life in this period.

Moreover, there is a new insistence that the history of Polish Jews in the nineteenth century should no longer be subsumed under the rubric of Russian Jewish history. As Marcin Wodziński and others have demonstrated,

---

23 On this last point, see the studies by Jurgita Šiaučiunaitė-Verbickiene and Maria Cieśla listed in the RAMBI Index.

there really was a distinctly *Polish* Jewish community between the partitions and 1918.

With regard to autonomy, the reigning subtheme has been to tone down the romantic, Jewish nationalist interpretation of the past. Some of the institutions of Jewish autonomy have come to be seen as more limited in scope and authority and more subservient to Polish institutions than previously thought. What would be useful now is more study of the parallels and points of articulation between the Jewish and Polish institutions, in order to arrive at a better understanding of the intricacies of governance of the Jews.

With regard to Hasidism, there has been a great deal of attention paid to Israel Baal Shem Tov and the origins of Hasidism; however, the most important trend has been to target Hasidism of the nineteenth century not as the degenerate stage of the movement, but rather as the mature and more interesting one.[24]

The struggles of the Jews for rights in the interwar period have been carefully documented and analyzed. At the same time, their efficacy and even the appropriateness of the term *struggle* have been questioned. The subjectivist versus objectivist view of Polish–Jewish relations and anti-Semitism are engaged in something of a struggle of their own. It is here that the ideological commitments of the historians of the various backgrounds described above are most apparent. The older "former Polish" school usually saw interwar Poland as the crucible where a secular, left-leaning, new Jewish society and culture were cultivated. Politically, interwar Poland demonstrated the national nature of the Jewish people and proved the need for a nationalist solution to the precariousness of their existence.[25]

Today's Polish historians—and others—tend to view the Jewish problem as one among many of the time. For them anti-Semitism was an unfortunate byproduct of a set of conditions that generated a host of social ills.

The younger "Sabras" and "Westerners," many of them committed to a religious outlook, include more sectors of Jewish society in the story. With regard to anti-Semitism, their own experience with pluralist and

---

24 On Israel Baal Shem Tov see, for example, Immanuel Etkes, *The Besht: Magician, Mystic and Leader* (Waltham, MA: Brandeis University Press; Hanover, NH: University Press of New England, 2005); Moshe Rosman, *Founder of Hasidism* (Berkeley: University of California Press, 1996). On nineteenth-century Hasidism, see the impressive oeuvre of both David Assaf and Marcin Wodziński as well as the new synthetic history of Hasidism edited by David Biale, (Princeton, 2017).

25 See sources in notes 5, 15, and 19 above.

majority–minority societies incline them to take the Polish analysis more seriously than their teachers did. Still, for them, anti-Semitism was not merely an unintended consequence of the operation of larger forces.

In general, the research focus on this period has changed from the secular, nationalist, and leftist groups to previously ignored groups among the Orthodox, the political right, and the assimilationists. There has also been a turn away from politics toward social life, economics, culture, and religion. In particular, we should probably expect more studies about the weakening of Jewish cultural institutions. To my mind, it would be desirable to pay more attention to unaffiliated, nonideological, moderately traditionalist Jews. One can easily get the impression from the historiography that there were few such people in interwar Poland; such a counter-intuitive conclusion surely bears examination.

GRAND SYNTHESES

The vast new corpus of scholarship has led to the fashioning of three syntheses of Polish Jewish history, each of which has as its foundation the scholarship of the past fifty years or so, its findings, its interpretations, and its spirit. Each belongs to a different scholarly genre and treats our subject in accordance with the canons of its characteristic style and tone. The first was Gershon D. Hundert's *The YIVO Encyclopedia of Jews in Eastern Europe*, 2 vols. (New Haven, CT, 2008); followed by Antony Polonsky's magisterial survey, *The Jews in Poland and Russia*, 3 vols. (Oxford, 2010–2012); and, most recently, the core exhibition of POLIN Museum of the History of Polish Jews, created under the direction of Barbara Kirshenblatt-Gimblett, which opened in Warsaw in October 2014.

All three of these works posit that Polish Jews were not passive, acquiescing in a fate determined by others. Within the framework and limits imposed by the Christian majority, they forged the nature, rhythm, and content of their lives: their autonomous community with its constituent institutions, their culture, religious life, social structure, and so on. They were conscious of their own worth, claimed what was coming to them, and negotiated the specific terms of their existence with their non-Jewish interlocutors.

In the early modern period, they navigated between the often reliable support of the king and nobility and the frequent hostility of the townsmen and many church institutions. In the nineteenth century, they fashioned a modern culture, including modern religious components, and attempted to establish a new political basis for their survival. In the twentieth century they demanded their rights and struggled to secure a better life for their children or—in times of catastrophe—just to survive. In general, Jews took the initiative in relations with the non-Jewish majority, aiming for a reasonable, lasting, and secure modus vivendi with them.

All three narratives gingerly approach the question of Jewish treatment of non-Jews. For example, Antony Polonsky's assertion in an *Encyclopedia* article "that Jews reciprocated the contempt in which their religious beliefs were held by the Christians," tempered by the true observation that "one should not equate the position of the two groups [Polish Jews and Polish Christians]. Effectively all power was in the hands of the Christians,"[26] is reiterated in his *History* and echoed in various places in the museum's core exhibit. There is no restatement, however, of Jacob Katz's pronouncement that the traditional early modern Ashkenazic Jewish community that included Polish Jewry practiced a double standard of morality vis-à-vis non-Jews.[27] Overall, not too much attention is paid to less than noble feelings or dishonorable actions of Jews toward their countrymen[28] lest these be taken out of context by people who still today are eager to give credence to anti-Semitic tropes.

All three syntheses strike a tone that is *sine ire et studio*, that is, there is a sincere attempt at academic objectivity. Successes are reported, not celebrated. Failures are analyzed, not defended. Moral judgments may be implied but are not made explicit. The mode of writing or displaying is neither justification nor condemnation, but explication.[29]

This approach is particularly noticeable when treating the sensitive subjects of Polish anti-Semitism and the Shoah, especially the issue of the complicity of Poles in the murder of Polish Jewry. These subjects are certainly

---

26 *The YIVO Encyclopedia*, s.v.: "Relations between Jews and Non-Jews," col. 1538; cf. History (e.g. 1:38).

27 Jacob Katz, *Tradition and Crisis*, trans. Bernard D. Cooperman (New York: New York University Press, 1993), 32–34; *Exclusiveness and Tolerance* (New York: Schocken Books, 1962), 3–12, 37–47, 143–55.

28 An exception to this is the museum's treatment of sporadic episodes of *Jewish* collaboration with the Nazis during the Shoah.

29 Of course, this does not preclude the presence of a certain meta-history underlying each of these narratives. For discussion of these see my reviews of Hundert's and Polonsky's books in *Gal-Ed* 23 (2012) and *Zion* 80 (2014) respectively, and my article about POLIN, "Categorically Jewish, Distinctly Polish: The Museum of the History of Polish Jews and the New Polish-Jewish Metahistory," *JSIJ* 10 (2012).

highlighted, but they do not dominate the narrative. All of these works make the point that the Shoah, as central as it is to Polish Jewish history, was not the "last chapter" of that history.[30]

The syntheses strongly emphasize Jewish creativity, vitality, and achievement in Poland, whether social organization as exemplified by Jewish autonomy institutions; cultural endeavors like schooling, journalism, literature, Torah learning, and theatre; or art and architecture as represented by the model of the Gwoździec synagogue.

While the three general narratives represent broad consensus in many areas, they also differ from each other in many ways (and not only in genres and resulting characteristics). For example, Polonsky casts the narrative of post-partition Polish Jewish history as a story of modernization and also stresses the crucial role of Jewish autonomous institutions, even in the modern period, all the way up to the Shoah. In his introduction to the *Encyclopedia*, Hundert states a commitment to portraying "all aspects of Jewish life." Indeed, one comes away from reading the *Encyclopedia* with an impression of kaleidoscopic variety and fractal complexity. In contrast to previous historiography, everyday life is particularly highlighted. The museum's core exhibition does not explicitly portray Jews as part of a larger Jewish context. They are, to be sure, wholly Jewish but simultaneously, if syncretistically, Polish.

CONCLUSION

The past two generations have witnessed an intense international discussion on the history of the Jews in Poland. It has involved a sizable number of scholars from several countries who engage each other at frequent conferences and on the pages of journals and volumes of collected studies. There are centers for the study of the history and culture of Polish Jewry on three continents. There are graduate students at all of these institutions and others besides, including a biannual joint Polish–Israeli workshop for doctoral candidates.

---

30 The by now standard criticism of the POLIN permanent exhibit and *The YIVO Encyclopedia* is that they do not devote *enough* attention to either Polish anti-Semitism or the Shoah and put too much emphasis on the salutary aspects of the history they depict. In my opinion this is a good example of the conflict between historical scholarship and historical memory enunciated by Yosef Hayim Yerushalmi in his *Zakhor*. The museum and encyclopedia follow the scholarship in placing both of these key topics in historical perspective and not allowing them to overwhelm the significance of other trends. Historical memory would dictate a different approach, giving them primacy.

In 1955, Jacob Shatzky, the historian of Warsaw Jewry, despaired:

> For whom am I slaving? For whom am I writing and about whom? My people is dead, my theme is a dead one and I am dead tired.

If only he could have seen the creations of Hundert, Polonsky, and Kirshenblatt-Gimblett—and all they represent.

POLIN, the Medieval and Early Modern Galleries
A Comment

KENNETH STOW[1]

My friend the sociologist Mitchel Duneier has told me of a small episode that occurred in POLIN Museum in the summer of 2013. Duneier's Princeton Global Seminar spent several weeks in Warsaw, including, of course, in the museum. Duneier reports, "One of my students asked the chief curator, Barbara Kirshenblatt-Gimblett, whether the museum was intended to be a celebration of Jewish life. 'To be able to say that what you see is an uplifting story is really fantastic,' Barbara replied."

To celebrate, not in the sense of a party, but a living memorial, a recognition—that is precisely what POLIN does. It revivifies the Polish Jewish experience, the experience of Jews in Poland. It presents, as Hanna Zaremska has

---

1   This brief essay is not annotated since it draws its inspiration directly from the medieval early modern exhibit and halls of POLIN, on which it is intended to comment. It has no pretensions to represent "new research." Comparative materials for Italy come from my own works on the Jews in the Middle Ages and early modern Rome, which are easily traced. I mention only Baron's "Ghetto and Emancipation," in *The Menorah Treasury*, ed. Leo Schwartz (Philadelphia: Jewish Publication Society, 1964) and Marcin Wodziński's essay, "Clerks, Jews and Farmers: Projects of Jewish Agricultural Settlement in Poland," *Jewish History* 21 (2007): 279–303, both of which this essay mentions. Further reference is to my *Anna and Tranquillo: Catholic Anxiety and Jewish Response in the Age of Revolutions* (New Haven, CT: Yale University Press, 2016) and its discussion of the confessional state. The best source on medieval charters is Vittore Colorni, *Legge ebraica, leggi locali* [Jewish Law, Local Laws] (Milan: A. Giuffrè, 1945), which explains the notion of *tuitio* in the sense of special privilege given to permanent residents. Readers will be interested in the various works of Adam Teller and Hanna Zaremska beside their major contributions to the museum and its catalogue, as well as essays on the museum by Moshe Rosman.

written, a visual recreation of what the historian describes in words, and often a more vivid one, which, as Barbara Kirshenblatt-Gimblett tells us, requires great care; for the visitor is in the museum, in the presence of the pictorial or artifactual recreation, in most instances but a single time. To the written word, which may also be lengthy, one may return. The pictorial/artifactual recreation must be succinct, but forceful as well. At moments, as I walked through the galleries, I felt that I myself had become momentarily a part of the Polish Jewish past.

The theme of POLIN draws on Moshe Rosman's pithy characterization: "categorically Jewish, distinctly Polish," a phrase that may be read in many ways. Let me convey my reading as I have come to it by visiting the galleries, but, I must add, also through reading the descriptions that Hanna Zaremska and Adam Teller have provided for the early through the early modern periods. What I celebrate—in this case, applaud—is the fluidity of the presentation, the ability to move through the galleries in whatever way, and order, the visitor desires. The experience becomes one, whole, integrated. It preserves memory alive.

I was immediately reminded, through both reading and viewing, of the classic *How Societies Remember* (Cambridge: Cambridge University Press, 1989) of Paul Connorton: How does a society preserve its identity—its integrity—through the written word, through ritual, and through social action (among others)? Memory, as I have written about Italian, especially Roman, Jews, can be conservative, in the positive sense that it urges its possessors not to discard the values or essences of the past. Roman Jews, who were highly acculturated—indeed, because of their millennial presence in the city from the time of the ancient Romans, it was sometimes a question of who was acculturated, who the cultural pacesetter, the Jews or the Christians—thus allowed change to occur, but never so greatly that the past was obscured, in all of these categories.

One thus argued, as did Yosef ha-Kohen (who did not live in Rome) that biblical Hebrew, not Latin, was the original language, to be revered as such, for it bore the lamp of true learning. By implication, Hebrew wisdom outshone that of the neo-Latin humanists. In like manner, Roman Jews might adopt Christian musical forms, but always within their own liturgical cycle, just as Jewish ritual shirked from achieving the kind of transcendental sacrality attributed to the sacraments, especially the Eucharist. Rabbis were not, nor did they wish to be, priests. The Jews of Rome used Italian as their daily language (sometimes mixed with highly italianized Hebraisms), but they would draw notarial texts (that were so important for communal harmony) in Hebrew, which, however, clearly betrays that they were *thinking* in Italian.

Much of this acculturation is attributable, as I said, to the Jews' longevity in Rome, but it is also attributable to urbanization, to the fact that Italy itself, as a whole, was highly urbanized (in its north, at least) from about the same time that Jews began to settle in Poland. It was an effect, too, of limited Jewish autonomy, which was forever being usurped by the growing integration of the Jews into the system of *ius commune*, Roman law as modified and applied in the Italian cities alongside local law. And of a common diet—Romans today, Jews and non-Jews alike, who wish to resurrect early modern Rome dining, frequent the restaurants of the (still so-called) ghetto.

Acculturation was, in addition, an effect of a contractual bargain with the papacy, certainly in Rome, which guaranteed Jewish life and limb (and even more), as long as Jews abided by canonical restriction. Most notably, Pope Sixtus IV in 1475 was furious at the pseudo-judicial execution of all the Jewish men in the town of Trent (which, note, was in the Empire) on a spurious charge (as such charges are always) of ritual murder. This world would come apart from 1555, although even then, until 1751, the essential bargain of protection (under drastically reduced conditions, to be sure) would be maintained.

The year 1751 is crucial, for it was events in Poland that brought the then Pope Benedict XIV, in the bull *A quo primum*, to the brink of abandoning Jewish protection; he never rejected it completely, but he, and his successors, continually wavered. This instability recalls the sometimes precarious volatility of Polish Jewish existence, with a Church that actively, through early university polemic or later support by important clergy, sustained the libels of blood and ritual murder; I wonder whether in the Paradisus Judaeorum exhibit of POLIN the phrase *Dominatus famulorum*, ruled by slaves or servants, does not really refer to the Jews, sons of the *famula* Hagar in the Christian tradition. Yet there were always leading churchmen who ignored the vilifications and willingly entered virtual partnerships with Jews: bishops depositing monies with Jews, who lent these monies at interest, effectively making the bishops parties to what was termed always usury. And it was over this practice that Benedict XIV exploded in *A quo primum*.

It is in the exhibits in POLIN that one senses this Polish Jewish difference, that which, indeed, created something "categorically Jewish, yet distinctively Polish." For whereas Italian—again, especially Roman—Jewry was so highly integrated, living with others in the city in a state of what I have called elsewhere a "tense intimacy," the path I see in Poland (with the emphasis on *I*) is one of intertwined destinies: Jews and Poles (and the other peoples of medieval and early modern Poland) almost, but not quite, symbiotic. I am certain that there will be disagreement with me, some persons preferring the direction of lesser blending, some that of greater. Yet is not that the point of the fluidity of the museum, its open-endedness, which also cautions that the kind of study of Polish Jewry which searches out commonality and interrelationship has only recently begun, the study *not* of two distinct peoples occupying the same place, but of two people constantly interacting and mutually influencing each other? As put by Hanna Zaremska: "Throughout the exhibition, the coupling of Jewish history with the history of Poland is repeatedly highlighted."

What I, again from personal perspective, observe in following the galleries, is that tracing the course of Jewish life in Poland is to trace the destiny of early modern Poland itself; what happened in the eras of modern nationalism, during the partition, and then after 1918 I will not address, although I do note that the path in post–French Revolutionary Poland seems to mirror that in Italy: when true integration became possible (in Italy, with the end of the ghettos), it occurred rapidly.

In Italy, and especially late premodern Rome, the Jews' civil integration brought legal minds to question the very existence of a confessional state, with an official religion, and separate laws for separate folks; they were pressing toward post-French and American Revolutionary modernity. In Poland, I espy—please do not be upset with me for saying this, even though I suspect that from the perspective of his extraordinary "Ghetto and Emancipation," Salo Baron would have agreed—a retreat into the Middle Ages, entrenching the concepts of the past into the social memory of Poles and Jews alike. Old patterns would, until the moment of radical change with the late eighteenth-century partitions, anchor and sustain Polish society.

Polish Jews, over time, were being made ever more dependent on charters, as once they had been in the West. They were the *iudaei nostri* of the kings and eventually the nobles; these words inserted by Duke Bolesław—*iudaeis nostris . . . declaranda statute eorum et privilegia*—in his 1264 charter of Kalisz intentionally imported patterns from early and later medieval predecessors. That the charter recalls, too, the need to observe the decree of Pope Innocent IV decrying blood libels leaves no doubt about the direct importation of the charter's clauses. In the West, the era of charters was coming to an end, which was one reason—the inability to find a firm "statute" (read: constitutional status) for the Jews—they were expelled in 1290 and 1306 from England and France.

In Poland, the Jews' direct attachment to the king or noble, before whom, alone, they were to be judged, reinforced the idea found first in Western charters of the ninth through eleventh centuries that Jews were to be permitted "to live by *statuta eorum*," an elusive phrase, which means not simply Jewish law, but a composite of Jewish law and special law and privileges for the Jews, known as Jewry law, and which the charters spell out. Likewise, Jews asked and received, as did the Jew Lewko in Kraków in 1370, and/or the community in Zamość in 1588, "defense and protection," wording identical, and not by accident with that contained in the just mentioned charters, known, appropriately, as charters of *tuitio*, or protection, given originally only to permanent residents. Isaac Troki thus emphasizes the enabling function of the Jews *kitvei kiyyumeihen*, the opposite of legal integration.

A further issue is the course of Jewish commerce, which the galleries so well represent. The early settlers, long-distance merchants, with the maps of their routes on display, supplying needs in a forming society (I would, though, much as scholars of the early medieval West have revised the idea that Jews monopolized the trade in slaves, suggest that in Poland, too, their role was perhaps not dominant). These merchants morphed over the centuries into small traders, but some became the confidantes of the upper nobility and even kings; the elegance of their wives, as seen in the portraits, says enormous amounts, in every sense, about the situation and the tenor of their lives. By contrast, the tavern keeper, which signals a whole new kind of Jewish existence, was most often elegance's contrary. Likewise, Jews were active in markets, but, most often, these were the Jews of small towns, or noble estates, serving peasants.

Poland as an entity was disintegrating; power was going to the nobles; the peasants (serfs) on the estates were tied to the soil. We have gone back to a social structure that characterized medieval Europe before 1300 (yes, of course, there were cities, as we see in the exhibits, but more characteristically, the exhibits feature the towns and noble estates). Thirteenth- and fourteenth-century Polish urbanization (with no city housing more than perhaps one hundred Jews) was yielding, giving way, as Poland reshaped its essential institutions. Unique Jewish districts were instituted, in accordance with canon law, as in the virtually Jewish city of Kazimierz, decreed in 1495, although, here—in distinction from the goal of the Italian ghetto—what occurred was the Jews' "extramission," paradoxically to enable their "intromission," enabling them the better to participate in Polish life. Indeed, "extramission," in the climate of growing localization in commerce, and governance, also allowed Jews to take advantage of decentralization, to consolidate, and create the Council of Four Lands (although this august body lacked formal governing powers). By contrast, in Italy, the ghetto increasingly strangled the Jews' social participation.

If, as an aside, it is asked why Jews did not engage in agriculture, we must beware. As much as this was impossible for reasons of law and labor supply, the idea that Jews should enter this field is, in fact, the product of a great myth stretching from the time of its invention by Thomas Aquinas (if not earlier), its adoption by King Louis IX, its repetition in arguments for closing Jewish banks in Rome in 1682, its reappearance in the *Oceana* of the seventeenth-century James Harrington, and finally in plans for Polish reform, as Marcin Wodziński has shown, in the late eighteenth century. The core of the myth was the belief that should Jews go back to the soil, they would, like the pristine Adam and Eve, be open to "regeneration," meaning, originally, conversion to Christianity (then, in Enlightenment regimes, the Jews' so-called "civic improvement"). We must not confuse myth with fact.

No wonder, then, that in defense against the potential effects of this, and so many other, even more dangerous myths, Jews set out to grow their institutional life, protecting tradition, including by spawning a distinct artistic and physical presence as realized in the growth of what I might call the Jewish *haram*, the holy district, which was the *shulhoyf*. The learning is distinctly Talmudic, halakhic, internally turned (the Vilna Gaon is the exception, is he not, but his specialty, mathematics, is, after all, culturally neutral). The art forms, embodied in the extraordinary wooden synagogue that calls our attention wherever we go through the galleries, are of the Jews, just as is the behavior of the household or the women. The unicity of Yiddish—it is a language unlike any other to which I have been exposed. Jews in Poland were setting their own limits, cultivating social and ritual memory as did those of Rome.

The formation of Polish Jewish society, to sum up, and, again, as the exhibits so well convey, was thus a function of the changes in Poland itself (its borders, its governmental organization, its ravishing by enemies, its exchange of what has been called early religious tolerance for Catholic rigidity). Rather than a move to international trade, as in the Jewish West, along with modernizing privilege, Poland's Jews experienced the reverse: from the international merchant of the thirteenth century, to the local one. Rather than being integrated into systems of *ius commune* (eventually overthrown by Napoleon's Code Civil of 1804, which alone enunciated legal equality), Polish Jews before the partition became ever more dependent on charters of privilege as they had in the immediate post-Carolingian West. As the Jews went, so went Poland; as Poland went, so did the Jews—a true mirror, one of the other. Should it not, then, be "distinctly Jewish, categorically Polish"? I leave this for the experts in the history of Polish Jewry to decide.

What is certain, however, is that as any other visitor, as I wandered back and forth through the galleries, I was taken inside this world of interactivity, of simultaneous Jewishness and Polishness. It is a world that no longer exists. But it is an existence we may celebrate, and in so many senses, as we celebrate, too, this magnificent museum, with all that has gone into its planning and execution—not to forget the planners themselves. All three have enriched us beyond measure.

Modernity and Identity: Polish Jews Facing Change in the Nineteenth Century

TOMASZ KIZWALTER

One of the basic issues giving the nineteenth-century gallery its shape concerns the transformations in Jewish identity. In the publication introducing the Museum of the History of Polish Jews, we read that we shall not find among the exhibits a "normative presentation of the Jews or of Judaism." Answers to the pressing questions of "Who are the Jews?" or "Who is a Polish Jew?" remain open. "Answers," writes Barbara Kirshenblatt-Gimblett, "provisional at best, are to be found in historically specific moments of the story, in actual situations."[1]

A visitor to the exhibit (especially someone who reads this book) will learn, however, that these concrete situations are arranged within a cycle of transformations in identity. The direction of these changes is clear: it ranges from the undisputed dominance of traditional religious identity to the diversity that modernity brings. The nineteenth century sees the appearance—in my view most important of all—of thinking along national lines, and alongside it arise basic dilemmas of identity. Questions such as "Are the Jews a nation?" were asked in the face of accelerating modernity: Enlightenment reform projects and various government regulations, then industrialization, the expansion of the great cities, and the development of nationalist movements.

This all appears obvious when we look at the issue of historical changes in identity from an academic perspective. The modernistic/constructivist

---

1 Barbara Kirshenblatt-Gimblett, "Theater of History," in *Polin. 1000 Year History of Polish Jews*, ed. Barbara Kirshenblatt-Gimblett and Antony Polonsky, Museum of the History of Polish Jews (Warsaw: Museum of the History of the Polish Jews, 2014), 33.

paradigm has become a key element in studies on "nations and nationalism," and in all discussions on the subject no scholar is now surprised by the idea that "nations are modern" (although not everyone agrees).[2] This is certainly not the case outside academic circles. Here the conviction that nations are a sort of natural phenomenon has certainly not disappeared. Of course, over the last few years the situation has been changing somewhat compared to half a century ago, since whatever might be said, the views of scholars slowly begin to affect the views of wider circles. Moreover, today we are dealing with far more diverse opinions than at the time of the flowering of nationalist historiography; nevertheless, the conviction that nations have always existed and are, in effect, immutable, still forms the public imagination to a significant extent. Several key factors contribute to preserving such a state of affairs. Although much has been said about the demise of nationalism, it is still present in world politics, and nationalistic tendencies strengthen during crises and wars. Time and again, nationalism seems a useful tool of integration and social mobilization. Current transformations in the intellectual climate undoubtedly exert a certain influence on proponents of nationalist tendencies, but the feeling that the nation should be firmly rooted in the past has weakened little in these circles. Hence, those who are attracted to nationalist views have a tendency to draw up long national genealogies and to accept as given that the essentials of a nation have undergone no changes over the course of this long history.

The durability of these views can in no way, however, be explained by the vitality of nationalism and the manipulations of political "establishments" alone. We are dealing here with several causes, social as well as academic. We must not underestimate the human thirst for "historical roots," even if they not infrequently encourage people to revere illusions. If we value a community, then the desire to learn about its ancestry is natural and understandable. Everything here points to a frequently appearing tendency to emphasize the historical immutability of such a community stemming from the conviction that immutability is a sign of value: the longer something lasts and doesn't change, then the more it is worth. The historian's task here would be to convince the wider public that change does not detract from any community's value; on the contrary, it testifies rather to its creative potential. At the same time, historians should not forget that nations arose as a result of the transformation

---

[2] See inter alia Umut Özkirimli, *Theories of Nationalism: A Critical Introduction*, 2nd ed. (Basingstoke, UK: Palgrave Macmillan, 2010).

of traditional communities. The use of constructivist interpretive models must also be linked to research into the premodern basis of modernizing processes.

The importance of taking this into account can be seen very clearly when we examine the nineteenth-century history of society in the former Polish–Lithuanian Commonwealth. This noble Polish nation or stratum, whose evolution did not follow the general pattern of the transformation of European state institutions,[3] was granted a long "life after death." To put it another way, the legacy of the pre-partition commonwealth to a significant degree defined the character of local early modernity. The traditional structure of relations between the two main social groups—the nobility and the peasantry—still had clear repercussions even in the twentieth century. The nineteenth century passed under the sign of attempts to deal with the reform of the rural economy: agrarian reforms, carried out at the time by the governments of the partitioning powers, produced only partially satisfactory results in terms of the economy; likewise, the inability to achieve an effective transformation of agriculture contributed to maintaining former social divisions and conflicts. Toward the end of the century, the gulf between the peasantry and the upper and middle classes was still significant, which meant that the peasants' national identity was slow to develop. Economic backwardness and the retention of traditional mental and cultural structures were responsible for the slow tempo of emancipation, understood as the introduction of the norm of social equality.[4]

In the case of the Jews, the associated dilemmas had an especially dramatic character. On the threshold of the nineteenth century, the Jewish community was a significant element in the population of the Polish Republic, differing from their non-Jewish neighbors in religion and culture, yet for centuries deeply integrated into the country's socioeconomic fabric.[5] The idea

---

3 Antoni Mączak, "Jedyna i nieporównywalna? Kwestia odrębności Rzeczypospolitej w Europie, XVI–XVII wiek" [The one and only, beyond compare? A question of the particularity of the Polish-Lithuanian Commonwealth in the sixteenth- and the seventeenth-century Europe], *Kwartalnik Historyczny* 4 (1993): 121–36.
4 Tomasz Kizwalter, *W stronę równości* [Towards equality] (Kraków: Universitas, 2014).
5 Moshe J. Rosman, *The Lords' Jews: Magnate-Jewish Relations in the Polish-Lithuanian Commonwealth during the Eighteenth Century* (Cambridge, MA: Harvard University Press for the Center for Jewish Studies, Harvard University and the Harvard Ukrainian Research Institute, 2005); Gershon D. Hundert, *Jews in Poland-Lithuania in the Eighteenth Century: A Genealogy of Modernity* (Berkeley: University of California Press, 2004); Jacob Goldberg, *Żydzi w społeczeństwie, gospodarce i kulturze Rzeczypospolitej szlacheckiej* [Jews in the society, economy and culture of the Republic of Nobles] (Kraków: Polska Akademia Umiejętności, 2012).

of emancipation appealed to part of the Jewish elite wanting to participate on equal terms in the country's economic and intellectual life. However, emancipation turned out to be a difficult and painful undertaking that could undermine traditional identity.

Today, there is nothing original in the thesis that throughout the world the expansion of modernity had and has significant, sometimes very high costs. Modernization brought the promise of a better life, but it also destroyed old, sometimes hallowed ways of life. At the start of the nineteenth century, for most Jews modernity meant above all external pressure threatening their traditional way of life.[6]

When we tackle this issue, the question arises to what extent a museum can transmit to visitors such complicated and hard-to-grasp issues as changes of identity. Clearly, authorial comments play a part here, including those that can be made available thanks to multimedia facilities; yet in the first place there should be a presentation of the reality of life. The museum's creators have indeed chosen this method.

The starting point here was obvious: the fall of the Polish Republic and the introduction by the new authorities of legal regulations on the lives of Jews. In the next part of the gallery, visitors are introduced to the debates on the "Jewish question," which were conducted in the circles of the elite of the last years of the Polish–Lithuanian Commonwealth, the Duchy of Warsaw, and the constitutional Kingdom of Poland. It can be seen here how Enlightenment reformist-cum-emancipatory tendencies were often linked to traditional anti-Judaism, creating policies at whose heart were demands for far-reaching changes to Jewish identity.[7]

This is an especially acute manifestation of the confrontation of modernity with tradition—a phenomenon that normally appeared in this period in less acute form. Governments and political elites, even if in ideological terms they represented conservative tendencies, were adopting modern methods of operating: they strove to increase state power, to improve methods of governing, and to control society more effectively. Given this state of affairs, various manifestations of the "old order" came under threat; efforts were made to marginalize them, to transform them thoroughly, and sometimes to remove them

---

6 Antony Polonsky, *The Jews in Poland and Russia: A Short History* (Oxford: Littman Library of Jewish Civilization, 2013), 40–42.

7 Richard Butterwick-Pawlikowski, "Jews in the Discourses of the Polish Enlightenment," eds. Glenn Dynner, Antony Polonsky, and Marcin Wodziński, *Polin. Studies in Polish Jewry: Jews in the Kingdom of Poland, 1815–1918* 27 (2015): 45–62.

altogether. On the whole, however, protective mechanisms worked quite well. What was old was considered anachronistic, or even evidence of "ignorance" and "superstition," yet was simultaneously seen on the whole as part of something innate. As such it could, after an appropriate preparation, form the basis of notions of a developing national culture. In the nineteenth century, the culture of the Polish Republic's nobility was the object of sharp criticism, but eventually—and not only thanks to the novels of Henryk Sienkiewicz—it provided rich material for the creators of modern Poland. The Polish upper and middle classes saw the ethnic Polish peasantry on the whole as a backward and primitive community; in the end, however, transformed peasant culture was appreciated from the nationalist point of view. In the case of the Jews, these types of mechanisms did not work. Their religious and cultural difference meant that criticism of the Jewish community became aggressive and virulent. Among the voices directed at the Jews, one demand, however, dominated: stop being different and when you have become like us, then we shall consider whether we can grant you the same rights to which we are entitled.[8]

I see the first section of the nineteenth-century gallery as key in cognitive terms, for it clearly depicts under what external conditions Polish Jews had to live, together with the approach of modernity (it is a pity that in visual terms the exhibition is less suggestive here than in other sections of the gallery). Visitors to the museum should be informed when formal emancipation did or did not come to specific parts of the former Polish–Lithuanian Commonwealth. They should also be made aware that, although formal emancipation did not mean real emancipation, this was indeed a real change, changing to a significant extent the situation of the Jewish population.

In further sections of the gallery, what I see as the essential issues linked to the "challenges of modernity" are effectively presented: the diversity of Jewish reactions to the processes of modernization, gradual integration into the modern world, and striving to retain one's identity in the face of ever rapider changes.

It should be emphasized here that insofar as for the start of the nineteenth century the modernizing efforts of governments and associated political elites had an essential meaning, in the second half of the century the dissemination

---

8 Artur Eisenbach, *Emancypacja Żydów na ziemiach polskich 1785–1870 na tle europejskim* [The emancipation of Jews in Poland, 1750–1870, in the context of Europe] (Warsaw: Państwowy Instytut Wydawniczy, 1988), 101–13; Glenn Dynner and Marcin Wodziński, "The Kingdom of Poland and Her Jews: An Introduction," *Polin. Studies in Polish Jewry* 27 (2015): 8–17.

of feeling and thinking along nationalist lines and the associated trajectory of nationalism became a factor of great import. It was then that the real revolution in collective life in the lands of the former Polish Republic began. Nationalism—the principle that in politics the ethnically defined interests of a given nation should come before anything else—initially seen as a radical ideology, with time entered the political mainstream. It molded the actions of the partitioning powers and the Polish political class, contributed greatly to the formation of Ukrainian, Lithuanian, and Belarusian nationalist movements, and to Zionism among the Jews. It grew in importance alongside advances in modernization and the weakening of traditional ties and social hierarchies. It initially had a democratizing aspect—the peasants were on the same level as the nobility at least as members of the nation—but later its exclusionary tendencies began to become more noticeable: those of alien ethnicity could not belong to the national community. The society that the Polish Republic left behind it—with its strongly delineated social divisions and complete mosaic of different communities—was now heading toward an example of a culturally homogenous and socially integrated nation.[9]

For Jews, this created a very difficult situation. When the Polish Lithuanian–Commonwealth disappeared from the map of Europe, it was a traditional society par excellence, focused on its religious content. The gallery shows well how its inhabitants adapted themselves in various areas to the pressures of modernization in the first decades of the nineteenth century and by degrees began to act in accordance with the "spirit of the age." This was not easy, but the most serious challenges still lay ahead, with industrialization, mass migration of populations to the cities, and accompanying cultural changes.

Jews now found themselves faced with the stress of greater pressure than they had hitherto experienced from governments and political elites. These were problems to a certain extent felt by all groups in a premodern society left to deal with the impact of modernity. In the case of the Jews, however, they became especially acute when faced with continuing deeply held religious resentments and a sense of cultural difference. Whatever we may say about the barriers separating the ethnically Polish nobility and the ethnically Polish peasantry (and they persisted long after the abolition of serfdom), the integration of these two groups began in the nineteenth century and progressed in the following

---

9 Tomasz Kizwalter, *O nowoczesności narodu. Przypadek Polski* [On the modernity of nations. The case of Poland] (Warsaw: Semper, 1999), 269–324.

century, although slowly and not without difficulty. Nineteenth-century projects for integrating Jews did not bring concrete results and it does not appear that they stood any great chance of success. In these changing civilizational circumstances, new, anti-Semitic notions, nationalistic in nature and based on racial stereotypes, were added to the traditional anti-Judaism widespread among the non-Jewish majority.

I think that the development of anti-Semitism could be put into a somewhat broader context than it has been in the gallery's final section. The issue appears rather suddenly in the presentation and discussion of the wave of pogroms at the beginning of the 1880s. Jan Jeleński now appears as a central character among the spokesmen of anti-Semitism; he is in fact a figure located outside the main current of public life, but one who undoubtedly catches the eye, even if his influence is overrated.[10] Meanwhile, at the turn of the century, anti-Semitism entered the political mainstream, and it is hard to understand this phenomenon without taking into account the spread of nationalist views. I do understand that encouraging them to expand the exhibition must be annoying for its creators, who grapple with selecting material and the inevitable limited size of the gallery, but all I have in mind is an addition requiring little space, which would make the visitor aware that in the last decades of the nineteenth century a very significant change began to appear in Europe in the area of imagination and political views—a change that had a powerful effect on the situation of the Jews. At the start of the gallery the significance of the lands of the former Polish Republic passing into the hands of ever more bureaucratic monarchies has rightly been strongly emphasized. The presentation of industrialization and urbanization—factors changing fundamentally the circumstances of life—plays a similar role in the second part of the exhibition. I think that it would be worth supplementing this context with the case of nationalism.

I concluded my several visits to the museum with the feeling that its creators have achieved a success. From the point of view of my interests, their

---

10 Andrzej Jaszczuk, *Spór pozytywistów z konserwatystami o przyszłość Polski, 1870–1903* [The dispute between the Positivists and Conservatives on the future of Poland, 1870–1903] (Warsaw: Państwowe Wydawnictwo Nauk, 1986), 210–15; Alina Cała, *Asymilacja Żydów w Królestwie Polskim (1864–1897). Postawy, konflikty, stereotypy* [The assimilation of the Jews in the Kingdom of Poland, 1864–1897: views, conflicts, stereotypes] (Warsaw: Państwowy Instytut Wydawniczy, 1989), 279–94; Grzegorz Krzywiec, *Chauvinism, Polish Style: the Case of Roman Dmowski (Beginnings: 1886–1905)*, translated by Jarosław Garliński (Frankfurt am Main: Peter Lang Edition, 2016).

principal task was—as is common in the case of a narrative of the history of a community spanning several centuries—to strike a balance between continuity and change. I believe they have succeeded in this, and if I pointed them along the path of one or two corrections it is only because when we see something good, we would like it to be even better.

Translated by Jarosław Garliński

Hasidism in the Museum: The Social History Perspective

DAVID ASSAF

"Hasidism is a movement of religious revival with a distinctive social profile. Originating in the second quarter of the eighteenth century, it has continued to exist without interruption up to the present day."[1] There is no need to explain the importance of the hasidic "experience" (whether one supports or opposes this movement) in modern Jewish history, or why it is essential to include aspects of this topic in any exhibition about Eastern European Jews. The question is *how* to do this. Here, I offer some thoughts on the difficulties of presenting Hasidism in a museum setting and describe some solutions that were offered in the past.

We should keep in mind that the question of how to portray Hasidism, particularly in a museum setting, is a modern and, naturally, a secular one. *Hasidim* would never have considered asking such a question, at least not until most recent times. A museum, like a zoo or a nature reserve, is a secular institution and space that has two modern purposes: to preserve worlds of content and knowledge, and to present them in a sophisticated and critical way to visitors. The museum and its aims are thus entirely alien to *Hasidim*. They do not see a need to preserve their world since from their perspective it is not in danger of extinction. On the contrary, they view their world as being very much alive and are not interested in presenting it to outsiders both because

---

1 David Assaf, "Hasidism: Historical Overview," in *The YIVO Encyclopedia of Jews in Eastern Europe*, ed. Gershon D. Hundert, 2 vols. (New Haven, CT: Yale University Press, 2008), 1:659.

they suspect that it is not possible to present it in an authentic way and because they have no real interest in explaining themselves to outsiders or doing so for purposes of propaganda.

Hasidism in a museum entails condensing both a long historical phenomenon—some 250 years at least—and a complex and multidimensional religious experience into a limited and prescribed physical space of galleries and walls. The space limitation compels making decisions about what *is* and *is not* important. *Hasidim* cannot take part in this exercise because—from their perspective—*all of it* is important. While experts outside of the world of Hasidism look only for what is unique and different in Hasidism, for the *Hasidim*, the similarities between them and other groups within the Jewish religion are as important as what differentiates them. The *Hasidim* could not agree to a viewpoint that contends that adoration of the rebbe, hasidic customs, or typical hasidic dress are more important to understanding their religious world and its uniqueness than following halakha according to the *Shulhan Arukh*, which is the practice for all observant Jews, *Hasidim* and non-*Hasidim* alike. The religious world of the Hasid is not divided into two parts, where in one part he is a Hasid and in the other he is an observant Jew like all others, but rather, being a Hasid is a complete entity that cannot accept such a dichotomy. Portraying the Hasid as someone who supposedly has an additional "story" atop the "communal building" is not precise and is opposed to the self-awareness of the Hasid who does not see being a Hasid as just an "addition" to his religious world. For him, it is an organic part and of equal status to other non-hasidic elements that comprise his religious world. Therefore, deciding the criteria of what *is* and *is not* important in presenting Hasidism in a museum can never be entrusted to *Hasidim* themselves.

Moreover, placing Hasidism within a museum framework de facto determines a certain formulation and canonization that is obligated to critical academic considerations, which may not always accord with Hasidim's concept of time. In the eyes of *Hasidim*, the history of Hasidism is an unimpeded harmonious continuum that began with Rabbi Israel Baal Shem Tov, the Besht (who was himself a link in the historical continuum of early *Hasidim* and kabbalists), and continues up to the present. However, the consensus among scholars of Hasidism is that in the history of the movement there are at least two basic periods during which the face of Hasidism radically changed: the first period, "early Hasidism," that originated with the Baal Shem Tov and continued with the Magid of Międzyrzecz and his disciples until the end of the eighteenth century; and the second period, "late Hasidism," which dates from the start of the nineteenth century and continues to our day. Scholars are also in agreement that the characteristics of late Hasidism differ considerably from those of early Hasidism, with the key identifying characteristics being formation of the hasidic dynasty and loyalty to it.

This scholarly approach also rightly influenced the planners of the new POLIN Museum of the History of Polish Jews; therefore, one can find Hasidism in the eighteenth-century gallery of Poland before the partitions and also in the nineteenth-century gallery. The focus of Hasidism in the latter gallery is the result of agreement among scholars that would not have been possible a few decades before, since today scholars of Hasidism concur that the "golden age," or the "mature period" of Hasidism, is not the eighteenth but rather the nineteenth century. I have trouble imagining the forefathers of the study of the history of the Jews of Eastern Europe, and especially the scholars of Hasidism then, such as Simon Dubnow, Shmuel Horodetsky, Ben-Zion Dinur, Raphael Mahler or Shmuel Ettinger, agreeing on that. From their perspective, the importance of Hasidism in Jewish history was centered in the eighteenth century, when Hasidism initiated a revolution in the Jewish religion. By contrast, the nineteenth century was, in their view, a period of corruption, stagnation, and decline, not worthy of investigation.[2]

In the last two generations, the trend has been completely reversed, not because of a lessening of the importance of Hasidism's period of emergence, but because of an understanding that the historical portrait of Hasidism, as it is known to us also today and for the foreseeable future, was not determined in the eighteenth century, but rather in the nineteenth. Also, the ways in which the hasidic experience was designed were reflected not only in the pages of the classic books of hasidic teachings written by the founders of Hasidism but also mainly in the social and economic life, which was the result of the dynamic meeting of ideology with the changing reality.

The question is how to present this in a museum. The solutions offered in earlier exhibitions were simple and easy, but missed the mark because they were neither truthful nor engaging.

In reviewing the short history of exhibitions about Hasidism, it is surprising to find that their origins were actually in a hasidic initiative that attempted to embrace the secular challenge of creating an "exhibition," but that went about it in a typically Orthodox way.

---

2 David Assaf, *The Regal Way: The Life and Times of Rabbi Israel of Ruzhin* (Stanford, CA: Stanford University Press, 2002), 8–11.

To the best of my knowledge, the first exhibition ever about Hasidism opened in *Beit Ha-Sofer* (The Writers House) in Tel Aviv on September 5, 1960. The date is not an accident: it was the two-hundredth anniversary of the death of the Besht. The exhibition was the initiative of the moderate Haredi politician Binyamin Mintz, then minister of the postal service, and himself a Ger Hasid. The members of the public steering committee who were behind it were all Orthodox rabbis. There was not a single academic among them, and certainly no secular person. Mintz's son organized the exhibition, and the advisor was the young Yitzhak Alfassi, who would later become a prolific hasidic author. This was most definitely an exhibition made by *Hasidim* about Hasidism, and to judge from the introduction to the catalogue that was published,[3] and the description of the items that were displayed, it was an exhibition with an agenda, governed over by a harmonious hasidic spirit and a heavy dose of nostalgia for the glorious past that had perished in the Holocaust. The fact that the exhibition was organized by Orthodox figures and enjoyed rabbinic approbation made it easier to secure loans of objects and documents from private collections, mainly in the possession of *Hasidim*.

The exhibition's catalogue rightly made much of the fact that it was "the first [exhibition] of its kind in the world" and that it included 193 objects, mostly printed hasidic books, manuscripts, autographs, pictures and letters of famous rebbes (some of the letters were taken from the forged collection known as *Genizat Herson*),[4] drawings, and photographs. There were also items of Jewish ceremonial art that supposedly belonged to various rebbes and included Hanukkah menorahs, kiddush cups, spice boxes for the Havdalah ceremony, clothing, pipes, and tobacco snuff boxes. The inventory even included pieces of furniture, such as the chair of Rabbi Nachman of Bratslav, which was disassembled in the Soviet Union and spirited out piece by piece and reassembled in Israel, and the chair of Rabbi Avraham Dov of Ovruch, brought from the synagogue bearing his name in Safed. There were other items, such as the tefillin (phylacteries) and a kiddush cup belonging to the Magid of Międzyrzecz, the snuff box of the Kotsker rebbe, and even the glasses of Rabbi Avraham Yehoshua Heschel of Apt (Opatów), and the walking stick attributed to Rabbi Yisrael of Ruzhin. All these items were included not because of their

---

3 *Katalog ta'arukhat ha-Hasidut* [Catalog of the exhibition on Hasidism], Tel Aviv, September 5–October 20, 1960), 42 pp. (including advertisements).

4 For a short summary on this forged collection, see David Assaf, *Derekh ha-malkhut: Rabbi Yisrael me-Ruzhin u-mekomo be-toldot ha-Hasidut* [The regal way: Rabbi Yisrael of Ruzhin and his place in the history of Hasidism], (Jerusalem: Zalman Shazar Center, 1997), 202–3.

visual or historical importance, but because they carried special religious value and evoked romantic and nostalgic memories for the visitors.

Contemporary Israeli newspapers reported that during the three weeks of the exhibition, about 25,000 visitors, among them 7,000 schoolchildren, came to see it. These numbers seem a bit exaggerated but, no doubt, it was a success.

Over the years, three additional hasidic exhibitions were organized, all in the Lubavitch library in Brooklyn, New York. We can assume from the venue and the identity of the exhibitions' organizers that all the exhibitions were from the treasures of the library and were connected mostly to the history of Chabad, its leaders, and their thought and activities. The first exhibition opened in summer 1993;[5] the second opened in 1998, on the three-hundredth anniversary of the birth of the Besht (according to Chabad tradition, which determined the year of his birth to be 1698). This exhibition comprised 130 items;[6] and the third opened on 19 Kislev (December) 1998, on the bicentennial anniversary of Rabbi Schneur Zalman of Liady's release from prison in Russia.[7] These exhibitions consisted of manuscripts, books, historical documents, and some pictures of the Chabad rebbes. Held in the Lubavitch library rather than in a neutral museum location, they are better compared to the content of an internal hasidic history book supplemented by many illustrations.

Clearly, the focus of these hasidic exhibitions is on the *text* (either handwritten or printed) and the *tzaddik* (his books, pictures of him, or objects that were his personal effects). It is worth noting that the 1960 exhibition in Tel Aviv was in a secular location (a literary club), which suggests that the organizers wanted to attract broader audiences than just *Hasidim*. It therefore stands to reason that the objects included in that exhibition were meant to appeal to a range of viewers, including secular first-generation Israelis who might have had some sentiments for the kinds of "Old World" objects displayed. The exhibitions from 1993 and 1998, on the other hand, were displayed in the Lubavitch library, suggesting that they were intended for an insular audience of Chabad *Hasidim*. Hasidic viewers may not have been impressed by religious artifacts which are used in their daily lives, whereas books and pictures of their leaders carried much more value and interest. Exhibition books and photographs or

---

5   *Ta'arukhat sifriyat Lubavitch* ... [Exhibition of Lubavitch books...], ed. Shalom Dovber Levin (New York: Otsar ha-Ḥasidim, 1994).
6   *In Celebration of the Ba'al Shem Tov's 300th Birthday Anniversary ... The Lubavitch Library Presents Chasidism on Display* (New York, 1998).
7   *Ta'arukhat rabenu ha-zaken* [Exhibition of our Old Rabbi], (New York: Otsar ha-Ḥasidim, 1998), 16 pp. See: www.chabadlibrary.org/exhibit/ex7/exheb7.htm.

portraits of famous rabbis is, of course, the conventional and easiest solution for portraying Hasidism in an exhibition: describe its history through its books and leaders. Yet the reason the organizers of these hasidic exhibitions chose this route was not because it was the easiest way to organize the material but because the subtext of this type of exhibition plan concealed within it a worldview and historiographic outlook that was connected to the hasidic identity of the exhibition's organizers. For critical historians, this approach is unacceptable. The issue can be viewed through two questions:

THE PRINTED BOOK OR THE ORAL EXPERIENCE?

The point of departure, shared by *Hasidim* as well as scholars of Jewish philosophy, is that hasidic teachings are mainly expressed in the homiletic literature of Hasidism's founders, that these teachings were familiar to masses of *Hasidim* from books, and that these texts were an important tool for the spread of Hasidism. Moreover, there is a museological tradition, unconnected to Hasidism, of treating books and manuscripts as museum-worthy "objects" such as incunabula and illuminated manuscripts.

From a social history viewpoint, the importance of the book in Hasidism is a debatable point. The texts of teachings, which are, in their own right, highly important for study, were not the deciding factor in the spread of Hasidism, either in the eighteenth century (keep in mind that the first hasidic book, *Toldot Ya'akov Yosef*, was only first printed in 1780, twenty years after the death of the Besht and eight years after the death of the Magid of Międzyrzecz) or throughout the nineteenth century. As regards the spread of hasidic ideas, important weight must be given to the oral culture that characterized Hasidism during its growth and diffusion. Showing the printed book as central to the movement's experience represents an outsider's viewpoint. The late hasidic scholar Haim Liberman already proved that the printed book did not have much importance in the spread of Hasidism, and in fact throughout the nineteenth century only three hasidic books were printed in Yiddish, the language of the masses.[8] Greater importance must be given to the huge corpus of hagiographic stories about the *tzaddikim*—a popular literature that began to be published in significant numbers of volumes in the 1860s, reaching a peak

---

8 Hayyim Lieberman, "Fiction and Truth Regarding the Hasidic Printing Houses" [in Hebrew], in *Zaddik and Devotees: Historical and Social Aspects of Hasidism*, ed. David Assaf (Jerusalem: Zalman Shazar Center, 2001), 186–209.

in the interwar period. Of course, from an internal hasidic perspective, this is not considered a high or sophisticated genre, but a low genre. *Hasidim* would sooner present to themselves and the outside world the classic treatises of the Magid of Międzyrzecz and his pupils, and not the collections of imaginary stories written and collected by rank-and-file *Hasidim*. A good example is the role of the book *Shivhei ha-Besht* (In Praise of the Ba'al Shem Tov), first published in 1815, among academic scholars and *Hasidim*. While scholars consider this book as a major, though problematic, source for the history of early Hasidism, the *Hasidim* tended to lessen its importance. In fact, they never considered it a canonic book but rather a leisure reading.[9]

In terms of the visual aspect of books in an exhibition, one must admit that there is nothing duller than looking at a book or manuscript from behind a glass case without being able to touch it or flip through its pages. The majority of hasidic books are of no particular artistic or graphic value and, therefore, their inclusion in an exhibition meant for a non-hasidic general audience must be kept to a measured minimum. An example of a book that is worthwhile exhibiting is the so-called "star edition" of *No'am Elimelekh*. This book was written by the famous tzaddik Elimelekh of Leżajsk and was first printed in Lwów (Lviv) in 1788, shortly after the author's death. The book, which contained homilies on the Pentateuch, is considered one of the classic hasidic writings, particularly for developing the role of the tzaddik and his spiritual qualities. The first edition of the book was, however, even more special, because, in place of the regular punctuation marks, which were apparently not available to the printer at the time, the symbol of the asterisk was substituted throughout the text, hence the book appeared as if it were strewn with stars. The *Hasidim* in Poland believed that it held kabbalistic secrets and some said that each star marked a place where Rabbi Elimelekh had experienced an epiphany of the prophet Elijah. This edition was attributed with magical properties, especially for women about to give birth and would be placed under their pillows. Since the first edition was published in a limited number, it was reprinted numerous times, each time with the asterisks. The fact that there are other books with asterisks is of no matter—this book was

---

9   There is a considerable literature on this book and its role, see for example: Moshe Rosman, "In Praise of the Ba'al Shem Tov: A User's Guide to the Editions of *Shivhei haBesht*," *Polin* 10 (1997): 183–99; Immanuel Etkes, *The Besht: Magician, Mystic, and Leader* (Waltham, MA: Brandeis University Press; Hanover, NH: University Press of New England, 2004), 203–48. For a Hasidic approach, see Yehoshua Mondshine's introduction to his edition of *Shivhei Ha-Baal Shem Tov: A Facsimile of Unique Manuscript, Variant Versions & Appendices* [in Hebrew] (Jerusalem, 1982), 52–57.

thought to have a special status that had nothing to do with its actual content. I would definitely include this book in an exhibition on Hasidism, not because of its teaching value, but because of its social impact.

TZADDIKIM OR HASIDIM?

From an internal hasidic point of view, Hasidism's historical portrait is embodied in its *tzaddikim*. *Hasidim* themselves are not important or interesting. This is why curators of hasidic exhibitions tended to exhibit the books written by *tzaddikim*, supplemented by pictures of them, their autographs, and objects that belonged to them. From the hasidic perspective, there is no visual meaning to these objects; it is their spiritual value that is important. Not only is there holiness in everything connected to a rebbe, but also loyalty to him and his dynasty are the essence of the hasidic experience. Ironically, this is also the attitude of the opponents of Hasidism—*mitnagdim* and *maskilim*—who viewed *Hasidim* as an illiterate mob blindly following a fraudulent rebbe. This is a view that social historians of Hasidism cannot accept: without taking away from the importance of the tzaddik, clearly *Hasidim* are a very important part of a balanced historical and social picture of Hasidism. But in the exhibitions about Hasidism, the *Hasidim* are almost never present, or perhaps at most are shown to be the passive flock following their shepherd. The hasidic court, where the rebbe resided, was without doubt an important place in the hasidic experience, but for most *Hasidim*, this encounter with the court and with the rebbe was a one-time event; most days of the year they lived in their own towns, far away from the rebbe and his presence. Therefore, the social historian of Hasidism will look for ways to expose and present the daily life and world of rank-and-file *Hasidim* in their localities—their activities in the hasidic *shtibl*, the emergence of the hasidic family and the status of the hasidic woman, the hasidic economy and the relationship of *Hasidim* in their town with other factions, including non-Jews and officials who represented the state—and not to be content only with examining the lives of *tzaddikim*.

OTHER EXHIBITIONS ABOUT HASIDISM

It is worthwhile to review briefly three other exhibitions about Hasidism that took place in the last decade,[10] and, as opposed to the exhibitions organized by

---

10 Before our decade, the first academic exhibition on Hasidism probably took place at Harvard University in 1982, curated by Abraham Foxbruner. According to the catalogue (16 pp.)

Hasidim, are modern, academic, and critical. The first important exhibition, titled *Czas chasydów* (Time of the *Hasidim*), opened in the historical museum of the city of Kraków in April 2005; the second, *In the Footsteps of the Besht*, in the National Library in Jerusalem, opened in June 2010 to commemorate the two-hundred-fiftieth anniversary of the death of the Besht and the two-hundredth anniversary of the death of Rabbi Nachman of Bratslav; and the third exhibition, which was also the largest and most comprehensive, titled *A World Apart Next Door: Glimpses into the Life of Hasidic Jews*, opened at the Israel Museum in Jerusalem in June 2012.

The exhibition in Kraków, curated by Elżbieta Długosz, was small in size but nevertheless pioneering and important. It was an academic exhibition organized in cooperation with scholars of Judaism from the Jagiellonian University.[11] In her preface to the catalogue, the curator was clearly aware of the dialectic that on the one hand Hasidism flourished in Polish territories and for that reason was an important and worthy topic for an exhibition in today's Poland, and on the other hand the distress that came from trying to mount an exhibition with a dearth of physical objects related to Hasidism after the Holocaust. For this reason, the exhibition's organizers had to make do mainly with archival material: photographs, maps, and about thirty books and twenty objects. Here, too, the organizers shared the outlook of the *Hasidim* regarding the importance of the book, and I quote from the catalogue: "Books have always been the greatest treasures of the *Hasidim* as they contain the ideas of their saintly leaders." In addition, the exhibitors constructed a kind of fictional study house (*beit midrash*), in which visitors could listen to hasidic tales.

The exhibition in the National Library in Jerusalem, curated by Esther Liebes, focused on the Baal Shem Tov and Rabbi Nachman of Bratslav.[12] The exhibition, which was quite small in terms of space, was designed like an

---

there were only forty-two items, all from the collections of Widener Library. The exhibition was prepared on the occasion of a colloquium on "Hasidism—Continuity or Innovation," and comprised only books of "key figures of the hasidic movement who flourished between c. 1740 and 1820," 3.

11 *Czas chasydów* [Time of the Hasidim] (Kraków: Muzeum Historyczne Miasta Krakowa; Katedra Judaistyki Uniwersytetu Jagiellońskeigo, 2005). This bilingual catalogue (Polish and English, 132 pp.) includes, along with many pictures and drawings, three scholarly articles on Hasidism.

12 *In the Footsteps of the Besht, Exhibition of Treasures from the Collections of the National Library of Israel* (Jerusalem: National Library of Israel, 2010). The catalogue (96 pp.) lists 108 items and includes four scholarly articles on Hasidism.

imaginary shtetl, within which was the Besht's study house in Międzybóż.[13] Like the Chabad exhibitions, the exhibition was held in a library and not a museum, and therefore it is not surprising that on view were mainly books, manuscripts, amulets, letters, paintings, photographs, and musical scores, almost all from the library's collections. Yet the treatment was academic and critical. The exhibition was a great success and was attended by large numbers of both Haredim and *Hasidim*. This in itself was not sensational news since for the ultra-Orthodox the National Library in Jerusalem is no longer considered a secular institution that cannot be frequented. Interestingly, a small scandal erupted regarding the exhibition, which shows the complexity of presenting Hasidism to *Hasidim*. Moshe Isaac Blau, a Haredi frequenter of the National Library, protested publicly, in the library itself and in the Haredi media, against the curator and the library's directors for what he considered a wrong interpretation as well as blasphemy of the Besht. Item no. 35 in the catalogue (p. 65) is a letter from the Besht to his disciple Ya'acov Yosef of Polonne (Połonne), which was loaned to the library by the Lubavitch library. The catalogue, as well as the label in the exhibition, claimed that the authenticity of this letter was in doubt and Gershom Scholem noted that, in his opinion, it was a forgery. Blau argued that the epistle, published in 1935, was authentic, having been approved by the previous Lubavitch rebbes. The case was publicized in the Haredi media and one of the Haredi Knesset members, Uri Maklev, also became involved and requested that the library change the exhibition label and the entry in the catalogue. Blau even brought the library to a rabbinical court (*din torah*) for blasphemy of the Besht's reputation. While the library ignored Blau's protest, they responded to Maklev that there was no incorrect information in the label text and the library would not accept any form of censorship.[14]

The exhibition at the Israel Museum, organized by curator Ester Muchawsky-Schnapper, was the largest and most lavish in terms of budget, size, and number of objects.[15] Nevertheless, the emphasis was clearly ethnographic

---

13 Ibid., 9; though Międzybóż at the time of the Besht was not a typical shtetl but a large town with approximately five thousand inhabitants. See Moshe Rosman, *Founder of Hasidism: A Quest for the Historical Ba'al Shem Tov* (Berkeley: University of California Press, 1996), 66–67, 234–35n17.

14 Some of the documents are provided in the Lubavitch site *Shturem*: www.shturem.net/index.php?section=news&id=44184. The library's response to Maklev (July 26, 2010) can be found at www.shturem.net/index.php?section=news&id=44329.

15 Ester Muchawsky-Schnapper, *A World Apart Next Door: Glimpses into the Life of Hasidic Jews* (Jerusalem: The Israel Museum, 2012). The catalogue, which is more a book than an exhibition catalogue, was published in separate Hebrew and English editions and comprised

and folkloric. The exhibition explicitly avoided dealing with history or theology, and instead placed the focus on ritual–ceremonial aspects of hasidic society and ethnography expressed in dress, daily life, the yearly rituals (Sabbaths and festivals), and the life cycle. Without the curators intending it, this exhibition's ahistorical approach was, in a way, close to the *Hasidim*'s own self-awareness and concept of time, for the *Hasidim*, as mentioned earlier, are not willing to differentiate between different periods in their history; for them it is all one continuous course. Here too, there was not much attention to periodization or historical changes. From a curatorial perspective, Hasidism is a united entity that exists above time and place with minor folkloric differences between the various groups. However, the exhibition was a tremendous success and many Haredim visited, including even a special private visit of the current rebbe of Karlin-Stolin *Hasidim*.[16] This was certainly a sensation, since the Israel Museum, which is open on the Sabbath and holidays, and publicly displays objects such as sculptures and drawings, some showing nudes, is viewed by the ultra-Orthodox as a secular and therefore dangerous institution.

THE EXHIBITION OF HASIDISM IN POLIN MUSEUM

The exhibition about *Hasidim* at the new Museum of the History of Polish Jews is conceptually different from anything that has preceded it in three main concepts: context, periodization, and social history.

Context – Hasidism is not exhibited as a lone phenomenon, out of touch with historical, social, and religious phenomena that preceded it or that developed alongside it. The subject is treated in the appropriate and broad historical context of the history of Poland and Polish Jews.

Periodization – Hasidism is presented in two different galleries: The Jewish Town, 1648–1772 (the Besht and the emergence of Hasidism) and Encounters with Modernity, 1772–1914 (the spread of Hasidism during the long nineteenth century).[17] Thus, there is awareness not only of the various historical metamorphoses of Hasidism throughout different periods, but also deliberate emphasis on the nineteenth century as the golden age of Hasidism.

---

dozens of high-quality pictures and scholarly articles by Arthur Green (short introduction on Hasidism) and the curator (on hasidic costume and dress).

16 www.haaretz.co.il/news/education/1.1783098.

17 *Polin: 1000 Year History of Polish Jews*, ed. Barbara Kirshenblatt-Gimblett and Antony Polonsky, Museum of the History of Polish Jews (Warsaw: Museum of the History of the Polish Jews, 2014), 168–69, 197–99.

Nevertheless, here the exhibition failed in its message in two main points: in the eighteenth-century gallery, the Besht, alongside Eliyahu ben Shlomo Zalman, known as the Gaon of Vilna, are presented as the two main figures of the Jewish spiritual world of that century. This is an uncritical adaptation of the old historiographic concept about the "three cultural heroes," each of whom changed the Jewish world at the same time: the Hasid (Besht), the *mitnaged* (Gaon of Vilna), and the *maskil* (Moses Mendelssohn, who, however, lived in Berlin). This subtext directly influenced the design of the nineteenth-century gallery where Hasidism is portrayed as equivalent and alongside the Lithuanian *yeshivot* and the Haskalah. While the historical setting is correct and important, the equal space devoted to each of these three trends is somehow misleading. Although we do not possess reliable statistical data about the numbers of *Hasidim*, *mitnagdim*, and *maskilim*, other literary and anecdotal evidence suggests that the number of *Hasidim* was much greater than any other faction among Eastern European Jewish communities, at least until the turn of the twentieth century. Therefore, if "gallery space" is equivalent to "importance," nineteenth-century Hasidism should have been given much more space in the exhibition.

Social History – In emphasizing the social components of Hasidism over its theological components, which are difficult to present to the museum visitor, the Museum of the History of Polish Jews indicated its preference for social history over theology.

There are many ways to tell the story of Hasidism and the limitations enforced by the museum setting complicate the task, especially within the framework of a permanent exhibition, such as in the Museum of the History of Polish Jews. It seems that the best way to make an exhibition about Hasidism appealing to viewers on the one hand and critically sound for museum professionals and the scholarly community on the other is to approach the subject from the perspective of social history. Social history offers a vivid perspective, which takes into account not only the elite, leadership, and the center but also the daily life of the rank and file in the periphery, which gives the story of Hasidism a vital connection to real life and perhaps a much more accurate portrait of what Hasidism is.

What's In, What's Out: A Critique of the Interwar Gallery

MICHAEL STEINLAUF

I would like to begin with some personal remarks. My connection to the museum—and first of all, to this site—goes back many years. When I first arrived in Poland on a Fulbright fellowship thirty-two years ago, one of the first things I did was to come to the Pomnik, the monument which faces where we now sit. My father survived the Great Deportation from the Warsaw Ghetto, then managed to survive on the "Aryan side"; my mother survived most of the war on the "Aryan side." Both my parents had adamantly rejected any notion of returning to "that ground soaked—*przesiąknięta*—with Jewish blood." When I first stood in front of Rapoport's monument and the countless times after when I visited, often sitting on the benches nearby, I felt the blood beneath my feet—how could one not?—but also something else—an extraordinary sense of peace that I'd never felt anywhere else. I felt intimately linked to this place, and more broadly to Warsaw as a whole. In a word, I felt that this was where I belonged. This feeling was later deepened, indeed validated, when I discovered generations of my father's family buried in the Okopowa cemetery. They were Gerer *Hasidim* who had created the hardware business—iron weights and scales—*ayzngesheft*—in Plac Grzybowski. Meanwhile, my mother, a graduate of the University of Warsaw, grew up on Nalewki, where her father had a *skład galanterii* (haberdashery shop). So yes, I belong to Warsaw.

Jerzy Halbersztadt was the first person I met in Poland. He had been sent to greet me at the airport by our mutual academic advisor, Jerzy Holzer. We became friends. In 1990, I was sent by the United States Holocaust Memorial Museum to begin the process of retrieving Polish Holocaust-era archives. Jerzy soon took over this work, and over the subsequent years, Shayke Weinberg, the creator of the USHMM, inspired Jerzy with the vision of a museum in Warsaw dedicated not to the Holocaust, but to a millennium of Polish Jewish life. Jerzy eventually took on this task exclusively. Through the latter half of the 1990s and into the new century, Jerzy and I and a growing group of consultants, including Marcin Wodziński, thought and rethought what such a museum should be. I worked at writing the so-called briefs, summarizing what we needed to show, at least for the periods I knew something about. Out of this came the Outline of the Historical Program and then the Masterplan, a storyline for the core exhibition that would be told in nine galleries, using state-of-the art digital technology. Then Barbara Kirshenblatt-Gimblett joined us and later Samuel Kassow and many others. Under Barbara's leadership, the galleries began to move from theory into reality. Eventually, my life in the United States pulled me away from this work.

During the years that Jerzy and I worked together, our major concern was how to tell a story that would speak to two very different audiences. On one hand, the museum was to reach Polish visitors with the story of an unknown civilization, a world that existed for centuries behind what interwar Polish writers called a Chinese wall. Today, the wall is gone, replaced by wooden figurines of bearded Jews with *peyes*, some holding coins. For Polish visitors, the museum was to open into a history beyond walls and dolls. It is a history, moreover, intended to contest the contemporary Polish historical narrative of Poles living in the Polish lands. Despite the centuries-old multinational character of the Polish Commonwealth, and the fact that little more than a century ago, the forebearers of most of those who now call themselves Poles did not have a clear sense of national identity and identified themselves as being "from around here [*tutejsi*]," Polish schools and media today inculcate a unitary narrative of Polishness stretching far into the past. What the museum was to display was a history of Jews living in the Polish lands—Jews who, as Gershon D. Hundert has noted, often identified themselves as Polish centuries before their neighbors did. It is a story of how Jews lived with one another and how, for better and for worse, they lived with their non-Jewish neighbors. In the history of Polish–Jewish relations, there are what have been called "dark corners," instances of anti-Jewish hatred and violence, but the main story was that of a flourishing civilization, a history of life. This story would not end with the Holocaust; a thin but significant thread continues into the present.

The other major group of visitors, American and Israeli Jews, arrive with very different assumptions. For some, there may be a bit of residual nostalgia for a Yiddish world, but above all Poland is a place of death, populated by eternal Jew-haters who helped the Nazis do their work. By and large Jews come to Poland to visit Jewish cemeteries and sites of mass murder, a modern version of the practice that used to be called *keyver-oves*. The many thousands of young people, for example, who arrive in Poland annually as part of the March of the Living enact a monochromatic storyline: here in Poland are the death camps, there in Israel is life. For these visitors, the museum was to serve as a powerful corrective, an experience that stresses life and not death, that demonstrates the vitality and diversity of a millennial Jewish civilization from which they can be proud to be descended.

So here we are, sitting in a completed museum discussing a completed core exhibition. And we can ask first of all: Does the core exhibition—in particular, the interwar gallery—speak to these two audiences? And what is the story it tells?

There is indeed a story. It is never explicitly stated, but is implied, implicit in all the material presented. This lack of what is called a "museum voice" is consistent with the rest of the core exhibition; it was a key concept in its planning. Visitors must draw their own conclusions without being told what to think. Nevertheless, the story here is inescapable: the interwar years were a period when Jewish life and Jewish creativity blossomed on all fronts.

On either side of the Jewish street—itself strangely empty, however—a great range of Jewish politics and culture hold sway. There is Vilna and the founding of YIVO in their own gallery alongside verses from Moyshe Kulbak's paean to Vilna. Next there is the journal *Literarishe bleter* and its echoes among Yiddish-speaking Jews throughout the world; the legendary Jewish writers' union at Tłomackie 13; and the pantheon of Yiddish writers inspired by Y. L. Peretz. In an adjoining room, there is Café Ziemiańska, Tłomackie 13's Polish-speaking counterpart; the literary journal *Wiadomości Literackie*; and, of course, Julian Tuwim, along with a gramophone playing the hits *(szlagiery)* of Jewish composers and bands. Scores of Jewish newspapers, Yiddish on one side, Polish-language on the other, line one long side of these galleries. Across the hall, there is homage to Jewish political parties: Zionists, Bundists, and the Aguda. Stairs lead to what may be the crown of this gallery: rooms devoted to families, shtetl life, social welfare organizations, and above all to Jewish youth. There are wonderful exhibits on courtyards with children's games and songs; Jewish schools in all their variety; and an exhibit on *Mały Przegląd*, the newspaper founded by Janusz Korczak and written by children of all ages. This exhibit exemplifies what the storyline of the museum is about at its best. We see

Korczak and his children engaged in activities that could be the envy of today's progressive educators. In other words, they are doing something extraordinary and it is something other than boarding death trains. All of this is presented using a fine variety of media: photographs, films, interactive animation, sounds of children at play, facsimiles of school journals. Here and there, the touch-screens don't work or work poorly, but that is relatively rare.

Here is a world of intense life speaking clearly and directly to both Jewish visitors from abroad and to Poles. To the former: no, Jews were not sitting, as Celia Heller put it long ago, on the edge of destruction. To the latter: no, Jews were not some nasty, exotic creatures living in darkness. The interwar gallery, in other words, succeeds magnificently in the mission first formulated decades ago of showing life and not death.

Something is missing, however—or better, is greatly understated, because the Jewish creativity that is displayed here developed amidst rising Polish anti-Semitism. The chief place to look for this is in the timeline section, which runs along one side of the room devoted to interwar politics. Compared to the vibrant exhibits on Jewish political parties in this room, the timeline is much less attractive. It begins and ends with a quotation from the Jewish journalist Bernard Singer in 1934 referring to the Treaty of Versailles: "So beautiful was the sound of the words 'All citizens of Poland, regardless of race, language or religion, will be equal before the law.' What happened to this article of the treaty, how it was put into effect—all of this relates to the history of Jews in Poland since 1919." The visitor, it seems, is expected to decide based on what is presented in the timeline. But there is not much to go on: burdensome taxes on Jews in the 1920s; Emmanuel Ringelblum's rejection from the University of Warsaw; then in the late 1930s, an attack on Professor Marceli Handelsman, ghetto benches, the ban on ritual slaughter, and the wave of pogroms. The pogrom in Mińsk Mazowiecki is mentioned as one of 150 following the pogrom in Przytyk. But there is nothing else on the Przytyk pogrom. Cardinal Hlond's statement that one should not beat the Jews even though they are guilty of all sorts of depravity is here, as well as something about priest Stanisław Trzeciak's extreme anti-Semitism. But that's it for the Roman Catholic Church.

Above all, however, there is not a word here about the National Democrats, the increasingly popular party that worked to provoke pogroms. Indeed, the name Roman Dmowski, its founder and leader, does not appear in the timeline, though certainly there is much about Piłsudski and his tolerant attitude to Jews. "As elsewhere in Europe," began the guide to a group of students pausing briefly in front of the timeline's last years, as the Bund anthem resounded, ironically, from the adjoining exhibit.

If one digs elsewhere into the interwar gallery one can occasionally find some startling references. Thus, on a map showing the reach of *Literarishe bleter*, there is a link to a correspondent in the town of Karczew, located an hour from Warsaw, who describes the sacking of its Jewish library, its books thrown into the *besmedresh* and set on fire, as well as accusations by priests against Jewish organizations that resulted in their members being jailed.

But to find a reference to Roman Dmowski, one needs to search earlier in the core exhibition. At the very end of the exhibit on the 1905 Revolution, there is mention of Dmowski's leadership of the boycott of Jewish businesses in 1912. His new party, the National Democrats, is mentioned, as is the "surprising popularity" of his newspaper *Gazeta Poranna Dwa Grosze* (Morning Newspaper Two Pennies). This information is to be found within little wooden doors that worked only half the time I tried them, and it is not followed up anywhere else.

There is one small installation devoted to modern anti-Semitism. It is built, however, around the Russian and not the Polish kind. In the nineteenth-century gallery, there is a space that includes material on the early anti-Semitic Polish journal *Rola* and on a blood libel in the town of Chojnice. But the core of this installation concerns the Russian pogroms of 1881. This material is bracketed by quotations from Eliza Orzeszkowa and Bishop Antoni Sotkiewicz asserting that nothing like that could ever happen in Warsaw, and a statement from *Ha-melits* stating that nothing has. But just months later, in December 1881, a pogrom did break out in Warsaw, which is alluded to here in a nearly illegible letter from Aleksander Kraushar.

Pogroms are mentioned in connection with the Revolution of 1905 and also in 1919. There is material on the murder of Rabbi Shapira in Płock and the Yiddish writer A. Vayter (Isaac-Mayer Devenishsky) in Vilna by Polish forces. But the exhibit is dominated by a disturbing film about the Polish–Ukrainian fighting in Lwów. At this time, the Jews of Lwów were attempting to maintain their neutrality in the fighting. In the documentary-style film about these events, the Polish command in Lwów demands no anti-Polish expressions from Jews and "decent and loyal behavior." This is followed by a list of pogroms. The sequence implicitly links the pogroms to Jewish disloyalty. As one moves into the "Jewish street," there is a prominent quotation from Sholem Asch in 1928: "Fate has joined us to the Polish people for good, and our wishes and hopes belong to both nations, to one road, to a common bright future."

Unlike the presentation of the accomplishments of Jewish culture in interwar Poland, which lead the visitor to draw clear conclusions, the presentation of the many kinds of Polish antagonism to Jews is haphazard. There could have been—perhaps there might yet be—an organizing principle here: the development of Eastern European nationalisms, and above all the Polish variety, and its intimate link to many forms of anti-Semitism. This could naturally segue into an implicit cautionary critique of today's Polish nationalism, a message that Polish visitors could imbibe alongside that of a beautiful unknown Jewish civilization. But as things stand, the visitor is given little but hints that are not enough to develop any sort of coherent narrative about Polish anti-Semitism.

What can one say? This is, after all, a Polish museum, partly funded by the Polish government. A degree of self-censorship on the part of some of the museum's creators, perhaps unconscious, may have played a role here. The result is indeed an inspiring story that will go far, both for Jews and Poles, in combatting the long-established stereotypes of Jewish life in Poland. At least for the interwar period, however, this narrative skirts some inconvenient historical truths. In other words, amidst the brightness of Jewish life in this moment of Polish Jewish history, the so-called dark corners remain pretty dark.

The Truth and Nothing But: The Holocaust Gallery of Warsaw POLIN Museum in Context

OMER BARTOV

The Holocaust Gallery in POLIN Museum of the History of Polish Jews, the seventh out of a total of eight galleries that constitute the core exhibition in this extraordinary structure, fits uneasily, indeed awkwardly, into the main narrative of the museum as a whole. This is not and should not be seen as surprising; the genocide of the Jews, indeed, as any other genocide, cannot fit easily into its historical context, and should not be normalized or simplistically explained as an inevitable result of identifiable causes. Genocide is not normal but an aberration; it is not a routine historical event but an exception. And yet, any genocide, including the Holocaust, does occur within a historical context and cannot be understood and explained outside of its specific circumstances.

To be sure, POLIN Museum, whose core exhibition was guided by the well-articulated vision of Barbara Kirshenblatt-Gimblett, asserts that it provides no master narrative but only a set of guiding principles. But taken as a whole, these principles constitute a specific historical as well as didactic perspective. The museum wishes to present Polish Jews as being *of*, and not only *in* Poland; it stresses that Jews had a continuous, one-thousand-year history in Poland that cannot be viewed only from the perspective of its tragic end; and it points out that Jews had created a uniquely Jewish, distinctly Polish civilization there, one that for several centuries became the center of the Jewish world and represented its numerically largest community. Implicitly, this exhibition displays what Kirshenblatt-Gimblett has explicitly expressed on many occasions, namely, that one should not view the history of the Jews in Poland as one that inevitably led to the Holocaust. In that sense, the Shoah is both inherent to the exhibition and does not fit well into it. Kirshenblatt-Gimblett has asserted, to the irritation of some contemporary Polish nationalists, that the history of post-1945 Poland is a historical anomaly, because it was then, and only then, that Poland became a homogeneous country, the vast majority of whose population were and remain ethnically Polish Roman Catholics; and that by resurrecting the history of a thousand years of Jewish Polish civilization, the museum also illuminates Poland's extraordinarily rich and diverse past as a political entity that included numerous ethnic groups and religions living side by side (although not necessarily in complete or constant harmony).

This view of the past, this attempt to create a counter-narrative that undermines the popular and false perception of the Holocaust in Poland as somehow being generated from within Polish society, and to shed a critical light on the tendency to view the centuries of Jewish–Polish coexistence only through the prism of violence and extermination, is doubtlessly valuable, providing an important corrective to a widespread yet distorted historical understanding among both Jews and Poles. But it also generates its own problems and contradictions. The genocide of the Jews was, of course, planned and organized by the Nazi regime in Berlin, and was led and executed by German perpetrators and their numerous helpers and auxiliaries. It was, that is, a German project, and the main reason that so much of it took place in Poland was that a large portion of European Jewry lived in Poland, and that Poland was conveniently situated on the map of German-occupied Europe for the construction of extermination camps in which large numbers of Jews transported from elsewhere could also be murdered. Clearly, without Nazi Germany there would have been no Holocaust. But this cannot obscure the fact that there were powerful forces in Poland, which hoped and worked for the removal of Jews from the country; that these forces reflected a prevalent and growing anti-Semitic sentiment; that this sentiment became part and parcel of much of Polish nationalism; and that as a result of a combination of factors, including prejudice, ideology, greed, fear, cowardice, and resentment, to name only some of the most prominent, the existence of Jews in German-occupied Poland became unsafe not only because of the German will to murder them but also because so many of their Christian neighbors were glad to see them go or were at least indifferent to their fate. The history of Poland under German occupation can be told, therefore, from many different perspectives. It was a heroic and horrendously costly history of resistance to occupation; it was also, with some important exceptions, an ignominious, wretched history of betrayal, dispossession, and erasure of precisely those people and that civilization that had existed in the heart for Poland for a thousand years.

Presenting genocide as either deeply rooted in a specific history or as being entirely imported from the outside is, of course, hardly a Polish invention. Shortly after the war, the British historian A. J. P. Taylor published a book that presented the course of German history as an inevitable progression from Luther to Hitler. Several generations of historians of Germany have grappled with this deterministic argument, both rejecting it wholesale and, at the same time, agreeing that Hitler, as some postwar German historians and politicians had argued, was also not some foreign import, an alien growth that had nothing to do with the land of Goethe and Schiller and much more with French fascism and Russian communism: the pendulum has swung time and again from such views as those of Ernst Nolte, who saw the gas chambers as evolving from Bolshevik terror, to Daniel Jonah Goldhagen, who insisted on Germany's unique brand of annihilationist anti-Semitism. Indeed, one of the major predecessors of POLIN Museum is the Jewish Museum in Berlin, which has similarly had to grapple with the rich and complex history of Jewish German civilization as well as with its destruction by the Nazi regime, a government that was, after all, made up of Germans and that succeeded in transforming German society from one to which Jews from Eastern Europe had for many decades hoped to immigrate to one that turned on its own Jewish citizens before spilling over the border to pour its wrath on the millions of Jews who came under German-Nazi rule. Does Nazism negate Jewish German civilization? Of course not. But can the emergence of violent anti-Semitism in Germany be entirely divorced from a pre-Nazi past? We know that such arguments can only be labeled as old-hat apologetics.

So how does one fit a Holocaust Gallery into a museum of a Jewish European civilization? Ironically, it is "easier" to do that in Berlin than in Warsaw. In Berlin, as in numerous Holocaust museums around the world, one can show Hitler's gradual rise to power and the spread of anti-Jewish legislation and propaganda over the period of several years, leading to the isolation and eventual "social death" of German Jewry even before the outbreak of war. Once the war broke out, the Jews of other countries invaded by the Third Reich remained far from the gaze of most German citizens and were caught in the maelstrom of total war and general destruction. Germans, and for that matter Western Europeans as well, saw "their" Jews concentrated in certain camps or parts of towns and then packed into trains and shipped off to the east. People could imagine what happened in those far-flung territories but were neither exposed to the killing nor inclined to spend too much time ruminating about it. The case of Warsaw is very different. The rise of anti-Semitism in Poland was directly linked to the rise of Polish nationalism. Talk of removing the Jews from Polish society became prevalent in the years before the German attack, in a Poland that had regained its independence after well over a century of dismemberment and occupation. But the Second Republic was not just diverse; it was a country that contained large minorities, constituting more than a third of the total population, who were unhappy, often furious, to find themselves under the rule of a nationalist and nationalizing Polish state, a state that had been forced to sign an agreement to protect minority rights of which it remained deeply resentful and which it eventually and unilaterally discarded. To be sure, this was also a time of thriving cultural life and often successful integration of Jews and other minorities into the mainstream of Polish society, but it was no golden age, and, by the 1930s, anti-minority, and especially anti-Jewish rhetoric, combined with numerous local and government measures and general economic impoverishment made life in Poland increasing intolerable for many Jews. And just as growing numbers of Jews wished to leave, so too growing numbers of ethnic Poles wanted to be rid of them. Had the gates of immigration not increasingly closed down on the eve of the Second World War, far larger numbers of Jews would have left, often with the blessing of their Christian neighbors.

The dilemma, then, is how to fit a story of growing resentment and exclusion into a narrative of coexistence and diversity, even as the entrance to the Holocaust Gallery is looming at the corner of the Second Republic's "Jewish Street" gallery. Anti-Jewish sentiment in Poland did not cause the Holocaust, but German extermination policies were not enacted on a harmonious social fabric. While many Poles fought the Germans, many Poles, often the very same ones, were anything but unhappy about the fact the Germans were at least resolving one issue that had plagued Polish nationalism until then, even if in a radical, uncivilized, and—for some—objectionable manner. Can the Holocaust Gallery be inserted into the narrative of coexistence as an unrelated, externally imposed event (and space), or should it be "integrated," however much that would also indicate a prior disintegration of coexistence independently of the penetration of genocidal violence from without?

What, then, is the main narrative being told by the Holocaust Gallery? Is it that the Germans murdered Polish Jewry? Is it that Polish Jews and Christians suffered and died together under German occupation? Or is it about Polish–Jewish relations—or more precisely, about the relationship between Polish Jews and

Christians—during the Second World War? Each of these options necessitates another approach and would frame the Holocaust Gallery differently within the general narrative of POLIN Museum. To my mind, the gallery as it stands now has not chosen which of these to represent, but is generally inclined toward the second, namely, that both communities suffered under the Germans. That is, of course, true, but it does not tell the whole truth, and largely evades the question of the relationship between the two communities under the extreme conditions of war, genocide, and internal intercommunal violence. The reason the Holocaust Gallery has difficulties in confronting this issue head-on, despite the fact that this is the only reason to have a Holocaust Gallery within a museum about Jewish life in Poland in the first place, is that doing so would make it necessary to modify the narrative presented in earlier galleries so as to reflect the growing anti-Jewish sentiment in prewar Polish society. Precisely because the museum wishes to avoid the sense of inevitability of genocide and the tunnel vision of Polish Jewish history as leading to Auschwitz, it ends up largely evading or marginalizing the issue of Polish anti-Semitism and violence prior to, as well as during, and, of course, also after the Holocaust.

Let me state here clearly that, generally speaking, I find POLIN Museum to be a remarkable accomplishment. Even only two decades ago, hardly anyone would have predicted the establishment of such a major museum of Jewish history in the heart of Warsaw, on the grounds of the ghetto and facing Natan Rapoport's memorial to the uprising, attracting thousands of Polish and international visitors. Those who know or remember the manner in which Jewish life was represented in communist Poland, or, for that matter, in the Second Republic, must concede that the establishment of this museum is a sign of tremendous progress in understanding Poland's past and the role played by Jews in Polish history, just as much as in underlining the importance of Poland for Jewish history. POLIN is also an educational institution of vast importance, whose main targets should and will, it is hoped, be Polish and Jewish youth, who are still exposed to false and self-serving nationalist and ethnocentric narratives of the past.

Having said that, let me elaborate on what I find to be the two framing hiatuses or problematics of the Core Exhibition and the manner in which they contribute to positioning the Holocaust Gallery as outside the main course of Jewish history in Poland. The first has to do with the representation of violence; the second with the representation of the *kresy*, Poland's eastern borderlands. Violence in the museum tends to be represented as largely coming from the outside. At the end of the *Paradisus Judaeorum* gallery, covering the fifteenth and sixteenth centuries, the Golden Age of Jewish life in Poland ends with the Khmelnitsky uprising of 1648, in which large numbers of the Jews living in the eastern parts of the Polish–Lithuanian Commonwealth, now in Ukraine, were massacred. To be sure, the roots of the uprising are explained and an appropriate citation from Natan Hanover's account of the uprising, *The Abyss of Despair*, appears on the panel. Yet the Cossacks are depicted on the painted murals as the embodiment of the European nightmare of invading Eastern hordes, complete with Asiatic features, handlebar moustaches, and curved scimitars. They are in that sense the barbarians that Poland had set out to civilize, rather than the hired soldiers of their Polish paymasters; they emerge from the "wild fields" of the East and their violence against Jews is the precise reversal of the paradise of prior Jewish existence under benevolent Polish rule. One cannot but be reminded of Henryk Sienkiewicz's *By Fire and Sword*, that constitutive romantic tale of nineteenth-century Polish nationalism. Yet in Encounters with Modernity, the gallery of that century, anti-Semitic violence similarly appears to come from the east, this time from tsarist Russia, where, we learn, the word *pogrom* was coined and traumatic events such as the Kishinev pogrom occurred outside of the Polish sphere. We find this again, as already mentioned, in the Holocaust Gallery and the last gallery on the postwar years, where cases of local violence such as the massacres of Jedwabne and Kielce are mentioned yet do not fit comfortably into a narrative of Soviet and German occupation and postwar communist rule. What were the causes of such eruptions of fraternal violence? Were they just the actions of local hooligans or part of a larger framing of the Jews as external to and enemies of the Polish nation, disloyal collaborators with its foreign rulers and beneficiaries of Polish suppression? In other words, the entire social, economic, intellectual, and cultural discourse on the Jewish presence in Poland as it evolved, especially since the second half of the nineteenth century in Poland, is left largely unexamined or is played down. Roman Dmowski, the founder and moving spirit of right-wing, anti-Semitic Polish nationalism, whose influence on Second Republic political discourse through the Endecja Party increased year by year, makes a fleeting appearance in the exhibition: if the interwar period was a second golden age for Polish Jewry, the Endecja was the dark cloud on the horizon, certainly and not unreasonably seen as such from the vantage point of the Jews. That second golden age began with the marauding troops of Józef Haller's Blue Army and the 1918 pogrom in Lwów (Lviv), and ended with the institution of Jewish benches at Polish universities and plans to deport Jews to Madagascar. We cannot understand the satisfaction expressed by some Poles about the removal of Jews from Poland by the Germans, and the opposition to the return of Holocaust survivors after the war, without identifying the many dark spots on that golden age specifically and the role that Jews played within the Polish nationalist imaginary more generally. This does not mean that the Holocaust was an inevitable outcome of Polish attitudes but that the way it unfolded and was experienced by Jews in Poland had to do with attitudes that long predated the German occupation and, indeed, the rise of Nazism.

This growing complexity of Jewish–Polish relations, which is partly obfuscated in the galleries preceding the Holocaust, could have been displayed much more clearly by paying attention to the fact that large parts of Polish Jewry lived, in fact, in the *kresy*. In those eastern borderlands, particularly in Galicia, relations were actually triangular, between Poles, Ukrainians (Ruthenians), and Jews. Recognizing this fact would also shed much more light on the effect of nationalism on the relations between the Polish nation state and its national minorities and the manner in which this evolving relationship redefined the place, space, and image of Jews within Polish society as well as the perception by Jews of the new Polish nation state.

What is crucial to understand in this context is that the increasing competition between Polish and Ukrainian nationalism in the *kresy*, and the rise of Jewish nationalism, or Zionism, in part in response to these earlier movements, substantially altered the position of Jews in Poland. Within the Polish and Ukrainian nationalist discourse and visions of the future, the Jews as a religious and ethnic or national group had no space; whether the *kresy* ended up in Polish or in Ukrainian hands, the Jews were seen by both as external to the land, a group that could either assimilate, leave, or at best remain as a suspect minority. This held true both to Dmowski, who would have liked to remove the Jews, and to Józef Piłsudski, who, despite the Jews' love and admiration for him, paid little heed to them in his plans for a greater Poland. It was also the case for the popular Ukrainian National Democratic Alliance (UNDO) party and later of the more radical Organization of Ukrainian Nationalists (OUN), who dreamed of a Pole- and Jew-free Ukraine and veered ever closer to the Nazi regime in the latter part of the interwar period.

If we view the events in the *kresy* in the immediate aftermath of the First World War—the Polish–Ukrainian War followed by the Russo-Polish War—we find many of the seeds for the Ukrainian and Polish view of the Jews as communist collaborators and Bolshevik insurrectionists, a perception that came to play a major role in Polish and Ukrainian violence against Jews in 1918–1921, 1941, and 1945–1946, independently of external violence by foreign armies and occupiers. This also explains why in 1944, while the few surviving Jews in Poland and western Ukraine saw the Red Army as their liberators, Poles in Poland and Ukrainians in western Ukraine largely saw them as occupiers, and tended to associate them with the Jewish victims of the Nazis and their local collaborators. The manner in which these groups had envisioned the future in the 1930s and the place they had allotted to their neighbors in that future determined their conduct at times of extreme violence as well as their response to postwar realities. The memory of the war by Poles and western Ukrainians was of a costly nationalist struggle that ended in defeat and occupation; they perceived themselves as the victims of history, foreign invasion, betrayal by allies, and treason from within. This memory, suppressed under the communists, has been resurrected in many parts of Eastern Europe today: it is the recollection of a double genocide, in which the Jews were murdered by the Nazis, and the "indigenous" population was murdered and enslaved by the communists, identified by many nationalists with the Jews. The Jewish memory of those years is of a time in which their enemies from without allied themselves with their neighbors, hunted them down and eradicated them; they had nowhere to run because the "indigenous" population had either turned its back on them or eagerly awaited their demise so as to take over their property. These are both divergent and irreconcilable memories; there has never been and will never be any compensation for either. Nor did things have to happen the way they did, and they would not have happened had the Germans not set out to occupy the east and murder the Jews, and the Soviets not won the war and established their rule over these territories. But neither the Wehrmacht nor the Red Army marched into paradise; the seething forces of nationalism, resentment, fear, and hatred had grown deep into people's hearts independently of these outside forces. They are raising their ugly heads again throughout Europe today. One cannot fight against them by painting an idyllic picture of the past but by looking it straight in the eye. Paradise, if it ever existed, was lost long before the Holocaust began, and can be regained only in fantasy and imagination. If POLIN Museum is to succeed in its educational mission, it must also expose the destructive forces of nationalism and stand at the forefront not of rewriting the past but of creating a more inclusive, diverse, and tolerant future.

Perspectives: A Lithuanian Visit to the POLIN Museum Holocaust Gallery

SAULIUS SUŽIEDĖLIS

In April 2015, in conjunction with activities commemorating the Shoah, an International Conference on Holocaust Education convened in Vilnius. A presentation by Piotr Kowalik about the exhibits of POLIN Museum raised some questions. Could there be a model here for something similar in Lithuania? What perspectives would the Warsaw museum's Holocaust Gallery unlock for contemporary Lithuanians that would provide an insight into their own past?

Discussing such questions is a highly subjective enterprise. No visitor to a museum arrives as an empty vessel. Everyone brings the filter of his or her expectations, suppositions, prejudices, as well as collective memories inculcated through family histories, social media, or the educational system. Visitors arrive with emotional and perceptional baggage. Discussing this is a highly subjective enterprise, and requires some assumptions. I suspect that the Lithuanian visitor will carry more of this luggage than most, especially in traversing the Holocaust Gallery. Over the past decade, Lithuania's International Historical Commission, charged with investigating the crimes of foreign occupiers and their collaborators, has sent more than three hundred teachers to Holocaust education programs at Yad Vashem, Auschwitz, and most recently, to POLIN. What might the gallery reveal to them about the Holocaust that would relate to their own experiences? Let us assume that the Lithuanian visitor is a person of average education, possessing an interest in the past (otherwise why go to a museum?), and having some knowledge of modern history. When I speak of Lithuanian perspectives on the Holocaust, I mean primarily the manner in which non-Jewish Lithuanians relate to the Shoah, not only in academia, but in the society's collective memory and understanding as well.

BRIEFLY: PAST AND PRESENT NARRATIVES OF THE HOLOCAUST IN LITHUANIA

The slaughter of Jewish communities during the summer and fall of 1941 represents the bloodiest page in the history of modern Lithuania. This genocide should thus logically occupy a central place in the memory of the nation's twentieth-century experience of wars and foreign occupations. This has not yet happened, even as views of the Holocaust have changed considerably during the past two decades. One likely reason is that, unlike in the West, the genocide of the Jews is embedded in a broader and more contentious landscape, affected by conflicting wartime narratives of the Soviet and Nazi occupations, which have acquired domestic and international political dimensions. A further complication is that three conflicting views of Lithuania's Holocaust dominated both historical writing and public perceptions until the late 1980s. Allowing for some simplification, they can be divided into Soviet, Lithuanian, and Western perspectives. In the eyes of many Lithuanians, each has proven inadequate as a convincing explanation of the Holocaust in their country.

Soviet historical works accentuated the service of Lithuanian "bourgeois nationalism" to the Nazi cause, thus seeking to discredit both the anti-communist diaspora in the West and the postwar guerilla campaign against the Soviet occupation. Inasmuch as the Soviet version suffered from its obvious political agenda, the selectivity of documentation, as well as the obfuscation of the Jewish specificity of the Holocaust, it gained only limited credibility outside Communist Party circles. The Soviet system also rigorously protected Lithuanian society from cultural processes in the West, including the transformative narrative of the Holocaust. An unfortunate side effect of the widespread allergy to Soviet historiography was the mechanical rejection of even those elements of the Party's account, which contained valuable historic insights, for example, the scale of Nazi atrocities. The Soviet legacy lingered perversely as the proverbial millstone, weighing down society and leaving behind obstacles to an understanding of the Holocaust.

The second narrative of the genocide emerged from within the postwar Lithuanian diaspora. The émigré story rested on a denial of substantive local participation in the murder of the Jews accompanied, at times, by open or disguised anti-Semitism. Accustomed to a self-perception as victims, the older generation in particular reacted vehemently to any insinuation of collective Lithuanian guilt, insisting that the native killers constituted but a handful of rabble. Some even suggested that the Jews, because of their alleged collaboration with the Soviet oppressor, did much to deserve the wrath of ethnic Lithuanians. Liberal voices questioning this narrative remained in the minority. Some aspects of the émigré storyline resonated among anti-Soviet dissidents and have continued to enjoy a diminished afterlife in the post-Soviet period.

Western and Israeli accounts of Lithuania's wartime history focused on the fate of the Jews, which inevitably turned the spotlight on native collaboration in the Final Solution. The inability of most non-Baltic researchers to utilize materials in the indigenous languages of the region denied them full access to important sources: the mass of primary documents now available on the 1940–45 period, as well as scholarly studies published in Lithuania since independence. Some Western accounts tended to be one-dimensional, while others contained easily recognizable factual errors, which reduced their credibility.[1] The flaws in Western accounts of the Shoah were unhelpful in promoting Holocaust awareness in Lithuania. It was only natural that even those willing to travel the vexing path in confronting the Holocaust with an open mind were unlikely to accept as guides authors who understood them so little. This situation, along with the censorship, whether imposed (Soviet) or self-inflicted (Lithuanian), created barriers to serious self-examination of Lithuanian behavior during the Nazi occupation.

These different Holocaust narratives continue to attract constituencies, perhaps due to simple inertia. The more egregious anti-Semitic canards still have currency and will likely be with us for some time. On the other hand, the pre-1990 schools of thought are losing relevance, particularly within Lithuanian academic circles and, somewhat more gradually, in public perceptions. During the past two decades, an increasing number of mostly younger scholars have taken up Holocaust research. The current bibliographic output of scholarly books and articles would number at least several hundred publications. Serious Lithuanian-language scholarship on the Holocaust is thus no longer a novelty. Yet, despite numerous studies of the genocide of the Jews, which have given the lie to the "handful of rabble" thesis, the collaboration of Lithuanians in this genocide of Jews has continued as the most contentious issue of wartime history for Lithuanian society. I mention these conflicting trends in recent

---

1   See the interesting critique of Western historiography on the Holocaust in Timothy Snyder, "Commemorative Causality," *Modernism/modernity* 20, no. 1 (January 2013): 77–93.

historical understanding to emphasize that any Lithuanian visitor to the gallery will have been exposed to a "cacophony of voices" (borrowing a phrase from Jonathan Webber), not all of them benevolent.

INTERWAR LIFE: "JEWISH STREETS," LITHUANIAN AND POLISH

Most Lithuanians are aware that Poland and Lithuania share a common, if contentious, history. While one can find historical evidence of Polish influence virtually anywhere in the country, the nexus of the Jewish–Polish–Lithuanian interaction is, of course, Vilna/Wilno/Vilnius. Certainly, the cultural visuals of Jewish Lithuania's interwar period will not seem much different from what we see at the "Street" exhibition: the intense economic activity, the lively cultural and political life reflected in the ubiquitous Jewish press, examples of anti-Semitic agitation. Yet there are important aspects that differentiate the Lithuanian case.

Unlike in Poland, Lithuanian-speaking society did not begin to encounter the Jews as a cultural and political factor until very late in its historical development. This is not surprising. For centuries, before the onset of modernity, Jewish relations with Lithuanians essentially denoted economic contacts with the peasantry, since the latter constituted the only numerically significant social class still speaking the native idiom. During the anti-tsarist rebellions (1831 and 1863), many Jews took the sensible view that "Russia is the father and Poland is the mother. When [the parents] fight, children must stay out of their quarrel."[2] What was missing in this bit of folk wisdom, of course, was any mention of Lithuanians. It was the emergence of the Lithuanian national movement in the second half of the nineteenth century that signaled the first significant changes in relationships among the various ethno-religious communities. In this context, the connections of the Jews to Lithuania's Polonized aristocracy, while an interesting topic in itself, is not a significant theme in the development of Lithuanian–Jewish relations. As the anti-tsarist movement matured, the anti-Catholic and anti-Semitic imperial regime came to be seen as the enemy, and there were interludes of political Lithuanian–Jewish cooperation in the struggle for social and national rights. At the same time, the secular Lithuanian intelligentsia encountered modern anti-Semitism, which had already emerged in Austria, Germany, and France. From the second half of the

---

2 Solomonas Atamukas, *Lietuvos žydų kelias: nuo XIV a. iki XXI a. pradžios* [The Lithuanian Jewish way: from the fourteenth to the beginning of the twenty-first century] (Vilnius: Alma litera, 2007), 70.

nineteenth century, a conundrum afflicted Lithuanian–Jewish relations: the concurrent yet conflicting processes of integration and alienation.

In any case, the establishment of the Lithuanian state after 1918 meant a more fundamental and wrenching social upheaval than in Poland. Before the Great War, not a single city in Lithuania had a majority of Lithuanian speakers.[3] By the mid-1920s, Lithuanians predominated in all the major towns, which had once been bastions of Jewish, Polish, and German economic and cultural influence. This transformation of Lithuania's urban demography underscored a broad social transformation. For the first time in history, the language spoken by most of Lithuania's population became official.[4] Previously marginalized Lithuanians now played a decisive role within the political, economic, and cultural structures. Many Lithuanians and Jews, long accustomed to ritualized interaction within a semifeudal structure, found the new situation problematic.

The interwar Jewish community generally supported Lithuania during its bitter conflict with Poland. As long as the country's Jews supported the Lithuanian position, they could expect some favorable public expressions of sympathy. During the 1929 upheavals in Palestine and the 1931 pogroms in Vilnius, supportive accounts of Jewish suffering found their way into the Lithuanian press. However, pragmatic philo-Semitism was never the norm and did not last. Economic anti-Semitism was reinforced by the global depression of the 1930s, as well as by the assertive nationalism among the younger generation of students and intellectuals. More ominous were the nascent signs of anti-Semitism with racial overtones, which became increasingly noticeable during the mid- and late 1930s, despite efforts by the government and intellectual leaders to discourage anti-Jewish rhetoric and behavior. Paradoxically, the interwar period also witnessed the gradual linguistic "Lithuanianization" of the younger generation of Jews and there were interethnic cultural contacts, ably described by Israeli historian Mordechai Zalkin.[5] Upon leaving the "Polish

---

3 For example, according to the imperial census of 1897, Lithuanians numbered 6.6 percent in Kaunas and 27.8 percent in Šiauliai. The Republic of Lithuania's comprehensive demographic survey of 1923 reported a 59 percent ethnic Lithuanian majority in Kaunas and a corresponding 70 percent figure in Šiauliai.
4 The exception was the public use of Lithuanian alongside German in some regions of East Prussia until late in the nineteenth century.
5 Saulius Sužiedėlis, "The Historical Sources of Antisemitism in Lithuania and Jewish–Lithuanian Relations during the 1930s," in *The Vanished World of Lithuanian Jews*, ed. Alvydas Nikžentaitis, Stefan Schreiner, and Darius Staliūnas (Amsterdam: Rodopi, 2004), 119–54; cf. Mordechai Zalkin, "Sharunas, Prince of Dainava in a Jewish Gown: the Cultural and Social Role of Hebrew and Yiddish Translations of Lithuanian Literature and Poetry in Interwar Lithuania," *Jahrbuch für Antisemitismusforschung* 21 (2012): 149–65.

Street" exhibit, the Lithuanian visitor might conclude that his own country had provided a relatively safe haven for Jewish cultural life.

The irony of interwar Lithuania was that a nationalist authoritarian regime (often wrongly dubbed "fascist") had not only protected the country against the most egregious political extremes of left and right, but also had, by and large, punished anti-Semitic violence, allowed cultural diversity, and eschewed official ethnic discrimination. Some Jews considered the Leader of the Nation, Antanas Smetona, as an "iron wall" against their enemies. There were no mass fascist movements as in Romania and France. The regime's political police reported numerous instances of ethnic tensions, street scuffles, and minor outbreaks, but there is no record of anyone killed in an anti-Jewish pogrom during the years when the republic's government was in effective control of the country (1920–40) or during the first year of Soviet rule (1940–41) (therefore, explaining the *why* of the Holocaust in Lithuania remains a daunting task). When independence was lost in 1940, the "Lithuanian street" did not suffer the physical destruction so painfully evident in Poland.

THE HOLOCAUST GALLERY: THE POLISH PARADIGM AND THE LITHUANIAN EXPERIENCE

The passage through the Holocaust Gallery is a devastating experience. From a Lithuanian perspective, several revelations come to mind: some in terms of the Holocaust in general, others quite specific to Lithuania. The exhibits showcasing Separation and Isolation confront the visitor with the relentless march of the process of destruction. The paradigm for the genocide as elucidated by Raul Hilberg in his seminal work on the destruction of the European Jews is here: 1) Definition; 2) Expropriation (including the abrogation of civil rights); 3) Concentration (Isolation); 4) Destruction. Hilberg focused mainly on a description of the bureaucratic and police apparatus of mass murder, but essentially his interest lay in the course of the Holocaust, the *how* rather than the *why*. The exhibit accentuates that the period from 1939 to 1941 paved the way for the genocide. Compared to Lithuania, the process took a considerable time to unfold: the closing of the Warsaw Ghetto took place more than a year after the Nazi occupation of western and central Poland. The history of Warsaw's Jews presents a chronologically inverse reality to the experience of the Jews of Vilna.

On the one hand, "life in the shadow of death" was the experience of the victims of both ghettos. They attempted to maintain social support and a health system under horrendous circumstances. The residents engaged in a frantic search for additional sources of food to stave off starvation, but they also strove to continue cultural and spiritual life, in order to uphold their human dignity, which was under constant assault. The phenomena of resistance and collaboration, as well as the ongoing political conflicts and divisions, were all parts of the reality.

However, if we are looking at the POLIN gallery from the point of view of the victims, there is an important distinction from the Lithuanian perspective. The Warsaw Ghetto, in which the city's Jews led a precarious existence, was a *prelude* to their annihilation. As noted by historians Barbara Engelking and Jacek Leociak, during the deportations to Treblinka, some Jews volunteered for the trains in response to the promise of bread. There was also "the constant illusion that there actually existed some sort of 'labor camp in the East.'"[6] In Vilnius, the social, economic, and cultural struggle in the ghetto constituted an *epilogue* to a giant wave of mass murder. By the time the Vilnius Ghetto Theater opened in January 1942, nearly three-fourths of Lithuania's Jews were already dead. Herman Kruk noted in his diary on March 8, 1942, that "life is once again pulsating in the Vilna Ghetto. In the shadow of Ponary, life is happening and there is hope for a better morning."[7] In Warsaw, Ringelblum wrote the following: "One is left with the tragic dilemma: are we to dole out spoonfuls to everyone, the result being that no one will survive? Or are we to give full measure to a few—with only a handful enough to survive?"[8] Here one immediately thinks of the tortuous and unimaginably cruel choices made by Jacob Gens, the ill-fated leader of the Vilnius Ghetto, a decorated Lithuanian army veteran of the war against Poland, and a personal example of the conundrum facing assimilated Lithuanian Jews. A Lithuanian visitor would gain a broader understanding of the Holocaust in Poland by proceeding through the exhibits on hiding, the section on Żegota (the Council to Aid Jews), and the Warsaw uprising.

Perhaps the most striking reality of the Holocaust is seen in the application of industrialized mass murder, the institution of the "death camps," which has no analogue in Lithuania and is, indeed, unprecedented in all of history. The overwhelming majority of Holocaust victims, perhaps as many as 98 percent of the dead, perished through the application of three modes

---

6 Barbara Engelking and Jacek Leociak, "Holocaust, 1939—1945," in *Polin. 1000 Year History of Polish Jews*, ed. Barbara Kirshenblatt-Gimblett and Antony Polonsky (Warsaw: Museum of the History of Polish Jews, 2014), 289.

7 As quoted in "Vilna during the Holocaust," http://www.yadvashem.org/yv/en/exhibitions/vilna/during/theatre.asp.

8 As quoted in the POLIN Holocaust Gallery.

of genocide: mass shooting operations, suffocation by gas, and systemic starvation. Large-scale shooting campaigns took place in Lithuania (Ninth Fort, Ponar), Latvia (Rumbuli), Belarus (Minsk), Ukraine (Babi Yar), as well as in Romania and elsewhere. All of the modern industrialized killing centers, the well-known death camps (Auschwitz, Sobibór, Treblinka, Majdanek, Bełżec, and Chełmno) were located in Poland. As a rule, the large ghettos, where disease and starvation reigned, were a feature characteristic of Nazi-occupied Eastern Europe.

Unlike Treblinka, Ponary was within earshot of the city's Jews. The power of illusive hope in the face of death may be impressive, but given the fact of close proximity to the killing site and the knowledge that most of the community had already perished, the Jews of Vilnius must have had a much stronger sense of what awaited them. The Einsatzgruppen, Lwów, and Jedwabne appear *before* one walks out to the postwar section, and *after* one has viewed ghetto life and the deportations. The chronology of the walk through the Holocaust Gallery can thus be somewhat startling. Lithuania was the place where the Holocaust as the genocide of European Jews began, even as the unfortunates in Warsaw struggled to survive. In Lithuania, Hilberg's four stages of destruction can still be discerned, but they arrived closely together, almost as a single explosion. In mid-August 1941, roughly 90 percent of Lithuania's Jews were still alive; by the end of October, in less than three months, more than two-thirds were dead.

A Lithuanian visitor would immediately note the exhibit on Ponary, as well as the dead registered in the infamous Jaeger Report, the detailed accounting of mass shootings in Lithuania which was forwarded to Berlin by Einsatzkommando 3 on December 1, 1941. As the names of towns scroll down the screen, one recognizes places that were once in Poland but are now in the Republic of Lithuania, such as Eišiškės (Ejszyszki), which has come to the attention of the world through the beautifully arranged photographic tower at the Holocaust Museum in Washington. The photographs of Jedwabne attempt to serve a similar function, but as events, Jedwabne and Ejszyszki are quite different. The first is connected to "pogroms in the East" (*pogromy na Kresach*) which are defined as "having occurred during the first weeks of the German occupation." It is reported that "in scores of pogroms in the eastern lands (*Kresy Wschodnie*), over ten thousand (*kilkanaście tysięcy*) Jews were murdered."[9] The Ejszyszki slaughter occurred more than two months later, on September 22 and 27, carried out by militarized mobile killing squads and their auxiliaries under conditions that cannot be properly described as a pogrom.

---

9 Engelking and Leociak, 32.

The issue of native participation in the genocide of the Jews is crucial and, by addressing the activities of the local population, the Holocaust Gallery provides contrasting perspectives. There were the Jewish police, who participated in the deportations, as well as collaborators such as Abraham Gancwajch and informers for the Gestapo. The Third Reich put all Jews, even the collaborators, on death row, so that one should make a clear distinction between the behavior of those waiting to be murdered and the reaction of non-Jews. The spectrum of Polish responses to Jewish suffering would be recognizable in all the occupied countries: from rescue, to sympathy, then to indifference, hostility, and even outright murder. Certainly, the behavior of many Polish gentiles left much to be desired: "The most widespread reaction to the fate of the Jews was indifference (in feelings) and passivity (in action)," write Engelking and Leociak.[10] Some Poles reacted with hostility, even approving the actions of the Germans. Some betrayed Jews to the Germans, while others exploited the situation of the unfortunates through blackmail, the infamous *szmalcownicy* of which there were thousands. The so-called "blue police" did their share of persecution. In the case of Jedwabne, dozens resorted to actual murder. However, without minimizing the crimes of the blackmailers and murderers, and while acknowledging the anti-Semitism, which persisted during the occupation, one reality stands out: nine-tenths of Poland's Jews were, indeed, annihilated, but most died at the hands of people who were not Poles.[11] Statistically, Jedwabne is an outlier.

Numbers *do* matter. By contrast, the distressing reality is that most of Lithuania's Jews died at the hands of Lithuanians, albeit under the indispensable planning, leadership, and direction of the Nazi occupiers. Germans who participated directly in the mass murder of Jews numbered at least several hundred, mainly members of different security and police organizations, including some Wehrmacht personnel. Local people, mainly ethnic Lithuanians, constituted a much larger number; at least several thousand acted directly as murderers, thus contradicting the myth about a handful of low-life "Jew-shooters."

---

10 Ibid., 28.
11 The canard that the Nazis chose Poland as the site of the death camps because of Polish anti-Semitism is still current in some circles. More perplexing is the claim by one noted scholar which ignores the context of the uniquely harsh Nazi occupation here: "Consider the Poles, who, deservedly proud of their society's anti-Nazi resistance, actually killed more Jews than Germans during the war." Jan Tomasz Gross, "Europe's Crisis of Shame," in the online journal *Social Europe* (September 14, 2015), http://www.socialeurope.eu/2015/09/eastern-europes-crisis-of-shame/.

The so-called National Labor Security (TDA) soldiers operating in Hamann's *Rollkomando* (mobile killing unit), the coopted local police or "white armbands," the Special Unit (*Ypatingasis būrys*) in Vilnius, and a number of hastily organized police battalions distinguished themselves in the mass murder. Furthermore, some Lithuanian units took their work outside the homeland to Belarus, Ukraine, and figure even in the deportations to Treblinka on July 22, 1942, as documented in the gallery. Other Lithuanian units performed guard and convoy duties. Was this many people, or a few? The historian Solomonas Atamukas has attempted to answer this question, admitting that determining the precise number of perpetrators is complicated by the problem of defining various degrees of complicity. In any case, his conclusion seems logical:

> Thousands of local people participated in the process of the persecution of Jews, by pogroms, robbery, herding Jews into ghettos, guarding them, concentrating them further, herding, transporting and shooting them. Although this was only a small portion of the [country's] more than 2.7 million inhabitants, it is still a significant number of people who committed crimes against humanity.[12]

For the victims, the fewest opportunities for survival existed in the occupied territories where the Nazis were able to control local administrative structures.[13] Collaborators and anti-Semites considerably facilitated the work of the Berlin planners, but they were not the decisive factor in the destruction of the Jews as a community. On the other hand, within the context of occupation, the lives of Jews in hiding depended almost entirely upon the attitudes and actions of local gentiles. Scholars have done considerable work in explaining the structure of the genocidal mechanism and even identifying its most important drivers. Historians may be able to clarify the *historical* responsibility of the executors of the genocide and to indicate crucial factors, which facilitated the course of the mass murders. The question of *moral* responsibility is a different matter. Local collaborators were not the planners and decision makers, but neither were they simply cogs in a machine. Inasmuch as they possessed free will and the ability to make decisions, their moral responsibility was no less than that of the organizers.

---

12 Atamukas, 261.
13 Survival rates were markedly higher in the Axis countries allied to the Reich, that is, where the prewar state structures still endured. An interesting perspective on this point is in Snyder, 85.

There is another juncture where Polish and Lithuanian collective memories diverge sharply and, while this variance is not directly related to the Shoah, it has had a significant effect on the reception of the Holocaust in Lithuania. Polish and Lithuanian encounters with the German occupiers were starkly different, perhaps even incomparable. Many Lithuanians understandably greeted the Germans as liberators in June 1941 (although this good feeling did not last). The Nazis' murderous attack on the Polish intellectual elite in the fall of 1939 and the subsequent mass murder of Polish gentiles has no analogue in the Lithuanian experience. It is noteworthy that in 1943 collaborationist Lithuanian leaders warned the populace that if they continued to resist German demands for mobilization, the Nazis would introduce a "Polish-style occupation." In all, about 5,000 ethnic Lithuanians perished at the hands of the Nazis. More than 70,000 were dragged into the RAD (*Reichsarbeitsdienst*), most of whom survived. Again, numbers matter.

In human terms (or just to put it bluntly), the German occupation was hardly the worst experience in the lives of elderly ethnic Lithuanians who still remember those years. By contrast, as KGB sources report, under the Kremlin's rule, more than a quarter of a million persons, predominantly Lithuanians, were "repressed" (as per Soviet terminology) resulting in violent deaths (ca. 50,000), deportations, and detentions, most during the postwar years (1945–53). Considerably more ethnic Lithuanians were killed after V-E day than during the Second World War. In the collective memory of victimhood and in public commemorations, this is what stands out in Lithuania.[14] This past contrasts sharply with the Polish reality. For many people, their particular (and different) experience of victimization can create an obstacle to imagining the agony of other victims. It may be necessary to put aside, at least for a time, one's own memory of anguish to acknowledge that of the Other and, in particular, never to forget the unprecedented suffering and loss endured by the victims of the Holocaust.

---

14 This and other themes are explored in more detail in my article, "Zagłada Żydów, piekło Litwinów" [Jewish genocide, Lithuanian inferno], in *Gazeta Wyborcza* (November 28, 2013). Full text in http://wyborcza.pl/magazyn/1,134731,15042881,Zaglada_Zydow__pieklo_Litwinow.html.

Polin: A Bildungsroman

MARCI SHORE

Jacek Leociak talked about this place where we are today as a *droga do śmierci*, a path toward death. During my first long stay in Warsaw in 1997, I came here night after night, just for this reason. I see here today many people whom I first met then—including Antony Polonsky and Dariusz Stola, who have been among my favorite conversation partners now for nearly two decades.

I also see many absences: of Jerzy Tomaszewski, Feliks Tych, Marek Edelman, Władysław Bartoszewski. Nineteen ninety-seven was the year, too, I began to read the books of Benjamin Harshav and Ezra Mendelsohn—who just so recently were still here. I read *Zdążyć przed Panem Bogiem* (Outwitting God) nearly in one breath in 1997.

"And you suggested that God was there, but on their side?" I asked Marek Edelman.[1]

"It was a joke," he told me. "Anyway, God is an invented thing."[2]

It was during this same year I first read Stanisław Krajewski's 1983 samizdat essay "Żydzi a komunizm" (Jews and Communism), his confrontation with the legacy of *żydokomuna*. That text was my point of entry into a topic that preoccupied me for the coming years.

I heard then, perhaps at 6 Twarda Street, conversations about plans for a museum. I could not have imagined, though, that something on the scale of POLIN would come into being—amidst the anti-Semitic graffiti then in Warsaw.

Barbara Kirshenblatt-Gimblett contextualizes the new museology in a broader skepticism about meta-narratives. The new museology is a kind of *obnażenie*—a "laying bare"—of what a museum does. It is the moment when narrative consciousness becomes self-conscious, when it reflects back upon

---

1 "Sugerował Pan, że wtedy Bóg był, ale po ich stronie?"
2 "To dowcipy. Bóg to w ogóle wymyślona rzecz."

itself with a determination to avoid the teleological deceptions embedded in grand narratives. The Holocaust has long been a test case of these teleological deceptions of retrospect: how can historians recreate the horizon of our protagonists, other than by erasing from our minds our knowledge of what comes afterwards? And how can such knowledge ever be erased? We "bracket" it, we try not to think about it, but it is only an exercise, by nature artificial and incomplete. The rejection of meta-narrative is a revolt against the teleological in favor of the recreation of a space for contingency.

The space for contingency is also a space for polyphony. Barbara describes quotations as artifacts. I accept this; I am a verbal person, for me the quotations are artifacts. It is understandable that not everyone accepts the museum's shying away from its own narrative authority in favor of a polyphony of the voices of the past. This is the essence of postmodernism: that no single, stable, determinate meaning is possible, that we are fated to live with a plurality of mutually contesting truths. This stance feels intellectually enlightened, but morally unsatisfying—too much like the indeterminate "relationship status" option on Facebook: "it's complicated" as a way of avoiding responsibility for making a choice. Yet an authoritative narrative exploiting all the Hegelian advantages of retrospect—the Owl of Minerva who spreads its wings only with the falling of the dusk—would feel self-righteous and condescending. I understand the dissatisfaction, but I see no better way.

I would like to add one more thought in response to Jacek's impassioned *samokrytyka* in his account of the Holocaust gallery for which he was partially responsible—which was less a principled opposition to self-praise than an *obnażenie rozpaczy*, a laying bare of despair. I was moved by his desire to end the Holocaust Gallery with an empty space where a person can see only his shadows, where we feel ourselves on the very path to death, where we confront nothingness.

Jacek is right. Yet it is not an easy thing to present nothingness.

The nineteenth-century German philosopher Wilhelm Dilthey described the task of the historian as understanding through *Nacherleben*—that is, understanding arrived at through a vicarious (re)experiencing—a kind of *Einfühlung*, or feeling into another, to use Edith Stein's word. To write history well is to achieve what great novelists and film directors do: the suspension of disbelief. The reader should be able to feel himself *there*. Good literature can transport you. I cannot answer the question as to whether this can happen in a museum, whether a visitor can be transported in this way. The constraints seem too great: there is too much breadth, too many characters, too many visitors, too little space. We walk too quickly. Perhaps a museum has to aspire to something different—or not.

The postwar gallery involved a challenge that was itself a kind of moral dilemma: how to portray life after death. The academic creators of the gallery know the period with enormous intimacy; they understand everything that happened only too well. The result is a gallery that feels to me too busy, over-populated. There is too much simultaneous media, too many films playing at the same time in a small room—there is not enough space to create *Stimmung*, to give us the chance to absorb one moment at a time, to feel Stalinist terror. The difficulties are less intellectual than physical: the sounds clash too much; the polyphony becomes cacophony. Everything goes by too fast. I love these poems by Antoni Słonimski and Stanisław Wygodzki. But they alternate too quickly, the words disappear too fast.

There is some wonderful material: the postwar poster glorifying the Warsaw Ghetto fighters in a socialist realist aesthetic; Władysław Gomułka's March 1968 speech granting exit visas to those who "regard Israel as their homeland"—and the crowd's response of "*śmielej! śmielej!*" (boldly! boldly!), as if encouraging him to act even more vigorously; Chris Niedenthal's photograph *Czas Apokalipsy* (The time of the Apocalypse) capturing the nihilistic onset of martial law. I was struck by Marta Petrusewicz's handwritten survey from 1966, recording which of her classmates had heard of Leszek Kołakowski, of Jacek Kuroń, of Adam Michnik. Especially poignant was the story of Wera Lechtman, whose communist mother was imprisoned and tortured during the Stalinist years while Wera and her brother grew up in an orphanage. This was in part so absorbing, I think, because of the space created to take in one story at a time: to sit alone, to listen to the recording of her voice, to look at the photographs of her two small children, to read the letter in which she learns that her husband will not join her.

I would like to conclude by circling back. In 1648, space narrows when we encounter the Bohdan Khmelnytsky revolt, the massacres of Poles and Jews. Afterwards space opens again. We emerge into a wooden synagogue in Gwoździec, where the colors of the reconstructed roof are so rich they could be tasted: port, walnut and honey, caramel and cinnamon, and wild blueberries. It is a breathtaking work of collective artistry, of what Krzysztof Czyżewski has named *praktykowanie pamięci*, a remembering that is not only mental and verbal, but also visual and corporeal, enacted with the eyes and the hands. Memory as praxis.

The reconstructed roof of the Gwoździec synagogue is dazzling not only as a finished work of art, but also as a project. It is a synecdoche for the museum as a whole: a project of Poland's owning of Polish Jewish history as its own. The returning of Jewish history to Poland is a coming-of-age story, and the two-decade long history of the museum's making could itself be written as a Bildungsroman of post-communist Poland. The museum is also—to use the language of the years between the wars—a posthumous triumph of *doikeyt*, the need to be active in the place where we find ourselves. We should all take a moment to appreciate the enormity of that accomplishment.

A Historian's Response. Comments on the Postwar Gallery

ANDRZEJ PACZKOWSKI

A historical museum of the narrative kind, if it does not cover certain concrete, chronologically or clearly defined territorial events, but instead represents a long continuum in time, becomes—seen in a certain light—something in the nature of a Biblia Pauperum, or "poor man's Bible," for those who cannot read. Or to put it another way—a comic strip. That is usually the destiny of a museum of this kind. It is not a place for seasoned experts; it is not intended for professors or post-doctoral scholars of "applied opinions." So, it is difficult for me to review a gallery as the organizers of this panel invited me to. I think the job would probably be better entrusted to Jolanta Ambrosewicz-Jacobs, who in her article describes the educational dimension of the exposition, and it might even be better for a museum docent, who sees how visitors react. Of course, a historian also has a right to comment because when galleries are created, their creators often refer to consultants, and, of course, they also base their work on their own historical knowledge, which as a rule is very sound. So, I would like to exercise my right to comment. And, above all, I want to exercise the right to ask a few questions, or voice a few doubts.

First, a somewhat marginal comment. The museum as a whole carries the name Museum of the History of Polish Jews. However, I am not sure that it would not have been more appropriately called "Museum of the History of the Jews in Poland." One may ask if a Jew who was born in Poland and lived here as his ancestors did ceases to be a "Polish Jew" when he leaves this country—after he leaves Warsaw, Drohobycz, or Chmielnik, and from the moment he finds himself in New York, Buenos Aires, or Tel Aviv?

And if he does cease to be one, at what moment does this occur? In brief, I miss in the museum a proper treatment of compatriots' organizations with ties to Polish lands, no matter where the organizations are based. My next remark is also related to naming, but is directly connected to the gallery with which I am concerned. It might have been better to name the gallery "After the Holocaust" than "After the War." Of course, the Holocaust was part of the war, but from the point of view of Jewish history it was its crucial part, far more important than any other elements of the cataclysm. It is not the war as such but the Holocaust that became a constitutive factor for Jews—for all Jews, not only for Polish Jews. You might say that the world as it is and humanity as it is in some sense always exists "after the war" because after all, wars do occur with a certain regularity. But there has been only one Holocaust. So, it is natural that this gallery opens with an image of what followed "after the Holocaust"—a terrifying sea of ruins. A sea almost in the literal sense, insofar as it is not ruined or burned buildings, but simply frozen waves of stone (or brick). It might even be possible to find a subtle difference between the rubble and ruins of Warsaw's Old Town and the stone sea left by the ghetto.

In accordance with the convention adopted for the entire museum, this gallery has a linear, chronological structure. Following the same convention, the gallery describes what things were like and what people were like. On the first, basic level, it simply describes or, rather, shows. It is difficult to analyze things on this level; to find any attempt at analysis or to try to relate artifacts, images, or texts to each other, you have to "go down one level," using the electronic links of various sorts that are provided. I did a little try-out in a few places, and I can affirm that this "underground" offers rich possibilities for widening one's knowledge and also certain new accents on the level of emotion. However, I do not know what proportion of visitors will make the journey in search of additional information. If a visit takes place in a group, there probably are not any opportunities for people to take a step aside, and the guide will naturally describe what all the visitors can already see. So, I looked over the gallery as if I were an ordinary museum-goer, more on the basic level, and only occasionally "descending." On the basis of this approach, I would like to present a few comments.

What are the main points that I remember, both looking at the exhibition as a whole and devoting my attention solely to the Postwar Gallery? The opening is extraordinarily powerful: I've mentioned the ruins of the Warsaw ghetto. But, for me, the items (photographs) showing the massacred city and the Monument to the Ghetto Heroes rising amid those ruins had special meaning.

This monument is in essence a symbol of the entry into a new era, but it is accompanied by the ruins of the former world, which is gone. The visual contrast between the landscape and the monument was for me truly devastating. So, the gallery starts from this "heavy blow," and this is a good way to deal with it. I would like to add in the margin that it might make sense to reflect on whether the "lower level" of the exposition should not direct attention to the fact that the Monument to the Ghetto Heroes was unveiled in 1948, whereas the monument to the Heroes of the Warsaw Uprising was erected forty-one years later. This could be a small footnote to the problem of Polish–Jewish relations.

Another noteworthy feature of the gallery, a segment that is striking both in its narration and its drama, is the Kielce pogrom. I do not know if it's a good or a bad thing, but for someone walking through the gallery, the Kielce pogrom delivers the second emotionally "heavy blow," after the sea of ruins and the ghetto monument. It may be unfair, or a sign of my distorted sensibility, but in fact the next, third, and essentially (for me) final "blow" is Gomułka's speech of March 1968. The hysterical cry of the communist leader coming from loudspeakers, and his half-cartoonish, half-demonic figure blown up on a screen, create the impression that this is the central point of the whole gallery. This impression is fortified by an excess of materials connected to March 1968 events. From the point of view of the history of Jews in Poland, this is a decidedly overinterpreted episode.

Do I miss anything on the level of facts in the gallery we're discussing? If you accept that a narrative museum is an educational comic strip or a poor man's Bible, I can say that I do not really miss anything. Perhaps there is even too much information, or rather it is too densely packed, and so I'd probably remove some items, in order to make the whole exposition more legible (more comic strip–like?). On the other hand, I miss some authentic object, although, obviously, there can't be anything as striking as the can holding the Ringelblum archive. But this is just a generalizing comment. Though the gallery is "stuffed," I still miss certain things. They may be imaginary, and they may not lend themselves to meaningful presentation. It is the museum specialist who has to decide if something I come up with can be presented. In the discussion of the Holocaust Gallery at the conference in May 2015, a controversy developed in which one of the historians who created the Holocaust Gallery took it amiss that what he wanted in the exhibition was not there. Luckily, I did not participate in setting up the exhibit, and so I cannot take anything amiss. Furthermore, I do not know if what I imagine is representable.

I miss something showing the continuity of the shrinkage of Polish Jewry after the war. There are exhibits about the successive waves of emigration—the one after Kielce, the one in 1956–57, the one after March 1968—but I would have liked some kind of synthesis. After all, in the history of Polish Jews after the Holocaust this was a basic phenomenon: the community simply disappears, and the shrinking—vanishing, really—of Polish Jewry results not only from emigration but also from assimilation and the emergence of the category Isaac Deutscher once defined as "non-Jewish Jews." Another problem, I think, also requires reflection. We find a lot of information in the exhibition about—to put it crudely—Jews in Jewish culture. That's obvious, because who creates Jewish culture? Only Jews. But there's another question the gallery fails fully to address, and it seems to me a pretty interesting one, though I am not sure how important it is. Joseph Conrad was a Pole, but he was not a Polish writer. He was an English writer—and of course a world writer, but that was because he was a successful one—and so he became a part of English culture. You can imagine that if Joseph Conrad wrote inferior novels he would not be a world writer, but would remain an English one. Julian Tuwim was a Jew, but he wrote in Polish, so Tuwim's place is more in Polish culture than in Jewish culture. Can we try to show this in some way? Polish culture is not Joseph Conrad but Julian Tuwim.

Another matter I want to raise is the space in the gallery dedicated to Jan Błoński's famous essay "Biedni Polacy patrzą na getto" (The poor Poles look at the ghetto). I have a problem with this: POLIN Museum is not a museum of anti-Semitism, nor is it a museum of the struggle against anti-Semitism, nor, of course, a museum of the history of Poland. And with this in mind I ask myself: what role do texts like Błoński's wonderful essay play in the story of the fate of Polish Jews? What Błoński wrote about is, above all, part of the history of Poland, not the history of Polish Jews (not to mention non-Polish Jews). The question he raised was—and still is—very important, but is its proper place in this gallery, in this museum?

And finally, the last thing: the Jewish presence in Poland after 1989. It has been—to use a colloquial expression employed by "illiterates"—virtually reduced to a joke. What is the "Jewish renaissance" in the third Polish Republic, a renaissance that really started in the mid-1980s? This renaissance manifests itself in a return to Jewishness—in a cultural or religious sense—by a handful of Polish citizens (probably up to this point mostly "non-Jewish Jews"), but quite frequently what is seen as this renaissance is the (former) Jewish culture displayed mainly in festivals and events of various kinds. It isn't Jews, though, who are present at such events; there are too lamentably few of them, there are just mementos of them, and these are turned into a kind of commercial folklore. I think that this problem should be taken into account in the gallery, and although there is no particular increase in Polish Jews, we should be prepared for the museum to last a long time—I hope—and for new things to arise for the museum to display, things happening now or things that happen in the next five or ten years.

Translated from Polish by Alissa Valles

Museums and Education

Jewish Tourism to Poland: The Opportunities for New Museum Narratives to Recontextualize Jewish Histories

JONATHAN WEBBER

INTRODUCTION: NEW MUSEUM NARRATIVES

In her key methodological introduction to the companion volume to POLIN Museum, Barbara Kirshenblatt-Gimblett has reminded us that museums in general (and POLIN Museum in particular) can act as major agencies of social and intellectual transformation.[1] In POLIN Museum, the new meta-history of Jewish Poland has reached very significant consolidation, offering at long last not just a benchmark but a veritable beacon, illuminating the way for a multiethnic historical narrative which, slowly but surely, will have powerful

---

1 Barbara Kirshenblatt-Gimblett, "Theater of History," in *Polin. 1000 Year History of Polish Jews*, eds. Barbara Kirshenblatt-Gimblett and Antony Polonsky (Warsaw: Museum of the History of the Polish Jews, 2014), 19–35. Kirshenblatt-Gimblett's main role at POLIN Museum was as leader of the team responsible for developing its core exhibition; besides her numerous interests and experience in a wide range in the humanities, including Jewish studies, cultural anthropology, folklore, and tourism studies, she is a particularly accomplished scholar in the field of museum studies.

educational repercussions and significantly transform the way that people both in Poland and elsewhere will think about this country and its Jewish history. The challenges of the subject are enormous, but POLIN Museum has faced up to them very directly, and all of us are profoundly grateful to Barbara and her team.

As far as the popular Jewish world is concerned, there is a lot of work to do. Many ordinary Jews visiting POLIN Museum, having little prior knowledge and realizing during their visit that the history of Polish Jews is a very much larger subject than they might previously have thought, will simply get absorbed in particular details that happen to catch their eye. It is likely that they will not quite get the point that the exhibition as a whole in fact frames a new meta-history. But the message will get through, slowly but surely. After the fall of communist rule in Poland in 1989 it took about a decade for foreign Jews even to think about coming to visit Poland at all; but now such visits have become hugely popular, even fashionable. During that decade, in the 1990s, foreign Jews confidently told each other in no uncertain terms that it would be a sin to spend money in Poland, even by staying in a hotel or buying a souvenir; but much of all that has changed in the past fifteen years, in a truly striking manner that is almost worthy of being identified as a paradigm shift.[2] So if the

---

2 During the late 1980s and 1990s, as an English Jew who regularly visited Poland (for my research on the surviving Jewish heritage, part of an ongoing project that later gave rise to the "Traces of Memory" exhibition at the Galicia Jewish Museum, described below), I was regularly lectured by fellow Jews that it was both morally reprehensible and physically dangerous to visit Poland, on the grounds that it was a deeply anti-Semitic country. That was the conventional wisdom then, disseminated (as I understood it) by Polish Jewish Holocaust survivors who, fifty years on, had still retained a strongly demonized view of Poland, based on their experiences in the late 1930s, as well as on profoundly negative stereotypes of Polish behavior they had witnessed or heard about during the Holocaust and postwar pogroms ("Why else was Auschwitz in Poland?"—to quote one common rhetorical question; "the Poles were worse than the Germans."). These stereotypes, which were commonly absorbed and then transmitted unquestioningly by the descendants of survivors, were later fueled also by recollection of the "anti-Zionist" campaign of 1968 and by a succession of rather acrimonious Polish-Jewish controversies, including the well-publicized Jewish protests in the 1980s against the Carmelite convent at the "de-judaised" memorial site at Auschwitz, and more recently during the debate over the Jedwabne massacre. For a study of this background, see, for example, Robert Cherry and Annamaria Orla-Bukowska, eds., *Rethinking Poles and Jews: Troubled Past, Brighter Future* (Lanham, MD: Rowman & Littlefield, 2007).

However, as the subtitle of this work indicates, a new atmosphere of dialogue has slowly developed, particularly with regard to competing Polish and Jewish narratives of the Holocaust. The paradigm shift is not complete (anti-Semitic episodes and sentiment continue to exist in Poland), but it is certainly very marked, based on numerous factors, including energetic work by Polish government and NGOs, significantly closer ties with Israel, the

Jewish tour groups that come now to Poland still largely focus their attention on the death camps rather than learning about or being inspired by narratives focusing on the colossal spiritual and cultural achievements of an illustrious Polish Jewry over 1,000 years, there are grounds for confidence that that model will slowly but steadily change as well.

One of the key modes of the way in which museums in general can bring about the transformation of ideas derives from the opportunities that they offer to supply new narratives for recontextualizing Jewish histories. "Narratives" and "histories" are deliberately here in the plural, echoing what Barbara Kirshenblatt-Gimblett calls "the chorus of voices" which are to be found in POLIN Museum.[3] Methodologically speaking, this is in any case by necessity. The essence of Jewish existence, even from ancient times, is diversity, as Moshe Rosman has noted; Jewish history must take the form of separate histories of numerous communities, each of which has constructed Jewishness differently—there cannot be one grand narrative that seamlessly integrates the sociocultural histories of all the Jewish communities that have existed in the Diaspora over the past two thousand years.[4] This is why it is better to speak about Jewish identities, in the plural,[5] and of Jewish cultures, also in the plural.[6] What Barbara Kirshenblatt-Gimblett's "chorus of voices" in POLIN Museum draws attention to is precisely the plurality of approaches which today's generation needs to absorb—specifically, of course, in counterbalancing the prevalent idea that popular knowledge of the Polish Jewish past, as based entirely in Yiddish-land or Shtetl-land, is adequate in order to make sense of it. It isn't.

---

    emergence of Poland from behind the Iron Curtain, important Polish–Jewish reconciliation initiatives in the USA as well as Catholic–Jewish reconciliation (especially as promoted by the Polish pope John Paul II), the rise of considerable interest among Poles in Jewish culture (and their participation in Jewish culture festivals), and the new Jewish cultural revival in Poland. Of particular importance has been the emergence of a new generation of historians, both in Poland and abroad, who in addition to specialist monographs have contributed papers to the annual *Polin: Studies in Polish Jewry,* following a landmark conference in Oxford in 1984; all this has facilitated the scholarly reexamination of Jewish prejudices, Polish apologetics, and of other competing or polemical narratives, together with the opening up of subjects that were sensitive or hitherto taboo under communism (see Antony Polonsky, "Polish-Jewish Relations since 1984: Reflections of a Participant," ibid., 121–33).

3 Kirshenblatt-Gimblett, "Theater of History," 34–35.
4 Moshe Rosman, *How Jewish is Jewish History?* (Oxford: Littman Library of Jewish Civilization, 2007), 53.
5 Certainly, as regards today's Jewish world; see *Jewish Identities in the New Europe,* ed. Jonathan Webber (London: Littman Library of Jewish Civilization, 1994).
6 Thus, David Biale's monumental *Cultures of the Jews: A New History* (New York: Schocken Books, 2002).

Polish Jews lived in Poland, and they were fully engaged in that environment, as part of the texture of Polish social life. There is no master narrative or simple stereotype available as an intellectual guide to find one's way through the complexity of the subject (stereotypes are pretty useless as a guide to reality, in any case); and so museum visitors are encouraged to become aware not only of different modes of behavior but also the spectrum of interpretations, especially as regards a wide range in the nature of Polish–Jewish relations in different contexts and especially during the Holocaust. This is what the museum wants to show.[7]

On the other hand, Rosman has wondered whether, in a museum context, alternative histories, competing narratives, or the presentation of historical vicissitudes and oscillations may simply confuse the ordinary visitor.[8] Maybe he is right, and maybe there are specific museums where it would not work; but in my experience ordinary museum visitors can often be deeply gratified when they are shown that the subject that they have come to learn about can be approached in different ways, perhaps each of them with some measure of truth, even if not the whole truth. For those who prefer the coherence of harmony in their understanding of the world, the exposure to competing narratives may (in theory) seem like a cacophony. But the dissonance of a cacophony may on the other hand challenge people to think again about their stereotypes, and to emerge from their museum experience feeling that they have had some profound encounter with the subject. So, in this context I find the notion of cacophony useful, and will be returning to it below.

I cannot go into any detail in this brief essay about the full range that is available in present-day Poland, including many temporary museum exhibitions, which offer new narratives. For example, a recent temporary exhibition in Kraków about the art of Maurycy Gottlieb (1856–79) was provocatively entitled "In Search of Identity"—and indeed it did make an effort to explain the complexity of Maurycy Gottlieb's thinking about being both Jewish and Polish.[9] A cacophony, perhaps; but ordinary Jewish visitors to that exhibition

---

7 Moshe Rosman, "Categorically Jewish, Distinctly Polish: The Museum of the History of Polish Jews and the New Polish-Jewish Metahistory," *JSIJ Jewish Studies, An Internet Journal* 10 (2012): 361–87, accessed April 1, 2016, www.biu.ac.il/js/JSIJ/10-2012/Rosman.pdf; I am grateful to Antony Polonsky for this source.

8 Ibid., 364.

9 "I am both Polish and Jewish," he wrote in a letter to a painter friend, "and I want to work for the two nations" (cited in Maria Milanowska, "Maurycy Gottlieb—In Search of Identity: The Artist's Biographical Outline," in *Maurycy Gottlieb: In Search of Identity* [exhibition companion volume] (Łódź, 2014), 48–67; at 59). The subject is further explored in a nuanced

would doubtless have learned something they previously didn't know. But to illustrate more broadly the scope of the new museum narratives I shall restrict myself here to two museums with which I am familiar—the Auschwitz museum and the Galicia Jewish Museum in Kraków—and briefly outline the alternative histories that these museums present.

MULTIPLE NARRATIVES AT THE AUSCHWITZ MUSEUM

The Auschwitz museum now has about 1.7 million visitors a year. It is of course impossible to say how many of them are Jewish, though Israelis account for about 61,000.[10] The principal purpose of Israeli tour groups to Auschwitz, and especially the 10,000 or so who come each year on the March of the Living, is (as is well known) to consolidate an ethnocentric, nationalist narrative which emphasizes the fragility of Jewish life in the Diaspora, a teleology which presupposes the historical inevitability of the genocide against the Jews, and the survival of the Jewish people after the Holocaust especially in the State of Israel. However, the Auschwitz museum does not really present that narrative at all; it has quite a different story to tell.

During communist times, the Auschwitz museum presented itself as a symbol of *Polish* victimhood under the fascist German occupation; and the Holocaust was deliberately marginalized. The former camp at Birkenau, which was where the overwhelming majority of the approximately one million Jewish victims of Auschwitz were murdered in gas chambers, was left to rot; it steadily became overgrown with vegetation, although a substantial monument was installed there, between the ruins of two of the gas chambers.[11] Since 1989,

---

essay by Ezra Mendelsohn, "Maurycy Gottlieb: A Jewish Artist?," (ibid., 116–25), where he weighs up the complex evidence showing that Gottlieb was a creative universalist living between two worlds, wishing (justifiably) to be accepted both as a Polish artist and also as a Jewish artist creating Jewish art.

10 The figures for visitor numbers have been steadily climbing for a number of years: they reached one million in 2007, 1.5 million in 2014, and most recently 1.7 million in 2015. These statistics are provided in the museum's annual reports, available on its website (http://auschwitz.org/en/museum); for the 2015 figures, including the number of visitors from Israel in 2015, see a news report posted on this website on January 4, 2016.

11 For a detailed study of the Auschwitz museum during this period, see Jonathan Huener, *Auschwitz, Poland, and the Politics of Commemoration, 1945–1979* (Athens, OH: Ohio University Press, 2003). The monument in Birkenau was architecturally designed in a grand manner, as a setting for important commemorative ceremonies, although there are also smaller monuments elsewhere at the site used by specific victim groups, such as the Gypsy (Sinti and Roma) monument in the former Gypsy camp.

however, the museum has steadily revised this ethnic Polish narrative. The International Auschwitz Council was established, mainly for the purpose of discussing and supervising these revisions. I was a member of the council for over 20 years, and in that capacity had the opportunity to propose and then implement a number of changes—for example, that the outdoor information plaques would be in Hebrew, alongside Polish and English. Although a long overdue new core exhibition is still in preparation, the rigorously trained official guides at the Auschwitz museum have now moved very substantially to incorporate a Jewish narrative alongside the Polish master narrative—and, as part of this process, Birkenau has been cleaned up and substantially museologized. The Auschwitz museum in that sense is an excellent example of the wider mainstream trend in the new generation since 1989 to present the Jewish experience as an integral part of the Polish historical narrative. This bifocal approach can be witnessed, for example, in the large official ceremonies in Birkenau marking the major anniversaries of the liberation of the camp in 1945. At the most recent of these, at the seventieth anniversary ceremony in 2015, three survivors were invited to speak: two of them were Jewish and one was Polish. They spoke powerfully, even if what they provided—alongside the presentation by museum staff of formal, historical facts—was merely episodic, disconnected fragments. Technically, it might be thought that to combine and indeed integrate survivor testimony with the results of the museum's historical research would yield an intellectual cacophony. However, even if an educated observer might notice the contradictions and incongruities as between the two methodologies and rules of evidence, I don't think ordinary people find this confusing—many tour groups routinely bring survivors with them for their additional comments, which are valued by their audiences in terms of the emotional layer they bring to the subject. After all, what survivors offer is simply their personal experience of the historical Auschwitz, what they say Auschwitz was "really like." Survivors' accounts are in a different linguistic register and are simply understood as complementary to the museum's bifocal historical narrative and identity.[12]

But there are at least another two kinds of narrative available at Auschwitz today—first, the museum's national exhibitions, presenting a mosaic of memories, including a Hungarian narrative, a French narrative, a Sinti and Roma narrative, a Jewish narrative, and so on; and, secondly, a humanist narrative,

---

12 This is not to say that the development of a bifocal narrative and identity has been without controversy—far from it, even if the post-1989 inclusion of the Jewish experience at the historical Auschwitz has certainly gone a long way to satisfy ordinary Jewish sensitivities. Details of such controversies, however, are beyond the scope of this brief essay.

presenting Auschwitz as a universal subject regarding the propensity of humanity in general to undertake state-sponsored genocide, not at all restricted to Jews, Poles, Hungarians, Sinti and Roma, and their respective narratives. Does the existence of these competing narratives and their chorus of voices confuse the visitors? I don't think so. If anything, this museological incoherence demonstrates not only the multidimensionality of the subject, but also it helps unpack the fundamentally subversive nature of genocide, which for a universalist-minded visitor cannot be adequately grasped in a smooth, unproblematized documentary style that follows just one narrative or frame of reference—that would be too neat, too simple, too domesticated. In that sense, the cacophony is entirely appropriate. The Auschwitz museum is a cemetery, but it is also not a cemetery; it is a symbol, but it is also a real place, not at all a symbol; and, in addition, it is a museum and also a theater for the enactment of memorial events.[13] The average Jewish visitor does not look for an inclusive, transcultural view of these multiple narratives, although the museum does its job correctly by making them available. Museums may indeed in general be well placed to provide such dissonant historiographies and alternative pasts; the cacophony is present, but it is not usually imposed on visitors at Auschwitz unless they seek it out by giving themselves a wider perspective of the site (for example, by visiting the series of national exhibitions). After all, the average Jewish visitors and their tour guides do what pilgrims do everywhere—they visit only those places and hear only those stories and commentaries which are of direct interest to them, and they ignore the physical and conceptual spaces in between. Even if they are physically surrounded at the Auschwitz museum by huge crowds of non-Jewish visitors, no contact is made with them. They tend to come as single-interest groups, rather than in multiethnic groups specifically to study alongside young Germans or Poles, or interested in obtaining a differently nuanced, recontextualized understanding through exposure to universalist approaches of Christian or Buddhist fellow visitors. But the important thing is that there are indeed agencies nowadays who do promote multiethnic visiting and multidimensional programming—and an educated interest in participating in such groups is markedly growing, even to some extent among Jews.[14] The awareness of multiple narratives

---

13 For an exploration of these dissonant attributes, see Jonathan Webber, "The Kingdom of Death as a Heritage Site: Making Sense of Auschwitz," in *A Companion to Heritage Studies*, ed. William Logan, Máiréad Nic Craith, and Ullrich Kockel (Malden, MA: John Wiley & Sons Inc., 2016), 115–32.

14 In Oświęcim, these agencies include the Auschwitz Jewish Centre, the Centre for Dialogue and Prayer, and the International Youth Meeting Centre.

and the chorus of voices at Auschwitz is an important new feature of the twenty-first-century realities.

MULTIDIMENSIONAL NARRATIVE AT THE GALICIA JEWISH MUSEUM

The Galicia Jewish Museum is a small private institution located in a prewar vernacular building in the Kazimierz district of Kraków; it opened in 2004, on a shoestring budget. It consists of a core photographic exhibition, as well as space for two temporary exhibitions and an education room, as well as a café and a large bookstore specializing in books on Jewish subjects and the Holocaust. I curated the core photographic exhibition, called "Traces of Memory," and wrote a companion volume.[15] It is not at all an exhibition of Polish Jewish history arranged chronologically. Rather, in line with my professional approach as an anthropologist, it portrays just the present-day realities, using color photos arranged thematically; there are no (black-and-white) historical photographs. The exhibition popularizes the subject for visitors, taking them not on a time journey back into the past but rather accompanying them in the present— and specifically to offer a post-Holocaust narrative focusing on the dramatic changes that have happened to Jewish culture in Poland, characterized by the simultaneity of contradictions and paradoxes as they exist today. Among the many disadvantages of offering a present-day approach to the subject is that by definition I could not show Polish Jewish history as such, though that is rectified as far as possible in my captions to the photos, including brief reference to such things as the historical "at-homeness" of Polish Jews in Poland alongside moments of anti-Jewish violence. On the other hand, one advantage was that I could present the persistence of popular stereotypes or simplified,

---

15 In 2016, the museum completed two major expansion initiatives: one was to take over and modernize an adjoining building, a project which enlarged its exhibition space and meeting rooms by 50 percent; the other was to expand and refresh the "Traces of Memory" exhibition, for which I updated the captions and selected more than fifty new photos taken by Jason Francisco, a film and media studies scholar from Emory University (Atlanta, Georgia). For the companion volume, see Jonathan Webber, *Rediscovering Traces of Memory: The Jewish Heritage of Polish Galicia* (Oxford: Littman Library of Jewish Civilization, 2009). "Polish Galicia" refers to that part of the former Austro-Hungarian province of Galicia which is within the present-day borders of Poland, occupying much of the southern part of the country today; what follows below refers only to this territory. Eastern Galicia, today in Ukraine, is the subject of a separate photographic exhibition in the museum; it was curated by Jason Francisco, who also prepared his own companion volume, *An Unfinished Memory: Jewish Heritage and the Holocaust in Eastern Galicia*, a bilingual Polish–English edition published by the Galicia Jewish Museum in 2014.

mythologized subjective memories of the imagined past, since they are part of the present-day realities; and that the exhibition could then go on to challenge and problematize them.

The exhibition is divided into five sections or themes; and the photos were taken in about fifty different places in southern Poland, inside the former borders of old Galicia. The opening section directly presents the popular Jewish stereotype that Poland is nothing but a vast Jewish graveyard. All that this first section includes is the raw, shocking sight of ruins and desolation—for example, photos of ruined synagogues or ruined Jewish cemeteries. But the following section of the exhibition then moves on from the ruins of the past and explicitly contradicts that theme—by showing photos which offer glimpses of the pre-Holocaust Jewish world that can still be seen today (for example, synagogues or Jewish cemeteries that are in reasonably good condition, either because they were never damaged or because they have been restored). In fact, to achieve its objective, the five sections of the exhibition are intended to articulate a multidimensional view—in other words, that today's realities encompass profound diversity in their range of meanings and so introduce the visitor to these different mental landscapes and messages. The diversity of modern Jewish identities is clear from the cemeteries. For example, we show tombstones with inscriptions only in Hebrew, some of them visited by Orthodox Jewish pilgrims who believe in the inherent sanctity of this country because of the outstanding rabbi scholars who lived here; but we also show that even in the early twentieth century (let alone today) there were Polish Jews who did not live in a Yiddish-land or Shtetl-land but were conscious of their *Polish* Jewish identity, as some of their tombstone inscriptions are in monolingual Polish, and some with both languages. We also show tombstones marking the graves of victims of Polish anti-Jewish violence. The third section, which shows photos of the different kinds of landscape settings where local events of the Holocaust took place, are in the center of the exhibition—in other words, the exhibition's narrative does not either begin with the Holocaust nor does it end with the Holocaust, something which of course POLIN Museum has consciously done as well.[16] What then follows the Holocaust section is a fourth section focusing

---

16 Kirshenblatt-Gimblett, "Theater of History," 30. Of course the idea of not ending with the Holocaust was operationalized in POLIN Museum by including a substantial section of its own on the post-Holocaust history of the Polish Jews. In the Galicia Jewish Museum, the thinking behind this was rather different: the "Traces of Memory" exhibition does not in any case follow chronological order, for, if so, the second section (glimpses of the pre-Holocaust Jewish world) would have come first, followed by the Holocaust section, followed by the

on the different ways people here have coped with a difficult past—including the erasure of memory in recent decades and also the opposite of that, for example, the sustained, multifaceted attempts at memorialization, made by Poles as well as Jews. The photos for these first four sections are totally without people, symbolizing Jewish absence. But the fifth and last section reverses all that. It consists entirely of portraits of the wide range of people who are positively involved as memory-makers—scholars, politicians, Holocaust survivors, souvenir dealers, pilgrims, tourists, and students, as well as those ordinary local people of Kraków who participate in the extensive activities of the city's JCC (Jewish Community Center, established in 2008) and the massive annual Festival of Jewish Culture (established in 1988) and thereby demonstrate an interest in, and even support for, what is widely understood nowadays as the renewal or revival of Jewish culture in present-day Poland.

Altogether, these five sets of photos offer an immediacy representing the conflicting truths and the chorus of voices that coexist with each other today. What they articulate is the highly complex nature of a country which has witnessed something as catastrophic as the Holocaust. It is certainly true that in Poland today one can find ruined synagogues, ruined Jewish cemeteries, sites of former concentration camps, and the erasure of the Jewish memory; but it simply is not true that that is all that one can find in this country. There is also active memorialization in many locations as well as Jewish revival and a strong sense of Polish nostalgia for the Jewish past alongside attempts at healing. Collectively, these clearly suggest open-ended, alternative futures. It is precisely the encounter with the multiple narratives, including the contradictions, paradoxes, and incongruities, that forms the cacophonous, central message. Visitor feedback indicates that such multidimensionality is appreciated as highly instructive and as a space for critical reflection; the museum has received many awards, and TripAdvisor has recently named it as one of the top ten museums in Poland.

---

section showing the ruins. I felt that quite a different narrative structure was needed to tell the story of the Holocaust today, in the particular context of this exhibition of the post-Holocaust realities. To put this very simply: genocide turns the world upside down, and to drive the point home I resisted chronology altogether and so started the exhibition with the post-Holocaust ruins as the key present-day reality (or, in other words, presenting the result before the cause) and then proceeded to show the surviving traces of pre-Holocaust Jewish culture. Only after that does the exhibition move to the Holocaust itself, which is displayed not in terms of the perpetrators but rather the local settings of Holocaust atrocities in the Polish landscape, i.e. in forests, in open countryside, and in cities—not only in the large death camps such as Auschwitz or Bełżec.

CONCLUSION: THE CASE FOR CACOPHONY?

It is a fairly unconventional approach for a museum, since there is no fixed interpretative model and (unusually for a Jewish museum) there are no Jewish ritual objects on display; but it is based on my belief in the need to be strongly inclusive, addressing also the central fact that models and explanations of Jewish culture have continued to undergo profound changes and transformations during the years since 1989. Visitors are thus attuned to the multi-thematic, multilayered realities by being taken on a present-day itinerary across many kinds of intellectual and emotional terrain. The core exhibition is tiny—occupying just 400 square meters, it is about one-tenth of the size of POLIN Museum, and all it shows are 140 fully captioned present-day photos in color. But visitors can easily walk through it in one hour and then emerge feeling they have learned something about this difficult and indeed incoherent, tangled, and chaotic subject. The photos are superb, taken by a professional photographer (the late Chris Schwarz), supplemented in 2016 by new photos taken by Jason Francisco, and their aesthetic is what visitors remember, along with the five simple and totally accessible messages we want to communicate; and the exhibition ends on an optimistic, upbeat note—that even the visitors, by coming to the museum, are themselves memory-makers. The museum is widely regarded as a Jewish space; it is a fully active civic institution, acting as a podium for intercultural dialogue by hosting numerous cultural events on Jewish themes of all kinds, including music, films, book presentations, lectures, workshops, and conferences. In these ways, it presents a chorus of dissonant, cacophonous voices that mingle and interlock with each other, all of them needing to be heard—including the voices of the Holocaust dead, the voices of the Jews who created an outstanding Jewish civilization here in Poland, and the voices of present-day remembrancers. Performing Jewish music in such a space is not just performing Jewish music; it functions also as a post-Holocaust tribute to the destroyed culture and as a contribution to the Jewish revival. Indeed, in making sense of any particular cultural situation, one always needs to be made aware of the problems, the contradictions, the questions, and the different moods; all that is what real life includes, in any case. So, from the modest perspective of the Galicia Jewish Museum there is no doubt now that new recontextualized narratives offered by a range of museums in Poland are acting as agencies for social transformation, contributing massively to new ways of thinking.

Jewish Museums in Moscow[1]

VICTORIA MOCHALOVA

Standing inside the splendid POLIN Museum, I have no intention of comparing it with museums in Moscow, especially in terms of the extent of its narrative content: the history of the Jews in Russia began just slightly more than two hundred years ago, and really started with the partitions of Poland. Jews did not go to Russia; rather, they found themselves in it, along with their centuries-old places of settlement, a factor that must be taken into account when examining curatorial concepts. As July Gessen wrote, "In the second half of the eighteenth century Russia annexed foreign territory on which a great many united, well-organized Jews had long been living; thus Jews appeared in Russia also in large numbers, remaining moreover in the same places where they had lived for centuries."[2]

Three Jewish museums exist in Moscow. Each is different in concept, was created at a different time along different lines, and is run by different people. All, however, date from the post-Soviet era; their development would have been out of the question earlier.

Chronologically, the first Jewish museum was established in 1998 on the grounds of the huge memorial to the Great Patriotic War (the Second World War, 1941–45) on the so-called Poklonnaya Gora. This is a hill in a western suburb of Moscow (historically, that is, since today it is an exclusive district relatively close to the city center), whose name appears in fourteenth- and sixteenth-century documents. It is held that the name derived from the fact that travelers would stop there to pay their respect to the famous churches of Moscow, which for the most part no longer exist, and a saying maintains

---

1 The paper was prepared due to the grant of the Russian Scholarly Foundation №15-18-00143.
2 July I. Gessen, *Istoria evreiskogo naroda v Rossii* [The history of the Jewish nation in Russia] (Petrograd: L. Y. Ginzburg, 1916), vol. 1. Quotation taken from a more recent edition: Moscow, Jerusalem, 1993, 5.

that there were "forty times forty" of them. It was here, on this suburban hill, that important guests and foreign emissaries were "respectfully" received, and so it was here that Napoleon waited fruitlessly for the "keys" to the Kremlin. Therefore, on the anniversary of the 1812 victory over Napoleon, a fitting memorial was planned on that very spot, but the project came to fruition only in 1968, and nearby on Kutuzovsky Prospect a triumphal arch was erected (it is a partial reconstruction of the 1834 arch by the famous architect Osip Bové, which had been dismantled in 1936).

In 1958, thanks to funds raised by the city's inhabitants and subsidies provided by the state and the Moscow city authorities, a 135-hectare victory park celebrating the Great Patriotic War was established here. It now is home to an architecture and sculpture park, which was opened on the fiftieth anniversary of the end of the war, May 9, 1995, and includes a statue of Victory, the Central Museum of the Great Patriotic War,[3] the Orthodox Church of St. George the Conqueror, a memorial mosque, a chapel in memory of Spanish volunteers, and an open-air exhibit of wartime military equipment, as well as sculptures.[3]

It was on this historic site that a Jewish memorial was erected (figures nos. 1a and 1b).

Figure 1a The Museum of Jewish Heritage and Holocaust at Poklonnaia Gora. The building houses the memorial synagogue and the museum.

---

3 Muzei Pobedy (The Museum of Victory). For its website, see http://www.poklonnayag-ora.ru/?part=11; http://www.poklonnayagora.ru/?part=5; http://vtour.cmvov.ru/vtour/.

Figure 1b The Museum of Jewish Heritage and Holocaust, interior view. *Photo courtesy of the Museum of Jewish Heritage and Holocaust.*

THE SYNAGOGUE, THE MUSEUM OF JEWISH HERITAGE, AND THE HOLOCAUST[4]

The idea of establishing a Jewish museum came initially to the Research and Educational Holocaust Center,[5] which was established in June 1992 as an independent charitable organization. Its first president was the Russian historian and philosopher Mikhail Gefter (1918–95); currently, it is led by Alla Gerber, a writer, journalist, and social activist and Dr. Ilya Altman, a well-known Russian historian of the Holocaust. Some two hundred academics, journalists, social activists, teachers, and students of various nationalities have come together at the center, and regional departments have been established in ten Russian cities, as well as in Belarus, Ukraine, and Israel. In 1994, the center became a member of the International Association of Holocaust Organizations; in 1997, an interregional fund to set up a Holocaust museum was established. Work now began

---

4 Khram pamiati evreev—zhertv Kholokosta [Sanctuary for the memory of Jews—victims of the Holocaust]; for its website, see http://www.rjc.ru/rus/site.aspx?SECTION-ID=415840&IID=416253; https://www.facebook.com/poklonnaya.

5 Research and Education Holocaust Foundation. See its website: http://www.holocf.ru/.

for collecting documents, as well as for finding items that would form the basis of the future museum's collections.[6] The Russian government allocated the center its own buildings; it now contains a library, a video library, a lecture hall, an exhibition hall housing a permanent display of documents, and an archive holding personal collections and possessions of former ghetto inmates, participants in the Great Patriotic War, and resisters. The guide to the center's archives[7] gives an idea of its permanently expanding holdings. The Claims Conference provides the center with financial support (from funds designated for research), as do the Russian Jewish Congress, the American Jewish Joint Distribution Committee (the Joint), as well as private individuals; the center receives specific grants from the president of Russia and the State Academic Fund.

Finally, in 1998 the dream became a reality, and a Holocaust museum (its full name is "The Museum of Jewish Heritage and Holocaust") was established by the Russian Jewish Congress, with support from city authorities. This was a significant event in modern Russia: President Boris Yeltsin and the mayor of Moscow, Yuri Luzhkov, who presented the synagogue with a Torah scroll, took part in the opening ceremony.

The museum's character suits the overall concept of a Great Patriotic War Memorial. The synagogue was designed by architects from Israel (Moshe Zarchi) and Russia (Vladimir Budayev), and the interior design work (with relief images of Jerusalem, Torah scrolls, and symbols of the twelve tribes of Israel) is by the well-known Israeli sculptor Frank Meisler. Three separate Jewish communities gather here for prayers (scheduled at different times) and holy days: Orthodox Ashkenazi, Reform, and Mountain Jews; there are concerts, lectures, and conferences held in conjunction with the Holocaust Center,[8] as well as other events.

The museum's display area occupies a gallery in the upper part of the synagogue and in a basement. The current director is Aleksander Engels and its principal curator is Natalia Anisina, who also coordinates educational programs at the Holocaust Center. The holdings assembled by the Holocaust Center (its co-president Dr. Ilya Altman is the museum's academic director) were a significant part in the exhibition, as was assistance from the State Historical Museum, the Museum of the History of Religion, and the largest Russian archives.

---

6 "Tsentr 'Kholokost'" [The Holocaust Centre], in *Nieprikosnovennyi zapas* [Iron rations], nos. 2–3 (40–41), 2005. On line see: http://magazines.russ.ru/nz/2005/2/ce44.html.
7 Kratkii putevoditel' po fondam [A short guide to the archives], see: http://www.holocf.ru/pages/48.
8 For instance, on June 22 (the day of the Nazi attack on the USSR), 2015 an international forum, "The Holocaust: 70 Years On" was held; see http://www.holocf.ru/news/1049.

Although the curatorial narrative is quite traditional, the museum has no parallels in Russia or the former USSR.

The exhibition display has two parts: the first (in the gallery) is devoted to the history of Jews in the Russian and Soviet empires, to religious and daily life (it holds displays of ritual items and traditional articles), and to the shtetl, where the display is influenced by Marc Chagall's paintings. Materials illustrate the history of the Jews from the time they settled in Russia, reflecting their contribution to Russian culture, their role in the country's economic development, and their defense of the tsarist army. The exhibition also covers tragic episodes in the history of Russia's Jews: their life in the Pale of Settlement, pogroms, persecution (in tsarist Russia more than four hundred regulations limited Jews' rights, their work, places of residence, culture, education, and religious rites).

The second—larger and principal—part of the museum (on the lower level) focuses on the war and the Holocaust: presented here are documents, photographs, lists of people shot, letters written from the ghettos, memoirs of Jewish soldiers and officers who fought at the front in the Great War (some 500,000, of whom more than 150 were awarded the superior Hero of the Soviet Union medal), material on the history of Jewish partisan groups, and mention of the involvement of Jews in resistance movements in occupied lands.

A film, produced for the museum by the Moscow Dixi Film Association using Nazi footage on the "final solution of the Jewish question," is shown in the restored cinema hall, which has six screens. One of the first films to be screened in this great hall was the Holocaust-themed *Free to Cry*, by the British film producer Garry Scott-Irvine and the Scottish composer and poet Bréon George Riddell, presented to the museum by its producers. It was filmed at the Berlin Holocaust Memorial and contains, as a soundtrack, Henryk Górecki's *Symphony of Sorrowful Songs* (No. 3, Op. 36).[9]

Another area focuses on the Righteous Among the Nations—Russians, Ukrainians, and Belarusians who saved Jews and thus put their own lives at risk. One example highlights Father Aleksey Glagolev, son of the famous theologian who spoke in defense of Mendel Beilis at his celebrated trial in 1913. Glagolev hid Jews in the bell tower of his church in occupied Kiev, while his wife gave her identity papers to a Jewish woman, living for a year without documents and thus exposing herself daily to mortal danger. The museum continues to do research to help identify people as Righteous Among the Nations.

"Without the past there is no future" states a motto on a wall of the synagogue. These words guide the museum's academic staff as they organize

---

9   Bréon Rydell, *Free to Cry*. This can be seen on: https://vimeo.com/77217903, accessed 12.20.2017.

commemorations of the war and the Holocaust, temporary displays, and conduct educational work and outreach, especially among school-age children.

The Museum of Jewish History in Russia (MJHR)[10] opened on May 18, 2011 (figures nos. 2a and 2b).[11] A private museum holding ethnographic material and historical documents, as well as works of art dating from the period when a significant proportion of the Jewish people lived in Russia, it is above all a museum of culture, art, and ethnology. Its founder and owner is the writer, journalist, businessman, and member of the Presidium of the Russian Jewish Congress, Sergei Ustinov (figure no. 3); its director since November 2012 has been Leonid Liflyand.

Figure 2a The Museum of Jewish History in Russia. *Photo courtesy of the Museum of Jewish History in Russia*

10　Muzei Istorii Evreev v Rossii [The Museum of the History of Jews in Russia]; for its website, see http://www.mievr.ru/; http://www.youtube.com/watch?v=6ecMAH6KZ8w, http://www.mievr.ru/exposition.html; https://www.facebook.com/jewishmuseumrussia/timeline.
11　In November 2012, MJHR became a member of the Association of European Jewish Museums.

Figure 2b The Museum of Jewish History in Russia. Display devoted to Beilis affair. *Photo courtesy of the Museum of Jewish History in Russia.*

Figure 3 Sergei Ustinov, founder and owner of the museum.

Its organizers (in addition to Ustinov, the MJHR has two academic consultants from Israel, both of them art historians: Hillel/Grigori Kazovsky and Dr. Boris Khaimovich; as well as an academic director, Dr. Maria Kaspina)[12] see their main role to be the preservation of the historical memory and story of Jewish culture and tradition, as these were almost completely destroyed in Europe during the Second World War. The museum is in the midst of dynamic development: its holdings include more than four thousand authentic items, of which only one thousand can be displayed in its relatively small gallery space. The collection is constantly growing, further additions are planned, and it is anticipated that new premises will be built.

The MJHR is divided into two main departments: *traditional culture*—illustrating the community's way of life, education, philanthropy, religion, and "holy works" (synagogues and religious sites). It contains a display representing the non-Ashkenazi Jewish community's traditions and culture; and *historical processes*—showing relations between Jews and society and the authorities; Jews' participation in the economy, culture, and science; and the Soviet attempt to create Jewish autonomy. The exhibition attempts to present more than two hundred years of Jewish history in Russia, displaying accounts of people who remained faithful to their beliefs and traditions, and also of those who abandoned Judaism in order to adopt Russian culture. This is a dramatic story not only of famous industrialists and financiers, who had an enormous impact on the development of the Russian economy, but also of ordinary craftsmen and engineers, lawyers and doctors. It is also a story of writers, artists, musicians, and scholars, without whom Russian literature, art, and science would be unthinkable. It is a tale of traditionalists and revolutionaries, liberals and conservatives, about people who at the end of the day created a specific type of Russian and Soviet Jewishness. This story is not well known to the outside world, and it continues to be hidden by a veil of myth and slander, which are food for prejudice and misunderstandings.

Specific subjects in the collection's departments[13] are *traditional Jewish life* (showing the life cycle and items in everyday use, the synagogue and religious life, holy days); *education, charity, and culture* (literature, art, the stage); *Jewish crafts and professions*; and *politics* (no national minority in tsarist Russia had as many political organizations as did the Jews). The political area includes sections

---

12   The staff names can be found at http://www.mievr.ru/page.html?id=3.
13   http://www.mievr.ru/exposition.html. See also: *Museum of Jewish History in Russia*. Edited by Hillel (Grigory) Kazovsky, Maria Kaspina, Boris Khaimovich. In 2 Vols. (Moscow: ///, 2015).

on Jews and the Russian throne, and on the Soviet period. Since from the second half of the nineteenth century Moscow was (and still is) a significant center of Jewish life in Russia, a special section is devoted to its community.

Although most of the exhibits highlight Ashkenazi Jewry, as early as May 2012 the MJHR opened a section devoted to the history and ethnography of non-Ashkenazi Jews (Bukharan, Mountain, and Georgian Jews).[14]

The MJHR also organizes temporary exhibits, on its own premises or, due to its limited gallery space, at other venues. Such exhibits have included "Pages of a Battlefield Album,"[15] an exhibition from its archival holdings devoted to Jewish participants in the war.[16] On February 10, 2013, the MJHR hosted representatives of the Association of the Jewish Historical Institute from Warsaw as well as POLIN Museum of the History of Polish Jews. Polish colleagues expressed admiration at the holdings and at the speed with which such a collection had been assembled.

The third institution, the Jewish Museum and Tolerance Center (JMTC),[17] was developed to be a form of "edutainment," as well as a widely appreciated cultural center. The idea for its creation belongs to the Federation of Jewish Communities of Russia (FJCR),[18] specifically to its president R. Alexander Boroda, to R. Boruch Gorin (the FJCR's head of public relations, the editor-in-chief of the magazine Lechaim as well as the Knizhniki publishing house), and to the chief rabbi of Russia, Berel Lazar. The story of its founding is neither simple nor short. In 2001, city authorities granted the FJCR the Bakhmetevsky bus depot, which was in a state of disrepair. The site is a Constructivist monument built in 1927 by architects Konstantin Melnikov and Vladimir Shukhov, containing more than 8,500 m^2 (figures nos. 4 and 5) and is located near the Moscow Jewish Community Center. Almost a century after the rise of the Russian avant-garde, this architectural masterpiece had been designated as the platform for a high-tech museum in Russia. The FJCR now faced an exceptional challenge, since this monument to Russian Constructivism had to be refurbished while retaining its historic appearance, and at the same time needed to install museum facilities carefully and solicitously (figures nos. 6–8).

---

14 http://www.mievr.ru/exposition.html?id=13; http://www.mievr.ru/page.html?id=38.
15 http://www.mievr.ru/page.html?id=49.
16 Ibid.
17 http://www.jewish-museum.ru/; http://www.jewish-museum.ru/about-the-museum/museum-staff/.
18 Federatsia Evreiskikh Obshchin Rossii; for its website see http://www.feor.ru/about/.

Figure 4 The Bakhmetevskii bus depot, before reconsruction.

Figure 5 The Bakhmetevskii bus depot, before reconstruction.

The restoration work was undertaken by the Iris Foundation for development and supporting the arts, established by Daria Zhukova, who is a board member of the JMTC foundation. Starting in 2008, the Garage Center for Contemporary Culture operated for a few years in the refurbished building. At the same time an international competition was held to suggest

Figure 6 The Bakhmetevskii bus depot, after reconstruction.

Figure 7 The Bakhmetevskii bus depot, after reconstruction.

ideas about converting the building, with a view to installing a contemporary arts museum and cultural center. The originators of the museum concept decided that Ralph Appelbaum Associates, which for years had been planning the JMTC exhibition, would be the lead contractor. Victor

Figure 8 The Bakhmetevskii bus depot, after reconstruction. The museum interior.

Vekselberg, Len Blavatnik, Roman Abramovich, and others contributed to the project.[19]

For more than ten years, work was carried out to establish the collection's vision, with gathering and sorting material under the direction of an international academic board led by Professor Benjamin Nathans, and including scholars from Russia, the United States, and Israel.

The fruit of these labors, the JMTC, was opened in the Bakhmetevsky depot on November 11, 2012 (figures nos. 9–11) as a cultural and educational complex, which in addition to the permanent collection has housed temporary exhibits: "Le Corbusier—Architect of Books," "Foreigners Everywhere" (pictures from the Pomeranz Collection as part of the 5th Biennale of Contemporary Art), "Performance Now" (curated by Rose Lee Goldberg, founder and director of the Performa Festival), and others.[20] Activities also take place in the

---

19   Evreiskii Muzei i Tsentr Tolerantnosti. See its website: http://www.jewish-museum.ru/fond/.
20   I shall give as examples just a few catalogues from these shows, organized in cooperation with various institutions: *Emmanuil Yevzerikin. Photos that Have Never Existed* (2013); *Moishe Appelbaum Atelier* (2014); *The Avant-Garde and Aviation* (2014); *Andy Warhol: 10 Famous Twentieth-Century Jews* (2014); *Alienated Heaven: Contemporary Chinese Art from the DSL Collection* (2014–2015); *Russian Jews and the First World War* (2014–2015); *Alfred Eisenstaedt—the Father of Photojournalism* (2015).

Part One • Museological Questions

Figure 9 The unveiling of the JMTC, November 11, 2012. *Photo by Victoria Mochalova.*

Figure 10 The unveiling of the JMTC, November 11, 2012. *Photo by Victoria Mochalova.*

Figure 11 The unveiling of the JMTC. Boruch Gorin, one of the Museum directors, speaks at the exhibition. *Photo by Victoria Mochalova.*

Research Center,[21] the Tolerance Center,[22] the Education Center,[23] and the Children's Center.[24] Extensive artistic programs (exhibitions, workshops, film demos, and publications) are put on by the Avant-Garde Center.[25] The Center is thus a multifunction cultural institution open to all (in 2014, some 170,000 people visited).[26] Its permanent collection recounts the history of Russia from Catherine the Great up to the present day (figures nos. 12–15).[27] Unlike traditional museums, the Museum and Tolerance Center contains interactive

---

21 http://www.jewish-museum.ru/research-center/.
22 http://www.jewish-museum.ru/tolerance-center/.
23 http://www.jewish-museum.ru/education-center/.
24 http://www.jewish-museum.ru/childrens-center/.
25 http://www.jewish-museum.ru/news/24-iyunya-v-evreyskom-muzee-i-tsentre-tolerant-nosti-sostoyalas-press-konferentsiya-na-kotoroy-byla-p/.
26 See, for instance, http://www.jewish-museum.ru/events/.
27 See the splendid publications on this exhibition: *Atlas istorii Evreev v Rossii. Po materialam Evreiskogo muzeia i Tsentra tolerantnosti* [Atlas of the History of Jews in Russia. Based on the Materials in the Jewish Museum and Center for Toleration], ed. Boruch Gorin, assisted by Maria Kaspina, Pavel Zhuravel, Anatolii Vorobiev, Uri Gershovich, and Ilya Barkussky (Moscow: Jewish Museum, 2013).

Figure 12 The JMTC permanent exhibition.

Figure 13 The JMTC permanent exhibition.

Figure 14 The JMTC interior.

Figure 15 The JMTC permanent exhibition.

exhibits. Twelve themed pavilions are equipped with panoramic screens and interactive audiovisual equipment (utilizing archival photographs and footage, documents, and interviews).[28]

An important event in the history of the JMTC occurred with the incorporation of Joseph Isaac Schneerson's library[29]—a set of Hebrew books and manuscripts from the famous Lubavitcher rabbi's collection. This collection had been held in the Russian State Library, and was the subject of a great many discussions, disputes, and U.S. court cases.

Moscow's Jewish museums cooperate extensively with other cultural institutions. An example was the exhibition "To See and to Remember: Sacral Aesthetics of Jewish Visual Culture" (September 21–October 14, 2012; figure no. 16),[30] organized on the premises of the M. I. Rudomino All-Russian State Library for Foreign Literature. A number of holdings were displayed: mizrahi, amulets, folk paintings, portraits of rabbis, and yahrzeit tables.

The MJHR was a partner in the exhibition "The High Points of the Habima and GOSET Jewish Theatres in Russia (1919–1949)" (February 20–March 19, 2015), at the Bakhrushin State Central Theatre Museum. One of the exhibition's consultants was the MJHR historian Hillel/Grigori Kazovsky. For the first time in Russia an exhibition on this scale of the history of Russian

---

28 http://www.jewish-museum.ru/about-the-museum/permanent-exhibition/.
29 http://www.jewish-museum.ru/libraries/schneerson-library/.
30 For the catalog see *Videt' i pomnit'. Estetika sakral'nogo v evreiskoj vizual'noj kul'ture. Kollektsia Muzeia istorii evreev Rossii* [To see and remember. The sacred aesthetic in Jewish visual culture. The collection of the Museum of the History of the Jews of Russia], eds. Grigorii Kazovsky, Boris Khaimovich, and Maria Kaspina (Moscow: Jewish Museum, 2012).

Figure 16 Poster of the exhibition "To See and to Remember".

theater was held. Six sections covered the eras from the "renaissance of Jewish culture" (the end of the nineteenth/start of the twentieth centuries) to the sad end of its theatrical age.[31] Another example—the exhibition "Good Luck in the New Year! Jewish Autumn Holidays in Decorative Art from the Collections of the Museum of Jewish History in Russia" (September 4–September 30, 2013)

---

31 http://www.mievr.ru/event.html?id=113; http://bakhrushin.theatre.ru/branches/gctm/ex/jewishtheatre/.

  GOSET is an acronym for Gosudarstvenny Evreiskiy Teatr (the State Jewish Theatre), which performed in Yiddish and whose end was tragic. After the brutal murder of its principal director from 1929—Solomon Mikhoels—as well as the arrest of many Jewish cultural activists, the theatre was closed down in 1949. Fate was kinder to *Habima* which performed in Hebrew. After a 1948 tour it did not return to the USSR and exists to this day in Israel.

Jewish Museums in Moscow | 167

Figure 17 Poster of the exhibition "Good Luck in the New Year!".

held at the JMTC, displaying exhibits, most of which had never been shown before in Russia or abroad (figures nos. 17–18).[32]

---

32 http://www.mievr.ru/page.html?id=51.

A major exhibition, "Contemporaries of the Future: Jewish Artists in the Avant-Garde" was held at the JMTC (March 30–May 24, 2015), in conjunction with the MJHR (curated by Josif Bakshtein, Hillel/Grigory Kazovsky, and Maria Nasimova). The exhibition displayed 140 works by thirty-four twentieth-century artists from the holdings of Russian museums and private collections, in three sections: "The First Russian Avant-garde" (1910–1930), "The Second Avant-garde" (1956–1970), and "Moscow Conceptualism and Soc-art" (1956–1970).[33]

The exhibition "Between Two Worlds: Personal Memory and Immortal Souls in Jewish Culture" (July 15–August 23, 2015) was a joint project of the MJHR and the JMTC. Yahrzeit cards and other ritual objects were displayed, as well as works of folk art linked to funerals and Jewish commemorative rites, expressing the idea of the continuity of "the two worlds," as well as the existence of the human soul. Most of the items had never been exhibited before.

Internal cooperation between the Jewish museums, as well as external cooperation with other cultural institutions, including those abroad, appears to be a highly positive factor that enriches the activities of each

Figure 18 At the exhibition "Good Luck in the New Year!" *Photo by Victoria Mochalova.*

---

33 See the catalogue *Sovremenniki budushchego. Evreiskie khudozhniki v russkom avangarde* [Contemporaries of the Future. Jewish Artists in the Russian Avant-Garde] (Moscow: Jewish Museum, 2015).

organization taking part in the cultural exchange. It is now possible to talk of a cycle of joint artistic and educational projects, whose aim is to popularize Jewish culture, history, and art, allowing us to overcome the barriers between cultures.

Translated from Polish by Jarosław Garliński

The Challenges of New Work in History and Education about the Holocaust in Poland

JOLANTA AMBROSEWICZ-JACOBS

During the postwar years through the 1990s, museums and places of remembrance in former death camps in Poland focused mainly on the occupation, the martyrdom of the Polish nation, and patriotic education. During the 1980s, the subject of the Holocaust began to appear more often in scholarly studies, publications, and, gradually, after the fall of communism, in school curricula and displays in museums and places of remembrance. A period of non-remembrance was followed by competition over who had suffered most, reinforced by Polish messianism of romantic lineage, an attitude among Poles that ascribed to the Polish nation moral superiority.[1] The hypothesis that this led to a competition in suffering, especially in relation to Jews, was put forward by a group of scholars in Warsaw, under the direction of Ireneusz Krzemiński and Aleksandra Jasińska-Kania, who studied the attitudes of Poles toward other nations. The hypothesis was supported by Marcin Kula, Antoni Sułek, Zdzisław Mach, Michał Bilewicz, and Anna Stefaniak.[2]

---

1 "Opowiadać o ludzkim cierpieniu" [Telling stories of human suffering], Andrzej Franaszek in conversation with Professor Maria Janion, *Tygodnik Powszechny*, no. 6 (November 2, 2007): 8.
2 See Ireneusz Krzemiński, ed., *Czy Polacy są antysemitami? Wyniki badania sondażowego* [Are Poles anti-Semites? Results of a public opinion survey] (Warsaw: Oficyna Naukowa, 1996); Aleksandra Jasińska-Kania, "Zmiany postaw Polaków wobec różnych narodów i państw" [Changes in the attitudes of Poles towards different nations and states], in *Bliscy*

This battle for victim status blocks empathy for the suffering of others and prevents the perception of the complexity of Polish attitudes toward Jews during the Holocaust; such complexity is revealed in recent historical scholarship, discussed later in this essay.

A report by the Center for the Future of Museums, under the auspices of the American Alliance (formerly Association) of Museums, titled "Museums and Society 2034," shows the evolution of the role of museums, pointing out factors that have led to changes in their relationship with visitors, and how passive museum narratives have been transformed into interactive ones.[3] POLIN Museum of the History of the Polish Jews has the opportunity to change the attitudes of Poles, especially younger ones, toward Jews, and toward the Holocaust and its memory, on the basis of careful planning and systematically applied research. The observations in this essay on the subject of the museum refer exclusively to the Holocaust Gallery and, in light of the writer's own research, to teaching about the Holocaust in Poland and the attitudes of young Poles. It should be pointed out that these observations, some in the form of suggestions, are less important than visitors' reactions to the gallery and the effects of visiting the exhibit. I imagine that for a great many young Poles, who cannot easily get to museums and places of remembrance connected with the Holocaust,[4] the Holocaust Gallery might be the only source of education on this subject, in addition to or in place of teaching in school. Indeed, many schools plan trips to Warsaw.

---

    i dalecy: studia nad postawami wobec innych narodów, ras i grup etnicznych [Near and far; studies on attitudes towards other nations, races and ethnic groups], ed. Aleksandra Jasińska-Kania, vol. 2 (Warsaw: Uniwersytet Warszawski, 1992), 219–46; Marcin Kula, *Nośniki pamięci historycznej* [The carriers of historical memory] (Warsaw: Wydawnictwo DiG, 2002); Antoni Sułek, "Zwykli Polacy patrzą na Żydów" [The Ordinary Poles look at the Jews], *Nauka* 1 (2010): 7–23, http://www.pan.poznan.pl/nauki/N_110_01_Sulek.pdf; Zdzisław Mach, "The Holocaust in Public Memory and Collective Identity of Poles," in *Fact and Lies in the Common Knowledge on the Holocaust. Conference Materials, 2005.11.17*, ed. Daria Nałęcz and Mariusz Edgaro (Warsaw: Oficyna Wydawnicza "Aspra-JR," 2006), 99–103; Michał Bilewicz and Anna Stefaniak, "Can a Victim Be Responsible? Anti-Semitic Consequences of Victimhood-based Identity and Competitive Victimhood in Poland," in *Responsibility: A Crossdisciplinary Perspective*, ed. B. Bokus (Warsaw: Studio Leksem, 2013), 69–77.

3 *Museums and Society 2034: Trends and Potential Futures*, Center for the Future of Museums (Washington, DC, 2008), http://www.aam-us.org/docs/center-for-the-future-of-museums/museumssociety2034.pdf.

4 Part of the problem is true not only in Poland and was discussed in a report based on studies by the Fundamental Rights Agency (FRA) in 2010. Attention should also be drawn to the lack of funds, despite a declaration by EU ministers of education and culture, to the need for parents to pay for visits, logistical problems, and lack of time during the school year.

Special attention should be devoted to teachers, partly because of the reform introduced by the minister of education in December 2008 that excluded the subject of the Holocaust from the secondary school history syllabus, while leaving it in the social studies and Polish literature syllabi. This change was prompted by the desire for an in-depth study of recent history once over the course of a school education, instead of relegating it to two more superficial topics at the end of the third form in academic secondary schools and then in postsecondary schools, where time was limited because of final examinations. Until systematic changes are made in this reform, it is clearly necessary to influence the group most affected by the 2008 reform—secondary school history teachers and postsecondary teachers of social studies and Polish. Certainly, despite the influence of the electronic media and peer groups, the attitudes of young people toward the Holocaust do depend on their teachers' attitudes, knowledge, competence, and teaching skills. Before visiting museums and places of remembrance, young people should be prepared in school by their teachers.

There is no one definition of the Holocaust or of education on the Holocaust agreed upon by state and nongovernmental institutions. Almost every significant Holocaust museum in the world adopts a slightly different definition—these are not in conflict but differ in their perspective, extent, and detail. Education about the Holocaust under the project of the European Union's Fundamental Rights Agency (FRA) has been defined as "education that takes the discrimination, persecution and destruction of the Jews by the National Socialist regime as its focus, but also includes Nazi crimes against other victim groups, both for the purpose of deeper understanding and contextualization of the Holocaust and out of a desire to acknowledge and commemorate the suffering of numerous non-Jewish victims of the Nazi era."[5]

The Holocaust Gallery at POLIN Museum rightly focuses on the fate of the Jews condemned to death, mainly on Jews from Warsaw, so its creators have adopted a different educational perspective on the history of the Holocaust from the FRA. Perhaps the UNESCO Chair for Holocaust Education at the Jagiellonian Museum, in cooperation with the museum, could examine the difference in impact between teaching about the Holocaust in the context of other victims and teaching focused exclusively on the fate of the Jews not

---

5 "Discover the Past for the Future: The Role of Historical Sites and Museums in Holocaust Education and Human Rights Education in the EU," European Union Agency for Fundamental Rights, 2011, 9, http://fra.europa.eu/sites/default/files/fra_uploads/1791-FRA-2011-Holocaust-Education-Main-report_EN.pdf.

only in terms of assimilating information but also in terms of understanding historical facts and changing attitudes. Describing the Holocaust Museum in Washington, DC, Anna Ziębińska-Witek uses the expression "the concept of imagined death."[6] Personalizing the commentary in the Holocaust Gallery in POLIN Museum, the gallery's small size (a simulacrum[7] of overcrowding in the ghetto), and the idea of the footbridge over Chłodna Street, all serve to stir the imagination and arouse empathy with the victims. Only research will show whether the exhibit's extremely effective presentation is also a useful pedagogical strategy for changing visitors' perceptions.

The variety of programs and projects on the Holocaust in Poland is rarely accompanied by reflection on the aims of teaching, program content, methodology, and evaluating their results. As Tomasz Kranz correctly observes in writing about museums located in former camps—although his remarks apply to all museums—visitors' needs and expectations require assessment:

> Recognizing and evaluating [its motivations, expectations and needs] is a key condition for improving communication with the museum-going public and, at the same time, making it possible for visitors better to absorb recent scholarship ... The experiences of traditional museums are proof of the need to conduct sociological studies on these issues.[8]

There is a lack, and not only in Poland, of constructive discussion about the following key questions: What are the aims of education on the Holocaust? Should teaching about the Holocaust be based on historical research and stress context, or it be conducted through the prism of civic engagement? What are the limits in framing the issues of Holocaust history in terms of investigations into the nature of society? What dangers are inherent in universalist approaches? What is the value of comparativist approaches?

Since the mid-1990s, I have been engaged in research into teaching about the Holocaust in schools and elsewhere (including places of remembrance). One aim of my research has been to analyze attitudes toward Jews and the

---

6 Anna Ziębińska-Witek, "Estetyki reprezentacji śmierci w ekspozycjach historycznych" [The aesthetic of representing death in historical displays at museums], in *Obóz-muzeum. Trauma we współczesnym wystawiennictwie* [Camp-museum. Trauma in contemporary display], ed. Małgorzata Fabiszak and Marcin Owsiński (Kraków: "Universitas," 2013), 39.
7 J. Baudrillard's phrase in Ziębińska-Witek, "Estetyki reprezentacji," 38.
8 Tomasz Kranz, "Muzea martyrologiczne jako przestrzenie pamięci i edukacji" [Martyrological museums as spaces of memory and education], in *Obóz-muzeum*, 59.

Holocaust in order to make possible the development of effective teaching strategies, especially where ethnocentrism, anti-Semitism, entrenched opinions, and, indeed, outright lies about Auschwitz are present in the minds of schoolchildren. My own research conducted in 1998 showed that not every educational project produces the desired positive effect in terms of attitudes toward Jews. In addition to a survey in 2008, between 2008 and 2010 I used quantitative and qualitative methods in my research into memory of the Holocaust.[9] This research focused, above all, on *postmemory* (Marianne Hirsch's term, now a key term in liberal arts research): memory is not "living" memory based on direct personal experience, but is inherited or borrowed. She also raises the question not only of how memory should be transmitted, but also of who can or should be a "guardian" of a traumatic past with which we have no personal or direct contact, but toward which we are not indifferent.

Post-memory, like memory, is not monolithic; it is full of zigzags, blank pages, oblique remarks, linguistic codes, and ubiquitous taboos. Historical facts are permanent; however, representations of them can vary, and even conflict with one another. The history of the Holocaust on Polish soil is remembered or recreated differently by Jews and by Poles. Jews remember Poles' attitudes toward Jews—the general indifference, the courage of a few, the fear of denunciations and murder. The Poles want above all to remember the courage of their ancestors and of the rescuers. They do not want to accept aspects of local memory and new research in history which show that the rescuers' attitudes were not common and that in towns under German occupation denunciation and blackmail were widespread, as was the hunting of Jews who had escaped from transports and were trying to survive in dugouts in the countryside.

Unfortunately, not enough research has been done to accompany theoretical thinking about postmemory. Postmemory is not about one's own memories, but about often traumatic memories felt by earlier generations. Since we ourselves do not return to our memories if they cause us pain, subsequent generations do. The return can be therapeutic; however, this is not the rule.

---

9 The research included a nationwide survey (N=1000, 17–18 year-olds), a focus group with eight teachers/experts (set up by the CEM Market and Public Opinion Research Institute in Kraków on April 17, 2009), an evaluation of written curricula into which the study of Jewish history and culture, as well as memory of the Holocaust, had been introduced (control group N=1110, school pupils above primary school, as well as students in tertiary education), observation of selected programs: Tykocin/Treblinka (23 pupils), Kielce (124), Lublin (11), Bodzentyn/Starachowice (54), Warsaw (15), and one-on-one interviews with teachers and NGO leaders (44) and pupils (61).

Limits of access to memory can be caused not only by self-censorship, but also by deliberate actions by state agencies. Deformation of memory is not solely a function of totalitarian systems, but can become a strategy of everyone armed with a laudable past who turns their backs on examples of shame, seeking in the past encouragement and/or compensation for real failures, or simply a lack of success. The myth of the honorable, heroic Polish past, particularly during the Second World War, is tenacious and ingrained, prevents a general group acceptance of the facts that undermine this myth.

Nevertheless, my own research demonstrates that "experimental" teaching about the Holocaust practiced by creative teachers and NGO activists that goes beyond the basic syllabus makes sense and produces statistically quantifiable effects, although they are smaller than those involved in teaching about the Holocaust expected. A greater percentage of respondents from experimental group E, when compared to control group K representing schoolchildren who had completed primary school, knew in 2008 what percentage of Poland's prewar population consisted of Jews (E, 18 percent; K, 5 percent). The average attitude on a scale of attitudes toward Jews was higher in group E (3.5) than in group K (3.2). A greater percentage of pupils from group E than in control group K defined the Holocaust as the Destruction of the Jews (E, 59 percent; K, 33 percent). A greater percentage of pupils in this group also correctly identified the number of Jewish victims of the Second World War (E, 34 percent; K, 14 percent).

From the point of view of a scholar of comparativist attitudes toward the Holocaust, the question as to whether the Holocaust Gallery in POLIN Museum will effect changes in viewing Poland's past in relationship to the Holocaust, especially among the younger generation of Poles, seems appropriate. Will it cope with the many years of absence of memory, the silences, the warping, the disfiguring, and the ubiquitous taboo on discussing individual and group collaboration on the part of Poles with the German occupier? Some Poles—and everyone was a victim during the time of the occupation's terror tactics—killed other victims, in other words, Jews in hiding. This historical fact represents a challenge for Poles' collective identity and often produces defensive reactions, including secondary anti-Semitism. How can we make this fact part of the educational process, given how often information contrary to our positive self-image is rejected, while maligned people are devalued and demonized?

Polish witnesses to the Holocaust manifest a memory that has been muffled, suppressed by a sense of guilt at the behavior of some members of their own national group and by the memory of their own victims. This memory does not include Polish Jews within the framework of the shared category of citizenship. Additionally, communist ideology denied Polish Jews the right to be present in the history of Poland. Postwar mourning embraced the Polish nation without its Jewish fellow citizens. In the studies mentioned above, nearly one-third of those surveyed felt that it was better that Poland now had fewer Jews than before the war. Among the remainder, the dominant opinion was that it was neither good nor bad (41 percent of respondents). One in four pupils had no opinion. In the postwar imagined community,[10] by now covering several generations, there is an absence of Polish Jews, outside the islands of memory created from the mid-1980s by academic institutions and NGOs, as well as local historians or involved educators.

If an historical narrative covering Polish–Jewish relations and the Holocaust began slowly to appear in transmitters of Polish memory, such as in post-1989 textbooks, this process was not accompanied by a parallel appearance of the Holocaust in ethnic Poles' collective group memory. It would be unfair to ignore the great many educational projects produced by historical museums, places of remembrance, or state institutions and NGOs, but it is too soon to speak of a community of memory, or of a common historical narrative of the Holocaust within Polish civil society. POLIN Museum has an opportunity to change the way in which Jews are perceived and bring them into civil society.

In my own research conducted in 2008, pupils were asked an open question: "What does the term 'Holocaust' mean?" A significant part of them failed to reply to the question or replied that they did not know (39 percent). Only one in three pupils identified the "Holocaust" as a term referring to the destruction of the Jews; 12 percent understood it as destruction of people in general, or of minorities in general. Over half the pupils responded that they did not know how many Jews had died during the Second World War. Barely 14 percent of those surveyed gave the correct number, and this figure leads us to speculate that the Holocaust is treated superficially in Polish schools, without deeper thought on the essence and extent of the crime. Antoni Sułek ascribes the fact that in 2011, a total of 41 percent of pupils aged fifteen through nineteen had not heard about

---

10 Benedict Anderson's phrase. See Benedict Anderson, *Imagined Communities: Reflections on the Origin and Spread of Nationalism*, rev. ed. (London: Verso, 1991).

Jedwabne (18 percent in 2002) not to a lack or a rejection of memory, but to a failure to absorb the facts.[11]

It is not impossible that this attitude toward Jews is, to some degree, the result of the perception of the Polish Jew as the Other, about which Alina Cała wrote in the 1990s, despite nearly a thousand years of common history.[12] Over the course of that common history, the Catholic church nurtured attitudes of mistrust and/or hostility toward Jews. "Father Franciszek B.," recalled Michał Głowiński,[13] "invoking the authority of the Church and the principles of faith taught that all Jews were responsible for the crucifixion, all without exception, irrespective of where and when they lived, responsible always and everywhere and that nothing could ever change that."

Only research will show what will and will not "register" with Polish schoolchildren visiting the Holocaust Gallery. To Aleida Assmann's question posed during a conference in Vienna in December 2014,[14] "Is the Holocaust still seen as a German project?" the gallery replies that it is. A large photograph of the conference hall in Wannsee, as well as photographs of participants at the conference—high-ranking officials of the Third Reich—leaves no doubt. The participation in the Holocaust of "helpers" of the Third Reich is also referred to; this essay will have more to say on the matter.

In the most recent Polish school textbooks published after the 2008 reform, the history of the Holocaust was presented in line with international scholarly standards, while the subjects of Poles' attitudes toward the Holocaust or the context of "the Righteous" raise serious concerns.[15] The newest research in history, above all the achievements of scholars at the Centrum Badań nad

---

11 Antoni Sułek, "Pamięć Polaków o zbrodni w Jedwabnem" [The crime in Jedwabne as remembered by Poles], *Nauka* 3 (2011): 39–49, http://www.pan.poznan.pl/nauki/N_311_02_Sulek.pdf.
12 Alina Cała, *The Image of the Jew in Polish Folk Culture* (Jerusalem: Magnes Press, 1995), 220.
13 Michał Głowiński, *Czarne sezony* [Black seasons] (Warsaw: Wydawnctwo Literackie, 1999), 148.
14 Seminar, "Remembrance of the Holocaust and Nazi Crimes in Post-1989 Europe: Reflecting on Competition and Conflict in European Memory International Workshop," Austrian Academy of Sciences, European Network Remembrance and Solidarity, Konstanz University, Vienna, December 15–16, 2014.
15 Jolanta Ambrosewicz-Jacobs and Robert Szuchta, "The Intricacies of Education about the Holocaust in Poland: Ten Years after the Jedwabne Debate, What Can Polish School Students Learn about the Holocaust in History Classes?," *Intercultural Education* 25, no. 4 (July 2014): 283–99.

Zagładą Żydów (Polish Center for Holocaust Research),[16] are not widely reflected in the educational process and are mentioned solely by individual educator-enthusiasts. Likewise, as Sławomir Kapralski has pointed out,[17] in the exhibit in the renovated synagogue in Dąbrowa Tarnowska there is no mention at all of Jan Grabowski's research presented in the book *Jugenjagd: Polowanie na Żydów 1942–1945*,[18] which deals with the district in which this town is located. In many European countries, there has arisen a divergence between history and memory of the Holocaust. In most but not all of them,[19] the history of the Holocaust, contrary to the latest research trends, passes over in silence the behavior of their fellow citizens toward the Jews. Historical scholarship does not penetrate public, collective memory since one of the transmitters influencing the processes of postmemory of the Holocaust, namely education, makes a large detour around the latest research. Thus, debates on Polish–Jewish relations at the time of the Holocaust as well as research in the field of education indicate that there is a gap between scholarly research and education. The

---

16 The most significant publications are Barbara Engelking, *"...szanowny panie gistapo". Donosy do władz niemieckich w Warszawie i okolicach w latach 1940-1941* ["Dear Mr Gistapo." Denunciations to the German authorities in Warsaw and the surrounding area in the years 1940–1941] (Warsaw: Wydawnictwo IFiS PAN, 2003); Jan Grabowski, *"Ja tego Żyda znam!" Szantażowanie Żydów w Warszawie 1939–1943* ["I know this Jew!" Blackmailing Jews in Warsaw 1939–1943] (Warsaw: Wydawnictwo IFiS PAN, 2004); Barbara Engelking and Dariusz Libionka, *Żydzi w powstańczej Warszawie* [Jews in Warsaw during the 1944 uprising] (Warsaw: Stowarzyszenie Centrum Badań nad Zagładą Żydów, 2009); Tadeusz Markiel and Alina Skibińska, *"Jakie to ma znaczenie, czy zrobili to z chciwości?" Zagłada domu Trynczerów* ["What difference does it make if they did it out of greed?" The murder of the Tryncer family] (Warsaw: Stowarzyszenie Centrum Badań nad Zagładą Żydów, 2011); Barbara Engelking, *"Jest taki piękny słoneczny dzień..." Losy Żydów szukających ratunku na wsi polskiej 1942–1945* ["It was such a beautiful sunny day..." The fate of Jews seeking shelter in the Polish countryside 1942–1945] (Warsaw: Stowarzyszenie Centrum Badań nad Zagładą Żydów, 2011); Jan Grabowski, *Judenjagd. Polowanie na Żydów 1942–1945. Studium dziejów pewnego powiatu* (Warsaw: Stowarzyszenie Centrum Badań nad Zagładą Żydów, 2011), English edition: *Hunt for the Jews. Betrayal and Murder in German-Occupied Poland* (Bloomington: Indiana University Press, 2013); *Zarys krajobrazu. Wieś polska wobec zagłady Żydów 1942–1945* [A sketch of the countryside. Polish village in the face of the mass murder of the Jews], ed. Barbara Engelking and Jan Grabowski and introduction by Krzysztof Persak (Warsaw: Stowarzyszenie Centrum Badań nad Zagładą Żydów, 2011); Dariusz Libionka and Laurence Weinbaum, *Bohaterowie, hochsztaplerzy, opisywacze. Wokół Żydowskiego Związku Wojskowego* [Heroes, swindlers and graphomaniacs. On the Jewish Military Union] (Warsaw: Stowarzyszenie Centrum Badań nad Zagładą Żydów, 2011).
17 A lecture at the Jewish Cultural Centre in Kraków, December 2014.
18 Grabowski, *Judenjagd. Polowanie na Żydów*.
19 In Scandinavian countries, the "black" history of the Holocaust, including collaboration, is mentioned in school textbooks (e.g., in Norway).

exceptions are committed teachers, including many graduates of the last ten years of the Center for Holocaust Studies of the Jagiellonian University and its International Summer Schools for the Study of the Holocaust.[20] Research conducted among young people in Poland in 2008 indicates that knowledge and understanding of the Holocaust in classes conducted by committed teachers who deepen their own education while working in a school are greater than in a representative sample.

Information on Poles' multiple attitudes toward Jews during the Second World War is available in the Holocaust Gallery and is visible thanks to the large size of the displays. However, accounts of cases of denunciation, murder, and death of Jews in hiding at the hands of Poles, as well as those of rescuers, are placed very low, so low that one has to bend down to read them. The intention of the exhibit's creators was to use space to convey how much the Jews in hiding suffered, how hard it was for them. But, paradoxically, it is also difficult to get information about the individual fates of those in hiding. The location of this information forces one to adopt such a contorted posture that many people may well pass through the gallery sparing themselves the difficulty of obtaining the information and thus not learning about the fate of Jews handed over to death by Poles. Ironically, the scholars (Barbara Engelking and Jacek Leociak) who placed this information down "beneath the surface" are those who are bringing the dark history of Polish attitudes during the Holocaust "to the surface" through their research and publications. But in the museum, the dark history can continue to lie undiscovered, pushed aside, rejected, and "unregistered."

The time devoted to absorbing this information is key. A pupil in Robert Szuchta's class at Warsaw High School No. LXIV stated that the important thing was that "You don't have to rush ... there's no hurry up, hurry up, no time to stop here, let's go, let's move on. There's a chance to feel it. Not just learn about it, but feel it." Will pupils visiting the museum have enough time to "stop here" in the Holocaust Gallery to learn the fate of the Warsaw Jews condemned to die,[21] for the commentary is principally directed at *them*? Will they have an opportunity *not just to learn, but also to feel*? This depends to a great extent on

---

20 The summer schools were organized jointly with the Chair for Holocaust Studies at the Institute of European Studies, Jagiellonian University, the Illinois Holocaust Museum and Education Center in Skokie, United States, and Yad Vashem, in cooperation with Polish institutions and NGOs in Kraków and Oświęcim.

21 The Holocaust Gallery focuses on the site of POLIN Museum. A similar idea (commentary on one former Nazi death camp) motivated the creators of the exhibit at the Museum-Memorial Site in Bełżec.

the educators at the Education Center and the guides at POLIN Museum, and also on the teachers, who will need to prepare young people before their visit to the museum and then discuss the visit afterwards. Also, young people demonstrate a need for empathy during the process of learning about the Holocaust. There is no agreement whether cognitive rather than affective components[22] are more effective in education. It may be that it is precisely empathy that will allow us to see Jews, both in the past and today, as part of the community of fellow citizens.

Tomasz Kranz, Robert Szuchta, Piotr Trojański, and other experts, as well as working teachers, [23] have written frequently about the theoretical, methodological, and logistical problems of education about the Holocaust. Apart from a lack of theoretical underpinnings and methodology, as well as the imprecision of the words "education about the Holocaust," on which, above all, Tomasz Kranz, director of the Majdanek Museum, has written, in my view

---

22 The Kraków-based sociologist Marek Kucia suggests an emphasis on strengthening the cognitive over the affective components in Holocaust education. See Marek Kucia, "Optymistyczne dane—niepokojące pytania—radykalne wnioski" (Optimistic data—unsettling questions—radical conclusions)," in *Auschwitz i Holokaust. Dylematy i wyzwania polskiej edukacji* [Auschwitz and the Holocaust. Dilemmas and challenges faced by Polish education], ed. Piotr Trojański (Oświęcim: Państwowe muzeum Auschwitz-Birkenau, 2008), 35–44. Trojański suggests in turn that we shift the center of gravity from transmitting information to forming attitudes as well as adding axiological ideas: he feels that education about the Holocaust ought to lay greater emphasis on prevention by including a psychological prism, with the aim of understanding the processes leading to genocide. See Piotr Trojański, "Edukacja o Holokauście w Polsce. Próba krytycznego bilansu" [Education on the Holocaust in Poland. An attempt to strike a critical balance], in *Edukacja muzealna w Polsce. Aspekty, konteksty, ujęcia* [Museum education in Poland. Aspects, contexts, undertakings], ed. Wiesław Wysok and Andrzej Stępnik (Lublin: Państwowe Muzeum na Majdanku, 2013), 129–50.

23 Tomasz Kranz, "Pedagogika pamięci jako forma edukacji muzealnej" [The pedagogy of memory as a form of museum education], in *Wizyty edukacyjne w Państwowym Muzeum na Majdanku. Poradnik dla nauczycieli* [Educational visits to the State Museum in Majdanek. A guidebook for teachers], ed. Tomasz Kranz (Lublin: Państwowe Muzeum na Majdanku 2012), 11–25; Tomasz Kranz, "Posłowie" [Afterword] in *Edukacja muzealna w Polsce. Aspekty, konteksty, ujęcia*; Jacek Chrobaczyński and Piotr Trojański, eds., *Holokaust—lekcja historii. Zagłada Żydów w edukacji szkolnej* [The Holocaust—a lesson in history. The genocide of Jews in school teaching] (Kraków: Wydawnictwo Nauk. Akademii Pedagogicznej, 2004); *Jak uczyć o Auschwitz i Holokauście. Materiały dydaktyczne dla nauczycieli* [How does one teach about Auschwitz and the Holocaust. Didactic materials for teachers], texts selected and ed. Jolanta Ambrosewicz-Jacobs, Krystyna Oleksy, and Piotr Trojański (Oświęcim: Międzynarodowe Centrum Edukacji o Auschwitz i Holokauście Państwowego Muzeum Auschwitz-Birkenau, 2007); *Auschwitz i Holokaust. Dylematy i wyzwania polskiej edukacji*, ed. Piotr Trojański (Oświęcim: Państwowe Muzeum Auschwitz-Birkenau, 2008).

teaching on the subject of the Holocaust in Poland has special limitations. What is important in teaching about the Holocaust in Poland? What is important is that the history of the Jews before the Holocaust, the Holocaust, and the renewal of Jewish life after the war be assimilated, "registered" as "everyone's" work, as the history of fellow citizens. A prerequisite is to abandon perceiving the nation and group identity in terms of ethnic categories. In Poland, this is a long and difficult process that requires the awareness of teachers and of other social agents of education, as well as bold strategic approaches to embrace the historical narrative in textbooks, as well as to encourage teachers to experiment in their teaching. According to contemporary experts Zehavit Gross and Doyle Stevick,[24] experimental teaching in the area under discussion is more effective within the framework of civic education than within history teaching. Scholars also suggest an increased emphasis on experimental education as opposed to education based on sedentary activities in school.

Museum discussions and visits to places of remembrance as well as projects belong to experimental education. Leaders in this type of education that aims at creating islands of memory about Polish Jews, such as Piotr Krawczyk, assert that "we owe the Polish inhabitants of Chmielnik something."[25] This historian from Chmielnik—like Artur Franczak from Nowy Sącz, Joanna Zętar from the Brama Grodzka NN Theater Center in Lublin, and Adam Musiał, a teacher from Kraków—is aware that many small Polish towns owe their existence to Jews and that Jews were co-founders of many of them. But in addition to a great many islands of memory in Poland, there are also islands of non-memory, *lieux d'oubli* (places of forgetfulness),[26] such as Izbica,[27] where there is no mention of the town's prewar Jewish inhabitants.

The report of the Center for the Future of Museums, "Museums and Society 2034," referred to at the start of this essay, speaks of museums' potential to inspire action within local communities through causative narratives.

---

24 Zehavit Gross and Doyle Stevick, eds., *As the Witnesses Fall Silent: 21st Century Holocaust Education in Curriculum, Policy and Practice* (Cham: Springer International Publishing, 2015).
25 A response during a panel discussion at the 10th International Summer School on Teaching about the Holocaust in July 2015 at the Center for Holocaust Studies at the Jagiellonian University.
26 A phrase used by Yoseph Haim Yerushalmi referring to concepts of "lieux de mémoire" [places of memory] of Pierre Nora. See Yoseph Haim Yerushalmi, ed., *Usages de l'oubli* [The uses of forgetting] (Paris: Le Seuil, 1988); Pierre Nora, "Between Memory and History: Les Lieux de Mémoire," *Representations* 26 (Spring 1989): 7–24.
27 Information provided by Robert Szuchta in July 2015.

Referring to this report, experts of the Małopolski Institute of Culture write openly: "The Museum creates new needs and does not just respond to its visitors' expectations, although it attaches great importance to them."[28]

POLIN Museum has an opportunity to make more widely known the new historiographical research in Poland, which, unfortunately, is not fully reflected in the educational process. I have high hopes that a visit to the museum will encourage many teachers and pupils throughout Poland to look for traces of a Jewish past in the towns from which they will have come to Warsaw, and will allow them to feel the emptiness that the Holocaust has left. And this feeling of emptiness will grow into a need to take care of memory of the Jews, those from Poland and those shipped in from the whole of Europe to be murdered on our soil. Polish group identity badly needs such guardians of memory.

---

28 Joanna Hajduk, Łucja Piekarska-Duraj, Piotr Idziak, and Sebastian Wacięga, *Lokalne muzeum w globalnym świecie—poradnik praktyczny* [The local museum in a global world—a practical guide] (Kraków: Małopolski Instytut Kultury, 2013), cover. See also 153–57, http://esklep.mik.krakow.pl/ebooks/lokalne_muzeum_w_globalnym_swiecie.pdf.

HISTORIOGRAPHIC QUESTIONS

Premodern Poland–Lithuania

Did the Polish Nobility Take Seriously the Teaching of the Catholic Church? Reflections on the Relations between the Nobility, the Church, and the Jews

ADAM KAŹMIERCZYK

Much has been written on the subject of close and manifold links between the Jewish population and the nobility in the Polish–Lithuanian Commonwealth. Older historiography emphasized the role of a king as the main protector of the Jews, but even exponents of "martyrological historiography," such as Simon Dubnow, noted that part of the nobility, particularly the magnates, favored them.[1] Subsequent generations of historians did not contradict this view.[2] The fate of Jews in the Polish–Lithuanian state depended on the attitude

---

1 Simon Dubnow, *History of the Jews in Russia and Poland. From the Earliest Times until the Present Day* (Philadelphia, PA: Jewish Publication Society, 1916), 54: "The Jews of Poland were favored by two powers within the state, by royalty and in part by the big Shlakhta."
2 However, Shmuel Ettinger, a historian of an older generation (but already of the twentieth-century Zionist Jerusalem School), stated that whereas the nobility provided Jews with the

of the dominant nobility. In 1539, the nobles forced the Crown to grant them judicial powers over their Jewish subjects. The consequences of this noble protection, and particularly that of the magnates, is eloquently illustrated by the fact that a clear majority of Jews settled in private estates. Of the sixteen towns in the commonwealth with a Jewish population in excess of two thousand, at least ten were owned by the nobility.[3]

The attitude of the Christian nobility was one reason behind this migration and demographic expansion into private domains. They may have well shared the predominant negative stereotypes of Jews, but were rather selective in their adherence to the articles of canon law relating to them. Naturally, it would be unreasonable to expect Protestant or Orthodox nobles to have concerned themselves with the intricacies of the canon law of the Roman Catholic Church. But even in the later period of the commonwealth, from the second half of the seventeenth century—that is, after the Khmelnytsky uprising, when the vast majority of the nobility subscribed to Catholicism—they were only marginally mindful of the Church's teachings.

Quite early on, men of the cloth drew public attention to the particular bond linking the nobility and the Jews. They highlighted the fact that the extraordinary position of the Jews in the state, which they deemed offensive to the church, resulted from the patronage of the nobility. This theme of Jewish expansion facilitated by noble protection recurred with greatest frequency in the eighteenth century, coinciding with the greatest triumphs of the Roman Catholic Church in the commonwealth.

After 1648, the commonwealth lost a large portion of its territory inhabited by the Orthodox, while later, especially under Jan Sobieski, the policy of the state led the remaining Orthodox bishops to accept union with Rome. In fact, outside the eastern borderlands, a majority of Ruthenians accepted the union and consequently acknowledged the supremacy of the Papal See and its local representative, the Papal Nuncio. The beginning of the eighteenth century witnessed not only the marginalization of Eastern Orthodoxy, but also Protestantism ceased to threaten the position of the Catholic Church. This may explain the new importance accorded to the Jewish question, especially following the Great Northern War. Jews and their perceived destructive

---

means of existence and shielded them from excesses of other estates (the clergy and the burghers), their patronage left them entirely dependent on the landowners, and exposed to their whim. Shmuel Ettinger, "The Modern Period," in *A History of the Jewish People*, ed. Hayim Hillel Ben-Sasson (Cambridge, MA: Harvard University Press, 1976), 751.

3 Gershon D. Hundert, *Jews in Poland-Lithuania in the Eighteenth Century: A Genealogy of Modernity* (Berkley: University of California Press, 2004), 23.

influence on the Christian community now had much greater significance for the clergy and bishops.

In the eighteenth century, the Catholic hierarchy maintained the traditional view that Jews should be tolerated within a Christian state, but, at the same time, should remain in a state of subjugation to and isolation from Christians.[4] This attitude found expression in the renewal of the *De Judaeis* clauses in the synodal statutes, as well as in pastoral letters from the bishops, such as that issued by Stefan Rupniewski, bishop of Łuck, in 1722. The letter clearly reflects his view that, upon his investiture, the situation of Jews in the Łuck Diocese was far from the ideal from the viewpoint of canon law. According to him:

> Not only have they almost shed in Poland their shameful, slavish name, openly carry on with their observances, holidays, and rites and have usurped every freedom, but they already aspire to rule over Christians, denying them their commerce, skills, trades, industries, and other means of earning a livelihood.[5]

In their eighteenth-century pastoral letters, Polish bishops commonly expressed their fear of the demographic expansion of Jewry, putting the blame on the mostly Catholic nobility. In 1717, Jan Skarbek, archbishop of Lwów, put it as follows:

> As we hear with the greatest sorrow in our heart and as we see with our own two eyes, the infidel Jewish nation in our archdiocese is multiplying daily and spreading wide through the favors and protection of the potentates to the detriment and uprooting of Christians.[6]

4　The so-called Augustine doctrine of a Witness Nation.
5　*Decretales Summorum Pontificum pro Regno Poloniae et Constitutiones synodorum provincialium et dioecesanarum Regni ejusdem ad summam collectae* [Collected Decrees of the Supreme Pontiff concerning the Kingdom of Poland and the Decisions of the Provincial and Diocesan Synods of that Country], vol. 3, ed. Zenon Chodyński (Poznaniae: J. Leitgeber, 1883), 118–22. First published in *Litera Pastoralis alias Instructio seu Monita Paterna ad Clerum et Populum: sibi commissum Operam et Studio Illustrissimi et Reverendissimi Domini D. Stephani Boguslai [...] Rupniewski [...]*, [Pastoral Letter otherwise Instruction or Paternal Warning to the Clergy and People entrusted to him: the work and study of the Illustrious and Reverend Bishop Stefan Bogusław (...) Rupniewski (...)], 1722, 118.
6　The Kraków Metropolitan Curia Archive [AKM], *Edicta et mandata dioecesis Cracoviensis 1737–1772*, 39 verso.

Such fears among churchmen reflected the real demographic expansion of the Jewish populace, particularly in towns, large and small, belonging to the nobles. Owners of ruined or freshly located settlements made attempts to populate them with new inhabitants, for the most part from among the Jews, particularly in the eastern reaches of the commonwealth.

Ensuring favorable conditions for the new arrivals was a *conditio sine qua non* of a successful settlement drive. In the case of Jews, quite apart from economic concessions, it was vital to provide them with a guarantee of freedom of worship. Charters issued to Jewish communities included licences to construct synagogues, establish cemeteries, use bathhouses, and maintain property free of taxation and other obligations for a rabbi, a cantor and so on.[7] Sometimes, an owner would attempt to obtain the local bishop's consent for the construction of a synagogue, but frequently church regulations were entirely flaunted.

The conditions imposed by the bishops in permits for the construction or refurbishment of a synagogue contained the same reservations as specified in diocesan statutes. However, a closer reading of Bishop Rupniewski's letter suggests that, perhaps, the real policies of the majority of church hierarchs were far more tolerant toward the Jews than their declared adherence to the traditional doctrine of the church would suggest. Even when it came to court cases against Jewish communities, these often ended in a compromise settlement, which usually meant only additional costs to the Jews. The bishops did not generally put obstacles to the settlement of Jews but assented, for a fee, to the construction of new synagogues or repairs to old ones and intervened only if their prerogatives were ignored.

Religious changes and the appearance of new prayer houses were also reflected in the charters issued by the landowners, even though they contradicted the laws of the Roman Catholic Church, which decreed that a settlement was entitled to only one synagogue. Even earlier, in 1629, Stanisław Koniecpolski, voivode of Sandomierz province, in a privilege issued to the settlers of Nowopol (Sieradz province), granted them the right to construct further houses of prayer should the need arise.[8] Sometimes, detailed instructions were issued, which on the one hand attested to some familiarity with Jewish rites, and on the other,

---

7 See introduction to Jacob Goldberg, ed., *Jewish Privileges in the Polish Commonwealth. Charters of Rights Granted to Jewish Communities in Poland Lithuania in the Sixteenth to Eighteenth Centuries. Critical Edition of Original Latin and Polish Documents with English Introductions and Notes* (Jerusalem: Israel Academy of Sciences and Humanities, 1985).

8 *Jewish Privileges*, vol. II, 153.

showed disregard for the laws of the church, which forbade public Jewish religious observance. Thus, Jan Paweł Dąmbski, lord of Lubraniec, allowed not only the customary synagogue, but also agreed to the creation of a Sabbath enclosure (eruv).[9]

This permissive approach of lay Catholics (the nobility) to the restrictions imposed by the canon law was bitterly opposed by the Roman Catholic Church. For centuries, it had attempted to place Judaism in the position of a tolerated but private faith. Hence the irritation of the clergy at the landowners, who more or less openly ignored the fact that their Jews were breaking canon law strictures by celebrating religious rites in public and failing to observe the limitations imposed on them during Christian holidays and fasts. Work on Sundays and holidays (and demanding work from Christians in Jewish employment), public funerals, and open merriment at wedding feasts during Christian periods of fast were the main issues. However, interventions by the church were treated as an encroachment on the freedoms of the noble estate, especially when such interventions were perceived as involving an element of economic competition.

As already discussed, landowning potentates often ignored the restrictive statutes of the canon law and state legislation. That said, some charters granted to Jews did contain regulations based on the law of the Roman Catholic Church. It is difficult, though, to be entirely sure of the motives behind such constraints as the prohibition to open windows or loiter outdoors during Easter Week or the Octave of Corpus Christi. They could well be repressive but, perhaps, were intended to save Jews from anti-Jewish violence, which has lingered in various parts of Europe right up to our time.[10]

An important field of contention, as seen by landowners, was the subject of Christians in Jewish service.[11] Numerous pastoral letters by eighteenth-

---

9   Ibid., vol. I, 166.
10 A tradition of the persecution of Jews during Easter did exist in Poland, as attested by a Jewish charter of Pniewy of 1648, in which Andrzej Karol Grudziński laid down as follows: "During the days of Easter, both my castle office, as well as the municipal one, ought to protect them [the Jews] in every way from the common man and his insolence, which is commonly directed against them at this time, with firm town and castle guard provided daily for three days of Easter," State Archive Poznań, *Księgi wojewodzińskie poznańskie* [Poznań Province Registry Books], W-3, 160–62, Pniewy (July 17, 1648).
11 Adam Kaźmierczyk, "The Problem of Christian Servants as Reflected in the Legal Codes of the Polish–Lithuanian Commonwealth during the Second Half of the Seventeenth Century and in the Saxon Period," *Gal-Ed. On the History of the Jews in Poland*, vol. XV–XVI (Tel Aviv, 1997): 23–40; Judith Kalik, "Jews in Catholic Ecclesiastical Legislation in the Polish–Lithuanian Commonwealth," *Kwartalnik Historii Żydów* 209 (2004): 26–39.

century bishops, as well as Diocesan Synodal Statutes, stressed the prohibition on the permanent employment of Christian servants by Jews. The issue of Christian servitude was highly important to the church because it negated one of its oldest anti-Jewish canons and also undermined the foundations of Christian theology toward Judaism. The church was also concerned that Christians who were subject to Jews would fail to observe their religious duties and thus not only expose their souls to eternal perdition but also scandalize the remaining flock. Such fears were legitimate insofar as there are known instances of Jewish proselytism in the eighteenth century.[12] In any case, church documents contain complaints against servants who neglected their religious duties and against Jews accused of preventing their laborers from attending to their religious rites out of hatred of Christianity. In a letter to the administration of the Zamoyski estates, the clergy of Zamość described the consequences of Jews employing Christians:

> Such communality with Jews brings about a thousand criminal acts, abominations and indecencies, such as non-observance of holidays, breaking fasts, non-attendance at church services on holy days and at spiritual instruction necessary to the soul's salvation, ignorance of even the central mysteries of the Faith, abandonment of the sacraments of Confession and Eucharist for a whole year and longer, carnal sins with Jews and Jewesses, services abhorrent to the Christian religion, such as lighting of Sabbath candles, carrying of Jewish books after Jews and Jewesses and carrying beverages that Jews are wont to use during their holidays and Sabbaths.[13]

---

12 Apart from the phenomenon of the return to Judaism of Jewish converts (see Adam Kaźmierczyk, *Rodziłem się Żydem… Konwersje Żydów w Rzeczypospolitej XVII–XVIII wieku* [I was born a Jew. The conversion of Jews in the Polish-Lithuanian Commonwealth in the seventeenth and eighteenth centuries] (Kraków: Księgarnia Akademicka, 2015), 165–97, there were instances of conversion of Christians to Judaism. There was a celebrated case of two women from Dubno sentenced to death for apostasy: *Arkhiv Iugo-Zapadnoi Rossii, izdavaemyi Kommisseiu dlia razbora drevnikh aktov* [The Archive of South-West Russia published by the Commission for the Examination of Old Documents], part V, vol. I, *Akty o gorodach* [Documents on towns] (Kiev, 1869), part III, vol. 4, 267–270. Magda Teter, "Kilka uwag na temat podziałów społecznych i religijnych pomiędzy żydami i chrześcijanami we wschodnich miastach dawnej Rzeczypospolitej" [Some observations on the topic of the social and religious divisions between Jews and Christian in the eastern towns of the Polish-Lithuanian Commonwealth], *Kwartalnik Historii Żydów* 3 (2003): 334–35.

13 State Archive Lublin, Sąd Kom. 8, 45–48.

In the Polish church pronouncements, the failure to observe such prohibitions was deemed to constitute one of the heaviest sins, with absolution or its denial reserved to the bishops. It can be questioned whether the bishops really approached this failure with such rigor, since they themselves admitted it was a common occurrence. In their *ad limina* reports to the Holy See, they unanimously blamed the nobility for instances of breaking this particular article of the canon law. It is worth noting, though, that only in the eighteenth century did bishops begin to pay greater attention to the problem of the Jewish population and the issue of Christians in their service. Among earlier extant reports, only the bishop of Przemyśl, Stanisław Sarnowski, in his letter dated October 30, 1666, noted this phenomenon, although he also confirmed his helplessness to act against it. Perhaps, because he came from a different part of the commonwealth, the bishop found relations in Red Ruthenia particularly galling. As he wrote, it was especially Orthodox Christians who were employed by Jews who were sheltered by the nobles.[14]

Attempts to institute a prohibition on Christian service were, indeed, frequently ignored by the landed nobility. The growing role of the Jews in the economy of the estates, especially those belonging to magnates (in trade, crafts, and, above all, in the sale of locally produced alcohol), provoked displeasure with the interventions of the clergy. Their attempts to force adherence to certain points of canon law were seen as economically harmful by owners, tenants, and administrators alike, all interested in maximizing profits. Jewish leaseholders could not cope without Christian laborers, either free, or serfs (assigned in a tenancy contract). Similarly, Jewish trade would have been significantly hamstrung if it lacked the chance to hire Christians, if only as drovers. Small wonder, then, that when Jan Skarbek, archbishop of Lwów, issued a decree forbidding his flock to work for Jews, the manager of Starosielsk estates, Józef Karetti, avoided making any decision and declared that he needed to refer the matter to the owner. He also suggested to Elżbieta Sieniawska, wife of the Kraków castellan, that she play a delaying game to check whether the archbishop would succeed in forcing his decree elsewhere.[15]

In this case pretence was at least maintained, probably out of reverence for the generally respected Metropolitan of Lwów. Elsewhere, attempts to impose

---

14　Archivio Segreto Vaticano [ASV], Congreg. Concil. Relat. Dioec. 667.
15　More on the subject in Adam Kaźmierczyk, "Jews, Nobles and Canon Law in the Eighteenth Century," *Biuletyn Polskiej Misji Historycznej* 9 (2014), 226, dx.doi.org/10.12775/BPMH.2014.009.

this point of canon law met with open resistance, and noble-owners and leasers had no intention of listening to officious priests. They viewed such interventions as attempts on the prerogatives of the noble estate. Stefan Żuchowski, the archdeacon and judicial vicar of Sandomierz, well known for his anti-Semitic books and especially for his role in the Sandomierz blood-libel accusations, collected cases of Jews breaking canon and state laws, quoting many such instances in his book. One of Żuchowski's correspondents quoted a reply he had received from the noble-owner of a village when he attempted to impose canon law: "You priests will never succeed in preventing Catholics from serving the Jews," said the owner, and allegedly added: "And I will even order my Jew to distill alcohol on a holiday, because the Jew should not observe Catholic holidays, as has always been right and proper."[16]

The fact that bishops reissued such prohibitions again and again shows, above all else, that they were difficult or even impossible to enforce, a consideration of which the hierarchs themselves were all too aware. Steps were taken to oblige the lower clergy at least to attempt to apply such strictures, for instance at Decanal Congregations. Active teaching, such as pastoral missionary work, was another avenue. During one such exercise, conducted by a priestly missionary order at Nowy Korczyn, fifty women deposited signed promises with a local vicar that they would refrain from serving Jews.[17] Outright criticism of the behavior of noble-owners was certainly difficult. Mikołaj Wyżycki, archbishop of Lwów, had to intervene on behalf of a missionary priest who, in the course of his mission, offended the sensibilities of Prince Michał Kazimierz Radziwiłł, and begged him not to forbid further such missionary work on his estates.[18]

An even greater challenge to the theologically and canonically grounded conviction of a rightful subjugation of Jews and Judaism to Christians was the fact that Jews were granted leases and employed as commissioners, foremen, and other manorial posts. It is worth bearing in mind that in earlier times, particularly in Ruthenia, Jewish tenants enjoyed all the owners' prerogatives over the serfs, including even the right to impose capital punishment. In later times, for the most part, tenancy agreements forbade Jews to sit directly in judgment over Christians, but this was not always adhered to. Even influential bishops could not countermand the practice of employing Jews as manorial clerks and

---

16 Diocesan Library at Sandomierz, AKKS 742, 70r. Wojciech Kaniewicz, parish priest of Grzegorzowice to Stefan Żuchowski, at Grzegorzowice, September 20, 1712.
17 Kaźmierczyk, "Jews, Nobles," 228.
18 Ibid.

administrators, even though this violated church laws. This is well illustrated by the case of the so-called tenants of Słuck, brothers Gdal and Szmujło Ickowicz. Szmujło, especially, styled a cashier to Anna Radziwiłł née Sanguszko, and later to her son Hieronim Florian, practically controlled their finances and accumulated enormous power, which was a general irritant, not just to churchmen. The Lithuanian nobility were also scandalized and envious to boot, but the might of the Radziwiłł family was such as to stop any schemes against the Ickowicz brothers or other influential Jewish factors in their service. Even the Catholic hierarchs in Lithuania could only afford to issue humble entreaties. In a letter to Anna Radziwiłł, dated January 22, 1741, Michał Zienkowicz, bishop of Vilna, conveyed his New Year's greetings and pleaded with her to keep an earlier promise to remove the Jews from the administration of her estates, appealing to her pity for her suffering Christian serfs.[19] Similarly, Franciszek Antoni Kobielski, the bishop of Łuck, stopped short of any direct steps against Jews, when visiting Biała (Anna Radziwiłł's seat), formally postponing any cases against Jews until he had a chance to talk to the owner.[20] The bishops' entreaties went unheeded and the subsequent fall of the Ickowicz brothers had entirely different causes, unrelated to the hierarchs' interventions.[21]

Since the magnates paid no attention to bishops, they were even less inclined to listen to lower clergy. If the bishops were often forced to suffer disrespect and open defiance from noble landowners, then rank-and-file vicars, who depended on their lay patrons in many ways, were clearly not in a position to enforce articles of church law relating to Jews. In one case, well attested in literary sources, the *starosta* (district head) of Kaniów, Michał Potocki, ordered the reopening of a synagogue sealed by a bishop and sent him a letter in which he denied him any right to interfere with his Jews. It could be assumed that such crass disrespect was, perhaps, exceptional, since Potocki was well known for his lawlessness, but a similar situation occurred in Przeworsk. While visiting the parish, Walenty Antoni Czapski, bishop of Przemyśl, felt offended by the behavior of the estate's foreman, the local burghers, and Jews, and sealed their synagogue. The owner, Teresa Lubomirska, sent him an exceedingly angry letter in which she wrote: "we call the Church our mother, but I can see

---

19 AGAD AR V, 18763/I p. 71, Michał Zienkowicz to Anna Radziwiłł, at Vilna, January 22, 1741.
20 Franciszek Antoni Kobielski to Anna Radziwiłł neé Sanguszko, at Równe, July 6, 1741, AR V 6905, 25–26.
21 Adam Teller, *Money, Power, and Influence in Eighteenth-Century Lithuania. The Jews on the Radziwiłł Estates* (Standford: Stanford University Press, 2016), 73-105.

it has now become an oppressor of our noble estates."[22] Lubomirska assumed that the bishop should have behaved as any other landowner and come to her in the first instance, so that she should adjudicate in the case of his displeasure with her subjects. However, Czapski did not intend to give way; he wrote her an equally offensive reply, including threats of sanctions, and, eventually, the lady had to concede. The question arises, though, whether Czapski would have shown as much severity and determination had he been dealing with a different magnate and not a widow and had he not secured a nomination to a higher church office, which allowed him to disregard local elites.[23]

Aware of the position of the landowners on the matter, administrators and tenants of the nobility also flouted anti-Jewish church regulations. Church wardens were ineffectual in their attempts to make Jews comply with the law, in part because manorial officials and militias shielded them. Sometimes this resulted in blows and even bloodshed, and the clergy complained of the loss of face in front of the serfs, which only emboldened the Jews. The bishop of Kraków, Kajetan Sołtyk, lodged a complaint against a certain Mirecki, administrator of Szydłowiec, who failed to prosecute local Jews for hiring a Catholic on Yom Kippur. When the local vicar intervened with his wardens, they were offended and thrown out of the synagogue. The bishop ordered his court to issue writs, but was prepared to forgo a trial, asking only that the Radziwiłłs punish the perpetrators.[24]

Certainly, examples can be found when manorial courts did try cases of breaking church law, usually brought by local clergy, and the verdicts passed reflected synodal and diocesan instructions. But were they always religiously motivated? Take, for instance, the circumstances of a decree relating to an important Jewish center in Międzybóż, which was also a hub of the Czartoryski holdings in Podolia. A local commissioner of the estates imposed heavy fines on Jews for staying outside their houses during a Corpus Christi procession and for holding private religious services in their homes. But the real reasons may have been more prosaic. These festivities had been arranged shortly before a planned visit by Wacław Hieronim Sierakowski, bishop of Kamieniec Podolski. He was expected to consecrate a new church in Międzybóż, an act which, doubtless, also carried political

---

22 BC 2066 IV, s. 48–49, Kopia listu Teresy Lubomirskiej do W.A. Czapskiego (Copy of Teresa Lubomirska's letter to W.A. Czapski), sine datum et loco.
23 More on this in Kaźmierczyk, "Jews, Nobles," 234–35.
24 AGAD, AR V 14847, 85–87, Kajetan Sołtyk, Bishop of Kraków to M. K. Radziwiłł, from Warsaw, December 15, 1760.

weight. During the procession, some of the assembled Catholic nobles caught a number of Jews in the streets of the town and both the local vicar, Łossowski, and the bishop demanded severe punishment of the culprits as criminals, citing the 1670 Act of the Sejm. Ensuing correspondence shows that both churchmen relented somewhat from their extreme demands, but the commissioner had to punish the local Jews with appropriate severity. Considerable time elapsed between the events and the final sentence, and the verdict bears a mark of a compromise between the bishop and the magnate. The Jews did receive their punishment from the Czartoryski administration, so that the magnate kept his reputation intact in the eyes of the nobility of Podolia.[25]

Although the bishops, such as W. H. Sierakowski, Stefan Rupniewski, and Franciszek Antoni Kobielski, achieved a degree of success, their contemporaries saw limited possibilities of enforcing canon law, and these particular bishops were seen as particularly zealous in comparison with the rest. Stanisław Wodzicki wrote in his memoirs from the second half of the eighteenth century that only the use of diocesan militias could break the opposition. But he also added that "such power reached only as far as the Jews; no bishop would have dared to enforce his rulings on the nobility."[26]

Small wonder, then, that the bishops regularly complained in their reports to the Apostolic See of the protection afforded the Jews by the rich and mighty and of their own inability to enforce canon law. This frustration and a sense of helplessness led some of them to suggest in their *ad limina* reports that the Apostolic See should issue an edict to the faithful of the kingdom, and particularly to its upper class.[27] In the end, these supplications prompted the Congregation of Councils to act, and the case ended up at the *Sanctum Officium*. Its decree, issued in May 1751, stressed in no uncertain terms that the matter reached Rome at the initiative of the Polish "zealot" bishops. That same decree provided a foundation of the papal encyclical of Benedict XIV of June 14, 1751, *A Quo Primum*, which faithfully repeated the overview of the

---

25 Kaźmierczyk, "Jews, Nobles," 237.
26 Stanisław Wodzicki, *Stanisława hr. Wodzickiego wspomnienia z przeszłości od roku 1768 do 1840* [The memoirs of Count Stanisław Wodzicki from 1768 to 1840] (Kraków: J. K. Żupański & K. J. Heumann, 1873), 125.
27 The last such suggestion before the issuing of the encyclical was submitted by the bishop of Kraków, Andrzej Stanisław Załuski in his *ad limina* of 1751, *Relacje o stanie diecezji krakowskiej 1615–1765* [An account of the state of the Kraków diocese in the years between 1615–1765], ed. Wiesław Müller (Lublin: Towarzystwo Naukowe Katolickiego Uniwersytetu Lubelskiego, 1978), 145.

position of the Jewish population, as presented by the Polish bishops. Based on the conclusions of his predecessors, the Pope naturally prescribed adherence to the canon law. On the issue of servants, he wrote:

> the sons of freedom should not serve the sons of servitude, so that the Jews, as servants held in contempt and rejected by the Lord, should feel, through their labors and subjugation, that they are serfs of those set free through Christ's death, just as they themselves were made slaves through it.[28]

The encyclical, both in the Latin original and in its Polish translation, was widely disseminated. Practically all Polish bishops included it in their pastoral letters. However, it does not appear that this last resort had any real effect at this time when the Enlightenment with its secularizing tendencies was taking root among the magnates. Even earlier, before any Enlightenment influence could be discerned, the Polish nobility notoriously failed to comply with anti-Jewish laws, not only church but also civil ones. This state of affairs prevailed despite their protestations of attachment to all forms of legality. This is very well illustrated by the case of the Masovian Exception, the law which excluded Jews from the Masovian Voivodship. Even earlier, local nobility argued for the removal of Jews and for severely punishing transgressors but, on the other hand, they quite pragmatically taxed them and their Christian servants.[29] Later, in the eighteenth century, neither the nobility-in-assembly (*sejmiki*), nor, even less, the church authorities, were in the position to enforce the law of the land or canon law. In the parish of Zielona (decanate of Przasnysz, Masovian Voivodship, land of Ciechanów), documents of an episcopal visit of 1781 show that despite a diocesan reform decree issued by the bishop of Płock of 1756, from the perspective of church authorities, nothing much had changed in the intervening twenty-five years.[30] The sole notable

---

28 Quote from Wacław Hieronim Sierakowski, *Epistola pastoralis celsissimi illustrissimi et reverendissimi Domini Domini Venceslai Hieronymi de Bogusławice Sierakowski Dei et Apostolicae Sedis gratia archiepiscopi metropolitani leopoliensis* [Pastoral Letter of the Most High, Most Illustrious and Most Reverend Lord Wacław Hieronim de Bogusławice Sierakowski by the Grace of God and of the Apostolic See Metropolitan Archbishop of Lwów], Leopoli 1761, T2v.

29 Adam Kaźmierczyk, *Sejmy i sejmiki szlacheckie wobec Żydów w drugiej połowie XVII wieku* [Sejms and sejmiki of the nobility on Jews in the second half of the eighteenth century], Warsaw: Wydawnictwo Sejmowe, 1994, 74–76.

30 *Materiały do dziejów ziemi płockiej. Ziemia przasnyska. Z archiwaliów diecezjalnych płockich XVIII wieku* [Documents on the history of the Płock region. The Przasnysk County. From the diocesan archives of Płock in the eighteenth century], vol. 7, compiled and prepared

improvement was better adherence to civil law, but only because the so-called Sejm constitution of 1775 allowed Jewish settlement in Mazovia (with the exception of Warsaw).[31] There is also proof that attempts to remove Jewish populations from royal cities were effectively used by the magnates and their officials for their benefit.[32]

The economic policies of the Polish magnates translated into active support of Jewish settlement on the greater part of the territory of the commonwealth. In 1753, Mikołaj Ignacy Wyżycki, archbishop of Lwów, wrote sarcastically, in a charter issued to a Jewish community of Stanisławów, that wherever a new town was established in the Polish Crown lands, the very first act was to lay the foundations of a synagogue.[33] Wyżycki used a similar phrase in two other permissions, registered in 1754 but issued earlier to the communities at Uście and Tyśmienica. Naturally, while copying the documents, chancellery scribes used an existing format, but the presence of this phrase shows that the phenomenon was persistent and common and that the encyclical *A Quo Primum* had not altered the attitudes of the nobility. Neither did any change occur in the matter of Christians in Jewish service, as desired by the clergy. Almost a decade after the publication of the encyclical, in a letter to Pope Clement XIII, Primate Władysław Łubieński explained in the name of the College of Polish

---

for publication by Michał Marian Grzybowski (Płock: Towarzystwo Naukowe Płockie, 1995), 163: "Jewish habitation having been forbidden in the inns, located too near the church, erected barely 15 paces away from it, which was severely forbidden by the Illustrious Szembek, Bishop of Płock, in person in the decreta reformationis in the course of a general visitation die 16 Junii 1756 anno, these same inns are now all full of Jews, who publicly perform their Jewish rites in breach of the law. Those same Jews, apart from performing their faith's rites in very near proximity of the church, serve drinks like possessed to all and sundry, and despite the vicar's many admonitions produce and sell the drink publicly on Catholic holidays and Sundays, even during the high Catholic mass. And whenever I talked to the lords of those Jews and inns, so that they would revoke licence for the Jews to serve during a Catholic mass, they would not listen, excusing themselves with the loss of revenue and the Jewish freedom to trade on Catholic holidays."

31 VL VIII, 148.
32 "I have news to report that the Christians of the city of Kowno won a case in a civil court against the Jews, who are obliged to vacate the whole city within a year. Whereas it must be noted that over the Wilia river, and adjacent to this city of Kowno, there lie Your good Grace's hereditary lands of Słobódka from Milkoln, very propitious for the erection of a new town, which could be located on the occasion of these Jews building their new houses," Kazimierz Wiszniewski to Hieronim Florian Radziwiłł at Rumyszki, October 11, 1753, AGAD AR V 17539, 186.
33 CGIA Lwów, Fond 5, op. 1, d. 263, 12 VI 1753, 1179–82. "Ut ubi oppidum aliquod originatur prima ponant fundamenta synagogae," 1180. At Uście (April 17, 1741), 1197–99 and Tyśmienica (November 22, 1740), 1214–16.

Bishops that it was impossible in Poland to meet the requirements as set out in the encyclical of Benedict XIV.[34]

All the above examples prove that economic necessities and not religious scruples were paramount in the shaping of the legal status of Jewry in the Polish–Lithuanian Commonwealth.[35] Moreover, this view is validated by the fact that the church in the commonwealth was surprisingly uninterested in missionary work among Jews. Characteristically, the Polish translation of Pope Clement XI's bull *Propagandae per universum* of 1704 omits the original's summary of Gregory XIII's bull *Sancta Mater Ecclesiae* of 1584, in which the Pope ordered compulsory preaching to the Jews. In addition, the first, very modest, Book of Catechism addressed to Jews was published in Poland as late as 1760. Franciszek Antoni Kobielski, bishop of Łuck who was the sole member of the Polish Episcopate engaged more actively in missionary work, complained in his *ad limina* report of the magnates' opposition to his campaign of preaching in the synagogues, which he had overcome with difficulty—not for long, though, because he probably gave up on it before his death.[36] One of the reasons was, doubtless, a lack of interest by the nobility, and particularly the magnates, in any anti-Jewish campaign (which did not preclude individual instances of support for missionary work or other anti-Jewish measures).

Throughout the duration of the Polish–Lithuanian Commonwealth, the Polish church had failed to impose on the Catholic nobility its own point of view on the Jewish question, partly because the clergy and the monastic communities also used Jews for economic reasons in their own estates.[37] In

---

34 Stanisław Librowski, "Konferencje biskupów XVIII wieku jako instytucja zastępująca synody prowincjonalne" [Bishops conferences in the eighteenth century as a substitute to provincial synods], *Archiwa, Biblioteki i Muzea Kościelne* 47 (1983): 276.

35 This is also an opinion expressed by the main creator of a gallery at the Museum of the History of Polish Jews, Adam Teller, "Telling the Difference. Some Comparative Perspectives on the Jews' Legal Status in the Polish–Lithuanian Commonwealth and the Holy Roman Empire," *Polin: Studies in Polish Jewry* 22 (2010): 141.

36 More on this subject in the chapter on Jewish conversions: Adam Kaźmierczyk, "Nawrócenie Żydów. Misja polskiego Kościoła. Prawda czy mit?" [The conversion of Jews. A mission of the Polish church. A fact of a myth?], *Rodziłem się Żydem...*, 219–48.

37 Kalik, "Jews in Catholic Ecclesiastic Legislation"; "Patterns of Contact Between the Catholic Church and the Jews in the Polish–Lithuanian Commonwealth: The Jewish Debts," in *Scripta Hierosolymitana*, vol. 38: *Studies in the History of the Jews in Old Poland in Honor of Jacob Goldberg*, ed. Adam Teller (Jerusalem: Zalman Shazar Center, 1998), 102–22; "'Zastaw' (Deposit) and 'Wiederkauf' in the Economic Activity of the Jews in Polish–Lithuanian Commonwealth" [in Hebrew], in *Jewish Entrepreneurship in Modern Times: East Europe and Eretz Israel*, ed. Ran Aaronsohn and Shaul Stampfer (Jerusalem: Magnes Press, 2000), 25–47.

addition, there was a tradition of anticlericalism among the nobility that was totally unrelated to the later trends in the Age of Enlightenment. Strongly jealous of their privileges, the nobles looked askance and with hostility on any interventions by the clerics, especially those entangled in political intrigue or fighting with them for tithes and other church income. (Incidentally, in no way did this preclude the declared, and frequently demonstrated, religiosity, or dislike of the Jews, or individual support for converts from Judaism.) All these factors facilitated the rapid growth of Jewish settlement, although it is worth noting that its expansion was greatest in these parts of the country where the structures of the Roman Catholic Church were the weakest. This was certainly an additional factor favoring this growth, but certainly not the decisive one.

Relations between Jews and Non-Jews in the Polish–Lithuanian Commonwealth Perceptions and Practices

JÜRGEN HEYDE

A history of Polish–Jewish relations in early modern Poland–Lithuania would be incomplete if we did not seek answers to the question about how Jews and non-Jews thought about one another. One might trace such attitudes by analyzing statements about the other in public discourse or literary works (perceptions) or by researching patterns of contact and communication in day-to-day encounters (practices). The first two parts of this chapter discuss research on these two aspects and show discrepancies in the ensuing picture of Polish–Jewish relations. Perceptions of the other—on both sides—tend to underline the features separating both groups, whereas practices focus on common interests. The difference between apparently exclusive perceptions and inclusive practices can be attributed to the way these phenomena are researched. In both cases, historical literature tends to treat Jews and non-Jews as two distinct groups interacting with each other, neglecting individual factors and agendas. Consequently, the third part of this chapter proposes a different approach, one that analyzes Jewish–non-Jewish relations as part of a multipolar framework of actors and agendas. It adopts a case study, discussing the anti-Jewish legislation that was passed at the Sejm of Piotrków in 1538 but never enforced in practice. By tracing the political debates in the first half of the sixteenth century, this study shows how even harsh anti-Jewish polemics could leave inclusionary practices unaffected. In fact, they were not even intended to do so, but were meant to send a message to other non-Jewish actors.

The argument is that relations between Jews and non-Jews in Poland–Lithuania cannot be analyzed using terms taken from the documents which are expressed in binary categories (Jews vs. non-Jews/Poles), but have to be taken as part of a polyvalent sociopolitical system with actors forming varying groups according to the necessities of their social or political agendas.

PERCEPTIONS AND ATTITUDES

The early modern period introduced a wide range of sources describing the "other" from Polish as well as Jewish perspectives. Such statements often claim to represent the opinions of a larger group, even Jewish or Polish society as a whole. Nevertheless, such attitudes were formulated (and published) by individual authors, whose viewpoints and agendas have to be taken into account.

The necessity of doing so becomes clear when we compare two classical historiographical studies on Polish attitudes about Jews in early modern Poland. Janusz Tazbir, in his articles on Polish images of Jews in the sixteenth through eighteenth centuries, focused on explicit statements that were made about Jews. He found these primarily in polemical literature written by burghers and priests, which led him to the obvious conclusion that the attitude of early modern Poles toward Jews was characterized by rejection and exclusion.[1] Jacob Goldberg, by contrast, framed the question differently: he examined attitudes of the two groups based on accounts of everyday contacts and encounters between Jews and non-Jews (Poles).[2] He concluded that on various levels intensive contacts between Jews and non-Jews could be found, a supposition that contradicted the suggestions of polemical literature of the time.

Basically, the same holds true from the Jewish perspective. Older research predominantly used normative texts, such as rabbinical responsa or community records, as sources. They drew a picture of Jewish–Polish relations that showed the Jewish population being legally as well as economically dependent

---

1 Janusz Tazbir, "Żydzi w opinii staropolskiej" [Jews in the public opinion of pre-partition Poland] in *Świat panów Pasków. Eseje i studia* [The world of the Paseks. Essays and studies] (Łódź: Wydawnictwo Łódzkie, 1986), 213–41; "Das Judenbild der Polen im 16.–18. Jahrhundert" [The Polish image of the Jews from the sixteenth to the eighteenth centuries], *Acta Poloniae Historica* 50 (Warsaw, 1984): 29–56.

2 Jacob Goldberg, "Poles and Jews in the Seventeenth and Eighteenth Centuries: Rejection or Acceptance," *Jahrbücher für Geschichte Osteuropas* [Yearbook for the history of Eastern Europe] 22 (1974): 248–82; "The Changes in the Attitude of Polish Society toward the Jews in the Eighteenth Century," in *From Shtetl to Socialism: Studies from Polin*, ed. Antony Polonsky (Oxford: Littman Library of Jewish Civilization: 1993), 50–63.

on their non-Jewish surroundings, but they could not acknowledge any cultural influence whatsoever. More recent historiography has called this dichotomy into question: Moshe Rosman has proposed to view relations between Jews and non-Jews in early modern Poland–Lithuania as a "polysystem," in which elements of segregation coexisted with creative appropriation of cultural elements from the non-Jewish society. Magda Teter has pointed out that the difference between normative demarcation and practical contacts is fundamental to Jewish–Polish relations.[3]

When sixteenth-century Jewish thinkers in Poland reflected on the conditions of Jewish existence in Poland, they mainly emphasized the contrast with persecutions and expulsions in middle and Western Europe. Frequently quoted are Moshe Isserles's words to a friend who was assigned to be a rabbi in the Holy Roman Empire but decided to return to Poland: "It is perhaps preferable to partake of dry bread crust, but in security, in this country [meaning Poland], where there is no fierce hatred of us like in Germany."[4] One might also recall the well-known phrase of Ḥayim Betsalel Friedberg: "It is known that, thank God, His people is in this land [i.e., Poland] not despised and despoiled. Therefore a non-Jew coming to the Jewish street has respect for the public and is afraid to behave like a villain against Jews, while in Germany every Jew is wronged and oppressed in every way."[5]

Reflections on the situation of the Jewish population in Poland underline the close ties to the king and the nobility as factors of stability, but in reality Isserles himself reveals some ambiguity about this subject: "The king and nobility favour us and desire us, thank God, so long as there are no tattlers in

---

3 Moshe Rosman, "A Minority Views the Majority: Jewish Attitudes Towards the Polish–Lithuanian Commonwealth and Interaction with Poles," in *Polin* 4 (1989): 31–41, here 35–36; on "Polysystem," "A Prolegomenon to the Study of Jewish Cultural History," *Jewish Studies. An Internet Journal* 1 (2002): 109–27 (also *How Jewish Is Jewish History. Writing Jewish History in the Postmodern Climate* (Oxford: Littman Library of Jewish Civilization, 2007, 131–53); Magda Teter, "Kilka uwag na temat podziałów społecznych i religijnych pomiędzy Żydami i chrześcijanami we wschodnich miastach dawnej Rzeczypospolitej" [Some remarks on the subject of the social and religious divisions between Jews and Christians in the eastern towns of former Polish-Lithuanian Commonwealth], *Kwartalnik Historii Żydów/Jewish History Quarterly*, 3 (2003): 327–35.

4 Moses Isserles, *She'elot u-tshuvot* [Queries and responses], ed. by Asher Ziev (Jerusalem, n. p.: 1971), no. 95; Bernard D. Weinryb, *The Jews of Poland. A Social and Economic History of the Jewish Community from 1100 to 1800* (Philadelphia, PA: Jewish Publication Society, 1972), 166; Moshe Rosman, "Jewish Perceptions of Insecurity and Powerlessness in Sixteenth–Eighteenth-Century Poland," *Polin* 1 (Oxford, 1986): 19–27, here 20.

5 Quoted after Weinryb, *The Jews of Poland*, 166.

the dark who stab like sharp swords."⁶ In the mid-eighteenth century, Rabbi Yaacov Yisrael of Krzemieniec pointed out that Jews were in danger of being harmed mostly during times of war and in interregna, for those times absorbed all the attention of the authorities. Then perpetrators gained the upper hand, and they plundered and mistreated the Jews. In quieter times, however, the government had the power to protect Jews from oppression.⁷

Again and again Jewish leaders justified their calls for modest behavior (imposing measures against ostentatious luxury, criticizing the "arenda"— Jewish lease-holding) with the need for consideration of the non-Jewish environment.⁸ To what extent such statements, which can be found in rabbinical responsa as well as in community records, reflected real concerns based on a specific situation, or to what degree they represented mental projections aimed at upholding social discipline, is only marginally reflected in historiography and may be difficult to prove in any particular case. Striking, however, is the contrast between the almost omnipresence of such scenarios of danger in rabbinical and communal sources on the one hand and the—admittedly few—testimonies of individual Jews, as found, for instance in the memoirs of Dov Ber of Bolechów or Moshe Wassercug from the second half of the eighteenth century, drawing a rather positive picture of contacts between the Jewish narrators and their non-Jewish environment.⁹

Early modern Jewish sources present a certain set of norms for encounters with non-Jews, which Rosman has characterized with the words *kabdehu ve-hashdehu* ("respect, but suspect").¹⁰ Distance was especially necessary in business dealings, where too close contacts might lead to the violation of religious requirements (Shabbat, kashrut). A degree of restraint in seeking to lease whole estates or parts of their activity (the arenda) was justified with regard to non-Jewish laws and the fear of antagonizing the non-Jewish population.¹¹ From yet another angle, early modern authors argued for restraint

---

6   Rosman, "Jewish Perceptions of Insecurity," 21n19.
7   Ibid., 20.
8   Examples: Rosman, "Jewish Perceptions of Insecurity," 21–23.
9   Mark Vishnitzer, ed., *The Memoirs of Ber of Bolechow (1723–1805)* (Oxford: Oxford University Press, 1922); Jacob Goldberg, ed., *Die Memoiren des Moses Wasserzug* [The memoirs of Moses Wasserzug] (Leipzig: Leipziger Universitätsverlag, 2001); Rosman, "A Minority Views the Majority," 36.
10 Moshe Rosman, "Innovative Tradition. Jewish Culture in the Polish–Lithuanian Commonwealth," in *Cultures of the Jews. A New History*, ed. David Biale (New York: Schocken Books, 2002), 519–70, here 524.
11 Dieter Fettke, *Juden und Nichtjuden im 16. und 17. Jahrhundert in Polen* [Jews and Non-Jews in the sixteenth and the seventeenth centuries in Poland] (Frankfurt: P. Lang, 1986), 38–41.

in sexual relations between Jews and non-Jews: here male authors (Jewish and non-Jewish alike) envisioned the females of their own group as potential victims of assaults by men of the other group, and appealed to their own men not to expose their wives and daughters to contact with "the other." The same arguments were used both by Jews and by Christians.[12]

In practice, close social relations between Jews and non-Jews were found in the realm of Christian servants in Jewish households (the so-called "shabbes Goy," or Christian maids or wet nurses) as well as in business contacts before Passover, when the Jewish partner gave his share in the common business to his non-Jewish partner to ensure the continuity of the business over the holidays.[13] Neighborhood contacts could be influenced by the community elders. Especially in larger communities, such as Poznań or Kraków, the kahal had the right of first refusal when a Christian sold real estate within the boundaries of the Jewish quarter.[14] Thus the Jewish community was able to strive for a certain coherence in Jewish settlement within towns. A different tendency, however, is evident in a response by Yoel Sirkes. He explicitly confirmed a ruling by the kahal in the small town of Luboml from 1558 that forbade the preemption of Christian property by Jews, as he saw the presence of Christians within the Jewish quarter as a factor shielding Jews against attacks from the outside.[15]

---

12 Judith Kalik, "Fusion versus Alienation. Erotic Attraction, Sex, and Love between Jews and Christians in the Polish–Lithuanian Commonwealth," in *Kommunikation durch symbolische Akte. Religiöse Heterogenität und politische Herrschaft in Polen-Litauen* [Communication through symbolic acts. Religious heterogeneity and political rule in Poland-Lithuania], ed. Yvonne Kleinmann (Stuttgart: Steiner, 2010), 157–69; Magda Teter, "'There Should Be No Love between Us and Them'. Social Life and Bounds of Jewish and Canon Law in Early Modern Poland," Polin 22: *Social and Cultural Boundaries* (2010): 249–270; Edward Fram, *My Dear Daughter. Rabbi Benajmin Slonik and the Education of Jewish Women in Sixteenth Century Poland* (Cincinnati, OH: Hebrew Union College Press; Detroit, MI: distributed by Wayne State University Press, 2007); *Ideals Face Reality. Jewish Life in Poland 1550–1655* (Cincinnati, OH: Hebrew Union College Press, 1997).

13 Jacob Katz, *The "Shabbes Goy". A Study in Halachic Flexibility* (Philadelphia, PA: Jewish Publication Society, 1989).

14 Majer Bałaban, *Historia Żydów w Krakowie i na Kazimierzu 1304–1868* [The History of Jews in Kraków and Kazimierz 1304–1868; Kraków: Nadzieja, 1931], vol. 1, 407 with note 3; Józef Gierowski, "Die Juden in Polen im 17. und 18. Jahrhundert und ihre Beziehungen zu den deutschen Städten von Leipzig bis Frankfurt a. M." [The Jews in Poland in the seventeenth and the eighteenth centuries and their relations to the German cities from Leipzig to Frankfurt on Main] in *Die wirtschaftlichen und kulturellen Beziehungen zwischen den jüdischen Gemeinden in Polen und Deutschland vom 16. bis zum 20. Jahrhundert* [The economic and cultural relations between the Jewish communities in Poland and in Germany from the 16th to the 20th centuries], ed. Karl-Erich Grözinger (Wiesbaden: Harrassowitz, 1992), 3–19, here 4.

15 Fettke, *Juden und Nichtjuden*, 84–87.

Similarly, again in a small town, Binyamin Slonik was asked whether it was acceptable for a Jew to lend a good coat to a Christian neighbor, when this Christian would wear the coat to church. Slonik confirmed that it was indeed acceptable, for the Christian neighbor would be wearing the coat to impress his neighbors, but not because of religious considerations (which would amount to idolatry).[16]

At no time did Jewish writers take the security of Jewish existence in early modern Poland–Lithuania for granted, although in the sixteenth century this had been constantly emphasized in contrast to treatment of Jews in the Holy Roman Empire and to the memory of the expulsions from Western Europe. In any dealings with non-Jews, Jewish normative sources appealed for restraint, portraying potential dangers in vivid colors. Sometimes, however, it is clear that such normative distance was not an absolute rule, and that under specific circumstances close relations between Jews and non-Jews were considered positive or at least not harmful.

A striving for distance is also characteristic in non-Jewish norms concerning Jewish–Christian coexistence. The majority of the sources reflect the opinion of the Roman Catholic Church; since the Middle Ages, ecclesiastical authors had been setting up normative guidelines for the coexistence of Jews and Christians. From the seventeenth century on, bourgeois writers discovered this topic as well, and like the ecclesiastical authors before them, they argued in polemical texts for the segregation between Christians and Jews and the marginalization of the latter.[17]

---

16 Benjamin Aaron Slonik, Responsum 86, in Nisson E. Shulman, *Authority and Community. Polish Jewry in the Sixteenth Century* (Hoboken: Ktav Pub. House; New York: Yeshiva University Press, 1986), 160; Magda Teter, "Kilka uwag na temat podziałów społecznych i religijnych," 331.

17 Judith Kalik, "Jews in Catholic ecclesiastic legislation in the Polish–Lithuanian Commonwealth," *Kwartalnik Historii Żydów* 209 (2004): 26–39; "Church's Involvement in the Contacts between Jews and Burghers in the Seventeenth–Eighteenth Centuries Polish–Lithuanian Commonwealth," *Kwartalnik Historii Żydów* 207 (2003): 342–48; "The Attitudes towards the Jews in the Christian Polemic Literature in Poland in the 16th–18th Centuries," in *Jews and Slavs*, vol. 11: *Jewish–Polish and Jewish–Russian Contacts*, ed. W. Moskovich and I. Fijałkowska-Janiak (Jerusalem: Hebrew University, 2003), 58–78; Hanna Węgrzynek, "Was the Catholic Church in Poland Afraid of Conversion to Judaism in the Early Sixteenth Century?" *Kwartalnik Historii Żydów* 1 (2005): 5–10; "The Attitude of the Catholic Church toward Jews in Poland at the Beginning of the Eighteenth Century," *Kwartalnik Historii Żydów* 4 (2006): 662–68; "The Catholic Church and the Jews in the Kraków Diocese during the Sixteenth Century," History.Pth.Net.Pl, http://www.history.pth.net.pl/articles, accessed November 9, 2016. Originally in Polish: "Kościół katolicki a Żydzi w Małopolsce w XVI wieku," in *Kościół katolicki w Małopolsce w średniowieczu i we*

From the Middle Ages on, religious differences had been demarcated by forcing Jews to wear distinguishing marks on their clothing, by spatial segregation, and by marginalizing them in economic as well as social life. During the sixteenth century, this issue found its way into political debates in the Polish Sejm (see below).[18] In the mid-sixteenth century, a new motif appeared: borrowing from anti-Jewish polemics in Western Europe, Polish authors integrated the accusation of ritual murder into their works, using the trial of Trent in 1475, which had been described at length in the chronicle of Jan Długosz, as a template.[19] At the same time, accusations of the desecration of the Host were aimed directly against Jews as well as (indirectly) against the rising Protestant movement. Whenever such allegations were taken to trial before ecclesiastical and secular courts, economic motives usually played a major role.[20] Accusations of an alleged host desecration took place mainly between the mid-sixteenth and the mid-seventeenth centuries. By then, the wave of trials lessened remarkably in the second half of the seventeenth century, when the leading role of

---

wczesnym okresie nowożytnym [The Catholic Church and the Jews in Lesser Poland in the Middle Ages and in the Early Modern Era], ed. Waldemar Kowalski and Jadwiga Muszyńska (Kielce: Kieleckie Towarzystwo Naukowe; Gdańsk: Officina Ferberiana 2001), 225–36. On the Orthodox Church, Judith Kalik, "The Jews and the various churches of the Polish–Lithuanian Commonwealth," in *Churches and Confessions in East Central Europe in Early Modern Times*, vol. 3, ed. Hubert Mikołaj Łaszkiewicz (Lublin: Instytut Europy Środkowo Wschodniej, 1999), 144–49; "The Orthodox Church and the Jews in the Polish–Lithuanian Commonwealth," in *Jewish History: Gzeirot Ta"h. Jews, Cossacks and Peasants in 1648 Ukraine* 17, no. 2 (2003): 229–37; examples for bourgeois polemical literature: Tazbir, *Żydzi w opinii staropolskiej*.

18 Judith Kalik, "Szlachta Attitudes towards Jewish Arenda in the Seventeenth and Eighteenth Centuries," in *Gal-Ed. On the History of the Jews in Poland* 14 (1995): 15–25, here 19; Adam Kaźmierczyk, *Sejmy i sejmiki szlacheckie wobec Żydów w drugiej połowie XVII wieku* [Sejms and sejmiki on Jews in the second half of the seventeenth century] (Warsaw: Wydawnictwo Sejmowe, 1994).

19 On the topic of "ritual murder": Susanna Buttaroni and Stanisław Musiał, eds., *Ritualmord. Legenden in der europäischen Geschichte* [Ritual Murder. Legends in European History] (Vienna: Böhlau, 2003); Daniel Tollet, *Accuser pour convertir. Du bon usage de l'accusation de crime rituel dans la Pologne catholique à l'époque moderne* [Accusing to convert. How the accusation of ritual crime was exploited in Catholic Poland down to the Modern period] (Paris: Presses universitaires de Fran, 2000); Robert Weinberg, "The Blood Libel in Eastern Europe," *Jewish History* 26 (2012): 275–285 (with further literature).

20 Hanna Węgrzynek, *"Czarna legenda" Żydów. Procesy o mordy rytualne w dawnej Polsce* [The "black legend" of the Jews: Trials for alleged ritual murder in old Poland] (Warsaw: Wydawnictwo Bellona; Wydawnictwo Fundacji Historia pro Futuro, 1995); Zenon Guldon and Jacek Wijaczka, *Procesy o mordy rytualne w Polsce w XVI–XVIII wieku* [Trials for ritual murder in Poland in the seventeenth and eighteenth centuries] (Kielce: Wydawnictwo DCF, 1995).

the Catholic church appeared no longer to be endangered by Protestant rivals. Allegations of ritual murder first peaked in the 1560s and 1570s, accompanied by trials against host desecration, where Jews were mostly accused of "mocking the Passion of Christ." During the seventeenth century, a series of trials took place in the southeastern provinces of Poland–Lithuania, mirroring the insecurity of the population before and after the Cossack uprising; in the eighteenth century, as well, most trials of this sort were held in that region.[21]

The seventeenth century also witnessed an increasing wave of polemical texts against the employment of Christian servants in Jewish households. "Shabbes goyim" found employment not only in private homes but also within communities, where their task was to extinguish the candles after the Shabbat service, or they served as cemetery keepers and undertakers. Most infuriating, in the eyes of these authors, however, was the employment of female servants to live together with Jews under one roof.[22]

The Catholic demands for marginalization and exclusion of Jews found their way into the public discourse not only by means of sermons or political incentives of the Catholic hierarchy. Jan Długosz's chronicle, with its copious amounts of anti-Jewish polemics, was used to train young noblemen in rhetoric, and his narration of Polish history heavily influenced the early modern political debate.[23] From the seventeenth century on, bourgeois authors such as Sebastian

---

21 Guldon and Wijaczka, *Procesy o mordy rytualne w Polsce*; "Procesy o mordy rytualne na Rusi Czerwonej, Podolu i prawobrzeżnej Ukrainie w XVI–XVIII wieku" [Trials for ritual murder in Red Ruthenia, Podolia and right-bank Ukraine in the seventeenth and eighteenth centuries], *Nasza Przeszłość* 81 (1994): 5–50; Jacek Wijaczka, "Ritualmordbeschuldigungen und -prozesse in Polen-Litauen vom 16. bis 18. Jahrhundert" [Ritual murder accusations and trials in Poland-Lithuanian from the sixteenth to the eighteenth centuries] in *Ritualmord*, Buttaroni and Musiał, 213–32; see also Jurgita Šiaučiūnaitė-Verbickienė, "Blood Libel in a Multi-Confessional Society: The Case of the Grand Duchy of Lithuania," *East European Jewish Affairs* 38, no. 2 (2008): 201–209.

22 Judith Kalik, "Christian Servants Employed by Jews in the Polish–Lithuanian Commonwealth in the Seventeenth and Eighteenth Centuries," *Polin: Focusing on Jews in the Polish Borderlands* 14 (2001): 259–70; Adam Kaźmierczyk, "The Problem of Christian Servants as Reflected in the Legal Codes of the Polish–Lithuanian Commonwealth during the Second Half of the Seventeenth Century and the Saxon Period," *Gal-Ed. On the History of the Jews in Poland* 15–16 (1997): 23–40.

23 Hans-Jürgen Bömelburg, *Frühneuzeitliche Nationen im östlichen Europa. Das polnische Geschichtsdenken und die Reichweite einer humanistischen Nationalgeschichte (1500-1700)* [Early modern nations in Eastern Europe. Polish historical thinking and the diffusion of a humanistic national history (1500-1700)] (Wiesbaden: Harrassowitz, 2006), 33–41; Jürgen Heyde, *Transkulturelle Kommunikation und Verflechtung. Die jüdischen Wirtschaftseliten in Polen vom 14. bis zum 16. Jahrhundert* [Intercultural communication and interconnection: the Jewish economic elites in Poland from the fourteenth to the sixteenth centuries]

Miczyński and Sebastian Śleszkowski, whose works reached a wide public and were reprinted several times, adapted Catholic polemics in their use of a bourgeois agenda.[24] Later in the seventeenth century, there was an intellectual and ideological feedback-loop: publications intended for burghers were responsible for a renewed interest in anti-Jewish polemics within the theological debate, and sermons and theological books were used as references in bourgeois works.[25] Consequently, the focus of theological polemics shifted. Until the seventeenth century, it was heavily influenced by the dispute with the Protestants over the doctrine of transubstantiation and focused on Eucharistic miracles around the topics of blood and the sacred host, but later these arguments faded into the background and gave way to a more general othering of the Jews.

Magda Teter has shown that Catholic teaching in this phase became more and more "polonized," meaning that confessional confrontation ceased to be a theological topic but became a part of the political and diplomatic battleground.[26] Identifying Protestantism and Orthodoxy with political enemies of the Polish–Lithuanian Commonwealth seemed in a way self-evident. Judaism, however, did not fit into such categories; therefore, the Jews were presented either as agents of the Swedes or the Ottomans, but always as an enemy force.[27] This was necessary to build a common ground with the political debates of the nobility, who appeared to have little interest in anti-Jewish polemics. From time to time parliamentary debates alluded to Catholic anti-Jewish rhetoric, especially during the reform debates of the sixteenth and again from the late seventeenth century onwards. In contrast to bourgeois authors, however, the nobles seemed not inclined to take this sort of polemics too seriously. It was a means of directing attention to certain topics, and had to be weighed against elements of—sometimes outspoken—anticlerical polemics. Despite all that, the noble discourse was neither anti-Jewish nor anti-Catholic.[28]

(Wiesbaden: Harrassowitz, 2014), 56–67; Hanna Zaremska, *Żydzi w średniowiecznej Polsce. Gmina krakowska* [Jews in Medieval Poland. The Kraków community] (Warsaw: Instytut Historii PAN, 2011), 267–92.

24 Tazbir, "Żydzi w opinii staropolskiej," 219–20.

25 Magda Teter, *Jews and Heretics in Catholic Poland. A Beleaguered Church in the Post-Reformation Era* (Cambridge: Cambridge University Press, 2006), 107.

26 Ibid., 52–58.

27 Hanna Węgrzynek, "The Attitude of the Catholic Church towards Jews in Poland at the Beginning of the Eighteenth Century," *Kwartalnik Historii Żydów* 4 (2006): 662–68; Judith Kalik, "Attitude towards the Jews and Catholic Identity in Eighteenth Century Poland," in *Confessional Identity in East Central Europe*, ed. Maria Crăciun, (Aldershot, UK: Ashgate, 2002), 181–93; Teter, *Jews and Heretics*, 107–13.

28 Heyde, *Transkulturelle Kommunikation*, 67–74; Teter, *Jews and Heretics*, 80–98.

There is a remarkable difference between the Jewish perception of their non-Jewish surroundings and the picture of Jews presented in the early modern Polish discourse. Jewish statements about the non-Jewish world display knowledge about and reflection on the legal and economic structures as well as political and cultural developments in Poland–Lithuania, whereas the picture of the Jews in the Polish public discourse seems curiously out of touch with the realities of Jewish life in the commonwealth. The most important topics and images of this debate were copied from medieval and Western European contexts and were unsuitable for communicating with the Jewish population. On the contrary, the main goal was to give testimony, to present their own point to their own audience; it was part of the political debate and political agenda-setting. The political debate "about Jews" in the early modern Polish–Lithuanian Commonwealth was not directed at the Jews, but appears as part of political and social negotiation processes within the non-Jewish elites. This might help to explain discrepancies between the basic tenor of those debates and the practical relations among Jews and non-Jews, characterized by social interconnection, pragmatic deal-making and, not infrequently, trustful interaction.

PRACTICES/ENCOUNTERS

Contacts between Jews and burghers occurred frequently in everyday life, ranging from business dealings to neighborly communication. Nonetheless, historiography describes the relations between those two groups traditionally as tense and conflict-ridden. Negative images appear in a variety of sources, including in bourgeois anti-Jewish literature, in the agitation of the towns' representatives at the Four Years' Sejm at the end of the eighteenth century, and in opinions of burghers in the province of Great Poland, when they were interrogated by German missionaries from the Institutum Judaicum in Halle, around the middle of the eighteenth century.

In fact, in early modern Poland–Lithuania institutional conflicts between burghers and Jews concerned mostly trade and crafts, but sometimes involved settlement rights within towns, mostly in royal towns governed by the Magdeburg law and less so in private towns, where the owners exercised their power to curb such conflicts.[29] But even in times of acute institutional

---

29 On conflicts, Heyde, *Transkulturelle Kommunikation*, 126–47; Jacob Goldberg, "De non tolerandis Judaeis. On the Introduction of Anti-Jewish laws into Polish towns and the Struggle against them," in *Studies in Jewish History. Presented to Professor Raphael Mahler on his Seventy-Fifth Birthday*, ed. Shmuel Yeivin (Merhavia: Sifriyat Po'alim, 1974), 39–52; on relations in

conflict, relations between individual burghers and Jews might not necessarily have deteriorated. When the magistrate of Poznań tried in the late 1530s to have the town's Jews expelled, the minutes of the town council again and again complained that Poznań burghers in spite of the magistrate's efforts were willing to rent rooms and houses to Jews (who had lost their homes in a fire in 1536).[30] In eighteenth-century Kozienice in the district of Radom, Jadwiga Muszyńska noted similar complaints from town officials against fellow burghers.[31] Furthermore, even though conflicts between "the burghers" and "the Jews" almost in every case were about (Jewish) trading rights, partnerships and companies between burghers and Jews in long-distance trade appeared to be mostly unaffected by these. Bourgeois merchants seemed not to have had major qualms about establishing relationships with Jews, as long as there was no direct pressure not to do so. Therefore, even in an atmosphere of tension between the magistrate and the kahal as representative bodies of burghers and Jews in town, such partnerships could be formed with Jewish merchants from towns in other countries or provinces (e.g., from Poland to the Grand Duchy of Lithuania or from Kraków to Volynia), or even, as Edmund Kizik has shown in the case of Gdańsk, coming from one of the suburbs under the rule of the bishop instead of the magistrate.[32]

---

private towns see Yvonne Kleinmann, "Städtische Gemeinschaft. Christen und Juden im frühneuzeitlichen Rzeszów," *Osteuropa* 62, no. 10 (2012): 3–24; "Normsetzung, Narration und religiöse Symbolik. Privilegien als Grundlage der Religionspolitik auf dem frühneuzeitlichen Latifundium Rzeszów" [Setting of norms, narratives and religious symbolism. Privileges as the basis for the religious policy in the Early-Modern latifundium of Rzeszów] in *Kommunikation durch symbolische Akte* [Communication through symbolic acts], 249–69; Gershon D. Hundert, *The Jews in a Polish Private Town. The Case of Opatów in the Eighteenth Century*, (Baltimore, MD: Johns Hopkins University Press, 1992). On direct negotiations between magistrates and Jewish communities as a form of conflict management, see François Guesnet, "Agreements between Neighbours. The 'ugody' as a Source on Jewish–Christian Relations in Early Modern Poland," in *Jewish History* 24 (2010): 257–270; Hanna Węgrzynek, "Jewish–Christian Agreements and Their Impact on the Legal Status of Jews in Polish Towns (the Case of Lublin)," *Kwartalnik Historii Żydów* 1 (2011): 107–112.

30 Rex Rexheuser, "Zurückdrängen oder Aussiedeln. Die Stadt Posen und ihre Juden 1518–1538" [Expulsion or resettlement. The city of Poznań and its Jews 1518–1538] in *Kulturen und Gedächtnis. Studien und Reflexionen zur Geschichte des östlichen Europas* [Cultures and Memory. Studies and Reflections on the History of Eastern Europe] (Wiesbaden: Harrassowitz, 2008), 13–38.

31 Jadwiga Muszyńska, "Żydzi i mieszczanie w sandomierskich miastach królewskich w XVIII wieku" [Jews and burghers in the royal towns of the Sandomierz Province in the eighteenth century], *Kwartalnik Historii Żydów* 207 (2003): 403–15.

32 Edmund Kizik, "Mieszczaństwo gdańskie wobec Żydów w XVII–XVIII wieku," [The Danzig burghers' attitude to Jews in the seventeenth and eighteenth centuries], *Kwartalnik*

In his study on Opatów, Gershon D. Hundert rightly concluded that everyday contacts between burghers and Jews were by far more intensive than is suggested by the traditional historiographical image with its emphasis on conflicts. For instance, knowledge of the Polish language must have been widespread and almost essential. But one has to bear in mind that the concept of separate social realms as an ideal was present not just on the side of the burghers, but for Jews as well.

In this respect, the contacts between Jews and nobles show remarkable parallels to those with burghers. Jewish involvement in the arenda entailed not only intensive economic ties, but also frequent personal contacts between leaseholders and nobles, as examples from eighteenth-century memoirs or correspondence show.[33] There are also traces in inner-Jewish sources. Both in noble and in Jewish sources the assessment of this situation varies significantly.

Decidedly negative is the image of a magnate portrayed in Salomon Maimon's description of his grandfather's estate.[34] Maimon's portrait long enjoyed acceptance in historiography because it fit so well with the idea of separate realms.[35] But a different impression prevailed in the memoirs of Dov Ber Birkenthal of Bolechów: the author describes close neighborly relations with nobles, who visited his home as well as received visits from him; Dov Ber explicitly calls one of his neighbors a friend.[36] His experiences conform to criticisms of the nobility from the southeastern parts of Poland–Lithuania by the journalist and politician Jędrzej Kitowicz. Kitowicz lamented that these nobles were raised among Jews and knew no other burghers than Jews, which would

---

Historii Żydów 207 (2003): 416–34; Judith Kalik, "Suburban Story. Structure of Jewish Communities in Largest Royal Cities of Eighteenth Century Crown Poland," *Kwartalnik Historyczny* 2 (2006): 47–74.

33 Goldberg, "Poles and Jews," 257–62; Moshe Rosman, *The Lords' Jews. Magnate–Jewish Relations in the Polish–Lithuanian Commonwealth During the Eighteenth Century* (Cambridge, MA: Harvard University Press for the Center for Jewish Studies, Harvard University and the Harvard Ukrainian Research Institute, 1990); Adam Teller, *Money, Power, and Influence in Eighteenth-Century Lithuania: The Jews on the Radziwill Estates* (Stanford, CA: Stanford University Press, 2016).

34 *Salomon Maimons Lebensgeschichte. Von ihm selbst erzählt* [The Life History of Salomon Maimon. Told by Himself], ed. Z. Batscha. (Frankfurt a.M.: Insel, 1995), 14–17.

35 Gershon D. Hundert, "The Kehilla and the Municipality in Private Towns at the End of the Early Modern Period," in *The Jews in Old Poland. 1000–1795*, ed. Antony Polonsky (London: I. B. Tauris, 1993), 172–85, here 174–75.

36 Goldberg, "Poles and Jews," 259; *The Memoirs of Ber of Bolechow*; cf. Gershon D. Hundert, "Bandits in Bolechów: Eighteenth-Century Jewish Memoirs in Context," *Jewish History* 22, no. 4 (2008): 373–85.

explain why they thwarted any effort of the Warsaw burghers to drive the Jews out the town and "screamed with all their might in their [the Jews'] defense."[37]

Social interactions between clergy and Jews appear to have been mostly limited to economic contacts. Credits raised by Jews from ecclesiastical institutions (not just Catholic clergy, but also Orthodox or Uniate, as well as religious orders, e.g., the Jesuits) enabled them to locate funds and acquire stable income from interest payments. Indirectly, a priest might become involved in conflicts around the lease of commodities by a noble to a Jew. Polemical literature quoted examples of churches, allegedly sealed up by a Jewish leaseholder in order to enforce payments; on the other hand, there are documented cases showing that ecclesiastical creditors enforced the sealing of a synagogue in analogous cases.[38] Representatives of the church themselves leased out commodities or real estate to Jews and made sure that their subjects met the obligations to the Jewish leaseholders. Thus, for instance, the bishop of Przemyśl agreed in an arenda contract from 1778 that the peasants of a certain village should work a "pańszczyzna" (compulsory labor tribute) of one day a week for the Jewish leaseholder.[39] Around the same time the parish priest of Chocz set up a partnership with a Jewish entrepreneur, who was to build an ironworks factory for him.[40]

---

37 Jędrzej Kitowicz, *Pamiętniki, czyli historia polska* [Memoirs—a history of Poland], ed. Przemysława Matuszewska and Zofia Lewinówna (Warsaw: Państwowy Instytut Wydawniczy, 1971), 441.

38 Judith Kalik, "Patterns of Contact Between the Catholic Church and the Jews in the Polish–Lithuanian Commonwealth: The Jewish Debts," in *Studies in the History of the Jews in Old Poland*, ed. Adam Teller (Jerusalem: Scripta Hierosolymitana 38, 1938), 102–22; "The Orthodox Church and the Jews in the Polish–Lithuanian Commonwealth," *Jewish History* 17, no. 2 (2003): *Gzeirot Ta"h. Jews, Cossacks and Peasants in 1648 Ukraine*, 229–37; "The Jews and the Various Churches of the Polish–Lithuanian Commonwealth," in *Churches and Confessions*, ed. Łaszkiewicz, 144–49; "Hafkadah u-widerkaf be-peilutam ha-kalkalit shel yehudei mamlekhet Polin-Lita" [Deposits and loans in the economic activity of Jews in Poland-Lithuania], in *Yazimut ha-yehudit be-et ha-hadashah. Mizrach Eiropah ve-erets* [Israel/Jewish entrepreneurship in Modern times. Eastern Europe and Eretz Israel] (Jerusalem: Magnes Press, 2000), 25–47.

39 Kalik, "Christian servants," 263.

40 Jacob Goldberg, "Jak ksiądz z Żydem zakładali manufakturę żelazną w Wielkopolsce. O przedsiębiorcach żydowskich w przemyśle polskim w XVIII w." [How a priest established an iron factory with a Jew in Wielkopolska. On Jewish involvement in Polish industry in the eighteenth century], in *The Jews in Poland*, vol. 1, ed. Andrzej Paluch (Kraków: Jagiellonian University, Research Center on Jewish History and Culture in Poland, 1992), 149–60; "Manufaktura żelazna księdza infułata Kazimierza Lipskiego i Szlamy Efraimowicza w Choczu (inicjatywy gospodarcze Żydów w XVIII wieku)" [The iron factory of Prelate

A peculiar problem in relations between clergy and Jews involved converts. Bringing Jews to accept Christianity was an important goal in Catholic policy toward Jews, but Catholic clergy also harbored deep-rooted distrust of people who changed their faith. In early modern times the Roman Catholic Church in Poland showed no inclination for systematic missionary work among Jews; some individual missionary undertakings competed rather with the efforts of Protestant missionaries (e.g., from the Institutum Judaicum in Halle). In general, Catholic clergy appeared very skeptical of the chances of converting Jews in Poland and Lithuania to Christianity.[41] For the converts themselves, such a step usually had far-reaching consequences, as they had to find a place within Christian society and were supposed to cut their ties to the Jewish environment. This was demanded by the church in order to prevent possible reversions to Judaism, but was often also enforced by the Jewish community so that family members of the converts might not be pressured to leave Judaism themselves.

RELATIONS IN A MULTIPOLAR FRAMEWORK[42]

The Sejm of Piotrków in 1538 represents one of the "darker" moments in Polish–Jewish relations, as a previously unheard of number of anti-Jewish

---

Kazimierz Lipski and Szlama Efraimowicz—economic initiatives of Jews in the eighteenth century], in *Żydzi w Wielkopolsce na przestrzeni dziejów* [Jews in Wielkopolska throughout the centuries], ed. Jerzy Topolski and Krzysztof Modelski (Poznań: Wydawnictwo Poznańskie, 1995), 83–99.

41 Adam Kaźmierczyk, *Rodziłem się Żydem… Konwersje Żydów w Rzeczypospolitej XVII–XVIII wieku* [I was born a Jew. The conversion of Jews in the Polish-Lithuanian Commonwealth in the seventeenth and eighteenth centuries] (Kraków: Księgarnia Akademicka, 2015)—with further literature; Jacob Goldberg, "Die getauften Juden in Polen-Litauen im 16.–18. Jahrhundert. Taufe, soziale Umschichtung und Integration," [Baptized Jews in Poland-Lithuania in the sixteenth-eighteenth centuries. Baptism, social restructuring and integration], *Jahrbücher für Geschichte Osteuropas* [Yearbooks for the History of Eastern Europe] 30 (1982): 54–98; Magda Teter, "Jewish Conversions to Catholicism in the Polish–Lithuanian Commonwealth of the Seventeenth and Eighteenth Centuries," *Jewish History* 17 (2003): 257–83; on Protestant missions, Jan Doktór, ed., *W poszukiwaniu żydowskich kryptochrześcijan. Dzienniki ewangelickich misjonarzy z wędrówek po Rzeczypospolitej w latach 1730–1747* [Looking for Jewish crypto-Christians. The diaries of Protestant missionaries travelling across the Polish Lithuanian Commonwealth in the years 1730–1747] (Warsaw: Tikkun, 1999); "Christian Missions among Jews in the Eighteenth Century: Motivations and Results," *Kwartalnik Historii Żydów* 1 (2012): 18–38.

42 The argument in this passage is more broadly developed in my article "Polemics and Participation—Anti-Jewish Legislation is the Polish Diet (Sejm) in the 16th Century and

measures were not only discussed but also passed as law. However, to add a positive note, afterward there were no traces of their implementation. The lack of implementation should not be attributed to incompetence or corruption, and the fierceness of the debated measures should not be interpreted merely as an anti-Jewish stance by the king and *szlachta*. In fact, this very coincidence makes it possible to reframe the analysis of Polish–Jewish relations by taking them as indications of an entirely different conflict.

The argument is as follows: the constitutions of 1538 were not enforced in juridical practice, but they fulfilled their goal nevertheless, for it was not the legal position of Jews that was meant to change—it was the political balance between the king and the nobility. In short, the anti-Jewish measures were part of the greater struggle for noble participation, known as the "execution of rights" movement. King Zygmunt realized this, and by giving in to the demands presented by the *szlachta* envoys and granting the constitutions of 1538, he sent out the right signals. Thus, the greater goal was achieved, and there was no need to dwell on the details. The anti-Jewish legislation of 1538 had a high symbolic value, but it was not supposed to have a major practical influence.

The events of the 1538 Sejm will be discussed under three headings. The first presents the major features of the Piotrków constitutions on the Jews, analyzes the sources from which they were drawn and their polemical impact. It is followed by a comparison of the Piotrków laws to earlier legislation on the Jews, namely, the constitutions passed at the Kraków Sejm of 1532 and several royal decrees issued to the burghers, when they demanded similar measures to those of the 1538 Sejm. Examining the Jewish legal position as a point of discussion at the Sejm of 1534 and the *sejmiki* afterward leads to an understanding of the polemical undertones; a decree issued by King Zygmunt August in 1551 makes it clear that there had not been any intention of implementing the anti-Jewish legislation of 1538. Based on these points, we can finally discuss the "value" of the Piotrków constitutions in terms of political communication.

The constitutions on the Jews of the Piotrków Sejm did not form a concise legislative program.[43] The first three points took up issues discussed

---

its Political Contexts," in *Religion in the Mirror of Law. Eastern European Perspectives from the Early Modern Period to 1939*, ed. Yvonne Kleinmann, Stephan Stach, and Tracie Wilson (Frankfurt: Vittorio Klostermann, 2016), 3–20.

43 "Konstytucje Sejmu walnego Piotrkowskiego 1538" [The Consitution of the General Sejm in Piotrków in 1538], in *Volumina Constitutionum*, vol. 1, part 2: 1527–1549, ed. Wacław Uruszczak, Stanisław Grodziski, and Irena Dwornicka (Warsaw: Wydawnictwo Sejmowe, 2000), 160–92, especially 169–70.

earlier at the forum of the Sejm. First, there was the claim that Jews were to be forbidden to hold public leases or offices of any kind.[44] That demand had first been brought up at the Sejm of Radom in 1505, but was not passed as a bill.[45] In Piotrków, the constitution added a polemical phrase motivating the ban, declaring that it would be unworthy and against divine law to allow people "of that kind" ("eius generis homines") to hold any honors or offices among Christians. The next phrase repeated a constitution from 1532, demanding that Jewish creditors register their pawns in the official record books. This passage referred to the Kraków Sejm of 1532, where it had been an incentive of Jewish creditors that led to this constitution—what the Jews then had asked for was now demanded of them. The third sentence revoked a passage from the first general privilege for the Jews, freeing a Jewish pawnbroker from responsibility for taking stolen goods on commission. From now on, Jews were to be held responsible and, as it was emphasized, should be compulsorily incarcerated under such an accusation.

The next paragraphs dealt with issues that had not been brought up in previous legislative discussions. They mirrored the conflict between burghers and Jews about Jewish trading rights in the large royal cities.[46] No longer should Jews be granted unrestricted trading rights, but Jews should be submitted to trading regulations—to be introduced in the future—in the whole kingdom, and should respect existing trading agreements with the burghers in some of the royal towns.

In the third paragraph, the constitution discussed an old demand by the Roman Catholic Church. It stated that the Jews were not observing an old regulation to place signs on their clothing distinguishing them from the Christians. Therefore, in the future they were to wear a yellow hat everywhere in the kingdom, except during travel, when they might take off these signs and hide them.

The various points mentioned in the constitution showed a pronounced and definitely biased picture of Jews. Anti-Jewish polemics of this sort in the Sejm constitution were exceptional, as we can see when comparing the

---

44 "Statuimus inviolabiliter observandum, Iudaeos teloneis quibuscunque praefici non debere neque posse, indignum et iuri divino contrarium censentes, eius generis homines aliquibus honoribus et officiis inter christianos fungi debere," in *Konstytucje Sejmu walnego Piotrkowskiego 1538*, 169–70.

45 Ferdinand Bostel, "Tymczasowa ustawa radomska z r. 1505" [The provisional Radom law of 1505], *Kwartalnik Historyczny* 3 (1889): 658–86, here 666, 679. A new edition of the project is printed in Stanisław Grodziski, Irena Dwornicka and Wacław Uruszczak, *Volumina Constitutionum*, vol. 1, part 1: *1493–1526* (Wydawnictwo Sejmowe, Warsaw, 1996), 143–47.

46 Heyde, *Transkulturelle Kommunikation*, 126–47.

proceedings of the 1532 Sejm, when the inscription of pawns in the local court records was introduced. The said constitution stated that it had become customary to oblige the seniors of the Jewish community with supervision of the pawns. Jewish creditors, however, thought this to be impractical, and in order to avoid uncertainties about a pawn or some public scandal or mischief, they asked to revert to the old custom of inscribing them in the court records.[47] By this means, the constitution restricted a part of Jewish communal autonomy, but it did so in support of a Jewish incentive and without polemical undertones.

The Sejm of 1532 discussed another project that might have affected Jews, but it was not passed as a constitution. The "correction of the laws" (*korektura praw*) was meant to provide an amendment and unification of law in the whole kingdom. In its parts affecting Jews, it was based on general privileges, but it also revoked some economic rights granted exclusively to Jews but not to Christians, such as the release from responsibility in accepting a pawn of stolen origin. On the other hand, it definitely maintained the paragraphs concerning protection from invading a Jew's house or abducting Jewish children for baptism, among others.[48]

But not all legal incentives were discussed at the Sejm. In matters concerning the Jews, Zygmunt asserted his rights as their supreme overlord, giving out privileges and issuing decrees without consulting the parliament. When the king issued a decree in 1532 confirming Jewish trading rights in the Polish kingdom, he issued a special order to the towns in Royal Prussia. In this decree, the king states that during the Sejm in Kraków a complaint was brought up by "the entirety of the Jews of the king as well as the Jews of his subjects in the Polish kingdom" that Prussian towns denied entry to Jewish merchants. At the instance of all estates of the kingdom, the king ordered Prussian towns to allow Jews to enter and provide trade unhindered.[49]

The king implies that there was no difference between him and the estates in the question of unlimited trading rights for the Jews. The burghers, however,

---

47 *Volumina Constitutionum*, vol. 1, part 2, no. 41: Sejm walny krakowski 1531–1532, 99.
48 Waclaw Uruszczak, *Korektura praw z 1532 roku. Studium historycznoprawne* [The correction of the laws of 1532. A historical-legal study], vol. I (Warsaw: Nakład Uniwersytetu Jagiellońskiego: Państwowe Wydawnictwo Naukowe, Oddział w Krakowie, 1990), 117–19; ibid., vol. 2 (Kraków, 1991), 91–92.
49 Vladislaus Pociecha, ed., *Acta Tomiciana per Stanislaum Gorski Canonicum ejusdem Petri Tomicii, post Serenissem Bone Sforce Regine Polonie Secretarium collecte* [Acta Tomiciana, collected by Canons Stanisław Górski and Piotr Tomicki, Secretaries of the Exalted Bona Sforza, Queen of Poland], vol. 14 (Poznań: Bibliotheca Kornicensis, 1952), 89–90. A similar decree was issued to all royal dignitaries and town magistrates in the kingdom (Ibid., 89).

had lobbied unsuccessfully for several decades for official restrictions on Jewish trade, but their complaints had been regularly rejected. In 1506, King Alexander explained his standpoint in an address to the burghers of Lwów: "It is true that the Jews of Lwów share the urban burdens just as well as the Christians and persons of other faiths . . . and therefore they are to enjoy the same freedoms as their fellow citizens."[50]

In the 1530s, however, the situation had somewhat changed. At the Sejm of 1534, for the first time representatives of the *szlachta* brought up a complaint that the Jews would soon monopolize the whole trade in the kingdom. They were said to hold commercial ties to other countries, buying up cattle, furs, or skins in Moldavia and selling them again to foreign merchants, thus driving up prices. The envoys demanded that Jews should be compelled to wear a yellow badge as a distinguishing sign, and should be made to provide hostages if stolen goods were to be found in a Jew's home.[51]

In its answer, the senate pointed out the following: Jews, as subjects of the king, paid ordinary as well as extraordinary taxes and were entitled to trade on behalf of their privileges; these rights could not be revoked without consent of the king.[52]

As the envoys returned home from the Sejm, they convened at regional dietines (*sejmiki*) to give accounts of their activity at the Sejm. As the envoys of Małopolska described the initiative concerning Jewish trade at the *sejmik* of Parczów, they were greeted with rejection and disbelief. The nobles of Małopolska, on the contrary, voiced their opinion that the diet should encourage Jewish trade, especially in Kraków, because the Jews provided goods at better prices than Christian merchants. To the nobles convened in Parczów, without doubt it was the Christian merchants of Kraków, and not the Jews,

---

50 "[...] verum cum judei Leopolienses cum cristianis et aliorum rituum personis illuc commorantibus equaliter civilia ferunt onera sumptusque pares ad reformacionem civilem tribuunt et impendunt, merito eadem libertate cum concolis sunt potituri." Sergey A. Bershadsky, ed., *Russko-evreiskii arkhiv: Dokumenty i materialy dlya istorii evreev v Rossii*, vol. 3: *Dokumenty k istorii pol'skich i litovskich evreyev v 1364–1569 gg.* [Russian-Jewish archive: Documents and materials on the history of Jews in Russia, vol. 3: Documents on the history of Polish and Lithuanian Jews in the years 1364–1569], St. Petersburg: Izdanie Obshchestva rasprostraneniia prosvieshcheniia mezhdy evreiami v Rossii, 1903), 71–72 (no. 48); Miron Kapral, ed., *Privileyi natsional'nych hromad mista L'vova XIV–XVIII st.* [The Privileges of national associations of the town of Lwów from the fourteenth to the seventeenth Centuries] (Lviv: Mis'ke Hromads'ko-Kul'turne Ob'jednannja "Dokumental'na Skarbnycja L'vova," 2000), 400–401 (no. 118).
51 *Acta Tomiciana*, vol. 16, part 1, 100–107 (no. 51), here 102.
52 *Acta Tomiciana*, vol. 16, part 1, 111–16 (no. 53), here 113–14 (§ 3).

who were to blame for the ruin of the nobility.[53] The answer of the *sejmik* of Małopolska shows clearly that the incentive to restrict Jewish trading rights did not arise in the first place from economic interests of the *szlachta*.

On the basis of these examples, one may formulate a sort of negative conclusion—it becomes quite clear what did *not* drive the anti-Jewish legislation at the Piotrków Sejm of 1538. First, there was no generally hostile attitude toward the Jews, so what was the source of the polemical wording? Second, one sees no direct economic motivation for restricting Jewish economic rights, so why was this so important in the constitution?

The *szlachta* initiative at the Sejm of 1534 and the answer to it indicate conflicting interests between *szlachta* and king. One should thus place the anti-Jewish legislation in a broader framework of the struggle for the "execution of rights." This conflict touches upon a basic problem of Polish parliamentarianism at the beginning of early modern times: What kind of decisions might the king make alone, and how far did parliamentary participation of power go?

During the reign of Zygmunt I there was a heated debate on these questions, when the king chose to declare his nine-year-old son Zygmunt August the grand duke of Lithuania, and enforced his election to be king of Poland in 1530. An election "vivente rege" reduced the right of the nobility to choose its monarch to a mere technicality, and was perceived as a demonstration of contempt for the nobility's political rights.

It was just one example of how the king and his main advisors reacted to the demands of the "execution movement," which ultimately led to an escalation of the conflict—in 1537, the troops who had convened near Lwów refused to follow the king's orders. The incident became known as the "chicken war" (*wojna kokosza*). The king had to look for ways to negotiate with the enraged nobles in order to find a lasting compromise. The Sejms of Piotrków and Kraków in 1538 and 1539 had to provide substantial signs that the king took the demands of the *szlachta* seriously.

It is against this background that the paragraphs of the 1538 constitution against the Jews reveal their sense: the points in the first part referred to former constitutions and projects and thereby underlined the importance of the Sejm debates for legislation. The second part was meant to show that it was not just the agenda of the nobility that the king had to acknowledge; the constitution took up the central points for which the burghers had been lobbying for a long time and integrated one of the core points in Catholic anti-Jewish polemics

---

53 *Acta Tomiciana*, vol. 16, part 2, 358–61 (no. 573), here 360.

since the Middle Ages. With this, the *szlachta* envoys gave a strong signal that they had a large backing for their demands.

To make this point, the policy concerning Jews seemed extraordinarily suitable, because the burghers were struggling to limit Jewish trading rights in order to compensate for their own deteriorating legal position, and the church took to anti-Jewish rhetoric as a means of demonstrating its authority in a time of insincerity because of the rising Protestant movement. Moreover, policy concerning Jews had been traditionally claimed as a prerogative of the king. By attacking the legal position of the Jews, the *szlachta* could claim political participation in a crucial point of the monarch's self-esteem as a ruler, while at the same time Zygmunt lacked means to deny the claim.

This was because in these years Zygmunt tried to enforce his image as a defender of the Catholic faith—in his decrees against the spread of the reformation as well as in the plans to wage a war against the Ottoman Empire. However, he had close ties to Jewish economic elites, for example, the Fiszel family of Kraków, whose members belonged to his and his wife's court. The religious polemics in the wording of the constitution was therefore a demonstration of power aimed at the king.

What does this mean in terms of *perceptions and practices*? The constitutions of the Sejm of 1538 and the incidents leading up to them did not mark the first time that anti-Jewish polemics were used to negotiate participation rights. Instead of directly demanding that the king consider the nobility's positions—which might have been interpreted as an insult to the monarch—the attack on the Jews drove home that point nicely without risking the wrath of the ruler. Similar tactics had been used by Cardinal Oleśnicki in his showdown with king Kazimierz Jagiellończyk in 1454—in the end, the king renounced the Jewish privileges, which he had confirmed just the year before, but afterwards there was no change in the king's policy toward the Jews.[54] Even earlier, passages about Jewish moneylending in the statutes of Kazimierz the Great, issued after and before his confirmations of Jewish privileges, do not make much sense when contrasted with the political practice of the time. On the contrary, the court records of the late fourteenth century reveal a strong commitment not to allow any discrimination against Jewish creditors. The statutes of King

---

54 Jürgen Heyde, "Szlachta polska a Żydzi 1454–1539" [The Polish nobility and the Jews 1454-1539] in *Żydzi i judaizm we współczesnych badaniach polskich* [Jews and Judaism in contemporary Polish studies], vol. 3, ed. Krzysztof Pilarczyk (Księgiarnia Akademicka, Wydawnictwo Naukowe: Kraków, 2003), 13–24.

Kazimierz were invoked in court on a few occasions, but each time, the judges left no doubt that any credit had to be paid back.[55]

After 1538, during the continued struggle about the political constitution of the commonwealth, anti-Jewish expressions and initiatives showed up several times in the years up to the 1560s, but after the union of Lublin these vanished from Sejm debates for more than a hundred years. Only in the early years of the reign of John III Sobieski was anti-Jewish rhetoric again used to influence the king's policy.[56]

Looking for political strategies rather than perceptions might prove useful as well in the interpretation of Jewish sources—taking, for example, the strict admonition on the dangers of the arenda in the charters of the Jewish community of Kraków from 1595, or the negative stance on Jewish encounters with non-Jews in some rabbinical responses.

However, this does not mean that one should neglect displays of anti-Jewish rhetoric as mere symbolic politics, because all those statutes and constitutions were recorded and published—and therefore could be used as arguments that an actual implementation of anti-Jewish measures was indeed nothing new but just a return to a previous legal situation. Such argumentation became politically pressing in the negotiations of the Four Years' Sejm in the end of the eighteenth and even more during the whole nineteenth century, when a new conception of law put such historical arguments out of their original context. On a local level, anti-Jewish measures were sometimes implemented, especially when private towns changed ownership, up to the point where whole communities were forced to take residence in nearby towns. There is little research on such local-level politics, and even less on Jewish responses to it.[57] It remains a task for future analysis to see how much a rhetoric displaying seemingly anti-Jewish attitudes in the end actually shaped perceptions of Jewish–non-Jewish encounters and—in consequence—their practice.

---

55 Heyde, *Transkulturelle Kommunikation*, 40–47, 97–113.
56 Stanisław Grodziski, Irena Dwornicka, and Wacław Uruszczak, eds., *Volumina Constitutionum*, vol. 2, part 1: *1550–1585* (Warsaw: Wydawnictwo Sejmowe, 2005), 172 (no. 68: Sejm of Piotrków 1565); ibid., 200 (no. 70: Sejm of Piotrków 1567); Anna Michałowska-Mycielska, ed., *Sejmy i sejmiki koronne wobec Żydów. Wybór tekstów źrodłowych* [Sejms and sejmiki on Jews. A selection of sources] (Warsaw: Wydawnictwa Uniwersytetu Warszawskiego, 2006), 196–210 (no. 116: Sejm of Grodno 1678/1679), here 109.
57 The only comprehensive study on this topic: Goldberg, "De non tolerandis Judaeis."

Agreements between Towns and Kahals and their Impact on the Legal Status of Polish Jews

HANNA WĘGRZYNEK

"By virtue of the above adjudication, the Starosta of Lublin assured the Jews that the agreements they reach with the town's Christians with regard to purchase of houses and land will stand and will be forever honoured: it applies also to trading in various kinds of alcohol."[1] This quotation comes from a document issued in 1676 by King Jan III Sobieski, addressed to the Lublin Jewish community, in which the ruler confirmed its rights and privileges as granted by his royal predecessors. The statement that the agreement was to be "forever honoured" was by no means unique in the royal legislation—one can often come across similar statements. In the privilege issued in 1675 by Michał Korybut Wiśniowiecki to the Jews of Lublin, the phrasing was even more explicit: "All pacts, or rather agreements—both from the past and now reached with full consent of Lublin burghers and pertaining to land, jurisdiction, trading in mead, beer, vodka and other affairs, I hereby approve of and confirm."[2] The purport of both

---

1   State Archive in Lublin, AmL 145; Biblioteka im. Hieronima Łopacińskiego in Lublin, ms 1397; Jan Riabinin, *Materiały do historii miasta Lublina 1317–1792* [Materials on the history of the town of Lublin, 1317–1792] (Lublin: Wydawnictwo Dziennik Zarządu M. Lublina, 1938), 131.
2   Jacob Goldberg, *Jewish Privileges in the Polish Commonwealth. Charters of Rights Granted Jewish Communities in Poland—Lithuania in the Sixteenth to Eighteenth Centuries* (Jerusalem: The Israel Academy of Sciences and Humanities, 1985), 160.

these documents is unequivocal—agreements made between the burghers and the Jews were as legally binding as royal privileges.

Even though the legal status of the Jewish population has always been and still remains of interest to many scholars, the question of such agreements has been considered only to a very small degree. The most extensive research on the subject has been conducted with regard to Kraków,[3] Lwów,[4] and Poznań,[5] to a lesser degree to Przemyśl,[6] and most recently also to Lublin, the consequence of the large amount of archival material available. One should particularly mention the studies of Ryszard Szczygieł,[7] Henryk

---

3 Hanna Zaremska, *Żydzi w średniowiecznej Polsce. Gmina krakowska* [Jews in Medieval Poland. The Kraków kahal] (Warsaw: Instytut Historii PAN, 2011), 493; Bożena Wyrozumska, *The Jews in Mediaeval Cracow. Selected records from Cracow Municipal Books* (Kraków: Polish Academy of Arts and Sciences, The Jagiellonian University in Cracow, The Israel Academy of Sciences and Humanities, 1995), 186; Bożena Wyrozumska, "Czy Jan Olbracht wygnał Żydów z Krakowa?" [Did Jan Olbracht expel the Jews from Kraków?], *Rocznik Krakowski* 59 (1993): 5–11; Majer Bałaban, *Historja Żydów w Krakowie i na Kazimierzu 1304–1868* [The history of Jews in Kraków and in Kazimierz, 1304–1868], 2nd ed., vol. 1 (Kraków: "Nadzieja," Towarzystwo ku Wspieraniu Chorej Młodzieży Żydowskiej Szkół Średnich i Wyższych w Krakowie, 1931), 57; Ignacy Schipper, *Studya nad stosunkami gospodarczymi Żydów w Polsce podczas średniowiecza* [Studies in economic relations of Jews in Poland during the Middle Ages] (Lwów: Fundusz Konkursowy im. Wawelberga, 1911), 338.

4 Jürgen Heyde, "Polityka rady Lwowa wobec Żydów i Ormian w XV wieku" [The politics of the Lwów Council toward Jews and Armenians in the fifteenth century], *Kwartalnik Historii Kultury Materialnej* [The quarterly of the history of material culture] 63 (Warsaw, 2015): 283–92; Majer Bałaban, *Żydzi lwowscy na przełomie XVI i XVII wieku* [The Jews of Lwów at the turn of the seventeenth century] (Lwów: H. Altenberg, 1906), 71; Majer Bałaban, *Dzielnica żydowska, jej dzieje i zabytki* [The Jewish quarter and its historic sites] (Lwów: Towarzystwo Miłośników Przeszłości Lwowa, 1909; reprint: Warsaw, 1990), 11, 61.

5 Jürgen Heyde, *Transkulturelle Kommunikation und Verflechtung. Die jüdischen Wirtschaftseliten in Polen vom 14. bis zum 16. Jahrhundert* [Intercultural communication and interconnection: The Jewish economic elites in Poland from the fourteenth to the sixteenth centuries] (Wiesbaden: Harrassowitz Verlag, 2014), 138; Rex Rexheuser, *Kulturen und Gedächtnis. Studien und Reflexionen zur Geschichte des östlichen Europas* [Cultures and memory. Studies and reflections on the history of Eastern Europe] (Wiesbaden: Harrassowitz Verlag, 2008), 13–38; Leon Koczy, "Studja nad dziejami gospodarczymi Żydów poznańskich przed połową XVII wieku" [Studies on the economic history of the Poznań Jewry prior to the mid-seventeenth century], *Kronika Miasta Poznania* 12 (1934): 334.

6 Mojżesz Schorr, *Żydzi w Przemyślu do końca XVIII wieku* [Jews of Przemyśl until the end of the eighteenth century] (Lwów: 1903, reprint: Jerusalem: The Hebrew University of Jerusalem, 1991), 15.

7 Ryszard Szczygieł, "Ugoda Żydów lubelskich z gminą miejską w sprawie udziału w życiu gospodarczym miasta z 1555 r." [The agreement of Lublin Jewry with the municipal office in regard to their involvement in the economic life of the town], in *Żydzi wśród chrześcijan w dobie szlacheckiej Rzeczypospolitej* [Jews among Christians during the Nobles' Commonealth], ed. Waldemar Kowalski and Jadwiga Muszyńska (Kielce: Instytut Historii

Gmiterek,[8] and my own.[9] The essay written by François Guesnet, in which he compares the situation in the Polish Kingdom and the German states, is also of great importance.[10]

Making agreements was a common practice in Polish towns and cities in the late Middle Ages and in the early modern era. Most often, these were agreements between municipal councils and ordinary people. Such agreements could widen access to civic rights[11] or ensure concessions for market stalls, which in turn implied consent for more people to engage in trade.[12] Agreements were also signed with merchants from other localities.[13] At times, such agreements were made between representatives of different denominations, such as the Russian Orthodox and Protestants in Lublin, who constituted a minority in relation to the Catholic majority.[14] Agreements between municipal authorities and Jewish communal bodies (kahals) were by no means unusual. The research conducted in both the Crown Archives (*Metrica Regni Poloniae*) and the archives of different towns, but most of all in the printed collections of documents, indicates that

---

 Wyższej Szkoły Pedagogicznej w Kielcach, Kieleckie Towarzystwo Naukowe, 1996), 43.

8 Henryk Gmiterek, "Z dziejów Żydów lubelskich. Ugoda na Podzamczu z 1642 roku" [On the history of the Jews of Lublin. The agreement in Podzamcze in 1642], in *W służbie Klio... Księga poświęcona pamięci Profesora Tadeusza Radzika* [In the service of Clio... Jubilee book in the memory of Professor Tadeusz Radzik], ed. Janusz Kłapeć et al. (Lublin: Uniwersytet Marii Curie-Skłodowskiej w Lublinie, Polskie Towarzystwo Historyczne. Oddział w Lublinie, 2012), 59–69.

9 Hanna Węgrzynek, "Jewish–Christian Agreements and Their Impact on the Legal Status of Jews in Polish Towns (the Case of Lublin)," *Kwartalnik Historii Żydów / Jewish History Quarterly* 237 (2011): 107–112; Hanna Węgrzynek, "Der Vergleich als Mittel der Kommunikation und Konfliktlösung. Lubliner Franziskaner und Judengemeinde im 17. Jahrhundert," [Comparison as a means of communication and conflict resolution. The Lublin Franciscans and the Jewish community in the seventeenth century] in *Kommunikation durch symbolische Akte. Religiöse Heterogenität und politische Herrschaft in Polen–Litauen* [Communication through symbolic acts. Religious heterogeneity and political authority in Poland-Lithuania], ed. Yvonne Kleinmann (Stuttgart: Frantz Steiner Verlag, 2010), 209–227.

10 François Guesnet, "Agreements between neighbours. The 'ugody' as a source on Jewish-Christian relations in early modern Poland," *Jewish History* 24 (2010): 257–70.

11 Tomasz Strzembosz, *Tumult warszawski 1525 roku* [The Warsaw riot of 1525] (Warsaw: Państwowe Wydawnictwo Naukowe, 1959), 24.

12 Jan Riabinin, *Rada miejska lubelska w XVII wieku* [The municipal council of Lublin in the seventeenth century] (Lublin: Towarzystwo Przyjaciół Nauk w Lublinie, Wydawnictwa Magistratu m. Lublina, 1931), 25.

13 Maria Trojanowska, *Dokument miejski lubelski od XV do XVIII wieku* [The Lublin municipal document in the fifteenth–eighteenth centuries] (Warsaw: Naczelna Dyrekcja Archiwów Państwowych, Wojewódzkie Archiwum Państwowe w Lublinie, 1977), 103.

14 Aleksander Kossowski, *Protestantyzm w Lublinie i w Lubelskiem w XVI–XVII w.* [Protestantism in Lublin and its province] (Lublin: Towarzystwo Przyjaciół Nauk w Lublinie, 1933), 142.

such agreements were common practice. I have come across texts and information on the signing of such documents in over fifty Polish towns, mainly royal, but also less frequently in private towns. These were usually single agreements, but sometimes there were several of them—as in the case of Przemyśl, or over a dozen—as in the case of Lublin. This data does not do justice to the scale of the phenomenon; it merely reflects the extent of research conducted, which, apart from published sources, has been undertaken only in selected localities. In many cases, the renewal of agreements and, by extension, their number depended on the period for which they had been concluded as well as their specific character.

The first known agreements between Christians and Jews were signed in Polish towns in the second half of the fifteenth century. They were the result of increasing conflict over the area of Jewish settlement and the range of Jewish economic activity as well as the burghers' struggle to uphold their rights. The agreements reached in Kraków in the years 1469, 1485, 1494, and 1502 have been discussed in the work of Majer Bałaban, Ignacy Schipper and, more recently, of Bożena Wyrozumska and Hanna Zaremska.[15] The Lwów agreements have been analysed by Majer Bałaban, Ignacy Schipper, and Jürgen Heyde.[16]

The practice of entering into agreements—often referred to as pacts, contracts, deals, settlements or combinations—between the municipal and the kahal authorities became common in the second half of the sixteenth century. This was related to the demographic growth of Jewish communities and, by extension, to their growing role in local economies which were bound to cause conflicts over areas of settlement and the right to engage in trade and crafts. The earliest agreements were signed in vibrant urban centers with powerful institutions of self-government, such as Kraków, Lwów, Poznań—places in which there existed large Jewish communities.

The increase in the number of agreements was also triggered by the political changes which took place at the turn of the sixteenth century and the legislative processes that followed, aiming at reorganizing the legal system of the Polish Kingdom. Among the provisions which were then established, there were regulations pertaining to agreements between municipal authorities and the Jews. These are mentioned for the first time in the *De Iudeis* constitution adopted during the Piotrków *Sejm* in 1538. This constitution stated that Jews did not possess full freedom to trade in all commodities. When trading in food products, they were to adhere to the rules that the king had previously laid down. The regulations conclude with the following statement: "And so let them keep in full

---

15 See footnote 3.
16 See footnote 4.

the pacts and contracts that they have agreed upon in some of the large cities of our Kingdom."[17] The provision thus standardized the hitherto existing practice while simultaneously resolving the legislative inconsistency. By virtue of royal privileges, Jews resided in towns and engaged in trade legally; however, in doing so they encroached on rights of burghers which were also guaranteed by royal legislation. Agreements were to serve as a solution for this complex problem.

As I have mentioned above, the earliest agreements with Jews were reached in Kraków and Lwów, and later in Poznań. The conflict between Jews and burghers, which had been becoming more intense from the beginning of the sixteenth century, most probably exerted a direct impact on the passage of the *De Iudeis* constitution. The conflict concerned the Jewish right to trade, especially retail merchandising, and the number of houses they could occupy. The situation deteriorated in 1536 in Poznań when a fire started in a Jewish house; it spread quickly and ultimately led to the destruction of a large section of the town.[18] The *De Iudeis* constitution might have been closely related to the conflict. In 1538, another agreement was reached in Poznań—it pertained to the area of Jewish settlement within the city borders.[19]

Without thorough investigation of the primary sources, it is indeed difficult to determine to what degree the provisions adopted by the *Sejm* in 1538 contributed to the practice of signing agreements between the municipalities and Jewish kahals. Aside from the settlement in Poznań, mentioned above, a similar agreement was signed in Brześć[20] in 1538, and in the 1550s in Bełz, Kazimierz, Lublin, and once again in Poznań.[21] In the second half of the sixteenth-century agreements were also signed in Kamionka Strumiłowa, Szydłów, Kołomyja, Kazimierz, Parczew, Łuck, Lwów, and Przemyśl.[22]

---

17 "Volumus praeterea, ut Iudei non habeant liberam mercandi in omnibus rebus facultatem. Sed modum per nos statuendum in mercimoniis ad victum quaerendum, ubique in Regno nostro teneant et deligenter observent. Atque etiam pacta et conventiones, quas cum nonnullis civitatibus maioribus Regni nostri habent, in toto teneant," *Volumina Legum*, vol. 1 (St. Petersburg: Jozafat Ohryzko Publishers, 1860), 259; *Sejmy i sejmiki koronne wobec Żydów: Wybór tekstów źródłowych* [Crown Sejms and Sejmics on Jews: selected documents], ed. Anna Michałowska-Mycielska (Warsaw: Wydawnictwo Uniwersytetu Warszawskiego, 2007), 32.
18 Mathias Bersohn, *Dyplomatariusz dotyczący Żydów w dawnej Polsce na źródłach archiwalnych osnuty (1388–1782)* [A collection of documents on the Jews in pre-partition Poland taken from archival sources, 1388–1782] (Warsaw: E. Nicz, 1910), 37; see also footnote 5.
19 Bersohn, *Dyplomatariusz dotyczący*, 67.
20 Ibid., 45.
21 Ibid., 49, 52, 62, 63; Szczygieł, "Ugoda Żydów lubelskich," 43; Trojanowska, *Dokument miejski lubelski*, 103.
22 Maurycy Horn, *Regesty dokumentów i ekscerpty z Metryki Koronnej do historii Żydów w Polsce 1697–1795* [Register of documents and excerpts from the Crown Registry pertaining to the

Throughout this period, the issue of agreements was raised three times in resolutions of the *Sejm*: in 1562/63,[23] 1565,[24] and 1567.[25] The provisions that had been agreed upon were frequently referred to during the era of the Polish–Lithuanian Commonwealth.[26] It is worth noting that the agreements were reached and signed not only in the principal towns, but also in small localities.

The laws passed by the *Sejm* in the sixteenth century which limited the freedom to trade were fueled by the burghers' resentment of competition from foreign merchants and artisans. The *Sejm* deputies accused Jews of being the cause of the decreasing income of the burghers.[27] Similar accusations were leveled at other groups of different religious denomination or ethnic origin. At the same period, and even during the same *Sejm* sessions—for instance, the Piotrków *Sejm* of 1562/63 and 1565—laws concerning foreigners were passed, especially relating to Scots and Italians, who were also accused of harming the interests of burghers.[28] The towns appealed to their former privileges: thus

---

history of Jews in Poland, 1697–1795], vol. 2: *Rządy Stanisława Augusta (1764–1795)* [The reign of Stanisław August, (1764–1795)], 1st part: *1764–1779* (Wrocław et al.: Zakład Narodowy im. Ossolińskich, Wydawnictwo Polskiej Akademii Nauk, 1984), 31, 38, 43, 88, 131; Maurycy Horn, *Regesty dokumentów i ekscerpty z Metryki Koronnej do historii Żydów w Polsce 1697–1795* [Register of documents and excerpts from the Crown Registry pertaining to the history of Jews in Poland, 1697–1795], vol. 2: *Rządy Stanisława Augusta (1764–1795)* [The reign of Stanisław August, (1764–1795)], 2nd part: *1780–1794* (Wrocław et al.: Zakład Narodowy im. Ossolińskich, Wydawnictwo Polskiej Akademii Nauk, 1988), 7; Łucja Charewiczowa, "Ograniczenia gospodarcze nacji schizmatyckich i Żydów we Lwowie XV i XVI wieku" [Economic restrictions on the schismatic nations and the Jews in Lwów in the fifteenth and the sixteenth centuries.], *Kwartalnik Historyczny* 39 (1929): 223; Schorr, *Żydzi w Przemyślu*, 96.

23 "A iż też Posłowie skarżą, że przez żydy wszystkie handle y żywności mieszczanom a poddanym naszym są odięte; roskazuiemy aby w tey mierze był zachowan statut anni 1538," *Volumina Legum*, vol. 2, (St. Petersburg: Jozafat Ohryzko Publishers, 1859), 20; *Volumina Constitutionum*, ed. Stanisław Grodziski, Irena Dwornicka, Wacław Uruszczak, vol. 2, 1st part *1550–1585* (Warsaw: Wydawnictwo Sejmowe, 2005), 114; *Sejmy i sejmiki koronne*, 36.

24 "Ale iż pakt, który miasta z niemi i oni z miasty maią ukazać teraz nie mogli, tedy nie derogując nic paktom miejskim, i owszem ie w mocy zosatwuiąc, odkładamy ie do drugiego przyszłego sejmu koronnego, tak iżby na drugim blisko przyszłym sejmie, byli mieszczanie i żydowie powinni kłaść pacta et conventiones, które maią z miasty, około kupiectwa żywności ich," *Volumina Legum*, vol. 2, 51; *Volumina Constitutionum*, 172; *Sejmy i sejmiki koronne*, 36.

25 "Żydowie imo pakta, które z miasty maią, aby kupiectwa mieszczanom nie odeimowali ani się nimi bawili," *Volumina Legum*, vol. 2, 68; *Volumina Constitutionum*, 200; *Sejmy i sejmiki koronne*, 36.

26 Horn, *Regesty*, vol. 2/2, 110.

27 See footnote 23.

28 "Co się tycze Włochów, Szkotów y innych cudzoziemców, przez których miasta nasze wielką szkodę a zniszczenie biorą, takowemu każdemu, któryby osiadłości a prawa mieyskiego nie miał, roskazuiem, aby im były miasta i handle zapowiedziane iuż ex nunc," *Volumina Legum*, vol. 2, 20.

Kraków referred to the laws passed by King Kazimierz Jagiellończyk in 1451.[29] Renewing old acts of law indicates that they were not being obeyed but also serves as a proof that the burghers were strongly determined to maintain the privileges that had once been granted to them.

The fact that similar arguments were directed at both Jews and foreigners bears testimony to the consistent municipal policy of which the sixteenth century laws concerning trade were a vital part. The policy was aimed at eliminating com-petition from outsiders—both in regard to religion and origin. Since the towns could not expel their Jews as they had been granted royal privileges to settle in them, they made efforts to protect their interests in other ways. Agreements were a means to achieve this goal. It is worth noting that first agreements were signed in main centers: Kraków, Lwów, Poznań, or Lublin, namely, places where the largest, economically active Jewish communities existed. In addition, already in the sixteenth century such documents were signed in a number of smaller localities, where the Jewish communities were rather low in numbers, but growing rapidly.[30] The change in the legal status of Jews must have exerted a considerable influence on the promulgation of agreements. The laws of 1539 transferred the jurisdiction over Jews residing in private towns to the landowners.[31] Thus, the royal privileges lost some of their relevance. Jewish kahals, both those in royal and private towns, therefore made attempts to obtain separate documents which would validate their rights. The content of such documents depended on the issuer's will, and the provisions made often encroached on the municipal rights that had already been granted. That was yet another reason for wanting to regulate the relation between the Christian and Jewish communities by way of separate documents. Agreements reached in towns, in line with the interested parties' intentions and with full knowledge of local conditions, were gaining in importance as far as everyday practice was concerned.

Such agreements dealt with the issue of trade, but also with other issues which were crucial to Jewish communities, such as the area of settlement and the possibility of purchasing properties from Christians. At times, there were also issues pertaining to the general functioning of a town, such as the Jewish share in the cost of maintenance of the city walls.[32] In the seventeenth century, agreements signed with guilds, especially tailors, shoemakers, butchers and belt makers, regulated in minute detail the production and sale of artisan

---

29 Ibid., *Volumina Legum*, vol. 2, 57.
30 See footnote 22.
31 *Sejmy i sejmiki koronne*, 33.
32 Schorr, *Żydzi w Przemyślu*, 96.

products.[33] Especially interesting were the agreements signed with church institutions, mainly monasteries, such as the Jesuits in Lwów, and the Jesuits and Franciscans in Lublin.[34]

The terms of such agreements were settled during negotiations between representatives of both communities,[35] sometimes referred to as electors, selected from among members of the Council or guilds or the Jewish Elders (i.e., the kahal).[36] When such negotiations failed to reach a consensus, the parties would appeal for help to a mediator.[37] In some documents, the equality and partnership of both sides was stressed. The signed agreements were referred to as "friendly,"[38] and the terms were confirmed and agreed to not merely by signatures but also by a handshake which symbolized consent. In one of the agreements from Lublin, we read: "We testify by our signature that we made a verbal promise and sealed it with a handshake."[39] Another document included even more polite statements: "let there be a neighbourly peace and love between the parties."[40]

The civil wording does not change the fact that agreements were entered into in cases of conflict, and meetings of representatives of the parties to the dispute were held in order to reach a lasting settlement. They were often preceded by assaults on Jewish artisans and merchants or by riots. Most of the agreements were of a restrictive nature and significantly limited the economic activity of Jews. Burghers agreed to Jewish presence and activity in town, but only on pre-set conditions. They were also sometimes granted financial or material benefits as compensation for restricting the rights reserved for citizens and members of guilds.[41]

Agreements were regarded as documents of great significance; they were announced publicly like any other legal act or read out at town halls in the presence of councilors, lay judges and guild masters.[42] The parties also sought royal approval. Such sanction was given not only to the previously quoted documents concerning Lublin, but also to many others. The kings frequently confirmed

---

33 Horn, *Regesty*, vol. 2/1, 53, 78, 88; Horn, *Regesty*, vol. 2/2, 8, 110; Gmiterek, "Z dziejów Żydów lubelskich," 59; Jan Riabinin, *Lauda miejskie lubelskie* [Municipal laws of Lublin] (Lublin, 1934), 157; Schorr, *Żydzi w Przemyślu*, 114, 147, 179.
34 Bałaban, *Żydzi lwowscy*, 79; Węgrzynek, *Der Vergleich*, 213.
35 Gmiterek, "Z dziejów Żydów lubelskich," 62.
36 Ibid., 64.
37 State Archive in Lublin, KGZ-CLMO 111.
38 State Archive in Lublin, KGZ-RLMO 64; Schorr, *Żydzi w Przemyślu*, 147.
39 State Archive in Lublin, KGZ-CLMO 111.
40 Gmiterek, "Z dziejów Żydów lubelskich," 62.
41 Horn, *Regesty*, vol. 2/2, 111; Riabinin, *Lauda miejskie*, 103.
42 Schorr, *Żydzi w Przemyślu*, 147.

agreements, sometimes together with privileges granted to Jewish kahals or to towns[43]; such documents were referred to as binding regulations.[44] This was important from a practical point of view. In a case the terms of an agreement were breached, the matter was put before the king as a mediator. The king subsequently summoned a commission to settle the dispute.[45] Disputes were also dealt with by courts of conciliation, which was sometimes made the subject of a special paragraph of the agreement.[46] Documents were entered in the municipal registers, council registers, and if they had been granted a royal confirmation, to the Crown Registers. The basic sanction to uphold such agreements, however, was the penalty clause which they contained.[47] The party which breached the agreement had to pay a large sum of money as compensation, sometimes as much as several thousand zlotys. This did not always prevent such breaches, and accusations of the failure to observe agreements occurred rather often. It is possible that at times such claims were abused in an attempt to get high financial compensation.

Agreements were either open-ended or signed for a specified period of time—this depended on the nature of a document and, particularly, on how detailed it was. In most cases, agreements were open-ended; sometimes the wording of the document suggested this, using such phrases as "eternal agreement" or "agreement forever binding."[48] In such cases, they were usually confirmed along with Jewish privileges, as in Przemyśl, where in the mid-eighteenth century the agreement signed one hundred years earlier was confirmed.[49] The situation in Kraków was similar.[50] Less often, an agreement was signed for a specified period of time—two, five, or ten years; after the specified period, the agreement was renewed. This was true especially of agreements with guilds, as in Lublin.[51] The municipal authorities and the kahal were thus able to update the terms of agreement in accordance with current situation and needs.

---

43 Horn, *Regesty*, vol. 2/1, 30; 42, 113.
44 Ibid., 162.
45 Horn, *Regesty*, vol. 2/1, 16; 53; Schorr, *Żydzi w Przemyślu*, 147.
46 Schorr, *Żydzi w Przemyślu*, 158.
47 Riabinin, *Lauda miejskie*, 103.
48 Gmiterek, "Z dziejów Żydów lubelskich," 59; Schorr, *Żydzi w Przemyślu*, 147.
49 Maurycy Horn, *Regesty dokumentów i ekscerpty z Metryki Koronnej do historii Żydów w Polsce 1697–1795* [Register of documents and excerpts from the Crown Registry pertaining to the history of Jews in Poland, 1697–1795], vol. 1: *Czasy saskie (1697–1763)* [The Saxon period] (Wrocław et al.: Zakład Narodowy im. Ossolińskich, Wydawnictwo Polskiej Akademii Nauk, 1984), 10.
50 Bałaban, *Historja Żydów w Krakowie*, 121.
51 Riabinin, *Lauda miejskie*, 157; Horn, *Regesty*, vol. 2/2, 31.

Documents which contained elaborate and detailed arrangements turned out to be much more long-lasting, as was the case in Przemyśl. The agreement reached there in 1645 encompassed over a dozen various branches of trade and artisan activity.[52]

The context of the process of signing agreements can be traced by analyzing several examples. As has already been stated, they were usually concluded—especially in larger towns and cities—in a hostile environment of growing economic disputes and conflicts. In Przemyśl, the agreement of 1645, which we have mentioned, was preceded by a complaint made to the king in which the burghers presented their objections to Jewish behavior in minute detail.[53] Over a dozen years earlier, the most affluent and powerful Jews of Przemyśl had been accused of desecrating the Host.[54] Religious allegations often served to reinforce economic arguments.

Sometimes, agreements accompanied the privileges recently granted to the Jews and had a very detailed character, as was the case of Trembowla.[55] They constituted general guidelines as to how privileges, which usually contained rather general provisions, were to be interpreted. For example, if a privilege dealt with trade, the subsequent agreement stated precisely what produce and goods it referred to. In some known cases, agreements were reached prior to the Jewish community privileges as in Łask[56] and Szydłów.[57] They thus indicated the basic rules governing Jewish presence in a given locality. Interestingly enough, a privilege of the Jewish kahal in Łask, granted almost 30 years later, was much more detailed. A clear and straightforward practice emerges—initial documents contained general rules, subsequent documents made them more specific.

At times agreements were the only documents regulating the rules according to which the local Jewish community functioned. This was the case in Kamionka Strumiłowa, where an agreement was signed in March 1589; it granted municipal rights to the Jews, which meant they could enjoy all the freedoms appertaining to the citizens, but also had to fulfil the same obligations.[58]

---

52 Schorr, *Żydzi w Przemyślu*, 147.
53 Ibid., 145.
54 Hanna Węgrzynek, "*Czarna legenda*" *Żydów. Procesy o rzekome mordy rytualne w dawnej Polsce* [The "black legend" of the Jews. Trials for alleged ritual murders in Old Poland] (Warsaw: Wydawnictwo Bellona, Wydawnictwo Fundacji Historia pro Futuro, 1995), 81.
55 Horn, *Regesty*, vol. 2/1, 19.
56 Ibid., 32; Goldberg, *Jewish Privileges in the Polish Commonwealth*, 120.
57 Horn, *Regesty*, vol. 2/1, 38.
58 Ibid., 32; Goldberg, *Jewish Privileges in the Polish Commonwealth*, 120.

Two weeks later, the document was confirmed by the king, and later by subsequent kings, as was the normal practice with privileges.

In many cases the wording of agreements was akin to that of Jewish community privileges. The substantial difference was the fact that they were written in the towns in which they would be in force and took local conditions into consideration and also that they were prepared by both parties involved, rather than one—as was the case with privileges. This does not mean that agreements were always fully original documents. Sometimes they were copied, which meant that their authors were following the pattern set by other towns—for example, in 1581 Lwów followed the template of the agreement which had been signed in Lublin in 1555.[59]

The importance of agreements was sealed with the constitution of 1768, titled *Warunek miast i miasteczek Naszych królewskich w Koronie i Wielkim Księstwie Litewskim* (The condition of our royal towns and townlets in the Crown and the Great Duchy of Lithuania). This constitution was linked to the municipal reforms in the Polish-Lithuanian Commonwealth and to the activity of the Good Order Commission—*Boni Ordinis*. Invoking the former legal acts of the years 1538, 1562, 1567, and 1588, it laid down that Jews were permitted to engage in trade in regions of and in ways agreed upon in the agreements signed with towns. In places where such agreements did not exist, they had to be reached according to the rules binding in other localities. If towns attempted to evade the terms of the 1768 constitution, the Good Order Commission was to act as mediator. If a person did not obey the terms of the constitution and allowed Jews to trade freely, sell alcohol, and deal with crafts without a prior signed agreement, that person was to pay a hefty fine of 5,000 grzywnas. The privileges issued to Jewish communities remained in force, and freedoms granted in them remained binding.[60] The statement can be interpreted as an

---

59 Szczygieł, "Ugoda Żydów lubelskich," 43.
60 "Aby po miastach i miasteczkach naszych Żydzi handle nie insze i na innych miejscach sprawowali, tylko co im z ułożenia paktów z miastami zawartych wyraźnie jest pozwolone. I dlatego Żydzi po wszystkich miastach i miasteczkach, gdzie przywilejów konstytucją aprobowanych nie mają, aby się podług paktów z miastami zawartych zachowali i więcej sobie wolności nie przywłaszczali, pod surowemi karami zakazujemy. Gdzie zaś przywilejów konstytucją aprobowanych lub paktów z miastami nie mają, tam pacta ad normam innych miast, gdzie są poczynione, poczynią, a gdzie by miasta takowych paktów robić nie chciały, ciż komisarze wysłuchawszy przyczyn sporów obydwóch stron, takowe pacta miedzy niemi mediante autoritate sua do ustanowienia jak najsprawiedliwiej przeprowadzą. Bez tych zaś handlów, ani szynków prowadzić, ani rzemiosł robić nie powinni pod rygorem wyżej opisanym, w czym nikt Żydom naprzeciw prawu niniejszemu protekcji dawać nie ma sub

acknowledgement of agreements as documents with the same status as privileges. For towns which did not have an appropriate legislation, it was agreements signed between their Christian and Jewish inhabitants rather than king's decision that regulated mutual relations. This means that towns were to have jurisdiction over what took place within them in a much broader way than before. This improved status was further confirmed by the royal recommendation to the Good Order Commission to inquire whether the agreements signed would not limit the town's development or Christian settlement.[61]

The constitution entitled "The conditions of our royal towns and townlets" contributed to agreements becoming widespread and commonly applied. In subsequent years, a large number of agreements were signed in accordance with the 1768 legislation, including in the towns of Krasnystaw, Płońsk, and Owrucza.[62] Many agreements were reached in Warsaw, in a situation of open conflict which required mediation. The fact that such mediation was resorted to demonstrates that there were appeals to the Associate Judges Court (*Sąd Asesorski*), which was the highest instance of appeals for towns.[63] Conflicts were solved also by other instances, such as the Crown Tribunal and the Crown Treasury Commission.[64]

The overall number of agreements as well as the fact that they were often referred and appealed to in cases of conflicts and disputes prove their significance. Their minute details allow us to become acquainted with daily life of Jewish communities and their relations with Christian communities. The main difference between privileges and agreements was the fact that the latter had been accepted in the given place and environment in which they were to come into force. Since agreements were often tailored to the local conditions, they clearly reflected the reality of everyday life. They therefore played a far more significant role than that which has up to now been attributed to them.

---

poena Piąciu tysięcy grzywien w sądach naszych windicanda. Żydzi jednak w miastach swoich żydowskich za przywilejami ulokowanych, według opisów tychże przywilejów w tych swoich miastach bez przeszkody handlować wolność mieć powinni," *Volumina Legum*, vol. 7, (St. Petersburg: Jozafat Ohryzko Publishers, 1860), 351; *Sejmy i sejmiki koronne*, 154.

61 Horn, *Regesty*, vol. 2/2, 108, 114, 119, 122, 123.
62 Horn, *Regesty*, vol. 2/1, 149; ibid., 121, 126.
63 Horn, *Regesty*, vol. 2/2, 147; ibid., 124.
64 Horn, *Regesty*, vol. 2/2, 130, 131; Bersohn, *Dyplomatariusz dotyczący*, 195.

The Role and Significance of the Jews in the Economy of the Polish–Lithuanian Commonwealth: The State of Research and Research Directions

JACEK WIJACZKA

INTRODUCTION

Research conducted in the nineteenth and early twentieth century on the participation of the Jewish population in the economy of the Polish–Lithuanian state in the sixteenth through eighteenth centuries was summarized in the 1930s in two studies by Ignacy Schiper. The first was a chapter in a collection, dealing with the economic history of the Jews of the Polish Crown and Lithuania in the pre-partition era.[1] The second was a monograph on the history of Jewish trade in the Polish lands.[2]

---

1 Ignacy Schiper, "Dzieje gospodarcze Żydów Korony i Litwy w czasach przedrozbiorowych" [The economic history of the Jews of the [Polish] Crown and Lithuania in the pre-partition era], in *Żydzi w Polsce Odrodzonej. Działalność społeczna, gospodarcza, oświatowa i kulturalna* [The Jews in Reborn Poland: Social, economic, educational and cultural activity], vol. 1: *Żydzi w dawnej Rzeczypospolitej Polskiej* [Jews in the former Polish Commonwealth], ed. Ignacy Schiper, A[rieh] Tartakower, and Aleksander Haftka (Warsaw: Wydawnictwo "Żydzi w Polsce Odrodzonej," 1932), 111–85.
2 Ignacy Schiper, *Dzieje handlu żydowskiego na ziemiach polskich* [The History of Jewish trade in the Polish lands] (Warsaw: Nakład Centrali Związku Kupców, 1937; reprint, Kraków: Krajowa Agencja Wydawnicza, 1990).

Research on Jewish history in Poland was interrupted by the outbreak of the Second World War, in the course of which many sources were destroyed, including records of Jews' economic activities. Among them were mass sources preserved at the Archive of the Crown Treasury in Warsaw, particularly customs records for the years 1509–1794. Fire also consumed 2,198 quarterly registers of various customs posts for the years 1718–90 at the Krasiński Library in Warsaw.[3] The loss to scholarship was irreparable since without that source material we will never be able to establish the scale of commerce in the early modern commonwealth. For that reason, some prewar studies, based on sources that no longer exist, still have evidentiary value; for example, Roman Rybarski's study of trade and trade policy in sixteenth-century Poland, based on customs books from that time.[4]

In the first decades after 1945, research on this subject was very limited. To be sure, many Polish historians did study the economic history of the Polish–Lithuanian Commonwealth in the sixteenth through eighteenth centuries, but the role of the Jewish population was rarely mentioned. The few articles that did appear were published almost exclusively in the *Bulletin of the Jewish Historical Institute* (*Biuletyn Żydowskiego Instytutu Historycznego*; hereafter Biuletyn ŻIH). Jan M. Małecki, in a paper presented in 1986 on Jewish trade in Kraków (published in 1991), described the postwar literature on Jewish trade in premodern Poland as "very modest," citing only four publications.[5] He overstated the case somewhat, however, since he did not mention such articles as Janina Morgensztern's on Jewish activity in Zamość, Moshe J. Rosman's on the

---

3 Janina Karwasińska, "Archiwa skarbowe dawnej Rzeczypospolitej" [The Treasury Archives of the former Polish Commonwealth] in *Straty archiwów i bibliotek warszawskich w zakresie rękopiśmiennych źródeł historycznych* [Losses of handwritten historical sources in Warsaw archives and libraries], vol. 1 (Warsaw: Państwowe Wydawnictwo Naukowe 1957), 88–90.

4 Roman Rybarski, *Handel i polityka handlowa Polski w XVI stuleciu* [Polish trade and trade policy in the sixteenth century], vol. 1: *Rozwój handlu i polityki handlowej* [The development of trade and trade policy] (Poznań: Towarzystwo Miłośników Miasta Poznania, 1928); vol. 2: *Tablice i materiały statystyczne* [Tables and statistical material] (Poznań: Towarzystwo Miłośników Miasta Poznania, 1929; photo-offset reprint, both vols., Warsaw: Państwowe Wydawn. Naukowe, 1958).

5 Jan. M. Małecki, "Handel żydowski u schyłku XVI i w pierwszej połowie XVII w. w świetle krakowskich rejestrów celnych" [Jewish trade at the end of the sixteenth and first half of the seventeenth century in the light of Kraków customs registers], in *Żydzi w dawnej Rzeczypospolitej. Materiały z konferencji 'Autonomia Żydów w Rzeczypospolitej szlacheckiej'. Międzywydziałowy Zakład Historii i Kultury Żydów w Polsce, Uniwersytet Jagielloński, 22–26 IV 1986* [Jews in the former Commonwealth: Materials from the conference "Jewish autonomy in the Nobles' Commonwealth," Interdisciplinary Institute for the History and Culture of the Jews in Poland, Jagiellonian University, April 22–26, 1986] ed. Andrzej Link-Lenczowski and Tomasz Polański (Wrocław-Warszawa-Kraków: Zakład Narodowy Ossolińskich, 1991), 214.

participation of Polish Jews in trade in Gdańsk in the late seventeenth and early eighteenth centuries, Maria Bogucka's on Jewish merchants in Gdańsk in the first half of the seventeenth century, or a book by Maurycy Horn on the Jews of Red Ruthenia in the sixteenth and first half of the seventeenth centuries, which includes an extensive chapter on trade.[6]

After 1980, as Rosman has noted, research by both Polish and Jewish historians focused primarily on "the history of the Jews of a given place, or micro-studies of a particular Jewish or Polish institution at the local level."[7] It must be noted, however, that at the same time sources began to be published that were directly related to the economic activity of the Jewish population of the former commonwealth, for example, on Jewish trade in Kraków,[8] or containing information on the subject. Here one must mention the source collections published by Adam Kaźmierczyk, Anna Michałowska-Mycielska, Jakub Goldberg, and Henryk Gmiterek.[9]

---

6 Janina Morgensztern, "O działalności gospodarczej Żydów w Zamościu w XVI i XVII w." [On the economic activity of the Jews in Zamość in the sixteenth and seventeenth centuries], Biuletyn ŻIH 53 (1965): 3–32; 56 (1965): 2–28; Moshe Rosman, "Polish Jews in the Gdańsk Trade in the Late 17th and Early 18th Centuries," in Danzig, Between East and West: Aspects of Modern Jewish History, ed. Isadore Twersky (Cambridge, MA: Harvard University, Center for Jewish Studies and the Harvard Semitic Museum: Distributed by Harvard University Press, 1985), 111–20; Maria Bogucka, "Kupcy żydowscy w Gdańsku w pierwszej połowie XVII wieku" [Jewish merchants in Gdańsk in the first half of the seventeenth century], Przegląd Historyczny 80, no. 4 (1989): 791–99; Maurycy Horn, Żydzi na Rusi Czerwonej w XVI i w pierwszej połowie XVII w. Działalność gospodarcza na tle rozwoju demograficznego [The Jews of Ruthenia in the sixteenth and first half of the seventeenth century: Economic activity against the background of demographic development] (Warsaw: Państwowe Wydawnictwo Naukowe, 1975), 83–159.

7 Moshe Rosman, "Między koniecznością a modą. Uwagi nad przeszłością i przyszłością badań nad dziejami Żydów w Polsce" [Between necessity and fashion. Observations on the past and future of research on the history of Jews in Poland], Małżeństwo z rozsądku? Żydzi w społeczeństwie dawnej Rzeczypospolitej [A marriage of convenience? Jews in the society of the Polish-Lithuanian Commonwealth], ed. Marcin Wodziński and Anna Michałowska-Mycielska (Wrocław: Wydawnictwo Uniwersytetu Wrocławskiego, 2007), 141.

8 Jan M. Małecki, ed., in collaboration with Elżbieta Szlufik, Handel żydowski w Krakowie w końcu XVI i w XVII wieku. Wypisy z krakowskich rejestrów celnych z lat 1593–1683 [Jewish trade in Kraków and the end of the sixteenth and in the seventeenth century. Entries in the Kraków customs registers from 1593 to 1683] (Kraków: Polska Akademia Umiejętności, 1995).

9 Adam Kaźmierczyk, ed. and intro., Żydzi polscy 1648–1772. Źródła [Polish Jews 1648–1772: Sources] (Kraków, 2001); Anna Michałowska, ed. and trans., Gminy żydowskie w dawnej Rzeczypospolitej. Wybór tekstów źródłowych [Jewish communities in the former Commonwealth: Selected sources] (Warsaw: Dialog, 2003); Anna Michałowska-Mycielska, ed., Sejmy i sejmiki koronne wobec Żydów. Wybór tekstów źródłowych [Sejms and sejmiki on Jews. A selection of sources] (Warsaw: Wydawnictwa Uniwersytetu Warszawskiego, 2006);

COMMERCE

In the late Middle Ages and the early modern era, the number of Jews living in the Polish–Lithuanian state was still quite small.[10] Their economic role was thus not very significant and their participation was limited to a few spheres. From the thirteenth to the fifteenth century, part of the Jewish population made their living from agriculture.[11] The activity of Jewish minters and bankers

---

Jakub Goldberg and Adam Kaźmierczyk, eds., *Sejm Czterech Ziem. Źródła* [The Council of Four Lands: Sources] (Warsaw: Wydawnictwo Sejmowe, 2011); Henryk Gmiterek, ed., and Adam Teller, intro., *Materiały źródłowe do dziejów Żydów w księgach grodzkich lubelskich z doby panowania Augusta II Sasa 1697–1733* [Source materials on the history of the Jews in the Lublin city records during the reign of Augustus II the Saxon, 1687–1733] (Lublin: Wydawnictwo Uniwersytetu Marii Curie-Skłodowskiej, 2001); Henryk Gmiterek, ed., *Materiały źródłowe do dziejów Żydów w księgach grodzkich lubelskich z doby panowania Michała Korybuta Wiśniowieckiego i Jana III Sobieskiego 1669–1697* [Source materials for the history of the Jews in the Lublin city records during the reigns of Michał Korybut Wiśniowiecki and Jan III Sobieski 1669–1697] (Lublin: Wydawnictwo Uniwersytetu Marii Curie-Skłodowskiej, 2003); Henryk Gmiterek, ed., *Materiały źródłowe do dziejów Żydów w księgach grodzkich lubelskich z doby panowania Władysława IV i Jana Kazimierza Wazów 1633–1669* [Source materials for the history of the Jews in the Lublin city records during the reigns of Władysław IV Vasa and Jan Kazimierz Vasa 1633–1669] (Lublin: Wydawnictwo Uniwersytetu Marii Curie-Skłodowskiej, 2006); Henryk Gmiterek, ed., *Materiały źródłowe do dziejów Żydów w księgach grodzkich lubelskich z doby panowania Zygmunta III Wazy 1587–1632* [Source materials for the history of the Jews in the Lublin city records during the reign of Zygmunt III Vasa 1587–1632] (Lublin: Archiwum Państwowe w Lublinie, 2014).

10 On the difficulty of calculating the size of the Jewish population in the early modern commonwealth, see Zenon Guldon, "Źródła i metody szacunku liczebności ludności żydowskiej w Polsce w XVI–XVIII wieku" [Sources and methods for estimating the size of the Jewish population in Poland in the sixteenth–eighteenth centuries], *Kwartalnik Historii Kultury Materialnej* [hereinafter KHKM] 2 (1986): 249–63; Zenon Guldon and Jacek Wijaczka, "Die zahlenmäßige Stärke der Juden in Polen-Litauen im 16.–18. Jahrhundert," [The numerical strength of the Jews in Poland-Lithuania in the sixteenth–eighteenth centuries], *Trumah* 4 (1994): 91–101; Zenon Guldon, "Osadnictwo żydowskie i liczebność ludności żydowskiej na ziemiach Rzeczypospolitej w okresie przedrozbiorowym. Stan i program badań" [Jewish settlement and the number of Jews on the territory of the Polish-Lithuanian Commonwealth in the period before the partitions. The state of research and a programme for its continuation] in *Żydzi i judaizm we współczesnych badaniach polskich. Materiały z konferencji, Kraków 21–23 XI 1995* [Jews and Judaism in contemporary Polish research. Materials from a conference held in Kraków on 21–23 November 1995], ed. Krzysztof Pilarczyk (Kraków: Księgarnia Akademicka, Wydawnictwo Naukowe, 1997), 145–54.

11 Maurycy Horn, "Wirtschaftliche Tätigkeit der polnischen Juden im Mittelalter unter Berücksichtigung des Siedlungswesens" [Economic activity of the Polish Jews in the Middle Ages seen in the light of their settlement patterns] in *Deutsche—Polen—Juden. Ihre Beziehungen von den Anfängen bis ins 20. Jahrhundert* [Germans—Poles—Jews. Their relations from the origins to the twentieth century], ed. Stefi Jersch-Wenzel (Berlin: Colloquium, 1987), 62.

should be stressed,[12] while until the end of the Middle Ages the role of Jews in commerce and crafts was much smaller.[13] That situation changed as the Jewish population grew. Certainly, there were many more Jews in the commonwealth by the second half of the sixteenth century, and by the mid-eighteenth century, on the basis of a census carried out between October 1764 and February 1765, the size of the Jewish population can be fairly reliably estimated at about 750,000,[14] out of a total population of 12.3 million.[15]

As to the participation and significance of the Jews in the commonwealth's economy at that time, we know the most about their role in commerce.[16] In the

---

12 Antony Polonsky, *The Jews in Poland and Russia. A Short History* (Oxford: Littman Library of Jewish Civilization, 2013), 22–24; Maurycy Horn, "Działalność gospodarcza Żydów polskich w średniowieczu na tle rozwoju osadnictwa" [The economic activity of Polish Jews in the middle ages against the background of their settlement patterns], *Biuletyn ŻIH*, 2/3 (1983): 73–84; "Chrześcijańscy i żydowscy wierzyciele i bankierzy Zygmunta Starego i Zygmunta Augusta" [Christian and Jewish creditors and bankers of Zygmunt the Elder and Zygmunt August], *Biuletyn ŻIH* 3/4 (1986): 3–11; Jürgen Heyde, "The Jewish Economic Elite in Red Ruthenia in the Fourteenth and Fifteenth Centuries," in *Polin: Studies in Polish Jewry* 22: *Early Modern Poland: Borders and Boundaries*, ed. Antony Polonsky, Magda Teter, and Adam Teller (2010): 156–173; *Transkulturelle Kommunikation und Verflechtung. Die jüdischen Wirtschaftseliten in Polen vom 14. bis zum 16. Jahrhundert* [Intercultural communication and interconnection: The Jewish economic elites in Poland from the fourteenth to the sixteenth centuries] (Wiesbaden: Harrassowitz, 2014).

13 Maurycy Horn, "Rola gospodarcza Żydów w Polsce do końca XVIII wieku" [The economic role of Jews in Poland until the end of the eighteenth century], in *Żydzi wśród chrześcijan w dobie szlacheckiej Rzeczypospolitej* [Jews among Christians in the period of the Republic of Nobles], ed. Waldemar Kowalski and Jadwiga Muszyńska (Kielce: Kieleckie Towarzystwo Naukowe, 1996), 20.

14 Rafał Mahler, "Żydzi w Polsce w świetle liczb" [Jews in Poland in numbers], *Przeszłość Demograficzna Polski* 1 (1967): 207. According to the 1765 census, the Jewish population of the commonwealth numbered 587,000 at that time; Andrzej Wyczański et al., eds., *Historia Polski w liczbach* [A history of Poland in numbers] vol 1: *Państwo, społeczeństwo* [State, Society] (Warsaw: Główny Urząd Statystyczny, 2003), 69, tbl. 51.

15 Cezary Kuklo, Juliusz Łukasiewicz and Cecylia Leszczyńska, eds., *Historia Polski w liczbach*, vol. 3: *Polska w Europie* [Poland in Europe] (Warsaw: Zakład Wydawnictw Statystycznych, 2014), 49, tbl. 2.

16 Gershon D. Hundert, "The Role of Jewish Commerce in Early Modern Poland–Lithuania," *Journal of European Economic History* 16, no. 2 (1987): 245–46: "Jewish participation in the economy of the Polish Commonwealth was characteristically entrepreneurial. Artisans often marketed the goods they produced, merchants resorted to artisans and lent money at interest, rabbis and other religious functionaries engaged in commerce, and arendars also pursued independent commerce. It can be shown, though, that the proportion of the Jewish population which was engaged primarily in commerce was greatest in the sixteenth century and declined slowly in the course of the seventeenth century and more rapidly during the eighteenth century."

late Middle Ages, Polish Jews were free to trade any goods under the privileges granted to them by Duke Bolesław the Pious of Kalisz in 1264. In Lithuania, similar possibilities were created by the privileges granted by Grand Duke Vytautas in 1388 and 1389. The burgher class, still very weak in the lands of the Polish Crown, could not mount an attack on the Jews' freedom to conduct trade until the late Middle Ages, when the patriciate of Kraków and Lwów succeeded in greatly limiting the commercial activities of the Jews in their cities. In 1485, the Jews of Kraków were forced to sign an agreement with the burghers, restricting their trade to caps and collars of their own manufacture: all other trade was punishable by fines and confiscation of goods. Similar restrictions affected the trading activity of the Jews of Lwów in 1488, although their right to conduct foreign trade was not questioned.[17]

In the early modern era, successive Polish rulers as well as the nobility supported the commercial activities of the Jews and granted them privileges.[18] At the Diet of Piotrków in 1527, King Zygmunt the Old issued a document equalizing customs duties for Jewish and Christian merchants, a privilege later confirmed by Zygmunt III Vasa in 1600.[19] In 1578, King Stefan Batory abolished all the privileges barring Jews from domestic trade that had been granted to particular cities, and introduced the principle that Jews were free to trade in all the cities of the commonwealth.[20] Numerous trade privileges were also granted to Jewish merchants by King Władysław IV, the most important in 1633, when he also reconfirmed all the freedoms granted by previous rulers.[21] Ten years later, in 1643, he released them from all transport dues, such as road and bridge tolls, throughout the commonwealth.[22]

The role of Jewish merchants and the extent of their participation in the commercial activity of the former commonwealth remains a subject

---

17 Horn, "Rola gospodarcza Żydów w Polsce," 18.
18 Jacek Wijaczka, "Szlachta a kupcy żydowscy i chrześcijańscy w dawnej Rzeczypospolitej" [The nobility versus Jewish and Christian merchants], *Kwartalnik Historii Żydów* 3 (2003): 349–62.
19 Janina Morgensztern, "Regesty dokumentów z Metryki Koronnej do historii Żydów w Polsce (1588–1632)" [Registers of documents from the Crown Registry on the history of Jews in Poland, 1588–1632], *Biuletyn ŻIH* 51 (1964): 61, note 5.
20 Mathias Bersohn, *Dyplomatarjusz dotyczący Żydów w dawnej Polsce na źródłach archiwalnych osnuty (1388–1782)* [A collection of documents on the Jews in pre-partition Poland taken from archival sources, 1388–1782] (Warsaw: E. Nicz, 1910), 162.
21 Ibid., 230; Morgensztern, *Regesty dokumentów z Metryki Koronnej*, 108.
22 Schiper, *Dzieje handlu żydowskiego na ziemiach polskich*, 63.

of debate.[23] Writing at the turn of the twentieth century, Roman Rybarski concluded that "at a time when Polish trade was already in full bloom, i.e. in the mid-sixteenth century, Jewish participation in it was generally still very weak."[24] He added that while "in the second half of the sixteenth century, their participation in trade was becoming ever more distinct," Christian merchants were still dominant.[25] Ignacy Schiper disagreed, writing that by the second half of that century, "thanks to their extensive relations with Jewish communities abroad, Jewish merchants had a decided advantage over non-Jewish ones."[26] According to him, this advantage was equally visible "in all the most significant branches of trade."[27]

In the light of recent research, Rybarski's view seems nearer the truth since studies of Poznań and Kraków indicate rather clearly that Christian merchants remained dominant until the mid-seventeenth century.[28]

---

23 Zenon Guldon, "*Żydzi w Polsce do końca XVIII wieku. Wybrane zagadnienia*" [Jews in Poland until the end of the eighteenth century. Selected topics], in *Z przeszłości Żydów polskich. Polityka—gospodarka—kultura—społeczeństwo* [On the history of Polish Jews. Economy —culture—society], ed. Jacek Wijaczka and Grzegorz Miernik (Kraków: Wydawnictwo Towarzystwo Naukowe "Societas Vistulana," 2005), 12.

24 Roman Rybarski, *Handel i polityka handlowa Polski w XVI stuleciu* [Trade and trade policies in Poland in the sixteenth century], vol. 1: *Rozwój handlu i polityki handlowej* [The development of trade and trade policies] (Poznań, 1928; here: reprint Warsaw, 1958), 227.

25 Ibid., 226.

26 Schiper, *Dzieje handlu żydowskiego*, 57.

27 Ibid., 58.

28 Daniel Tollet, "Entreprise commerciale et structures urbaines en Pologne au XVIe et XVIIe siècles (1588-1668). L'exemple des Juifs de Poznań" [Commercial enterprises and urban structures in Poland from the sixteenth to the eighteenth centuries (1588-1668). The example of the Jews of Poznań], *Studia Historiae Oeconomicae* 16 (1981): 117-47; "Typologie des marchands et les hommes d'affaires juifs de Poznań et de Cracovie l'epoque des Vasa (1588-1668)," [A typology of Jewish merchants and business men in Poznań in Kraków under the Vasas (1588-1668)] *Studia Historiae Oeconomicae* 23 (1998): 121-38; *Marchands et hommes d'affaires juifs dans la Pologne des Wasa (1588-1668)* [Jewish merchants and business men in the Poland of the Vasas (1588-1668)] (Paris: Champion, 2001); Małecki, "Handel żydowski u schyłku XVI," 214-25; Jacek Wijaczka, *Handel zagraniczny Krakowa w połowie XVII wieku* [Foreign trade of Kraków in the mid-seventeenth century] (Kraków: Towarzystwo Naukowe "Societas Vistulana," 2002), 120; Zenon Guldon, Szymon Kazusek, "Rola Żydów w handlu polskim w pierwszej połowie XVII wieku" [The role of Jews in Polish trade in the first half of the seventeenth century], *KHKM* 3 (2004): 287-303; Szymon Kazusek, *Żydzi w handlu Krakowa w połowie XVII wieku* [Jews in the trade of Kraków in the middle of the seventeenth century] (Kraków: Towarzystwo Naukowe "Societas Vistulana," 2005); Józef A. Gierowski, "Die Juden in Polen im 17. und 18. Jahrhundert und ihre Beziehungen zu den deutschen Städten von Leipzig bis Frankfurt a. M.," [The Jews in Poland in the seventeenth and the eighteenth centuries and their relations

The state of commerce in the commonwealth during the second half of the seventeenth and during the eighteenth century is less well known, but the role of Jewish merchants seems to have increased significantly. Until the mid-seventeenth century, "the Jews were active in all branches of the Commonwealth's economy, and that state of affairs was not affected by changes in the occupational structure and material situation of Jewish society in the second half of the seventeenth and the eighteenth century."[29] According to Jakub Goldberg, these changes were the result of three factors: the ravages of war, from the Khmelnytsky uprising and the Swedish Deluge in the seventeenth century to the Great Northern War of the early eighteenth century; the general economic decline of the Polish–Lithuanian state; and competition from the burghers, together with new restrictions imposed on Jews. Jews had no choice but to adapt to these new economic conditions, "and above all to changes in the economic structure of the small towns, which underwent ruralization during that period."[30]

The events of the mid-seventeenth century—war, insurrection, and epidemics—caused great economic damage and led to a significant decline in population. It should be added, however, that signs of economic crisis in the commonwealth were already evident before 1648.[31] Changes in the agricultural situation in Europe generally, which also began in the mid-seventeenth century and were first reflected in a decline in Polish grain exports to Western Europe, also contributed to deepening the economic crisis in the Polish lands.

In this situation, nobles and magnates who were engaged in grain production switched from export to the production and sale of liquor distilled from grain. Jews took advantage of this change and began playing a significant role

---

to the German cities from Leipzig to Frankfurt on Main] in *Die wirtschaftlichen und kulturellen Beziehungen zwischen den jüdischen Gemeinden in Polen und Deutschland vom 16. bis zum 20. Jahrhundert*, ed. Konrad E. Grözinger [The economic and cultural relations between the Jewish communities in Poland and Germany from the sixteenth to the twentieth centuries] (Wiesbaden: Harrassowitz, 1992), 10.

29 Jacob Goldberg, "Dzieje Żydów w dawnej Rzeczypospolitej – próba syntetycznego spojrzenia," [History of the Jews in the Polish-Lithuanian Commnowealth—an attempt at synthesis], in *Między wielką polityką a szlacheckim partykularzem. Studia z dziejów nowożytnej Polski i Europy ku czci profesora Jacka Staszewskiego* [Between great politics and noble particularism. Studies on the history of modern Poland and Europe in honor of Professor Jacek Staszewski] (Toruń: Wydawnictwo Mikołaja Kopernika, 1993), 343.

30 Ibid.

31 Stanisław Śreniowski, "Oznaki regresu ekonomicznego w ustroju folwarczno-pańszczyźnianym w Polsce u schyłku XVI w." [Signs of economic regress in the feudal-estate system in Poland at the turn of the sixteenth century], *Kwartalnik Historyczny* 61 (1954), 165–96.

in this new organization of the nobles' economy. As Antoni Podraza, among others, has noted: "the role of Jews in the nobles' economy grew in the second half of the seventeenth and in the eighteenth century in all the lands of the Commonwealth, though it seems never to have reached the same importance as in the lands of the south-east" (in other words, in Ukraine, Volynia, Podolia, and Ruthenia).[32] It was primarily the Jews who were the lease-holders (*arendarze*, arendars), while the inns and breweries they leased "constituted an integral part of the economy of the landed estates and linked the activities of the arendars to the feudal economic system."[33] Jerzy Topolski further concluded that from the second half of the seventeenth century, the Jewish population that was concentrated in the eastern part of the commonwealth "was an element in introducing the latifundial economic system. Without it, we would have had something like a living organism without blood-flow."[34]

Surely for the same reason, researchers in the past thirty years have been especially interested in the economic ties between Jews and magnates.[35]

---

32 Antoni Podraza, "Żydzi i wieś" [Jews and the village], in *Żydzi w dawnej Rzeczypospolitej*, 254.
33 Jakub Goldberg, "Żyd a karczma wiejska w XVIII wieku" [The Jew and the village inn in the eighteenth century], *Wiek Oświecenia* 9 (1993): 210; "Żyd a karczma miejska na Podlasiu w XVIII wieku" [The Jews and the rural tavern in Podlasie in the eighteenth century], *Studia Podlaskie* 2 (1989): 27–38; "Władza dominialna Żydów arendarzy dóbr ziemskich nad chłopami w XVII–XVIII" [The domainal authority of Jewish leaseholders over peasants in the seventeenth and eighteenth centuries], *Przegląd Historyczny* 81, nos. 1/2 (1990): 189–98; "Arenda i kredyt. Arendarz żydowski wobec Żydów, mieszczan i władzy dominialnej w małopolskim miasteczku w XVIII wieku" [Leaseholding and loan. The Jewish leaseholder versus Jews, burghers and the estate authority in a town in Małopolska in the eighteenth century] in *Rozdział wspólnej historii. Studia z dziejów Żydów w Polsce* [The divisions of a common history. Studies on the history of the Jews in Poland], ed. Jolanta Żyndul (Warsaw: Cyklady, 2001), 85–96; Judith Kalik, "Jewish Leaseholders (Arendarze) in 18th Century Crown Poland," *Jahrbücher für Geschichte Osteuropas* 54 (2006): 229–40; Paweł Fijałkowski, "Między starostą, burmistrzem i plebanem. Żydowscy arendarze w mazowieckich miastach u schyłku XVIII wieku" [Between a starosta, a mayor and a parson. Jewish leaseholders in the towns of Mazovia at the end of the eighteenth century], *Kwartalnik Historii Żydów* 4 (2014): 737–48.
34 Jerzy Topolski, "Uwagi o strukturze gospodarczo-społecznej Wielkopolski w XVIII wieku, czyli dlaczego na jej terenie nie było żydowskich karczmarzy" [Remarks on the economic-social structure of Wielkopolska, or why there were no Jewish inn-keepers in that area], in *Żydzi w Wielkopolsce na przestrzeni dziejów* [Jews in Wielkopolska over the ages], ed. Jerzy Topolski and Krzysztof Modelski (Poznań: Wydawnictwo Poznańskie, 1995), 81.
35 See inter alia: Moshe Rosman,"*Izrael Rubinowicz: Żyd w służbie polskich magnatów w XVIII wieku*" [Izrael Rubinowicz: a Jew in the service of Polish magnates in the eighteenth century], *Sobótka* (1982), no. 3/4: 497–507; Gershon D. Hundert, *The Jews in a Polish Private Town. The Case of Opatów in the Eighteenth Century* (Baltimore, MD: Johns Hopkins University Press, 1992); Adam Teller, "Radziwiłłowie a Żydzi w czasach saskich" [The

Contributing to this interest is also the fact that the most extensive surviving sources pertain to the large estates, the latifundia, sometimes including very rich economic archives such as those of the Radziwiłł family.

Commerce fulfilled three important functions in the economy of the great aristocratic estates: it supplied residents with goods, and yielded both tax revenues and export income. The magnates were, of course, aware of the role of commerce in the economy of their estates, and therefore supported all those who were occupied in it, including, and perhaps, above all, the Jews.

In the eighteenth century, the number of Jewish merchants in the great estates increased significantly in proportion to the number of Christian ones.[36] No wonder, then, that the Sobieskis[37] and Radziwiłłs supported the Jewish merchants, whose activities invigorated the economy of the latifundium and brought additional income from the fees they could levy on any form of mercantile activity. For that reason, the magnates rejected requests by Christian townspeople to restrict Jews' activities in retail trade.[38] Further, as Adam Teller has observed, in the eighteenth century these activities not only generated revenues for the magnates, but also sustained the functioning of markets in the towns themselves.[39]

The magnates facilitated extensive access to credit for the Jewish merchants in their estates, sometimes guaranteeing their loans.[40] Representing the magnates also opened up credit to Jewish merchants, from bankers and other

---

Radziwiłłs and the Jews in Saxon times], in *Rzeczpospolita wielu narodów i jej tradycje* [The Republic of many nations and its traditions], ed. Andrzej K. Link-Lenczowski and Mariusz Markiewicz (Kraków: Towarzystwo Wydawnicze "Historia Iagellonica," 1999), 149–61; Moshe Rosman, *The Lords' Jews: Jews and Magnates in the Polish-Lithuanian Commonwealth* (Cambridge, MA: Harvard University Press for the Center for Jewish Studies, Harvard University and the Harvard Ukrainian Research Institute, 1990); Adam Kaźmierczyk, *Żydzi w dobrach prywatnych w świetle sądowniczej i administracyjnej praktyki dóbr magnackich w wiekach XVI–XVIII* [Jews on private estates in the light of the legal and administrative practices of magnate estates from the sixteenth to the eighteenth century] (Kraków: Uniwersytet Jagielloński, Katedra Judaistyki, 2002).

36 Teller, *Radziwiłłowie a Żydzi*, 157.
37 Stefan Gąsiorowski, *Chrześcijanie i Żydzi w Żółkwi w XVII i XVIII wieku* [Christians and Jews in Żółkiew in the seventeenth and eighteenth centuries] (Kraków: Polska Akademia Umiejętności, 2001), 134–51.
38 Teller, *Radziwiłłowie a Żydzi*, 157.
39 Ibid., 159.
40 Juliusz Bardach, "Żydzi w Birżach radziwiłłowskich w XVII–XVIII wieku" [Jews in Birże under the Radziwiłłs], *Przegląd Historyczny* 1/2 (1990): 216.

merchants: for example, the Itzkowitz brothers, Shmoyle and Gadol Yakov, acting for the Radziwiłłs, could obtain credit in Königsberg.[41]

It can be agreed that in the second half of the eighteenth century Jews played a dominant role in domestic trade and an important one in foreign trade.[42] Research, to cite only Jakub Goldberg's study, has confirmed that in the eighteenth century "retail and petty trade, in small cities as well as large ones, was to a great extent in the hands of the Jews."[43] By the reign of Augustus II (1697–1733), at meetings of dietines in various parts of the country, the lesser nobility were already accusing Jewish merchants of displacing Christian ones.[44]

In writing about commerce in the early modern period, smuggling must also be taken into account.[45] When import and export duties were imposed, the Jews of Kazimierz, the Jewish district of Kraków, petitioned the king for an exemption. They were opposed by the royal treasurer, Jan Daniłowicz, who in 1640 filed a complaint against them for nonpayment of their duties and demanded payment in arrears.[46] The case was settled in 1643 by a judgment in the Assessors' Court, ordering Jews to pay duties on goods imported from abroad, while releasing them from paying road

---

41 Teresa Zielińska, "Kariera i upadek żydowskiego potentata w dobrach radziwiłłowskich w XVIII wieku" [The career and fall of a Jewish tycoon in the Radziwiłł estates in the eighteenth century], *Kwartalnik Historyczny* 3 (1991): 33.

42 Jacek Krupa, *Żydzi w Rzeczypospolitej w czasach Augusta II (1697–1733)* [Jews in the Polish-Lithuanian Commonwealth during the reign of August II, 1697–1733] (Kraków: Uniwersytet Jagielloński, Katedra Judaistyki, 2009), 143–51.

43 Jakub Goldberg, "Żydowski handel detaliczny w Polsce w XVIII w świetle polsko-hebrajskiego porządku kramarzów miasta Zasławia 1771 anno" [Jewish retail trade in Poland in light of the Polish-Hebrew ordinance for traders in the town of Zasław in 1771], *Przegląd Humanistyczny* 37, no. 4 (1993): 45. On Kraków recently: Przemysław Zarubin, *Żydzi w aglomeracji Krakowa w czasach stanisławowskich. Przemiany prawne, gospodarcze i społeczne* [Jews in the Kraków agglomeration during the times of Stanisław August. Legal, economic and social changes] (Kraków: Księgarnia Akademicka, 2012), 129–47.

44 Krupa, *Żydzi w Rzeczypospolitej w czasach Augusta II*, 143–51.

45 Klaus Heller, *Die wirtschaftliche Lage der Juden unter polnischer und russischer Herrschaft vom 16. bis zum 19. Jahrhundert* [The economic situation of the Jews under Polish and Russian rule from the sixteenth to the nineteenth centuries], in *Die wirtschaftlichen und kulturellen Beziehungen*, 26.

46 Majer Bałaban, *Historja Żydów w Krakowie i na Kazimierzu 1304–1868*, vol. 1: *1304–1655. Wydanie nowe rozszerzone i przerobione* [History of the Jews in Kraków and Kazimierz, vol. 1: 1304–1655] (New enlarged and revised edition, Kraków: Nadzieja, 1931; reprint: Kraków: Austeria, 1991), 235.

and bridge tolls and other transport and trading fees.[47] Still wanting to avoid customs duties, the Jews of Kraków avoided border posts and smuggled goods through the wilderness. To prevent this, all the importers in Kazimierz, twenty-seven in number, were summoned on May 22, 1645, and ordered to swear an oath that "with respect to goods that I have imported or will in the future import from foreign countries, I will not bypass the customs posts, but will pay duties to the Commonwealth."[48] Smuggling, in which Jewish merchants among others took part, also flourished in the last decades of the eighteenth century along the Polish–Russian border.[49]

CRAFTS

Crafts were an important area of economic activity for the Jews of the former commonwealth. As Daniel Tollet rightly pointed out some years ago, "the relative abundance of sources on merchants and business people should not obscure the fact that most of the Jews in Poland were involved in crafts."[50] While in 1539 there were about 3,200 merchants in the Polish Crown, Jewish craftsmen numbered some 10,000.[51] It must be noted, however, that in the mid-1770s, among Jews living in cities, 35–38 percent were engaged in commerce, and only 30–32 percent in crafts.[52]

At first, Jewish craftsmen were mainly butchers, bakers, tailors, soap-makers and bookbinders, providing for the Jewish community. Many fewer Jews took up crafts such as ceramics, wood- and metal-working, and the building trades.[53] In time, the number of crafts in which Jews were engaged increased.[54] In the 1770s, two-thirds of Jewish craftsmen worked in the clothing industry and in making fashion accessories.[55] We know a great deal about Jewish craftsmanship in the former

---

47 Ibid., 235–36.
48 Ibid., 236.
49 Josef Reinhold, *Polen-Litauen auf den Leipziger Messen des 18. Jahrhunderts* [Poles/Lithuanians at the Leipzig Fairs in the eighteenth century] (Weimar: Böhlau, 1971), 108.
50 Daniel Tollet, *Histoire des juifs en Pologne: du XVIe siècle à nos jours*, [The history of Jews in Poland: From the sixteenth century to our days] (Paris: Presses Universitaires de France, 1992).
51 Bernard Mark, "Rzemieślnicy żydowscy w Polsce feudalnej" [Jewish artisans in feudal Poland], *Biuletyn ŻIH* 9–10 (1954): 9.
52 Artur Eisenbach, *Z dziejów ludności żydowskiej w Polsce w XVIII i XIX wieku. Studia i szkice* [On the history of the Jews in Poland in the eighteenth and nineteenth centuries. Studies and essays] (Warsaw: Państwowy Instytut Wydawniczy, 1983), 21.
53 Guldon, *Żydzi w Polsce do końca XVIII wieku*, 13.
54 Polonsky, *The Jews in Poland and Russia*, 27.
55 Eisenbach, *Z dziejów ludności żydowskiej*, 22.

commonwealth, mainly through the research of Brand Wischnitzer,[56] Maurycy Horn,[57] Władysław Ćwik,[58] and Anatol Leszczyński.[59] Horn's study of Jewish craft fraternities in the years 1630–1850, published shortly before his death in 2000, and based on many years of archival research, deserves particular notice.[60]

AGRICULTURE

While in the western part of the commonwealth only a small fraction of the Jewish population lived in villages, eastward the proportion increased.[61] In the mid-eighteenth century, 30.5 percent of the Jews in the Lublin district lived in villages, and 55 percent in Podlasie.[62] According to Rafael Mahler's calculations, in the second half of the eighteenth century more than 25 percent of Jews lived in the countryside,[63] and by the end of the century, about

---

56 Research on this subject is summarized in Mark Wischnitzer, *A History of Jewish Crafts and Guilds*, foreword by Salo W. Baron, introduction by Werner J. Cahnman (New York: J. David, 1965), 206–86; bibliography, 314.

57 Maurycy Horn, "Rzemieślnicy żydowscy na Rusi Czerwonej na przełomie XVI i XVII w." [Jewish artisans in Red Ruthenia at the turn of the sixteenth and seventeenth centuries], *Biuletyn ŻIH* 34 (1960): 28–70; "Nowe szczegóły o rzemiośle żydowskim w województwie bełskim na przełomie XVI i XVII wieku" [New details on Jewish artisan trade in the Bielsk voivodeship at the turn of the sixteenth and seventeenth centuries], *Biuletyn ŻIH* 55 (1965): 85–92; *Żydzi na Rusi Czerwonej*, 83–159; "Usługi chrześcijańskich i żydowskich rzemieślników i przedsiębiorców na rzecz dworu królewskiego w Polsce i na Litwie za ostatnich Jagiellonów (1506–1572)" [The services of Jewish and Christian artisans and traders at the royal court in Poland and Lithuanian during the rule of the last Jagiellonians—1506–1772], part 1: *Biuletyn ŻIH* 2 (1990): 3–22; part 2: ibid., 1991, no. 2: 3–9.

58 Władysław Ćwik, "Ludność żydowska w miastach królewskich Lubelszczyzny w drugiej połowie XVIII wieku" [The Jewish population of royal towns in the Lublin area in the second half of the seventeenth century], *Biuletyn ŻIH* 59 (1966): 29–62.

59 Anatol Leszczyński, "Rzemiosło żydowskie ziemi bielskiej od połowy XVII do 1798 r." [Jewish crafts in the area of Bielsk form the middle of the seventeenth century to 1798], *Biuletyn ŻIH* 101 (1977): 17–39; idem, *Żydzi ziemi bielskiej od połowy XVII do 1795 r. (Studium osadnicze i ekonomiczne)* [Jews in the area of Bielsk from the middle of the seventeenth century to 1795—a study in settlement and economics] (Wrocław: Zakład Narodowy im. Ossolińskich, 1980).

60 Maurycy Horn, *Żydowskie bractwa rzemieślnicze na ziemiach polskich, litewskich, białoruskich i ukraińskich w latach 1613–1850* [Jewish artisan gilds in Poland, Lithuania, Belarus, and Ukraine in the years 1613–1850] (Warsaw: Żydowski Instytut Historyczny, 1998).

61 Stefan Cackowski, "Wiejscy Żydzi w województwie chełmińskim w 1772 r.," [Rural Jews in the Chełmno Province], *Acta Universitatis Nicolai Copernici. Historia* 28 (1993): 61–72.

62 Schiper, *Dzieje gospodarcze Żydów*, 179.

63 Raphael Mahler, *Yidn in amoylikn Poyln in likht fun tsifern* [Jews in Old Poland in numbers] (Warsaw: Yidish bukh, 1958), 49.

40 percent of the Jews of Mazovia are thought to have lived in villages.[64] Most were not engaged in agriculture, however, but mainly in crafts, trading, and innkeeping.[65] In 1765–91, nearly 90 percent of the rural Jews in Podolia and Ukraine made their living by managing inns or other leaseholds.[66] Mordechai Nadav has provided some information about their land ownership and farming activity in sixteenth-century Lithuania.[67] In 2007, Hanna Węgrzynek wrote: "Agriculture has rarely been the livelihood of the Polish Jews, but in the complex economic situation that the Commonwealth faced, especially in the eighteenth century, it became a kind of necessity, providing for their families wherever they lived."[68] In a later article, she described the role of Jews in the rural economy of the Zamoyski estates at the turn of the seventeenth and eighteenth centuries, concluding that "inn and mill leaseholds were a kind of multi-branched enterprise" and that Jewish tenants received "probably entire villages or parts of them."[69]

Projects and attempts (mostly unsuccessful) undertaken in the late eighteenth century to transform Polish Jews into farmers have recently been discussed by Marcin Wodziński.[70]

---

64 Paweł Fijałkowski, "Osadnictwo żydowskie na Mazowszu północnym i wschodnim w świetle wizytacji kościelnych z lat 1775–1781" [Jewish settlement in northern and eastern Mazovia in light of church visitations in the years 1775–1781], *Kwartalnik Historii Żydów* 2 (2002): 161; "*Żydzi w mazowieckich wsiach od czasów najdawniejszych do początków XIX wieku*" [Jews in the villages of Mazovia from the earliest times to the beginning of the nineteenth century], in *Żydzi na wsi polskiej. Sesja naukowa, Szreniawa, 26–27 czerwca 2006* [Jews in the Polish countryside. Scholarly session, Sreniawa, June 26–27, 2006], ed. Wojciech Mielewczyk, Urszula Siekacz (Szreniawa: Muzeum Narodowe Rolnictwa i Przemysłu Rolno-Spożywczego, 2006), 17–30.

65 Jacob Goldberg, "Rolnictwo wśród Żydów w ziemi wieluńskiej w drugiej połowie XVIII wieku" [Agriculture among Jews in the area of Wieluń in the second half of the eighteenth century], *Biuletyn ŻIH* 27 (1958): 62–89.

66 Schiper, *Dzieje gospodarcze Żydów*, 179.

67 Mordechai Nadav, "Jewish Ownership of Land and Agricultural Activity in 16th Century Lithuania," in *Studies in the History of the Jews in Old Poland. In Honor of Jacob Goldberg*, ed. Adam Teller (Jerusalem: Magnes Press, 1998), 161–65.

68 Hanna Węgrzynek, "Zajęcia rolnicze Żydów w Rzeczypospolitej w XVI–XVIII wieku" [Agricultural activities of Jews in the Polish-Lithuanian Commonwealth from the sixteenth to the eighteenth centuries] in *Małżeństwo z rozsądku?*, 102.

69 Hanna Węgrzynek, "Rola Żydów w gospodarce Ordynacji Zamojskiej w drugiej połowie XVII i na początku XVIII wieku" [The role of Jews in the economy of the Zamoyski entail in the second half of the seventeenth and the first half of the eighteenth centuries], in *Żydzi w Zamościu i na Zamojszczyźnie. Historia—kultura—literatura* [Jews in Zamość and the Zamość area. History—culture—literature], ed. Weronika Litwin, Monika Szabłowska-Zaremba, and Sławomir Jacek Żurek (Lublin: Towarzystwo Naukowe Katolickiego Uniwersytetu Lubelskiego, 2012), 49.

70 Marcin Wodziński, "*Wilkiem orać.* Polskie projekty kolonizacji rolnej Żydów, 1775–1823," ["To plough with a wolf." Polish plans for Jewish agricultural colonization] in *Małżeństwo z rozsądku?*, 105–29.

INDUSTRY AND MANUFACTURING

The Jews of the commonwealth played only a minor role in industry, but industry in general was not particularly developed there at that time. Most manufactories, founded primarily by magnates, quickly fell into bankruptcy. Jews nevertheless tried their hand in this sphere of the economy, though in practice only when they could find Christian partners. Thanks to the research of Shmuel A. Cygielman, we know of a Polish–Jewish salt extraction enterprise that operated between 1577 and 1580.[71] Jakub Goldberg, in turn, described how a priest and a Jew built and managed an iron foundry in the town of Chocz in western Poland (Wielkopolska).[72] In the second half of the eighteenth century, Jacob Izraelowicz of Przytyk prospected for ore and salt deposits in a few places in the fork of the Vistula and Pilica rivers, and for salt in Rączki near Przedbórz (in the former district of Chęciny).[73] His activities await their historian. It should be added that Izraelowicz was not the only Jew in the Polish–Lithuanian state who was trying to find salt deposits.[74]

Concerning the Jews' participation in industry during the reign of Stanisław August Poniatowski (1764–95,) still relevant are Emanuel Ringelblum's observations that Polish Jews played a smaller role than they would in the nineteenth century for the following reasons:

a) the general rise in the country's economy, hence of trade, which was largely in the hands of the Jews;
b) lack of sufficient capital to introduce new industries;
c) lack of manpower, since Jewish entrepreneurs essentially did not have the right to employ Christian workers, thus neither guild craftsmen

---

71 Shmuel Arthur Cygielman, "Polish Jewish partnerships for the extraction of salt 1577–1580" [in Hebrew], *Zion* 51, no. 2 (1986).
72 Jacob Goldberg, "Jak ksiądz z Żydem zakładali manufakturę żelazną w Wielkopolsce" [How a priest and a Jew founded an iron foundry in Wielkopolska] in *The Jews in Poland*, vol. 1, ed. Andrzej K. Paluch (Kraków, 1992), 149–60; "Manufaktura żelazna księdza infułata Kazimierza Lipskiego i Szlamy Efraimowicza w Choczu (inicjatywy gospodarcze Żydów w XVIII wieku)" [The iron foundry of Prelate Kazimierz Lipski and Szlama Efraimowicz in Chocz—economic initiatives of Jews in the eighteenth century], in *Żydzi w Wielkopolsce na przestrzeni dziejów*, 83–99.
73 Zenon Guldon, Lech Stępkowski, "Jakub Izraelowicz z Przytyka, nieznany geolog z XVIII wieku," [Jakub Izraelowicz of Przytyk, an unknown geologist of the eighteenth century], *Biuletyn ŻIH* 3–4 (1987): 123–25.
74 Emanuel Ringelblum, "Projekty i próby przewarstwowienia Żydów w epoce stanisławowskiej (Dokończenie)" [Projects and attempts to restructure the Jews' social structure in the eighteenth century—conclusion], *Sprawy Narodowościowe* 8, no. 2/3 (1934): 210.

nor state serfs, even in those branches of production in which there were no Jewish specialists;

d) the lack of the proper education and skills needed to introduce modern factory equipment;

e) the risk connected with the introduction of new industries, as best demonstrated by the widespread bankruptcy of factories founded by magnates.[75]

Despite these unfavorable conditions, Jews did own, for example, textile factories.[76]

RESEARCH DIRECTIONS

The participation and significance of the Jewish population in the economy of the commonwealth undoubtedly require further detailed study, which must be conducted in parallel with studies on the economic history of the Polish–Lithuanian state. That may be difficult, however, since in the last twenty years the number of Polish historians specializing in the economic history of the sixteenth through eighteenth centuries has declined drastically. Why that has happened is a subject for a separate article.

I have already mentioned the huge losses of source material on the history of Polish Jews incurred during and even before the Second World War. It is thus all the more necessary to work with what remains. I have in mind primarily the records of the Chancellery of the Royal Chamber at the Central Archives of Historical Records in Warsaw, which contain 1,819 quarterly registers of more than 200 customs posts and sub-posts for the years 1738 and 1763–67 in the entire Crown (excluding Royal Prussia).[77] Only some of these records have been employed so far in studies on Polish trade in the mid-eighteenth century; namely, in Anatol Leszczyński's study of the participation of Jewish merchants in the cities of the Bielsko region on the basis of the customs registers for 1766,[78] and Wiktor Ojrzyński's on the Jewish merchants of Przedborze

---

75 Ibid., 181–82.
76 Ibid., 188–90.
77 Zenon Guldon, Lech Stępkowski, "Rejestry komór celnych z terenu Korony z lat 1738–1767" [The register of customs registers from the Crown in the years 1738–1767], *KHKM* 33, no. 3, (1985): 215–28.
78 Anatol Leszczyński, "Kupcy żydowscy miast ziemi bielskiej w aktach komór celnych z 1766 r." [Jewish merchants in the Bielsk district in the documents of the customs] *Biuletyn ŻIH* 106 (1978): 91–100; *Żydzi ziemi bielskiej od połowy XVII w. do 1795 r. (Studium osadnicze, prawne i ekonomiczne)* [The Jews of the Bielsk region from the

in Mazovian commerce.[79] Also interested in these registers was Gershon D. Hundert, who reported that in twenty-three of sixty customs registers for the years 1764–67, a total of 11,485 transports were recorded, of which 5,888 were Jewish.[80] On that basis, he concluded that "generally, 50–60 percent of internal trade was in the hands of the Jews, recalling at the same time that the great majority of Jews lived in the eastern lands of the commonwealth."[81]

Taking as an example the registers of customs post in Ostrołęka (and its sub-post Myszeniec) for 1765: in the former, 141 Jewish transports and 146 Christian ones are recorded, while in the latter the numbers were twenty-four and seventy-nine, respectively.[82] There were thus more Christian transports than Jewish ones, which might be taken to indicate a predominance of Christian merchants. Nothing could be further from the truth since the records clearly indicate that in the quantity of merchandise and the customs duties paid, it was Jews who were predominant. For example, on February 14, 1765, Herszko Leybowicz from Ciechanowiec appeared at the customs post in Ostrołęka, having carried, most likely from Gdańsk, the following goods: six (Polish) stone (150 lbs.) of pepper, four stone (100 lbs.) of Dutch coffee, two stone of ginger, one stone of Venetian cumin, one stone of rice, one stone of almonds, four stone of brown sugar, two stone of Gdańsk gunpowder, fifteen parcels of plain woolen belts, six tallisot, one lot of scarves, three kopy (fifteen dozen) printed cloths, one Gdańsk kuczbaja (an item of clothing made of shaggy woolen cloth), four jachras [?] of suede skins, and five stone of Spanish olive oil. The duty amounted to six zlotys twenty groszy; the fee for four horses, eight groszy. In contrast, the well-known Wojciech Wieczorkowski of Szczuczyn brought in two barrels of perch and six barrels of roach from Prussia, for which he paid fifteen groszy at the Myszeniec sub-post. Similar examples from this post and sub-post can be multiplied.

In my opinion, however, we should publish not just the entries for Jewish merchants and transports, as has been done in the case of Kraków,[83] but

---

middle of the seventeenth century to 1795—a study of settlement, legal rights and economic activity] (Wrocław, 1980).
79 Wojciech Ojrzyński, "Żydzi z Przedborza w handlu mazowieckim w świetle akt komór celnych z lat 1764–1766" [Jews from Przedbórz in Mazovian trade in the light of customs records from 1764–1766], Biuletyn ŻIH 121–122 (1982): 71–76.
80 Hundert, Żydzi w Rzeczypospolitej, 56.
81 Ibid.
82 Archiwum Główne Akt Dawnych w Warszawie (Central Archives of Historical Records in Warsaw), Archiwum Kameralne, Komora celna Ostrołęka, 1765, sygn. AKam. III/1629/5, author's calculations.
83 Małecki, "Handel żydowski u schyłku XVI."

the entire registers, since only then will it be possible to determine the ratio between Jewish and Christian merchants and compare the kinds and quantities of goods traded. The information contained in these records will provide material not only for studies that place Jewish commerce in the overall picture, but also for micro-histories of commerce generally in a given locality. An example is the city of Brody. While it is true that a monograph on the economic activity of the Jews in Brody has been published, the author did not make use of the city's customs records, though they contain numerous references to the city's Jewish dealers.[84]

The names of Jewish merchants listed in customs records, such as those for Ostrołęka in 1765, can be compared with those that appear in lists of writs of safe passage issued by the Gdańsk city council to Jewish merchants coming to the city.[85] Jan M. Małecki and Zenon H. Nowak drew attention to these Gdańsk writs some years ago,[86] both of them stressing the uniqueness of this source, but knowing only of the list for 1641. In fact, many more such lists survived,[87] such as those of Jewish merchants who arrived in Gdańsk in 1588–89 (among them, eight Jews from Kraków).[88]

On the basis of the lists and customs registers from the early mid-eighteenth century, it is possible to study the export trade—both Jewish and Christian—going to Brandenburg Prussia (mainly Gdańsk). The scale of this

---

84 Dawid Wurm, *Z dziejów żydostwa brodzkiego za czasów dawnej Rzeczypospolitej Polskiej (do R. 1772). Z przedmową prof. dra Majera Bałabana* [On the history of the Jewish community of Brody during the Polish-Lithuanian Commonwealth—to 1795. With a foreword by Dr. Majer Bałaban] (Brody: Gmina Wyznaniowa Żydowska, 1935; microfilm in Jewish Historical Institute); Tadeusz Lutman, in *Studja nad dziejami handlu Brodów w latach 1773–1880* [Studies on the history of trade in Brody in the years 1773–1880] (Lwów: Drukarnia Naukowa, 1937), 167n1, felt that Wurm's assessment of the decline of commerce in Brody in the 1760s was unjustified, perhaps because he did not take the customs registers into account.

85 Edmund Kizik, "Mieszczaństwo gdańskie wobec Żydów w XVII–XVIII wieku" [The attitude of the burghers of Gdańsk towards Jews in the seventeenth and eighteenth centuries], *Kwartalnik Historii Żydów* 3 (2003): 417; "Żydzi przed gdańskim Sądem Wetowym w połowie XVIII wieku" [Jews in the face of the Gdańsk prohibition on settlement in the middle of the eighteenth century] in *Z przeszłości Żydów polskich*, 53–54.

86 Jan M. Małecki, *Związki handlowe miast polskich z Gdańskiem w XVI i pierwszej połowie XVII wieku* [Trade links between Polish towns and Gdańsk in the sixteenth and first half of the seventeenth centuries] (Wrocław: Zakład Narodowy im. Ossolińskich, 1968), 53; Zenon H. Nowak, "Dzieje Żydów w Prusach Królewskich do roku 1772. Charakterystyka" [The history of Jews in Royal Prussia to 1772. Its main features] in *Żydzi w dawnej Rzeczypospolitej*, 141–42.

87 Kizik, "Mieszczaństwo gdańskie wobec Żydów," 420.

88 Archiwum Państwowe (State Archive) in Gdańsk, 300, 12/312, 70 and 76.

trade must have been considerable, since Jerzy Woyna-Okołów, the Polish consul in Königsberg, reported at the beginning of January 1794 that in his opinion, "counting lightly," 15,000 Jews were traveling to Prussia from the commonwealth to conduct trade.[89] The trade must also have been very profitable, since each Jewish merchant leaving for Prussia had to pay a 20-zloty "escort fee," which in theory covered a one-month stay, but had to be paid even if the stay was only a single day.[90] The Polish consul believed that the commonwealth was losing at least one million zlotys annually thereby.

In view of the destruction of most of the registers of the state customs posts, the books of the city posts have become an especially important source. As Jan M. Małecki has written: "Historians of commerce deprived of this source [the state customs books], usually relying on material taken from city books, [charters of] privileges etc., can indicate general developmental tendencies, trade links between various centers and the goods traded, and can support their arguments with sometimes interesting examples; but it is difficult for them to study the movement of goods in detail, the quantitative relationships between various groups of goods, the amount of trade between cities, the rise and fall of exchange rates in different periods; in a word, without customs registers it is almost impossible to carry any of the statistical studies that are so important in economic history."[91]

Of the surviving customs books of the former commonwealth, historians at least have those of Kraków at their disposal. On the basis of those records, Janina Bieniarzówna provided a sketch of Jewish commerce in Kraków from

---

89 Jacek Wijaczka, ed., *Relacje Jerzego Woyny-Okołowa, przedstawiciela Rzeczypospolitej w Królewcu w latach 1792–1794* [The account of Jerzy Woyna-Okołow, representative of the Polish-Lithuanian Commonwealth in Königsberg in the years 1792–1794] (Toruń: Towarzystwo Naukowe w Toruniu, 1999), 64.

90 Ibid.

91 Jan M. Małecki, "Krakowskie księgi celne i problem ich wydania" [The customs books of Kraków and the difficulty of publishing them], *KHKM* 9, no. 2 (1961): 251. The significance of these municipal customs books was emphasized again in 2014 by Szymon Kazusek, "Rola Żydów w handlu polskim w XVI–XVIII wieku. Szkic do badań" [The role of Jews in Polish trade in the sixteenth to the eighteenth centuries. Research outline], in *Rola Żydów w rozwoju gospodarczym ziem polskich* [The role of Jews in the economic development of the Polish lands], ed. Janusz Skodlarski (Łódź: Wydawnictwo Uniwersytetu Łódzkiego, 2014), 25–38. In his article, Kazusek did not focus so much on the role of the Jews in commerce in the early modern commonwealth as on pointing out that in research on the participation and role of Jewish merchants, "mass sources remain unpopular and are still insufficiently appreciated," among which customs books occupy a significant place. Further in the same article, he discussed the state of preservation of these sources and their use in research since 1945.

the mid-seventeenth to the mid-eighteenth century.[92] She noted that in Kraków in 1751 there took place "a complete separation between Polish and Jewish trade, while the routine use of the term *infidus* [infidel] is evidence of worsening mutual relations."[93]

There seems to be some possibility of studying the participation of Jews from the commonwealth in foreign markets, especially in the second half of the seventeenth and the eighteenth centuries. It is known that between 1675 and 1699, a total of 11,959 independent Jewish merchants took part in the Easter and Michaelmas fairs in Leipzig, of whom 982 (i.e., one-twelfth) came from Poland.[94] In the second half of the eighteenth century, Jewish merchants regularly attended the Leipzig fairs, and were among the largest wholesalers from Poland–Lithuania. Besides Christian merchants—the Heryng brothers from Warsaw and a Bogdanowicz from Lwów—one should mention Nathan Chaim from Szkłów, along with Feyvel Herz, Jacob Nathan, and Henan Landau from Brody.[95] Of these, Nathan Chaim conducted the largest commercial operations at the Leipzig fair in the 1780s, bringing goods worth almost 500,000 *Reichstalers* to the Michaelmas fair in 1786.[96] In November of that year, the wealthiest merchants of Leipzig supported his petition to the Elector of Saxony to allow his agent to remain in Leipzig between fairs;[97] we do not know whether the elector responded positively to his request.

It must further be kept in mind that the commercial activity of the Jews in those two centuries was limited by the debts that burdened Jewish communities. As an example, the Poznań kehillah had a debt of 32,000 guldens in 1626, which by 1700 had grown to 109,278 guldens.[98] The debts of the Jewish communities had an adverse effect on Jewish trade: Christian creditors confiscated goods from Jewish merchants, and often imprisoned the merchants

---

92 Janina Bieniarzówna, "Handel żydowski w stuleciu upadku Krakowa" [Jewish trade in the century of Kraków's decline], in *Żydzi w dawnej Rzeczypospolitej*, 226–35.
93 Ibid., 235.
94 Max Freudenthal, *Leipziger Messgäste. Die jüdischen Besucher der Leipziger Messen in den Jahren 1675 bis 1764* [People present at the Leipzig Fair. Jewish visitors at the Leipzig Fairs in the years 1675 to 1764] (Frankfurt am Main: J. Kauffmann, 1928), 17.
95 Reinhold, *Polen-Litauen auf den Leipziger Messen*, 148.
96 Ibid., 149. The Reichstaler was nominally worth about 26 grams of silver [GSP].
97 Ibid., 7.
98 Marcus Breger, *Zur Handelsgeschichte der Juden in Polen während des 17. Jahrhunderts. Mit besonderer Berücksichtigung der Judenschaft Posens* [On the history of Jewish trade in Poland during the seventeenth century. With particular reference to the Jewish community of Poznań] (Berlin: Buchhandlung R. Mass, 1932), 7.

themselves. For that reason, Jewish merchants from Poznań often had to pay the kehillah's debts, or avoid certain markets, so as not to lose their freedom or their goods. The communities' debts also impoverished merchants, leading to bankruptcies and eventually the financial collapse of Jewish communities in the eighteenth century.[99] There already exists a fairly extensive literature on the debts of individual communities; Krzysztof Modelski[100] and Moshe Rosman,[101] among others, have recently written on the subject, but so far as I know there is no synthetic study even of the Crown.

CONCLUSION

The question of the participation and significance of the Jewish population in the economy of the Polish–Lithuanian state in the sixteenth through eighteenth centuries is a complex one, and, given the current state of research, clearly impossible to answer. For that reason, it is hardly surprising that historians writing on the subject have sometimes avoided clear statements and taken refuge in general formulations. For example, Janina Bieniarzówna, summarizing the role of the Jews in Polish foreign trade in the years 1648–1764, wrote: "Foreign trade in Poland was very feeble in the period studied here. Jews took the export of raw material into their hands, thanks to the support—not disinterested—of the noblemen. They played a large role in Polish exports."[102]

For decades, assessments of the role and significance of the Jews' economic activity in the Polish–Lithuanian state in the early modern period have remained inconclusive. Contemporaries most often accused the Jews of driving the country, especially the towns, to ruin. Sporadically, opinions were expressed such as those of an anonymous Pole who wrote in 1774: "the Jews are mainly engaged in active trade, the only kind that brings benefit to the country; the *szlachta* also carry on trade of that kind. The trade that the Christians conduct

---

99 Ibid., 7.
100 Krzysztof Modelski, "Z dziejów gminy żydowskiej w Wolsztynie (finanse gminy w XVIII wieku)" [On the history of the Jewish community in Wolsztyn—the finances of the community in the eighteenth century], in *Żydzi w Wielkopolsce*, 100–114.
101 Moshe Rosman, "The Indebtedness of the Lublin Kahal in the 18th Century," in *Studies in the History of the Jews in Old Poland. In Honor of Jacob Goldberg*, ed. Adam Teller (Jerusalem: Magnes Press, the Hebrew University, Center for Research on the History and Culture of Polish Jews 1998), 166–83.
102 Janina Bieniarzówna, "The Role of Jews in Polish Foreign Trade, 1648–1764," in *The Jews in Poland*, 109.

is passive, rather destructive trade."[103] In turn, a nobleman writing under the pseudonym Stężycanin ("man from Stężyce") had the courage to admit that "we wanted to have more, so we brought in the Jews. It was not they, but we ourselves who mauled the peasants, just using Jewish claws."[104] That the magnates and wealthy nobility used Jews to do their dirty work was confirmed by another anonymous Pole, who in 1791 wrote to a German friend in Saxony: "Die Geschäfte des vornehmen Pohlen besorgt entweder die Geistliche oder der Israelite. Der Erste machte eine Art. Vom Haushofmeister, vom den letzteren bekannt ist, dass die mehrersten Professionen in Pohlen treiben."[105] (The business of the high-ranking Poles is conducted by either the clergy or the Israelites. The former do one kind of work. Of the arendars, of the latter, it is admitted that they carry out most of the main professions in Poland.)

Negative conclusions about the destructive role of the Jews in the economy of the nobles' commonwealth were also repeated by historians such as Roman Rybarski, who wrote: "their participation [in trade] grows ever greater when the economic situation of the urban population worsens, when towns decline. The Jews in Poland were not the yeast required for a more buoyant economic life to flourish; they were the ferment that destroyed the old economic organization but did not create in its place something that would increase the country's economic strength."[106] One cannot agree with his opinion.

Maurycy Horn, in his work on the Jews in Ruthenia in the sixteenth and first half of the seventeenth century wrote: "The significance of Jewish trade lay not only in organizing retail markets, but proved to have an equally strong influence on the organization of cottage industries. The Jews' commercial activity influenced the activation of the internal market, and by drawing peasants and the inhabitants of small towns into the money economy, stimulated

---

103 Cited after Nathan Michael Gelber, "Ogólny obraz stosunków społeczno-gospodarczych żydostwa polskiego z końcem 18 wieku" [The general picture of the social-economic situation of Polish Jewry at the end of the eighteenth century], *Moriah. Miesięcznik młodzieży żydowskiej* 14, no. 2 (1919): 59.
104 Cited after Emanuel Ringelblum, "Projekty i próby przewarstwowienia Żydów w epoce stanisławowskiej" [Projects and attempts at shifting social classes of Jews in the eighteenth century], *Sprawy Narodowościowe* 8, no. 1 (1934): 6.
105 *Über Pohlen überhaupt und besonders über die glückliche Staats-Revolution am 3ten May 1791. Briefe eines Pohlen an seinen Freund in Chursachsen* [On Poland and especially and particularly about the happy state-revolution of 3 May 1791. Letters of Pole to his friend in Saxony] (Warsaw, 1791), 55.
106 Rybarski, *Handel i polityka handlowa*, vol. 1, 227.

the economic development of these centers, and brought about their gradual transformation from agrarian settlements into small market towns in which crafts and commerce also played a role."[107] Without doubt, the Jewish population was an agent of urbanization. For that reason, to take one example, Michał Antoni Radziwiłł, the owner of the town of Szydłowiec, which was very run down in the late seventeenth century, began efforts in 1711 to gain the consent of the bishop of Kraków, Felicjan Konstantyn Szaniawski, to build a synagogue in the town so as to keep the Jews from leaving.[108] His son, Leon Michał Radziwiłł, whenever a dispute arose between Catholics and Jews, quickly settled the issues of contention, believing that conflict led to the economic deterioration not only of the Jewish community, but also of the town itself.[109] As Zenon Guldon noted, "after the destructive wars of the mid-seventeenth and early eighteenth century, the Jews played an important role in the economy of some of the central and eastern of the Commonwealth, though a much smaller one in Royal Prussia and western Wielkopolska."[110]

Writing at the beginning of the nineteenth century, Tadeusz Czacki, in *Rozprawa o Żydach* (A discourse on the Jews), was persuaded that in the final years of the commonwealth, before the partitions, three-quarters of exports and one-tenth of imports remained in the hands of Jewish merchants.[111] At the meeting of the Sejm on December 30, 1791, Jacek Jezierski, the castellan of Łuków, said: "I take the Jews as Polish citizens, and useful ones, because I know no merchants but Jewish ones, since to me the only merchant is one who exports the country's products, not one who brings fashionable things into the country and exports ready cash."[112]

---

107 Horn, *Żydzi na Rusi Czerwonej*, 191.
108 Jacek Wijaczka, "Żydzi w Szydłowcu do końca XVIII wieku" [Jews in Szydlowiec to the end of the eighteenth century], in *Żydzi szydłowieccy. Materiały sesji popularnonaukowej 22 lutego 1997 roku* [The Jews of Szydłowiec. Materials from a popular-scholarly session, February 22, 1997], ed. J. Wijaczka (Szydłowiec: Muzeum Ludowych Instrumentów Muzycznych w Szydłowcu, 1997), 13–14.
109 Ibid., 18.
110 Guldon, *Żydzi w Polsce do końca XVIII wieku*, 12.
111 Tadeusz Czacki, *Rozprawa o Żydach* [A discourse on the Jews] (Wilno, 1807; reprint, Kraków: Wydawn. Biblioteki Polskiej, 1860), 217–18.
112 Schiper, *Dzieje gospodarcze Żydów*, 181; Krystyna Zienkowska, *Jacek Jezierski, kasztelan łukowski (1722–1805). Z dziejów szlachty polskiej XVIII w.* [Jacek Jezeierski. Castellan of Łukow 1772–1805, On the history of the Polish nobility in the eighteenth century] (Warsaw: Państwowe Wydawnictwo Naukowe, 1963), 192.

In the current state of research on the participation and significance of the Jewish population in the economy of the commonwealth in the sixteenth through eighteenth centuries, one can certainly agree with Gershon D. Hundert that in the early modern era, "the Jews became an indispensable part of the economic structure of the Commonwealth."[113]

Translated from Polish by Gunnar S. Paulsson

---

113 Gershon D. Hundert, *Jews in Poland-Lithuania in the Eighteenth Century: A Genealogy of Modernity* (Berkeley: University of California Press, 2004), 55.

Reassessment of the Jewish Poll Tax Assessment Lists from Eighteenth-Century Crown Poland

JUDITH KALIK

In my book titled *Scepter of Judah: Jewish Autonomy in the Eighteenth-Century Crown Poland* (Leiden, 2009), which was based on an analysis of the assessment lists of the Jewish poll tax in 1717–64 in Crown Poland, I drew attention what I call a "rotation schedule" of tax assessment, that is, an increase of taxation burden in some communities and simultaneous reduction of this burden in other communities. Since during this period the Jewish poll tax for Crown Poland was fixed at a permanent sum of 220,000 złotys, which was about half the real Jewish population of the country, the Council of Four Lands and the regional councils had relatively broad freedom of choice to assign the taxation burden to various communities in rotation.

The claim was raised in the course of further discussion on my conclusions that in practice every individual Jewish taxpayer paid annually the same sum of money, the poll tax being only a fraction of this sum, while the rest covered other expenses of Jewish communities and councils. Thus, the reduction of the poll tax for a certain community did not mean that this community paid less, but that the sum reduced from the poll tax was diverted for other needs. Of course, the poll tax assessment lists do not reflect all the expenses of the Jewish communities, but the usual level of the poll tax, regardless of periodical changes and tax exemptions for all communities of Crown Poland combined together, would produce what I called the "tax potential," which does reflect the actual size of the Jewish population.

One of the ways to solve this controversy is to compare the assessment list presented in my book with the sporadic documentation reflecting the relations between the Council of Four Lands with the regional councils and Jewish communities. Thanks to the wonderful edition by the late Mordechai Nadav of the minute book of the Tykocin autonomous major community,[1] we have a relatively rare opportunity to look into the nearly complete set of documents of one of such regional councils (the major autonomous community of Tykocin functioned in practice as a regional council). In this essay, I would like to clarify the picture, showing some examples of the hidden mechanism behind the fluctuations of poll tax assessment.

The matter is that the assessment lists are systematic records covering the entire Crown Poland, but the pattern of periodical changes in assessment of the poll tax level is reflected also in sporadic Jewish documentation. Let us look at some of these documents. Thus, we find that in 1731 the community of Orly (now Orla) reached an agreement with the major community of Tykocin that the annual poll tax of Orly would be set at 1350 złotys,[2] which was, in fact, a sum paid by Orly in 1733–34 according to the assessment lists.[3] However, the agreement includes the following clause:

> But if the poll tax (*kharga*) will increase by the assessment of the Council of Four Lands beyond our present estimate, the value of the addition shall be cleared from the assessed expenses of the above holy community on behalf of Council of Four Lands or to Warsaw etc., [but] the holy community of Orly shall be exempted from a payment of even one *grosz* (*pruta*) during the validity of this assessment.

A similar clause is found in an agreement between the community of Boczki (now Boćki) and the major community of Tykocin on which it was dependent in 1745, which set the poll tax of Boczki at the level of 500 złotys,[4] but in this case provision was only made for raising the community's contribution if the

---

1 *Pinkas kahal tiktin 5301–5566, haskamot, hahlatot vetakanot kfi shehe'etikan min hapinkas hamekori sheavad bashoah Israel Halperin* [The minutebook of the Tiktin community between 5301 and 5566, decisions, resolutions and regulations reconstructed by Israel Halperin from the original minutebook lost in the Shoah], ed. Mordechai Nadav, vol. 1 (Jerusalem, 1996), vol. 2 (Jerusalem, 2000).
2 *Pinkas kahal tiktin*, vol. 1, 878.
3 Judith Kalik, *Scepter of Judah: Jewish Autonomy in the Eighteenth-Century Crown Poland*, vol. 2 of *Studia Judaeoslavica*, ed. A. Kulik (Leiden: Brill, 2009), table 3b, 165.
4 *Pinkas kahal tiktin*, 523, according to the assessment lists that Boczki paid this sum from 1738 to 1754; Kalik, *Scepter of Judah*, table 3b, 165–66.

poll tax were raised, not for lowering it: "But if our poll tax will increase by assessment of the Council of Four Lands beyond our present assessment, the value of assessment shall be according to the addition imposed on this holy community." Both cases show clearly that an unexpected increase of the taxation burden as result of the reassessment of the Jewish poll tax by the Council of Four Lands was a real possibility, which should be taken into consideration in negotiations between the communities and regional councils.

Even more interesting is that some documents provide us with the reasons for tax reduction. Thus, for example, in 1732 the community of Orly, which, as we see in our first example, had to pay in the following year 1,350 złotys as a poll tax, but asked for and received a reduction of 200 złotys as compensation for the loss of income from a rural tavern (*shenk* in Yiddish), which was attached to another community.[5] According to the assessment lists, this reduction was implemented only in 1737, when the community of Orly indeed paid 1,050 złotys as a poll tax—exactly 200 złotys less than the original assessment.[6] This case shows, among other things, that villages in the rural periphery of Jewish urban communities were indeed transferred from one community to another because of poll tax considerations, as I claimed on the basis of the situation in the neighboring Węgrów community that is reflected in the assessment lists, but without the support of any direct evidence. In 1756, the agreement between the same community of Orly and the major community of Tykocin set the poll tax of Orly at the level of 1,100 złotys for the next four years, but Orly received a reduction of 100 złotys for the purpose of repairing their synagogue, which was split into three equal installments of 33 złotys over three years.[7] In practice, we know from the assessment lists that Orly paid 1,100 złotys continuously from 1742 to 1764.[8] During that period, the sum increased in 1743 to 1,200 złotys and was reduced twice: to 900 złotys in 1749 and to 1,066 złotys in 1759. The last reduction obviously corresponds to the reduction for repair of a synagogue agreed upon in 1756, but contrary to an agreement this reduction was valid for just one year.

The reference to the other expenses of the Jewish communities mentioned in our first example is significant, since they could be used for coverage of the poll tax and vice versa. As Adam Kaźmierczyk remarked in his review on my book,[9] in 1744 the regional councils of the Ordynacja Zamojska and

---

5 *Pinkas kahal tiktin*, 881.
6 Kalik, *Scepter of Judah*, table 3b, 165.
7 *Pinkas kahal tiktin*, 112.
8 Kalik, *Scepter of Judah*, table 3b, 165–68.
9 Adam Kaźmierczyk, (Review of) Judith Kalik, *Scepter of Judah. Jewish Autonomy in the Eighteenth-Century Crown Poland*, in *Kwartalnik Historyczny* 118 (2011): 578.

Wołyń agreed that the council of the Ordynacja Zamojska would pay a debt of Wołyń to father Maciej Pawołowicz, the dean of Zamość, in a sum of 8,000 złotys, and the council of Wołyń in return would pay the poll tax of Ordynacja Zamojska.[10] I am grateful to Adam Kaźmierczyk for this wonderful example, which shows clearly the direct connection between the assessment lists and the occasional documents. According to the assessment lists, the poll tax of the Ordynacja Zamojska was indeed reduced in 1744 from 9,640 złotys to 920 złotys.[11] An increase of the poll tax assessed for Wołyń in 1744 was much more modest: it was raised from 28,399 złotys to 30,150 złotys,[12] but Wołyń was a very large regional council and it had broad space for distribution of the tax burden between its constituent major communities in order to diminish an overall tax increase on Wołyń as a whole. Thus, the Kowel community, which was tax exempt in 1743, was obliged to pay 2,950 złotys in the following year,[13] and the poll tax of the Ostróg major community increased in 1744 from 16,425 złoty to 18,404 złotys,[14] while the taxation burden of Krzemieniec, Łuck, and Włodzimierz was simultaneously reduced.[15] This is exactly what I call a "rotation schedule" in my book, the term which was sometimes misunderstood.

Some communities were totally exempted from taxation, permanently or temporarily. The reasons for these exemptions can be found in occasional documents. Thus, quoting Kaźmierczyk again,[16] the community of Lublin was tax exempt in 1739 on account of its expenses in the sum of 1,400 złotys for maintenance of the rabbinical High Court of Lublin.[17] We find in the assessment lists that indeed the community of the city of Lublin proper, called "Lublin synagogue," was tax exempt in 1739, but two suburbs of Lublin, Kalinowszczyzna and Krakowskie Przedmieście, together paid 1,450 złotys as a poll tax for this year,[18] which means that the taxation burden was simply transferred from Lublin proper to the suburban communities.

Does all this mean that the assessment lists are irrelevant for the reconstruction of the demography of the Jewish population in Crown Poland? The answer is no! The continuous and systematic records uninterrupted for nearly

---

10 *Sejm Czterech Ziem. Źródła* (The Council of the Four Lands. Sources), ed. Jacob Goldberg and Adam Kaźmierczyk (Warsaw: Wydawnictwo Sejmowe, 2011), 214.
11 Kalik, *Scepter of Judah,* table 9, 260.
12 Ibid., table 14h, 354.
13 Ibid., table 14a, 317.
14 Ibid., table 14f, 346.
15 Ibid., tables 14b, 14c, 14h, 320, 325, 354.
16 Kaźmierczyk, *Kwartalnik Historyczny*, 578.
17 Goldberg and Kaźmierczyk, *Sejm Czterech Ziem*, 139.
18 Kalik, *Scepter of Judah,* table 2, 54.

half a century enable us to apprehend the tax potential for every community regardless of periodical tax reductions and exemptions. This hypothetical tax potential stands consistently at 17.5 percent above the figures in the census of 1764. This observation demonstrates the advantages and shortcomings of systematic and sporadic records: systematic records (assessment lists, in our case) provide an overall picture of continuous fluctuations in poll tax figures, but do not disclose the reasons behind every reduction or increase in taxation burden, or tax exemptions, while the sporadic documents reveal these reasons, but do not show their long-term context and significance. Quite naturally, both groups of sources complement each other.

We have seen that every change in poll tax assessment for every community had some hidden reason behind it. I did not deal with these reasons in my book, with the sole exception of the case of Wierzbowiec in Podolia, whose poll tax was reduced in 1761 by half from 324 złoty to 160 złotys because of the destruction caused by Hajdamaks, indicated in the assessment list itself.[19] Some of these reasons are surely indicated in numerous other documents related to the Council of Four Lands. The solid basis for the search after such documents already exists in the published source collections. These are, first of all, the major collection of Hebrew documents in Halperin's *Pinkas va'ad arba' aratsot* (Minutes of the Council of the Four Lands)[20] and the collection of Polish documents that Jacob Goldberg and Adam Kaźmierczyk recently published, *Sejm Czterech Ziem. Źródła* (The Council of the Four Lands. Sources).

The expected second part of the collection of Hebrew documents is currently being prepared by Israel Bartal. Numerous letters attached to the assessment lists in the files of the military treasury remain thus far unexploited. I began to work with these letters only now in the framework of Bartal's new research project conducted in cooperation with me, and sponsored by the Israeli Academy of Sciences. The period before the fiscal reform of 1717 is also of great interest, as seventeenth-century documents issued before the setting of the fixed sum of the Jewish poll tax contained tax assignments (*asygnacja*) for every taxation unit with references to all other communal expenses, written often in Hebrew on the margins of the same sheet of paper by several persons.

This combination of tax assessment with detailed accounts of reasons for its level in one document reveals the full spectrum of financial considerations standing behind the fiscal policy of the Council of Four Lands.

---

19 Kalik, *Scepter of Judah*, 6.
20 *Pinkas Va'ad Arba' Aratsot*, ed. Israel Halperin (Jerusalem, 1945; a new edition revised and edited by Israel Bartal, Jerusalem: Mossad Bialik, 1990).

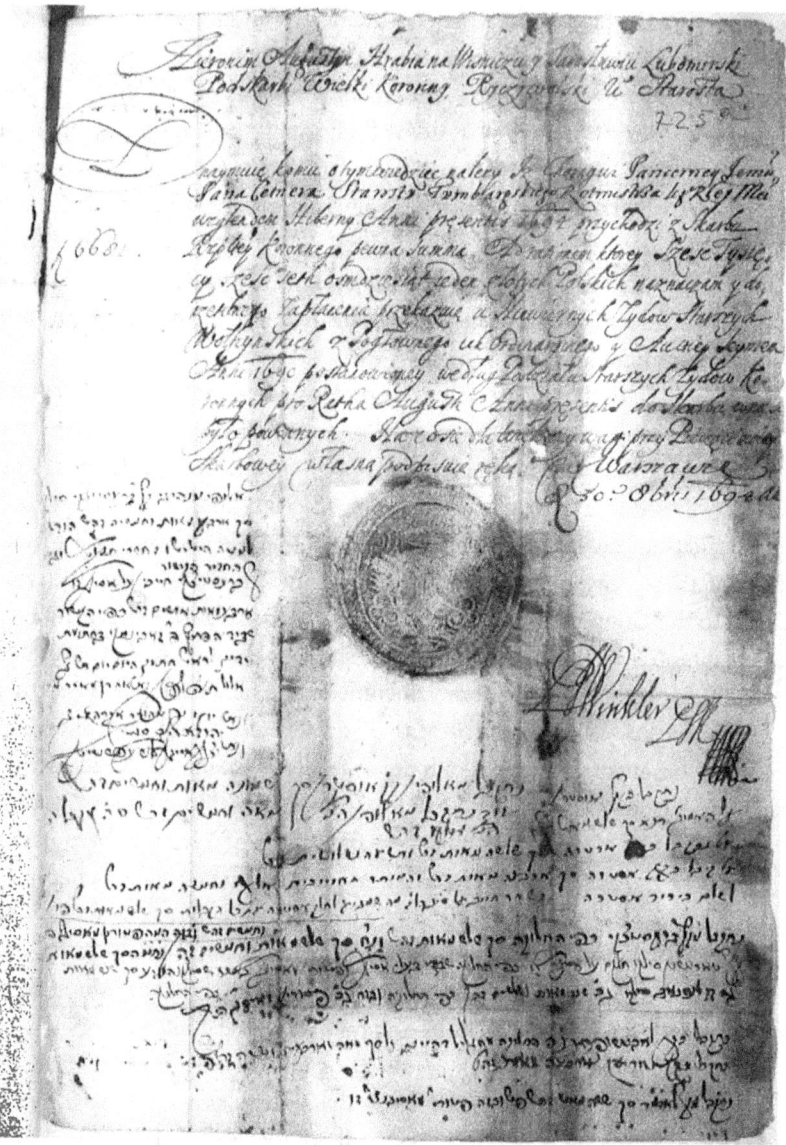

The search for such sporadic documents with explanations of the oddities of the Jewish poll tax assessment in other archival collections seems to me a very promising and challenging direction of research. I believe that only such combinations of systematic and sporadic records will make possible the production at last of a synthetic study of how the Council of Four Lands functioned, a record that presently is still lacking.

Frankism: The History of Jacob Frank or of the Frankists

JAN DOKTÓR

In the literature on the subject—even the most up to date—the history of Frankism is presented as the story of a charismatic messianic pretender and his followers, and not as the history of the development of Jewish messianism, which in the mid-eighteenth century emerged—in the southeastern borderlands of the Polish Commonwealth—out of the Sabbatean underground.[1]

---

1 This was already well expressed by the title and contents of the very first historical piece on the subject of Frankism, written by Hipolit Skimborowicz, *Żywot, skon i nauka Jakuba Józefa Franka* [The life, death and teaching of Jakub Józef Frank] (Warsaw: J. Unger, 1866), who simply assumed that the history of Frank and Frankism are identical. The literature on the subject of Jacob Frank and Frankism is vast. The best and most fully documented volume is by Aleksander Kraushar, *Frank i frankiści polscy 1726–1816. Monografia historyczna osnuta na źródłach archiwalnych i rękopiśmiennych* [Frank and the Polish Frankists 1726–1816. A monograph based on archival and manuscript sources] (Kraków: G. Gebethner i spółki, 1895). Another work which is still valuable today is Meir Balaban's *Letoldot hat-nu'a hafrankit*, 2 vols. (Tel Aviv: Dvir, 1934–35). There is a very important collection by Gershom Scholem: *Mechkarim umekorot letoldot ha-shabta'ut vegilguleha* [Researches and documents on the history of Sabbateanism and its transformation] (Jerusalem: Mossad Bialik, 1974). The latest books on Frankism are by Ada Rapoport-Albert, *Women and the Messianic Heresy of Sabbatai Zevi 1666–1816* (Oxford: Littman Library of Jewish Civilization, 2011), and by Paweł Maciejko, *The Mixed Multitude: Jacob Frank and the Frankist Movement, 1755–1816* (Philadelphia: University of Pennsylvania Press, 2011; Polish translation: *Wieloplemienny tłum. Jakub Frank i ruch frankistowski 1755–1816*, [Warsaw: W podwórku, 2015]). My own works about Frank and Frankism are mainly *Jakub Frank i jego nauka na tle kryzysu religijnej tradycji osiemnastowiecznego żydostwa polskiego* [Jakub Frank and his teaching against the background of the crisis of religious tradition of eighteenth-century Polish Jewry] (Warsaw: Instytut Filozofii i Socjologii PAN, 1991) and *Śladami mesjasza-apostaty. Żydowskie ruchy mesjańskie w XVII i XVIII wieku a problem konwersji* [In the footsteps of the Messiah-Apostate. Jewish messianic movements in the seventeenth and eighteenth centuries and the problem of conversion] (Wrocław: FNP, 1998). At

Thus it was supposed to have begun with Jacob Frank's arrival in December 1755 in the commonwealth, when he was caught performing sectarian rites with some other Jewish messianists. It was to end with his death in 1791 or else (according to the modern literature on the subject) with the death of his daughter Eva in 1816. Such a take on Frankism can be partly explained by the state of the sources, which are focused or even fixated on the charismatic character of Frank. His sectarian comrades and rivals have virtually disappeared from the records of history. Instead, his daughter Eva emerged as his alleged messianic successor. But, to be fair, his contemporaries were not really interested in preserving the truth about the beginnings of the sect and its intricate fate. In this essay, I present the most significant moments in the history of Frankism, whose image in the historiography (including my own earlier works) requires revision.

THE ARRIVAL OF JACOB FRANK IN THE COMMONWEALTH, AND THE INCIDENTS IN LANCKOROŃ

There is no doubt that the events of January 27, 1756, in Lanckoroń[2] near Kamieniec Podolski, when a number of messianic sectarians, including Frank, ostentatiously manifested their Sabbatean faith, can be accepted as the founding act of the movement that later came to be called Frankism.[3] After being revealed, the sectarians were assaulted by Jews gathered at the market, denounced to the local authorities, and arrested. This began a spiral of events, which culminated in two public debates with rabbis and in hundreds of sect members joining the Roman Catholic Church. We still do not know, however, why and with whom Jacob Frank traveled to the Polish Commonwealth. We also do not know whether the incidents in Lanckoroń were accidental events that brought about totally unexpected results, fraught with consequences—or if this was, rather, a planned demonstration, if not a provocation. These are

---

the end of the twentieth century I published the most important Frankist sources: *Rozmaite adnotacje, przypadki, czynności i anekdoty Pańskie* [Various divine annotations, cases, actions and anecdotes] (Warsaw: Tikkun, 1996], quoted further as RA, and *Księga słów Pańskich. Ezoteryczne wykłady Jakuba Franka* [A book of the words of the Lord. Esoteric lectures by Jakub Frank] (Warsaw: Semper, 1997), second complete edition: *Słowa Pańskie* [Words of the Lord] (Warsaw: Żydowski Instytut Historyczny, 2016), quoted further as SP.

2   Today, Zaričanka in Ukraine.

3   I write at length about the Lanckoroń incident in my article, "Lanckoroń in 1756 and the Beginnings of Polish Frankism: An Attempt at a New Outlook," *Kwartalnik Historii Żydów / Jewish History Quarterly* 3 (2015): 396–411.

important questions, because the answers could help us determine Frank's actual role in the movement, the extent to which Frank was its initiator and actual leader in the initial phase (his leadership in the final phase is unquestionable), and the degree to which his image as founder was created and mythologized.

Yaakow Yosef ben Leib, known as Frenk and later as Frank, was born in Podolia in 1726 but left with his parents for Wallachia when he was barely a year old. He saw himself as a Sephardic Jew, he did not know Yiddish (his mother tongue was Ladino), and—as he admitted himself—he had no affinity with Poland and the Polish Jews. Until the autumn of 1755, there was nothing to indicate his messianic mission in Poland, particularly nothing coming from him. The circumstances of his arrival in the commonwealth and his removal a few weeks later are among the most important and least explained facts in the history of Frankism. Frank did not come alone but with a large (more than ten) group of Balkan sectarians. It included only one Polish Jew—his matchmaker Naḥman ben Samuel from Busko, who had accompanied him during his campaign in the Balkans after Frank's wedding in 1752. We do not know whether he came on his own initiative or was sent by someone. In the latter case, in my view more probably, he could only have been instructed to make such a journey by the Koniosos of Thessalonica, the descendants of Sabbatean converts to Islam, whose authority was accepted at that time by the majority of the followers of Sabbatai Zevi, including those in Poland.

The course of events that followed suggests that Frank arrived with his companions to take part in a demonstration, which had been planned over a period of time by the sectarians of Podolia in agreement with the area's church hierarchy. Having gathered in Czernowitz in Bukowina,[4] the sectarians from Wallachia (Frank was believed to be one of them) made their way first to Korolevka, where Frank's uncle resided, and from there on to Lwów (Lviv) for talks with the clergy. Frank himself was not let into the curia. We do not know the subject matter, the participants, or the development of the talks, except for the fact that they were conducted on behalf of Frank by Naḥman

---

4 "In 1756, having collected the necessary funds, he went accompanied to Poland, to Czerniowce—a town in Wallachia, located a few miles from the Polish border. There he found another dozen Jews from his company"; Konstanty Awedyk, *Opisanie wszystkich dworniejszych okoliczności nawrócenia do wiary świętej Contra-Talmudystów albo historia krótka, ich początki i dalsze sposoby przystępowania do wiary świętej wyrażająca* [An account of all the conditions of the conversion to the holy faith of the anti-Talmudist, or a short history describing their origin and reception of the holy faith] (Lwów, 1760), 10.

of Busko.[5] The church sources pass over this episode in silence. It is easy to guess that the church simply did not agree to allow the foreigners led by Frank to take part in the forthcoming operations. There is still the open question of the Podolian sectarians' attitude toward them and whether they shared any objectives with Frank's group.

Certainly, Frank decided to join in the game with his companions, probably expecting that the other participants would have to accept them. On January 27, he arrived with a group of his supporters, mainly from Wallachia,[6] in "Lanckoroń where about twenty sectarians from Podolia had already gathered."[7] According to church sources, this assembly was reported to have been singing mystical songs; according to Frank's sources, they were singing and dancing; and according to Jewish sources they were caught performing an orgiastic ceremony that involved a naked woman (who, however, was not present among the detainees). The multiplicity and diversity of the records concerning the incident are symptomatic for the historiography of Frankism, and they show how ideologically skewed and distorted is the documentation that was produced about the movement from almost its very beginnings.

Everyone present at the inn was arrested by the town's administrator, but three days later the foreigners with Frank at their head were released and expelled from the commonwealth.[8] Most probably, they were simply transported across the border to Chocim, where a Turkish garrison was stationed. Thus, they were not interrogated in the Kamieniec consistory, where the remaining detainees were taken, and neither were they present among the signatories of the sectarian "Manifesto," which preceded the debate with the rabbis in 1757. It is true that Frank returned to the commonwealth in April of that year,[9] but he was almost immediately rearrested and then definitively removed. So, he made his way to Turkey, where he converted to Islam with a group of supporters. A further game was then conducted solely by the Polish sectarians, who were not particularly distraught after their guests had departed;

---

5 Skimborowicz, *Żywot, skon i nauka*, 7.
6 RA 17 mentions only the following as his Polish followers: "Jakubowski [Nah.man of Busko] and Jakób Lwowski [Natan ben Aaron]," which means that the remaining Podolian sectarians present in the inn, including Elisha Shor with his sons (renamed Wołowski after baptism), were not yet among his followers.
7 Awedyk, *Opisanie wszystkich dworniejszych*, 13. Twenty names of Podolian sectarians arrested at the inn are found in the documents of the later Inquisition in Kamieniec.
8 "On the second day, Frenk and his staff, who assisted him in Turkish dress, [were] released from prison"; Awedyk, *Opisanie wszystkich dworniejszych*, 15.
9 See RA 19 and 20.

but we shall not deal here with their independent activities, which led to the Kamieniec Debate in 1757 and the condemnation and public burning of copies of the Talmud in the central square of Kamieniec Podolski.

THE RETURN OF FRANK TO THE COMMONWEALTH, AND THE DEBATE IN LWÓW

Barely a fortnight after the debate, the death of Bishop Mikołaj Dembowski—who was in charge of the case of the Jewish sectarians—opened an opportunity for Frank to embark on a new mission in Poland.[10] In 1758, he finally managed to win over the Catholic hierarchy, most significantly the new Archbishop of Lwów and the future primate Konstanty Władyslaw Łubieński. Intriguingly, he managed to do this as a Muslim, when he and his supporters were serving in the Turkish garrison in Giurgiu on the Danube. This outlaw and convert to Islam was invited to the commonwealth along with his Balkan supporters—also Muslims—and spent many months living on the estate of the bishop of Kamieniec. This indicated a radical change in the policies of the church and state toward the sectarians. Just a few months prior to this, on June 11, 1758, King August II issued a letter of safe conduct to the "counter-Talmudists," some of whom had recently fled to Bukovina, taking them under his protection. The letter guaranteed safety and even the right to claim compensation in common courts—but only to the Polish Jews. It ostentatiously called upon the Polish counter-Talmudists to continue the work commenced the year before in Kamieniec Podolski, thus excluding Frank and his Balkan supporters, some of whom, like him, were already Muslim.

This time Frank had clearly been invited to the commonwealth since he settled with his Muslim companions on the estate of the bishop of Kamieniec. The reasons for this turn are not clear. What is clear is that the hierarchy had plans in connection with Frank. Perhaps they were not happy with the conduct of the Polish sectarians who—after their return—were delaying, staying on the bishop's estate, before taking the expected action. It was they whom Frank joined, along with the Balkan supporters, some of whom were Muslim converts. But, for the second time, Frank arrived in Poland in a new role and

---

10 Toward the end of his life, in Brno and Offenbach, as he was recalling his messianic way, he believed his mission in Poland began with his return to the commonwealth and with his teaching in Iwanie in 1759, when he persuaded the sectarians to undergo a collective conversion. The disgraceful Lanckoroń episode does not even once appear on the pages of *Słowa Pańskie*!

with another—already messianic—legitimization. This is why in his *Słowa Pańskie* (*The Words of the Lord*, i.e., Frank himself), he presents his arrival on January 7, 1759,[11] as the beginning of his messianic mission in Poland; it was followed by several months of teaching on the bishop's estate in Iwanie, where he managed to persuade the sectarians into a collective conversion. But it is doubtful whether the new messianic legitimization warranted him the position of leadership among the Polish sectarians. There are many indications that he only managed to attract a minority. Nevertheless, it was Frank who came out with the new initiative, set the direction, and imposed the pace of the messianic march of the Podolian sectarians.

Frank and his Balkan supporters initiated the second public debate with the rabbis, which on this occasion was to extend across state borders. The written proposal for the debate was put forward not by the Podolian sectarians—as was the case before the Kamieniec debate—but by those from Hungary and Wallachia. Their delegation went to Lwów, where on February 20 they made an appropriate supplication to the consistory. Here they declared their readiness to be baptized in the Roman Catholic Church and requested that another public debate be organized with the rabbis (after that at Kamieniec Podolski), in which they wished to raise the question of ritual murder: "We make a request to Your Excellency for a field, on which we wish to carry out a second battle with the enemies of Truth, and to demonstrate openly from the Holy books the appearance in the world of God in human form, His sufferings for the nation of mankind, the need for universal unity in God, and to prove their godlessness, gross lack of faith, their worse than pagan desire for innocent Christian blood, its spilling and its abuse."[12] Although the signatories wrote in their introduction that they were acting on behalf of Jews from the states of "Poland, Hungary, Turkey, Multenia, Wallachia and others," the supplication to the Archbishop of Lwów, Konstanty Łubieński, was signed exclusively by sectarians from abroad: Moshe ben Israel from Sighet,[13] his nephew Anczel (Ansel) Shloma and Major ben David from the same town, Esdras ben Israel, Aaron ben Shmul from Czerniowitz, and Moshko ben Yaakov from Bucharest.

Initially, the Polish sectarians were reluctant about the initiative. How else can one explain the absence of their signatures under the supplication, which must have drawn the attention of the authorities and of public opinion

---

11 Skimborowicz, *Żywot, skon i nauka*, 45.
12 Awedyk, *Opisanie wszystkich dworniejszych*, 26–27.
13 Syhot Marmaroski on the Cisa River on the current border between Romania and Ukraine.

(the supplication was printed and widely circulated by order of the primate, including his positive response). However, they were taken by surprise first by Frank and then by the hierarchy, and when the foreign initiators withdrew—for reasons unclear to us—they had to continue by themselves. Putting it simply: the Polish sectarians stepped into the shoes Frank had made for them. As for Frank himself, he used the initiative to make himself—at least temporarily—the sectarians' leader. It was not his only initiative to this end. His position in the sectarian community was greatly enhanced by the funds his Hungarian and Balkan supporters collected, which he stewarded and oversaw. It was Frank who for several months supported hundreds of Podolian sectarians living on the estate of the bishop of Kamieniec,[14] and it was he who imposed the direction of the messianic way, which led to the Roman Catholic Church.

THE CZĘSTOCHOWA "ARREST"

Shortly after the baptism, some mysterious events took place, as the result of which Frank was taken to Częstochowa and imprisoned in the Jasna Góra monastery. However, the sources on this subject are highly problematic. Both the church documents and the Frankist sources agree that the cause was Frank's denunciation to the church authorities by his own supporters. Gaudenty Pikulski, to whom for unknown reasons the denunciation was delivered, published it in its entirety (while Konstanty Awedyk provided a detailed discussion). The denunciation, which was made by sectarians from Frank's closest circles, provided the formal grounds for starting the inquisition by the Warsaw consistory.[15]

---

14 It was admitted in the supplications to the Primate and the King, dated May 16, 1759, by their signatories Shloma Shor and Jehuda Leib Krysa: "Several hundred souls of both genders, in the villages belonging to the table of the Kamieniec diocese, with no means to feed ourselves, we rent accommodation and survive universally on charity which was sent to us by our brothers from the kingdom of Hungary, from Wallachia and other towns." Quoted after Kraushar, vol. 1, 140. See also the following reproach by Frank in 1784: "I told you in Iwanie and I asked you: Where shall we find the money for our needs? You advised me to send out to Hungary" (SP 176).

15 Gaudenty Pikulski, *Złość żydowska przeciwko Bogu i bliźniemu, prawdzie i sumieniu na objaśnienie talmudystów. Na dowód ich zaślepienia i religii dalekiej od prawa Boskiego przez Mojżesza danego* [Jewish spite towards God, their neighbors, truth and conscience on the basis of the revelations of the talmudists. As proof of their blindness and how far their religion is from God's truth as revealed through Moses] (Lwów, 1760), 334–38.

Doubts arise not only from the contents of the denunciation—they depart widely from what we know about Frank's teachings at that time (and we know quite a lot thanks to the many references to it in the *The Words of the Lord*)—but also from the signatories, who stayed with Frank even after he was imprisoned in the monastery and whom he did not reproach for the denunciation. Even in 1866 the Frankist sources of Hipolit Skimborowicz did not want to reveal the truth about these events. Frank indeed spoke about treason, but he directed his accusation at entirely different individuals, whose names Skimborowicz did not want to or could not reveal in public. Skimborowicz only wrote that in the manuscript that was in his possession, Frank "names six traitors who denounced him in Lwów, and mentions another six, whose confessions threw him into the Częstochowa monastery. Indeed, the names we have given above [the signatories of the denunciation submitted to Pikulski] are not listed in the manuscript, but there are many other names, which again we would not like to reveal here."[16]

If his most faithful companions submitted a written denunciation of their leader, proving that his teachings departed widely from Catholic orthodoxy, and that he saw himself as a Jewish messiah, then what did they hope to achieve with the denunciation? The sectarians' spiritual guardians were not surprised by the fact that the informers remained faithfully alongside his wife, moving step by step with her, until they ended up in Częstochowa alongside Frank. We can guess that they delivered the document with Frank's agreement because the church needed it as formal grounds for pursuing the steps agreed on with Frank, and as a way of explaining their decisions to the public. Apart from this, after the baptism a group of sectarians headed by Jehuda Krysa made their way to Warsaw, independently of Frank,[17] conducting talks there. It was they whom Frank later accused of treason or at least of disloyalty.

Frank's status in the fortress of Jasna Góra is not clear. The word *arrest* to define Frank's stay in the monastery is used only in Frankist sources (the Jewish historians talk about imprisonment, while the church sources only mention "residing"). The term *arrest* is surprising in the context of the events associated with Frank's stay in the fortress, as they are described in the same sources. And so, two months before the announcement of an appropriate decision by the church authorities, Frank arrived in Jasna Góra on February 4, 1760, with his personal cook Kazimierz (probably due to fears of being poisoned), in his own

---

16 Skimborowicz, *Żywot, skon i nauka*, 60.
17 Kraushar, vol. 1, 162.

coach—drawn by six horses purchased especially for this journey[18]—which he then placed in storage with the bishop's curia in Kraków, as if he expected to leave soon afterward. Moreover, he was escorted by soldiers who were clearly there for his security.[19] He spent his first four days in the officers' chamber, then moved to dwellings especially prepared for him. Judging from these circumstances, it is hard to avoid the conclusion that his stay in Jasna Góra took place with the knowledge and approval of the hierarchy—and, more than that, resulted from some arrangements made between the hierarchy and Frank. Bishop Kajetan Sołtyk's takeover of the costs of maintaining Frank, his close circle, and thirty families was probably part of those arrangements.

In this context, it is not surprising that he was quickly (though not immediately) joined by his wife and children, who came to live with him, as well as by his closest supporters, who settled in a nearby town for several years. He was free to use the Hebrew writings he had brought with him and to stay in contact with his circle. All this looks more like a residence in the safest (for Frank) place in the commonwealth.

There is no church document mentioning a judicial trial at the consistory or a sentence passed upon Frank. The only document that has survived is the record of Frank's interrogation—and only his, although reportedly his twelve supporters who confirmed everything were also interviewed.[20] On March 1, 1760, the priest Feliks Turski, the judicial *officialis*, circulated a document to the clerical authorities; this was not the court ruling, but a proclamation (later it was also published),[21] in which he presented the official position of the church in this matter. He stated enigmatically that "the Warsaw clerical authorities, having called upon the light of the Holy Spirit, have deemed it necessary that the said Jacob Josef Frank from the community with others who are drawn to the Holy Catholic Faith, be removed, and be put in a separate and safe place

---

18 "Going into arrest I bought myself a coach with horses" (SP 327). He must have done so with the knowledge and assistance of the Church authorities, because after all he was staying in the care of the Camaldolese Monastery in Bielany. In doing so he must have believed he was not departing for very long.
19 "He had a convoy of royal lancers. A lieutenant sat with the Lord" (RA 58).
20 According to Awedyk, *Opisanie wszystkich dworniejszych*, 106, the first witness, Nahman of Busko, confirmed the denunciation, "and the other eleven agreed with the first in their answers."
21 *Uwiadomienie Zwierchności duchownej co do osoby Józefa Franka i żydów przechodzących na wiarę chrześcijańską* [Informing the religious hierarchy about the person Józef Frank and Jews who converted to Christianity], Druk Biblioteki Ossolińskich, 1760, No.: 54874; see Kraushar, vol. 1, 18 and 318.

until a further Judgment of the Holy See in Rome, which is suited to judge questions of faith."

Some very interesting details of Frank's stay in Jasna Góra were noted by Cardinal Giuseppe Garampi (1725–92), who was the apostolic nuncio in Warsaw from 1772. When he learned at the beginning of 1776 that he was appointed the apostolic nuncio in Vienna[22] and that Jacob Frank—who after leaving the commonwealth settled in Brno, Moravia—would be in his "care," the nuncio made his way to Jasna Góra to question the Pauline monks about their long-term ex-resident. He could expect that, three years after Frank's departure from Częstochowa, they would speak of him quite openly. This is how he summed up his conversations with the Paulines in his diary:[23]

> I asked around about the behavior of Frank, the neophyte, who had already been removed [*relegate*]. He took part in the Holy Mass every day, was very godly and devoted; he spent the rest of his day in the study of Hebrew books and writing. General Bibikov, who stayed there at the time [after the fortress was seized by the Russians], talked to him a great deal. And so did Prince Golitsyn. They talked even more with his daughter, whom Frank had beside him. However, she did not part from her father and turned out to be highly virtuous [*onestissima*]. Later Bibikov returned to Warsaw and made an order to release [*reliascatio*] Frank, which did

---

22 Giuseppe Garampi was a confidante of Pope Clement XIV and represented him in 1764 at the coronation of Joseph II Habsburg in Frankfurt am Main. In 1772, he became the papal nuncio in Warsaw, and from 1775 he held the office of the nuncio in Vienna until 1785, that is, throughout Frank's stay in Brno. In the same year, Frank left for Offenbach. It is highly probable that they met personally during Frank's several visits to Vienna. It is puzzling that this great clergyman and intellectual was a nuncio only in Warsaw and Vienna, and precisely at the time when Frank was staying in Poland and Austria. Was he perhaps supervising him and his case on behalf of the Holy See? It was probably Frank who mediated the arrangements with regard to his new residence in Brno, Moravia, and who secured the Emperor's protection. He knew a good deal about Frank, but he was clearly surprised by what he heard from the Pauline monks in Jasna Góra.

23 Extensive excerpts from the diary were published by Ignaz Philipp Dengel, *Nuntius Josef Garampi in preussisch Schlesien und in Sachsen im Jahre 1776. Quellen und Forschungen aus italienischen Archiven und Bibliotheken* [Nuncio Josef Garampi in Prussian Silesia and in Saxony in the year 1776. Sources and studies from Italian archives and libraries], vol. 5 (Rome: Loescher & Co., 1903), 223–68. The only scholar to pay attention to those notes was Jakub Szacki, "An unbekanter makor tsu Jakob Franks biografye" [An unknown source to the biography of Jakob Frank], *Yivo bleter, Journal of the Yiddish Scientific Institute* 34 (1950): 294–96.

happen. He is now staying in the lands of Austria and lives in opulence, because again swarms of supporters are running to him with gifts.[24]

The monks had no reservations about the behavior of Frank and his daughter and did not treat them as prisoners but residents.

THE EXILE IN BRNO AND THE UNIFICATION OF THE NEOPHYTE CAMP UNDER FRANK'S LEADERSHIP

When the confederates surrendered the monastery to the Russians on August 18, 1772, after the two-year siege and eighteen days of intensive fighting, together with the residents Frank and his family, General Bibikov—having consulted with the Russian mission in Warsaw—ordered Frank to leave the monastery. Frank, by then an unwanted resident, returned to Warsaw but "took the back roads"[25] in his own coach, which he collected from the bishop. But not for long.

One might wonder, did Frank want to leave the commonwealth or was he forced to? Nobody wanted him there—neither the Jews, the church, nor the neophytes whom he had convinced or forced to change religion. This is how he reproached the remorseful neophytes in 1784 in Brno: "Having left detention and arrived in Warsaw, I found none of you, and hence you blasphemed to the rulers, I had to leave the country that is God's succession. After all you had heard from me that I would go for Poland, and I had to go to another country, until this day."[26] We can conclude from these bitter words that it was the sectarians and neophytes who did not want Frank among them and it was they who persuaded the authorities to throw him out of the country. It is interesting that to the end of his life Frank regretted leaving not just Poland but even the Jasna Góra monastery—"It would have been better for me to remain detained in Częstochowa till this moment"[27]—and he did not think of the time he spent

---

24 "Rochiesi quel che ne fu del neofito Frank giá quivi relegato. Questo sentiva la S. messa ogni giono e mostravasi divoto; nel resto della gioranata studiava libri ebraici e scrivea. Il generale Bibicov, allorchèfu qui, si compiacquè molto Della sua conversazione, come se ne compiaceva il principe Galiczin, e piu ancora della foglia che Frank avea seco, la duale però non si discontáva mai dal fianco del padre ed era onestissima. Bibicov tornado poi a Varsavia mandò l'ordine, acciò Frank fosse rilascatio, e così seguì. ora è nei stati austriaci e si trata sfarzosamente, giachè dai suoi seguaci raccoglie frequenticontribuzioni." I. Ph. Dengel, vol. 5, 239.

25 RA 83.
26 SP 114.
27 Ibid., 595.

there as wasted: "I spent time in Częstochowa, and I took from there what I needed."[28]

It is very telling that the Polish authorities refused to grant Frank a passport to leave the country, which in fact meant that he would have no right of return to the commonwealth. However, he was issued passports by the envoys of the three states partitioning Poland: Russia, Prussia, and Austria. Neither of his two surviving passports mention Frank's nationality or his origins. They emphasize, instead, that he was a merchant, therefore leading an itinerant life. Though he was leaving the commonwealth, there was no question of his being a subject of the Polish king.[29]

Almost immediately after Frank crossed the southern border of the commonwealth, the Austrian imperial court began to receive the first denunciations of him—even before the informers knew his place of abode. The authorities in Vienna and then Brno set up investigating proceedings, from which a large proportion of the documentation has been preserved.[30] A particularly strong impact was made (though seemingly mainly on historians) by the denunciation of a Jacob Galiński and sent first to Vienna and then—in virtually unchanged form—to Brno, when Frank's presence in the city became publicly known. Preserved in the Viennese archive, and published first in translation by Aleksander Kraushar and then in the original German by other historians, it was and still is treated as a primary source of knowledge about the history and doctrine of the sect—originating as it does from the sect's heart. Like other denunciations of Frank that were sent to the Austrian authorities—and treated by them as devoid of any foundation or credibility—it did not have an impact on the history of Frankism. The credibility of Galiński's denunciation, and indeed of its author, is highly questionable. There are many signs indicating that it is not the work of a rebel neophyte from Frank's camp, but of the heresiarch's Jewish opponents.[31]

The rift in the sectarian-neophyte camp did not last forever—they had too much in common, and solidarity in a new environment was too great a value to sacrifice on the altar of the faction leaders' personal ambitions.

---

28   Ibid., 474.
29   The text of the two preserved passports was published by Kraushar, vol. 2, 3–4.
30   An extensive section was published by Oskar K. Rabinowicz, "Jacob Frank in Brno," *JQR*, New Series 57 (1967): 429–45.
31   I have written on this subject in "Historycy frankizmu i ich źródła: fałszerze, wydawcy i interpretatorzy" [The historians of frankism and their sources: forgers, publishers and interpreters], *Kwartalnik Historii Żydów / Jewish History Quarterly* 1 (2014): 101–6.

We do not know the circumstances under which Frank managed to win over the hearts and minds of the majority of the messianic neophytes, but this almost certainly happened after the death of Dominik Antoni Krysiński and on the wave of the new messianic proclamations. We learn a little about the course of events from this note included in *Rozmaite adnotacje* (Various annotations):

> In 1784 a messenger arrived in Brünn and then the Lord gave an order to write this letter, saying that *the lambs will be led through the hands of the shepherd*.[32] On 7 November the Lord gave a sign and said: this week begins a new year for the company; blessed be the one who lasts, that one will be signed into the register, even though they had signed long ago but are still hesitating. At the same time he demanded that even those who had been to Brünn should sign into the register, and the Lord himself signed his and [his wife's] names. On the 26th the register returned from Warsaw and everyone was signed in.[33]

We are clearly dealing here with a breakthrough moment in the sect's history, which was marked by the arrival in Brno of the mysterious messenger. We can guess that the messenger brought from Warsaw a loyalty declaration from the sectarians who so far had not recognized Frank's leadership and mandate. Now this was confirmed by personal enrollment in a new "register" of the faithful, which was to guarantee salvation.

In 1784 Frank accused the repentant sectarians, who had come to Brno, saying that for twenty-five years they had been following some (unnamed) rival of his, and only recently found shelter under his wing:

> You should have said, we were going to that state [i.e., baptism] behind our leader, why should we listen to another man? . . . but you instantly turned your backs on me, and were opposed to me, and followed the blind, and said that a soul was already in the world and that you recognized who had what soul, and you gave support and searched for other foreign gods, which I did not order you to do; I understood I would have a vineyard, but here only dry bushes remained. Lastly, after leaving

---

32 Jeremiah 33:13. This chapter of the prophesy announces the renewal of the covenant and forgives the apostates their sins: *I shall purify them of all the sins with which they transgressed against Me and I shall forgive them all their misdeeds with which they sinned against Me and disobeyed Me* (Jeremiah 33:9).

33 RA 100.

> detention and reaching Warsaw, I did not find any of you, and hence you had blasphemed to the rulers, I had to leave the country that was God's succession; after all you had heard from me that I would go for Poland, and I had to go to another country, until this day, and this for you, so you would not perish eternally. God save and I with you together [*sic*]. From this day at least stay united.[34]

It was at that time, in 1784, when—clearly on Frank's own instructions—they began recording his "chats" (which is what Frank calls his speeches in the oldest known manuscript of *Słowa Pańskie* [Words of the Lord], quoted extensively by Hipolit Skimborowicz); these were addressed primarily—as is clear from their content—to new followers from the until then rival sectarian-neophyte faction. This meant breaking up with the till-then strictly observed sectarian tradition that forbade recording in writing not only the doctrine but also any inside details regarding the sect's way of life.[35]

To strengthen his authority, particularly among newly recruited followers, Frank ordered that same year, 1784, that "each man should appear three times a year."[36] However, he could not see larger groups of Polish neophytes in the modest house in Brno's Petersburgerstrasse without attracting police attention. Immediate efforts were therefore made to find a new residence, where Frank could set up a court appropriate to the new requirements.[37] He finally found such a place in the castle of Wolfgang Ernst II of Isenburg in Offenbach, which had been abandoned since the Thirty Years' War. Here, after refurbishing it, he spent the last years of his life surrounded by crowds of followers, mainly from the commonwealth.[38] There are no grounds to support the view, popular in the

---

34 SP 114.
35 On the circumstances of the origin and history of the edition of *Words of the Lord* see J. Doktór, "The Words of the Lord: Jakub Frank at the crossroads of esotericism," *Kwartalnik Historii Żydów / Jewish History Quarterly* 3 (2016): 583–603.
36 I.e., at Frank's court; SP 424.
37 Echoes of these efforts can be found in RA 108: in 1785 "Franciszek and Michał Wołowski took a letter to [Teodor] Wessel the treasurer, announcing that the Lord wished to stay at his residence. They wished to go and view his palace in Pilica [Libartowska Wola near Pilica] on his estate, but the Lord wrote [telling them] not to go there until such time as the Lord lets them know about it."
38 Werner estimates that sometimes up to four hundred resided there: Klaus Werner, "Versuch einer Quantifizierung des Frank'schen Gefolge in Offenbach am Main 1788–1818" [An attempt to quantify Frank's adherents in Offenbach am Main 1788–1818], *Frankfurter Judaistische Beiträge* [Frankfurt Judaic Studies] 14 (1986): 153–212, and by the same author: "Ein neues 'Frankistendokument,'" *Frankfurter Judaistische Beiträge* 17 (1990): 201–11.

literature, that for some reason the Holy Roman Emperor Joseph II expelled Frank from his territories. It was Frank himself who abandoned his current protector and moved over to a more convenient place. The Austrian archives contain no documents regarding the circumstances of his departure. *Rozmaite adnotacje* gives the laconic information that in June 1786, "the Lord and the Emperor had a great skirmish in Laxenburg. The Emperor told the Lord to send away all the people and pay all the debts."[39] This note can be interpreted in various ways, but the earlier efforts to find a better location for Frank abroad suggest that this is how the emperor reacted to the information that the neophyte had scorned his care and protection.

FRANKISM AFTER FRANK'S DEATH

The image of the charismatic patriarch of the neophytes and his court in Offenbach was later extrapolated by historians and feature writers and applied to both the earlier and later history of the movement. This is particularly true with regard to the court of his daughter Eva, who remained in Offenbach for twenty-five years after Frank's death and was promoted by historians to the rank of the sect's leader. Mysterious documents—which appeared under extraordinary circumstances several decades after her death and disappeared straight after publication—were very helpful to this end.[40] First came the memoirs of Moses Porges, describing the Frankist courts in Offenbach in two versions: one was related by Leopold Stein on the basis of Porges's story, and the other was allegedly written by Porges himself. Added to this are the wonderfully discovered records of the interrogations of three Frankist fugitives from Eva's Offenbach court—one of them Porges—conducted in 1800 in Fürth. There is also a similar record of an interrogation from Kollin. These testimonies corroborate one another as well as Porges's memoirs, and thus lend each other credence. However, they do not agree with historical facts and the documents preserved in the city archives of Offenbach. It is worth taking a closer look at these documents, which are still regarded by historians as the primary and indeed only sources of knowledge about the court of Frank's children.

The first to come to light were the memoirs of Porges von Portheim in the journal *Achawa. Vereinsbuch* [Love. A Book of the Association]. They were

---

39 RA 103.
40 See Doktór, "Historycy frankizmu," 95–101.

published there by the Prague rabbi Leopold Stein, who maintained that it was the verbatim account—recorded by the rabbi himself—of a respected Prague factory owner, unnamed but still alive, who had spent a year and a half in the court of Eva Frank in Offenbach at the end of the eighteenth century.[41] However, the issue of these memoirs' authorship—both those published by Stein and the later reworked and expanded version—remains unclear. This is because of the involvement of two von Portheim brothers, the sons of Gabriel Porges, who were to stay at Eva Frank's court between 1798 and 1799: Moses (1781–1870) and Leopold (1785–1869). In Stein's account the matter seems straightforward: his interlocutor says that "after half a year my younger brother arrived in my wake"[42]—so it appears that the author of the account is Moses, and his younger brother is Leopold. But other documents say otherwise.

Stein ended his story with an announcement that he would provide a more extensive written testimony.[43] And indeed such a testimony did come into being, though quite late. It did not find its way into the hands of historians until 1929, and one can doubt whether its author is Moses Porges, as was claimed by its first publisher Natan M. Gelber. The "original" manuscript of Porges's memoirs, written in German, was supposedly in the possession of the von Portheim family. Gelber translated the text into Yiddish and published it.[44] He admitted in the introduction that he had never seen the original and only had at his disposal a copy of a fragment, prepared in Vienna by the scholar and collector Max von Portheim. The manuscript containing the complete memoirs was said to be in the possession of Mrs. Augusta Portheim in Smichov near Prague. But Gelber did not even try to get hold of it and was satisfied with a copy, which he deemed credible.

Three years later the "original" German text of Porges's memoirs, or, strictly speaking, the fragments concerning the court of Eva Frank, was published by the rabbi of Frankfurt am Main, Caesar Seligmann.[45] The text does not differ from Gelber's translation, but we are told by the publisher that it certainly did not originate from the Viennese Portheim family. The rabbi was to discover it in

---

41 Leopold Stein, "Mittheilung über die Frankistensekte" [A pilgrimage to Offenbach], in *Achawa Vereinsbuch* [Love. A book of the association] (1868), 154–68.
42 Stein, "Mittheilung über die Frankistensekte" [Information of the Frankist sect], 159.
43 Ibid., 160.
44 Natan M. Gelber, "Di zikhroynes fun Moses Porges" [Memoirs of Moses Porges], *YIVO Historishe Shriftn* I (1929) col. 253–296.
45 Caecar Seligman, "Eine Wallfahrt nach Offenbach," *Frankfurter israelitisches Gemeindeblatt* [The communal bulletin of the Frankfurt Jewish community] 6–7 (February–March 1932): 121–23 and 150–51. This edition has one paragraph missing, which was published by Gelber in the Yiddish translation.

Frankfurt itself in the collection of the Meyer family ("Frankfurter Freiherrlich von Meyerschen Familie"). The author of those memoirs, supposedly, was not Moses but—according to Kraushar—Leopold Porges. Nor does the publisher mention the fact that the published memoirs of the stay at the court of Eva Frank were a fragment of a greater whole.

Gelber not only published Porges's "memoirs" in Yiddish but also other documents concerning the Offenbach court translated by him from the Hebrew manuscript; this too was not the original, but merely a copy. Scores of years earlier, in 1877, the documents had been published in German translation by Rabbi Samuel Back.[46] The story of their origins and publication is very unclear, not to say suspect. Back took them from the archives of the Prague council. As he wrote in his introduction, they belonged to Podiebrad, the secretary who had received them from the descendants of Landau; now the council board had decided to make them available to the historian for the purposes of publication. There is no other confirmation that these documents existed in the Prague archive, and if they did ever exist, they mysteriously disappeared from there immediately after their publication.[47] However, copies were discovered in the archive of Max Portheim and from there they found their way to Gelber. As in the case of the Porges memoirs, neither the original records of the interviews nor the copies on which their publication was based have survived.

The Porges story takes place in 1798 and 1799 in the castle at Offenbach, where the Frank siblings (Eva and her brothers Roch and Joseph) were to live, along with a large number of servants, guards, teachers, resident Frankists from Warsaw and the Czech area, and, finally, guests. Similarly, in the second version of the memoirs, published by Gelber and Seligman, we read of the "residents of a castle" that had a huge courtyard and was surrounded by walls. In reality, after her father died and the Polish Frankists left Offenbach, Eva moved with a small number of courtiers (maids) to a fairly small house, "Zu den drei Schweizern," at the corner of Frankfurter and Canalstrasse (now Kaiserstrasse), and in 1796 a two-story house at the junction of Canalstrasse and Judenstrasse, which

---

46 Samuel Back, "Aufgefundene Aktenstücke zur Geschichte der Frankisten in Offenbach" [Frankist court documents found in Offenbach], *Monatsschrift für Geschichte und Wissenschaft des Judenthums* [Monthly for the history and study of Jewry] (1877): 189–92 and 232–40. Aleksander Kraushar either did not know this publication or ignored it.

47 Gershom Scholem in *Encyclopaedia Judaica*, vol. 7 (Jerusalem 1971), col. 70 says: "The important file on the Frankists in the Prague community archives was removed by the president of the community at the end of the nineteenth century, out of respect for the families implicated in it."

could not contain such a large company as Porges described, and where there would be no space for military exercises and parades. Similarly, there were no walls on which they were to keep guard, and which the three runaways were supposed to leap over. In fact, we do not know how many of them there were. In Stein the only escapees are Moses Porges and his brother. In the reports from Fürth there are already three of them: besides the Porges brothers, there is Jonas Hofsinger, which is why in the second version of Porges's memoirs, published by Gelber and Seligman, there are also three.

The same is true with regard to other details. The description of the teachings that were allegedly conducted at Eva's court by three elders with long beards wearing Polish outfits is purely fantastical. In *Encyclopedia Judaica*, Gershom Scholem even identified the elders by name, seeing in them the editors of *Słowa Pańskie*.[48] The description comes from Porges's account published by Stein. Then it was simply copied from that publication into the later memoirs he allegedly wrote up himself. The tale of the elders dressed in the Polish way, wearing long beards and giving lectures in Hebrew—according to the second version of Porges's memoirs—is quite striking in its absurdity. We know from other sources that before being baptized Frankists shaved off their beards and never grew them again. It is also doubtful if any of them would have been able to lecture in a language of which they did not have active command even in their Jewish youth.

The authors of the documents had only a faint idea of what went on at Eva's court and even of where it was located. It is also certain that Porges never stayed at Eva Frank's court in Offenbach—he would at least have known where she resided at the time. Besides, it would defy reason for the young sectarians from Prague's prominent Jewish families, allegedly escaping from conscription, to make their way to the "Polenhaus" in Offenbach—as Eva Frank's house was colloquially known—whose residents were closely watched by their neighbors, the authorities, and the police. The presence of young Jews from Prague in the small town (at the time it had about five thousand residents), and their weekly

---

48 Cf. entry "Frank Jacob" in *Encyclopaedia Judaica*, vol. 7, 69: "The literary activity of the sect began at the end of Frank's life, and was centred at first at Offenbach in the hands of three learned 'elders', who were among his chief disciples: the two brothers Franciszek and Michael Wołowski (from the well-known rabbinic family Shor) and Andreas Dembowski (Yeruham Lippmann from Czerniowitz). At the end of the eighteenth century they compiled a collection of Frank's teachings and reminiscences, containing nearly 2,300 sayings and stories, gathered together in the book *Słowa Pańskie* [The words of the Lord; Heb., Divrei ha-'adon] which was sent to circles of believers."

attendance at the Holy Mass for as long as a year and a half, would have been quickly noticed and noted.

The fixation on these documents of questionable value (they could reasonably be described as fake) is even more surprising when we consider that other Frankist documents that emerged after Frank's death are either ignored or treated in a cursory manner. The most significant of these are the letter from Frank's last secretary, Antoni Czerniewski, to the Warsaw *machna*;[49] the anonymous "Isaiah Prophesies";[50] and the so-called "Red Letter."[51] These three documents are the only credible Frankist testimonies that emerged after Frank's death. They deserve careful and critical analysis because the circumstances of their origin are not entirely clear, and their clarification could expand our knowledge of the final period of the history of the sect. Another key could and should be the analysis of all the fully preserved or quoted fragments of the manuscripts of *Słowa Pańskie*. The story (very tangled, so it seems) of their editing; the chronological order of the making of copies; the removal, addition, and encoding of inconvenient information; the internal polemics (e.g., "The letter from Jakubowski of Warsaw" in the so-called *Brulion Lubelski*—the Lublin Notebook)—all these can reveal the history from another perspective.

To recapitulate: we have an exceptional number of sources concerning the history of Frankism but these are of an extremely varied degree of credibility and are often dubious. Further, the way in which historians make use of them gives rise to doubt. Consequently, the depiction of Frankism in the literature on the subject is still very imperfect and—as I hope this text has illustrated—requires considerable revision.

Translated from Polish by Barbara Howard

---

49 It was published by Kraushar, vol. 2, 94–96, who however dated it incorrectly, believing that it regarded Czerniewski's actual diplomatic mission from an earlier period, when Frank was living in Brno, Moravia.

50 Extensive excerpts were published by in his monograph, *Frank i frankiści polscy*, vol. 2, 186–218.

51 The letter was published on several occasions. First, Peter Beer published a German translation of the letter addressed to the kahal of Prague. Peter Beer, *Geschichte, Lehren und Meinungen aller bestandenen und noch heute bestehenden religiösen Sekten der Juden und der Geheimlehre oder Kabbalah* [The history, doctrine and opinions of all former and still existing religious sects among the Jews and the secret doctrine of the Kabbalah], vol. 2 (Brno, 1923), 319–39. Second, Mark Wisznicer published the letter in the original Hebrew and Russian translation addressed to the communities of Crimea (Tataria)—Mark Wisznicer, *Posłanie frankistow 1800 goda* [A letter from the Frankists of 1800] (Petersburg, 1914). Third, the letter was published along with a facsimile by Ben Zion Wacholder, *Hebrew Union College Annual* 53 (1982): 265–93. All three letters sound almost identical and differ only in minor detail.

The Nineteenth Century

Modern Times Polish Style? Orthodoxy, Enlightenment, and Patriotism

ISRAEL BARTAL

In this short essay, I examine the gap between historiography and collective memory as far as nineteenth-century Jewish history in Eastern Europe is concerned—and I have deliberately used the term *Eastern Europe* rather than *Poland*. Was there a singular track of modernization in Jewish history, or was the case of Polish Jewry different from that of other Jewish communities in the nineteenth century? These questions are highly relevant for the presentation of Jewish history in Poland in the nineteenth century as set out in this magnificent museum. One of the issues that most concerns me is the continuity of premodern institutions, mentalities, and ways of life well into the nineteenth century. This issue is closely related to that of Jewish individual and collective responses to the changes experienced by society in general and Jewish society in particular as a result of the impact of *modernities* (in the plural)—a process that took place in the nineteenth century. These responses can broadly be described as ranging from rejection, indifference, in many or most cases, to identification with and encouragement and support of those processes. Every modern Jewish movement emerged as a result of choices involving all these options. In addition, they acted together, operated simultaneously, and had their impact on the process.

The second issue is that of voluntary continuity in a post-corporative environment—of alternative collective Jewish entities, whether real—such as the hasidic community as a sociological institution—or imagined, or reinvented such as, to be blunt, modern Jewish nationalism. This also involves geopolitical concepts, such as the emergence of something claiming to be a Galician Jewish identity in the second half of the nineteenth century, the emergence of a Russian imperial Jewish identity, and also the many forms taken by modern Jewish national identity that were invented, created, and fostered from the second half of the nineteenth century until well into the twenty-first century. In addition, one should never forget that all these identities overlap, are blurred, and simultaneously go hand in hand.

Another issue is how premodern Jewish ethnocultural transnationalism coped with the emerging imperial Jewish identities during the nineteenth century. This process is not unique to partitioned Poland–Lithuania—it is part and parcel of a general European development that took place from the second half of the eighteenth century well into the beginning of the twentieth century, if not later. I am referring here to what used to be described as the all-European premodern Ashkenazi identity and what happened to it in the nineteenth century. This phenomenon similarly affected the Sephardi transnational identity that also preceded all the geopolitical national identities that began to emerge in the early nineteenth century.

Finally, there is the question concerning the uniqueness of Polish Jewry in the nineteenth century. What was specific to the Polish Jewish community compared to other Jewries in relation to all these issues? These can be summed up under two headings, which are frequently referred to in this volume. One is the *size*—both demographic and geographic—of this community and the other is the *intensity* and *diversity* of these developments within it. The result is that, in the nineteenth century, this community gave rise to a whole spectrum of responses, ranging from social radicalism on the one hand and to extreme religious radicalism on the other, and everything in between.

The second issue is that of Western influence. Most Jews in the nineteenth century understood the challenge of coping with modernity in terms of European or Western influence. Both those who supported the Haskalah and those who favored the emerging phenomenon of religious Orthodoxy spoke explicitly about Europe, about the West. Within the lands of partitioned Poland, the impact of Western developments differed over the area in both its pace and its effect. There was a great difference in how this was experienced in villages and small towns as compared to cities. There was also a major difference between center and periphery, while the understanding of the relationship between center and periphery also changed in the period. This was related to the question of political identification—for some, St. Petersburg was the center and Warsaw the periphery, for others Warsaw the center and St. Petersburg the periphery. One can cite other similar cases throughout the long nineteenth century.

An important aspect of the impact of modernities on Polish Jewish life is the effect of the imposed social and cultural engineering initiated by imperial regimes, which was embraced by some Jewish modernizers and rejected totally or partially by the more traditional sections of Jewish society. Another was the transformation of social organizations, starting with the family and of institutional, cultural—that is linguistic—communication; cultural creativity, such as literature or literatures in the plural; and the emergence of modern Jewish art and of Jewish philanthropy.

It is well known—and this is clear from the presentation of the nineteenth century in POLIN Museum—that there were at least four alternative major channels of acculturation available to the Jews of Poland from the late eighteenth century. Using shorthand, one could describe these as German, Russian, Polish, and the Jewish Western channel, the latter of which has been studied least. The partitions were, of course, a watershed in Jewish history, but the impact of the partitions on the Jewish-inspired Westernizing process has been least studied, since historiography has tended to stress either the imperial channel or the specifically Polish and Russian channels. The Jewish channel has been seen rather as part of the traditionalist rejectionist reaction to the impact of new developments.

All four options merge. They tend to work simultaneously. Most importantly, the Russian, the Polish, the German, the French, the British, and all others work together in Eastern Europe and merge, in a very interesting way, with the Jewish Westernizing option. The emergence of the modern Jewish identity and modern Jewish *cultures* (in the plural) actually encompassed all other options, whether translated, adapted, or rejected. What is striking about the modernizing process is its multiple character.

I should like to refer to a very interesting text by Y. L. Peretz, who wrote in Hebrew, Yiddish, and Polish. In his memoirs, published in 1913, very late in his life, he describes the emergence of the Haskalah in Zamość. He argues that it came from Warsaw, but that when concrete cultural decisions had to be made—and I quote him deliberately in Yiddish—when the exponents of the Haskalah wanted to identify with concrete social groups "un es iz nishto mit vemen" (and there was nobody with whom one could relate). He spends a whole chapter enumerating the options. He discusses the Polish option, but the Polish backward intelligentsia of Zamość was not attractive to Jews who looked for enlightenment. He discusses the rural population, which was becoming increasingly socially conscious. However, although identification with peasants seemed to be an option, Peretz spends half a page describing why there is no way to identify with the peasant society. He then deals with the Russian imperial option, describing at length the relations between its representatives and politics in Zamość; he describes Russian soldiers and officers stationed there, who would like to have a good time with Jewish girls in Zamość. Effectively the only thing that he can say about Russian culture in that context is that it is not an option. Indeed, already in Peretz's lifetime one can detect the hybridity of the emerging modern Jewish culture and Jewish identity in post-partition Poland—the mutual interaction of all options. This interaction had to do, on the one hand, with conscious decisions about cultural options, and, on the other hand, with spontaneous developments. This is a good paradigm for the processes of modernization, which did not proceed in the way prescribed by ideologues, whose views have been echoed, until recently, by historians.

Historiography has tended to read the twentieth century back into the nineteenth century. In this reading, three major trends have shaped the development of Polish Jewish modernity—Enlightenment (Haskalah), nationalism, and social radicalism. All have shaped collective memories and created politicized versions of the past. However, while historians in recent decades have, partially at least, shifted away from the previous ideologically dominant trends and the political systems derived from them, collective memory still lags. Let me very briefly note three trends, which differ, at least in part, from the now traditional understanding. The first is Haskalah, redefined. Today most historians understand the Haskalah not simply as part of the European Enlightenment but as a belated conservative version of the moderate Enlightenment. This means that today one can view the Haskalah as a mostly traditionalist and conservative phenomenon, in contrast to how it was understood by most scholars until some thirty years ago. Most importantly, the Haskalah overlaps—according to our understanding today—with both traditionalism and radical Jewish movements. This paradox confirms my argument that most of the trends that we are now examining are more complex than their unidimensional perception might be in the contemporary collective Jewish memory.

The second is Orthodoxy. It is well established in recent scholarship that Jewish Orthodoxy has been a *modernizing* response to modernity. Let me cite just one short example: the role of the train. Modernity clearly encouraged traditionalism. In fact, transportation and modern media made Jewish traditionalism, including traditionalism in Eastern Europe, a major force with a modern politicized consciousness. The train, and I am reminded of the special railway line that led the Góra Kalwaria, the Gerer *Hasidim*, from Warsaw to Ger, to Góra Kalwaria, called in Yiddish the *rebbes koleyke* (the rebbe's train), is an example of how, in the nineteenth century and early twentieth century, city life actually became part and parcel of Jewish emerging Orthodoxy. Surprisingly, Orthodoxy would end up in the twentieth century as a city phenomenon exposed to modernity, challenged by modernity, coping with modernity, and responding to modernity.

Finally, yet importantly, the most delicate issue of all in the Polish lands of the nineteenth century is Polonization—I call it the unfinished symphony. This was not assimilation as understood even today by some observers. It was, in the understanding of some historians, yet another version of emerging modern Jewish identity. It is a hybrid identity, of course, like any other modern hybrid identity. This hybridity emerges clearly, for instance, when one examines the impact of Polish culture and the identification of some Jewish intellectuals and political activists with the Polish cause, be it from a left-wing, liberal, or even sometimes right-wing standpoint. In addition, modern Jewish nationalism had been shaped enormously by the Polish nationalist discourse. Similarly, modern Jewish historiography Polish-style that emerged in Poland can, in many ways, be described as a Polish–Jewish cultural project leading to a unique Polish Jewish identity, not necessarily a Polish-assimilated identity, but rather, a Polish Jewish modern identity that could be counted among other modern Jewish hybrid identities of the twentieth and twenty-first centuries.

In conclusion, the modern Jewish identities that have been reshaped from the corporative identity of the Jews in pre-partition Poland–Lithuania should be situated among other post-corporative Eastern European identities that emerged in partitioned Poland. What I really miss in terms of scholarship and also redefining Jewish identities in the nineteenth century is the issue of continuity of premodern corporative components well into modernity. What really happened to the kahal? How did old institutions gradually transform into new ones? What really happened to the communal identity in times when premodern political and socioeconomic surrounding powers ceased to exist and Jewish collectives were left alone to cope with all kinds of alternative identities?

Jew-Hatred and Anti-Jewish Violence in the Former Lands of the Polish-Lithuanian Commonwealth during the Long Nineteenth Century

DARIUS STALIŪNAS

One can find many examples of how growing anti-Jewish sentiments or anti-Semitic propaganda triggered anti-Jewish pogroms (e.g., Father Stojałowski's activities in West Galicia and the pogroms of 1898).[1] Yet increasingly in scholarly literature attempts have been made to distinguish between conflicts and the outbreaks of violence, seeing such outbreaks as not primarily the result of a conflict but rather as themselves a specific type of conflict—"as a form of social or political action in [their] own right."[2] As Rogers Brubaker and David D. Laitin have pointed out, there is a lack of

> strong evidence showing that higher levels of conflict (measured independently of violence) lead to higher levels of violence. Even where violence is clearly rooted in pre-existing conflict, it should not be treated as a natural, self-explanatory outgrowth of such conflict, something that

---

1 On this see Daniel Unowsky, "'The Jews Want to Kill Us!': Imagining Anti-Jewish Violence as Self-defense during the 1898 riots in Western Galicia," unpublished in the possession of the author.
2 Rogers Brubaker and David D. Laitin, "Ethnic and Nationalist Violence," *Annual Review of Sociology* 24 (1998): 425.

occurs automatically when the conflict reaches a certain intensity, a certain "temperature."[3]

In this essay, I analyze three regions of the former Polish–Lithuanian Commonwealth that in the "long nineteenth century" exhibited quite strong anti-Semitism but which experienced only a very small number of pogroms. I will examine the Kingdom of Poland, East Galicia, and Lithuania,[4] where anti-Semitic ideology gained strength in late imperial period; however, at the same time the number of anti-Jewish pogroms was very small compared to other regions with a significant Jewish minority (e.g., West Galicia[5] and other parts of the Jewish Pale of Settlement).[6] I first present a short outline about anti-Semitism in each case, and then discuss the number of pogroms and their dynamics in these territories. In the final section, I confront current historical literature and offer an explanation.

Anti-Semitism was quite strong in all three regions in the late nineteenth and early twentieth century. In the Kingdom of Poland, the journalist Jan Jeleński was the first to call himself an "anti-Semite" and seek to "defend" Polish society from Jewish "exploitation" and the "infection" of Polish culture.[7] While in 1863 many Poles saw Jews as allies, at the turn of the century an increasing number of Polish political groups began to regard Jews as an alien and very often not a friendly part of the society. As Theodore R. Weeks points out, "By the eve of World War I, aside from the socialists and the aristocratic conservatives ('realists'), Polish society had nearly entirely turned its back on the idea of integrating Jews into the Polish nation."[8] Many factors influenced this deteriorating situation: modernization and especially urbanization increased friction between Jews and Christians in the cities; the "Litvak invasion" was

---

3 Ibid., 426.
4 Lithuania is understood in this case as Vilnius, Kaunas, and Suwałki provinces in Late Imperial Russia.
5 More than four hundred pogroms took place in West Galicia in 1898.
6 Existing studies assert that during the 1905 Revolution between six hundred and seven hundred pogroms took place in the Romanov Empire; see Shlomo Lambroza, "The Pogrom Movement in Tsarist Russia, 1903–06" (PhD diss., Rutgers University, 1981), 117.
7 Maciej Moszyński, "'A Quarter of a Century of Struggle' of the *Rola* Weekly: 'The Great Alliance against the Jews,'" in *Quest. Issues in Contemporary Jewish History. Journal of Fondazione CDEC*, no. 3, July 2012, www.quest-cdecjournal.it/focus.php?id=297.
8 Theodor R. Weeks, "Russians, Jews, and Poles: Russification and Antisemitism 1881–1914," in *Quest. Issues in Contemporary Jewish History. Journal of Fondazione CDEC*, no. 3, July 2012, www.quest-cdecjournal.it/focus.php?id=308.

perceived as a threat to Polish culture and language as Jews coming from the Pale of Settlement were seen as agents of Russification; a growing national consciousness among Jews and new political phenomena (Zionism and the Bund) clearly showed Jewish unwillingness to integrate into the Polish society; the 1912 elections to the Russian State Duma in Warsaw saw Jewish electors supporting the socialist candidate Eugeniusz Jagiełło, who promised to support equal rights for Jews; and, finally, an anti-Semitic press initiated the policy of anti-Jewish boycott that lasted until the First World War. According to Weeks, a major reason for the worsening interethnic situation was Polish statelessness and the policy of Russification: Polish society felt endangered and the Jewish willingness to push their own agenda was perceived as an enemy act.[9]

In the late nineteenth century, anti-Semitism was also strong within the Lithuanian national movement. Animosity toward Jews was motivated mainly by economic reasons, and to a lesser degree by religious, cultural, and political factors. The palette of economic anti-Semitism can be divided into several categories: Jews as exploiters of Lithuanians; Jews as dishonest in trade; and the need for Lithuanians to engage in trade and crafts themselves and to advance their economic interests by boycotting Jewish stores and to buy only from "their own kind."[10] Blood libels also occurred in Lithuania from time to time, and this superstition was also supported by some periodicals; Jews were accused of spreading Russian culture in Lithuania. Catholic-oriented publications featured another claim typical of the anti-Semitic discourse then popular in Europe: that Jews aimed to control the world or already almost did so. However, starting from 1900, anti-Semitic texts decreased very significantly in the Lithuanian press which was partly related to a pragmatic calculation: Lithuanians needed allies in their struggle against their main enemies—Poles and Russians.[11] Nonetheless, anti-Jewish attitudes were still present in a latent form among the grassroots support for liberal trends. Anti-Jewish moods were also strong among Poles in Lithuania. Very similar arguments were put forward by Polish National Democrats in Lithuania to those in their propaganda elsewhere in the Polish lands. *Gazeta Codzienna* (The daily newspaper)

---

9 Ibid.
10 Darius Staliūnas, "Lithuanian Antisemitism in the Late Nineteenth and Early Twentieth Centuries," *Polin: Studies in Polish Jewry 25: Jews in the Former Grand Duchy of Lithuania since 1772* (Oxford: Littman Library of Jewish Civilization, 2013): 135–49.
11 For more on Jewish–Lithuanian political cooperation, see *Pragmatic Alliance: Jewish–Lithuanian Political Cooperation at the Beginning of the 20th Century*, ed. Vladas Sirutavičius and Darius Staliūnas (Budapest: Central University Press, 2011).

thus asserted that all the problems in France were connected with the fact that power in that country had been seized by Jews and Masons. Some Polish publications accused Jews of spreading Russian culture in the region: "The old concept of the 'capitalist Jew' is giving way to that of the 'russifying Jew.'"[12] Even Bishop Edward von der Ropp of Vilna (Vilnius) did not hide his antipathy toward the Jews. One of his pastoral letters revealed his prejudice against Jews to his flock clearly: one should be on guard against their trickery, but not harm them physically. Thus, the collective image of Jews in von der Ropp's rhetoric was clearly negative:

> Jews also dwell among us. These unfortunates do not know Christ and devote little time to God and eternity, although internally they pray often, but only profit and money are most important to them. Therefore they often harm us and deceive us and in recent times they have been inviting us to join in sedition and disturbances.[13]

A similar dynamic was found in East Galicia. John Paul Himka has observed that Ukrainian nationalism in the second half of the nineteenth century had a distinctly anti-Jewish component, and that animosity was motivated by economic and political factors. But in the early twentieth century the Ukrainian national movement changed, when the influence of Russophiles diminished. Now it was dominated by liberal democratic and socialist ideas. Yet, as in the Lithuania, there were groupings that were anti-Semitic.[14]

Despite these anti-Semitic trends, there were very few pogroms in all three areas under discussion. Answers to the question of whether there were pogroms in a particular region, and if so, how many, depend very much on what expressions of collective violence we define as pogroms. Here I rely on the definition of the German sociologist Werner Bergmann that a pogrom is a one-sided and non-governmental form of social control, a form of "self-help" by a group that occurs when no remedy from the state against the threat which

---

12 Stanisław Staniszewski, "My i Żydzi" [We and the Jews], *Tygodnik Suwalski* 12 (1907): 5.
13 "List pasterski," *Dziennik Wileński* 35 (1906), 1.
14 John-Paul Himka, "Ukrainian-Jewish Antagonism in the Galician Countryside during the Late Nineteenth Century," in *Ukrainian-Jewish Relations in Historical Perspective*, ed. Peter J. Potichnyi and Howard Aster (Edmonton Canadian Institute of Ukrainian Studies, University of Alberta, 1988), 111–58; John-Paul Himka, "Dimensions of a Triangle: Polish-Ukrainian-Jewish Relations in Austrian Galicia," *Polin* 12: *Focusing on Galicia: Jews, Poles, and Ukrainians 1772–1918*, ed. Israel Bartal and Antony Polonsky (Oxford: Littman Library of Jewish Civilization, 1999): 25–48.

another ethnic group poses can be expected. The pogrom is different from other forms of control, such as lynching, terrorism and vigilantism, in that the participants in a pogrom hold the entire out-group responsible and therefore act against the group as a whole, and also in that it usually displays a low degree of organization.[15]

This definition allows us to discern common features between expressions of violence which at first sight appear to be different, such as the 1881–82 and 1903–6 pogroms in the Russian Empire. While the former were directed mostly against Jewish property, the anti-Jewish violence at the beginning of the twentieth century, according to some historians, already showed features of genocide and are similar what Donald Horowitz has called "deadly ethnic riots."[16] I consider that Bergmann's stress on the feeling of being abandoned by the government also fits examples of violence against Jews in many such cases in Central and Eastern Europe; in other words, pogroms often erupted here when a portion of Christian society felt it had been hurt by Jews in some way and that the authorities were unwilling to do anything about this. Furthermore, I consider, like Bergmann, that violence committed by the authorities belongs to quite a different category. Finally, this definition distinguishes between a pogrom as violence against a whole group and other expressions of violence. I supplement Bergmann's definition by adding dimensions of time, scope, and space in order to distinguish between small-scale conflicts between individuals and pogroms. Although historians have stressed on several occasions that pogroms were not an everyday phenomenon, in Lithuania, as in neighboring lands, small-scale conflicts between Jews and Christians, such as clashes between young people on market days, quite frequently erupted into violence. For this reason, we must distinguish clearly between such everyday conflicts and larger-scale violence. In this article, I define as pogroms acts of violence against another group which last for at least a few hours (although time spans are difficult to determine unless they are specified in historical sources) with at least a few dozen participants, where violence takes place in a place of mass

---

15 Werner Bergmann, "Ethnic Riots in Situations of Loss of Control: Revolution, Civil War, and Regime Change as Opportunity Structures for Anti-Jewish Violence in Nineteenth- and Twentieth-Century Europe," in *Control of Violence: Historical and International Perspectives on Violence in Modern Societies*, ed. Wilhelm Heitmeyer, Heinz-Gerhard Haupt, Stefan Malthaner, and Andrea Kirschner (New York: Springer, 2011), 488.

16 Donald L. Horowitz, *The Deadly Ethnic Riot* (Berkeley: University of California Press, 2001).

assembly (such as at a market square) or spreads within a certain inhabited area.

Using this definition, there were approximately ten pogroms in Lithuania from the early 1880s until the First World War. The most important reason for collective anti-Jewish violence in Lithuania was religious Judeophobia. The blood libel was an important trigger for mass collective anti-Jewish violence in Lithuanian shtetls. The fact that no pogrom took place in a large city was one factor protecting Lithuanian Jews from larger outbreaks of ethnic violence. Usually most of the perpetrators or members of the crowd watching the pogrom were peasants from local villages who had come to town for a religious holy day, a Sunday, or a market day. In the evening, they had to go home, to work on their farms. Thus, anti-Jewish violence in small towns lacked the conditions to continue for several days; usually, it lasted for a few hours.[17]

In Eastern Galicia under Austrian rule, as in Lithuania, there were very few pogroms. Historians mention only a few, mostly in 1898 in Tłuste, Bursztyn, Borszczów, and Przemyśl. However, even during these outbursts those responsible were not the local Ruthenians but "Mazurians," that is, immigrant Catholic workers from Western Galicia (i.e., Poles). Jewish property was ravaged and attempts were made to steal as much of it as possible, while in cases of violence against persons we see no attempts to kill Jews.[18] In other words, these riots remind us more of the 1881–82 pogroms in the Russian Empire than those of 1903–6. There were smaller cases of collective violence or at least increases in tension in other periods. Often fights, where opponents divided along ethno-confessional lines, developed in towns that had sprung up as a result of the development of the oil extraction business. Particular panic arose in Jewish communities in 1903 when news reached Eastern Galicia of the Kishinev pogrom; and rumors began to spread in this region too that accounts were about to be settled with Jews.[19]

---

17 For more on pogroms in Lithuania, see Darius Staliūnas, *Enemies for a Day: Antisemitism and Anti-Jewish Violence in Lithuania under the Tsars* (Budapest: Central European University Press, 2015).

18 Tim Buchen, *Antisemitismus in Galizien. Agitation, Gewalt und Politik gegen Juden in der Habsburgermonarchie um 1900* [Anti-Semitism in Galicia. Agitation, violence and anti-Jewish politics in the Habsburg Monarchy in 1900] (Berlin: Metropol, 2012).

19 Buchen, *Antisemitismus in Galizien*, 190–91, 330. On the "Boryslav wars," when first an anti-Jewish pogrom, and then an act of vengeance, in which approximately three thousand Jews participated, took place, see Alison Fleig Frank, *Oil Empire: Visions of Prosperity in Austrian Galicia* (Cambridge, MA: Harvard University Press, 2005), 128–30.

In an article written in 1907, and published in 1910, Itzhak Grünbaum counted up to six pogroms that had occurred in the Kingdom of Poland, but his own description of events already showed very clearly that at least some of these incidents could not qualify as pogroms.[20] Recently, this topic was analyzed in volume 27 of *Polin* by Artur Markowski, who argued that there were ten pogroms in total in the Kingdom of Poland (not counting the one in Siedlce in 1906)—two of them were in ethnic Lithuanian areas (Suwałki province).[21] Of the other eight incidents, only in four cases (Kalisz 1878, Warsaw 1881, Gąbin 1882, and Częstochowa 1902) did anti-Jewish violence reach the level of a pogrom; the other cases reflected day-to-day violence, which I would claim happened quite often and was not recorded in written sources.

The number of pogroms in all three regions was thus very small compared to many parts of the Jewish Pale of Settlement in the Russian Empire or West Galicia. One may raise the question whether it is appropriate to look for reasons why something (in this case, anti-Jewish pogroms) did not happen. I believe this is a legitimate question for at least two reasons. First, in other cases, as mentioned at the beginning of this essay, one can see a clear link between anti-Semitic ideology and mass anti-Jewish violence. Second, pogroms were taking place in neighboring regions of the territories under discussion, and in some cases members of the same ethnic group were quite actively involved in anti-Jewish violence (as in Ukraine in the 1880s and during the 1905 revolution).

This is not the first time such a question has been raised. Historians offer several explanations for the low level of anti-Jewish violence in Eastern Galicia. Himka asserts that the reason lies in the politicization of the Ukrainian–Jewish conflict. In other words, the Ukrainian national movement impressed upon the peasantry, which formed its base, the idea that civilized means should be used to fight the Jews, namely, that the movement should set up educational and commercial institutions and boycott Jewish trade. Himka suggests that this

---

20   Izaak Grünbaum, *Die Pogrome in Polen, Die Judenpogrome in Russland. Herausgegeben im Auftrag des Zionistischen Hilfsfonds in London von der zur Erforschung der Pogrome Eingesetzten Kommission* [The pogroms in Poland. The anti-Jewish pogroms in Russia. Published under the auspices of the Zionist Assistance Fund in London on the basis of the research of the commission to investigate the pogroms] (Cologne, 1910), 134–86.
21   Artur Markowski, "Anti-Jewish Pogroms in the Kingdom of Poland," in *Polin. Studies in Polish Jewry 27: Jews in the Kingdom of Poland, 1815–1918,* ed. Glenn Dynner, Antony Polonsky, and Marcin Wodziński (Oxford: Littman Library of Jewish Civilization, 2015): 219–55.

propaganda was effective. Tim Buchen, for his part, stresses the significance of the fact that Jews were numerically dominant in Eastern Galician towns and cities, while the Christian segment of urban and rural society was split along confessional lines (city dwellers were mostly Latin Rite Catholics, while rural communities were mostly Eastern Rite Uniates). As a result, Jews in Eastern Galicia answered violence with violence much more often. In other words, they felt much more confident than their coreligionists in Western Galicia, where Latin Rite Catholicism dominated in both towns and villages.[22]

In the case of the Kingdom of Poland, Grünbaum suggests that there were two reasons behind the small number of pogroms: the "higher" culture of Poles as compared to Russians, and the fact that Poles were fighting against the imperial government so they did not need additional enemies inside the kingdom.[23] A similar argument was recently formulated by Artur Markowski, who stated that "at least up to the autumn of 1905—there was a spirit uniting Poles and Jews in their common struggle against the tsarist empire."[24] Markowski also formulated some other arguments, namely, that the small number of pogroms could be explained by the efforts of local officials who did their best to prevent pogroms. In addition, in contrast to the 1880s, in 1905 "[some] powerful Jewish political groups, capable of standing up to the pogroms not just ideologically, but also politically and physically, had made an appearance in the political arena and social structures."[25]

It is difficult to take seriously Grünbaum's argument about Polish cultural superiority that prevented Poles from "bestial" attacks against Jews. The 1919 pogrom in Vilnius and other places showed the falsity of such reasoning. Markowski's argument about the role of the government is also questionable. One might challenge this explanation because tsarist officials in the Congress Kingdom took the same measures as their counterparts in the Pale of Settlement. The argument about the role of the imperial government would be even more questionable in the case of Lithuania and Belarus, where there were brutal pogroms in Grodno province (including the notorious Białystok pogrom in 1906), whereas almost none happened in Vilnius province, while both of these provinces were under the rule of the

---

22 Buchen, *Antisemitismus in Galizien*, 191.
23 Grünbaum, *Die Pogrome in Polen*, 135, 186.
24 Markowski, "Anti-Jewish Pogroms," 254–55.
25 Ibid.

same governor-general. Indeed, if we go further and compare the actions of the local governments in Ukraine, Belarus, or Lithuania we see that tsarist officials took, if not the same, then very similar measures everywhere with very different outcomes.[26] Certainly, from the perspective of the imperial capital, these regions had a similar (or even higher) geopolitical importance as the Kingdom of Poland.

The argument about the impact of Jewish political groups is also problematic since these groups were quite powerful in many provinces of the Jewish Pale of Settlement, but pogroms occurred there, while some historians claim that the activity of some Jewish self-defense groups led even to more violence.[27] Yet the emergence of strong Jewish political groups was important in another aspect: Lithuanians, like Ruthenians (Ukrainians) in East Galicia, needed allies in their struggle against their main enemy—the Poles—so, at times, they formed a pragmatic alliance with Jewish political groups.[28] This led to a decline of anti-Semitic agitation which seems to be one reason why there were so few pogroms in these areas.

The second argument, presented by Grünbaum, is worth considering, although I think it should be slightly corrected. There were certainly Polish as well as Lithuanian political groups that saw Jews as their allies, but there were also Polish political trends which were openly hostile to the Jews. I would rather formulate this argument in a somewhat different manner: the numerically dominant national groups in the three areas under discussion—Poles, Lithuanians, and Ukrainias/Ruthenians—did not feel that they were masters; they were not yet strong enough to achieve national emancipation and

---

26 Theodore R. Weeks, "Pasakojimas apie tris miestus: požiūris į 1881 m. pogromus Kijeve, Varšuvoje bei Vilniuje" [The story of three cities: an approach to 1881 pogroms in Kiev, Warsaw, and Vilnius] in *Kai ksenofobija virsta prievarta. Lietuvių ir žydų santykių dinamika XIX a.—XX a. Pirmoje pusėje* [When xenophobia turns into violence. Dynamics of Lithuanian-Jewish relations in the nineteenth and the twentieth centuries. century. Part 1], ed. Vladas Sirutavičius and Darius Staliūnas (Vilnius: Lietuvos istorijos institutas Leidykla, 2005), 25–50.
27 Stefan Wiese, "Jewish Self-Defense and Black Hundreds in Zhitomir. A Case Study on the Pogroms of 1905 in Tsarist Russia," in *Quest. Issues in Contemporary Jewish History. Journal of Fondazione CDEC*, no. 3 (July 2012), www.quest-cdecjournal.it/focus.php?id=304.
28 Joshua Shanes and Yohanan Petrovsky Shtern, "An Unlikely Alliance: The 1907 Ukrainian–Jewish Electoral Coalition," *Nations and Nationalism* 15, no. 3 (2009): 483–505; *Pragmatic Alliance: Jewish-Lithuanian Political Cooperation at the Beginning of the 20th Century*, ed. Vladas Sirutavičius and Darius Staliūnas (Budapest, 2011).

therefore they preferred other methods in their struggle with Jews. At same time, neither Poles nor Lithuanians had anything to gain by defending the tsarist regime while a large number of the pogroms during the 1905 revolution sought to punish "Jewish revolutionaries." This was not a goal supported by many Lithuanians and even by many Poles. These factors are probably the reasons for the relative absence of pogroms in these three areas, in spite of the strong hostility in all of them to Jews.

Those Who Stayed: Women and Jewish Traditionalism in East Central Europe

GLENN DYNNER

In her day, Grandmother Yente Sarah was an interesting example of a "primitive," independent woman, a stray spark of an ancient matriarchy.

—**Puah Rakovsky**, *My Life as a Radical Jewish Woman*—

One Saturday afternoon around 1904, a Jewish high school student named Bernard Singer attended a theater performance near Warsaw's Old City. To his surprise, seated in the row right in front of him was his relative Srulówna, daughter of his mother's extremely pious cousin. Bernard promised Srulówna that he would not reveal her secret—in his house, such an escapade might earn a scolding; but, in her house, it would be treated as a "crime against God and man." The two became covert theater partners, attending a string of performances that included Shakespeare's *Romeo and Juliet*. Eventually, they fell out of touch. Years later, Bernard ran into Srulówna on the street accompanied by her children. Now she was "stooped, with a wrinkled face and dim eyes." They chatted a bit about her father's store, which she now ran, and of course made no mention of their past exploits. Then Srulówna was called away sharply by her husband, a bearded Jew with a long kapota. At this point the narrative abandons her and resumes Bernard's youthful journey into secularist freedom.[1]

---

1 Bernard Singer, *Moje Nalewki* [My Nalewki] (Warsaw; Czytelnik, 1959), 65–66. Thanks to Moshe Rosman as well as the Scholars' Working Group in Jews and Gender at the Center for Jewish History for their helpful comments to earlier drafts. Thanks as well to the Memorial Foundation for Jewish Culture and the NEH Senior Scholar Fellowship for generous support of this research.

On the surface, this episode would seem to justify our expectations about gender, tradition, and Jewish "traditionalism," the latter term invoked by Jacob Katz to describe modern Jews whose "loyalty to tradition . . . was the result of a conscious decision" in the face of other Jews' "rejection of tradition," nonobservance, and acceptance of new, alternate lifestyles.[2] Women like Srulówna would appear to have had much to lose by embracing this cultural option. Bernard hints at a weary life consigned to heeding their husband's commands, dragging the children around, and—echoing a literary trope invoked by earlier Haskalah writers—aging prematurely.[3] Srulówna's eyes were more than just physically dim; her choice to enter a state of virtual servitude after having tasted freedom implies metaphorical blindness as well.

Yet a closer look at the episode reveals certain countervailing details. Srulówna seems to have chosen her own path, and her earlier exposure to secular western culture suggests, upon further reflection, that it was an educated decision. It almost certainly helped preserve her relationship with her parents, considering their abhorrence of that culture. And though we do not have access to Srulówna's inner spiritual life, which may have been richer than Bernard imagined, we do have passing mention of a significant mundane factor: Srulówna had assumed the daily operation of her father's store and may have, in fact, inherited it. These economic assets and skills suggest a kind of agency—in the worst case, Srulówna could consider divorce without having to fear destitution. What was intended as a mere plot foil divulges intriguing details about one of secularism's female detractors.

Such memoirs and autobiographies are rich but potentially misleading, since they usually present the main subject's break from tradition as the sole means of obtaining agency and legitimacy.[4] Recovering the perspectives of

---

2 Jacob Katz, "Orthodoxy in Historical Perspective," *Studies in Contemporary Jewry* 2 (1986), esp. 3–4. On the rise of Orthodoxy in Germany and Hungary, see Adam Ferziger, *Exclusion and Hierarchy: Orthodoxy, Nonobservance, and the Emergence of Modern Jewish Identity* (Philadelphia: University of Pennsylvania Press, 2005); Michael Silber, "The Emergence of Ultra-Orthodoxy," in *The Uses of Tradition: Jewish Continuity in the Modern Era*, ed. Jack Wertheimer (New York: Jewish Theological Seminary of America, 1992), 23–84.

3 See, for example, Judah Leib Gordon, "*Kotso shel yod*" (The tip of the [Hebrew letter] Yud), 1875. Thanks to Naomi Seidman for this insight.

4 Theorists of modernity increasingly argue that many modern men and women willingly join movements that promote humility, discipline, asceticism, and other more traditional means of self-fulfilment, form an important part of modernity, and should not be delegitimized by modern historians. See Talal Asad, *Genealogies of Religion* (Baltimore, MD: Johns Hopkins University Press, 1993), 17–19; Saba Mahmood, *Politics of Piety: The Islamic*

minor, tradition-oriented actors like Srulówna, who were much less inclined to write in genres that celebrated individual autonomy, requires reading most memoirs and autobiographies against the grain. Fortunately, their perspective can be more directly accessed, albeit from a slightly earlier period, using a large collection of petitions (*kvitlekh*) to the late nineteenth century non-hasidic miracle worker Rabbi Elijah Guttmacher of Grodzisk Wielkopolski (1796–1874), many of which were written by or about women.[5] While there is also abundant evidence that women visited hasidic *tzaddikim* over the course of the nineteenth century, their petitions have not been preserved for the perusal of historians.[6] The Guttmacher petitions therefore provide unique glimpses of tradition-oriented Eastern and East Central European Jewish women's lives in their own voices, mediated through scribal transcription, or refracted from appeals by their spouses and parents. Unlike autobiographies, which tend to be

---

Revival and the Feminist Subject (Princeton, NJ: Princeton University Press, 2005), 5, 17, 45. On autobiography in Eastern and East Central Europe, see Paula Hyman, *Gender and Assimilation in Modern Jewish History* (Seattle: University of Washington Press, 1995); Marcus Moseley, *Being for Myself Alone: Origins of Jewish Autobiography* (Stanford, CA: Stanford University Press, 2005); Gershon Bacon, "Woman? Youth? Jew? The Search for Identity of Jewish Young Women in Interwar Poland," in *Gender, Place and Memory in the Modern Jewish Experience: Re-placing Ourselves*, ed. Judith Tydor Baumel and Tova Cohen (London: Vallentine Mitchell 2003), 3–28; Shulamit Magnus, "Sins of Youth, Guilt of a Grandmother: M. L. Lilienblum, Pauline Wengeroff, and the Telling of Jewish Modernity in Eastern Europe," in *Polin* 18, ed. ChaeRan Freeze, Paula Hyman, and Antony Polonsky (Oxford, 2005): 87–120. See also Karen Auerbach, "Bibliography: Jewish Women in Eastern Europe," in *Polin* 18, ed. ChaeRan Freeze, Paula Hyman, and Antony Polonsky (Oxford, 2005): 273–306. Examples of female defectors' self-narratives include Ita Kalish, *Etmoli* (Tel Aviv: Hakibbutz Hameyuhad, 1970); Puah Rakovsky, *My Life as a Radical Jewish Woman* (Bloomington: Indiana University Press, 2008).

5 The petitions cited here are found in the Elijah Guttmacher collection, YIVO Archives in New York (file no. RG-27). Another, smaller portion of petitions is held in the National Library in Jerusalem. On Guttmacher, see Glenn Dynner, *Yankel's Tavern: Jews, Liquor and Life in the Kingdom of Poland* (New York: Oxford University Press, 2014), ch. 5; and "Brief Kvetches: Notes to a Nineteenth-Century Miracle Worker," *Jewish Review of Books* (Summer 2014): 33–35.

6 For recorded examples of women visiting and bringing petitions to hasidic *tzaddikim*, see Yizhak Isaac Yehudah Jehiel Safrin, *Megilat Setarim*, ed. Naftali Ben-Menahem (Jerusalem, 1944), 9; Eleazar Hakohen of Pułtusk, "Etz Avot" [Tree of the fathers], in *Hidushei Maharakh* [The Innovations of the Maharakh (Rabbi Abraham Hakohen)] (Warsaw, 1898), 1; Glenn Dynner, *Men of Silk: The Hasidic Conquest of Polish Jewish Society* (Oxford: Oxford University Press, 2006), 175 and 183. There are many more examples of female petitioners to *tzaddikim* throughout Yaakov Aryeh of Radzymin, *Ma'asyot nora'im* [Fearful tales] (Piotrków, 1904), e.g., 7–8; thanks to Elly Moseson for this latter reference.

written by those who strayed, the Guttmacher petitions bring us into the lives of those who stayed.

The period of most Guttmacher petitions, the early 1870s, was one of wrenching transition. Increased mobility and urbanization resulting from the momentous technological and legislative changes of the 1860s encouraged more and more Jews of partitioned Poland to break away from their communities.[7] Passively traditional Jews were increasingly confronted with friends, business competitors, spouses, and children who had "mingled with the Gentiles and learned their ways," as well as those who had "deviated from the proper path," no longer followed "the ways of the Jewish religion at all," preferred the company of non-Jews, or had gone so far as to convert to Christianity, each presenting what Katz has called a "possible alternative" lifestyle.[8] These instances of deviance set off a veritable moral panic, reflected in outraged appeals to Rabbi Guttmacher to change the transgressors' hearts, to help petitioners divorce them, or to "cause their downfall." While some petitioners may have occasionally indulged in the new freedoms themselves, the wives of wayward soldiers, veterans, and traveling merchants often experienced the threat in such a personal way that they came to regard themselves as defenders of piety, emerging as some of the region's first conscious Jewish traditionalists.[9]

The Guttmacher petitions are not likely to change our sense of injustice regarding the many systematic limitations imposed on Jewish women, especially in realms like education, public ritual, and betrothal. Many petitions simply reinforce our empathy for the women who chose to escape those societal strictures by breaking with their communities.[10] Nevertheless, many other

---

7 Among such changes were peasant emancipation, the abolition of anti-Jewish legislation like residential restrictions in 1862, and improvements in rail transport.

8 Katz, "Orthodoxy in Historical Perspective," 4; Guttmacher collection, YIVO Archives, New York (file no. RG-27). On witnessing fellow Jews profane the Sabbath, see 309. "Zawlocze," 572. "Village of "Olgaszew," on spouses' "Gentile ways," 763. Klodawa (KP), 11. "Ozarkow, 87. "Biala," on children and spouses who converted, 848. "Sieradz," 2; 826. "Raszkowice n. Chrzanow," 300. "Warsaw" 9.

9 Their responses may be contrasted with Pauline Wengeroff's grudging acceptance of her husband's nonobservance. See *Rememberings: The World of a Russian-Jewish Woman in the Nineteenth Century*, ed. Bernard Dov Cooperman, trans. Henny Wenkart (Potomac; University Press Maryland, 2000), esp. 208–209.

10 For discussions about Jewish women's spiritual status, see Chava Weissler, *Voices of the Matriarchs: Listening to the Prayers of Early Modern Jewish Women* (Boston: Beacon Press, 1998); Moshe Rosman, "The History of Jewish Women in Early Modern Poland: An Assessment," *Polin* 18 (Oxford, 2005): 39–40; and Ada Rapoport-Albert, "On Women and Hasidism: S. A. Horodecky and the Maid of Ludmir Tradition," in *Jewish History: Essays in*

petitions remind us of what women who made that choice may have had to give up: the empathic ear of a rabbinic sage like Guttmacher, family relationships, kinship networks, and empowerment deriving from their economic enterprises, often familial or kin-based. The importance of this latter mode of empowerment should not be underestimated: unlike in bourgeois culture, where women's work was discouraged as being unladylike, traditional women's economic enterprises were fully socially sanctioned, providing them with both agency and an economic safety net in the event of divorce.

AREAS OF EXCLUSION: EARLY EDUCATION AND MATCHMAKING CONVENTIONS

Before addressing the available modes of female empowerment in traditional Jewish society, however, it is imperative that we acknowledge those social structures that tended to undermine female agency, beginning with early education. Notwithstanding attempted reforms like private Jewish girls' schools and the attendance of lower-level *heders* for boys or non-Jewish schools by girls from better-off families, the education of most Jewish girls in the nineteenth century remained informal and more focused on penmanship than on reading comprehension.[11] Girls from wealthier families had unique access to belles lettres, but this was not considered prestigious within a traditional Jewish context, and was sometimes deemed heretical.[12] The Guttmacher petitions reveal, in addition, a basic lack of parental encouragement: requests for blessings for children's

---

Honour of Chimen Abramsky, eds. Steven Zipperstein and Ada Rapoport-Albert (London: Peter Halban, 1988), 495–525.

11 No girls, apparently, attended communal-run Talmud Torahs for the poor. See Avraham Greenbaum, "The Girls' *Heder* and Girls in the Boys' *Heder* Eastern Europe Before World War I," *Response: A Contemporary Jewish Review* 18 (1973): 32–45. On educational reform in the Tsarist Empire, see Elyana Adler, "Women's Education in the Pages of the Russian Jewish Press," *Polin* 18 (2005): 121–32; *In Her Hands: The Education of Jewish Girls in Tsarist Russia* (Detroit, MI: Wayne State University Press, 2011). Memoir accounts of religious girls' education include Hayya Huberman, *Tsurikgemishte bletlekh: zikhrones* [Assorted writings: Memoirs] (Paris: Shipper, 1966), 5–6; and Helen Londinski, *In shpigl fun nekhtn: zikhrones* [In the mirror of yesterday: Memoirs] (New York, 1972), 11–12.

12 On girls studying in non-Jewish schools, see Shaul Stampfer, "Literacy among Jews in Eastern Europe in the Modern Period," in *Families, Rabbis, and Education: Traditional Jewish Society in Nineteenth-Century Eastern Europe* (Oxford: Littman Library of Jewish Civilization, 2010), 190–210; Iris Parush, *Reading Jewish Women: Marginality and Modernization in 19th-century East European Jewish Society*, trans. Saadyah Sternberg (Waltham, MA: Brandeis University Press; Hanover, NH: University Press of New England, 2004).

educational success were exclusively written on behalf of sons.[13] This sense of systematic discouragement of female sacred study is confirmed in memoir accounts. Helen Londinski's attempts to continue her education inevitably ended with her father yelling, "I already said it, enough learning!" When Haya Huberman expressed her wish to be "learned," her parents assumed she was possessed by a *dybbuk*.[14] It almost goes without saying that those barriers to female Torah education precluded formal, public female spiritual leadership, even without the additional ritual legal proscriptions.

The toll of such barriers to girls' religious education also became evident during matchmaking procedures. In principle, and often in practice, men were valued for their mastery of Talmudic study, in addition to their *yihus* (familial prestige) and wealth. In some cases, a poor young man without *yihus* who possessed the self-discipline to achieve Talmudic expertise might be sought after by wealthy unlettered heads of families and achieve upward mobility, which provided much added motivation for study. Potential brides, in contrast, were valued mainly for their promised dowries, economic skills and assets (including crucial knowledge of non-Jewish languages), *yihus*, physical beauty, and reputations for chastity.[15]

One result of these gendered educational expectations during matchmaking was a courtship ritual in which parents frantically pursued scholarly young men on their daughters' behalf, attempting to outbid each other with dowry offers and years of room and board that would enable the groom's future studies. Parents often employed the language of suitors, promising to support the "lovely" potential groom and attempting to "speak to his heart." Shlomo ben Devorah sought to marry his only daughter, Pesa bat Esther, to "a certain boy who is diligent in Torah, and to support (*lahzik*) him. And now God has enabled a match with a boy who is diligent in Torah." Inconveniently, the lad

---

13 I did not find a single request for a blessing for a daughter's educational success. The situation would only improve with the establishment of the Bet Yaakov school system during the interwar period. See Naomi Seidman's forthcoming *Sarah Schenirer and the Bais Yaakov Movement: A Revolution in the Name of Tradition* (Littman Library of Jewish Civilization, forthcoming).
14 Huberman, *Tsurikgemishte bletekh*, 6; Londinski, *In shpigl fun nekhtn*, 12.
15 Jacob Katz, "Nisuim Ve-Hayyei Ishut," [Marriage and Sexual Relations] 33–48; Dynner, *Men of Silk*, ch. 4; ChaeRan Freeze, *Jewish Marriage and Divorce in Imperial Russia* (Waltham, MA: Brandeis University Press; Hanover, NH: University Press of New England, 2002), 36–41. On changing courtship criteria in modernizing segments of East European Jewish society, see Naomi Seidman, *The Marriage Plot: Or, How Jews Fell in Love with Love, and with Literature* (Stanford, CA: Stanford University Press, 2016).

was already "attached to another match, but he wants to get out of the match because he realizes that it will give him no free time to study Torah."[16] A tavernkeeper named Eliezer Lazer ben Hannah had the opposite problem: he wanted to marry his daughter Rekhel to Shmuel ben Beila, but another man had "spoken to the youth's heart" by promising a huge sum of money.[17] In these scenarios, the scholarly young man was rendered an object of desire by the parents, the actual suitors, while their daughter was treated merely as part of a suit of enticements.

In the scramble for scholarly grooms, parent-suitors often promised more dowry than they could deliver. Many had their wealth invested in informal loans, often to non-Jews, and sometimes found it difficult to collect their debts in time for the wedding:

> I made a match for my daughter Pesa bat Rikla, and the boy is one of the lovely boys, Uziel ben Bluma. And my obligations for the dowry are a total of 400 rubles cash with books and a number of years for meals at my table for the couple. And my sole intention is to enable him in Torah. But this is my worry: that I don't have the ability to discharge my obligations, because the aforementioned sum is in loans with a certain man from our town. And it is hard for me to get it from him. And in addition, I have debts with the gentiles the miller Marcin Wegner in the amount of 200 zlotys, and with the miller Maciej Jariciek in the amount of 52 rubles. And it's been very hard for me to collect from them. And what to do? For they repel me repeatedly."[18]

Some had already squandered the dowry money when the time for betrothals and weddings arrived. One petitioner admits that he drank away both of his daughters' intended dowries because he "didn't have the strength to overcome the desire . . . And my household cries and complains about their situation, and when the wine is removed from me for any amount of time, I cry about it too."[19]

---

16 YIVO Archives, Guttmacher Collection, RG-27, 58. "Blaszki". Invariably, the mother's name is given in these petitions, in accordance with the Zoharic formula (Bereshit 84a).
17 YIVO Archives, Guttmacher Collection, RG-27, 56. "Oswiecim".
18 YIVO Archives, Guttmacher Collection, RG-27, 58. "Blaszki".
19 YIVO Archives, Guttmacher Collection, RG-27, 88. "Biezun". On Jewish drinking practices and the myth of Jewish sobriety, see Dynner, *Yankel's Tavern*, ch. 1; "'A Jewish Drunk is Hard to Find': The Myth of Jewish Sobriety in Eastern Europe," *Jewish Quarterly Review* 3 (2013): 9–23.

The most serious predicament was that of the female orphan, who had "no money for a dowry and no one to turn to; only the blessed God can help her."[20]

Beyond economic obstacles to a potential bride's match were any number of threats to her reputation for mental stability or chastity. Episodes of spirit possession tended to occur, inconveniently enough, just as young women reached the marriageable age. One father complained to Rabbi Guttmacher that "five weeks ago, an evil spirit possessed Perl bat Malkha so that she can't sleep at night. And it broke her fingers. And she clapped her hands until her fingers bled. And she sits for two hours at a time and does not say anything. And the time of her wedding is approaching!" Yet as Yoram Bilu has noted, spirit possession was an important and accepted way for women on the verge of marriage to "temporarily escape . . . the confines of their social roles" and claim some agency.[21]

Parents of girls who had suffered an accident that resulted in a broken hymen were sure to register the accident with a well-known rabbinic authority, lest their daughters' virginity be doubted on their wedding night.[22] In cases of alleged sexual indiscretion involving non-Jews, parents felt they had little choice but to ship their daughter abroad:

> Kalman ben Rivka and his spouse Golda bat Rivka [inquire] whether to send their daughter Leah bat Golda to America because she had a suspicion of wrongdoing (*safek issur*) among the Goyim, and her brother saved her from their hands. And her second brother wants to send her a ticket. Whether to permit her or not, especially since if she is in a place where they know her they will not make a match with her.[23]

---

20 YIVO, Guttmacher Collection, RG-27, 69. "Baluty (Lodz)". See also 306. "Warsaw" 15.
21 YIVO, Guttmacher Collection, RG-27, 118. "Berzyin / Berezhany, Ukr." On spirit possession, see Matt Goldish, ed., *Spirit Possession in Judaism* (Detroit, MI: Wayne State University Press, 2003); Yoram Bilu, "Dybbuk and Maggid: Two Cultural Patterns of Altered Consciousness in *Judaism*," AJS Review 2 (1996): 341–66, esp. 346–48. According to Christine Worobec, in nineteenth-century Russian Christian society spirit possession had become an "overwhelmingly female phenomenon." See Christine D. Worobec, *Possessed: Women, Witches and Demons in Imperial Russia* (De Kalb, IL: Northern Illinois University Press, 2001), 64, 66, 99.
22 For a surviving registry of *mukat etz*, as such accidents are called, see "Collection of R. Abraham Meir Gitler of Sosnowiec (1843?–1925)," 233, in the Central Archives of the Jewish People, Jerusalem. A total of twenty-two cases are recorded there, referring to girls between the ages of four and fourteen. See also Freeze, *Jewish Marriage and Divorce*, 36.
23 YIVO, Guttmacher Collection, RG-27, 626. "Piotrkow (Kujawski?)".

Occasionally, a daughter ran off with a non-Jew and converted, a decision that could undermine the matchmaking prospects of any unwed siblings and cousins. One father of an apostate actually requested "that God quickly kill her, may her name be forgotten." He then reconsidered, requesting rather that "she greatly regret this [conversion]," and that Rabbi Guttmacher "persistently give her advice about how to leave this religion [Christianity]."[24] Another father was less equivocal, informing Rabbi Guttmacher that "the evil one, her name be blotted out, is pregnant. So during the birth would be a fitting time to uproot her from this world, so that her parents will have peace and remove the shame and disgrace and sorrow, and to avenge God on the Goyim so that they know and recognize it."[25] These petitions, though relatively rare and composed by unsympathetic parents, illustrate how some women attempted to claim agency by severing their familial, communal, and religious bonds altogether.[26]

JEWISH DIVORCE AND FEMALE STATUS

Divorce presents a more complicated picture of traditional female disabilities and modes of empowerment. In the most harrowing cases, a wife might find herself divorced after ten years of apparent infertility. While prominent rabbinic authorities denied the ability of a court to compel a man to divorce his wife after that period of time, some rabbis upheld the practice.[27] Indeed, a number of childless male petitioners asked Rabbi Guttmacher whether they should consider divorcing their wives.[28] Some women did whatever they could to stave off this cruel eventuality. When Shlomo ben Sarah's wife Miriam bat Hinda remained childless after thirteen years of marriage, he "spoke with her tenderly to convince her to appear before the rabbinical court (bet din), and several times the rabbinical court sent her an invitation." Miriam not only refused to appear, but also "opened her mouth and insulted me and the rabbinical court."

---

24 YIVO, Guttmacher Collection, RG-27, 848. "Sieradz 2".
25 YIVO, Guttmacher Collection, RG-27, 826. "Raszkowice n. Chrzanow".
26 Another example, blamed on a young woman's employment as a domestic servant in the house of a Jew who "resides among the Goyim," is found in YIVO, Guttmacher Collection, RG-27, 437. "Village Lachowa n. Dobrzyń".
27 See Moshe Isserles (Remu) and Shmuel ben Uri Shraga Phoebus, *Bet Shmuel* (1794) on *Shulhan Arukh*, Even Ha-ezer, Halakhot Gitin 154. However, Yaakov Gesundheit, the Chief Rabbi of Warsaw during Guttmacher's last years, expressed "wonder" that any rabbi should hesitate to compel divorce in cases of infertility. See *Tiferet Yaakov* vol. 3 (Warsaw, 1926), 281.
28 YIVO, Guttmacher Collection, RG-27, 163. "Grochow"; 293. "Warsaw II"; 783. "Radom"; 69. "Kalisz 5. Baluty (Lodz)". In the latter case, the divorce occurred.

Shlomo now turned with a "bitter spirit" to Rabbi Guttmacher, asking that he "send into her heart the good will to accept a writ of divorce (*get*) from me," adding damningly that he could not, in any case, live with her anymore because "her way is not at all the way of the daughters of Israel according to Torah law, for she is always in the company of gentiles."[29]

Miriam's defiance, while understandable, was risky. If she continued to evade the rabbinical court, her exasperated husband might simply abandon her without granting a writ of divorce, rendering her an *aguna* (literally, "chained woman"), who was unable to ritually remarry.[30] Such a status could prove, at very least, economically debilitating, since husbands were also business partners in many cases. The *aguna* phenomenon reached alarming proportions during this period. One cause was military recruitment, which separated married couples for long periods of time either due to a husband's distant military service or his flight abroad to evade service.[31] Another cause of the increase in *agunot* seems to have been the famine of 1867–70, which sparked a westward migration that separated numerous husbands and wives.[32] Finally, technical improvements in steamship and rail transit made it much easier for husbands to flee to America and other distant locales without issuing a writ of divorce. Tova bat Pesa had been married to Yosef ben Tifra for ten weeks, when "his heart turned evil towards her, and he left her and she was made an *aguna*." Yosef became vindictive, spreading "false slanders, so that she was ashamed to go outside." Finally, he departed for America, leaving her destitute, shamed, and unable to remarry.[33] A pregnant woman named Basha bat Frieda was blackmailed with a threat of *aguna* status by her husband, who had absconded to Berlin with their daughter and converted to Christianity. He threatened to withhold her writ of divorce unless she brought him the baby to be converted

---

29 YIVO, Guttmacher Collection, RG-27, 87. "Biala".
30 On *agunot*, see Haim Sperber, "Tofa'at ha-nashim ha-agunot ba-hevra ha-yehudit be-mizrah eyropa u-bituya ha-itonut ha-yehudit, 1857–1896" [The Phenomenon of the Aguna in Jewish Society in Eastern Europe and its Treatment in Jewish Newspapers, 1857–1896], *Kesher* 40 (2010), 102–8. Sperber counts 3,398 *aguna* cases during those years.
31 YIVO, Guttmacher Collection, RG-27, 453. "Lubicz 2" (in this case, the husband feared that his long military service might render his wife an *aguna*); 635. "Praga n. Warsaw".
32 Mark Baker, "The Voice of the Deserted Jewish Woman, 1867–1870," *Jewish Social Studies* 2:1 (1995): 98–123. An editorial by Eliezer Lipmann Silbermann of *Ha-magid* reports that, as a result of the famine, "crowds of people diseased and disfigured, blind, lame, and having all sorts of illnesses . . . travel to seek healing and cures from the healers of Germany," a likely reference to Guttmacher, who resided in Prussian Poland (106). The editorial appeared in *Ha-magid* on June 30, 1869, 1.
33 YIVO, Guttmacher Collection, RG-27, 873. "No location".

once it was born.[34] In many of the collection's *aguna* cases, however, letters from husbands simply ceased to arrive. Most rabbis tried to pressure recalcitrant husbands to grant writs of divorce, and were as lenient as possible in determining *aguna* status.[35] Nevertheless, the anguish conveyed in some petitions is shattering—Sirka Hadas, daughter of a widowed female tavernkeeper, "suffered greatly from it and went out of her mind from it." Even when her husband relented and gave her a writ of divorce, she remained "very angry." Meanwhile, her practical mother reminded Rabbi Guttmacher that Sirka Hadas needed to be matched again "so that she can be normal."[36]

Yet in the vast majority of cases, where both spouses consented to rabbinic authority, Jewish women were much less captive to marital misalliances than their non-Jewish counterparts. For although Jewish divorce rates in specific cities in the tsarist empire have been overestimated by some scholars, the rates were, of course, higher than those of Polish Catholic and Russian Orthodox women, thanks to Judaism's relative tolerance of divorce.[37] Technically, Jewish ritual law (halakha) gave husbands the sole right to initiate divorce. However, rabbinic authorities attempted to mitigate the law, effectively giving women "more rights and a higher status than that accorded them by the Torah," to quote Judith Hauptman.[38] The rabbis stipulated numerous circumstances under which a rabbinical court might compel a husband to grant a writ of divorce, including a husband's offensive odor as a result of his occupation; his repulsive appearance; his inability to support her; his inability to impregnate her owing to lengthy military service or sexual dysfunction ("he cannot shoot straight"); his madness or epilepsy; and instances of domestic abuse (striking one's wife "is not the way of Israel; it is the way of Gentiles," unless, according

---

34 YIVO, Guttmacher Collection, RG-27, 300. "Warsaw IX".
35 See, for example, Jay Harris, *How Do We Know This? Midrash and the Fragmentation of Modern Judaism* (Albany: State University of New York Press, 1995), 211–34.
36 YIVO, Guttmacher Collection, RG-27, "Kaluszyn 696".
37 See Freeze, *Jewish Marriage and Divorce*, 148–159. The figures on divorce in the cities recorded there have evidently been misread, since those cities often served as centers for "destination divorces" by Jews from the provinces. The same may be said of the data in Shaul Stampfer, "Love and Family," in *Families, Rabbis, and Education*, 45–46, where Stampfer himself expresses misgivings. See Marc Shapiro's review of Stampfer's *Families, Rabbis, and Education* on H-Judaic (November 2010). Divorce was rare among Christians in late Imperial Russia (allowed mainly in marriages to political criminals) and almost nonexistent among Catholic Poles, though annulments did occur.
38 Judith Hauptman, *Rereading the Rabbis: A Woman's Voice* (Boulder, CO: Westview Press, 1998), 4.

to some opinions, she cursed him without cause or denigrated his parents). In several instances, a wife was permitted to reclaim her dowry.[39]

The Guttmacher collection contains many cases of women attempting to effectively divorce their husbands with a frequency that suggests he had gained a reputation for helping women extricate themselves from misalliances. In the case of one woman who was "practically raped" by her husband, Guttmacher joined "great sages of Poland such as the *admorim* of Płock, Kutno, and Ciechanów" in pressuring the husband to give her a writ of divorce.[40] A male petitioner appealed to Guttmacher to help prevent his being effectively divorced by his wife as a result of sexual dysfunction. They had been married for over three years, but he had still not been with her "in the way of all men, for he could not finish his coming (lit.) and remove her virginity, for his member is weak." During the first two years, the young couple had not understood the proper "method"; but then his wife, after talking to her friends, realized that what they were doing was "not according to the customs of marriage." After numerous nocturnal emissions, consultations with doctors, and treatments at the baths, the petitioner realized he had "a mental block (*ma'atzor ruah*)." Expelled from his father-in-law's house "empty-handed," he now asked Guttmacher for "virility like everyone else, and that his wife will have a desire to consummate," and that her father and mother would become favorably disposed to him again.[41]

Military recruitment was perhaps the most common stressor on marriages, since it involved long periods of absence in distant locales. Moreover, husbands often returned home after their years of army service as changed men. Feigel bat Hadas's husband, who had been "taken by the soldiers" for twenty years, had finally returned home. But Feigel complained that he now walked "the improper path, is quarrelsome, and constantly plays cards and does other profane things that are impious." When she protested, he would beat her. Feigel therefore asked R. Guttmacher to "pray to our fathers in Heaven to turn his heart to good, or to arrange a proper divorce." Either penitence or divorce

---

39 Moshe Isserles (Remu) on *Shulhan Arukh*, Even Ha-ezer, Halakhot Gitin 154. See also Freeze, *Jewish Marriage and Divorce*, 140–42; Shaul Stampfer, "Was the Traditional Jewish Family Patriarchal?" in *Families, Rabbis, and Education*, 130–31.
40 Cases of men being forced to divorce their wives are found in YIVO, Guttmacher Collection, RG-27, 411. "Janow"; 447 (due to military service); "Lask 3" (due to sexual dysfunction); 56. "Oświęcim" (due to sexual dysfunction, instructed to divorce her by Sanzer Rebbe).
41 YIVO, Guttmacher Collection, RG-27, 447. "Lask 3".

would suffice, so long as her husband's repeated transgressions were banished from their home.[42]

THE SAFETY NET: WORKING WOMEN AND ECONOMIC-BASED AGENCY

Divorce was intricately related to Jewish gender norms in the economic sphere, since a female divorcee would not have to resign herself to poverty if, like many Jewish women, she had a trade.[43] However, determining the actual extent of women's work is no easy matter. Both the tsarist census of 1897 and a study under the auspices of the Jewish Colonization Society put the proportion of working women at little more than twenty-one percent, estimates which have been dismissed as "myth-making" by one historian on the grounds that they failed to incorporate the large numbers of women who "worked for themselves and produced small amounts sold locally" in market stalls.[44] At the other extreme is the popular image of the Jewish wife as the sole breadwinner and "enabler" of her scholarly husband's fulltime studies, a situation that is now considered to have been rather exceptional.[45]

It appears that, censuses and popular images aside, most traditional Eastern European Jewish women worked, as did their husbands. A common arrangement was a kind of economic partnership between husbands and wives in a single enterprise like a mill or tavern, though this would change

---

42 YIVO, Guttmacher Collection, RG-27, 8; "Uniejow"; 847. "Sieradz". Additional cases of domestic abuse are found in 763. "Klodawa (KP)"; 764. "Krasnik"; 824. "Rem[ę]blielice village n. Dzialoszyn"; 847. "Sieradz"; 880. "No location" (also infected her with venereal disease).
43 Stampfer, "Love and Family," 45–46.
44 Charlotte Baum, "What Made Yetta Work? The Economic Role of Eastern European Jewish Women in the Family," *Response* 18 (1973): 32–35. Baum has in mind the report by Isaac M. Rubinow, "Economic Condition of the Jews in Russia," *Bulletin of the Bureau of Labor* XV, no. 72 (September 1907): 523.
45 For this claim, see Parush, *Reading Jewish Women*, esp. 39; and Daniel Boyarin, *Unheroic Conduct: The Rise of Heterosexuality and the Invention of the Jewish Man* (Berkeley: University of California Press, 1998), esp. 156. An early version of this stereotype appears in *Izraelita* 51 (1869): 421. For a critique of that image, see Moshe Rosman, "The History of Jewish Women in Early Modern Poland." Mark Zborowski and Elizabeth Herzog argue that "the earning of livelihood is sexless, and the large majority of women, even among the sheyneh [elites], participate in some gainful occupation if they do not carry the chief burden of support. The wife of a 'perennial student' is very apt to be the sole support of the family." Mark Zborowski and Elizabeth Herzog, *Life Is with People: The Culture of the Shtetl* (New York: Schocken Books, 1995), 131. See also the Introduction by Barbara Kirshenblatt-Gimblett.

with the decline of lease-holding by the end of the century. Certain women, particularly widows, could become quite economically powerful as international merchants, a phenomenon familiar to us from the early modern period in the case of Glückel of Hameln. Temerel Sonnenberg-Bergson and Blumke Wilenkin became premier patrons of hasidic courts and Lithuanian yeshivas, respectively, and Temerel seems to have become a veritable king-maker in the Polish hasidic world.[46] Before the abolition of residential restrictions in 1862, in towns and cities with Jewish residential restrictions their lack of beards, sidelocks, and other male Jewish markers that officials found so odious meant that Jewish women often became the public faces of their businesses and were more likely to apply for licenses and exemptions in their names. Widowed women and divorcees exercised ultimate authority not only in their family businesses but also in matchmaking decisions for their unmarried children.[47]

Debates over the meaning of Jewish society's substantial female workforce began in the nineteenth century. Maskilic reformers like Moshe Leib Lilienblum spoke in favor of women's work and compared non-working nihilist women to "dolls;" while other maskilim criticized women's work as "unnatural."[48] Debates among historians have centered around the question of female work and agency. Eli Lederhendler doubts whether traditional female Jewish breadwinning can be equated with "economic independence," a more

---

46 See Rosman, esp. 55; Teresa Kozłowska, "Rodzina żydowska w świetle akt notarialnych powiatu skalbmierskiego z lat 1817–1835" [The Jewish family in the light of notarial acts in the powiat of Skalbmierski in the years 1817–1835], *Kwartalnik Historii Żydów* 202 (2002): 231; Dynner, *Yankel's Tavern*, 91. For cases of widows serving as patrons to study houses and prayer houses, see the *pinkasim* held in YIVO Archives, Sutzkever Kaczerginski Collection, Part II: Collection of Literary and Historical Manuscripts RG 223.2, series 7 (my thanks to Eliyahu Stern for sharing this source with me). For a description of a hasidic Rebbetzin's daily management of a hasidic Court, see Malka Shapira, *The Rebbe's Daughter: Memoir of a Hasidic Childhood*, trans. Nehemia Polen (Philadelphia: Jewish Publication Society, 2002), esp. 137–139.

47 See, for example, YIVO, Guttmacher Collection, RG-27, 772. "Krzepice 2"; 696. "Kaluszyn".

48 For the original source, see Moshe Leib Lilienblum's letter "Mikhtav el ha-mo'l" [Letter to the Editor], *Ha-melitz* 10 [not 12 as cited in Feiner] (1872), 64–68. For analysis, see Shmuel Feiner, "Ha-ishah ha-yehudiyah ha-modernit: Mikra'-mivḥan be-yaḥasei ha-haskalah veha-modernah" [The modern Jewish woman: A test-case in the relations between the Haskala and modernity], in *Eros, erosin ve-isorim: miniyut ve-mishpaha be-historiya* [Eros, betrothal, and suffering: Sexuality and the family in history], ed. Israel Bartal and Yeshayahu Gafn (Jerusalem: Zalman Shazar, 1998), 253–303, esp. 273; and David Biale, "Eros and Enlightenment: Love Against Marriage in the Eastern European Haskalah," *Polin* 1 (Oxford, 1986): 59–67.

"worldly" role, or any actual career preparation, seeing it more as a consequence of economic desperation within the declining Jewish "petit-bourgeoisie."[49] Susan Glenn argues somewhat similarly that, "although women were looked upon as breadwinning partners in the Jewish family, they remained second-class citizens" as a result of their exclusion from realms like higher Jewish education and public ritual.[50] Shaul Stampfer, however, surmises that "the economic contribution of the wives limited the authority of their husbands," and warns scholars against a "superficial or casual use of the term 'patriarchy'" to describe Jewish society.[51]

Most Guttmacher petitions refer only vaguely to the female petitioners' "livelihood," but around one hundred identify specific women's occupations. The most commonly stated endeavor is trade, usually in a store or market stall (forty-eight times), followed by lease-holding, usually of a tavern or liquor distilling monopoly (twenty-one), an occupation that demanded a lot of grit.[52] However, the latter respondents are, suspiciously enough, all widows and divorcees, suggesting that the wives of living male tavernkeepers—who typically dealt with customers while their husbands traveled to suppliers or worked on the side as coachmen—did not identify themselves as "tavernkeepers" in petitions. As there are 114 identifiably male tavernkeepers, it seems plausible to increase the number of female tavernkeepers by nearly that amount. Charlotte Baum notes a similar problem in censuses with women who "minded the store" in their husbands' places, but did not explicitly identify themselves as storekeepers, which would make it necessary to substantially enlarge the category of "trade," as well.[53] The next largest category, after trade and leaseholding, is moneylending (sixteen), which was usually a side endeavor. The remaining female endeavors in the Guttmacher petitions include small-scale industry (five), partnerships inherited by widows (four), crafts (three), and a single clerk and agent. Consonant with recent reassessments, only four women described themselves as their

---

49 Eli Lederhendler, *Jewish Immigrants and American Capitalism, 1880–1920: From Caste to Class* (Cambridge: Cambridge University Press, 2009), 13 and 146n43.
50 Susan A. Glenn, *Daughters of the Shtetl: Life and Labor in the Immigrant Generation* (Ithaca, NY: Cornell University Press, 1990), 8.
51 Stampfer, "Was the Traditional Jewish Family Patriarchal?," 129.
52 One tavernkeeper claims he had to give up his tavern because "my spouse, may she live, has a weakness of constitution." YIVO, Guttmacher Collection, RG-27, 673. "Kazimierz". Several male petitioners had to leave the occupation because of their own sensitivities; see Dynner, *Yankel's Tavern*, 145.
53 Baum, "What Made Yetta Work?," 36.

families' sole providers, either because their husbands were full-time Torah scholars or were physically unable to work.[54]

These economic skills and resources better enabled women to demand divorces, and the agency possessed by such women is reflected in their tendency to compose their petitions themselves. A female tavernkeeper named Sarah bat Feiga claimed she had married a widower who turned out to be a gambler and "a drinking man" who did not contribute financially. "So I divorced him through the *bet din*," Sarah reported. However, the rabbis had only gotten Sarah's husband to agree to grant her a divorce on the condition that she compensate him financially, and Sarah grumbled that until she came up with her part of the financial settlement she would have to provide him with meals while he continued to wander around drinking and gambling.[55] Another petitioner, Pesel bat Mirel, claimed to have left her husband because "he does not walk the straight path." She wondered whether she should "return home to her husband's house or wait until her husband comes after her?" Then she revealed an economic factor: Pesel had owned orchards, but in her absence her husband had proceeded to sell the land on which they lay to a nobleman for mining use. The fact that he waited to do so until after she had left the house is telling—would he have dared to do so while she was still living with him? In any case, Pesel ended her petition with an appeal that she find favor with a certain nobleman so that he would agree to sell her his barn, an indication that the separation was not too debilitating.[56]

Of course, working provided no guarantee of financial security. A bad husband could be the ruin of a woman with even a substantial dowry and experience in trade:

> I am the woman of afflicted spirt Feiga bat Zlota. For ten years I was married to my husband Avraham ben Miriam, and my husband betrayed me several times. For he took all the money, more than one thousand rubles that remained from my childhood, from my trade in the store, and my dowry, and scattered it in different places, until [I and my] four children were left with nothing. And I support myself now by going around with oil to houses, and compassionate people buy from me. And I separated from him because he beat me several times and infected me with his evil illness

---

54 YIVO, Guttmacher Collection, RG-27.
55 YIVO, Guttmacher Collection, RG-27, 772 "Krzepice 2".
56 YIVO, Guttmacher Collection, RG-27, 455 "Modrzew".

[venereal disease?]. And now he wants to live with me again, but I fear lest he deceive me. Even if he is a man who can support himself, does he have the desire to be like honest people?

Feiga asked Rabbi Guttmacher to advise her and pray for her, reminding him that "presently my livelihood is awful."[57] Nevertheless, despite Feiga's apparently horrific suffering at the hands of her husband, phrases like "my trade" and "my dowry," her doubts about his ability to "support himself," and her own economic resourcefulness in a time of crisis seem to illustrate the advantages of economic-based agency.

CONCLUSION

While the Guttmacher petitions often enhance our sense of traditional society's restrictions on women, they occasionally highlight important economic sources of agency and empowerment. Ironically, it was the modern embrace of European bourgeois cultural norms that tended to draw Jewish women out of the workforce and relegate them to the domestic sphere.[58] As Marion Kaplan has argued, the higher a woman was placed on a pedestal, the farther she was removed from power.[59] This sense is reinforced by a walk around the Warsaw Jewish cemetery on Okopowa street, where the Polish epitaphs on acculturated Jewish women's tombstones read "Doctor's wife," "wife of a merchant," "wife of a teacher in the Warsaw Rabbinical School," and so on, emphasizing the women's merely contingent status. The small amount of agency reclaimed by serving on charitable boards and other volunteer organizations was but little recompense.[60]

It remains tricky to gauge the degree to which economic endeavor truly affected traditionalist women's status, however. A woman's economic utility to her family unit may have enhanced her roll in decision-making and her range

---

57 YIVO, Guttmacher Collection, RG-27, 880. "No location".
58 Feiner, "Ha-ishah ha-yehudiyah," 253–303.
59 Marion Kaplan, *The Making of the Jewish Middle Class* (Oxford: Oxford University Press, 1991), 17. See also Julius Carlebach, "Family Structure and the Position of Women," in *Revolution and Evolution, 1848 in German-Jewish History*, ed. Werner Eugen Mosse, Arnold Paucker, Reinhard Rürup (Tübingen: Mohr, 1981), 170.
60 See Agnieszka Jagodzińska, "Does History Have a Sex? On Gender, Sources, and Jewish Acculturation in the Kingdom of Poland," *Gal-Ed* 22 (2010): 84. It should be noted that some highly acculturated Jewish women found work in secular-oriented schools as both teachers and principals. See, for example, Londinski, *In shpigl fun nekhtn*, 13–14.

of life options, and wealthy widows seem to have garnered enormous influence. But female economic influence never seems to have threatened male communal and spiritual hegemony. The main point that these petitions collectively make, rather, is that working provided a potential for empowerment that bourgeois women seem to have often had to give up. Seen in this light, Srulówna's decision to forego the theater and similar secular pursuits in order to inherit her father's store in Warsaw begins to look less strange.[61]

---

61 On women's work and autonomy in a contemporary context, see Graham Dawson and Sue Hatt, *Market, State and Feminism: The Economics of Feminist Policy* (Northampton, MA: Edward Elgar, 2000), 68. For a revealing collection of contemporary accounts by traditionalist women, see Gina Messina-Dysert, Jennifer Zobair, and Amy Levin, eds., *Faithfully Feminist: Jewish, Christian, and Muslim Feminists on Why We Stay* (Ashland, OR: White Cloud Press, 2015).

Pauline Wengeroff: Between Tradition and Modernity, East and West

SHULAMIT MAGNUS

POLIN Museum is an extraordinary monument to complexity and a refusal to compromise with the complexities of history or of the present. It is very fitting that Pauline Wengeroff and her memoirs form part of the museum's permanent exhibit on social and cultural change in Jewish modernity in Eastern Europe, not only because Wengeroff is an immensely rich source on that subject but also because she is anything but a simple protagonist of one version of Jewish culture, or a simple embodiment even of geographic, linguistic, or ethnic placement.[1]

In the wing of POLIN Museum dedicated to modernization of Polish-Jewish society in the nineteenth century, Wengeroff serves as a *shamash*—a facilitator— her *Memoirs of a Grandmother* providing source material to illustrate social and cultural change. It is a function—and a prominence—she would relish. My purpose in this essay, however, is to bring her out of relief so we begin to see her in her own right and grasp who this woman was. The museum's use of her might contribute inadvertently to stereotyped gender associations: Wengeroff as a source about dress, marriage. This is not at all to denigrate these categories, so critical to social history, anthropology, folklore;

---

1 This article is based on my unabridged translation and critical edition of Wengeroff's memoirs: *Pauline Wengeroff, Memoirs of a Grandmother: Scenes from the Cultural History of the Jews of Russia in the Nineteenth Century*, 2 vols. (Stanford, CA: Stanford University Press, 2010, 2014), cited here as Magnus/Wengeroff, and my biography of Wengeroff and her work, *A Woman's Life: Pauline Wengeroff and Memoirs of a Grandmother* (Oxford: Littman Library of Jewish Civilization, 2016). All citations of Wengeroff are from Magnus/Wengeroff.

I have mined her myself about these and other, related issues to which Wengeroff indeed devotes considerable space in the first volume of her *Memoirs*. But I do wish to get beyond the seemingly apparent in Wengeroff to her complexity—and to the reasons her complexity has eluded attention until now.

The title of Wengeroff's work is *Memoirs of a Grandmother*—which would lead us to expect a straightforward project with a personal and familial focus. The lie is given to any pretense to simplicity in the work's subtitle—"Scenes from the Cultural History of the Jews of Russia in the Nineteenth Century." Wengeroff's coupling of the personal and the historical was an extraordinary proposition coming from a Jewish woman born in 1833; we have nothing comparable to it in claim or scope from the pen of a woman prior to this in the annals of Jewish literature.[2] Wengeroff gives a full-fledged account of the transformation of Jewish society from traditional to modern during the nineteenth century, in two volumes totaling more than four hundred printed pages, in which she uses her and her family's experience of modernity to refract Russian Jewry's passage from traditionalism to modernity, and that large story to make sense of her family's odyssey. Indeed, Wengeroff's historical consciousness is remarkable, expressed in writing which consistently places her story in historical context. As I argue in my work about her, aside from being a clear proclivity of hers—and testimony to maskilic influence, about which, more below—her historicizing has a personal purpose: it lessens the severity of her sense of personal failure and guilt for the losses of Jewish modernity, including the radical assimilation of her own children, to which she knew she had contributed.

Wengeroff's work is remarkable in many ways. It gives a rich portrayal of traditional Jewish society in Russia with a particular focus on women's religious practices and piety. It tells a dramatic tale of the dissolution of traditionalism in this society, then the world's largest Jewish community (more than five million people at the time she wrote), from the perspective of women, marriage, and families. Wengeroff's writing is unprecedented, too, in treating men as subjects of inquiry: she does not simply and unconsciously render them as generic Jews whose experience is universal and normative but as a specific case, whose behavior differs from that of women—who have their own ways of behaving—another focus of her work.[3] Wengeroff, of course, does not use the term

---

2   For a comparison of Wengeroff's *Memoirs* with the *zikroynes* of Glikl Hameln, see my introduction to Magnus/Wengeroff, I:13–14.

3   To be clear: Wengeroff does treat men as "generic Jews," but she also considers them as specific and separate in observed behavior from women.

gender, but her woman-centered narrative is profoundly gendered, asserting that women and men had very different experiences of modernity and that there was a power shift between them that led to the loss of Jewish tradition. According to this reading, not just the opening of outside cultures to Jews and Jewish receptivity to those cultures, but dynamics between women and men led to the loss of Jewish tradition. Men, she claims, modernized rashly, thoughtlessly abandoning tradition, then coerced women to do the same, taking from them their traditional domestic control and mandate to transmit Jewish culture to the next generation, with catastrophic results. In short, hers is an argument for the cultural power of women, albeit, I maintain, not from a feminist stance.

Memoirs is a carefully crafted and beautifully written narrative by a brilliant woman who "loved books" and was very well read in Jewish, German, Russian, and even English literature (the latter in translation). From the beginning, Wengeroff intended her work to be published, that is, to have a public, not just a private readership, one of the distinctions between her and the premodern Glikl of Hameln, and a mark of her singularity as a female writer. She achieved this goal during her lifetime, to wild acclaim in scores of reviews in the Jewish and non-Jewish press, which she preserved, some of which are published in her volumes, I believe at her prompting. Her talent, ambition, and success are extraordinary.[4]

Wengeroff's title, *Memoirs of a Grandmother*, I believe, was a disingenuous ruse, intended to allow this female author to pick up the pen and write—and get published. It was a strategy that ambitious women writers needed to employ at the turn of the twentieth century, let alone earlier. Wengeroff uses several such strategies for this purpose. She claims that she is no writer, that it is only because her subject is so important and because she has a steel-trap memory that she allows herself to write. Supposedly, she writes just to record. She also claims to write for her children—altruism, not the need or desire for self-expression, driving her. The first claim is patently absurd, as anyone who reads these memoirs in either the (largely) German original (with some Hebrew, Yiddish, and some Polish phrases) in which the published work appeared, or my unabridged English translation, will readily see. Wengeroff was a gifted, born writer. But quite the contrary to male Jewish culture, either traditional or modernizing, which held intellectual accomplishment and innovative thinking and writing in highest esteem—for men—Jewish women had to justify the audacity to think, let alone write—that is, to pronounce, literally, with authority. Much as Glikl

---

4   I treat Wengeroff's ambitions, successes, and disappointments in detail in *A Woman's Life*.

of Hameln claimed to write for her children, some of whom were too young to know their father when he died, and to assuage loneliness—claims we should by no means dismiss—but who in fact wrote because she was a robust raconteuse, ethicist, and theologian, Wengeroff, too, makes use of prevailing cultural tropes that allowed her to pronounce—as a mother and "Grandmother." With her subtitle comes the "left hook," to use boxing language, with which Wengeroff delivers the "punch" of what she is really about—which is not writing for her children, three of seven of whom she omits from the work; or for her grandchildren, biological ones at least, not one of whom Wengeroff mentions in her published work.

So: simple? No.

Indeed, Wengeroff's supposedly transparent work is surprisingly subject to variant readings, and to outright misreadings. Her son, Semyon (Simon), a noted Russian literary historian, Pushkin scholar, intimate of Nabokov and other Russian writers—that is, a man familiar with literature and, presumably, his mother—characterized her as a defender of "Orthodoxy."[5] Not long after publication of her first volume, in Berlin, in 1908, the Jewish Publication Society of America (JPS) came very close to publishing an English translation. No less a figure than Solomon Schechter, president of the Jewish Theological Seminary of America, championed an English edition, calling *Memoirs* "the greatest human document" he had ever read—and Schechter, one of the foremost Judaica scholars of his time, had read a great deal. *Memoirs* had the warm endorsement of the scholars and communal leaders Rabbi Israel Friedlaender and Cyrus Adler, and, initially at least, of the financier Jacob Schiff and of Judge Mayer Sulzberg—in short, of many of the most prominent leaders of US Jewry at the turn of the twentieth century. Some members of the publication committee of JPS also read the work as an apologia for Orthodoxy. A sufficient number of them, however, went from reading *Memoirs* as a testament to traditionalism to reading it as an apologia for assimilation and conversion that JPS ultimately rejected it.[6] How could the same work be read in these contradictory ways? At JPS, *Memoirs* seemed to have functioned like a Rorschach test of anxious projections about Jewish communal prospects in America, but that means that its meaning was somehow ambiguous.

---

5 See Semjon Wengeroff's entry in Salomon Wininger, *Grosse Juedischer National Biographie* [Large Jewish national biography] (Cernăuți: Druck "Orient," 1925–36), 6:257, signed, "Ihr Sohn."

6 On this, see my article, "Wengeroff in America: A Study in the Resonance of Conversion and Fear of Dissolution in Early Twentieth Century American Jewry," *Jewish Social Studies* 21, no. 2 (2015): 142–87, and my *A Woman's Life*.

Wengeroff's cultural positioning is indeed not a simple matter. Despite her passionate and poignant defense of traditional Jewish culture, she was a fervent adherent of Haskalah, the Jewish Enlightenment. She depicts the coming of Haskalah not only as inevitable but also as a positive good. She richly evokes the intergenerational conflict and marital tensions which Haskalah provoked. But in her depictions of the struggles of the 1830s and 1840s, she is sympathetic not only to traditional parents but also to the young adherents of Haskalah— of whom she herself was one. In her first volume, Wengeroff tells us of her brothers-in-law spiriting Schiller's *Don Carlos* into their study room, planting it within the folios of their Talmud tomes, and chanting it to the sing-song of traditional study. She neglects to note there that it was she who made Schiller available to the would-be *maskilim*—whose surreptitious activity her horrified mother discovered. She notes her own role as an aside—a volume away, in her second volume, a composing decision I believe was driven by unacknowledged feelings of guilt at being a chief agent of modernization in her parents' household and a cause of her revered mother's anguish.[7]

Wengeroff evokes traditional culture and society with love, reverence, and nostalgia but not uncritically. Even her politics was in line with that of the Haskalah—a distinctly minority position. She writes an astonishingly positive recollection of a visit by Tsar Nicholas I to Brisk (Brest/Brześć) in the 1830s when she was a young child. Her account focuses on Nicholas's looks (he was known to be handsome and well-built), and that of the tsarevich, the future Alexander II.[8] While Jews were generally warm about Alexander II for his reforms, Nicholas was reviled by the Jewish masses, above all for his cantonist policy which devastated Jewish society; there are reports of Jews rejoicing openly at news of his death. Wengeroff details several of his decrees that caused immense distress—her first volume ends with a dramatic account of sadistic abuse by tsarist officials of Jews for wearing traditional dress after a decree forbidding this; in her second volume, she includes folk songs about the horrors of the cantonist era. But she never criticizes Nicholas for these policies, or even attributes them to him. The only Jews who had anything positive to say about Nicholas were *maskilim*.[9]

---

7 See Magnus/Wengeroff, I:180–181; II:33–34, 43.
8 On Wengeroff's age and the reliability of her memory at the time of the tsar's visit, see Magnus/Wengeroff, I:61–75.
9 On this in particular and Wengeroff's cultural positioning altogether, see my introduction to Magnus/Wengeroff, I:61–72. On Wengeroff as an agent of secularization in her own family, see my introduction to Magnus/Wengeroff, II:14–15, and at length in Magnus, *A Woman's Life*.

Wengeroff's terminology about Jewish and European culture also reveals her identification with Haskalah. Writing of Friedrich Schiller, she says that his "poetry pierced the stifling, dank atmosphere of the ghetto like a breath of spring." For all her esteem for and attachment to traditional Jewish culture, Wengeroff met an essential requirement for a maskil, a stance that separated modern Jews from those who created ultra-Orthodoxy: she believed that traditional Jewish culture was not self-sufficient; that the best of European, but especially of German enlightenment culture, conveyed noble ideals of which Jews were in need.

We see this maskilic positioning clearly in one of several places in which Wengeroff gives her gendered reading and indictment of Jewish modernity full voice. Here, she laments that men "in this transitional era" left child-rearing to women only in children's infancy, but "brutally [shoved] the mother ... aside," ending her authority once "the time for moral education arrived." She writes:

> The woman, who still clung to tradition with every fiber of her being, wanted to impart it to her children, too: the ethics of Judaism, the traditions of its faith, the solemnity of the Sabbath and festivals, Hebrew, the teachings of the Bible ... She wanted to transmit this whole treasure to her children, in beautiful and exalted forms—together with the fruits of the Enlightenment, together with the new that *west European* culture had produced.
>
> But to all pleas and protests, they received always the same answer from their husbands: "The children need no religion!" The young Jewish men of that time knew nothing of moderation and wanted to know nothing of it. *In their inexperience, they wanted to make the dangerous leap instantly from the lowest rung of culture straight to the highest* [my italics].[10]

First, note that Wengeroff extols the best that Western—not Eastern—European culture had produced. But more fundamentally, in this passage, we see an explicit cultural taxonomy which places enlightened Western European culture at the apex and unenlightened, traditional Jewish culture well below it, in a stale, inferior sphere.

Even Wengeroff's Jewish ethnicity is more complicated than one might think. It might seem clear that she was an *Ostjüdin*. She was born in Bobruisk

---

10   Magnus/Wengeroff, II:43–44.

and raised in Brest-Litovsk ("Brisk," in Jewish parlance), in a region she and other Jews called *Lite* (Lithuania). She lived most of her life within the Russian Empire, most of it inside the northwest of the Pale of Settlement. Her mother tongue was Yiddish.

Wengeroff's work, however, comes to us as not as *zikhroynes fun a bubbe* [Memoirs of a (traditional Yiddish) grandmother] but as *Memoiren einer Grossmutter: Bilder aus der Kulturgeschichte der Juden Russlands im 19. Jahrhundert*, published by the Poppelauer House in Berlin. Wengeroff's attachment to the German language and cultural things German began early and was profound. She learned German and Russian and other secular subjects through tutors and became her husband's German tutor after their marriage—that is, she was a central, if not the sole, agent of his secularization, whose effects (but not her own role in them) she decries in *Memoirs*. And yes, that makes the second time she, supposed defender of "Orthodoxy," has, by her own testimony (how else would we know any of this?) functioned as an agent of secularization within her own family circle, subverting traditional norms.[11]

The question of Wengeroff's chosen language for *Memoirs* is an obvious, central one. Why German? Why not Yiddish? Or Russian? Wengeroff refers to Yiddish as jargon, which derogatory usage, employed by writers of the emerging Yiddish literature as well as by the language's many detractors, does not itself alone indicate her contempt for it. Yet, in describing what she depicts as primitive, simple Jews, she notes pointedly that they "spoke the purest jargon"—the language fit the type. She, the highly literate daughter of two literate parents, from a wealthy, prominent home, was not this "type." Yiddish was the language of the "ghetto."[12] It was her mother tongue but not her language of self-presentation.[13] Writing in Yiddish would have consigned her work to the East, whereas Wengeroff was profoundly oriented westward; she expended considerable effort to publish her work in Germany and the United States and, her papers attest, strove for publication in England, too.[14] Although there was a large and growing Yiddish-reading diaspora in the United States and England

---

11 On Wengeroff as an agent of secularization in her marital family, see my introduction to Magnus/Wengeroff, II:14–15, and at length in Magnus, *A Woman's Life*.

12 Wengeroff, as we have seen, uses this term to refer to traditional Jewish culture; there were no physical ghettos in Russia.

13 For Wengeroff's associations of "jargon" with "common" and poor people and those with basic traditional, but not enlightened learning, see Magnus/Wengeroff, I:115, 117, 173, 178, 196.

14 Wengeroff's papers are preserved in the Pushkin Archive, Archival Division, fond 39, St. Petersburg, Russia, cited henceforth as PD, with archival number and, when available, date.

by the time she published, clearly neither this nor the Yiddish-reading masses in the Old Country were her desired audience.

Wengeroff was fluent in Russian. She left behind an archive of her correspondence, much of it in that language, including with her husband and children.[15] Russian, then, was a language of intimacy for her and her family, not just an instrument for business contacts. Intimate use of Russian by itself marks her as anything but a simple traditionalist: the vast majority of Jews under Russian rule lived in the Pale among Polish and Ukrainian-speaking populations, did not need Russian even for business, and therefore did not know it. The Haskalah would come to make Jewish acquisition of Russian a centerpiece of its program; this was a central goal of Russian Jewry's main organization, the Society for the Promotion of Culture among the Jews of Russia, founded in 1863, and it was a priority of the Russian government from the beginning of tsarist rule over a substantial Jewish population.[16] Wengeroff and her family were well ahead of these efforts.

Indeed, in the course of my research, I discovered that Wengeroff did not compose her memoirs in German, and certainly not in the fluent, flawless German of the published work, but largely in Russian—with German, some Yiddish and Hebrew, and some Polish phrases. Why did she labor, working with a translator, to publish her life's work in German and conceal the fact that the work had undergone translation?

Wengeroff regarded Germany as *the* site of high culture, and the German language as its vehicle of expression, not only in Germany but also in the world she knew and above all respected in Russia. In his reminiscences of German literature evenings in his parents' home, in which he recalls an elderly Wengeroff nodding in pleasure to the declaiming of either Goethe or Schiller (he does not recall which), Vladimir Medem remarks: "there was something ... characteristic in the fact that within this circle only German authors were read, and only in the German language." German, he says, served "as the vernacular" among "the genteel-intellectual environment" of Minsk, of which Wengeroff was an integral part during her many years in that city.[17] In comments about the substitution

---

15 Other letters are in German; many include some Yiddish/Hebrew words or phrases.
16 On the language issue, see Benjamin Harshav, "Language," in *The YIVO Encyclopedia of Jews in Eastern Europe* (New Haven, CT: Yale University Press, 2008), I:977–96; Michael Stanislawski, *For Whom Do I Toil? Judah Leib Gordon and the Crisis of Russian Jewry* (Oxford: Oxford University Press, 1988); and Benjamin Nathans, *Beyond the Pale: The Jewish Encounter with Late Imperial Russia* (Berkeley: University of California Press, 2002).
17 *The Life and Soul of a Legendary Jewish Socialist: The Memoirs of Vladimir Medem*, trans. and ed. Samuel A. Portnoy (New York: KTAV Publishing House, 1979), 21.

of Russian for German in Jewish schools in the 1860s (a policy change she ties, correctly, to the aftermath of the Polish rebellion of 1863–64 and the administrative reforms of Alexander II), she links the weakening of Jewish instruction to this change. "Russification" to Wengeroff meant confinement to a specific culture, however much that culture presented itself as "general" (remarkably, the use of quotation marks around this term, signaling awareness that this privileged positioning was constructed, is hers). Clearly, to her, German was the language of the universal but was simultaneously so profoundly associated with things Jewish in her mind that a flourishing symbiosis was possible.

After her husband's death in 1892, Wengeroff spent significant time in Germany—she had two sisters in Heidelberg and composed at least part of *Memoirs* there; in a most poignant construction, she refers to the writing table her sister Helene had provided as her "homeland."[18] Letters she wrote to Theodor Herzl, in German, also emanate from Heidelberg.[19] She spent three years in Vienna, from 1881 to 1883, while her husband was still alive, and considerable time in Berlin, where her publisher was located. From letters she wrote from there, however, we see that Wengeroff lingered in Berlin not just for business but by preference: she liked it there. In Berlin, she felt free from the terror of pogroms and the pervasive Jew-hatred that plagued her in Minsk, and basked in respect and acceptance as a cultural figure.

When Wengeroff sought to publish *Memoirs*, she did not send it to any of the Jewish journals published in Russia, though she read them, had family links to some, and had even published excerpts from what would become *Memoirs* in one of them (*Voskhod*).[20] Instead, she sought serialization in the *Allgemeine Zeitung des Judentums* (General journal of Jewry), German-speaking Jewry's premier organ, whose editor, Gustav Karpeles, was a pioneer of Jewish literary history. Recognizing the quality of what he read, Karpeles told her that it merited publication as a book. Ultimately, she secured publication by Poppelauer, which published Karpeles's own work.

---

18 Magnus/Wengeroff, II:26. Wengeroff's use of this expression may be a borrowing from Heine, who coined the term "portable homeland" in reference to the Jews' relationship to the Hebrew Bible; Heine, *Sämtliche Werke* [Complete works] (Leipzig: Philosophisches Institutut, 1890), VI:57. Many thanks to Sidney Rosenfeld for identifying the source.
19 PD, archival number 975; Letter from Wengeroff to Herzl, January 27, 1904 (4 Shevat 5664), and Herzl to Wengeroff, dated February 1, 1904, in the Central Zionist Archives, Jerusalem, file ZI/354, and in *Theodor Herzl Briefe* (1996), no. 5487, 6:520 and 7:520.
20 See introduction, Magnus/Wengeroff, I:18–19.

Wengeroff evinces considerable sympathy for oppressed, repressed Poland, writing a notable account of the terrorized aftermath of the failed Polish rebellion of the 1860s as she experienced it, in Vilna. Yet she also denounces Jewish involvement in the Polish nationalist cause.[21] Wengeroff was a Jewish nationalist, specifically, a Zionist, sympathetic to Ḥoveve Tsiyon but a fervent supporter of Herzl. (She titles her inquiry a depiction of Jewish cultural change in nineteenth-century "Russia," clearly, in my opinion, because Russia was a state, with evident power, while Poland was no such entity. Rightly, the creators of this museum look beyond such limited, political criteria for inclusion of Wengeroff as a source of the history of the Jews in Poland.)

To return, in conclusion, to Wengeroff and how she was read: *Memoirs* was reviewed widely in the Jewish and non-Jewish press in Russia, Germany, Austria, and even the Netherlands. I saw about forty such reviews, all wildly enthusiastic. Surely, the most remarkable of them appeared in the *Berliner Tageblatt*, a mass-circulation (ca. 250,000), liberal daily, which employed many Jews or people of Jewish origin but was not a Jewish organ.[22] After expressing relief that a book about life in Russia, let alone Jewish life, was not simply a "Jobiade," but was "radiant" with a "warm hearted piety," the reviewer ("J.E.P.") states that the reader

> listens to the old narrator as *if she were the little grandmother of us all* telling us marvelous fairy tales … ; tales that we ourselves once beheld and experienced, when we were young … One's heart celebrates memories in this reading and one's soul laments *all that we moderns have lost in the battle for a better life—* … What a naïve, spirited book that has no other purpose but to hold up to us the mirror of *our own past* [my italics].[23]

In this extraordinary reading, a German reviewer looks beyond the Jewishness of Wengeroff's story and sees in it an evocation of the *temps perdu* that Germans, and indeed all "moderns," have undergone by dint of their modernity. This perception is all the more remarkable because the experience she portrays was not just of Jews but of *Ostjuden*, objects of such scorn and hostility in fin-de-siècle Germany, and these representative Jews losing their moorings in modernity

---

21 See Magnus/Wengeroff, II:117–120; 191, n19, 192, n1.
22 On the *Berliner Tageblatt*, see Walter Laqueur, *Weimar: A Cultural History* (New York: Capricorn, 1976), 73, 260.
23 Review of April 15, 1908, in issue number 194, among Wengeroff's papers; PD 39, archival number 970.

were undergoing transformation under the banner of Enlightenment emanating from Berlin.

Wengeroff herself represents an interesting case in this dialectic: on the one hand, she was clearly an *Ostjüdin*. On the other hand, she published in Berlin, in flawless, idiomatic German, giving the impression that this was her natural language of expression. Wengeroff could thus pass simultaneously as a spokeswoman for Jewish Eastern "authenticity" and for Jewish, Westernized modernity. Surely, this was one key to her success in the early twentieth century, by which time nostalgia for the Jewish past and idealization of *Ostjuden* were live currents in Jewish cultural life. Wengeroff was uniquely positioned to serve as translator of East to West, and West to East, even as a bridge between them: other, yet familiar; sympathetic, accessible, relatable.

In sum, Wengeroff is the perfect embodiment of cultural complexity enacted by this museum; may it succeed and prosper in its mission.

The Interwar Years

One Jewish Street? Reflections on Unity and Disunity in Interwar Polish Jewry

GERSHON BACON

It is a commonplace to speak of "Polish Jewry" in the interwar period, as if it were possible to treat a community of more than three million people as one entity. While this may be a convenient narrative shorthand, it is worthwhile to step back for a moment to contemplate the complexity of the Jewish community of the Second Polish Republic. Polish Jews were far from united regarding practically every political, social, or economic issue of the day. In this most political of Diaspora Jewish communities, a wide spectrum of political parties clamored for the support of Jewish voters and for a dominant voice in defining the nature of Jewishness, particularly for the younger generation. And yet, with all the diversity and strife, there remained a commonality that transcended politics, class, gender, and religious belief, and, beyond the fractious reality, there was an aspiration here and there for unity to meet the challenges of life in reborn Poland. This chapter aims to explore both the contemporary realities on the ground and the ideological views and critiques of those realities, offering both a perspective on past events and on the limitations of narrative discourse in describing those realities.

Any discussion of the unity or disunity of Polish Jewry must take into account the realities and challenges of the newly independent Polish state, most prominent among them the task of forging a unified state out of three regions that had lived under the rule of the former German, Russian, and Austro-Hungarian empires. To cite but one example, it took more than a decade for the legal system of Poland to become more or less unified, finally replacing the legal legacy of the partition regimes in the various regions of the country. The same was true regarding the legal basis for Jewish communal bodies, which reached a uniform legal standard only in the late 1920s. Tsarist discriminatory legislation against Jews also remained on the books for more than a decade into the period of the Second Polish Republic. In Galicia, formerly ruled by Austria-Hungary, the Yiddish language did not enjoy legal status, and thus in the early years of the Polish Republic, when older laws remained on the books, local authorities could, on occasion, prevent the convening of political gatherings held in that language. In the Vilna and Białystok area, new election regulations for the kehillot, the Jewish communal bodies, were issued only in the late 1920s, thus postponing for a full decade the holding of elections whose results would reflect the major political realignment the communities had undergone in the interim.[1] The delay in rectifying such anomalies stemmed from the more general challenges of unifying the country's institutions, but also from particular issues regarding the status of the Jewish minority.

Just as Poland had to undergo a period of reintegration of the regions that had lived under the differing partition regimes, so too there had to be an integration of the varied elements of Polish Jewry. Interestingly, this process proved even more difficult for Jews than for the country as a whole. Regional traditions and styles remained palpable and engendered no small amount of tension, as in the differing political traditions and styles of Zionist politics in the former Congress Poland as compared to that in Galicia. In fact, throughout the interwar period, the General Zionist movement in Poland, the largest Zionist faction, remained divided into a series of regional federations, and would never unite in one countrywide framework.[2] Regarding the period up until the Russian Revolution,

---

1 For a contemporary news report noting the government order for holding kehillah elections in the region, see "Kehillah Elections for Sixty-Four Jewish Communities in Poland Are Ordered," Jewish Telegraph Agency, April 27, 1928, http://www.jta.org/1928/04/27/archive/kehillah-elections-for-64-jewish-communities-in-poland-are-ordered.
2 Ezra Mendelsohn, *Zionism in Poland: The Formative Years, 1915–1926* (New Haven, CT: Yale University Press, 1981), 178–79.

Eli Lederhendler has noted the difficulty, both conceptually and organizationally, of crystalizing an entity that would encompass the more than five million Jewish subjects of the Russian Empire into something that could rightly be called "Russian Jewry."[3] The much smaller geographical expanse of reborn Poland encompassed within its borders (in Ezra Mendelsohn's felicitous term) "Jewries" of varying nature,[4] whose differences found expression in their political styles, their economic profiles, in their educational systems (where, for example, the Hebrew-language Tarbut schools were concentrated in the Kresy region, as opposed to Congress Poland or Galicia), or in the use of Polish versus Yiddish in polite conversation among younger intellectuals.[5] Despite this, among Polish Jews there was a consciousness of possessing some sort of common identity, and certainly the political situation created a need for cooperation in the face of common challenges, even though that cooperation was not always forthcoming.

Politically, at least at the outset of the interwar period, it is difficult for another reason to regard Polish Jewry as one entity, namely, that not all the Jews who came under Polish rule had expected that to be the case. Those of the Vilna region had enjoyed an extremely positive and encouraging relationship with the emerging Lithuanian leadership, who promised the Jewish minority significant national rights under an independent Lithuanian state, including the existence of a minister for Jewish affairs in the government.[6] The Polish conquest of Vilna, the city the Lithuanians regarded as their capital, changed the situation overnight. The Jews of Białystok had an antagonistic, even subversive attitude to being included within the borders of Poland. In 1919, the editorial staff of the leading Yiddish daily in the city, *Dos naye lebn* (The New Life), advanced the idea that since Poland had never clearly defined its eastern borders at the peace conference, the inclusion of Białystok in the Second Polish Republic represented no less than an illegal annexation. Emboldened

---

3 Eli Lederhendler, "Did Russian Jewry Exist before 1917?" in *Jews and Jewish Life in Russia and the Soviet Union*, ed. Yaacov Ro'i (Ilford, UK: Frank Cass, 1995), 15–27.
4 Ezra Mendelsohn, *The Jews of East Central Europe between the World Wars* (Bloomington: Indiana University Press, 1983), 17–23.
5 See, for example, Haskell Nordon, *The Education of a Polish Jew: A Physician's War Memoirs* (New York: Grossman, 1982), 176–77.
6 See Antony Polonsky, *The Jews in Poland and Russia*, vol. III: *1914 to 2008* (Oxford and Portland, 2012: Littman Library of Jewish Civilization), 45–46; Dov Levin, "Lithuania," *The YIVO Encyclopedia of Jews in Eastern Europe*, http://www.yivoencyclopedia.org/article.aspx/Lithuania. This "honeymoon" between Jews and Lithuanians, however, proved short lived, as the independent Lithuanian state become more and more ethnocratic in nature by the mid-1920s.

by the unquestioned support of émigré philanthropists, even several years into Polish rule, the press organs of the Jews of Białystok continually questioned the very inclusion of their city in Poland, a most idiosyncratic viewpoint for Polish Jews of the era.[7] In this region annexed to Poland, becoming Polish involved adjustment on the part of the Jews, and their integration into the larger collectivity of Polish Jewry also took time.

While the disunity of Polish Jewry was the reality, the language of unity and aspirations to achieve such unity still resonated in the interwar period. First of all, it can be claimed that Jewish culture carried with it a perception of factionalism and strife among Jews as the precursor of national disaster, most notably in attributing the fall of Jerusalem and the destruction of the Second Temple to baseless hatred, whether on the political or the personal level.[8] Such ideas were not lacking in the discourse of the interwar period. Beyond any cultural predilection toward unity as an ideal, the very process of politicization that led to the formation of the wide variety of Jewish parties active in interwar Poland carried within it at least the nucleus of an ideal of political unity. Modern Jewish politics in Eastern Europe stemmed from the concept of minority rights and minority autonomy. In the eyes of the proponents of such autonomy, there was envisioned some sort of recognized representative body of the Jewish minority that could speak in the name of the Jewish community as a whole in its dealings with the larger state government, whether it be the Austrian or Russian authorities, or later the nascent national states formed after the First World War. The autonomous Jewish minority was also supposed to receive state funding for its educational and cultural activities, and here too some sort of Jewish national committee would be charged with allocating funds to schools and cultural institutions. Among the Jewish parties, we find almost unanimous support for national autonomy, with some differences over questions of language (Yiddish, Hebrew, Yiddish and Hebrew), on the related issue of education, and on the question of the nature of the kehillah, the local Jewish organized body, which some parties wished to secularize, while Orthodox groups naturally opposed such a change. In other words, despite deep divisions in their views, Jewish political parties did share a concept of Jewish national existence that carried a potential for a unified framework for carrying on the fractious debate between them.

---

7   Rebecca Kobrin, *Jewish Białystok and Its Diaspora* (Bloomington: Indiana University Press, 2010), 145–47.
8   Babylonian Talmud Yoma 9b and Gittin 55b.

This potential, however, would never be realized. In the early days of Polish independence, a series of meetings was held, looking toward the establishment of a unified Jewish representation in dealings with Polish leadership and officialdom. A so-called Temporary Jewish National Council (Tymczasowa Żydowska Rada Narodowa) was set up under Zionist leadership, but not all Jewish parties participated in the preparatory meetings (e.g., the Orthodox group Agudat Ha'ortodoksim, later known as Agudat Yisrael), or they refused to recognize the authority of the body once it was set up (Aguda, assimilationist groups, the Bund).[9]

Nor was the general political atmosphere congenial to such efforts, as the Polish government refused to recognize Jews as a national minority eligible for autonomy. Characteristic of this atmosphere were the reactions in the Constituent Sejm chamber on the first "Jewish day" (February 24, 1919), when members of the three Jewish parliamentary clubs presented their programs and demands, with these speeches constantly interrupted by critical, oftentimes mocking remarks. Even the moderate program for religious and cultural autonomy presented by the Orthodox representative, the aged Rabbi Avraham Tsevi Perlmutter, who interspersed patriotic declarations throughout his address, was greeted with catcalls asserting that this amounted to a state within a state ("państwo w państwie"), and hence was unacceptable.[10] Proportional funding for Jewish educational and cultural institutions, called for by the Minorities Treaties signed by Poland, would never be forthcoming.

Nor would the internal Jewish political situation change in the 1930s, even in the face of growing anti-Semitism in Poland. To take one prominent example, in its party program of 1935, the socialist Bund rejected outright the notion of cooperating with bourgeois Jewish parties out of a sense of Jewish solidarity:

> The reactionary role of the Jewish bourgeoisie, however, is not limited to attempts to impede the Jewish masses in their struggle against their class enemies by stupefying them with dreams of Palestine or with religious fanaticism. All segments of the Jewish bourgeoisie directly support

---

9 On these efforts, see Shlomo Netzer, *Ma'avak Yehudei Polin al zekhuyotehem ha'ezrahiyot ve'ha'leumiyot [1918–1922]* [The struggle of Polish Jews for their civil and national rights, 1918–1922] (Tel Aviv: University of Tel Aviv Press, 1980), 47–72.

10 *Sprawozdanie Stenograficzne z 5. posiedzenia Sejmu Ustawodawczego z dnia 24 lutego 1919 r.* [The Stenographic Report of the Fifth Session of the Constitutional Sejm, 24 February 1919], cols. 181–184, http://dlibra.umcs.lublin.pl/dlibra/docmetadata?id=11543&from=publication.

the fascist regime and are for their part supported by it alone. On the Jewish street, then, the struggle against fascism means the struggle against all bourgeois Jewish parties. And this is exactly what the Bund is doing by rejecting any *klal yisroel* politics and any compromise with "our own" bourgeoisie.[11]

Of the major Jewish parties, the most consistent advocate of a united Jewish political front (at the beginning, demanding a Jewish electoral curia) was the Folkist group, but this remained a goal in theory, while the Folkists themselves indulged in shifting alliances with other parties. In a classic article, Ezra Mendelsohn spoke of the dilemma of Jewish politics, setting out four possible political options open to Jews in Poland: an alliance with a Polish party, an alliance with other national minorities, a loyalist stance toward the regime in power, and a united Jewish electoral list that would maximize Jewish representation and push for national and cultural autonomy.[12] Of these four paths, the latter, that of Jewish unity, would remain the only path not taken.

This extreme factionalism did not go without criticism, both at that time and in retrospective accounts. In a speech during his 1933 visit to Poland, Nahum Sokolow, president of the World Zionist Congress, characterized Poland as a "factory for parties" that unfortunately struggled against one another, thus dissipating the energies of the Zionist movement in Poland. In the past, he lamented, Jews sharpened their wits through Talmudic debate, but now they wasted that sharpness on political infighting.[13] This factionalism dismayed many foreign visitors, making them despair of anything positive emerging from the undeniably great political energies of Polish Jewry. Even in the dark days of the late 1930s, the political leadership of the community could never agree on forming a united representative body or formulating a plan of action for the emergency period. The then–political commentator Moshe Kleinbaum noted in the daily *Haynt* that while the external atmosphere of enmity toward Jews would seem to dictate Jewish internal unity, what he

---

11 Cited by Gertrud Pickhan, "*Yiddishkayt* and Class Consciousness: The Bund and Its Minority Concept," *East European Jewish Affairs* 39, no. 2 (August 2009): 258.
12 Ezra Mendelsohn, "The Dilemma of Jewish Politics in Poland: Four Responses," in *Jews and Non-Jews in Eastern Europe, 1918–1945*, ed. Bela Vago and George Mosse (New York: Wiley, 1974), 203–20.
13 *Haynt*, November 23, 1933, 4, http://jpress.org.il/Olive/APA/NLI_heb/SharedView.Article. aspx?parm=I9lYr1RkFQPzpSh6VpzI7CxfzKdvMdohpqcqTBz1Q%2Bq1z3j0QYElB62S63K-m78v3Yw%3D%3D&mode=image&href=HYT%2F1933%2F11%2F23&page=4&rtl=true.

termed the "unbridled sovereignty" of the small political factions rendered impossible any chance for a fitting Jewish response.[14] Citing calls for unity by the Jewish public and Jewish press after the March 1936 pogrom in Przytyk, Joseph Marcus criticized the response of political parties of that era:

> The call for unity expressed the popular belief that unity is a pre-condition of effective self-defense and political improvement. It was also seen as necessary to preserve Jewish dignity vis-à-vis the non-Jewish population. It is possible that many of the anti-Jewish measures of the post-1935 years would never have taken place if the government had been faced by a resolute and united Jewish leadership. Even the attitude of Jewish leaders abroad to the needs of Polish Jews might have been different if the Polish leadership had been united.[15]

Of course, historians cite the same political divisiveness and combativeness as signs of the vitality of Polish Jewry, but the undercurrent of criticism remains.

While this political divisiveness characterized Polish Jewish life in the interwar period, it did have some self-imposed limits. A representative body of Polish Jews never came into being, but the Koło Żydowskie, the Jewish club in the Sejm, despite its inner tensions, did function as an unofficial "address" for the community, whether in the eyes of the Polish government that negotiated with it or in the eyes of individual Jewish citizens who sought redress for discrimination on the part of government bureaucracy. The ideological struggle between Zionists, Bundists, and Agudists did on occasion paralyze Jewish community councils in Warsaw, Łódź, and other kehillot. To cite but one example, the debate over funding secular and religious Jewish school networks witnessed strange temporary coalitions, where Agudists and Zionists united to deny funding to Bundist schools, Zionists and Bundists united to deny funding to Orthodox schools, and then Agudists and Bundists voted together not

---

14 Cited by David Engel, "'Masoret Negaim?'—Hearot al ha'megamot ha'politiyot ve'ha'tarbut ha'politit shel Yahadut Polin bein shtei milhamot ha'olam," ["'A tradition in crisis?' Reflections on the political trends and the political culture of Polish Jewry between the two World Wars"] in *Kiyyum ve'Shever: Yehudei Polin le'dorotehem* [The Broken Chain: Polish Jewry through the ages] ed. Israel Bartal and Israel Gutman, vol. 2 (Jerusalem, Zalman Shazar Center, 2001), 650.

15 Joseph Marcus, *Social and Political History of the Jews in Poland 1919–1939* (Berlin: Mouton, 1983), 359.

to fund Zionist schools. In the end, however, in most cases practical considerations enabled common sense and compromise to prevail, and all the schools received funding.[16]

In our consideration of phenomena of unity and disunity in interwar Polish Jewry, we must recognize that this issue went far beyond the realm of politics alone and touched almost every aspect of Polish Jewish life. For brevity's sake, we divide our discussion into five main subtopics.

1. SOCIAL AND CLASS DISUNITY

Historical research of the last generation, as well as memoir literature, stressed the difficulties encountered by even the most acculturated Jews to find their way into general Polish society. As Theodore Hamerow put it:

> Those Jews who tried assimilation ... soon discovered that becoming Polish was by no means as easy as they had been led to believe. Talking, dressing, and behaving like Poles were not enough. There was always something about them that was not authentic, something which was alien or spurious or suspicious. Some of them did manage to win positions of prominence in Polish society and culture. But even they were always aware of whispered and sometimes loud complaints about their foreignness or pushiness or shiftiness. As it turned out, ceasing to be a Jew was almost as difficult as being one.[17]

Thus, those Jews aspiring to join Polish society were still part of an ascribed Jewish collectivity, but within this Jewish society there existed yawning social gaps, to the point that such Jews felt complete alienation and social and cultural distances from other Jews. Again, we cite Hamerow, who recalled his curiosity about a hasidic rebbe who rented a house near that of his parents in Otwock:

---

16 *Der Yud* (Warsaw), December 21, 1927, 3; Robert Moses Shapiro, *Jewish Self-Government in Poland: Lodz, 1914–1939* (PhD diss., Columbia University, 1987), 294–98; Lucy Dawidowicz, *From That Place and Time: A Memoir, 1938–1947* (New York: Norton, 1989), 156.

17 Theodore S. Hamerow, *Remembering a Vanished World: A Jewish Childhood in Interwar Poland* (New York: Berghahn Books, 2001), 138. On this group in general, see Anna Landau-Czajka, *Syn będzie Lech: Asymilacja Żydów w Polsce międzywojennej* [Your son will be called Lech: the assimilation of Jews in interwar Poland] (Warsaw: Wydawnictwo "Neriton," 2006).

> Almost all the Jews I knew were secular in dress, locution, and belief. Even the few who were devout, my grandfather, for example, were unobtrusive, almost subdued, in their religiousness. But there was nothing restrained about the devotion displayed by the rabbi's followers, who would gather in his house every Friday evening to begin their celebration of the Sabbath
> ... *They appeared to me almost as strange, almost as exotic, as the whirling dervishes of Turkey I had read about ... I felt that an invisible but insurmountable barrier separated me from them.* (emphasis added)[18]

Hamerow also noted the sharp social distinctions within the Jewish community, particularly between the affluent and those who lived literally on the other side of the railroad tracks.[19]

2. GENERATIONAL DISUNITY

Much has been made in recent scholarship of the vast gap between the generations in interwar Polish Jewry, mostly based on analyses of the youth autobiographies submitted to competitions held by the YIVO Institute for Jewish Research in the 1930s.[20] Young people felt alienated from their parents, particularly from their fathers, who represented the old-fashioned ways of tradition, or who, through their inability to provide for their families in the face of economic crisis, left their children adrift and without hope of finding a way out of poverty. Alternative models of authority and acculturation were sought in the public school or private modern Jewish school, or in the "better world" of the Jewish youth movements, or in revolutionary socialist, Zionist, or communist activity. Despite the tremendous ideological differences separating the various youth movements, they shared the common purpose of providing a social, political, and cultural refuge for young people frustrated by the poverty and perceived impotence of their parents' generation. The younger generation, educated for the most part in Polish public schools, identified more and more with Polish language and Polish culture, going through the same process

---

18 Hamerow, *Remembering a Vanished World*, 155.
19 Ibid., 91–92.
20 Barbara Kirshenblatt-Gimblett et al., "Introduction," in *Awakening Lives: Autobiographies of Jewish Youth in Poland before the Holocaust*, ed. Jeffrey Shandler (New Haven, CT: Yale University Press, 2002), xii–xiii.

of acculturation, if a bit delayed, as their Jewish contemporaries in the United States or the Soviet Union, and moving toward a new type of Jewish identity.[21]

In this reading, then, the younger generation and the older generation represented disunited and often antagonistic worlds. On further reflection, while granting this reality, we can point to evidence that the older generation gave its support, whether enthusiastic or grudging, to some aspects of this gap. Both Celia Heller and (in his memoir) Isaac Bashevis Singer cite the phenomenon of Yiddish-speaking parents making a conscious decision to bring up their children in the Polish language (including parents whose spoken Polish was relatively weak), including the children of leading Yiddish writers.[22] Apologizing to his nephew in America for his son's lack of knowledge of Yiddish, Wolf Lewkowicz, an unsuccessful Jewish businessman from central Poland who had an extensive correspondence with his deceased sister's son in the United States, wrote to him that he could not afford to send his son to a Jewish school, and, besides that, it was right for his son to learn the language of the land, despite the fact that civil service jobs were denied to Jews, and "what good does their language, their Polish, do me?"[23]

3. RELIGIOUS–SECULAR DISUNITY

A phenomenon that emerges again and again both in memoirs and scholarly literature is the clear trend of secularization and abandonment of tradition (although more exacting analyses of the pace and extent of the phenomenon are lacking, and the traditional community remained a significant sector in the

---

21 See, for example, Kamil Kijek, "Polska akulturacja, żydowski nacjonalizm? Paradygmat 'akulturacja bez asymilacji' a świadomość polityczna międzywojennej młodzieży żydowskiej na podstawie autobiografii YIVO" [Polish acculturation, Jewish nationalism? The paradigm of "acculturation without assimilation" versus political consciousness of interwar Jewish youth on the basis of the YIVO autobiographies] in *Wokół akulturacji i asymilacji Żydów na ziemach polskich* [On the acculturation and assimilation of Jews in the Polish lands], ed. Konrad Zieliński (Lublin: Wydawnictwo Uniwersytetu Marii Curie-Skłodowskiej, 2010), 85–112; "Was It Possible to Avoid 'Hebrew assimilation?' Hebraism, Polonization and Tarbut Schools in the Last Decade of Interwar Poland," *Jewish Social Studies: History, Culture, Society* 21 (Winter 2016): 105–41.
22 Celia S. Heller, *On the Edge of Destruction: Jews of Poland between the Two World Wars* (New York: Columbia University Press, 1977), 213–17; Isaac Bashevis Singer, *Love and Exile: An Autobiographical Trilogy* (New York: Farrar, Straus and Giroux, 1986), 186–87.
23 Wolf Lewkowicz collection, letter from December 20, 1931, http://web.mit.edu/maz/wolf/65-179/wolf127.txt.

Jewish community).²⁴ This was an unending source of tension within families and between the various Jewish parties. The meetings of kehillah councils were often witness to bitter debates and occasional violence surrounding these issues. With all the tension, however, the basic institutional unity of the community structure remained. The *kehillah*, or *gmina żydowska*, retained its basically religious nature (as stipulated by Polish law), despite the stated goal of many groups to remake it into a secular national body, but in practice it served as a wider Jewish political forum. The only group to opt out of participation in kehillah politics, for part of the interwar period, was the socialist Bund, but it too returned to participation in kehillah elections in the mid-1930s.

4. INTRA-RELIGIOUS DISUNITY

The heritage of decades of internal strife within the religious community continued in the interwar period. The long-standing rift between *Hasidim* and *mitnagdim* persisted, if in muted form. Within hasidic circles, rivalries and tensions between the largest hasidic courts, those of Ger, Aleksander, and Belz, also left their mark on individual communities and on national Jewish politics, reflected in the struggle between Agudat Yisrael, the religious Zionist Mizrahi, and so-called nonpartisan religious groups, as well as those rabbis and their flocks who supported the Piłsudski camp, the Bezpartyjny Blok Współpracy z Rządem (BBWR—Nonpartisan Bloc for Cooperation with the Government). Here, too, however, there is evidence of cooperation despite tensions, as exemplified by the participation of both hasidic and *mitnagdic* elements in the rabbinic and political leadership of Agudat Yisrael, of national and even international cooperation in the establishment of the great yeshiva in Lublin and the Bais Yaakov school network, and in the legendary 1930 delegation of rabbis from all sectors who personally lobbied the Polish government to prevent government-initiated changes in qualifications for heder teachers and for rabbis.²⁵

---

24 Heller, *On the Edge of Destruction*, 232–38. For a first attempt at providing an empirical framework for the discussion of secularization of Polish Jews, see Asaf Kaniel, "Bein hilonim, ortodoksim u'masortiyim: shemirat mitzvot be're'i hahitmodedut im 'gezeirat hakashrut,' 1937–1939" [Between secular Jews, the orthodox and the traditional: The observance of the mitzvot as reflected in the coping with the 'kashrut decree,' 1937–1939], *Gal-Ed* 22 (2010): 75–106; "Al milhama u'shemirat mitzvot: Vilna, 1914–1922" [On war and the observance of the commandments, Vilna, 1914–1922], *Gal-Ed* 24 (2015): 37–74.

25 See *Der Moment*, February 5, 1930, 2; February 6, 1930, 2; February 7, 1930, 10; http://www.jta.org/1930/02/07/archive/ask-10-year-respite-in-law-that-rabbis-know-polish.

Recent research has also highlighted attempts by hasidic rebbes to deal with abandonment of religion and with the generation gap by a new emphasis on youth. Institutional frameworks were set up for them, and, in a startling change in this most conservative of Jewish groups, there were alterations in the concept of "who is a Hasid," as children were accepted as full-fledged members of the groups and were even granted special attention at rebbes' courts.[26]

5. GENDER DISUNITY

It is difficult to speak of Polish Jewry as a whole when the historical narrative has, until recently, ignored 52 percent of the Jewish population, namely, the women. When the community spoke with one voice, that voice was male. Throughout the period, women were denied the vote in kehillah elections, and rectifying this situation was never a major priority for the secular Jewish parties. Of the dozens of Jews elected to the Sejm and senate, only one, Róża Melcer of the General Zionists, was a woman.[27] Here and there we can see opinions of a feminist nature and short-lived feminist groups making their way into public discourse, but this was the exception rather than the rule.[28] Changes, however, were in the making. In Orthodox circles, the Bais Yaakov schools for girls provided formal Jewish education, and also tried to foster the notion that a girl was a religious personality in her own right. In the women's movements and youth movements of the Bund and Zionists, including at the training farms of the latter, we can see a growing sense of full inclusion of women, even if not always on completely equal terms.[29] If we are to talk of Polish Jewry, it is incumbent upon historians to make these voices heard and to include women

---

26 See Moriah Herman, *Ha'yahas li'vnei hanoar ba'hasidut ba'tekufa she'bein milhamot haolam: ha'hiddushim ha'hagutiim ve'ha'maasiim be'hasidut Polin ba'yahas li'vnei ha'noar ke'teguva la'azivat ha'dat* [The attitude to young people in Hasidism in the interwar period: ideological and practical innovations in Polish Hasidism in the attitude to young people as a response to abandonment of religion among youth] (PhD diss.: Bar-Ilan University, 2014).

27 See "Melcer, Róża," *The YIVO Encyclopedia of the Jews in Eastern Europe*, http://www.yivoencyclopedia.org/article.aspx/Melcer_Roza.

28 See Paula E. Hyman, *Gender and Assimilation in Modern Jewish History: The Roles and Representation of Women* (Seattle: University of Washington Press, 1995), 83–92; Eva Plach, "Feminism and Nationalism on the pages of *Ewa: Tygodnik*, 1928–1933," *Polin* 18 (2005): 241–62.

29 See, for example, Daniel Blatman, "Women in the Jewish Labor Bund in Interwar Poland," in *Women in the Holocaust*, ed. Dalia Ofer and Lenore J. Weitzman (New Haven, CT: Yale University Press, 1998), 68–84.

in the historical narrative in dealing with political, demographic, economic, and social issues.[30]

The rifts and splits in Polish Jewry were real, but, as we have shown, never complete. In addition, though, it is important to point out other trends and forces, both from within and without, that led to a semblance of unity of the community. First of all, the reestablishment of the Polish state and the inclusion of the largest Jewish community in Europe within its borders could be seen as "creating" Polish Jewry. Gershon D. Hundert and Moshe Rosman have shown the long-standing identification of Jews with Poland, to the point that Hundert could famously speak of "Jews and other Poles."[31] Citizenship in a modern national state, however, goes beyond those feelings, and, despite clear manifestations of rejection and antipathy on the part of some Poles, we can see by the end of the period a growing sense among many Jews of linguistic acculturation and identification with the modern Polish state. First and foremost among the factors present in interwar Poland that had a profound effect on Jews was the Polish public school, where the vast majority of Jewish children were educated. In what we call "the victory of schooling," what had been the unfulfilled dream of Jewish *maskilim*, Jewish assimilationists, and Polish reformers alike became the social reality for the younger generation of Polish Jews.[32] That feeling of belongingness to the land and its historical sites was also fostered by Jewish organizations, for example the *landkentenish* movement.[33] The pressure from without of anti-Semitism, branding all Jews no matter what their level of acculturation, brought about a reidentification with Jewishness on the part of some Jews.[34]

Within the Jewish community, we can also see trends of unity. Philanthropic and charitable organizations, such as TOZ and Centos, interest-free loan banks set up by local communities and often subsidized and coordinated by the American Joint Distribution Committee, in addition to the social welfare

---

30 For a summary of findings, see Gershon Bacon, "Poland: Interwar," in *Jewish Women: A Comprehensive Historical Encyclopedia,* ed. Paula Hyman and Dalia Ofer (Jerusalem:Shalvi Publishing, 2006) and the bibliography cited there, http://jwa.org/encyclopedia/article/poland-interwar.

31 Gershon D. Hundert, *The Jews in a Polish Private Town: The Case of Opatów in the Eighteenth Century* (Baltimore, MD: Johns Hopkins University Press, 1992), 36–39.

32 Gershon Bacon, "National Revival, Ongoing Acculturation—Jewish Education in Interwar Poland," *Simon Dubnow Institute Yearbook* 1 (2002): 89–92.

33 See "Landkentenish," *The YIVO Encyclopedia of Jews in Eastern Europe,* http://www.yivoencyclopedia.org/article.aspx/Landkentenish.

34 See, for instance, the autobiography of J. Harefuler in Shandler, *Awakening Lives,* 376–77.

budgets of the kehillot, add up to an impressive effort by Polish Jews to help their community weather the difficult political and economic storms of the interwar period. The usually critical Joseph Marcus claims that the basic economic and social viability of Polish Jewry and the maintenance of minimal conditions for existence for much of the Jewish population were made possible through transfer payments from the upper half of the community to the lower half; he estimated that these payments accounted for almost 10 percent of the former's national income in 1929.[35] Although plagued on occasion by interparty wrangling, the struggle against anti-Semitism—whether the boycott of Nazi Germany or the protests against pogroms in Poland, against violence and "ghetto benches" in the universities, and against legislation to restrict Jewish methods of animal slaughter (*sheḥitah*)—did unite wide sectors of Jewish society in Poland.

This, then, was the complex reality of Polish Jewry in the interwar period: a community riven by internal fissures and ideological and political rivalries, but still exhibiting social solidarity in the face of economic crisis, growing poverty, and government inaction; a community unable to unite even in the face of serious political threats, but with a strong sense of a separate identity along with a growing feeling of belongingness to Poland. Hamerow's description of the Passover seder at his pious grandparents' home conveys much of this complex reality:

> And on both sides sat their sons and daughters, all of them in secular attire, all talking in Polish, all confirmed freethinkers, none of them believing in the miraculous liberation of the Jews from Egyptian bondage, none believing in the long march through the desert to the promised land, none believing in the Bible, none even believing in God. But all of them were taking part in a solemn religious observance, partly out of filial duty, but partly also as an expression of loyalty, perhaps unconscious loyalty, to a culture, a history, a tradition, and a community.[36]

---

35 Marcus, *Social and Political History of the Jews in Poland*, 47.
36 Hamerow, *Remembering a Vanished World*, 113.

Not Just Mały Przegląd: The Ideals and Educational Values Expressed in Jewish Polish-Language Journals for Children and Young Adults

ANNA LANDAU-CZAJKA

In the interwar period, some two hundred Jewish periodicals were published in the Polish language.[1] It is impossible to provide an exact figure. In addition, there were eighty-seven children's periodicals published in Polish, excluding one-off issues.[2] Usually these journals, whether for adults or children, did not see many editions, some of them folding after only a few issues.

The first magazine to come up with the idea of publishing a supplement for its readers' children was the Lwów-based *Chwila* (Moment). The first issue appeared at Hanukkah in 1925. Initially, the editor was Runa Reitmanowa, a social worker in Lwów whose focus was on children. This particular supplement

---

1 Alina Cała, *Żydowskie periodyki i druki okazjonalne w języku polskim. Bibliografia* [Jewish periodicals and occasional prints in the Polish language. Bibliography] (Warsaw: Biblioteka Narodowa, 2005). It is hard to make an exact count of the number of titles, not least because some of the publications disappeared after only one or two editions. In many essays the number of periodicals is not fully estimated, for example, a website generally very reliable concerning the interwar period states that "Jews issued 160 different newspapers and periodicals with a daily print-run of 790,000 copies," http://www.izrael.badacz.org/zydzi_w_polsce/dzieje_rzeczpospolita.html.

2 Izrael Szajn, "Bibliografia żydowskiej prasy młodzieżowej wydawanej w Polsce w latach 1918–1939" [A bibliography of the Jewish press for youth in Poland in the years 1918–1939], *Biuletyn Żydowskiego Instytutu Historycznego* 2 (Warsaw, 1975): 103–19.

was fairly conventional, and included the usual sorts of contents that appear in children's magazines: stories, poems, a variety of popular science items, and puzzles. There were also items written by readers, but they were marginal, not the main contents.[3] It was possible to subscribe just to *Chwilka* (Little moment), at the price of forty groszy per issue (the average newspaper price was ten to twenty groszy per issue).[4] The second children's magazine was established by the most popular Polish-language Jewish daily, *Nasz Przegląd* (Our review), which in 1926 invited Janusz Korczak to work with them—this was the origin of *Mały Przegląd* (The little review), the most famous of the children's magazines to be issued as a supplement to an adult periodical. Last to join in was the Kraków-based *Nowy Dziennik* (The new daily) which issued a supplement in 1926 called *Dzienniczek dla dzieci i młodzieży* (The little daily for children and youth) every two weeks, known for short as *Dzienniczek*.

All three magazines began as supplements to Polish-language dailies that were Zionist, or at least connected with the Zionist milieu. They were thus aimed at the same group of readers—acculturated Jewish children whose parents had a good command of the Polish language, held Zionist or similar views, and could afford to buy a daily newspaper. One would therefore imagine that the message addressed to such a closely related group of children and young people would be more or less consistent, whatever the newspaper.

Yet it was not quite so simple. Above all, their consistency was disrupted by an unconventional editor-in-chief—Janusz Korczak—and the innovative concept of a magazine edited by its own readers. Indeed, in practice this concept was not fully implemented (or certainly not while Korczak was running the magazine), but even so, the result was that the views appearing on the pages of *Mały Przegląd* were incomparably more diverse, debatable, and ambiguous than those featured in *Chwilka* or *Dzienniczek*, both of which had a clearly delineated educational purpose.

As a result, it is very difficult to compare the themes which appear in the *Mały Przegląd* with any other newspaper for children. While the other journals printed texts ordered by the editors on specific topics, *Mały Przegląd* consisted of letters to the editor, polemics, and reports written by the readers themselves. There were therefore no precise themes and no specific line—

---

3 Barbara Łętocha, "*Chwila*. Gazeta Żydów Lwowskich" [*Chwila*. A newspaper of the Jews of Lwów], http://www.lwow.com.pl/rocznik/chwila.html.

4 Answers from the editor, *Dzienniczek* (Little daily; hereafter Dz) 24 V 1929, no. 11, 6.

letters concerned various topics, sometimes frivolous, sometimes purely private, but also general issues, including Polish–Jewish relations, Jewish identity, and schools. However, there is no specific vision of the school, the homeland, Palestine, religion—each correspondent has his or her own opinion on various subjects, and *Mały Przegląd* is the only organ in which he or she can present his or her views.

This chapter is about two of the three periodicals mentioned above: *Dzienniczek* and *Mały Przegląd*. In many ways *Chwilka*—above all on the issues of Palestine and Zionism—held the same opinions as *Dzienniczek*.

The original editor of *Dzienniczek* was Runa Reitmanowa, the woman who had founded *Chwilka*. Until 1933, she edited both magazines. There were connections—apart from the person in charge—between *Chwilka* and *Dzienniczek*, because in 1929 the editors assured their readers that the items they sent in would appear in both journals. Starting in 1934, a new editor emerged, Marta Hirschsprunżanka, whose own articles had begun to appear at the end of 1933.

After the change of editor-in-chief, the journal, evidently undergoing a crisis, endeavored to be just like *Mały Przegląd*. More and more items were written by readers, and above all the magazine was aimed at younger readers than before—under the age of fifteen. Older teenagers complained that the magazine wasn't for them, but, as the editors explained, it was unfortunately not possible to fit items that would be relevant to children as well as to older teens in a one-page magazine.

For older teens, the journal had an idea undoubtedly modeled on *Mały Przegląd*. It proposed that teens collaborate to form Young People's Editorial Committees that would publicize the magazine and expand direct contacts with readers. Perhaps it was to disguise that the idea to establish such committees came from adults that the names of two readers were issued as its authors: Rel and Otto Blaustein.

The magazine was to have permanent "associates":

> Any children or young people who show their talents by publishing at least five articles in *Dzienniczek*, counted from today's date, can become permanent associates (correspondents or reporters) for *Dzienniczek*. We also propose that at our schools and at various foundations and organizations (not just in Kraków) young people and children (with the consent of those in charge, of course) should select someone among them to be a correspondent for *Dzienniczek*, charged with the task of informing the

magazine about important events at their particular school or organization. The chosen correspondents would then be able to join the permanent young people's editorial committee.[5]

Here it is worth drawing attention to the phrase about the consent of those in charge with regard to the choice of correspondent. Here the journal clearly diverged from the policy of *Mały Przegląd*, which taught its readers to be independent from adult guidance. But what follows is a further connection to the more popular periodical. The editor stresses that as most of the items in *Dzienniczek* are written by young people, the contents are far from perfect: "It is not our task to increase the number of future 'literary geniuses,' which would only enable a proliferation of scribblers. Above all, we are more concerned about 'what someone writes,' and only then about 'how someone writes.' We want *Dzienniczek* to be a mirror of the life and aspirations of the young, a personal platform by, and also for, children and young people."[6] This final statement refers to the subtitle of *Mały Przegląd: Pismo dzieci i młodzieży* (the newspaper of children and youth, and not for children and youth). Similarly, based on the model of the more popular publication, the editors of *Dzienniczek* decided not only to print items written by the readers, but also to drop everything that wasn't a report or a news feature—in other words, any attempts to write literature: "We cannot include any fairy tales, fables, or novellas. But we do publish short articles and interesting letters, and are also happy to include interviews and features."[7] Despite these grand announcements, poems and short stories by the readers did appear in most issues of the magazine. Thus, the similarities to *Mały Przegląd* were only superficial.

However, the new formula did not suit everyone. A major stir was caused by a letter in which a reader claimed that some stories that had won prizes in a competition were written by an adult, and that the editors had shown their naïveté. And, he wrote, *Dzienniczek* contained no up-to-date news on the latest in technology, and no interesting stories, so adults should be writing for it, as they did for *Płomyk* (Little flame), the youth journal of left-leaning teachers' trade union.[8] In other words, at least some of the readers preferred better-written

---

5 M. H. [Marta Hirschsprunżanka], "Porozmawiajmy sobie" [Let's talk], 3 V 1934, no. 24 (121): 9.
6 Ibid.
7 Answers from the editors, 1 XI 1934, no. 35 (299): 9.
8 L. L. K. B, "Oskarżam!" (I accuse!), 18 X 1934, no. 34 (285): 7.

articles to the outpourings of their own generation. Yet the idea of publishing works by adults was rejected.

> We, however, are of the view that *Płomyk*, which ... so strongly appeals to us, is of a different character and cannot be considered a magazine for us. Of course it is interesting, but we prefer *Dzienniczek*. In *Dzienniczek* we can boldly express our thoughts, and it is far more interesting to write and discuss articles produced by young people and children *for* young people and children than to read nothing but works by adults.[9]
>
> We are opposed to the suggestion that older people should write for *Dzienniczek*. Older people aren't needed in *Dzienniczek*![10]

Whether that really was the general opinion, or whether the editors selected letters to suit their own needs is hard to tell, but they clearly had no intention of changing the publication's policy. Yet judging by the very long deadlines for various competitions—because too few replies came in—the magazine was not particularly successful.

The next steps toward linking *Dzienniczek* with *Mały Przegląd* were editorial duty rosters and an invitation to readers to participate actively in the work of the editorial team: "Aiming for the most direct contact with our readers, the editors of *Dzienniczek* have established 'open hours' for readers of *Dzienniczek* on Thursdays between three and four p.m. We extend a warm invitation to all those who wish to communicate with us in person, but lack the courage."[11]

Mały Przegląd was a specific kind of journal, created by children—or maybe it is more accurate to say that it was created on the basis of correspondence from children. Korczak and his successor, Igor Newerly, were adults, but the rest of the editorial team were of the same age as the readers and correspondents. The filing system maintained by a fourteen-year-old resident of the Orphans' Home was—according to Newerly—worthy of two venerable archivists and one notary.[12] The "editor's right hand" was a fourteen- or fifteen-year-old schoolgirl named Madzia

---

9 "W odpowiedzi L. L. K. B.," 1 XI 1934, no. 35 (299): 8.
10 Ibid., 8–9.
11 Dz, 6 II 1935: 8.
12 Igor Newerly, *Rozmowa w sadzie piątego sierpnia. O chłopcu z bardzo starej fotografii* [A conversation in the court on 5 August. On a boy in a very old photograph] (Warsaw: Czytelnik, 1984), 20.

Mazurke,[13] whom Korczak often cited for her invaluable assistance; her brother worked with the editorial team, too. It is hard to state the entire list of the editorial team, because none was ever issued. When Korczak's name was withdrawn from the masthead, the new editor's name was not substituted. Furthermore, an official version that states that Korczak had too much work to do does not seem to be true, as he not only stopped editing the magazine, but also no longer contributed texts to it either—although he had not stopped writing. There can be no doubt, however, that in 1936, after a stormy debate between the "old" and "new" editors, mainly concerning the age group at whom the magazine was aimed, there was a return to Korczak's concept, and from then on his work appeared in the magazine again, though not as often as before.[14]

The main aim of this essay, however, is not so much to compare the two periodicals as to consider to the extent to which *Mały Przegląd*, regarded as a unique phenomenon, actually differed from other periodicals aimed at the same readers. Previous studies have focused mainly on the earliest period of the journal's existence, when Korczak edited it himself and passed on his own initiatives and ideas. They are more concerned with the fight for children's rights and topics involving relationships between children and adults. They often simply forget that *Mały Przegląd* was aimed at Jewish children and young adults, and as a result it featured themes relevant to this group. Apart from that, *Mały Przegląd* has mainly been studied by scholars of Korczak's ideas, experts on education and on children's literature. In analyzing *Mały Przegląd*, the authors refer to Korczak's educational achievements rather than to analogous periodicals for Jewish children, and make no comparisons with other periodicals for Jewish children, especially children from Zionist families. As a result, although the innovative nature of *Mały Przegląd* has been noticed, the similarities between certain educational ideas and Zionist thinking has been overlooked.

The problem is that although many people have researched *Mały Przegląd*, they have done it in a very specific way. Analysis of this magazine is weighed down by knowledge about the future of its editors and readers, and above all the fate of Korczak. It is hard to forget that almost the entire editorial team, including Janusz Korczak, and most of the readers, were killed during the war. Another problem is that *Mały Przegląd* has chiefly been regarded as source

---

13 Ibid., 36.
14 "Narada przełomowa" [The breakthrough session], *Mały Przegląd* [hereafter MP], 6 XI 1936: 1.

material for analyzing Korczak's educational ideas. Thus, the authors have focused on the texts he wrote and published there (perhaps also because these texts are included in his collected works, making them easier to access), but they overlook the main body of the magazine—the articles written by children. Many of the essays repeat references to the same trivial episodes, described in the first few issues of the periodical. None includes a shadow of criticism or doubt about whether everything that was presented to the children on the pages of *Mały Przegląd* was first-rate and flawless.

The editors of both supplements faced the problem of trying to publish a journal that would appeal to very small children as well as to adolescents. When it first appeared, *Dzienniczek* aimed to reach a very wide age group. It included stories for the smallest preschool children, as well as replies from the editors to letters sent in by readers who were close to adulthood. At first the magazine was very conservative, the articles were instructive, and the items for the youngest readers took the form of nineteenth-century cautionary tales. The older readers must have found them quite annoying. Most articles did not focus on Jewish matters, but instead stressed the development of positive character traits, above all caring for those weaker than oneself, being charitable, and helping the sick and the poor (surprisingly, it was rarely the so-called "acts of politeness," but mischievous children, especially boys, who were treated with sympathy). The editors responded to the readers' complaints: "*Dzienniczek*'s goal is not just to foster ethnic awareness (though we do put it in first place), but also to have an educational influence on children and friendly coexistence with them. It is not only young adults who read *Dzienniczek*, but also the youngest generation, so we have to include a variety of articles, for older and younger readers."[15] Yet despite such a convincing argument, moral tales soon disappeared from the magazine.

Mały Przegląd faced a similar problem, and explained its difficulty to its readers in a similar way. The readers (whom Korczak called the associates) included very small children who dictated their letters to their parents, or sent in just a few lines scrawled on postcards, as well as adolescents on the verge of adulthood. There can be no doubt that the former were better suited to Korczak—he was interested in the problems of children, not maturing adolescents. In one of the earliest issues of the magazine he responded to the charges of older readers (which were first included in issue number four) that it wasn't a magazine for them, and that it should be split into a section for children and a

---

15 Letters to the editors, Dz, 18 X 1928, no. 12 (279): 6.

section for adolescents. Korczak explained that adolescents had more opportunities to express themselves—they had books, discussion groups, and theatres, and were less controlled by adults, so did not have as great a need for the magazine as did the younger children. But in view of the fact that the magazine's name implied that it was also for adolescents, it would feature a corner specially designed for them. However, Korczak did not feel competent to decide how this corner should appear, so a competition was announced for an "adolescents' prospectus."

The periodicals followed the same path. In the 1930s, especially in the latter part of that decade, both aimed their contents at older readers, practically forgetting the youngest children. The articles grew longer and longer (especially in *Mały Przegląd*), related to specific problems, and were written in increasingly complex language. The ordinary, domestic topics were more and more often replaced by standard journalism and social issues. *Mały Przegląd* almost entirely ceased to publish short, one-sentence letters from readers.

The attitude toward parents is very interesting. In both *Mały Przegląd* and *Dzienniczek*, mothers are especially present; they are usually shown as protective people whose intentions are good, but not always well implemented, and—for the youngest children in particular—irreplaceable. But although mothers are appreciated, loyalty to them is not obligatory—which is especially striking in *Dzienniczek*. Young people not only have the right to their own choices in life (in both periodicals), but additionally in *Dzienniczek* they have a moral obligation to abandon their family, even when it needed their support, in order to leave for Eretz Israel. In this regard, *Mały Przegląd* is immeasurably more traditional. Young people, even those who emigrate to Palestine, maintain contact with their families, and above all—which is crucial—they miss them, and regard the necessity of abandoning them as a very painful loss. The new homeland can never fully compensate for having to leave one's closest relatives behind in Poland—family is no less important a value than homeland. But the attitude to mothers expressed in *Mały Przegląd* is also complicated. On the one hand, it is often much more traditional than in *Dzienniczek*. Each year *Mały Przegląd* published a special issue for Mother's Day. From the items included in it, a rather nineteenth-century image of mothers emerges—tired, worn out, and utterly devoted to their children. Thus, the women's task is to bring up the children (which, as we should note, is contrary to openly promoted gender equality), and at the same time this upbringing is generally presented as a string of sacrifices that has no reward, for children go their own way in any case, and a mother's authority ends as soon as they reach adolescence. However, by contrast with other children's periodicals, the mothers in *Mały Przegląd* very often cannot understand their own children and unwittingly cause them grief by failing to meet their basic needs—for example, they don't respect their children's studies, and prevent them from doing their homework, because their own concerns are more important. Yet almost every letter that is critical about mothers ends with the conclusion that essentially Mama is good, loving, and caring, but she isn't aware of the child's feelings.[16]

The next problem involves gender—in the interwar period, sexual equality had rising significance in education. Many of the children's and young people's periodicals contributed to the equality debate, including the popular *Płomyczek* (a newspaper for younger children, edited together with *Płomyk*). Much space is devoted to this issue in *Mały Przegląd*—throughout its existence it included debates on the duties of girls and boys, their merits and faults, their social roles, and the superiority of one sex over the other. In other words, this important question is discussed—naturally, at the level of children's debate, but the reader is shown that it exists and matters. However, in *Mały Przegląd*, even during these debates, the correspondents usually stress the "difference" between the sexes. Girls and boys differ in many features (though there is no ultimate agreement about which). They can do the same things, and can be friends, yet girls are frequently ascribed typical women's roles. Among other places, the differences in approach to the roles of women and men are apparent in the one-sentence references to Palestine. The boys dream of becoming soldiers, doctors, or engineers there, while the girls don't think about their professional future—either they simply want to go to Palestine, or else they write about their dream of Eretz Israel becoming a homeland for the Jews. Yet from its earliest years *Mały Przegląd* explained to its readers that certain features of the way women were treated were a remnant of the past, and should be forgotten in the modern day—so-called "chivalry toward women," for example. It is absurd when adults insist that boys should be "nice to little girls." You should be nice to everyone. A badly treated boy won't feel any better than a badly treated girl. Today, girls and boys study together, and women go to work, just as men do. So, there is no reason to treat girls differently. Another very interesting detail here is the example cited—some boys had rebelled against having to set out the benches before lessons, while the girls were let off this task; the teacher had conceded that the boys were right. Thus, total gender equality and nondiscrimination was being

---

16 "O naszych matkach" [About our mothers], 26 V 1933, no. 146 (3846): 2.

encouraged.[17] In 1933, a female reader called for the debate to stop, because everything had already been said by now: "There's no need to keep going on about the differences, to keep evaluating the opposite sex—but now there is a need to consider in longer and more reasoned articles the way the genders treat each other, because they are both going to exist—like it or not, we're all entering adult life together. The further we go, the more common tasks we shall have, common aims, efforts and difficulties to surmount."[18] And, indeed, topics to do with gender appear slightly less often in the second half of the 1930s, when the magazine was aimed at older readers and began to touch on a far greater number of "serious" political and cultural topics. But that doesn't mean such issues disappeared entirely. In 1934, a female reader complained that it's fashionable to be a tomboy, and that girls despise typical women's occupations, such as needlework:

> I realize that nowadays "masculinity" is in fashion ... Frankly it's nothing but a herd instinct—girls declaring themselves en masse to be tomboys, as if they'd been conscripted. A girl who doesn't know how to darn and crochet is "masculine," meaning a positive type, and she's pleased. But it's a pity. Because there's a very great deal that women could accomplish without losing their special characteristics.[19]

Yet one might wonder whether *Dzienniczek* didn't go a step further in promoting equality. In fact, it contains no debate about the role of women, and no articles directly concerned with the topic, but the attitude that emerges from its articles on completely different topics is unambiguous. There are no differences in the aspirations, duties, or opportunities in life for both sexes. In *Dzienniczek*, the girls and boys who are going to the Land of Israel are destined for identical roles. If equality isn't put into practice, the result will be discrimination against the girls—and this is presented as an injustice, a mistake on the part of the organizers. In a report from a kibbutz near Haifa the author complained that for eighteen months the girls did nothing but the simplest jobs on the farm; additionally, they had few opportunities for advancement: "The boys learned crafts in the city, or worked on the farm, but the girls never went further than domestic occupations: cooking, cleaning, doing the laundry, and that was

---

17 "Rycerskość dla kobiet" [Chivalry for women], MP, 4 II 1927, no. 35 (1475): 8.
18 Lila, "My—dziewczęta" [Us—girls], 24 XI 1933, no. 329 (4029): 1.
19 Wia, "Pobór na chłopczyce" [A call-up for tomboys], MP, 8 VI 1934, no. 152 (4232): 1.

their entire job, to tell the truth, a ghastly one." Only building their own house with their own hands led to the girls finding reasonable and useful occupations, and they started taking turns at work in the kitchen or the garden, although the Arabs—who would stop by for a friendly chat with the kibbutzniks—were surprised to see them doing typically men's jobs.[20] Nor, however, were any mothers sacrificing themselves for their children—both parents brought up their children at the kibbutz collective, and both derived satisfaction from doing so.

Evidently, both periodicals broke with tradition, while at the same time they did their best to foster that tradition, in order to prevent the assimilation of their readers, who were in any case already acculturated. One element that maintained tradition was the celebration of festivals, and both *Mały Przegląd* and *Dzienniczek* observed all the major Jewish holidays. Paradoxically, however, it was *Mały Przegląd* that stressed their religious significance from the start. *Dzienniczek*, until the mid-1930s at any rate, told its readers that celebrating festivals had a traditional rather than a religious dimension—with every candle he or she lights, a Jew connects with other Jews all over the Diaspora, and cherishes the memory of the Land of Israel. Purely religious tones, in any case secondary to those relating to identity, only appeared toward the end of *Dzienniczek*'s existence. One might ask if this was intentional, or if differences in educational tone were due to differences between potential readers. *Mały Przegląd* was distributed in Warsaw, home to a large number of traditional, religious Jews, while *Dzienniczek* was a journal for the far more assimilated residents of Kraków.

But the real difference that leaps out at us is in their educational aims. *Mały Przegląd* tried to educate its readers above all to be responsible, independent people who thought for themselves. In fact, the attitude toward independent thinking took various forms in Korczak's day—he could be highly critical of a child whose views he disagreed with, but a diverse range of political, religious, and moral choices was allowed. The magazine included continuous debate on how to behave, but without providing unambiguous answers. In this regard, *Mały Przegląd* was unique, offering a multitude of solutions, but never a one and only correct path.

Dzienniczek's ideology, by comparison, was to raise young Jews to be Zionists, future citizens of Eretz Israel. Everything was subordinate to this purpose. Here there was no room for personal views or even debate of any

---

20   The Ahawar youth group, Haifa, "Praca w troskach i radości. Reportaż palestyński" [Labour full of concern and joy. A reportage from Palestine], Dz, 3 II 1939, no. 34: 9–10.

kind. This is curious, considering that both periodicals were aimed at the same young people.

For readers of *Dzienniczek* in the first period, from 1928 to 1934, Poland was totally "nonexistent." Readers of *Dzienniczek* only had one homeland—Palestine. That is exactly how it was always defined: "the homeland," "our homeland," and never, as in many other Jewish periodicals, "the second homeland," "the old homeland," or even "the long-awaited homeland." There was never the faintest suggestion that the reader might also identify with Poland as his or her country.

Even when they received letters on apparently neutral topics—for instance, the correspondent would write that he preferred summer to winter—the editors would instantly try to find some reference to Palestine. They would reply that they too prefer the summer, and that in our homeland it lasts much longer.[21] When a little girl wrote that the spring is not a sorceress but a season, the editors replied: "You are right, little girl, the spring is not a lady out of a fairy tale, but a season of the year. The poets, who have a gift for beautiful expression, extol its charm and loveliness. Our poetry is the spring that is present in Eretz Israel."[22]

The most frequent device was to show the contrast between flourishing Israel and the inhospitable, not very lovely, gray reality of *Golus*, or exile. In a story titled "The Passover Picture," some children from an impecunious family in Palestine hear adults' tales about "the tough lot of our Jewish brothers for many a long century. Ever more frequently the children utter the words: 'Eretz,' 'Land.' And on the canvas of the story images gradually blossom forth about our own settlements in our own Land, within a ring of flower gardens and orange-tree orchards."[23] The descriptions of Palestine are designed to build a myth. Not only is there is nothing ugly there, but there is also actually nothing ordinary, everyday, or banal. It is the land of our dreams, described in a poetic way, rather than any kind of true reality. "I cherished you, O land of my fathers, in never-ending, sun-scorched days when the sand burned the soles of our bare feet, and the air was aglow, as in the bowl of a smelting crucible, when the whole world was consumed by eager longing. I came to love you in the transparency of bright luminous nights, when the world was wrapped in a veil of lights and shades. I fell in love with you on days of unbridled joy, when I long to sing

---

21   Dz, 4 I 1929, no. 1 (4): 6.
22   Answers from the editor, 7 III 1931, no. 5 (65): 6.
23   Blanka Hollaendrowa, "Obrazek Pesachowy" [An image from Pesach], Dz. 16 V 1932, no. 7 (104): 11.

and dance without end. And on days of gloom, when my eyes are misted with tears."[24]

Another standard feature is to describe life in Palestine as collective activity at all times—every single description involves people working together or playing together. No one does anything on their own, and the basis for life to function is the collective. This contrasts with the reality of the Diaspora, where the loneliness of the Jews is stressed above all. Other journals and memoirs very often stressed "duality"—a sense of having two homelands, or at least an attachment to "the minor homeland." Not only is this never featured in the pages of *Dzienniczek*, at least in the initial phase, but the completely alien nature of one's present environment was directly emphasized. In an article about *Chwilka* and the way Palestine is depicted there, Agnieszka Karczewska has drawn attention to a very interesting issue: "Eretz was spoken about ... by exploiting the very positive, high-value categories of light or its brightness, and also through comparison with the rising sun, or daybreak.... This sort of imagery appeared quite regularly and relied on contrasting the night, darkness, and evil, equated with the diaspora ('Golus'), with the radiant, friendly Palestinian earth."[25] The readers of *Dzienniczek* were given exactly the same image, even after Ruta Reimanowa had left the editorial team—and so there was more to it than just a particular editorial approach.

However, from 1935 to 1936 this perspective changed, as a result of news about Arab attacks on kibbutzim. But that was probably not the only factor. The approaching end of peace in Europe could also have prompted people to start to perceive the threat of war, and to feel the need to prepare young people to fight—not just against the Arabs. Something returns that was mentioned at the very start of the magazine's existence—the Arabs as a source of danger. But now fighting against the Arabs was not merely information on the front page. For the first time, young people were informed that in Palestine they would not just have to work, but also fight—and that they must prepare themselves for this too. Why did the magazine's outlook change? Perhaps it was simply because of the change of editor, or it reflected a change of attitude toward Poland, too.

---

24 Ester Cahnanit, VIII year [elementary/common] school pupil in Jerusalem, "Ojczyzno!" [Oh, my homeland!], Dz, 19 XI 1932, no. 18 (314): 11.
25 Agnieszka Karczewska, "Stary-nowy kraj—obraz Erec Israel w *Chwilce* Dzieci i Młodzieży (1925–1937)" [Old-new country—the image of Eretz Israel in *Chwilka* for Children and Youth"]: 305–6, in *Stare i nowe—czasopisma dla dzieci i młodzieży* [Old and new—periodicals for children and youth], ed. Bożena Olszewska, Elżbieta Łucka-Zając (Opole: Uniwersytet Opolski, 2013), 305–6.

Or an increasing number of emigrants, who instead of dreaming about Palestine had come up against the real living and working conditions there—although their enthusiasm may not have waned, they must have replaced the poetic vision of the homeland with experience of real life in it, which was always far from the ideal.

And here *Mały Przegląd* differs from *Dzienniczek*. Its readers were meant to regard Poland as their homeland first and foremost, and in the later years, when Palestinian patriotism appears, too, their lives still went on in Poland, and Polish problems were very relevant. Of course, leaving for Palestine, at any rate in the later years, was supported in every respect, but this had no effect at all on Polish patriotism. In Korczak's day, denying Polish patriotism was regarded as downright reprehensible. To a letter sent in by a reader, in which she describes how she went on a school trip to a synagogue on November 11, 1927, and when Rabbi Szor (as his name appears in the text—it is usually spelled Schorr) ended his sermon with the cry "Long Live the Polish Republic, long live independence," she sat down and twice made a rude gesture at him, Korczak reacted sharply. He mentioned Poland's misfortunes, the uprisings and wars, and to conclude he wrote:

> Whom did you insult, silly little Celinka, so arrogant and capricious? Do you think that if Poland ever puts up a monument to this dismal century—alongside the commanders and peasants, the worker and the priest, don't you think there will be a Jew? He was here, he lived, suffered, died, has blended with the earth and circulates in the tree sap ... There's always a scoundrel who'll thumb his nose or stick out his tongue, but you must break free and reject all this, because what will be must be. Unless you are faking your surprise and joy that Palestine is rising from the rubble, you cannot be indifferent to the resurrection of Poland.[26]

In *Mały Przegląd*, Palestine is no longer a bright land flowing with milk and honey, but a very real country. It had its pluses and minuses, some people lived pretty well there, while others gave up after a time and came back to Poland. The most striking feature of the articles in *Mały Przegląd* is that Palestine is regarded as just one of many foreign countries—a bit closer to the readers than others, but only sporadically regarded as their homeland. It is a country where

---

26 MP, 11 XI 1927, no. 58, quoted in: Janusz Korczak, *Dzieła. Prawidła życia. Publicystyka dla dzieci* [The works. The precepts of life. Journalism for children], vol. 11, part II.

many people had relatives, and which a surprisingly large number of children had visited, or were planning to visit as soon as possible. Here Palestine is not just a country to which you emigrate—an idea found in other Zionist magazines, too—but which you come back from. It is also a country you can visit as a tourist, just like many others: "A pupil in the sixth form would like to travel to Palestine where there are lots of ancient relics, and all over the world as well."[27]

All the published texts by correspondents expressed hope that an independent Jewish state would be created. Successes were a cause for joy and fighting against the Arabs and the attitude of the British were causes for concern. But leaving for Palestine was just one potential choice, admittedly worthy of respect, but neither a necessity nor a duty. Even the totally unquestionable issue, both in *Dzienniczek* and other Zionist magazines for children, of love for Palestine is challenged by some readers. Here one can plainly see the magazine's lack of a uniform policy and its presentation of extremely varied, often controversial opinions. In 1934, in a letter about issues to do with war and nationalism, a correspondent questions whether Polish Jews really can be attached to Palestine as a homeland. Palestinian nationalism, even affection for Palestine, is sheer ideology, and yearning for it is a form of subordination to its demands:

> Yearning for one's homeland as for a place with which a person has become intimate is innate, but only if it is real yearning for a place to which a person is properly tied. Yearning for a country which one has never seen at all is quite another matter. And yet in *Mały Przegląd* there have been letters, and even poems, expressing a great yearning for Palestine, although their authors wrote that they only knew the place from descriptions. I do not mean to regard these doubtful nostalgia-lovers as hypocrites. They have been persuaded, even given orders to yearn for it, so they have come to believe it, and they really do yearn for it.[28]

According to another letter in the same issue:

> I go about the streets like a sleepwalker, stiff and indifferent to everything, resigned to all, except for one thing. I want to go to *hakhshara*, and to Palestine. O God, as I utter the word *Eretz* can't you see the tears welling in my eyes, the sobs that are choking me? Can't you see that they're tears

---

27 "Z kraju" [From the homeland], 25 III 1927, no. 84 (1504), no. 25: 10.
28 Szmul R., "Wojenko, wojenko...," ["Oh war, my war..."], MP 18 V 1934, no. 140 (4210): 2.

of despair and torment? I am no longer capable of any action. All I can so is dream...."²⁹

Thus, in the late 1930s the readers of both magazines wrote of two homelands, although *Mały Przegląd* emphasizes Poland, while *Dzienniczek* longs for Eretz Israel.

It is generally accepted that *Mały Przegląd* was a unique magazine, with entirely innovative educational solutions—or, rather, a magazine that did not state solutions, and was written by its own readers, providing questions and problems but giving no unambiguous answers. In other words, it was a magazine that couldn't be compared with any other. However, this evaluation is not entirely correct. A great deal has been written about the fact the *Mały Przegląd* was a journal for children, about children's problems. That is true. But on closer inspection the values it promoted cease to be quite so exceptional and innovative.

What is stressed above all in *Mały Przegląd*—both in Korczak's time and later—is the call to challenge the authority of adults. Adults could be both good and bad. Trusting them, carrying out their instructions, heading in the directions shown by them depended on a judgment—often made by the children themselves—of whether or not their stances were right. Children were supposed to make decisions about their own lives to a far greater extent than was generally accepted at the time, and even these days, too. They were to be treated as thinking beings, but above all as people who made decisions about communal matters. *Mały Przegląd*, which aimed for its readers to remain in Poland, shows young people rebelling against adults. Especially in its first phase, when Korczak was its editor, this rebellion was fully understandable. Even at a later stage, it published numerous letters against teachers who had offended young people, or who had taken revenge on children for alleged misdeeds and insults. Parents were slightly better, but they too did not fully understand the new times and their children's aspirations. Thus, a critical attitude toward the older generation was usually fully approved. However, there was no promotion of individualism. Children's collective organizations and autonomous bodies were regarded as the ideal decision-making teams for issues affecting young people. This too was regarded as a total innovation. Yet it ceased to be quite so unambiguously new within education when we look at other magazines for children from the same

---

29 Heniek ze Świętojerskiej, "Myślą Marzą" [Heniek of Świetojerska Street, "They think, they dream"], "Do Erec" [To Eretz], MP, 18 V 1934, no. 140 (4210): 3.

environment. The point is not that, in its clumsy attempt to model itself on *Mały Przegląd*, *Dzienniczek* also introduced the principle of publishing its readers' works or tried to create a group of "correspondents." In an entirely different way from *Mały Przegląd* (and perhaps to an even greater extent), *Dzienniczek* promoted the independence of young people from adults, family, and tradition. In fact, in the stories it published in its earliest years for the youngest readers, we do find a few fables about obedience, and in the editors' replies to letters we find the statement that parents make the decisions about their children's upbringing. But in later years, this message entirely disappeared. The educational ideal promoted by *Dzienniczek* stressed life among one's peers preparing to leave for Eretz Israel, and doing as your scout leaders say—people almost as young as their subordinates. Parents, family, school, and teachers—all these ceased to matter. "Young and healthy"—this phrase is constantly repeated. I do not think that this is just a device to show young readers that their age is not an obstacle to leaving the country (even sixteen-year-olds were encouraged to go), but rather that it is a way of breaking away from the classic image of the experienced old Jew, sitting over his books. Youth and physical health become incomparably more important than theoretical studies (apart, perhaps, from the study of Hebrew). A young person should be independent and self-reliant, and should choose to live in Palestine. And Palestine is shown as a land of exclusively young people, a land without hierarchy, including within the family. The families there are ideal, the young parents (and not just the mothers!) take care of the children, although they usually live apart. It was strongly stressed that in Eretz Israel children and adults do not live in separate worlds. The kibbutz is a world of nothing but young people, managing independently. In other words, though in an entirely different way, both magazines showed their readers that the world of young people, fundamentally different from the world of adults, should matter to them, and that they must build this new world for themselves, without looking back at tradition or the demands of the older generation. In fact, this was never written about directly, but *Mały Przegląd*, by contrasting the two worlds, and *Dzienniczek*, by showing the unsuitability of the old norms to a future life in Palestine, unambiguously cut themselves off from traditional Jewish life. Thus, both magazines became part of the educational model that was extremely popular in the 1920s, and was promoted by the left as well as the right—and definitely in Zionist circles—of forming a "new man," and counting on youth to do it. The young—not purely in the biological sense, but young people as opposed to fossilized "old" ones—were the world's future. They had to—more so in the case of *Dzienniczek*, less in the case of *Mały Przegląd*—mentally separate themselves from the old world, the old traditions, and elaborate a new and better world (the only difference was their vision of this future ideal).

This essay has offered a very general outline of the issues concerned, but examining the place of *Mały Przegląd* among other, similar periodicals for Polish-language Jewish youth requires a new approach and further research.

Translated from Polish by Antonia Lloyd-Jones

Legitimizing the Revolution: Sarah Schenirer and the Rhetoric of Torah Study for Girls

NAOMI SEIDMAN

By the time Sarah Schenirer died in 1935, the movement she had started in 1917 to provide Orthodox girls with a rigorous Jewish education was already well established, with over 200 schools and 38,000 students throughout Poland and beyond.[1] These students were enrolled in a wide range of

---

1 These numbers are taken from Alexander Zusya Friedman, "Foreword," in Hillel Seidman, *Dos yidishe religyeze shul-vesn in di romn fun der poylisher gezetzgebung* [Jewish religious schools in the context of Polish legislation] (Warsaw: Horev, 1937), 8. See also Joseph Carlebach, "Keren Hathora-Fahrt zu Jüdischen Kultur-Stätten des Ostens" [The trip of the Keren Hathora group to Jewish cultural centers in the East] in *Ausgewählte Schriften: Band II* [Selected writings: Volume II] (Hildesheim, New York: G. Olms Verlag, 1982), 1103–83, which documents a trip undertaken in July and August of 1934 by the German Jewish leadership of Keren Hatorah, the educational wing of Agudat Israel, to Eastern Europe, which lists 187 Polish Bais Yaakov schools, seminaries, and colonies (some still in the process of being formed), and another 23 in Austria (including the teachers' seminary in Vienna), Czechoslovakia, Romania, and Hungary. Such figures, as Yosef Friedenson acknowledges, are hard to establish with any certainty, given the number of schools (especially the afternoon schools in smaller towns) that opened and closed and contradictory figures provided by the movement and those who studied it. Friedenson himself tentatively relies on internal Bais Yaakov figures from 1935 of 225 schools with 27,119 students in Poland; 18 schools with 1,569 students in Czechoslovakia; 18 schools with 1,292 students in Romania; 16 schools with 2,000 students in Lithuania, and 11 schools with 950 students in Austria. See Yosef Friedenson, "Batey hasefer levanot beyt-Yaakov bepolin" [The Beit Yakov girls' schools in Poland], in *Hahinukh vehatarbut ha-ivrit be-eyropa beyn shtey milkhamot ha'olam* [Jewish education and culture in Europe between the two World Wars], ed. Tzvi Sharfstein (New York, 1957), 71.

programs: full-time elementary and high schools, in which Jewish as well as secular subjects were taught, thus allowing Orthodox girls to fulfill compulsory education requirements in a Jewish setting; afternoon religious schools; vocational training programs, in which students could study both Jewish subjects and dressmaking, secretarial skills, bookkeeping, or even nursing (these vocational schools were later called Ohel Sarah, after Schenirer); and the crown jewels of the system, the teachers' seminaries in Kraków, Vienna, and Czernovitz. Schenirer also co-founded the youth movement Bnos Agudas Yisroel and was instrumental in establishing the women's organization of Aguda. Schenirer thus invented what has been described as the single most important development of twentieth-century Orthodoxy: the Bais Yaakov student, whose knowledge of and passion for Torah reinvigorated Orthodoxy as a whole at a moment of great danger. While the radical spirit of its origins had already diminished by the 1930s, the Bais Yaakov movement saw a rebirth after the Holocaust and continues to flourish throughout the Jewish world.

The role of Schenirer as founding figure is central to contemporary Bais Yaakov culture, as it was at its origins. Bais Yaakov girls everywhere know the story of the pious seamstress who saw the need to teach girls Torah, lest they be swept away from Orthodoxy by the lures of modern life. Orthodox hagiography often presents these beginnings as a creation ex nihilo, in which a simple woman sought to bring the garments of Torah to the "naked" souls of Orthodox girls. Yet Schenirer's modesty hardly explains the distinctive features of the movement or its astonishingly rapid success. Bais Yaakov succeeded despite a formidable set of obstacles, including a 1903 rabbinical decision against organized religious education for girls; arbitrary legislation by the Polish government concerning religious schools; and, as Schenirer lamented, the hostility to religion among the Jewish girls of her time. As I will argue, the achievements of Bais Yaakov should be traced not to a rejection of these challenges from the right and left, but rather to their dialectical incorporation; in revolutionizing Orthodoxy in the name of tradition, the movement brought together innovative and conservative impulses to create an unprecedented culture.

When Schenirer assembled twenty-five girls in her seamstress's studio in 1917, the Orthodox Jewish world lacked not only an established framework for educating girls, but also a coherent rhetoric that could establish Jewish girls' Torah study as legitimate and valuable, or which placed value on youth, women, or innovation. While Torah study—often read as Talmud—is central to masculine identity, various rabbinic passages explicitly forbid such study for girls. Despite the deep suspicion of innovation among traditionalist Jews, the community not only accepted but even embraced this new movement. How can we explain this? Agnieszka Oleszak has recently argued that the success of the movement followed from a number of critical developments in Poland: the granting of women's right to vote in 1918, the Aguda's involvement in Polish politics and recruitment of Jewish voters, and "the 1919 compulsory education law."[2] Political factors paved the way for Orthodox support, but without Schenirer's rhetorical and organizational genius, the movement could hardly have taken off. Bais Yaakov functioned, in the early years, as a missionary movement in which graduates of the summer teacher-training course were sent out "into the field" to found new schools. Among Schenirer's accomplishments was the construction of a discourse that could energize these social entrepreneurs, drawing on their youth (some were as young as fifteen) as a mobilizing factor and finding Jewish resources for female empowerment.

The distinctive culture that Schenirer helped create was a confluence of contradictory cultural influences. Schenirer's writings attest not only to her deep piety but also to her cosmopolitan sensibility. According to her memoir, the vision of religious education for Jewish girls emerged from a fateful encounter Schenirer had in Vienna, where her family had fled during the First World War. Attending the Orthodox synagogue in the Stumpergasse of Rabbi Moshe Flesch, Schenirer was inspired at hearing the rabbi deliver a sermon directed to women congregants, something unknown in her hasidic milieu. As Shenirer relates in her memoir, *Bleter fun mayn lebn* (Pages from My Life), the rabbi spoke passionately about the figure of Judith, "calling on contemporary women to follow the example of this historical heroine." Schenirer continues,

> I felt immediately that the main thing missing is that our sisters know so little about their past and this alienates them from our people and their traditions. In my mind, at that moment, were born various grandiose plans.[3]

---

2 See Agnieszka M. Oleszak, "The Beit Ya'akov School in Kraków as an Encounter between East and West," *Polin* 23 (2010): 281. For support for Oleszak's argument that the Agudat Israel adoption of Bais Yaakov was partly motivated by electoral concerns, see the many political advertisements in the Bais Yaakov journal, urging readers to vote for Aguda in local and national elections.

3 Sarah Schenirer, "Bleter fun mayn lebn" [Pages from my life], in *Gezamlte shriften* [Selected works] (Brooklyn: Bais Yaakov Teachers Seminary in America, 1956), 9.

This debt to German-Jewish neo-Orthodoxy, following the teachings of Samson Raphael Hirsch, is duly recorded as the very origin for the project of educating girls.

A second influence was cosmopolitan Kraków, with its public lectures, youth movements, and political activism. Schenirer often described herself as *competing* with these cultural options. In fact, Schenirer both resisted and borrowed from the atmosphere that celebrated youth, self-education, and cultural engagement. This influence is particularly evident in the Bnos movement, which adapted a host of practices from socialist and Zionist youth movements, including self-governance, hiking and nature activities, summer camps, and even "kibbutzim."

A third influence was Hasidism. Schenirer, who was raised in a Belzer hasidic family and proceeded with her plans only after receiving the blessing of the Belzer rebbe, recreated some of the atmosphere of the hasidic court in the ecstatic singing and dancing that were a part of Bais Yaakov, as well as in the social networks of graduating teachers, who were sent to small towns to spread the Bais Yaakov word.

Perhaps the most salient model for the Bais Yaakov movement was the yeshiva. The Bais Yaakov movement followed, in accelerated fashion, the pattern of growth of the yeshiva, from small study groups reliant on local community support to well-endowed institutions in major cities that attracted students from throughout Europe and even America. It is no surprise that the first Bais Yaakov high school was established in Poniewież (Ponevezh/Panevėžys), site of the world-famous yeshiva, or that the same Aguda conference that adopted Bais Yaakov also founded the elite Yeshivat Hokhmei Lublin. Schenirer herself avoided such comparisons, carefully maintaining the separation between girls' and boys' education in terminology and refraining from teaching Talmud.

While the Bais Yaakov movement borrowed freely from both traditionalizing and modernizing currents of its environment, its discourse strategically left some of these currents unstated. Schenirer framed her project as a traditionalist response to the lures of the modern city, underplaying the degree to which modernization was both a *threat* to Jewish culture and a *resource* for combating this threat. Bais Yaakov was a *product* of Jewish modernity, beginning with the influence of the neo-Orthodox slogan "Torah im Derekh Eretz," Torah with secular/practical education, a program that found initial expression in the Hirsch school system and was adopted by Bais Yaakov. The innovations introduced by Bais Yaakov included formal curriculum, teacher training, improved textbooks, the daily schedule of classes and the ringing of bells to mark the change of classes, the modern appearance of the schools, the emphasis on hygiene, the kindergarten as a unit, the introduction of secular studies and, particularly, of vocational training, physical education as a part of the curriculum, the use of modern facilities such as gymnasia and laboratories, the exposure to world literature and art, and, lastly, the conceptualization of "Judaism" as a subject area.

Indeed, after the 1923 adoptions of the movement by the Aguda, Bais Yaakov schools were staffed by educators and administrators brought from Germany, Austria, and Switzerland, including most prominently Judith Rosenbaum, who was working on a doctorate in education from the University of Frankfurt when she was recruited to train Bais Yaakov teachers in Kraków; Schenirer also raised funds among Central European Jews.

Perhaps ironically, the modern educational methods established by Schenirer may well have served to secure a place for Jewish girls' education within Orthodoxy because Bais Yaakov also reaffirmed the traditional principle of sexual segregation. Sarah Schenirer could provide a "modern" Orthodox education to early twentieth-century Jewish girls because as long as traditional sexual segregation was maintained, what went on in women's spheres—as long as it made no inroads into the male sphere—need not overly concern the rabbis.

In fact, Bais Yaakov schools produced not female counterparts of their learned brothers, but a distinct culture of gendered learning practices. The denominational distinction between centrist and neo-Orthodoxy, or the geographical distinction between German Jewish and Eastern European Jewry, thus reappears as a *gender* distinction within Eastern European Orthodoxy, with girls inhabiting a more "modern" and "Central European" world than their male counterparts.

In this sense, sexual segregation marked the limits of the Bais Yaakov revolution; in another sense, it was the most powerful tool in the movement, enabling Schenirer to harness the energy of same-sex community in clubs, summer courses, retreats, and camps. Memoirs of the early years attest to the strong connections forged among the Bais Yaakov girls in ceremonies, anthems, special holidays and celebrations, literature, and songs.

Schenirer was not only the revered founder of these movements, but also wrote its first textbooks, sewed lace collars for early classes as a kind of badge or uniform, composed plays to be performed at Jewish holidays, and spoke at meetings and graduations. She was often referred to as "the mother" of the movement, but she just as frequently referred to her students as "sisters," stressing not the maternal connection that located these relationships within the traditional terrain of the Jewish family but rather the spirit that linked her project to the youth movements of her day. In one speech to a Bnos group, Schenirer exhorted the girls: "Youth means: Happiness, courage, optimism, and faith in ancient ideals! Pessimism, doubt, sadness is anti-Youth! Youth means: enthusiasm, living and striving! Our youth movement must have life!"[4] The radical elements in this discourse also differentiated Bais Yaakov from the German Jewish neo-Orthodox discourse on femininity, which was strongly influenced by the bourgeois culture of the period. Rabbi Samson Raphael Hirsch mobilized a discourse of women's special religious feelings and their responsibility to raise Jewish children in the 1850s, as part of his own campaign for girls' education. Such family-oriented ideologies were not entirely absent from early Bais Yaakov literature. But equally prominent, especially in Schenirer's own writings, were motifs that emphasized sisterly solidarity and the school as a *replacement*, rather than a building block, for the building of Jewish families.

Despite the apparently radical nature of Schenirer's revolution, she did find support among the Orthodox leadership. Such rabbinical opinions could rely on the distinction, by now canonical in the literature of Bais Yaakov, between the study of "written Torah," which is permissible for girls and women, and the study of "oral Torah" (primarily the Talmud), which is forbidden to them. It is striking, then, that although such arguments were in principle available, the best-known responsa took an entirely different approach. Rabbi Yisroel Hacohen, the Chofetz Chayim, issued a responsum on Beis Yaakov first in 1918 and then in 1933:

> To the esteemed champions and lovers of Torah, the God-fearers [*haredim*] who are in the city of Fristik, may God bless them and protect them.[5]
>
> When I heard that God-fearing [*haredim*] people had volunteered to establish Bais Yaakov schools in the cities to teach Torah and piety, moral virtues and secular/practical studies [*derekh eretz*] and Torah to Jewish girls, I pronounced their enterprise praiseworthy and prayed that God would bring their efforts to fruition. Theirs is a great and necessary endeavor in these times, as the tide of heresy and all manners of miscreants are lurking and hunting for Jewish souls. Anyone who is concerned about

---

4 Schenirer, *Gezamelte shriftn*, 43–44.
5 Fristik is a small town in Galicia, known in Polish as Frysztak.

> piety should consider it a mitzvah to enroll his daughter in such a school. Those who have fears and doubts because of the prohibition against teaching their daughters Torah should not concern themselves with that in these times, and this is not the place to explain this at length, for our own times are not like those that have past, when there was a strong tradition of mothers and fathers to go in the path of Torah and religion, and to read the *Tse'ena re'ena* [Bible translation for women] every Sabbath. Due to our many transgressions this is no longer the case. Therefore every effort should be made to establish as many schools of this type as possible and to rescue what can still be rescued.[6]

The Chofetz Chayim's letter is testimony to the principles by which Orthodox authorities overcame their doubts about the value or permissibility of teaching girls Torah. From this perspective, educating Jewish girls, despite being an innovation, is justified because of *hora'at sha'ah*, the needs of the moment; in these times, when long-established practices no longer served as a bulwark against the temptations of modernity, religious schools for girls become an unfortunate necessity.

Schenirer only rarely described her accomplishments as a regretfully necessary response to contemporary conditions. Schenirer's largest and most attentive audience was comprised of girls and women, who required not an apologetic on the legitimacy of their enterprise but rather a rousing call to arms. Thus, at the first International Congress of Orthodox Women, Schenirer began by speaking of modernity as a moment of awakening:

> The Orthodox woman has awakened from her long, lethargic sleep and begun to organize.... Not long after we created the Bnos organization in Poland, the powerful voice of the religious Jewish woman rings out on the world stage. The intellectual Jewish woman is no longer isolated. In every corner of the world she is closely bound to her sisters.
>
> I know well that many religious Jews will view this with suspicion. We hold sacred the ideal of women's modesty. "She is in the tent" [*hineh*

---

6 For the text of this letter, dated 23 Shvat 5693, see Schenirer, *Gezamelte shriftn*, 1, where it serves a secondary function of approbation of Schenirer's writings, alongside the more institutional function of legitimating the movement. The name of the town in which families asked him to rule on the permissibility of Bais Yaakov is often omitted in other Bais Yaakov publications, presumably to widen the reach of the Chofetz Chayim's ruling.

ba'ohel]. Probably a portion of the Orthodox world views our Congress as, God forbid, a transgression. But these Jews need to understand that this conference is an outgrowth of the dangers Jewish women face from various secularist [*freye*] directions. *Es la'asos la'hashem*, It is a time to act for God—from this perspective must our public efforts be understood.[7]

The tensions of Schenirer's project appear in unusually close proximity here. Schenirer begins by celebrating the new visibility of Jewish women, after their long sleep and cultural isolation. She then acknowledges that Jewish tradition prefers Jewish women's modesty and invisibility, coded here in the biblical passage in which Abraham relays to the angels that Sarah is in her tent. Only in addressing these traditionalist doubts does Schenirer refer to the doctrine of "the needs of the hour."

In speaking of girls' formal Torah study, especially to girls, Schenirer rather crafted a discourse that deemed girls' Torah study *inherently* valuable. This is evident even from the name of the movement, Bais Yaakov, which locates textual warrant for the project in Exodus 19, the story of the revelation on Sinai that in Judith Plaskow's groundbreaking feminist manifesto provides painful evidence for women's exclusion from this revelation.[8] Exodus 19:3, which reads "Ko tomar levet ya'akov vetaged levenay yisrael" (Thus shall you say to the house of Jacob and declare to the children of Israel, as quoted from the JPS Tanakh) has long been taken to refer to a kind of double revelation—first to the women (as "the house of Jacob") and then to the men (as "the children of Israel"). Bais Yaakov not only found in this midrashic reading evidence for God's giving the Torah, through Moses, *first* to women, but it also read its own history—also midrashically—into the verse. A trope in the literature is the discovery of the first Bais Yaakov class of twenty-five students embedded in the first word of the verse—*ko*, which in gematriya adds up to twenty-five! This intertextual play extends as well to the ritual realm: among the distinctive holidays of the movement, and the one with no historical precedent, is the celebration of Sivan 3 (three days before the Sinai event, and thus the date of God's message to Moses to teach Torah to women), which became for a time

---

7 Schenirer, "Arum unzer velt-kongres," *Gezamelte shriftn*, 38. The verse in Psalm 119:126 (It is a time to act for the Lord, for they have violated Your teaching) is midrashically and boldly understood as allowing for the violation of the Torah when required for the sake of God. It is interesting, in this regard, that Schenirer leaves the second part of the verse unquoted.

8 See Judith Plaskow, *Standing Again at Sinai: Judaism from a Feminist Perspective* (New York: Harper & Row, 1990).

a Bais Yaakov holiday. In such intertextual and ritual performances, the very innovations of the movement become occasions for discovering traditional precedent, just as the Torah is shown to foresee the rise of the movement at the very moment of Sinaitic revelation.

Another ubiquitous and particularly rich intertextual locus is the association between Sarah Schenirer and her biblical forebear, the matriarch Sarah. Such a connection is evident in the naming of the movement's vocational schools "Ohel Sarah," a reference to the tent in which the biblical Sarah sits (Genesis 18:9), traditionally a sign of her modesty, and also to Schenirer, whose own occupation as a seamstress was among the courses of study at the school. In this name, the tensions between modesty—with which Schenirer is also often associated, precisely through this proof text—and economic self-sufficiency are resolved. Even more regularly, Schenirer is connected with the biblical Sarah in her "barrenness," a description that is regularly qualified with the sentiment that although she "unfortunately had no children of her own," she nurtured thousands of daughters. This rhetoric, too, conceals a submerged tension, since unlike the biblical Sarah, who was indeed long barren, Schenirer was not barren but rather unmarried during the formative years of the movement. The trope of Schenirer as a modern-day Sarah thus not only grounds her life in biblical precedent, but it also obscures her personal choices and domesticates the radical social and cultural practices of the movement she founded in the traditional Jewish language of reproduction, family, and lineage.

The problem of researching Orthodox Jewish women is enormously complicated, and not only for the usual reasons: the neglect of women's history and the paucity of materials on such topics, on the one hand, and the apologetic or hagiographic nature of Orthodox sources, on the other. Certain topics of great interest have been entirely out of bounds, including almost everything about Schenirer's personal life: we know she was married twice, but the name of her first husband and the reasons for the divorce have remained outside the historical record; whether she was compelled to remarry late in life or chose to remarry remains unclear. More generally, the Bais Yaakov story transcends national borders; Central European neo-Orthodoxy was crucial for Schenirer and for Bais Yaakov, and the board of Bais Yaakov included, for example, both Bertha Pappenheim (the German-Jewish Orthodox feminist) and Sara Ann Delano Roosevelt (the mother of FDR). Finally, many neglected records of the movement are probably available in Polish archives and remain to be studied.

One way to conceptualize these challenges is to recognize the degree to which scholarship on Bais Yaakov has commenced in several different spheres: feminist and Yiddishist activists and academics in the United States were among the first to view Schenirer's work as pioneering. Serious research is now taking place among Bais Yaakov teachers and former students throughout the world, some of whom are committed to recapturing some of the energies of the movement in its prime as well as memorializing its founder. And with the work of Polish scholars such as Oleszak, Joanna Lisek, and others, we are finally beginning to put the Bais Yaakov movement in its interwar Polish context.[9] Much remains to be done in all these areas, and collaboration among scholars with different areas of expertise will be critical in the decades to come. But the work will be worth it: that all these research agendas should direct their attention to one woman and the movement she founded is the strongest testimony of the importance and complexity of Schenirer and Bais Yaakov.

---

9 See, for instance, Joanna Lisek, "Orthodox Yiddishism in *Beys Yaakov* Magazine in the Context of Religious Jewish Feminism in Poland," in *Sprach- und Kulturkontakte in Europas Mitte* (Vol. 2: *Ashkenazim and Sephardim: A European Perspective*), ed. Andrzej Kątny, Izabela Olszewska, and Aleksandra Twardowska (Frankfurt am Main: Peter Lang Edition, 2013), 127–54.

Contested Jewish Polishness: Language and Health as Markers for the Position of Jews in Polish Culture and Society in the Interwar Period

KATRIN STEFFEN

The period between 1918 and 1939 was one of transition in Poland. These years were dominated by the complex transformation of the different areas that had formerly been ruled by Prussia, Austria-Hungary, and Russia. The new Poland, as defined by the Versailles Treaty and the Treaty of Riga which ended the Polish–Soviet War, was not a nation-state, but rather, with 30 percent of its population made up of national minorities, to use the terminology developed by Roger Brubaker, a nationalizing state.[1] Nevertheless, for many people—especially those on the political right—and increasingly after the assassination of President Gabriel Narutowicz in November 1922, who was accused of having been elected by minorities, the state was mainly conceptualized as an ethnic nation-state—the kind that the elite of the country, the *inteligencja*, had desired for a long time.[2] And like other nation-states of the region that emerged from the breakup of the tsarist, Habsburg, and German

---

1 Rogers Brubaker, "Nationalizing States in the 'Old New' Europe—and the New," *Ethnic and Racial Studies* 19, no. 2 (1996): 411–437.
2 Denis Sdvižkov, *Das Zeitalter der Intelligenz. Zur vergleichenden Geschichte der Gebildeten in Europa bis zum Ersten Weltkrieg* [The era of the intelligentsia. A comparative history of the educated classes in Europe down to the First World War] (Göttingen: Vandenhoeck & Ruprecht, 2006), 135–36.

empires, this state, as a political entity, had constantly to prove its superiority to the empires that had formerly ruled its territories. The almost always contested states of the region felt a strong need to prove their legitimacy, and there was considerable pressure to ensure that this was accomplished successfully. In addition, the interwar years constituted an "area of possibility," a space full of opportunities and challenges, in which established social, political, economic, ethnic, and gender relations could be ordered anew. In this way the interwar period became, in Samuel Kassow's words, "a living laboratory" for experiments in modern life, for Jews and non-Jews alike, producing new models of politics, self-help, culture, and identification.[3]

When we take a closer look at the quite diverse Jewish community in Poland, one of those phenomena was the increasing use of Polish as a first language by a growing number of Jews, sometimes alongside Yiddish and sometimes replacing it. The majority of Polish Jews who underwent this linguistic transition continued to regard themselves as Jewish, thereby creating a cultural and political space of "Jewish Polishness."[4] When it comes to research about the life of Jews in Poland during the interwar period, the questions of Polishness and the use of the Polish language within Polish Jewry still needs further investigation since we need to know more about what language change meant for ways of thinking and for social and cultural relations between all citizens of Poland, including Ukrainians, Germans, and Belarusians. In addition, the question of what Jews thought about Poles, directly linked to the question of their Polishness, and how they perceived the Polish nation and the Polish people, has not yet been in the center of historical investigation.[5] We still know more about

---

3 Samuel Kassow, "Oyf der yidisher gas/On the Jewish Street 1918–1939," in *Polin: 1000 Year History of Polish Jews*, ed. Barbara Kirshenblatt-Gimblett and Antony Polonsky (Warsaw: POLIN Museum of the History of Polish Jews, 2014), 227–85, 227.

4 See Katrin Steffen, *Jüdische Polonität. Ethnizität und Nation im Spiegel der polnischsprachigen jüdischen Presse 1918–1939* [Jewish Polishness: Ethnicity and nation in the light of the Polish-language Jewish press 1918-1939] (Göttingen: Vandenhoeck & Ruprecht, 2004), 11; and Katrin Steffen, "'Żydowska polskość' jako koncepcja tożsamości w polsko-żydowskiej prasie okresu międzywojennego i jej dziedzictwo w 'Naszej Trybunie' w latach 1940–1952" ["Jewish Polishness" as a conception of identity in the Polish-Jewish press of the interwar period and its inheritance by *Nasza Trybuna* in the years 1940–1952] in *Żydowski Polak, polski Żyd. Problem tożsamości w literaturze polsko-żydowskiej* [Jewish Pole, Polish Jew. Problems of identity in Polish-Jewish literature], ed. Alina Molisak and Zuzanna Kołodziejska (Warsaw: Dom Wydawniczy Elipsa, 2011), 140–53.

5 Those questions have been raised in my book, *Jüdische Polonität* (2004), but they still need further investigation. In that book, I acted on the assumption that the mutual perception of Jewish Poles and non-Jewish Poles cannot be separated. I took an integrative

how Poles thought about Jews and also what divided Jews and Poles rather than what united them—for example, when they met at markets, in courts or shops, when they studied together, and when they played on the same soccer field. One important but under-researched area is the field of public health. Here it quickly becomes apparent that Polish Jewish history during the interwar period was deeply affected by transnational entanglements and transfers of knowledge especially (but not exclusively) from neighboring countries, which should be taken into account in explaining many developments within Polish Jewry to a greater extent than has so far been the case. Although there are some integrated perspectives on the interwar period as a whole, for example, in urban or local history, in other fields such as the history of public health, simultaneous developments both in the majority population and within minority communities have not yet been adequately linked.

In this essay, I first reflect on the different contexts of the phenomenon of language change within Polish Jewry. I understand these contexts as one part of a discourse on the position of Jews in Polish culture and society, a discourse made up of components created by Jews and non-Jews alike.[6] Following this, I attempt to extend the discourse on Polishness in the interwar period by highlighting a further component, namely the "Jewish body" and Jewish health. Jewish bodies in a very concrete, anthropological sense, but also as a metaphor, can be seen as collective projections about Jews in Poland and their position in society. Finally, I attempt to unite both components in their relationship to Polishness.

---

approach, including the question about how Jews perceived Poles, Polish politics, Polish anti-Semitism, and Polish history, because this perception formed an important and integral part of "Jewish Polishness." So the assumption by Anna Landau-Czajka, who takes up similar questions in her recent publication *Polska to nie oni. Polska i Polacy w polskojęzycznej prasie żydowskiej II Rzeczypospolitej* [Poland is not them. Poland and Poles in the Polish-language Jewish press of the Second Republic] (Warsaw: Żydowski Instytut Historyczny im. Emanuela Ringelbluma, 2015), that I had shown only the "second side" of the medal, namely, how Jews presented Jewish life to a Polish audience (8), seems to be a crucial misunderstanding.

6 Partly, this articles translates from Katrin Steffen, "Umstrittene jüdische Polonität: Sprache und Körper als Unterscheidungsmythen in der polnischen Kultur" [The debated Jewish Polishness: Language and bodies as myths of difference in the Polish culture], in *Aleksander Brückner revisited. Debatten um Polen und Polentum in Geschichte und Gegenwart* [Aleksander Brückner revisited. Debates about Poland and the Poles in the past and present], ed. Yvonne Kleinmann and Achim Rabus (Göttingen: Wallstein Verlag, 2015), 99–122.

JEWISH POLISHNESS AND LANGUAGE CHANGE IN A MULTILINGUAL ENVIRONMENT

The term *Jewish Polishness* was coined retrospectively in 1946 by the Polish Jewish journalist Jakób Appenszlak, former chief editor of *Nasz Przegląd* (Our Review), the leading Jewish Polish-language daily newspaper of the interwar period in Warsaw, while he was living in exile in New York. After arriving in New York in 1939, Appenszlak quickly returned to his prewar occupation as a journalist for the Polish Jewish press. In November 1940, together with the sociologist Aryeh Tartakower, he founded the Polish-language paper *Nasza Trybuna* (Our Tribune), a paper with a print run of some two thousand copies that circulated in the United States and elsewhere until 1952. As an editor, Appenszlak received many letters from his readers that testified to the existence of a community of interpretation, grounded in the readership of the former *Nasz Przegląd*. In those readers, Polish Jews from all over the world, and in himself, Appenszlak recognized many sentimental feelings for Poland. He analyzed them as follows:

> In spite of everything, the number of subscribers of *Nasza Trybuna* in the world, the yearning with which the readership is waiting for the next issue to appear, the letters of gratitude ... all of this demonstrates how deeply one part of our intelligentsia has grown into Polishness, or into this specifically Jewish Polishness [żydowska polskość].[7]

For Appenszlak the devotion of the readership to his émigré journal was an incentive to continue his work in exile and to try again and again to find financial support for the newspaper. In the letter in which he coined the term "Jewish Polishness," he admitted: "I am working very hard to keep alive this irrational project, a Polish Jewish newspaper in America. Naturally it pales in comparison to the *Nasz Przegląd*, but I cannot break my ties to Poland...."

It is very difficult to define exactly what Polishness is and to know if it relates mainly to the nation, the state, society, religion, culture, or history, or to each one of those components. In addition, we do not know what Appenszlak had in mind by speaking of "Jewish Polishness." However, he named as one—if not the most important part—the Polish language, which he used for his articles throughout the interwar period in Poland and after 1939 also in the United

---

7 Steffen, *Jüdische Polonität*, 11.

States. Certainly, the Polish language seems to constitute a fundamental part of Appenszlak's self-understanding. Already in 1915 he began his poem "Mowie polskiej" (To the Polish Language) with "O Polish Language! Language of Mickiewicz and Norwid, you are also my language, the language of the Jew who dreams of Zion on the shores of the Vistula!"[8] In *Nasz Przegląd*, he once emphasized the influence the Polish language had exerted on Polish Jews like himself because of its musicality, its rhythm, and its romantic character (*romantyczność*).[9] So it is not surprising that while living in New York, he thought life in exile to be especially difficult for those Polish Jews, the journalists, lawyers, and writers, whose life had mainly been based on the language.[10] In exile this connection to the Polish language also constituted not a small problem for acceptance into the new environment. This is evident from a speech delivered in 1952 by the social scientist and editor of *Jewish Social Studies*, Abraham G. Duker, equally a Jew from Poland, at the funeral of Appenszlak. Duker, while looking back on Appenszlak's life, was quite aware of the problem the Polish language could constitute for individuals like Appenszlak in Poland and in the United States:

> American Jews who have been active in Jewish life could hardly figure out what appeared to them as the puzzle of the Polish speaking Jew. Jews from Germany were naturally expected to speak German. Hungarian Jews understandingly were supposed to use the tongue of the Magyars. … In contrast, Polish Jews were expected to speak Yiddish only. Those who couldn't were viewed in the same light as those who wouldn't … and Apenszlak[11] was no exception to this rule … Jacob Apenszlak was a product of this sociological assimilation process who never confused it with or succumbed to the ideological assimilationist sentiment or movement, which he had fought since his early youth. Born in 1894 in Warsaw, Apenszlak was raised almost completely in a Polish culture environment. His knowledge of Yiddish was negligible when he began his editorial work in his early twenties. He acquired it later. . . .

---

8 Jakób Appenszlak, *Mowie Polskiej* [To the Polish language] (Warsaw, 1915).
9 Pierrot, "Między wierszami. Na emigracji" [Between the lines. In emigration], *Nasz Przegląd*, November 11, 1924; also G. Jampoler, "Ogólno-polski zjazd polonistów o mniejszościach narodowych" [The All-Polish congress of Polonists on the national minorities], *Nasz Przegląd*, May 2, 1924.
10 Steffen, *Jüdische Polonität*, 373.
11 While in the United States, Appenszlak spelled his name with only one *p*.

Duker then was convinced that

> Apenszlak considered Polish his language as an individual.... His right to write in that language was disputed by some self-proclaimed "true" possessors. The Lebensraum allotted in Polish culture to Jews who refused to go through the polonization ceremonial of baptism was a narrow one, indeed.... It comes as a shock to American Jews to learn that the majority of the Jewish children in Poland attended Polish schools and that a sizeable proportion of them received little or no Jewish education. The schools, the motion pictures, the radio, the theatre, the street were continually and increasingly changing the language of Polish Jewish youth from Yiddish into Polish. With the language also came changes in culture and in ways of thinking....[12]

I will now turn to the complex process of language change, described here thoughtfully by Abraham Duker. The process as a slowly growing mass phenomenon began in the middle of the nineteenth century and reached its peak after 1918. In 1938, Tartakower estimated that 750,000 Jews in Poland used Polish as first language, which was still a minority, but not at all a marginal number, if we take into account that in the neighboring Weimar Republic in 1918 there were about 600,000 Jews.[13] Language change in Poland took place within a very "heterogeneous and multilingual milieu: between acculturation and *yidishkeyt*, between Zionism and socialism, between a secularized identification and Orthodoxy we find fundamental differences of Jewish self-perceptions and a multilingual environment of Yiddish, Polish, and Hebrew, as well as Russian and German."[14] One also has to take into account substantial regional differences caused by the impact of the partitions—while Polish-speaking Jews in Kraków or Lwów were no exception, in the former Russian parts of Poland the situation was different.[15] But the phenomenon of linguistic Polonization had found its way also into the strongholds of the Yiddish language in the northeast

---

12 Steffen, *Jüdische Polonität*, 376–77.
13 Arieh Tartakower, "Język żydowski i hebrajski" [The Yiddish and Hebrew languages], *Nasza Opinja* 145, 272 (1938).
14 See Chone Shmeruk, "Hebrew–Yiddish–Polish: A Trilingual Jewish Culture," in *The Jews of Poland between Two World Wars*, ed. Israel Gutman, Ezra Mendelsohn, and Chone Shmeruk (Hanover, NH: University Press of New England/Brandeis University Press 1989), 285–311.
15 See, for example, Sean Martin, *Jewish Life in Cracow 1918–1939* (London: Vallentine Mitchell, 2004).

such as in Vilna, Białystok, Brest, or Baranovichi.[16] The northwestern district of Warsaw around Nalewki Street was also affected by this process. In 1934, the journalist Szmuel Lejb Sznajderman observed:

> The children of the booksellers from Nalewki do not speak Yiddish. Thanks to money made on Jewish books, they have learned the most eloquent words of Mickiewicz and Wyspiański, which they use even when they have to address the most mundane matters. More and more often, they clean out of the displays the Jewish books and substitute them with, say, arithmetic textbooks in Polish.[17]

The linguist Mosze Altbauer, who researched the mutual influences of Yiddish on Polish and vice versa, confirmed this situation in 1929 and asserted that Polish had become the colloquial language for the Jewish *inteligencja* in Poland and that the command of Polish was spreading also among the lesser educated. About the knowledge of Polish among Jews in Poland he observed: "Of course they knew it, some better, some worse, because they had to know it for their relations to the Christians."[18] The development of language change therefore mirrored a long-time relationship of Christians and Jews in Poland, but also a cultural integration and a desire for participation in Polish institutions of higher learning and for social advancement. Policies of Polonization pursued by the Polish governments during the interwar period should also not be underestimated. By the concept of state assimilation they intended to turn the country into a distinctly national Polish state—in this way Polishness became the touchstone of respectability, as Shimon Redlich has described.[19] But the increase in the use of the Polish language cannot be reduced alone to the desire for social advancement, state policies, education, or the necessity to attend Polish schools. During the period of the partitions, a Jewish elite started

---

16 Nathan Cohen, "Reading Polish among Young Jewish People," in *Polin* 28: Jewish Writing in Poland, ed. Monika Adamczyk-Garbowska, Eugenia Prokop-Janiec, Antony Polonsky, and Sławomir Jacek Żurek (2016): 73–186, 177.

17 Szmuel Lejb Sznajderman, "Smutna geografia Nalewek" [The sad geography of Nalewki], *Literarishe Bleter* 37, 540 (1934): 604–6; 38, 541 (1934): 623–24.

18 Mosze Altbauer, "Polszczyzna Żydów" [The Polish language of Jews, first published 1932], in Mosze Altbauer, *Wzajemne wpływy polsko-żydowskie w dziedzinie językowej* [Mutual Polish-Jewish linguistic influences], ed. and selected by Maria Brzezina (Kraków: Nakładem Polskiej Akademii Umiejętności, 2002), 121–63, 134.

19 Shimon Redlich, *Together and Apart in Brzezany: Poles, Jews and Ukrainians, 1919–1945* (Bloomington: Indiana University Press 2002), 38f.

to take over the language of a society without its own state. This process was an idealistic and romantic one, influenced by the writings of Adam Mickiewicz or Juliusz Słowacki and identified with the liberation of the divided Polish nation.[20] The Polish language and culture then gained a high emotional value and were associated with the hope of equality for all citizens in the anticipated future nation-state. When it came increasingly clear by the end of the nineteenth and throughout the first decades of the twentieth century that those hopes would not be fulfilled, because Jews would not be accepted as equal in Poland despite their linguistic acculturation, many turned away from a far-reaching assimilation and embraced Jewish political movements such as Bundism or Zionism. Their attachment to Polish culture and language was not given up, not only for the mentioned social reasons. This attachment also stayed effective because the heritage of the early modern, multi-confessional Rzeczpospolita and the struggle for independence were still seen as a link between Poles and Jews. The recourse to Polish history and its "best elements," such as tolerance and the struggle for independence, was a way to create an opportunity to formulate a concept for living together with the Christian Poles, that somehow proved to be resistant against the anti-Semitic violence and disappointments Jews experienced in daily life during the interwar period. The journalist and politician Abraham Insler put this into words: "They," meaning right-wing, anti-Semitic Poles, "they are not Poland."[21] Beyond that, the successful Polish struggle for independence fulfilled the role of a model for those Jews who aimed to build their own Jewish state.[22] In any case, the Polish language had been transformed into a legitimate means to express Jewish culture and politics, or, in the words of the writer Roman Brandstaetter: "We unite the word of Mickiewicz with the holy word of the Bible."[23]

Nevertheless, this development was controversial from the very beginning, for Jews and for non-Jews. When in 1854 the supporters of Antoni Eisenbaum, the long-standing head of the Warsaw Rabbinic School and a vehement supporter of the Polish language who had died recently, wanted to erect

---

20 Ezra Mendelsohn, "A Note on Jewish Assimilation in the Polish Lands," in *Jewish Assimilation in Modern Times*, ed. Bela Vago (Boulder, CO: Westview Press, 1981), 141–49; Steffen, *Jüdische Polonität*, 125–43.
21 See Abraham Insler, "Oni—to nie Polska" [They are not Poland], *Nasza Opinja* 20 (June 1937), cited in Steffen, *Jüdische Polonität*, 131.
22 Yaacov Shavit, "Between Piłsudski and Mickiewicz: Policy and Messianism in Zionist Revisionism," *Studies in Zionism* 6 (1985): 229–46.
23 Roman Brandstaetter, "Sprawy poezji polsko-żydowskiej, III: Kłody pod stopami" [The question of Polish-Jewish poetry, III: logs underfoot], *Opinja* 25 (1933).

a monument in the Jewish cemetery with an inscription in Polish: "To Antoni Eisenbaum, Principal of the Rabbinic School," the Orthodox who controlled the cemetery as well as the congregational board objected the use of Polish on the monument.[24] From then on, linguistic Polonization repeatedly led to discussions as to if and how it was compatible with Jewish identification. Many Yiddish-speaking Jews in Poland were convinced that the decrease of Yiddish (although it still *was* the first language for the majority) led inevitably to a decline of Jewish culture as such. The journalist Szmuel Stupnicki interpreted the adoption of the Polish language in 1930 as the first and most important step to a "truthful assimilation."[25] What he meant was a transition of Jews to Polish nationalism and, ultimately, to Catholicism—a far-reaching assumption that was not at all supported, for example, by numbers of converts during the interwar period. In addition, it can be doubted whether language constitutes a universally applicable criterion of nationality, and, as mentioned, we probably do not know enough about those processes.

A different source of conflict over the Polish language was sparked by Polish nationalists and right-wing thinkers and journalists. Once Jews had begun to write in the Polish language, they were considered by those circles as representatives of a "typical Semitic" literature. The Jewish poet, journalist, and translator Izydor Berman summarized this constellation in 1937:

> A Jewish poet and writer has nothing to say here. About the question, who he is and who he should be, others decide, namely the authoritative ones: the hosts. And so we find the following views: 1. A Jew cannot be a Polish writer, because he creates only a undefined [*niejaki*], worthless literature. 2. Exceptionally, and only in rare cases, a Jew can be a Polish writer and create culturally and nationally valuable works. Those Jews we acknowledge. 3. It happens that Jews are good Poles and good writers, but that's a fact we regret. One can survive without these Jews.[26]

In certain right-wing circles, but not only there, it was obsessively discussed to what extent Jews in Poland, who counted mainly as "guests" and "foreigners," were able to speak Polish at all. It was a common prejudice that Jews could never

---

24 Antony Polonsky, *The Jews in Poland and Russia, Vol. 1: 1350 to 1881* (Oxford: Littman Library of Jewish Civilization, 2010), 312.
25 Samuel Hirszhorn, "Czy istotnie asymilacja triumfuje?" [Will assimilation actually triumph?], *Nasz Przegląd*, 4.1.1930.
26 Izydor Berman, "Dyskusje literackie" [Literary discussions], *Nasza Opinja* 92, 219 (1937).

be as proficient in speaking and writing in Polish as "true," that is, Christian Poles. In this context, Jews as an imagined collective were not only accused, but their presumably "asiatic psyche" would make it difficult for them to understand the language of a "European people," as the *Gazeta Warszawska* noted on September 30, 1933. In addition, it was quite common during the interwar period to claim that Jews would corrupt the Polish language by introducing elements of the so-called żargon, the Yiddish language. Above that we find many statements asserting that Jews and especially Jewish Polish writers would "violate" the language—"poison," "contaminate," or "decompose" it.[27] With the use of this organic and biological terminology, the discourse advanced beyond questions of grammar or accent: language was ethnicized and identified with an imagined "purity" and, going beyond that, with the nation itself. Language was thus integrated into a discourse in which Polish ethnicity counted as the dominant marker of belonging to the Polish nation and ultimately also to the Polish state.[28] In this conception, represented by the National Democrats and their leader Roman Dmowski, who succeeded in winning over large parts of the Polish population to this concept, ethnicity counted for everything and loyalty for nothing. This constellation meant that Jews could never belong to the Polish national body because if they used Polish as a precondition for such an integration, they at the same time "decomposed" the supposedly healthy nation.

JEWISH BODIES—POLISH BODIES: CREATING DIFFERENCES

The concept of the healthy nation enjoyed high priority in the Polish nation-building process after 1918. After the long period of being a nation without a state, concern over national existence in a biological sense also played an important role in discourses about modernization—matters of health went along with striving for modernization in Poland. As a result, health issues also always served ideological ends by enhancing social and ethnic cohesion and setting normative values in terms of behavior, consumption, physical fitness,

---

27 Samuel Hirszhorn, "Ankieta w sprawie żydowskiej" [An enquiry on the Jewish question] *Nasz Przegląd*, December 14, 1933; Irina Kamińska-Szmaj, "Judzi, zohydza, ze czci odziera. Język propagandy politycznej w prasie 1919–1923" [Goading, shaming, which deprives you of honor. The language of political propaganda in the press 1919–1923] (Wrocław: Towarzystwo Przyjaciół Polonistyki Wrocławskiej 1994), 128.
28 See also Paul Brykczynski, "A Poland for the Poles? Józef Piłsudski and the Ambiguities of Polish Nationalism," in *Pravo: The North American Journal for Central European Studies* 1 (2007), 1–20.

gender relations, and relations of the majority toward minority groups. Public health was an arena in which meaning and relevance were produced for and in complex interaction with an audience for which this meaning was clearly understandable—or else had to be made understandable.[29] Some voices in Poland went so far as to call for a kind of biological order of the state since they viewed the nation as an "organization based on a biogenetic community"[30] and in this way wanted to discipline bodies and regulate the population, sometimes in the context of a postulated "overpopulation." Those were classical issues of biopolitics that were not specific to Poland. Discussions about the "healthy body of the nation" and about an "improvement of the people" in the context of eugenic thinking were a transnational phenomenon discussed by scientists and politicians from the nineteenth century in both Eastern and Western Europe.[31]

Those discussions found their way also to Poland, a very interesting case in this respect, because of the great variety of experiences its elites gained before the First World War in three state traditions or outside those traditions, which later had to be included in the new state structure.[32] A large transfer of knowledge into the new state took place, observable in many areas of Polish life after 1918, in politics and administration, in the economy, and in science. What followed was an outstanding ability for many representatives of the *inteligencja* to move and communicate in a multilingual and multi-confessional environment. This created a transnational space for the formation of the state that was absent in most Western countries, and should be taken into account as one factor forming Poland during the interwar period. But one also has to examine how this was transformed during the interwar period into ever more nationalization of this space, in this way following trends elsewhere in Europe.

Within the framework of those trends, politicians and scientists after 1918 were eager to create "a new breed of men," as was stressed by Poland's first minister of health, the physician Tomasz Janiszewski, in a letter to the president of

---

29 Katrin Steffen, "Experts and the Modernization of the Nation—the Arena of Public Health in Poland in the First Half of the 20th Century," *Jahrbücher für Geschichte Osteuropas* 61, no. 4 (2013): 574–90.
30 Adam Paszewski, "Znaczenie biologji dla społeczeństwa" [The significance of biology for society], *Czasopismo Przyrodnicze* 7–8 (1931): 1–8.
31 See, for example, *Blood and Homeland: Eugenics and Racial Nationalism in Central and Southeast Europe, 1900–1940*, ed. Marius Turda and Paul Weindling (Budapest: Central European University Press, 2007).
32 Katrin Steffen and Martin Kohlrausch, "The Limits and Merits of Internationalism: Experts, the State and the International Community in Poland in the First Half of the Twentieth Century," *European Review of History* 16 (2009): 715–37.

the United States in 1921.³³ But in the minds of some Polish politicians and scientists not all Polish citizens were suitable for this ambitious goal. While, for example, representatives of the Polish Army advocated a policy of assimilating Ukrainians or Belarusians, Jews were not seen as eligible to participate in the project the of "new man," the project of recovery, of "Sanacja," as the regime in Poland described itself following Piłsudski's coup d'etat in May 1926. In descriptions and reports from military circles from 1922 on, Jews count as "lousy," as physically weak and constantly threatened by illnesses such as cardiac insufficiency or dizziness, while Ukrainians, for example, were perceived as "excellent physical material."³⁴ Renowned scientists were ready to back up those opinions with their expertise: the most famous Polish anthropologist Jan Czekanowski commented on the findings of a large anthropological mass examination of soldiers in Poland in the 1920s as follows:

> Our experience allows us to state that particular racial components of the people are not suitable for military service, and that the value of a soldier depends above all on his physical fitness. We all know that the Jews are physically inferior and that they are the worst soldiers. And we also know that the Nordic blond type constitutes the best material for the army, physically as well as mentally.³⁵

Another anthropologist and student of Czekanowski, Karol Stojanowski, stated as follows in 1927, after he had studied the writings of German anthropologists: "By the way, not without good reason German science interprets Jews as a threat for the Nordic-European type ... you do not have to persuade anyone in Poland that the Germans in their findings are totally correct...." And he concluded: "From a eugenic standpoint the assimilation of the Jews is not desired. They either have to emigrate or to restrict their natural growth or simply to die out."³⁶ In a different text, he denied Jews as "guests" and "foreigners" any

---

33 Tomasz Janiszewski, "The Versailles Treaty and the Question of Public Health," *International Journal of Public Health* 2 (1921): 140–51.
34 Tadeusz Kowalski, *Mniejszości narodowe w siłach zbrojnych Drugiej Rzeczypospolitej Polskiej (1918–1939)* [National minorities in the armed forces of the Second Republic, 1918–1939] (Toruń: Wydawnictwo Adam Marszałek, 2008), 157.
35 Jan Czekanowski, "Nauki antropologiczne" [Anthropological studies], *Nauka Polska* 5 (1925): 146.
36 Karol Stojanowski, *Rasowe podstawy eugeniki* [The racist bases of eugenics] (Poznań: Drukarnia św. Józefa, 1927), 68.

political rights in Poland and any influence on the fate of the country, thereby totally ignoring the fact that they had also built up the country.[37]

Stojanowski tried to back up his opinions with anthropological field work under his supervision. Under his direction, students at the university in Poznań carried out an examination of Jews in the Polish army. Those soldiers, all born between 1901 and 1906, came from different parts of Poland but were serving their time in the Poznań area. Initially, forty-one soldiers were selected for the study, but only eighteen were participating regularly in exercises and were therefore eligible to be studied. The project aimed to compare their level of physical fitness to that of Polish sports instructors. When the results were published, the author concluded that the physical fitness of the Jewish soldiers was not equal to that of the instructors, and was in fact far beneath their level. This was explained, on the one hand, by the fact that the instructors had access to special training and engaged in more exercise, but on the other hand, the results were taken to be a "confirmation of the popular and in the army well-known opinion that the Jewish material in physical respect is less valuable than the Polish." It was also argued that the poor results of the Jewish soldiers were a consequence of faked illnesses and dissimulation among the soldiers to avoid exerting themselves during their service (this constituted a common accusation made against Jewish servicemen during the interwar period). Even if this was taken into consideration, the article concluded, the level of physical fitness of the Jewish soldier in the Polish Army was very low.[38]

Stojanowski's views as a scientist might have been extreme, but his arguments fit quite well into forming bio-political anti-Semitism in Poland and clearly connected to the discourse on the construction of a social, national, or "racial" other, excluded from a supposedly "clean" and "healthy" national body. As part of this, the propaganda against Jewish doctors and medical students was particularly vehement. The medical professions had long provided a unique possibility for upward social mobility and, as a result, many Jews in Poland chose this profession: in 1931, a total of 46 percent of all doctors in Poland were Jews, and 55 percent of all practicing physicians. In Lwów, their number reached 65 percent.[39] Many non-Jewish doctors, students, and

---

37 Karol Stojanowski, *Rasizm przeciw Słowiańszczyźnie* [Racism against Slavism] (Poznań: Głos, 1934), 137.
38 Zofja Walicka, "Przyczynek do sprawności fizycznej Żydów żołnierzy W.P." [A contribution to the phyisical fitness of Jewish soldiers in the Polish Army], *Wychowanie fizyczne* 7–8 (1929), 217f.
39 Antony Polonsky, *The Jews in Poland and Russia, Vol. III: 1914–2008*, 61.

journalists made a veritable problem out of this situation, calling vehemently for a *numerus clausus* for Jewish medical students and enforcing a so-called Aryan paragraph into the Union of Doctors of the Polish State in 1937.[40] Above that, the medical faculties in the 1920s and 1930s witnessed a bitter conflict over the question of whether Jewish students should be allowed to dissect Christian cadavers, since Jewish religious law forbade Jews to dissect Jewish bodies.[41] Christian students demanded that Jews be denied access to "their" bodies because even dead bodies could be contaminated and profaned. In the same way that this argument was applied to the question of language, supposedly "foreign" and "impure" Jews were accused of violating the—utopian—construction of a "pure national body," and this, in the logic of the anti-Semites, had to be stopped.

Jewish writers and journalists, physicians and anthropologists, responded in many ways to their verbal or factual exclusion in terms of language or health and medicine matters. On an institutional level, they began the initiatives mentioned at the beginning of this essay (which were *not always* but sometimes a reaction to anti-Semitism and exclusion) and created their own structures such as the Jewish publishing house for Polish-language works, Cofim, and the Polish-language Jewish press as a forum for Polish-speaking writers and journalists. In questions of health, the Society for Safeguarding the Health of the Jewish Population, shortly TOZ (for its Polish name: Towarzystwo Ochrony Zdrowia Ludności Żydowskiej w Polsce) emerged as part of the transnational Jewish health network OSE/Obshchestvo Zdravookhraneniia Evreev (Society for the Protection of Jewish Health). The Polish branch of this organization was as unique as the Polish Jewish press. By 1939, TOZ was in charge of 368 hospitals and institutes in seventy-two towns all over the country and employed 1,000 physicians, nurses, and social workers. The goals of TOZ did not differ very much of those of the Polish health ministry: its work focused on the welfare and well-being of Jewish citizens in independent Poland, promoting their health and the health of their children and providing welfare for needy families. Many of their representatives such as the physician and longtime president

---

Ignacy Einhorn, *Towarzystwo Ochrony Ludności Żydowskiej w Polsce w latach 1921-1950* [The Society for the protection of Jewish health in Poland in the years 1921-1939] (Toruń, Wydawnictwo Adam Marszałek, 2008), 60.

40 Einhorn, *Towarzystwo Ochrony*, 58.
41 Natalia Aleksiun, "Christian Corpses for Christians! Dissecting the Anti-Semitism behind the Cadaver Affair of the Second Polish Republic," *East European Politics & Societies* 25, no. 3 (August 2011): 393-409.

of TOZ, Leon Wulman, had received their professional training in Germany, Switzerland, France, or Russia, just as their non-Jewish colleagues with whom they quite often had studied and also worked with on a daily basis.[42] After 1918, they continued to work in transnational health networks such as OSE and published frequently in the German-language OSE-Review (OSE-Rundschau). In this journal, Wulman stated in 1931, TOZ should identify the reasons for the "inferiority of the bodies of the Jewish masses and to develop a way to raise the biological fitness of the Jewish population." For Wulman, so it seems, an "inferiority" of Jewish bodies constituted a rather unquestioned fact.[43] A similar assessment of the health status of Jews in Poland came from the director of the Department of Internal Medicine of the Jewish Hospital in Berlin, Hermann Strauss. He traveled around Poland in 1930 and took his impressions to Berlin: "Those who come from Germany to Poland find all the ideas on the misery of the Jewish masses in Poland they already had in mind from various accounts, far surpassed by reality." However, Strauss was confident that Jews in Poland would succeed in a "complete transformation of the physical and mental condition of the Jewish masses."[44]

In order to achieve such goals, members of TOZ produced many brochures promoting hygiene, founded information centers for families and parents, and organized summer camps for children. In addition, they conducted medical examinations in order to find specific features of Jewish health in Poland and published their results in their own journals and publications, partly also in Polish. They also tried to connect doctors from all over the country, organizing in June 1928 the nationwide Doctors Congress of TOZ on social medicine, whose lectures and resolutions were published in a book in 1929.[45] Some 250 physicians from fifty-eight towns gathered in Warsaw and listened to forty-six lectures in six different sections on tuberculosis, contagious diseases, social hygiene, eugenics, medical care for children, and hygiene in schools. In those

---

42 Katharina Kreuder-Sonnen, "Grenzen ziehen und überschreiten. Ärzte und das Jüdische im Königreich Polen während der Choleraepidemie 1892/93" [To establish and breach borders. Doctors and the Jews in the Kingdom of Poland during the Cholera Epidemic of 1892–93], *Zeitschrift für Ostmitteleuropa-Forschung* 64, no. 3 (2015): 330–55.

43 Leon Wulman, "Das jüdische Krankenhauswesen" [Jewish hospital provision], *OSE-Rundschau* 6 (1931): 3–9, 3.

44 Hermann Strauß, "Medizinisch-soziale Reiseeindrücke in Polen" [Social-medical impressions of a trip in Poland], *OSE-Rundschau* 7 (1930), 1–4.

45 Księga pamiątkowa I Krajowego Zjazdu Lekarskiego "TOZ-u" (24.–25. czerwca 1928) [Memorial book of the first national doctors' conference of TOZ, 24-25 June 1928] (Warsaw, 1929).

sections a variety of topics were touched upon, mostly by doctors who routinely faced those problems. Among the many topics discussed were the impact of racial factors for a lower disposition to tuberculosis within the Jewish population, the role of eugenics under the living conditions of the Jewish masses, eugenics in the Bible and Talmud, the Jews' birth rates and mortality rates due to different illnesses, birth control, the mentally ill in Poland, the health of Jewish youth and children, and the question of circumcision. In addition, the reason why certain diseases or mental illnesses like schizophrenia appeared more frequently among Jews in Poland than among non-Jews was the subject of debate. In this context, the psychiatrist Rafał Becker, director of Zofjówka, a home for the mentally ill in Otwock near Warsaw, called for the popularization of the slogan: "The reproduction of the disabled has to be eliminated with the help of an adequate regulation of fertility."[46] He further demanded: "We, the Jewish community, do not have the opportunity to introduce adequate legislation, but we can do one thing, and this is to conduct energetic propaganda in order to introduce all the basic principles of eugenics to the broad Jewish masses."[47] Similar beliefs were shared by Henryk Higier, a physician from Warsaw, who was convinced that "good human material is the base for the richness of a people and decides the further development of the nation." Higier himself in his lecture at the congress developed a eugenics program to improve the hygienic situation of the "Jewish masses." Thus it is clear that most of the lecturers had a common approach: as long as a so-called "ghetto" existed, meaning an economic ghetto forced upon the Jewish population from the outside and a Jewish working class that supposedly lived in overcrowded dirty dwellings, these conditions would exert a negative influence on the Jewish psyche and the Jewish body. Today we know, however, that the living conditions of Jews in Warsaw, for example, were not much worse than those of non-Jews—they rather were bad for all inhabitants.

In order to substantiate the "findings" postulated at the conference, Jewish bodies were also measured by Jews. In Lwów, Salomon Czortkower, a student of Jan Czekanowski, carried out such examinations on a broad scale, and in Warsaw Henryk Szpidbaum tried to find out on the basis of 5,079 Jews from ten voivodships, where the fair-haired Jews in Poland came from—a question he could not really solve. But he ventured (given the time, a probably not very popular thesis) that fair-haired Jews in Poland were found exactly there, where

---

46 Rafał Becker, "Umysłowo chorzy Żydzi w Polsce i opieka nad nimi" [Mentally ill Jews in Poland and their care], in *Księga*, 112–117.
47 Rafael Becker, "Die Bedeutung der Rassenhygiene für die jüdische Familie" [The significance of racial hygiene for the Jewish family], *OSE-Rundschau* 3 (1928): 13–16.

the blond element also dominated among non-Jewish Poles. He therefore considered this phenomenon the result of the mixture of Jews and non-Jews.[48]

The congress also dealt with anthropological studies and the parameters of the Jewish body—the shape of noses, faces, and skulls compared to those of non-Jewish fellow countrymen. Donatella Lipcówna, an anthropologist from Warsaw, had examined five hundred Jews from Warsaw anthropometrically, in order to be able to fight diseases, but also to achieve "racial improvement," as she stated at the congress.[49] Lipcówna had compared certain characteristics of the examined Jews to those of non-Jewish Poles and wanted to show the "racial differences between Jews and Poles." She chose twenty-eight characteristics such as height, weight, chest measurement, or arm's length and found out that Poles were "superior" in twenty of those characteristics.

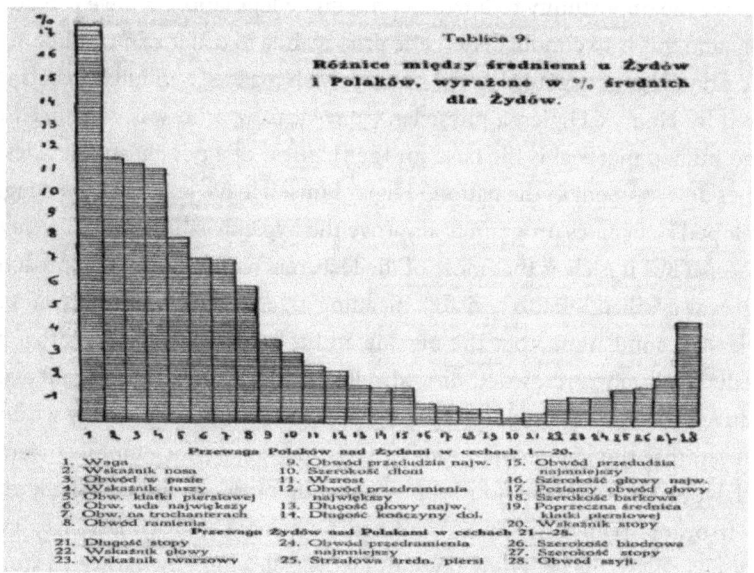

Figure 1 Graph from Donatella Lipcówna's anthropological research (in *Księga*, 48): Differences between the averages of Jews and Poles, shown in percentage of the average for Jews. Shows advantages of Poles to Jews in characteristics 1–20, and advantages of Jews to Poles in characteristics 21–28.

---

48 Henryk Szpidbaum, "Hellfarbige jüdische Typen in Polen," [Light-skinned Jewish types in Poland], *OSE-Rundschau* 6 (1930): 1–12.

49 Donatella Lipcówna, "Rezultaty badań antropologicznych na 500 Żydach woj. warsz." [The results of the anthropological investigation of five hundred Jews in the Warsaw province], in *Księga*, 48.

Besides "deficits" such as a lower height or a lower chest measurement, and a higher predisposition for cardiac diseases or diabetes, some "advantages" were found in similar examinations, for example a lower mortality among Jews in Poland than among non-Jews, as well as higher resistance to contagious diseases such as tuberculosis and typhus.[50] In spite of such findings, physicians like Henryk Higier or Rafał Becker were convinced that in Poland eugenic institutions had to emerge to improve the living conditions of the "Jewish masses" and to level the differences between the bodies of the Jewish and the non-Jewish population. The bodies of the latter thereby typically were set as the standard. And although most of those writers were convinced that environmental, cultural and social reasons were the principal reason for pathologies among Jews, some authors argued explicitly for the existence of a Jewish race, and many operated with the biologist terminology of the time. The physician Gershon Lewin, for example, argued that the rather dark pigmentation of the "skin, the hair and the eyes that we find with 85 percent of the Jewish population, is a very important racial factor in fighting tuberculosis."[51]

CONCLUSION

Consciously or unconsciously and in a context of a potentially hostile and excluding environment, where many felt a need for defense, but also a desire for inclusion, Jews took up some anti-Semitic interpretations. They adopted the view that too many Jews in Poland lived in overcrowded "ghettos" (which of course was partly also a politically motivated, Zionist argumentation, although not all of the doctors were Zionists), and described scenarios in which the "Jewish masses" appear as physically inferior and as carriers of bacteria, as if existent hygienic problems were specifically Jewish characteristics and not a social problem for all Polish citizens, resulting, above all, from the country's poverty. Many Jews tried to find complex answers to the accusations of Jewish inferiority—in this way their eugenic ideas often mirrored the biologist ideas of their social environment, a natural development given that Jewish and non-Jewish doctors in Poland did not live in separate, parallel societies, but met in the same or similar spaces of practice and knowledge. In addition, for the question of language, the myth that Jews were physically or

---

50 Einhorn, *Towarzystwo Ochrony*, 55.
51 Gershon Lewin, "Rola czynnika rasowego w większej odporności Żydów przeciw gruźlicy" [The role of racial factor in the greater resistance of Jews to tuberculosis], in *Księga*, 19–27.

mentally unable to be fluent in Polish, a myth that was created for the purpose of exclusion and stigmatization, was sometimes confused with reality. In the Polish Jewish press, we find repeated demands by Jewish writers and journalists to achieve perfection in Polish grammar and to speak Polish without any accent. Jakób Appenszlak, for example, protested against the Polish-language performance of the Yiddish play *The Dybbuk*, in which some of the actors imitated a Jewish accent. He considered this "yiddishizing" (*żydłaczenie*) to be a cardinal mistake and a mutilation of the Polish language. So, he picked up the idea that the input of a Yiddish accent or of Yiddish phrases into Polish actually could be evaluated as a "mutilation" of the Polish language. A perfect command of the Polish language was considered so crucial that the issue developed into one of the most sensitive places for criticism and attacks against Jews. The situation with Jewish bodies was comparable—they were, when compared to non-Jewish Polish bodies, often considered inferior, although from a medical point of view this could not be proved. Both perceptions reveal a dilemma: by orienting themselves to the Polish hegemonic culture, and the concept of Jewish Polishness included such an orientation, Jews were inevitably faced also with the anti-Semitic attributions of this culture.

Jewish Polishness, which included a commitment to the Polish language, culture, and to all Polish citizens who could be interpreted as representatives of the "good," tolerant, and multiethnic Polish past on the one side, and committed also to Jewish traditions and Jewish nationality on the other, was ambiguous and contested. It was attacked by both Jews and non-Jews, as it was directed against the national homogeneity that various groups were striving for during the interwar period. The programmatic title of an editorial by journalist and politician Abraham Insler in the newspaper *Nasza Opinja* in 1936 "Poland—this is also our country!" embodied an attitude that called for acceptance by non-Jewish Poles, but offered also loyalty and the fulfillment of obligations in Poland. While numerous Jews in Poland could identify with such a view, a large proportion of non-Jewish journalists, politicians, and scientists could not. They had dedicated themselves to a discourse on national purity in which thinkers like the national democrat Zygmunt Wasilewski saw anti-Semitism as a natural reaction of a body trying to heal an infection caused by invading bacteria. The issue of the Polishness of Jews was artificially connected to the allegedly pathological characteristics of the Jewish body and the supposed inability of Jews to speak Polish; the Polish language as well as Jewish bodies were exploited as a myth of physical separation between Jews and non-Jews in Poland. Biological terminology was used in order to suggest those supposedly pathological characteristics were given by nature and were unchangeable markers, making it impossible for Jews to claim Polishness for themselves. In this way, the body was used as a site, where—following Foucault—regimes of discourse and power inscribed themselves. It is probably no coincidence that the writer Karol Hubert Rostworowski in 1929 called for a "recovery" of Polish literature, by which he meant the exclusion of all Jews writing in Polish.[52] This, of course, did not work because it was neither possible to reverse the long-standing mutual Polish–Jewish influence in literature and in society as a whole. But it would probably also be too optimistic to say that the idea of an incompatibility of Polishness and Jewishness, which we find in the debates presented here, had had no impact on the thinking of Poles and Jews.

---

52   Karol H. Rostworowski, "O uzdrowienie literatury polskiej" [How to cure Polish literature], in *Polonia*, 1876, 1929.

The Holocaust Historiography on the Holocaust in Poland: An Outsider's View of its Place within Recent General Developments in Holocaust Historiography

DAN MICHMAN

The "Holocaust" has undoubtedly acquired a central status, or even more so a key status, in the contemporary public imagination; it has become, to use Alon Confino's definition, a foundational past "in modern European history," together with the French Revolution, and consequently of the Western mind-set.[1] In European societies, interest in and research on the Holocaust have become central to national identity struggles, to education, and to collective memory. In Poland, this aspect has been at the frontlines in recent decades.

Indeed, it would be audacious for a scholar who does not know Polish to claim to be able to present a well-balanced comprehensive analysis of the historiography of the Holocaust in Poland. Therefore, in this essay I will present an outsider's view of the place of this historiography within the larger picture of

---

1 Alon Confino, *Foundational Pasts: The Holocaust as Historical Understanding* (Cambridge: Cambridge University Press, 2012), 1.

recent developments in the historiography of the Holocaust, basing myself on some overviews of Polish historiography by experts,[2] on publications on this issue by Polish and non-Polish scholars in other languages, and on my acquaintance with Holocaust historiography in general.

In recent years, several analyses of Holocaust historiography have been published.[3] And as it is impossible to present a detailed comprehensive picture of the current state of research on the Holocaust within the limits of this writing, I will limit myself to depicting in large brush-strokes some of the major developments since the beginning of the 1990s—of course, according to my personal sense of the state of affairs.

---

2 See Shlomo Netzer, "The Holocaust of Polish Jewry in Jewish Historiography," in *The Historiography of the Holocaust Period*, ed. Yisrael Gutman and Gideon Greif (Jerusalem: Yad Vashem, 1988), 133–48; Natalia Aleksiun, "Polish Historiography of the Holocaust— Between Silence and Public Debate," *German History* 22, no. 3 (2004): 406–32; Havi Dreifuss, *Changing Perceptions on Polish–Jewish Relations during the Holocaust* (Yad Vashem: Jerusalem, 2012); Feliks Tych and Monika Adamczyk-Garbowska, eds., *Jewish Presence in Absence: The Aftermath of the Holocaust in Poland 1944–2010* (Jerusalem: Yad Vashem, International Institute for Holocaust Research, 2014), especially the articles in the section "Remembering and Forgetting"; and several articles in David Bankier and Dan Michman, eds., *Holocaust Historiography in Context: Emergence, Challenges, Polemics and Achievements* (New York and Jerusalem: Yad Vashem and Berghahn Books, 2008).

3 The earliest overviews of Holocaust historiography appeared in the 1980s, but they tended to map what had been done until then, and present mainstream conclusions—hardly analyzing the social, political, professional, and emotional contexts that shaped the paths and directions of historiography; see Lucy Dawidowicz, *The Holocaust and the Historians* (Cambridge, MA: Harvard University Press, 1981); Gutman and Greif, *The Historiography of the Holocaust Period*; Michael Marrus, *The Holocaust in History* (New York: Meridian, 1989); Abraham Edelheit, "Holocaust, Historiography of," *Encyclopedia of the Holocaust* (New York: Macmillan, 1990), 666–72. Since the beginning of the twenty-first century, and in the wake of much more self-reflection within the historical profession, more books on Holocaust historiography have been published and several authors proposed more sophisticated analyses; see Dan Michman, *Holocaust Historiography: A Jewish Perspective: Conceptualizations, Terminology, Approaches and Fundamental Issues* (London: Vallentine Mitchell, 2003); Dan Stone, *Constructing the Holocaust: A Study in Historiography* (London: Vallentine Mitchell, 2003); idem, ed., *Historiography of the Holocaust* (Basingstoke, UK: Palgrave Macmillan, 2004); *Histories of the Holocaust* (Oxford: Oxford University Press, 2010); Tom Lawson, *Debates on the Holocaust* (Manchester: Manchester University Press, 2010); Peter Hayes and John K. Roth, eds., *The Oxford Handbook of Holocaust Studies* (Oxford: Oxford University Press, 2010); Jonathan C. Friedman, ed., *The Routledge History of the Holocaust* (Abingdon, UK: Routledge, 2011); Frank Bajohr and Andrea Löw, eds., *Der Holocaust. Ergebnisse und neue Fragen der Forschung* (Frankfurt am Main: Fischer Taschenbuch, 2015).

THE IMPACT OF THE DOWNFALL OF THE COMMUNIST BLOCK AND THE CRYSTALLIZATION OF THE EUROPEAN UNION

The political developments in Europe around the end of the 1980s and the beginning of the 1990s had an enormous impact on Holocaust research—in several ways, *first* of all on the possibility to access vast archival collections that were hitherto inaccessible or restricted, and on the geographical perspective. The change of regimes in Eastern Europe enabled the opening of archives in the former communist countries (including East Germany). The newly discovered material included local German documentation and documentation of local non-German institutions, organizations, parties, and movements; German documentation that was captured in 1945 in Germany and was brought to the Soviet Union; materials of the special wartime Soviet inquiry committee (Extraordinary State Commission—Chrezvychainaia Gosudarstvennaia Komissia, Ch.G.K); and records of postwar trials. Altogether, the amount of this documentation runs into many thousands of documents. Additionally, the political change also made sites of the Holocaust in Eastern Europe much more easily accessible for foreigners, giving them the option to interview local inhabitants and experience the sites.

As a result, research on a series of issues had to be restarted or at least to be rethought and reconceptualized. One can fairly say that the turn in the understanding of the development of the decision-making on the Final Solution resulted to a large extent—along with the maturing of a new generation of scholars—from the new findings emerging from those materials. It became clear that there was a dynamic interaction between center and periphery, an ongoing process of "working toward the Führer" (as Ian Kershaw has called it), and an important contributing aspect of local collaboration, which altogether gradually—but rapidly—transformed the so-called Final Solution of the Jewish Question from a vague, not well-planned but much desired vision before June 1941 into a coordinated program which also affected survival prospects for Jews in hiding. That is, the Final Solution crystallized through the trying out of the feasibility of the idea of the comprehensive murder of the Jews through many petty initiatives that were undertaken at the grassroots level.[4]

---

4 The literature that has been produced in this field is enormous and still pouring out; it would be audacious and superfluous to describe this literature here. However, it is not superfluous to state that the widely acknowledged most important studies on the emergence of the Final Solution in general and in certain areas in particular (those written by Christopher Browning and Jürgen Matthäus, Ian Kershaw, Saul Friedländer, Peter Longerich, Chistian

Second, the change of regimes in formerly communist Eastern Europe and the process of broadening the newly emerging European Union to include those formerly communist countries that border with the initial EU, changed the research climate in those countries. More research on the Holocaust—which had previously been very limited and restricted in those countries—could now be done, and former tacit questions could now openly be asked, sometimes resulting from outside pressure (such as by the United States on the Baltic states to establish inquiry committees about the Second World War), the major topic being the extent of local participation in the persecution and murder of Jews. On the other hand, the same context has also had a negative impact. In many of the states that were liberated from the yoke of decades of communism, a renewed, often extreme, nationalism has emerged, which in many cases aspires to hail interwar and wartime nationalist leaders and movements that were anti-Semitic and participated in the persecution and murder of Jews (this has been especially apparent in Ukraine, but not only there). This atmosphere has provided a stage for attempts at downplaying the enormity of the Holocaust and the role of local participation, and sometimes to block serious research through administrative measures. This has been exacerbated even more by the "double dictatorship" paradigm, which aspires entirely and superficially to equate the so-called "Hitler crimes" and "Stalin crimes," sometimes by hinting at the myth of "Judeo-communism" that would explain collaboration with the Nazis as a form of justified revenge for "the Jews" being to a large extent responsible for the crimes of communism.

Third, the status of Auschwitz (with its iconic picture) as the ultimate symbol for the Holocaust, representing the supposed core meaning of the event as the modern, industrial "death factory," an image which triggered a constantly growing number of visitors during the first years after the downfall of communism in 1990,[5] has been challenged in recent research literature through a growing emphasis on the killing sites in Eastern Europe,

---

Gerlach, Dieter Pohl, Konrad Kwiet, Wendy Lower, and many more), which dramatically changed our overall understanding, could not have been written without the newly accessed materials. When, in a conversation with Christopher Browning several years ago I mentioned having found in the protocols of Yad Vashem's academic committee from March 1983 that he had promised to submit the manuscript of his book *The Origins of the Final Solution* (Lincoln: University of Nebraska Press; Jerusalem: Yad Vashem, 2004) in 1990 (!), he responded by saying that had he done so, the book would no longer have value.

5   See the annual reports of the Auschwitz museum.

where about half of the victims of the Holocaust were murdered in the most primitive and brutal ways.[6] From the perspective of today, one can say that the pendulum has even moved so far in emphasizing Eastern Europe from June 1941 onward, and first and foremost its killing sites as *the* locus of the Shoah, that one will find recent studies which entirely marginalize or even disregard the importance to the Holocaust of such essential issues as the 1930s in Germany and Austria; the persecution and murder of Western and Southern European Jewry; first steps of persecution in Tunisia and Libya; and other aspects of the Holocaust such as the enormous spoliation and the cultural warfare aimed at exorcising the *jüdische Geist*.[7] Perhaps the bluntest example for this development is Timothy Snyder's book *Bloodlands*,[8] which has been hailed on the one hand for its innovative perspective, but also extremely criticized by world-renowned experts on both Nazism and Stalin's Soviet Union.[9] Important for the current presentation is that Snyder views

---

6 See Yitzhak Arad, *The Comprehensive History of the Holocaust: The Soviet Union and the Occupied Territories* (Lincoln: University of Nebraska Press; Jerusalem: Yad Vashem, 2010); Patrick Desbois, *The Holocaust by Bullets: A Priest's Journey to Uncover the Truth Behind the Murder of 1.5 Million Jews* (New York: Palgrave Macmillan, 2008); Yad Vashem: The Untold Stories: The Murder Sites of the Jews in the Occupied Territories of the Former USSR; www.yadvashem.org/untoldstories/homepage.html.

7 For an extensive analysis of this phenomenon, see Dan Michman, "The Jewish Dimension of the Holocaust in Dire Straits? Current Challenges of Interpretation and Scope," in *Jewish Histories of the Holocaust. New Transnational Approaches*, ed. Norman Goda (New York: Berghahn Books, 2014), 17–38.

8 Timothy Snyder, *Bloodlands: Europe between Hitler and Stalin* (New York: Basic Books, 2010).

9 For praise see the long list of endorsements and quotations from reviews in the soft-cover reprint of his book; for very critical reviews see "Forum *Bloodlands*—eine Debatte über europäische Geschichte zwischen Hitler und Stalin" [The *Bloodlands* forum—A debate about European history between Hitler and Stalin], *Journal of Modern European History* 10 (2012), issues 3 and 4, with contributions by Manfred Hildermeier ("Montagen statt Mehrwert" [Montages instead of composite picture]), Dariusz Stola ("A Spatial Turn in Explaining Mass Murder"), Dietrich Beyrau ("Snyders Geografie" [Snyder's geography]), Sybille Steinbacher ("Befriedung der Erinnerung?" [The pacification of memory]), Dan Michman ("*Bloodlands* and the Holocaust"), and Johannes Hürter ("Gewalt, nichts als Gewalt" [Violence, nothing but violence]). An extremely critical review is Thomas Kühne, "Great Men and Large Numbers. Undertheorizing a History of Mass Killing," *Contemporary European History* 21, no. 2 (2012): 133–43, who says that "The book's dilemma is the way it presents history, or, more precisely, its obsession with large numbers and its resorting to great men when it comes to understanding what happened. 'For the time being', the reader is briefed at the end of the book, 'Europe's epoch of mass killing is overtheorised and misunderstood'. Rather than drawing 'theoretical conclusions' and thus confirming a 'disproportion of theory to knowledge', says Snyder, 'we must understand what actually happened,

the murder of the *physical* Jews not as having extraordinary characteristics but as a part of—what he calls—the Eastern European "Bloodlands event" (even though he admits that the Jews consist a disproportional 40 percent of the entire number of the civil victims as calculated by him). Consequently, and this is important for the Polish perspective, Snyder dedicates much of the preface of his book to counter the central place of Auschwitz as standing for the Holocaust or for the "Bloodlands event."[10]

THE BURGEONING OF GENOCIDE STUDIES AND ITS CONTROVERSIAL IMPACT

The term *genocide*, coined by the Polish Jewish lawyer Raphael Lemkin in 1943, was rapidly embraced in the legal world, including the United Nations (in December 1948), in order to prevent future such atrocities. However, in historiography and the social sciences this concept and studies on non-Holocaust cases were very limited, until the end of the 1970s. From then on, and at the initiative of a series of mostly Jewish Holocaust scholars, the field of genocide studies has burgeoned, especially in the past decade and a half. Since the end of the 1980s, the expression "Holocaust and Genocide Studies" has become a commonly embraced title for academic chairs, periodicals, conferences, and studies. If in the beginning the Holocaust was viewed as a starting point for broader research and that that research also contributed to a better understanding of certain ingredients of the Holocaust, the relationship between the study of the Holocaust and that of other genocides has recently become troubled, at least within one quite dominant subcurrent of genocide studies.[11] Some scholars started a crusade against the notion of "uniqueness"

---

in the Holocaust and in the Bloodlands generally' (p. 383). This is a strong statement. It distorts the relationship between theory and knowledge and marks a decisive setback in the historiography of 'Europe's epoch of mass killing.'"

10 Snyder, *Bloodlands*, xiv: "Mass killings in Europe is usually associated with the Holocaust, and the Holocaust with rapid industrial killing. The image is too simple and clean. At the German and Soviet killing sites, the methods of murder were rather primitive.... Starvation was foremost not only in reality but in imagination.... After starvation came shooting, and then gassing.... The Jews killed in the Holocaust were about as likely to be shot as to be gassed.... For that matter, there was little especially modern about gassing."

11 In a recent critical article, Clark University scholar Tomas Kühne has demonstrated that almost all of the studies that try to compare colonial genocides and the Holocaust or claim that some of them, especially that of the Nama and Herrero by the Germans in Southwest Africa in the beginning of the twentieth century, paved the way to the Holocaust—are perhaps knowledgeable about their colonial cases of research, but

often attributed to the Holocaust; according to Australian scholar Dirk Moses, the claim for uniqueness is an issue of "Jewish identity politics."[12] Another Australian genocide scholar, Colin Tatz, noticed an enmity in the camp of genocide scholars toward the "status" of the Holocaust and a tendency to marginalize it; he urged his colleagues to admit that "[t]he judeocide is an ally, not an enemy, and not on the margins."[13] Beyond the misunderstood meaning of the very common noun *uniqueness* and adjective *unique*, which points to an extraordinary combination of elements and is often used in common as well as historical discourse to point to most unusual conditions, the whole crusade is to be lamented because the notion of uniqueness by itself has not been an obstacle to compare and contextualize the Holocaust in its entirety or parts of it to other historical cases of genocide; on the contrary, the high profile of the Holocaust in public discourse and its relevance to other cases of mass atrocities have caused many a donor to fund chairs and projects carrying out research on a variety of genocides. On the other hand, the anti-"uniqueness" approach, by imposing certain definitions of genocide on the Holocaust ("the Holocaust is the genocide, i.e., comprehensive mass murder of the Jews"), has resulted in the exclusion of important aspects of the Shoah that are beyond the act of murder, and consequently caused distortions of the overall picture and of the comprehension of the deeper nature of this event—such as its contours (a global intention), its time span (1933–1945), and other issues (such as the campaigns for self-purification of the German language and legal thinking from "Jewish influence").[14]

---

are poorly acquainted with the Holocaust. See Thomas Kühne, "Colonialism and the Holocaust: Continuities, Causations and Complexities," *Journal of Genocide Research* 15, no. 3 (2013): 339–62.

12 Anthony Dirk Moses bluntly claimed in 2002 that "whether similarities [between the Holocaust and other genocides] are more significant than the differences is ultimately a political and philosophical, rather than a historical question. ... Uniqueness is not a category for historical research; it is a religious or metaphysical category." Anthony Dirk Moses, "Conceptual Blockages and Definitional Dilemmas in the 'Racial Century': Genocides of Indigenous Peoples and the Holocaust," *Patterns of Prejudice* 36, no. 4 (2002): 7–36; the quotation is from 18.

13 Colin Tatz, "Genocide Studies: An Australian Perspective," *Genocide Studies and Prevention* 6, no. 3 (December 2011): 232.

14 For an extensive elaboration on these issues, see Michman, "The Jewish Dimension of the Holocaust in Dire Straits?" For a concise conceptual summary see "Is the Holocaust Different from Other Genocides?" in Jewish Holocaust Centre, Melbourne, *Centre News* (April 2014): 18–19.

THE DEMISE OF THE HILBERGIAN CATEGORIZATION OF HOLOCAUST PROTAGONISTS

Several decades ago, the influential Holocaust scholar Raul Hilberg introduced the by now well-known and widely used tripartite categorization of protagonists in the Holocaust arena: perpetrators, victims, and bystanders.[15] This categorization has been growingly criticized from a variety of angles. As for the bystanders, it is quite clear that the array of modes of behavior to be found among the non-Nazi and non-Jewish populations is extremely broad and varied. First, one should distinguish between "bystanders" outside and those inside Germany and the occupied territories. Those outside included governments, organizations, and individuals—whether close or far away, more or less powerful—but also Jews. The Jews inside the Nazi-controlled territories did not belong, of course, to that category, but among the non-Jews one will find individuals, institutions, and organizations who helped Jews *pro deo*, paid helpers, denouncers, ideological collaborators (individuals, organizations, but also governments)—and even those who acted along more than one of these modes: some, for example, crossed borders (such as helpers who were also denouncers); there were also resisters to the Nazis who were at the same time anti-Semites and killed Jews themselves. As for those who joined in with the Nazis in the implementation of the anti-Jewish enterprise—should they be defined as "bystanders" or as "perpetrators"? And there were more shades. Research on these issues has mainly been done by scholars in the countries occupied by Nazi Germany, not so much by Germans. This happened first in Western Europe, mainly as a result of the shift of the mind-set happening after the violent 1968 student uprisings.[16] In Eastern Europe, this research venue started mostly after the collapse of the communist regimes around 1990.[17]

---

15 Raul Hilberg, *Perpetrators, Victims, Bystanders: The Jewish Castastrophe, 1933–1945* (New York: Aaron Asher Books, 1992).

16 Michman, *Holocaust Historiography*, 339.

17 For an excellent article with theoretical implications for this issue in Nazi-occupied Europe in general, see Jan Grabowski, "The Role of 'Bystanders' in the Implementation of the 'Final Solution' in Occupied Poland," *Yad Vashem Studies* 43, no. 1 (2015): 113–32. For an impressive study that uses Hilberg's categorization for closely examining the causes for the great differences of victimization (in percentages) between the Western European countries of the Netherlands, Belgium, and France, but shows the deep and changing interplay between them, see Pim Griffioen and Ron Zeller, *Jodenvervolging in Nederland, Frankrijk en België 1940–1945* [Jewish persecution in the Netherlands, France and Belguim, 1940–1945] (Amsterdam: Boom, 2011).

As for the perpetrator category: research on this aspect, as said, has been extremely intensive in the past two-and-a-half decades. From the 1960s through the second half of the 1980s, German perpetrator research was dominated by the "intentionalist"–"functionalist" debate. With the emergence of a younger German generation of researchers, the collapse of communist Eastern Europe, and with the input of many non-German researchers, the picture has changed. It has become quite clear that a sophisticated version of intentionalism can be combined with clearly existing functionalist modes of action. Kershaw's concept of "working towards the Führer" definitely contributed much to this understanding,[18] but more can and should be done. The important question that surfaced with the moving beyond the intentionalism–functionalism debate was this: How were the Nazi goals actually achieved so successfully? Altogether, the Nazi regime existed just twelve years and ninety-eight days—an extremely short moment in historical terms. And yet, the (evil) achievements were enormous. This could only happen as the result of an amazingly broad willful and creative participation in Germany and throughout Europe. The participation and contribution came from architects, environmental planners, economists, university professors, railway officials, judges, and others, all going beyond what was actually expected from them in bureaucratic terms; and there were those who were not part of the bureaucracy at all. Hilberg's view of the Holocaust as a purely bureaucratic "event" *cannot* explain as such the amazingly rapid transformations and results of the Nazi enterprise, a process not characteristic of bureaucracies. Scholars, mostly German ones, have tried to understand this phenomenon through delving into the personal and collective biographies of these people before 1933 and their careers during the Nazi period. They have also concluded that the Nazi regime, and especially the SS, intentionally left much maneuvering space to those who were ready to serve it creatively,[19] and, in general, the regime allowed for many to benefit in a variety of ways from the situations of occupation of other countries and of the deportations of the Jews.[20] Additionally,

---

18 Ian Kershaw, *Hitler 1889–1936: Hubris* (New York: Allen Lane, 1998), 527–89.
19 See, for example, Michael Wildt, *Generation de Unbedingten. Das Führungskorps des Reichssicherheitshauptamtes* (Hamburg: Hamburger Edition, 3., durchgesehene und aktualisierte Neuausgabe, 2003) [English version: *An Uncompromising Generation: The Nazi Leadership of the Reich Security Main Office* (Madison: University of Wisconsin Press, 2010)].
20 Götz Aly, *Hitlers Volksstaat. Raub, Rassenkrieg und nationaler Sozialismus* (Frankfurt am Main: S. Fischer, 2005) [English version: *Hitler's Beneficiaries. Plunder, Racial War, and the Nazi Welfare State* (New York: Metropolitan, 2007)].

recent years have seen a broad wave of research on grassroots activities by both Germans and locals, and it has become clear that the Holocaust—the comprehensive Nazi anti-Jewish enterprise—though German-initiated and led by Hitler, was in fact a Europe-wide project and has to be researched as such, and not just as a German one. And thus, the demarcation line between the perpetrator and bystander categories often blur. This has brought up in its wake again the question of the many shades of anti-Semitism in European culture and social life and its mobilizing potential as being a combining and driving factor, which could attract a broad variety of nationally, politically, and socially different people, among them also non-Nazis, who were ready to have their share in the eradication of "Jewish" presence. In this context the enormous extent of economic persecution and spoliation has got renewed attention, especially since the mid-1990s; the many historians' committees that were established throughout Europe in the wake of the Swiss dormant bank accounts affair which exploded in 1994 have shed much detailed light on this aspect, which was *not* a by-product of the Final Solution or—as Hilberg has it—a step or phase leading to it, but a feature by itself, another side of the higher goal of the Nazi project: to extinguish everything "Jewish."[21] Recent research has also looked into the ways persecuted Jews perceived the perpetrators; from this perspective a distinction between "perpetrators" and "fellow-travelers" has been proposed.[22]

As for the third Hilbergian protagonist, the so-called "victim"—this category also underwent an interesting development. In the first decade after the end of the war, an extremely comprehensive effort was made by Jewish historians and activists to collect survivor testimonies. This was accompanied by first attempts to write the history of the Holocaust through the Jewish angle, which, while it did not mean neglect of the perpetrator aspect, put its emphasis

---

21 Recent years have seen many studies in this field. Next to the publications of the findings of inquiry commissions in many countries, such as Austria, Belgium, France, and the Netherlands, leading scholars in this field are Frank Bajohr and Adam Tooze. A most important conference on this issue, whose proceedings, unfortunately, were not published, was organized by the Departmental Archives of the city of Grenoble on June 1–3, 2010, under the title: "'Aryanization' and the Spoliation of Jews in Nazi Europe (1933–1945)"; in order to see the broad variety of topics that were dealt with in this conference, it is worth accessing the program on the Internet: http://www.fondationshoah.org/FMS/IMG/pdf/Prog_Colloque_Grenoble_Engl.pdf.

22 Mark Roseman, *Barbarians from our "Kulturkreis": German-Jewish Perceptions of Nazi Perpetrators* (Jerusalem: Yad Vashem, 2016).

on the Jewish experience and Jewish society.[23] Due to a variety of reasons, which cannot be analyzed here, this endeavor was overshadowed by massive research on the perpetrators based on the vast amount of perpetrator documentation that was available and accessible in Germany after 1945, and mainly carried out in (West) Germany.[24] However, since the beginning of the 1980s, new testimony programs were initiated, and since the 1990s the awareness of the rich earlier collections grew. A growing number of contemporary diaries and correspondences have been published, too. Consequently, the voice of the Jews has been integrated into narratives of the Holocaust in various ways. Nevertheless, this important development is still limited to the individual aspect—to the voices of the individuals. The aspect of *Jewish* history, one that sees the reactions and behavior of the Jews as part of the broader context of modern Jewish history on the one hand and as a tool to grasp aspects of the perpetrator protagonist not revealed in perpetrator documentation, is not yet fully understood by many scholars dealing with the other categories.[25] Also in

---

23 Frank Beer, Wolfgang Benz, and Barbara Distel, eds., *Nach dem Untergang. Die ersten Zeugnisse der Shoah in Polen 1944–1947. Berichte der Zentralen Jüdischen Historischen Kommission* [After the destruction. The first witnesses of the Shoah in Poland 1944–1947. Reports of the Central Jewish Historical Commission] (Berlin: Metropol Verlag, 2014); Laura Jokusch, *Collect and Record: Jewish Holocaust Documentation in Early Postwar Europe* (Oxford: Oxford University Press, 2012); Boaz Cohen, *Israeli Holocaust Research: Birth and Evolution* (London: Routledge, 2013); Bankier and Michman, eds., *Holocaust Historiography in Context*.

24 To be sure, this research was characterized by many problems because scholars from the perpetrator society, themselves often involved in the Nazi regime in one way or another, now wrote the history of that period. See Nicolas Berg, *Der Holocaust und die westdeutschen Historiker. Erforschung und Erinnerung* (Göttingen: Wallstein, 2003). An abridged English version appeared recently: *The Holocaust and the West German Historians: Historical Interpretation and Autobiographical Memory* (Madison: University of Wisconsin Press, 2015). See also Chris Lorenz: "Border-crossings: Some Reflections on the Role of German Historians in Recent Public Debates on Nazi History," in Dan Michman, ed., *Remembering the Holocaust in Germany, 1945–2000: German Strategies and Jewish Responses* (New York: Peter Lang Inc., 2002), 59–94.

25 On these issues see Dan Michman, "The Jewish Dimension of the Holocaust: The Context of Modern Jewish History," in *Holocaust Historiography*, 59–88; "The Jewish Dimension of the Holocaust in Dire Straits?"; "Handeln und Erfahrung: Bewältigungsstrategien im Kontext der jüdischen Geschichte" [Behaviour and experience: Strategies for coping in the context of Jewish history], in Bajohr and Löw, *Der Holocaust*, 257–79; Yehuda Bauer, "Teguvoteihem shel kibbutzim yehudiyim lamediniyut hanatzit be'et hashoah lenochah morashoteihem hameyuhadot: mabat kelali mashveh" [Reactions of Jewish communities to Nazi Policy during the Shoah in connection with their unique backgrounds: A general comparative analysis] in *Hashoah Bahistoriya Hayehudit: Historiografiya, Toda'ah Ufarshanut* [The Holocaust in Jewish history:

the field of modern Jewish history, there has been an attempt by many scholars to sever the Holocaust period from earlier developments (i.e., that when one deals with the eighteenth and nineteenth centuries, one has totally to avoid thinking about the later occurrence of the Holocaust in order not to distort the picture)—an issue criticized by David Engel in his *Historians of the Jews and the Holocaust* (2010), which stirred a fierce discussion.[26]

THE CONTRIBUTION OF NEW METHODOLOGIES

As said in the beginning of this essay, it is impossible to deal here in an in-depth way with all the major developments in the field of Holocaust studies, a field that is vibrant and expanding constantly. Nevertheless, some of the new approaches and methodologies that have become popular in general historical studies and were applied to Holocaust studies in recent years have to be mentioned.

The concept of collective memory, a term first used in the second half of the nineteenth century, but which became popular with the theoretical study of sociologist Maurice Halbwachs in the mid-twentieth century,[27] has conquered center stage in general historical research since the 1970s. The Holocaust, because of its role in the immediate past and in the current identity struggles of European, Jewish, and Israeli societies, has been a fertile test case for this venue. The ways in which the Holocaust is remembered and memorialized (and manipulated) by states, organizations, and groups is by now a burgeoning subfield of Holocaust studies, often overtaking (and sometimes

---

    Historiography, consciousness, interpretations], ed. Dan Michman (Jerusalem: Yad Vashem, 2005), 109–28.

26 David Engel, *Historians of the Jews and the Holocaust* (Stanford, CA: Stanford University Press, 2010); Hebrew version: *Mul Har Haga'ash* (Jerusalem: Zalman Shazar Center, 2009). For some voices from the variety of reactions and reviews running from praise to criticism, see Dan Stone on H-Judaic, April 2010, https://networks.h-net.org/node/28655/reviews/30764/stone-engel-historians-jews-and-holocaust; Yerachmiel (Richard) Cohen, "Heker hahistoriya hayehudit leahar hashoah—Keitzad?" [Research into Jewish history after the Holocaust. How should this be done?] *Zion* 75, no. 2 (2010): 201–15; Guy Miron, "Bridging the Divide: Holocaust versus Jewish History Research—Problems and Challenges," *Yad Vashem Studies* 38, no. 2 (2010): 155–93; Norman J. W. Goda in *Central European History* 44, no. 3 (September 2011): 585–87; David Cesarani in *Jewish Quarterly Review* 102, no. 1 (Winter 2012): 91–95; Dmitry Shumsky, "The Cracks in the Wall: Toward a Neo-crisis Paradigm of Jewish Historiography? David Engel, "Historians of the Jews and the Holocaust," Yad Vashem Studies 40, no. 1 (2012): 275–300.

27 Maurice Halbwachs, *La mémoire collective* (Paris, 1950) [English version: *On Collective Memory*] (Chicago: University of Chicago Press, 1992).

overshadowing and blurring) research on the Holocaust itself. This explosion of interest is definitely a result of the expanding interest in the Holocaust worldwide since the mid-1970s—a topic that draws attention because of its high profile in the public sphere and its intertwining with politics. Yet the result is often a combination of the interest in the Holocaust on the one hand with a lack of knowledge of the needed languages for research on the core period (the 1930s and 1940s) on the other; memory studies usually do not require knowledge of several (and especially lesser known) languages and thus serve as a solution for this problem.[28]

Recently, the cultural, linguistic, and spatial turns in historiography as well as gender studies have also had their impact on Holocaust studies,[29] though not yet enough. And archeology has also entered the picture, clarifying certain material aspects, especially regarding the extermination camps in Poland, but through that angle raising certain new questions.[30]

---

28 Googling the words *collective memory* and *Holocaust* will provide more than half a million hits.

29 For a discussion of this approach see Dan Stone, "Holocaust Historiography and Cultural History," *Dapim: Studies on the Holocaust* 23, no. 1 (2009): 52–68; and the responses by Dan Michman (69–75), Carolyn J. Dean (76–80), Wendy Lower (80–86), Federico Finchelstein (87–88), and Dominick LaCapra (89–93). For an excellent study using cultural tools, see Alon Confino, *A World without Jews* (New Haven, CT: University Press, 2014). For a study of the emergence of the Nazi ghetto phenomenon using the tool of the history of concepts and changing semantics, see Dan Michman, *The Emergence of Jewish Ghettos during the Holocaust* (Cambridge: Cambridge University Press, 2011). For a general theoretical essay tackling this issue with relevance to the Holocaust, see Guy Miron, "A People between Languages—Towards Jewish History of Concepts," *Contributions to the History of Concepts* 7, no. 2 (Winter 2012): 1–27. For the spatial approach, see: Tim Cole, *Holocaust City: The Making of a Jewish Ghetto* (New York: Bloomsbury Continuum, 2003); and Guy Miron, "'Lately, almost constantly, everything seems small to me': The Lived Space of German Jews under the Nazi Regime," *Jewish Social Studies*, new series 20, no. 1 (Fall 2014): 121–49. Gender studies in the field of Holocaust historiography have their origins in the 1980s, but only since the end of the 1990s has a body of research, both on Jewish women and perpetrator women, established itself; see Marion Kaplan, *Between Dignity and Despair: Jewish Life in Nazi Germany* (Oxford: Oxford University Press, 1998); Judy Tydor Baumel, *Double Jeopardy: Gender and the Holocaust* (London: Vallentine Mitchell, 1998); Wendy Lower, *Hitler's Furies, German Women in the Nazi Killing Fields* (Boston: Houghton Mifflin Harcourt, 2013). For a combination of some of the approaches mentioned here see Janet Jacobs, *Memorializing the Holocaust: Gender, Genocide and Collective Memory* (London: I. B. Tauris, 2010).

30 Yoram Haimi and Wojciech Mazurek, "Uncovering the Remains of a Nazi Death Camp: Archaeological Research in Sobibor," *Yad Vashem Studies* 41, no. 2 (2013): 55–94.

RESEARCH ON THE HOLOCAUST IN POLAND WITHIN THIS PICTURE

Research on the Shoah in Poland has a special place in the overall picture. Much of the earliest conceptualizations of the Holocaust originated in the mid-1940s, as a result of the immediate post-liberation research and documentation activities on Polish soil, carried out by Polish Jewish survivor historians. Even during the communist period, Poland was the only Eastern European country in which there was serious research—even though limited and colored—and important analyses were carried out—by, for example, the people around the Jewish Historical Institute (Żydowski Instytut Historyczny—ŻIH). Moreover, some of the Polish-born Jewish historians and authors (such as Philip Friedman, Isaiah Trunk, and Nachman Blumental) emigrated afterwards to the United States and Israel and their interpretations of the Holocaust in general and of particulars in it—even if they had only limited access to archival materials in Poland—have left deep imprints in Holocaust historiography in general. Materials and studies were also published in the many *yizkor-bikher*, whose largest component deals with Polish Jewish communities. Since the 1960s, the Polish arena has had an important place in German perpetrator research too.[31]

But since the downfall of communism, which was in Poland a gradual process starting in the early 1980s, Poland has been the country where the scholarly and public debates about the Holocaust period have been most poignant, in-depth, and comprehensive—more than in any other East-Central or Eastern European country, and their intensity has also gone beyond that of the debates in many other European countries. Yet this has also led to the fact that Polish research has entirely focused on Poland, and we do not see Polish Holocaust scholars involved in more general debates raging in Holocaust studies. Jan Błoński's article "Biedni Polacy patrzą na getto" [Poor Poles Look at the Ghetto] (1987)[32] and Jan T. Gross's book *Neighbors*

---

31 The influential historian Martin Broszat, director of the Institut für Zeitgeschichte in Munich for many years (and who in the 1980s became controversial), dedicated a considerable portion of his research to Poland: *Nationalsozialistische Polenpolitik 1939–1945* [National Socialist policy towards Poland 1939–1945] (Stuttgart: Deutsche Verlags-Anstalt, 1961); *Zweihundert Jahre deutsche Polenpolitik* [Two hundred years of German policy towards Poland] (München: Ehrenwirth, 1963); *Der Staat Hitlers: Grundlegung und Entwicklung seiner inneren Verfassung* [Hitler's state: The foundation and development of its internal constitution] (München: Deutscher Taschenbuch Verlag, 1969) (this last book, in which the conquest and occupation play an important role, has had no less than fifteen reprints!).

32 Jan Błoński, "Biedni Polacy patrzą na getto" [The poor Poles look at the ghetto], *Tygodnik Powszechny*, January 11, 1987.

(2000)³³ were milestones in a painful but also healing discussion, which is still going on. An impressive volume of research has been pouring out in recent years by several groups of scholars, mainly in Warsaw and Kraków. Some of this research is path-breaking and sets standards for Holocaust research outside Poland too. I will just mention here the research project on the Polish countryside in the years 1942–44, conducted by a team of scholars headed by Barbara Engelking and Jan Grabowski. One can also see extensive fruitful cooperation between Polish and non-Polish scholars with Polish origins or with Polish background—from Germany, France, the United States, Canada, and Israel. An impressive body of studies by the younger German generation who matured in the past twenty-five years has contributed a critical mass to our knowledge about many aspects of the complicated picture of the Holocaust in the different parts of Poland which underwent different trajectories of persecution from the very first moment of the invasion on September 1, 1939, through the final liberation in 1945. Moreover, leading scholars of the overall picture of the Third Reich and the Shoah (such as Christopher Browning, Ian Kershaw, and Saul Friedländer) have done important work integrating the events on Polish soil into the larger picture. Projects at Yad Vashem and the USHMM, especially the two encyclopedias of the ghettos,³⁴ have also added much knowledge and contextualization. Indeed, the volume of impressive research has also raised controversy in the political arena, in which there has been made attempts to deny unpleasant findings regarding behavior of Poles and to counter with putting an emphasis on help and rescue activities;³⁵ but the seriousness of the above-mentioned scholarship cannot be contested.

---

33 Published in Poland in 2000; English version: Jan T. Gross, *Neighbors: The Destruction of the Jewish Community in Jedwabne, Poland* (Princeton, NJ: Princeton University Press, 2001).

34 Guy Miron and Shlomit Shulhani, eds., *The Yad Vashem Encyclopedia of Ghettos during the Holocaust* (Jerusalem: Yad Vashem, 2009); Geoffrey P. Megargee (General Editor) and Martin Dean (Volume Editor), *The United States Holocaust Memorial Museum Encyclopedia of Camps and Ghettos, 1933–1945.* Volume II (Parts A and B): *Ghettos in German-Occupied Eastern Europe* (Bloomington: Indiana University Press in association with the United States Holocaust Memorial Museum, 2012).

35 See Katrin Stoll, Sabine Stach and Magdalena Saryusz-Wolska, "Verordnete Geschichte? Zur Dominanz nationalistischer Narrative in Polen" [Imposed history? On the domination of the nationalist narrative in Poland] *Zeitgeschichte-Online*, June 2016, www.zeitgeschichte-online.de/thema/verordnete-geschichte-zur-dominanz-nationalistischer-narrative-polen#_ftnref64, accessed on September 4, 2016.

Yet one important thing is still missing: a comprehensive study of the Holocaust in Poland, which could be used as a handbook for university teaching and as an orientation point for scholars. For most countries of Europe at least one such volume, and often more than one, exists.[36] The reasons for this lack—or neglect—are various, yet they can hardly serve as a serious excuse. I hope that this challenge will be picked up by one or more people from the quite extensive community of scholars working on this important topic—a topic that is essential for the understanding of the Holocaust in general, from a variety of perspectives, not only that of Polish and Polish Jewish history.

---

36 There are such volumes for France, Belgium, the USSR, Bohemia-Moravia, Greece, Germany, Lithuania, Latvia, Hungary, Italy; a volume about Bulgaria is to be published soon. For the Netherlands, there are already six (!), the first account having appeared in 1947.

The Dispute over the Status of a Witness to the Holocaust: Some Observations on How Research into the Destruction of the Polish Jews and into Polish–Jewish Relations during the Years of Nazi Occupation Has Changed since 1989

ANDRZEJ ŻBIKOWSKI

Over the past quarter of a century, the topic of the ordinary Pole as a witness to the Holocaust has been discussed in at least fifty major historical monographs written by Polish authors, a great number of collective works, numerous post-conference reports, and the ten substantial volumes of *Zagłada Żydów. Studia i Materiały* (Genocide of the Jews. Studies and documents) produced by the Center for Research on the Destruction of the Jews, issued by the Philosophical and Sociological Institute of the Polish Academy of Sciences (Instytut Filozofii i Socjologii Polskiej Akademii Nauk—IFiS PAN). There is no space in a short essay even to list these works and their authors, let alone space for even the shortest of commentaries on their content. This has certainly greatly increased our knowledge on the changing situation of the

Jewish population under the German occupation, on the actual course of the Holocaust itself and on Polish–Jewish relations during the occupation. Above all, there is not enough space to discuss all the debates and arguments that these works have inspired. One detail, however, is certain: the community of Polish historians, often with the assistance of representatives of other disciplines in the humanities, has not slept through the last decades, and to the extent that this was possible has made good use of the new conditions after 1989 to depoliticize Poland's recent history in the area that interests us..

My goal in this article is to propose a personal systematic approach to the newest Polish historical writing that focuses mainly, although not exclusively, on assessing Polish–Jewish relations during the years of the Second World War. In point of fact, the issue is not so much Polish–Jewish relations, since a certain symmetry would be required and only Havi Ben Sasson[1] and indirectly Samuel Kassow[2] have written on the attitudes of Jews toward Poles, but of the attitudes of the Poles, of their underground institutions and the émigré government to their fellow countrymen, the Jews and their destruction, as well as their own self-assessment as to what extent Polish citizens succeeded in evading the obligations imposed by the Nazi occupier to collaborate and cooperate in the destruction of their Jewish fellow countrymen. Bartłomiej Krupa, in his article "Historia krytyczna i jej 'gabinet cieni'. Historiografia polska wobec Zagłady 2003–2013,"[3] has analyzed this same corpus of more recent Polish historical works on the Holocaust in much greater detail. It seems to me that what connects us is a conviction of the persistence of two basic contradictory scholarly trends in the historiography of the mass murder of Polish Jews, accurately categorized by Krupa as a critical historiography and a historiography glorifying Poles' wartime attitudes. Krupa has also ably demonstrated the influence of Jan T. Gross's important works on attempts to refashion regional historiography, specifically its "peasant trend."

---

1 Havi Ben-Sasson, "'Chcemy wierzyć w inną Polskę.' Stosunki żydowsko-polskie w podziemnej prasie żydowskiego getta warszawskiego" ["We want to believe in a different Poland". Jewish-Polish relations in the underground press of the Warsaw ghetto], *Zagłada Żydów. Studia i Materiały* 1 (2005), 96–113.

2 Samuel Kassow, *Who Will Write Our History? Emanuel Ringelblum, the Warsaw Ghetto, and the Oyneg Shabes Archive* (Bloomington: Indiana University Press, 2007); Polish edition, *Kto napisze naszą historię? Ukryte archiwum Emanuela Ringelbluma* (Warsaw: Wydawnictwo Amber, 2010).

3 "Critical history and its 'cabinet of secrets'. Polish historiography on the Holocaust, 2003–2013," *Zagłada Żydów. Studia i Materiały* 10 (2014), vol. 2., 721–67.

Jean-Yves Potel, in the foreword to his very interesting book *Koniec niewinności. Polska wobec swojej żydowskiej przeszłości*,[4] has observed that the people with whom he discussed these matters emphasized that "one day they became so aware of the tangible, physical reality of their received inheritance that they recognized that this subject was the prime topic to which they should devote all their time. They asked themselves to Polish identity more than about Polish–Jewish relations. They placed the responsibility of witnesses at the center of remembrance and public debate." This is certainly the case.

I might add that the category of witnesses (bystanders) to the Holocaust, "invented" by Raul Hilberg, is now often challenged, and not only by Polish historians. Omer Bartov, in his article "Wołanie krwi brata twego. Rekonstrukcja ludobójstwa w lokalnej skali" (regarding Buczacz in the Kresy borderlands),[5] writes: "Studying the Holocaust at the local level, we quickly come to the realization that the category of witnesses (bystanders) ceases to have any meaning. When an invader allies with local forces to murder a segment of the population, one can distinguish only specific levels of involvement, from total cooperation to complete opposition."

The debates mentioned by Potel can be dated back to 1985 when Claude Lanzmann produced his film *Shoah*, and when, out of a nine-hour film, Polish public television selected less than sixty minutes of footage showing his Polish respondents as heartless, bloodthirsty barbarians. Two years later, Jan Błoński published in *Tygodnik Powszechny* his disturbing essay "Biedni Polacy patrzą na getto,"[6] dealing with the pervasive indifference during the occupation on the part of Poles to the murder of their Jewish fellow countrymen. Writing on the quite widespread anxiety among Poles about their "good name" in the context of the Holocaust, he opined: "We must quite openly, quite honestly face the question of joint responsibility." The Rubicon had been crossed.

The year 1994 saw a controversial article by Michał Cichy in *Magazyn Gazety Wyborczej* (The magazine of the electoral newspaper) on the murder of several scores of Jews by insurgents in the Warsaw uprising and on the first academic publication devoted to the Kielce pogrom.[7] However, the watershed came in 2000 with the publicizing of the issue of Jedwabne, mainly due to

---

4 The end of innocence. Poles in the face of their Jewish Past (Kraków: Znak, 2010).
5 The cry of your brother's blood. Reconstructing genocide on a local scale, *Zagłada Żydów. Studia i Materiały* 10 (2014), vol. 1, 319–53.
6 The poor Poles look at the ghetto, *Tygodnik Powszechny*, January 11, 1987.
7 *Gazeta Wyborcza*, January 29–30, 1994. I mentioned this murder some time ago also in a review in *Więź* of Icchak Rubin's *Żydzi w Łodzi* [Jews in Łódź], as well as in the foreword to a volume of Samuel Willenberg's memoirs, *Bunt w Treblince* [Revolt in Treblinka] (Warsaw, 1991).

the reception of Jan T. Gross's book *Sąsiedzi*.[8] The following two years saw the publication of more than two thousand newspaper articles on the subject of relations between Poles and Jews during the occupation. An important stage in this debate was the publication by Instytut Pamięci Narodowej (IPN) of a two-volume collection of papers and sources, *Wokół Jedwabnego*,[9] covering both the crime in Jedwabne itself and other such events in several dozen small communities in the area. As I was one of the authors of this publication I can state, with complete confidence, that we differed greatly among ourselves in our assessment of the Polish population's attitude and behavior toward its Jewish fellow countrymen under both the Soviet and the Nazi occupation. Nevertheless, the years 2000–2002 seem to me to have been a watershed in setting a completely new direction for research. By degrees we began to include in our research an unknown, or perhaps "unacknowledged," body of sources hidden in the archives, as well as to develop new methodological assumptions. In terms of sources, we delved deeper into the collections of documents amassed during the occupation, created either by the German authorities (Polish magistrates' courts and German courts), or by the Polish underground state, studying not only the underground press but also the documentation of regional administrative structures.[10] Secondly, in cross-referencing, translating from the Yiddish, and comparing accounts of Jews who were saved, we felt more trust in their testimony. Thirdly, research into the "Jedwabne affair" resulted in the discovery of court cases and investigations connected with the 1944 August degree "on punishing war criminals and traitors to the Polish nation"—in other words, trying wartime collaborators. Detailed analysis of this material revealed that a substantial majority of investigations and trials were not political in nature and did not involve members of the wartime pro-London resistance movement but quite ordinary town and

---

8   Jan T. Gross, *Sąsiedzi. Historia zagłady żydowskiego miasteczka* (Sejny: Pogranicze, 2000). English version, *Neighbors: The Destruction of the Jewish Community in Jedwabne, Poland* (Princeton, NJ: Princeton University Press, 2001).

9   Concerning Jedwabne, eds. Paweł Machcewicz and Krzysztof Persak, vols.1–2, (Warsaw: IPN, 2002).

10 We also became better acquainted with Jewish sources from the years of occupation. I have in mind here, above all, the successive volumes of the Ringelblum Archive, published by ŻIH (vols.1–13, Warsaw, 2000–2013), as well as a great many wartime memoirs from this archive. Lately, the Centrum Badań nad Zagładą Żydów (CBnZŻ) has also begun to publish memoirs held in the archives at Yad Vashem. Most of these sources have been used by Barbara Engelking and Jacek Leociak in *Getto Warszawskie: Przewodnik po nieistniejącym mieście* (Warsaw: Wydawn. IFiS, 2001). English version, *The Warsaw Ghetto: A Guide to the Perished City*, trans. Emma Harris (New Haven, CT: Yale University Press, 2009).

country dwellers, who for various reasons had decided to collaborate with the Nazi occupier. Some 10–20 percent of these cases had a Jewish angle, including participation in a German roundup, denunciations, thefts of property, or taking part in the killing of people who were in hiding. Furthermore, the accused were not for the most part local officials or Polish "blue" policemen, but ordinary farmers with families. This was a startling discovery by scholars of recent history brought up on Aleksander Kamiński's *Kamienie na szaniec* [Stones against the ramparts] and the legend of the Warsaw uprising.

Put simply, and paraphrasing the words of Jan Karski, the central character of my last book,[11] we became aware of the narrow path of Polish–German cooperation during the occupation, directed against Polish Jews. Hence we began to study "negatives" from the occupation.

Not everyone did so, of course. The preceding decades had trained the community of modern-period historians (during the Polish People's Republic their numbers were small, due to constant ideological and administrative pressures) to present the subject of Polish–Jewish relations during the occupation solely in terms of the Polish people's supposed mass support of persecuted Jews. This purported assistance was usually characterized as disinterested and always heroic because of constant threats of death sentences, the help being widely supported in the underground by Żegota—the Council to Aid Jews. In those years, there was no place for the examination of shameful, let alone criminal attitudes and behavior. The beginning of this heroic-martyrological discourse was marked by the publication in 1966 by the Kraków publishing house Znak of a collection of accounts edited by Władysław Bartoszewski and Zofia Lewin titled *Ten jest z ojczyzny mojej. Polacy z pomocą Żydom 1939–1945*, better known to the public from the 1969 edition supplemented by documents from the Polish Underground.[12] A great many other authors wrote in a similar vein, as shown by Szymon Datner's *Las sprawiedliwych. Karta z dziejów ratownictwa Żydów okupowanej Polsce*,[13] Stanisław Wroński's and Maria Zwolakowa's *Polacy Żydzi 1939–1945*,[14] Marek Arczyński's and Wiesław Balcerak's

---

11 I have in mind his 1940 report for the government in Angers, titled "Zagadnienie żydowskie w kraju," in *Raport Jana Karskiego o sytuacji Żydów na okupowanych ziemiach polskich na początku 1940 r.* [Jan Karski's report on the situation of the Jews in the occupied Polish lands at the beginning of 1940], ed. Artur Eisenbach, *Dzieje Najnowsze* 1989, no. 2, 179–200.

12 He is from my fatherland. Poles who aided Jews 1939–1945, 3rd ed. (Warsaw: Świat Książki and Żydowski Iinstytut Historyczny, 2007).

13 A Forest of Righteous. Pages from the history of the rescue of Jews in occupied Poland, (Warsaw: Książka i wiedza, 1968).

14 Poles and Jews 1939–1945 (Warsaw: Książka i Wiedza, 1971).

Kryptonim Żegota. Z dziejów pomocy Żydom w Polsce 1939–1945,[15] Władysław Smólski's *Za to groziła śmierć. Polacy z pomocą Żydom w czasie okupacji*,[16] and Teresa Prekerowa's *Konspiracyjna Rada Pomocy Żydom w Warszawie 1942–1945*.[17] Strong support for these writers came from London from Kazimierz Iranek Osmecki, a former senior officer in the Home Army High Command,[18] and much later from the representative of the Government Delegate Stefan Korboński.[19] Literature on aid to Jews is discussed by Dariusz Libionka in his article "Polskie piśmiennictwo na temat zorganizowanej i indywidualnej pomocy Żydom 1945–2008."[20]

This current of historical thought has not died, although it has not flourished greatly since the debate over Jedwabne. A number of historians wrote in similar vein in a collection of papers issued in 2006 by IPN, which I edited, titled *Polacy i Żydzi pod okupacją niemiecką 1939–1945. Studia i materiały* (Poles and Jews under German occupation 1939–1945. Studies and materials). I have in mind here Marcin Urynowicz's essays on assistance for Jews and on the Warsaw Ghetto,[21] Aleksandra Namysło's writing on help for Jews in the Katowice district, Krystyna Samsonowska writing about Kraków, Elżbieta Rączy's writing about Polish–Jewish relations in the Rzeszów area, and Jan Żaryn's study about the nationalist camp which, in his view, was active in helping Jews. Two of these writers have devoted separate studies to related subjects. Leaving on one side the controversial work of Ewa Kurek-Lesik[22] and the useful, though

---

15 Code name Żegota. On the history of aid to the Jews in Poland 1939–1945 (Warsaw: Czytelnik, 1979).

16 This was punished by death. Poles who aided Jews during the occupation (Warsaw: PAX, 1981).

17 The Underground Council for Aid to Jews in Warsaw 1942–1945 (Warsaw: Państwowy Instytut Wydawniczy, 1982).

18 Kazimierz Iranek-Osmecki, *Kto ratuje jedno życie... Polacy i Żydzi 1939–1945* [He who saves one life... Poles and Jews 1939–1945] (London: Orbis, 1968).

19 Stefan Korboński, *The Jews and the Poles in World War II* (New York: Hippocrene Books, 1989); *Polacy, Żydzi i Holocaust* (Warsaw: Instytut Pamięci Narodowej—Komisja Ścigania Zbrodni przeciwko Narodowi Polskiemu, 2011).

20 Polish writing on the topic of organized and individual aid to the Jews 1945–2008, *Zagłada Żydów. Studia i Materiały* 4 (2008).

21 Urynowicz is also the author of a biography of Adam Czerniaków: *Adam Czerniaków. Prezes getta warszawskiego* [Adam Czerniaków, President of the Warsaw ghetto] (Warsaw: Instytut Pamięci Narodowej—Komisja Ścigania Zbrodni przeciwko Narodowi Polskiemu, 2009), in which, however, he devotes little space to Polish–Jewish relations.

22 Ewa Kurek-Lesik, *Dzieci żydowskie w klasztorach. Udział żeńskich zgromadzeń zakonnych w akcji ratowania dzieci żydowskich w Polsce w latach 1939–1945* [Jewish children in nunneries. The role of female religious orders in saving Jewish children in Poland in the years 1939–1945] (Kraków: Wydawnictow "Znak," 1992; 2nd ed. Lublin: Wydawnictwo "Klio," 2001).

somewhat one-sided source publication edited by Andrzej Krzysztof Kunert titled *Żegota—Rada Pomocy Żydom 1942–1945*,[23] I should devote a few words to the no less controversial book by Gunnar S. Paulsson, *Secret City: The Hidden Jews of Warsaw 1940–1945*.[24] Paulsson claims that quite a high number of Jews were hiding in the "Aryan side" (altogether 28,000, some 17,000 before the outbreak of the Warsaw uprising, of whom 8,900 were under the direct care of aid organizations), and that many Poles were involved in aid (70,000–90,000, figures which other historians have argued are exaggerated). In Paulsson's view, three-quarters of so-called individual selfless acts went undocumented, not to mention that, in addition, while Poles certainly could easily recognize assimilated Jews concealing themselves under a Polish identity, they did not turn them in to the occupying forces, with the exception of a rather narrow group of extortionists, whose actions led to the deaths of about 4,000 people. The occupying forces on their own initiative captured a similar number of Jews hiding in the city, in different types of roundups.

According to Paulsson, the fact that memoir writers always mention encountering extortionists suggests that the writers would be even more eager to describe theft carried out by someone known and trusted. Yet their accounts say almost nothing about this angle. In his view, anyone claiming that the majority of Poles in this situation exploited Jews, and basing this claim solely on entries about a certain number of blackmailers, displays an inadequate knowledge of psychological motivation.[25]

Paulsson also optimistically assesses reality under the occupation, writing that "networks of contacts on which Jews relied wove themselves into different shapes creating a single hidden city," of whose existence the Germans were completely unaware. Likewise, a general statement such as "Polish 'blue' police officers were rather cautious about turning in suspected Jews to the Germans, since there had been cases of Poles being taken for Jews" does not inspire confidence. We should also remember that at the end of the day the writer too strongly stresses the small number of memoirs of Jews, and does not discuss the court cases resulting from the August decree, mentioned above.

Summing up this aspect of Polish historical writing—I might add that it continues, although it is none too popular—we may state that up to the year

---

23 Żegota—the Council to Aid Jews 1942–1945 (Warsaw: Rada Ochrony Pamięci Walk i Męczeństwa, 2002).
24 English edition (New Haven, CT: Yale University Press, 2002), translated into Polish as *Utajone miasto. Żydzi po aryjskiej stronie Warszawy 1940–1945* (Warsaw: Znak, 2007).
25 Ibid., 54.

2000 so-called Polish witnesses to the Holocaust were for most part perceived to be the Righteous, people fighting German terror tactics and willing to help those in danger. There were supposedly many, many more than noted in underground documents and postwar accounts. The remaining Poles were supposedly equally supportive of Jews, although owing to the anti-Polish regime of terror, and fearful for their own families, they remained passive. However, no mention was made of collaboration with the Nazi occupier, even if collaboration was caused by fear, in achieving the complete liquidation of the Jewish population. The Jedwabne debate, the founding of the Polish Center for Holocaust Research (Centrum Badań nad Zagładą Żydów), and its initial publications forced a revision of the prevailing paradigm, and also spurred to action and somewhat emboldened communities beyond Warsaw. As a result of this process there have appeared in the last fifteen years a great many innovative historical studies that illustrate the complex wartime reality from various perspectives. In this work, we can distinguish several historical narratives, usually resulting from the authors' different historical methodologies.

TREND NO. 1—A CONTINUATION OF THE MARTYROLOGICAL LINE, POLISH NATIONALISTS

As historians began to uncover a growing number of examples of hostile behavior on the part of the Polish population toward Jews both during the time of the ghettos and during the mass deportations when there were a great many attempts to escape ahead of the deportations to death camps, the number of supporters of continuing the martyrological/merciful narrative has systematically dwindled. Only clearly defined proponents of the Polish nationalist/national democratic tradition have persevered, focusing mainly on the nationalist underground movement and the most recent history of the Roman Catholic Church. The leaders of this group are Jan Żaryn (referred to above) and the American historian of Polish descent Marek Jan Chodakiewicz. They are both associated with *Fronda*, as well as with *Glaukopis*—a publication that has arisen mainly to rehabilitate unconditionally the wartime activities of the Narodowe Siły Zbrojne (NSZ). The manifesto of this narrow and often attacked group has been Chodakiewicz's very controversial book *Żydzi i Polacy 1918–1955. Współistnienie—zagłada—komunizm*.[26] If we were to use just one descriptor

---

26   Poles and Jews 1918–1945. Coexistence—mass murder—communism (Warsaw: Fronda, 2000). His other work, *Po Zagładzie. Stosunki polsko-żydowskie 1944–1947* [After the

we could call this trend of writing the school of "parity," since the key to these people's writings is an interchangeably applied selection of examples of good and reprehensible behavior by both Poles and Jews during the Second World War. Many years ago, I devoted a number of remarks to characteristic features of Chodakiewicz's method.[27] He accuses exclusively the Nazi occupier for the development of a number of pathologies in Poles' attitudes toward persecuted Jews, and emphasizes the effectiveness of the Nazis' anti-Polish propaganda. It was terror tactics or circumstances that compelled Poles to collaborate with the Germans, such as, for instance, the fact that Jewish fugitives from the ghettos were unable to pay for the food needed for their survival and often simply stole from the fields. He sees denunciations to the authorities by peasants as a legitimate form of self-defense. However, he objects to and considers unjustified the generalizations claimed by rescued Jews that the Polish provinces were fundamentally anti-Semitic. One seeks in vain in Chodakiewicz's book expressions of empathy with the murdered Jews; he equates German terror tactics toward Poles with those toward Jews, which in his opinion justified the reluctance of representatives of Polish underground structures to undertake action to help Jews. Chodakiewicz blames the growing dislike of Jews during the years of occupation on their supposed mass collaboration with the Soviet occupier between 1939 and 1941. He does not take consider these accusations as convenient justification for passivity during the years of trial, but treats them literally as a fact supposedly widely known throughout occupied Poland. He does not even consider how rumors of conflicts beyond the Bug might have reached the provinces in central Poland, where radio information was not available and where both the gutter press and the underground press were difficult to obtain.

It should be noted, too, that in the first decade of this century several books have supported the continued tales of Righteous Poles who were murdered for assisting Jews, or who were simply forgotten after the war. These semi-academic, semi-literary works—and I have in mind here the works of Grzegorz

---

Holocaust. Polish-Jewish relations 1944–1947] (Warsaw: Instytut Pamięci Narodowej—Komisja Ścigania Zbrodni Przeciwko Narodowi Polskiem, 2008), which has been quite widely recognized as not meeting academic standards, has played a smaller part.

27 Andrzej Żbikowski, "Antysemityzm, szmalcownictwo, współpraca z Niemcami a stosunki polsko-żydowskie pod okupacją niemiecką" [Anti-Semitism, blackmailing, cooperation with the Germans and Polish-Jewish relations during the German occupation], in *Polacy i Żydzi pod okupacją niemiecką 1939–1945. Studia i materiały* [Poles and Germans under German occupation 1939–1945. Studies and materials] (Warsaw: Instytut Pamięci Narodowej—Komisja Ścigania Zbrodni przeciwko Narodowi Polskiemu, 2006), 462–63.

Łubczyk, *Polski Wallenberg. Rzecz o Henryku Sławiku*[28]; Elżbieta Isakiewicz, *Czerwony ołówek. O Polaku, który ocalił tysiące Żydów*[29]; Anna Mieszkowska, *Matka dzieci Holocaustu. Historia Ireny Sendlerowej*[30]; Jacek Młynarczyk and Sebastian Piątkowski, *Cena poświęcenia. Zbrodnie na Polakach za pomoc udzielaną Żydom w rejonie Ciepielowa*[31]; Mateusz Szpytma, *Sprawiedliwi i ich świat. Markowa w fotografii Józefa Ulmy*[32]—are discussed in detail by Dariusz Libionka in the article mentioned above.[33]

TREND NO. 2—INDIFFERENCE TO THE HOLOCAUST AS A RESULT OF JEWS' ATTITUDES TOWARD THE POLES AND THE DESTRUCTION OF THE POLISH STATE UNDER SOVIET OCCUPATION, 1939–41

It is not easy to generalize about this discourse, since not only do historians studying this subject differ greatly in their assessment of the phenomenon, but some have also radically changed their attitude toward the behavior of the Jewish population. The telling example is Krzysztof Jasiewicz; in *Pierwsi po diable. Elity sowieckie w okupowanej Polsce 1939–1941*,[34] who decisively rejected as unjustified the general accusation that Jews in the Kresy borderlands had collaborated on a large scale with Soviet authorities. In a second important work, *Rzeczywistość sowiecka 1939–1941 w świadectwach polskich Żydów*,[35] Jasiewicz clearly and decisively distanced himself from his own earlier views. He has accused Jews who tried to join the Anders Army of insincerity in their patriotic declarations before its officers when testifying to their experiences under Soviet occupation. This was supposedly confirmed by a wave of desertions when the army was in Palestine. Among the statements of eighty-three Polish Jews associated with the Anders Army, only one person was not

---

28 The Polish Wallenberg. A study of Henryk Sławik (Warsaw: Oficyna Wydawnicza Rytm, 2003).
29 The Red Pencil: On a Pole who saved thousands of Jews (Warsaw: Niezależne Wydawn. Polskie, 2003).
30 The mother of the Holocaust children. A history of Irena Sendler (Warsaw: Warszawskie Wydawn. Literackie MUZA SA, 2004).
31 The price of devotion. Crimes against Poles providing help to Jews in the Ciepielów region (Kraków: Instytut Studiów Stategicznych, 2007).
32 The Righteous and their world. Markowa in the photographs of Józef Ulma (Warsaw: Instytut Pamięci Narodowej, 2007).
33 Libionka, "Polskie piśmiennictwo," 72–74.
34 The first after the devil, Soviet elites in occupied Poland 1939–1941 (Warsaw: Rytm, 2003).
35 The Soviet reality 1939–1941 in the testimonies of Polish Jews (Warsaw: Rytm, 2009).

indifferent to the collapse of the Polish state; in Jasiewicz's view, this was "the most characteristic feature of Polish Jewry and this indifference, it appears, was then reciprocated by a great number of Poles during the Jewish national catastrophe, motivated additionally by the Jews' hostile attitude toward the Poles in the Kresy between 1939 and 1941 and toward the Polish nation and its citizens' dramatic circumstances."[36] Jasiewicz's and Chodakiewicz's views on this issue are now in complete harmony, although they had differed completely six years earlier.

To a lesser extent, the change of views in the assessment of Jewish collaboration, this time in the opposite way, is evident in the work of Marek Wierzbicki who, in *Polacy i Żydzi w zaborze sowieckim. Stosunki polsko-żydowskie na ziemiach północno-wschodnich II RP pod okupacją sowiecką (1939–1941)*,[37] emphasized the widespread nature of collaborationist attitudes toward the Soviet occupier and specifically the participation of Jews in sabotage directed against the Polish population in September 1939. However, in an article in English in a post-conference report from Ludwigsburg[38] he was far more cautious in generalizing about the extent of such collaboration in Jewish communities. More cautious, in any event than Bogdan Musiał—the author of *Rozstrzelać elementy kontrewolucyjne!*[39] This book could easily have appeared in the Fronda Library alongside Chodakiewicz's work for its equally strongly polonocentric and apologetic stances.

The research discourse into Polish–Jewish relations under the Soviet occupation mentioned above includes several of my works, with the book *U genezy Jedwabnego. Żydzi na Kresach północno-wschodnich II Rzeczpospolitej 1939–1941* in first place.[40] In all of them I have stressed the somewhat limited scope of strictly collaborationist attitudes toward Jews in the Kresy, apart from rather obvious expressions of indifference toward Poland's loss of independence, pointing out too the economic basis of the growing Polish–Jewish

---

36 Ibid., 74.
37 Poles and Jews in the Soviet partition. Polish-Jewish relations in the north-eastern territories of the second Polish republic under Soviet occupation (1939–1941) (Warsaw: Stowarzyszenie Kulturalne Fronda, 2001).
38 *Genesis des Genozids—Polen 1939–1941*, ed. Klaus-Michael Mallmann and Bogdan Musiał (Ludwigsburg: Wissenschaftliche Buchgesellschaft, 2004).
39 Counterrevolutionary elements should be shot (Warsaw: Stowarzyszenie Kulturalne "Fronda," 2001).
40 Andrzej Żbikowski, *U genezy Jedwabnego. Żydzi na Kresach północno-wschodnich II Rzeczpospolitej 1939–1941* [On the origin of Jedwabne. Jews in the north-eastern provinces of the Second Polish Republic 1939–1941] (Warsaw: Żydowski Instytut Historyczny, 2006).

conflict. This indifference was to a certain extent an attempt to mask fear of the Soviet authorities, but it also derived from a conviction held by many Jews that Poland had let them down, especially with the deeply anti-Semitic atmosphere of the 1930s.

TREND NO. 3—JEWS AND THE POLISH UNDERGROUND STATE

Like the previous trend, this trend in historical writing is based on a common topic and database, but does not reflect agreement on the issues discussed either in the evaluation of the subjects investigated or in the tone in which they are discussed. The eminent American historian David Engel—author of a two-volume study on the Polish Government-in-Exile's at best indifferent attitude toward the murder of the Jewish population on Polish soil—raised the bar very high for this branch of Polish historiography on the Holocaust, a topic that developed startlingly late.[41] Dariusz Stola, in his book *Nadzieja i zagłada. Ignacy Schwarzbart—żydowski przedstawiciel w Radzie Narodowej RP (1940–1945)*,[42] argued with Engel rather persuasively, pointing out the practical problems that limited the London authorities' ability to react swiftly to the tragic news of the Jewish population's fate; such information arrived only irregularly from Poland, as well as émigré circles' evident astonishment at the German decision on *Endlösung*. Both historians based their conclusions mainly on documents left by the Home Army and the Government-in-Exile. The final word in this discussion is Adam Puławski's *W obliczu Zagłady. Rząd RP na Uchodźstwie. Delegatura Rządu RP na Kraj, ZWZ-AK wobec deportacji Żydów do obozów zagłady 1941–1942*.[43] The somewhat too long subtitle indicates that the writer has placed the reactions of the Polish Underground and émigré circles to news of the Holocaust in a much broader context than did his predecessors. Puławski demonstrates that Polish communities' and institutions' own priorities, as well as the irregularity and fragmentary nature of incoming information, had an equally significant influence on the belated, if not ambivalent

---

41 David Engel, *In the Shadow of Auschwitz: The Polish Government-in-Exile and the Jews, 1939–1942* (Chapel Hill: University of North Carolina Press, 1987); *Facing the Holocaust: The Polish Government-in-Exile and the Jews 1943–1945* (Chapel Hill: University of North Carolina Press, 1993).

42 Hope and Mass murder. Ignacy Schwarzbrt—a Jewish representative on the National Council of the Republic of Poland (Warsaw: Oficyna Naukowa, 1995).

43 In the face of the Holocaust. The government of the Republic of Poland in exile, the government delegatura in occupied Poland and the ZWZ-AK on the deportation of the Jews to death camps in 1941–1942 (Warsaw: IPN, 2009).

and inconsistent reactions to the news of the mass murder of Jews. This was the case specifically of the London government, de facto considering itself to be a national government, relieved by virtue of exceptional wartime circumstances of responsibility for the national minorities who had been living in prewar Poland. We should also mention that Libionka's extensive and perceptive study "ZWZ-AK i Delegatura Rządu RP wobec eksterminacji Żydów polskich"[44] predated and perhaps inspired Puławski's work.

The German historian Klaus-Peter Friedrich, in *Der nationalsozialistische Judenmord und das polnisch-jüdische Verhältnis im Diskurs der polnischen Untergrundpresse 1942–1944*,[45] has provided the most detailed discussion to date on the issue of the destruction of Polish Jews as portrayed in the Polish underground press. In seven chapters, Friedrich analyzes several hundred newspaper articles produced by all the political groupings. He has conducted the most extensive survey of this source material; to recognize that this was a very difficult task we need only recall that in Warsaw alone in 1943 as many as 343 underground publications were issued. This is a much more extensive work than Paweł Szapiro's pioneering source book, *Wojna żydowsko-niemiecka. Polska prasa konspiracyjna 1943–1944 o powstaniu w getcie Warszawy*.[46] In this connection we should also mention an essay on anti-Jewish incidents that occurred in Warsaw around Easter 1940 by Tomasz Szarota, included in his *Zajścia antyżydowskie i pogromy w okupowanej Europie. Warszawa, Paryż, Amsterdam, Antwerpia, Kowno*.[47] At this time, his work is the only comparative study by a Polish historian on this subject.

What connects all these works is the acceptance of the status of Poles as conscious witnesses to the mass murder of their Jewish neighbors. All frankly—with no further discussion—accept the idea that not much more could have been done to save the Jewish population, since the underground authorities did not want to allow fugitives from the ghettos into their ranks. With such an extent of anti-Semitic prejudice, supporting operations to help the ghettos as they were being liquidated were too risky and volunteers could not be found.

---

44 The ZWZ-AK and the Delegatura of the government of Poland on the mass-murder of Polish Jews, in *Polacy i Żydzi* [Poles and Jews], ed. Andrzej Żbikowski (Instytut Pamięci Narodowej—Komisja Ścigania Zbrodni przeciwko Narodowi Polskiemu, 2006), 15–208.
45 PhD diss., Marburg, 2003.
46 The Polish-German war. The Polish underground press 1943–1944 on the uprising in the Warsaw ghetto (London: Aneks, 1992).
47 Anti-Semitic violence and pogroms in occupied Europe. Warsaw, Paris, Amsterdam, Kovno (Warsaw: Sic, 2000).

It was also hard to take action against blackmailers, who perhaps were numerous. Writers avoid answering the question about whether the Polish population on a large scale simply observed the deportation of the Jews to their deaths, or perhaps also accepted it.

TREND NO. 4—THE EMPIRICAL DISCOVERY OF "NEGATIVES"

The process of uncovering further Polish crimes against Jews during the Second World War moved like an avalanche after the publication in 2000 of Gross's account of it and continues to this day. I doubt if it will end soon. Studies and articles of various lengths have been devoted to these criminal episodes, and references to them appear in regional studies on the Holocaust ever more frequently.[48] It is impossible to list all these works here, so I shall mention only those which have made the most impact.

The first work after Gross's *Sąsiedzi* and Anna Bikont's *My z Jedwabnego* (We from Jedwabne) was *Wokół Jedwabnego* (Concerning Jedwabne), published by IPN in 2002; I included in that publication an extensive study titled "Pogromy i mordy ludności żydowskiej w Łomżyńskiem i na Białostocczyźnie latem 1941 roku w świetle relacji ocalałych Żydów i dokumentów sądowych" (Pogroms and murders of Jews in the Łomża and Białostok areas in the light of court documents). A year later, Jan Grabowski published in *Zeszyty Historyczne* (Historical notebooks) the first version of his important work, titled *"Ja tego Żyda znam." Szantażowanie Żydów w Warszawie 1939–1943*, later published as a book.[49] Using wartime judicial documents (from Polish magistrates' courts and German courts), he demonstrated that the blackmailing of Jews began at the same time as the Nazi occupier introduced the first discriminatory acts against the Jewish population, in other words, from the moment that it became compulsory for Jews to wear an armband with the Star of David. Blackmail continued when the Germans organized massive contributions and confiscations of property, prohibited Jews from leaving the ghettos, up to mass escapes from them at the time of deportations to sites of mass murder. The blackmailers were not exclusively people on the social margins, but were often also young men from so-called good families.

At the same time as Grabowski, Barbara Engelking published her slim but extremely significant work titled *"Szanowny panie gistapo." Donosy do*

---

48 For example, Adam Kopciowski, *Zagłada Żydów w Zamościu* [The mass murder of the Jews in Zamość] (Lublin: Wydawnictwo Uniwersytetu Marii Curie-Skłodowskiej, 2005).

49 "I know this Jew!" The Blackmailing of Jews in Warsaw 1939–1943 (Warsaw: Wydawnictwo IFIS PAN, 2004).

władz niemieckich w Warszawie i okolicach w latach 1940–1941.⁵⁰ The publication of both these works was possible within a year after the establishment of a small but very active institution—the Polish Center for Holocaust Research, attached to IFiS PAN. One of the Center's most important achievements was to establish the yearbook *Zagłada Żydów. Studia i Materiały* (Holocaust. Studies and Materials). Its first volume appeared in 2005 and included among others the important and widely quoted article by Alina Skibińska and Jakub Petelwicz, "Udział Polaków w zbrodniach na Żydach na prowincji regionu świętokrzyskiego" (Polish participation in crimes against Jews in the Świętokrzyskie province). How rarely, I think, does a title so clearly and unambiguously indicate the authors' field of interest and become a benchmark for a whole direction of empirical research. We have already come a long way from Jan Błoński's "Poor Poles look at the ghetto," amid various forms of Polish–Jewish relations and so-called symbiotic perceptions of Jews and their fate, to the straightforward killing of Jews by Poles. Not all scholars are satisfied by such accentuation of complex historical material, even though some are. Let me repeat that Jan T. Gross stated, "I see their—Skibińska's and Petelwicz's—article as a breakthrough in the understanding of the history of the third phase of the Holocaust in Poland, for suddenly everything takes shape there."⁵¹ It went on to describe the quite widespread social practice of catching fugitives from the ghettos hiding from deportation to centers of mass murder; once caught, they were killed or often taken to a German gendarmerie post, or a Polish "blue" police station. However, the problem remains to assess the scale of this phenomenon, and we historians continually dispute the extent of this social practice and its principal motivation: lust for plunder, religious and ethnic hatred, or perhaps fear of the Nazi occupier.

I have also devoted one of my longer works to seeking "negatives" in the complex process of interpreting the Polish population's observation of the Germans' anti-Jewish policies over several years, titled *Antysemityzm, szmalcownictwo, współpraca z Niemcami a stosunki polsko-żydowskie pod okupacją niemiecką*, which IPN bravely published in 2006.⁵² This trend of historical writing has been, as I have mentioned, continued by the authors cited above, and in this

---

50 "Dear Mr Gistapo". Denunciations to the German authorities in Warsaw and the surrounding area in the years 1940–1941 (Warsaw: Wydawnictwo IFiS PAN, 2003).
51 *Zagłada Żydów. Studia i Materiały* 7 (2011), 499.
52 Anti-Semitism, blackmail, cooperation with the Germans and Polish-Jewish relations under the German occupation (Warsaw: IPN, 2006).

connection it is impossible not to mention Jan Grabowski's *Hunt for the Jews. Betrayal and Murder in German-Occupied Poland* (Bloomington, 2013) and Alina Skibińska's (jointly with Tadeusz Markiel) *"Jakie to ma znaczenie, czy zrobili to z chciwości?" Zagłada domu Trynczerów* ("What is the difference if they did it from greed": The murder of the Trynczer Family) (both published by IFiS PAN).

What connects the studies belonging to the perhaps somewhat artificially created category of empirical works is their authors' relatively limited interest in the mechanisms for the destruction of Polish Jewry that were planned and implemented by the Nazis. Researchers are also not too interested in the main agents of the extermination of the Polish Jews—the German SS-man, the field policeman, the soldier, or the policeman, or the dominant elements in the process of liquidation—the ghetto, the camp, the selections, the executions. They work on the assumption that these are already well-known matters on which scholars have focused their attention for several decades. Instead, they are attracted by empiricism—familiar collections of sources, the ignored testimony of victims of and witnesses to Jewish suffering. They do not believe that it was possible not to be aware of the Holocaust—if only because people continually turned away when walking past the walls of a ghetto. They find irritating the unspoken postwar consensus to forget about the tragic and shameful wartime episodes and to bury them in dusty archives. For these writers, a Pole living during the occupation in the General Government could not have been an indifferent, passive witness to the Holocaust, since it surrounded him on all sides; Poles had to speak up either for the victims—there were not many who did—or at least accept the fact that in their community Jews were hated and that any act of mercy was publicly condemned, since it threatened the community and hindered collaboration with the Germans in their Holocaust policy. These writers react—understandably—very emotionally to descriptions of crimes discovered in the archives. Summing up a description of pursuits of Jews escaping from the ghettos which were being liquidated, Grabowski writes:

> Jewish [but Polish too, as the quote makes clear] descriptions of this initial phase of looking for fugitives provide testimony of unbelievable, even animal brutality, turning into an orgy of murder. For the local population this was a lesson in obedience. The Germans were masters of life and death, and compared to others' Jewish lives lost all value . . . It was more or less at that stage that witnesses to German bestiality stopped talking about "murdering" Jews, but rather began to use the more impersonal phrase "shooting Jews." . . . It was symptomatic that

only Jews were "shot"; witnesses used other verbs when referring to murders of the Polish population.[53]

Summing up, Grabowski asks an important question: Could the Nazis have "carried out the deed of the Holocaust as successfully, as thoroughly and as precisely as they did" without the help of local collaborators? He is surely aware that we are unable today to provide a reliable answer to this ostensibly simple question. He agrees that the "attitudes of the local population had at least for some of the Jews a critical significance"—those (their numbers are hard to calculate) who had been condemned to death and were trying to escape. Today we can say that the Poles were complicit in their deaths—and there were perhaps about a quarter of a million of them. We still don't know how many such Poles there were—thousands or tens of thousands—or whether their main motive for murder or denunciations was lust for property or rather fear of the occupying Germans—who had, after all, forbidden on pain of death any assistance to Jews. Or, as Grabowski writes, was it the fact that "helping a Jew was seen by many as a sin or worse—a crime"?

We shall not have long to wait for new work. The seventh volume of *Zagłada Żydów* contains several introductory studies, by Dariusz Libionka, Alina Skibińska, and Joanna Tokarska-Bakir, on Jews being murdered by insubordinate soldiers of the Polish underground.

TREND NO. 5—DECONSTRUCTIVIST

A critical analysis of narrative sources would catch errors and simple forgeries; such a route is undoubtedly essential for progress in historical research and also, and perhaps above all, peers into the very recent past. However, not all historians are as attracted to this method as is Dariusz Libionka— the coauthor of two important volumes, one with Barbara Engelking titled *Żydzi w powstańczej Warszawie*,[54] the other with Laurence Weinbaum titled *Bohaterowie, hochsztaplerzy, opisywacze. Wokół Żydowskiego Z wiązku*

---

53 Jan Grabowski, *Hunt for the Jews. Betrayal and Murder in German-occupied Poland*, (Bloomington: Indiana University Press, 2013), 59. This first appeared in Polish as Jan Grabowski, *Judenjagd. Polowanie na Żydów 1942–1945. Studium dziejów pewnego powiatu* (Warsaw: Stowarzyszenie Centrum Badań nad Zagładą Żydów, 2011).
54 *Jews in Occupied Warsaw* (Warsaw: Stowarzyszenie Centrum Badań nad Zagładą Żydów, 2009).

Wojskowego.[55] The inevitable consequence of applying this method is that the deconstructionist element greatly exceeds in volume the reconstructionist one. In a word, if earlier we blundered in a maze of falsehood—such as studies showing that various Polish veterans' circles invented nonexistent aid organizations, ones that even took an active part in the Warsaw Ghetto Uprising, then after reading the literature we realize at most how little we know about nonheroic events that occurred.

TREND NO. 6—EXISTENTIALIST

Barbara Engelking dominates in providing this type of historical narrative in our area of interest, although Alina Skibińska successfully adopts Engelking's method in *Dom Trynczerów*. Engelking's most recent work is called *Jest taki piękny słoneczny dzień . . . Losy Żydów szukających ratunku na wsi polskiej 1942–1945*.[56] She writes in the foreword:

> Helplessness in the face of someone else's pain leads to a violent urge to turn away, to withdraw, to flee. . . . But of course the conviction that we can avoid that which we fear to face is illusory. And although we did not want to and we still do not want to be witnesses to the Polish Jews' humiliation, torment, and death we are such witnesses, not by our own choice but by virtue of our place of birth.[57]

Engelking courageously faces up to the unspeakably painful memory of frequent killings of Jews who were trying to hide in the countryside. As she admits:

> I focus on the fate of the Jews and their existentialist experience. . . . I look at the countryside through the eyes of the Jews who were looking for shelter there, and I present a simplified and uncomplicated image of the Polish countryside under the occupation.

Engelking emphasizes that among the documents she has examined, she has come across no instance of appealing to a German for mercy: "such efforts were

---

55 Heroes, Swindlers, Graphomaniacs. On the Jewish Military Union (Warsaw: Stowarzyszenie Centrum Badań nad Zagładą Żydów, 2011).
56 "It was such a beautiful sunny day . . ." The fate of Jews seeking shelter in the Polish countryside (Warsaw: Stowarzyszenie Centrum Badań nad Zagładą Żydów, 2011).
57 Ibid., 8.

quite pointless and probably no one had illusions on that score. However a Pole, precisely because he had a choice, could show mercy."[58]

Nonetheless Engelking does not ignore the collective fear which overcame the villages and their inhabitants. This was a fear of German reprisals, reinforced by sporadic public executions of people who had been found to have been sheltering Jews, the aim of the occupying forces being to sow widespread fear among the population.

In her opinion a frequent motive for murder was avarice of the peasants over Jewish property that they had acquired. She sees murder as a crime of passion often emerging from a liking of evil. Hatred of Jews was the result of anti-Semitism that had been passed down from generation to generation. In analyzing the killing methods employed by people in the countryside, Engelking concludes that unlike the Germans who killed on the whole "calmly, without anger, systematically and in cold blood," Polish peasants killed in anger, with passion, haste, and cruelty.

This is not a pleasant image for Polish country-dwellers to confront. In summing up, Engelking recalls "the more or less voluntary collaborators in the German undertaking," the Holocaust. She states that "Polish peasants were volunteers in the task of murdering Jews."[59] And in this instance, as in Jan Grabowski's work, we don't know how many Polish peasants, or what proportion of them, were involved. Engelking recalls the more than 2,500 Jews murdered or turned in within the Polish provinces, and she adds that other historical sources known to her, but not analyzed, could at least double this figure. She does not, however, say how the number of survivors corresponds in comparison to the group of victims. It seems that it was many times smaller.[60]

One cannot avoid generalizations of a very high order when we speak of a truly reprehensible phenomenon, which is well documented and which has unambiguous consequences. The judgment "Polish peasants" and not, for instance, "many Polish peasants," defines quite differently the phenomenon of local murders of Jews in hiding, making this type of activity the norm and not the fringe, even if a very broad one. In the author's opinion in this third stage of the Holocaust, peasants, or simply perhaps Poles, ceased being witnesses: "their status changed" when "the Hilbergian triad of the roles of executioner, victim and witness broke down."

---

58 Ibid., 14.
59 Ibid., 257.
60 Ibid., 258.

TREND NO. 7—SYNTHESIZING

In this section I mention two collective grant-funded monographs by the team at the Polish Center for Holocaust Research: *Prowincja noc. Życie i zagłada Żydów w dystrykcie warszawskim*[61] and *Zarys krajobrazu. Wieś polska wobec zagłady Żydów 1942–1945*.[62] The books are too extensive to be able to discuss in any detail, so all I can do is emphasize that they are very different from each other not only in their range of subjects, but also, perhaps more importantly, in their methodology. The first of these works is denser, linking classic historical and statistical studies with a perspective on sociological and literary criticism. The authors have also used more types of sources. The second book is dominated by an analysis of court documents from trials provoked by the so-called August decree, in other words the 1944 decree of the Polish Committee of National Liberation (Polski Komitet Wyzwolenia Narodowego—PKWN) on "pursuing war criminals and traitors to the Polish nation," which greatly focuses a scholar's perspective.

TREND NO. 8—REJECTING ATTEMPTS TO CONTEXTUALIZE THE HOLOCAUST

In their recent works, Timothy Snyder—*Bloodlands: Europe Between Hitler and Stalin*,[63] and Marcin Zaremba—*Wielka trwoga. Polska 1944–1947*[64]—have drawn attention to the idea, which is anything but new, that the destruction of the Jews should be studied in a broader context: that the Poles' attitude toward it should be discussed alongside an analysis of daily life on the "Aryan side," as well as alongside a description of German policies of repression and economic exploitation of the Polish population. Admittedly this is not their main theme, yet from their perspective—Snyder is writing about a broader area and about a great many national and social groups affected by terror tactics, while Zaremba is concerned with the extensive spectrum of consequences emanating from the Holocaust—it is clear that the actual Holocaust lasted a relatively short time on Polish lands, and that its third phase of hunting fugitives from the ghettos did

---

61 Night in the province. The life and mass murder of Jews in the Warsaw district, eds. Barbara Engelking, Jacek Leociak, and Dariusz Libionka (Warsaw: Wydawnictwo IFiS PAN 2007).
62 An outline of the landscape. The Polish village in the face of the mass murder of the Jews, ed. Barbara Engelking and Jan Grabowski (Warsaw: Stowarzyszenie Centrum Badań nad Zagładą Żydów, 2011).
63 New York: Basic Books, 2010; Polish edition: Warsaw: Świat Książki, 2011.
64 The great fear. Poland 1944–1947 (Kraków: Znak, 2012).

not have to affect equally all parts of Poland. Hitherto, these attempts to draw attention to the need to increase the distance to the phenomena studied and to expand the research perspective have not generated a broader discussion. I had a similar feeling after publishing *Karski*.[65] In many quarters the Holocaust is still a very current topic, intertwined with the still-unfinished grieving for those murdered and the still-unfinished accounting for their possessions, which were partly taken over by the Polish state from the Nazi occupier, and to an unknown degree were plundered by the co-participants in and witnesses to the crime. It would appear, too, that for some time to come no one will pick up the torch of the interesting attempts to contextualize Polish–Jewish relations, such as, for example, Grzegorz Berendt's article "Cena życia—ekonomiczne uwarunkowania egzystencji Żydów po aryjskiej stronie."[66] However, not only scholars of the history of the Polish Jews are to blame, but also simply historians of the Second World War, especially those Polish ones who are unwilling to cede part of their research territory and undertake interdisciplinary research, without which we shall not learn what part of the social history of Poland under the occupation in reality was linked to the tragic experiences of the Jewish people.

Translated from Polish by Jarosław Garliński

---

65 Andrzej Żbikowski, *Karski* (Warsaw: Świat Książki, 2012).
66 The price of life—the economic aspect of Jewish survival on the Aryan side, *Zagłada Żydów. Studia i Materiały* 4 (2008).

Beyond National Identities: New Challenges in Writing the History of the Holocaust in Poland and Israel

DANIEL BLATMAN

I

About two decades have passed since Holocaust historiography received a second look, both in Israel and in Poland. In Israel, the 1990s saw the development of critical approaches to the history of the Zionist Movement and the State of Israel, which had direct ramifications for the assessment of the Holocaust's place in the crystallization of the Israeli national identity and Israeli collective memory.[1] The extensive debate provoked by this discussion was, as is common for controversies that examine a nation's history through the lens of collective identity and consciousness—for example, the *Historikerstreit* in Germany in the mid-1980s—left behind much in the way of writing but presented a very thin contribution to true historiography. It did, however, reinforce the mainstream approach of Holocaust studies in Israel by overemphasizing

---

1 Idith Zertal has written the most important works on that issue. See Idith Zertal, *From Catastrophe to Power: Holocaust Survivors and the Emergence of Israel* (Berkeley: University of California Press, 1998); *Israel's Holocaust and the Politics of Nationhood* (Cambridge: Cambridge University Press, 2005); see also Yael Zerubavel, "The Death of Memory and the Memory of Death: Masada and the Holocaust as Historical Metaphors," *Representations* 45 (1994): 72–100; Yechiel Klar et al., "The 'Never Again' State of Israel: The Emergence of the Holocaust as a Core Feature of Israeli Identity and Its Four Incongruent Voices," *Journal of Social Issues* 69, no. 1 (2013): 125–43; Dan Bar-On, "Israeli Society between the Culture of Death and the Culture of Life," *Israel Studies* 2, no. 2 (1997): 88–112.

the specifically Jewish aspect of the Holocaust and rejecting a multicontextual and comparative approach to the history and meaning of the Holocaust.

The roots of the view of the Holocaust as an event of deterministic significance in the history of the Jewish people, and the national meaning derived from this, are found in one of the founding fathers of Israeli historiography and initiators of Yad Vashem, Ben-Zion Dinur. Dinur's 1943 article, "Diasporas and Their Destruction," seems to contain the seeds of a view of the Holocaust from a uniquely Jewish perspective.[2] He argued for a fixed pattern of Jewish life in the Diaspora: the rise of a Jewish center in a specific place (Babylonia, Ashkenaz, Spain, Poland and Lithuania, Germany), which achieves a glorious economic and cultural life, until the moment when its existence becomes a thorn in the side of the host society or the local ruler. As a consequence, the center collapses and disintegrates, the Jews are expelled or murdered, and the place of the destroyed center is taken by a new center that develops elsewhere. In other words, Jewish life in exile has a deterministic and periodic nature, with cycles of migration or expulsion, consolidation, a flourishing zenith, and then collapse and destruction, followed by migration to another place where the community is renewed. In that view, the destruction of European Jewry in the Holocaust is the most horrific and tragic proof of the need to break this cycle of Jewish history by creating a national home for the Jewish people in the land of Israel.

Like every historical argument that deals with questions of national identity, the debate that took place in Israel in the 1990s about the Holocaust's place in the justice of the Zionist project and the blurring of its injustices to others did not take place in isolation from the political identity of those involved. Dan Michman, an Israeli Holocaust scholar, vigorously assailed the idea that the Holocaust serves instrumental purposes in the State of Israel's nation-building process, shaping historical consciousness or justifying aggression toward the Palestinians. In one of his articles, he wrote as follows:

> Those who hold this perspective, and aspire to change the State of Israel into a civil and "just" society that has no particular relationship to Zionism and Judaism, use the myth [that the establishment of the State of Israel is a historical product of the Holocaust] to undermine the legitimacy of the existence of a Jewish state as such. It supposedly emerges from this myth that the State of Israel "was conceived in sin"—the sin of forcibly

---

2 Ben-Zion Dinur, "Diasporas and Their Destruction" [in Hebrew], in *Historical Writings*, vol. IV (Jerusalem: Mossad Bialik, 1976), 175, 181.

imposing its establishment both on the Palestinians and the Jewish survivors of the Holocaust in Europe, perpetrated by an ultranationalist Zionist movement that used the Holocaust in a manipulative way.[3]

In another publication, Michman wrote "that in light of these declarations, it is easier to understand the contemporary political positions of the 'post-Zionists': we find them among the supporters of Hadash (the new Israeli communist party supported mainly by Israeli Palestinians) and Meretz (the small leftist Zionist party)."[4]

It is of course possible to maintain that this rule holds in both directions. In other words, we can say that those who attack the critics of Israeli Holocaust historiography are motivated by a nationalist outlook and are striving to preserve the significance of the Holocaust as a unique historical event that lies outside the boundaries of postmodern critiques; they can be found among supporters of the right-wing or centrist parties or religious movements in Israel. The political implications of this controversy have some significance, of course. In his book on the mid-1980s *Historikerstreit*, Richard Evans tries to understand the encounter between historical understanding and political action:

> How people regard the Third Reich and its crimes provides an important key to how they would use political power in the present or future. That is why the neo-conservatives' reinterpretation of the German past is so disturbing.[5]

The challenge to national narratives that would shield history from any reexamination in order to sustain a preferred pattern of national memory usually comes from the outside. It will be recalled that the revolution in French historiography of the Vichy period was initiated by Robert Paxton in his *Vichy France: Old Guard and New Order, 1940–1944*.[6] When the book was published

---

3 Dan Michman, "Holocaust to Rebirth! Holocaust to Rebirth? The Historiography of the Causal Connection between the Holocaust and the Birth of Israel—Between Myth and Reality" [in Hebrew], *Iyunim Bitkumat Yisrael* 10 (2000): 234–58.
4 Dan Michman, "The Zionism Busters: Current Outlook on Post-Zionist Thought in Contemporary Israeli Society" [in Hebrew], www.amalnet.k12.il/sites/commun/.../200323.doc, accessed April 15, 2016.
5 Richard J. Evans, *In Hitler's Shadow: West German Historians and the Attempt to Escape from the Nazi Past* (New York: Pantheon Books, 1989), 138.
6 Robert O. Paxton, *Vichy France: Old Guard and New Order, 1940–1944* (New York: Knopf; distributed by Random House, 1972).

in France in 1973, it put all the traditional myths entertained by the Gaullist right about the Vichy regime and the period of German occupation to a critical test. The Gaullist establishment, which still maintained substantial control of the media, research institutions, and state bureaucracy, attacked the book viciously. Paxton was castigated for two aspects of his book in particular. The first was thematic—his conclusion that elements of the Third Republic that collapsed in 1940 continued to exist in Vichy France, both in its institutions and in its legislative mechanisms; hence Vichy should not be seen only as an imposed regime of collaborationists. The second was methodological—Paxton's refusal to make use of the testimony of members of the Resistance (in contrast to his extensive use of German documentation) and the doubts he expressed about these testimonies. The French historical establishment was unanimous in its opposition to this revisionism from across the Atlantic.[7] But the younger generation of historians who grew up in France after 1968 welcomed Paxton with open arms. In the 1970s and 1980s, his book was a seminal text in the reconstruction of French national memory and its ability to cope with *les années noires*.[8] Tony Judt discussed this singular phenomenon in European history after the Second World War, and especially after the fall of the Berlin Wall in 1989: the need for an external historiographic catalyst to shake up the conventions of national memory and present new insights about the nation's past, and notably its more problematic chapters.[9]

In Israel, too, the challenge to the traditional directions in Holocaust research came from the outside. None of the critical academics who came to be denominated "post-Zionist" were Holocaust historians; most of them were sociologists or political scientists. The real external challenge to the direction of Holocaust studies in Israel came in the early twenty-first century from a group of young historians, mainly English-speaking and German, who blazed new paths in modern genocide studies and proposed new syntheses for linking the Holocaust with other genocides.

---

7 See John Sweets, "Chaque livre un événement: Robert Paxton et la France, du briseur de glace à l'iconoclaste tranquille" [Every book an event: Robert Paxton and France, from ice-breaker to peaceful iconoclast], in *La France sous Vichy, Autour de Robert O. Paxton* [France under Vichy, On the views of Robert O. Paxton], ed. Sarah Fishman et al. (Brussels: Complexe, 2004), 31–47.

8 Henry Rousso, *The Vichy Syndrome: History and Memory in France since 1944* (Cambridge MA: Harvard University Press, 1991).

9 Tony Judt, "The Past Is Another Country: Myth and Memory in Postwar Europe," *Theoria* 87 (1996): 36–69.

Several directions for research emerged from this synthesis. One of the most prominent relied on developments in colonial studies. Two scholars, among others, proposed ways to examine the Holocaust in this perspective—Dirk Moses and Jürgen Zimmerer. The former found common ground among the various instances of genocide that took place from the mid-nineteenth to the mid-twentieth century, a hundred-year period that he labeled the "Century of Race." Moses proposed examining three interwoven elements that laid the foundations for genocide then: nation-building, imperialist rivalries, and conflicts with an ideological and racial character. Many of the genocides perpetrated inside Europe during these years, as well as the colonial genocides that took place in the same period, combined these factors, which of course were part of the Nazi genocide.[10]

Zimmerer, a leading scholar of German colonialism, argues for continuity between the genocide carried out by the German Imperial Army in southwest Africa between 1904 and 1908 and the Nazi genocide in Eastern Europe around four decades later:

> This makes the Namibian War the first genocide of the twentieth century and the first genocide in German history. Studying the Herero and Nama genocide therefore is not simply an end in itself, but is of interest for a general history of genocide. It is also an important link between colonialism and the Nazi policy of extermination. After all, the German war against Poland and the Soviet Union can be seen as the largest colonial war of conquest in history. Never before were so many people and resources mobilized by a conqueror, and never before were war aims so expansive. Millions of people were to be murdered in order to conquer "living space" in the East and to establish a colonial empire.[11]

There has been extensive writing about the appropriate integration between the Holocaust and genocide studies; these are only a few examples.[12]

---

10 Anthony Dirk Moses, "Conceptual Blockages and Definitional Dilemmas in the Racial Century: Genocide of Indigenous Peoples and the Holocaust," *Patterns of Prejudice* 36, no. 4 (2002): 7–36.

11 Jürgen Zimmerer, "Annihilation in Africa: The 'Race War' in German Southwest Africa (1904–1908) and Its Significance for a Global History of Genocide," *German Historical Institute Bulletin* 37 (2005): 51–57, here: 53–54. See also *Von Windhuk nach Auschwitz? Beiträge zum Verhältnis von Kolonialismus und Holocaust* [From Windhoek to Auschwitz? Essays on the relationship of colonialism and the Holocaust] (Berlin: Lit, 2011).

12 For a comprehensive summary and analysis of the various approaches, see Dan Stone, *Histories of the Holocaust* (New York: Oxford University Press, 2010), 203–44.

The conclusions reached by these and other scholars can be subjected to critical scrutiny, of course, but it is doubtful whether it is possible to countenance the outright rejection of all attempts to remove the study of the Holocaust from the sphere of Jewish national memory and to set it in the context of broader historical phenomena. All the same, Holocaust studies in Israel remain within the consensus of the national narrative. The complex dialectic of this issue is represented by Yehuda Bauer, who was originally identified with the traditional uniqueness paradigm but has been trying for many years to release the Holocaust from the shackles of Jewish particularistic memory, seeking to juxtapose it with other instances of genocide while also preserving its particular aspects. In a recent lecture, he stated that

> There are ... parallels among genocides, and scholarship must endeavor to identify them. By the same token, we need to examine the differences among them, and this can be done only through comparison to other genocides. This is particularly essential in Holocaust studies, because only a comparison can clarify the extent to which there are unique elements. Was the Holocaust unique? I will argue that it was not—because if I say that it was unique, that is, that it was a one-time event that will never be repeated, it can be forgotten, because there is no danger that an identical event will take place in the future...
>
> I will also argue that I am not aware of any factors that led to any genocide other than the Holocaust that cannot be found in other genocides, including the Holocaust. But certain elements of the Holocaust are not found in any other genocide.[13]

Later, he enumerates those unique elements: totality, universality (that is, the desire to murder the Jews in every place the Nazis reached), and the Nazi ideology.

When he defines the Holocaust as "unprecedented" rather than "unique," Bauer is modifying the traditional concept of uniqueness that he wrote about in the 1970s and 1980s, but he essentially leaves the traditional argument in place. In other words, the Holocaust is not unique because we have seen that genocides similar to the mass murder of the Jews have recurred (in Rwanda, for

---

13 Yehuda Bauer, "Holocaust and Genocide" [in Hebrew], *Igeret* 34 (December 2012): 38–39, http://www.academy.ac.il/data/egeret/96/EgeretArticles/34_Igeretigeret%281%29.pdf. Accessed April 1, 2016.

example), but in its essence it is indeed unique, because it is the only one that combines all three of the traditional components—even though many scholars are skeptical about their absolute character or the extent to which they existed only in the Nazi genocide. His argument is tautological because he believes that the comparison of the Holocaust to other genocides indeed points to the existence of elements not found in other cases and thus attests to its unprecedented nature. In the end, though, the Holocaust remains an event with historical aspects that existed elsewhere and can accordingly be released from the chains of Jewish history.

II

Israeli scholarship about the Holocaust in Poland does not diverge from the general trend, of course. This domain, which was the main area of Holocaust studies in Israel until about twenty-five years ago, has gradually lost its centrality over the last two decades. This is not the place to go into the many reasons for this, but today Poland is the most important venue for study of the fate of Polish Jewry during the Holocaust and perhaps of Polish Jewish history as a whole. In Israel, the number of scholars who focus on the annals of Polish Jews in the Holocaust can be counted on the fingers of one hand. Among the most important books and dissertations that have been written by Israeli scholars in recent years, we can find a research study on the refugee problem in the Warsaw Ghetto, a study on Jewish medical care in occupied Poland, one on the ghettos and labor camps for Jews in the Kielce district, a book about the Jews of Lublin province in the Holocaust, a study of Jews' attitudes toward Poland and the Polish people during the Holocaust, and one about labor camps for Jews in the *Generalgouvernement* between 1939 and 1943.[14]

---

14 David Silberklang, *Gates of Tears: The Holocaust in the Lublin District* (Jerusalem: Yad Vashem, 2013); Witold Wojciech Medykowski, *Between Slavery, Extermination and Survival: Forced Labor of Jews in the General Government during the Years 1939–1943* (PhD diss., Jerusalem: The Hebrew University, 2014); Havi Dreifuss (Ben-Sasson), *"We Polish Jews?" The Relations between Jews and Poles during the Holocaust—The Jewish Perspective* [in Hebrew] (Jerusalem: Yad Vashem, 2009); Sara Bender, *In Enemy Land: The Jews of Kielce and the Region, 1939–1946* [in Hebrew] (Jerusalem: Yad Vashem, 2012); Lea Pries, *The Impact of the Refugee Problem on Jewish Communal Life in the City of Warsaw and the Warsaw Ghetto (September 1939–July 1942)* [in Hebrew] (PhD diss., Jerusalem: The Hebrew University, 2006); Miriam Offer, *White Coats inside the Ghetto: Jewish Medicine in Poland during the Holocaust* [in Hebrew] (Jerusalem: Yad Vashem, 2015).

Do these studies have a common denominator? Beyond the obvious—Polish Jews in the Holocaust—all of them are affiliated with the historiographic perspective instituted by the founders of Israeli Holocaust studies. Holocaust scholarship in Israel strongly reflects what several historians have already noted with regard to Holocaust studies as a whole: it is one of the most conservative fields in the study of history. There is almost no desire to deviate from traditional methodologies and writing style. These studies are marked by the meticulous and precise collection of documentation, which is cited in a descriptive and positivistic fashion with almost no interpretation or conceptualization. The main goal is a description and detailed recreation of the situation that prevailed in those years—the Jews' lives and fate—and nothing more. Not only is there no attempt at a comparative inquiry, but also almost none of the research orientations that are prominent today in historical scholarship in general, and in genocide studies in particular, including cultural history, gender history, spatial history, anthropological history, the history of social peripheries, and so forth, have found their way into Holocaust studies in Israel, including studies of the Holocaust of Polish Jewry.

In contrast to the difficulty of breaking out into new directions of research in Israel, Poland has seen a dramatic revolution in Holocaust studies in the last two decades. It liberated Polish Holocaust historiography from decades of restrictions, rooted mainly in the political system that controlled the country, but it is doubtful whether it has actually moved in a truly integrative direction. And like all breakthroughs in research, this one, too, requires review and reexamination after the passage of almost a full generation because of the danger that it will calcify into a reflection of the old trends that it strove to modify.

The starting point, of course, is Jan Błoński's 1987 article.[15] As will be recalled, the argument that erupted in its wake did not focus on the facts, but on its assumptions about the moral and ethical ramifications of Polish society's treatment of the Jews. Antony Polonsky rightly asserted that the moral controversy ruled out any possibility of discussing the facts and the problems they raise.[16] It would not be far off the mark to claim that the moral question continues to accompany Holocaust research in Poland. The study of Polish–Jewish relations and of Polish responses to the Holocaust has become the basis for

---

15 Jan Błoński, "The Poor Poles Look at the Ghetto," in *"My Brother's Keeper?" Recent Polish Debates on the Holocaust,* ed. Antony Polonsky (London: Routledge in association with the Institute for Polish-Jewish Studies, 1990), 34–52.
16 Antony Polonsky, "Introduction," ibid., 32.

exchanges with an ethical subtext, leaving no room for historians' traditional tools, according to Dariusz Stola.[17]

For around four decades, Polish historiography tended to blur the difference between the fates of the Jews and the Poles during the Nazi occupation; in other words, it did not explore the "unique" aspects of the Holocaust. The differences between the oppression and murder of the Poles and the extermination of the Jews were left in a gray area that no one tried to study because of the nature of the regime in Poland from 1945 to 1989. It was only in the 1980s that attempts began to address the fate of the Jews during the Holocaust and the history of Polish Jewry in general, including initial efforts to memorialize the Jewish past by renovating and reconstructing its ruins. It was a classic dissident expression of the rejection of the reigning narrative and a challenge to the long years of the obscuring of what young Polish intellectuals and scholars of the 1980s saw as the need to assess the national past and the Jews' place in it accurately.[18] But these efforts never broke through to what could be defined as "a historical reckoning." That came only after 1989, and it dealt with the question that continues to accompany Polish Holocaust studies: How did the Polish nation, including the underground organizations, respond to the extermination of the Jews? Paradoxically, Poland is probably the only country in the world, other than Israel, where non-Jewish historians who deal with the Nazi genocide treat the Holocaust as unique. The fact that so many Poles witnessed the catastrophe that played out on their soil is not enough to explain the way that the Holocaust has become an event with such meaningful roots in the Polish national identity and memory. After all, there were many witnesses in many countries—France, Hungary, Romania, Lithuania, the Netherlands—but the Holocaust has not become such an important element in their national histories.

The historiographic perspective on this process is broader than Holocaust studies alone. Young scholars who matured after 1989 saw the history of Polish Jewry as part of Polish history, in the national sense, but in a completely different way than what has been written in Israel. Polish historians see the Holocaust as inseparable from their country's history, which views prewar Poland as a complex and heterogeneous national unit, but a national entity shared by all its citizens, whatever their ethnic differences. This is the approach that took root

---

17 Dariusz Stola, "New Research on the Holocaust in Poland," in *Lessons and Legacies* VI, ed. Jeffry M. Diefendorf (Evanston, IL: Northwestern University Press, 2004), 264.
18 See Iwona Irwin-Zarecka, *Neutralizing Memory: The Jew in Contemporary Poland* (New Brunswick, NJ: Transaction, 1989).

in the extensive historical writing of recent decades about national minorities in Poland. The attention to Jews is only one aspect, albeit prominent, of this abundance.[19] Moshe Rosman wrote that the orientation of these studies is that "Polish Jewry was first and foremost Polish, and the general Jewish context is much more amorphous and much less essential."[20] Against this background, it is fascinating that alongside the aspiration to incorporate the annals of Polish Jews into the history of the national society in which they lived, it is actually the study of the Holocaust that isolated the Jews from the Polish history of those years.

The notion of the uniqueness of the Holocaust, as part of the overall history of Poland in the Second World War, made its appearance in Polish historiography in the mid-1990s. Its core is the conclusion that the conflict between Poles and Germans during the Second World War was different from that between Jews and the Germans. Jews were a national minority living outside the Polish national circle. Before the war, Jews lived in a closed and demarcated sphere, locked in their separate identity; or were sometimes torn between their aspiration to integrate and their desire to maintain their own lifestyle, on the one hand, and the arguments for emigration, on the other. The "outsider's" identity is never the same as the host's. The Jews were dependent on the Poles, inasmuch as their existence was influenced by the Poles' hostility or willingness to accept Jews as equal citizens; but the Poles were not dependent on the Jews. The relations between the two groups were not symmetrical.

This asymmetry was most salient during the war. There was nothing the Poles needed from the Jews in those years. By contrast, the Jews—if they wanted to avert the death sentence pronounced against them—could not do

---

19 The literature on this topic is voluminous. See, among others, Ewa Grześkowiak-Łuczyk, ed., *Polska—Polacy—mniejszości narodowe* [Poles—Poland—national minorities] (Wrocław: Zakład Narodowy im. Ossolińskich, 1992); Agnieszka Kolasa, *Ukraińcy w powiecie Biała Podlaska w latach 1918–1948* [Ukrainians in the Biała Podlaska powiat in the years 1918–1948] (Toruń: Wydawnictwo Adam Marszałek, 1997); Dariusz Maciak, *Próba porozumienia polsko-ukraińskiego w Galicji w latach 1885–1895* [Attempts at Polish-Ukrainian understanding in the years 1885–1895] (Warsaw: Wydawnictwo Uniwersytetu Warszawskiego, 2006); Paweł Samuś, ed., *Polacy—Niemcy—Żydzi w Łodzi w XIX–XX w., sąsiedzi dalecy i bliscy* [Poles—Germans—Jews in Łódź in the nineteenth and twentieth centuries, distant and near neighbours] (Łódź: Ibidem, 1997); Bronisław Makowski, *Litwini w Polsce 1920–1939* [Lithuanians in Poland 1920–1939] (Warsaw: Państwowe Wydawnictwo Naukowe, 1986).

20 Moshe Rosman, "The Historiography of Polish Jewry: 1945–1995," [in Hebrew] in *The Broken Chain: Polish Jewry through the Ages*, vol. II, ed. Israel Bartal and Israel Gutman (Jerusalem: The Zalman Shazar Center, 2001), 721.

so without the Poles. This dependence on the Poles is why the Jews' situation during the war was so tragic. For Poles living in the territories occupied by the Germans, there was only one enemy. But Jews faced one enemy who persecuted and murdered them, along with a public at large that was generally apathetic and indifferent to their fate and not infrequently turned into a second enemy, betraying or killing Jews themselves. In other words, Jews had to contend with more than one enemy, and that is a situation unique among the victims of all genocides in history.[21]

This notion that the Jews were unlike any other group of genocide victims, because they had to face more than the German persecutors, is shared by several Holocaust scholars.[22] In fact, a look at other instances of genocide detects that this situation existed elsewhere, too. From the Armenian massacres in the 1890s and the genocide of 1915–1917 to Darfur, the victims faced death at the hands of more than one agent, and the multiple persecutors did not necessarily share the same motives.[23] But what is interesting is that this "lack of symmetry"—a definition that effectively shaped the concept of the uniqueness of the Holocaust in Poland—diverted the focus of historiography toward writing in which the ethical characterization is so prominent—a trend that, as noted, can be traced back to the late 1980s.

This process is rooted in the revolution initiated by Jan T. Gross's *Neighbors*.[24] In the public arena, the events described in his book created the familiar effect that has frequently been discussed and written about: victims of mass violence, proud of their supposed tradition of tolerance toward minorities

---

21 Barbara Engelking, *Holocausts and Memory: The Experience of the Holocaust and Its Consequences. An Investigation Based on Personal Narratives* (London: Leicester University Press in association with the European Jewish Publication Society, 2001), 20–29.
22 See, for example, Yehuda Bauer, *The Death of the Shtetl* (New Haven, CT: Yale University Press, 2009), 156–57.
23 See Jelle Verheij, "'Les frères de terre et d'eau': sur le rôle des Kurdes dans les massacres arméniens de 1894–1896" ["Brothers of Land and Water": On the Role of the Kurds in the Massacre of Armenians in 1894–1896], *Les Annales de l'Autre Islam* [Annals of the other Islam] 5 (1998): 225–76; Raymond Kévorkian agrees that one cannot ignore the participation of local minorities, mainly the Kurds, in the massacres. However, Turkish and Western historiography seem to overestimate their part. Raymond Kévorkian, *The Armenian Genocide: A Complete History* (London: I. B. Tauris, 2011), 810; Mahmood Mamdani, *Saviors and Survivors, Darfur, Politics, and the War on Terror* (New York: Pantheon Books, 2009), 231–70; Gérard Prunier, *Darfur, A 21st Century Genocide*, 3rd ed. (Ithaca, NY: Cornell University Press, 2008), 91–116.
24 Jan T. Gross, *Neighbors: The Destruction of the Jewish Community in Jedwabne, Poland* (Princeton, NJ: Princeton University Press, 2002).

(here, the Poles) victimize a different ethnic or national group (the Jews).[25] The debate that Gross set off in Poland is effectively the same as that triggered by critical scholars in Israel, who asserted that the reigning national paradigm in Israeli writing about the Holocaust prevents an authentic treatment of the issue of the victims (here the Jews) who victimize another national group (the Palestinians). Gross's book opened a new direction in Holocaust studies in Poland. His call for a new historiography of the fate of Polish Jewry in the Holocaust lit the spark of the Polish national historiography of the Holocaust that has developed in the last decade, which is, of course, different from the model familiar in Israel but has no less of a unique national meaning. Still, the image is inverted: whereas the new trend in Israel challenged the traditional national insights and called for a more universal take on the meaning and lessons of the Holocaust, in Poland it moved toward a call for looking inward at the national history in order to understand it correctly.

The scholarly literature of the last two decades on Polish Jews during the Holocaust is extensive and important.[26] But it would not be inaccurate to say that the history of Polish Jewry during the Holocaust as written in Poland is mainly the history of the Poles' treatment of the Jews during the Holocaust.

---

25 See on that, Ilya Prizel, "Jedwabne: Will the Right Questions Be Raised?" *East European Politics and Societies* 16, no. 1 (2002): 278–90.

26 See, among others, Małgorzata Melchior, *Zagłada a tożamość. Polscy Żydzi ocaleni na "aryjskich papierach"* [The Holocaust and identity. Polish Jews saved on the "Aryan" papers] (Warsaw: Wydawnictwo IFiS PAN, 2004); Joanna Nalewajko-Kulikow, *Strategie przetrwania. Żydzi po aryjskiej stronie Warszawy* [The strategies of survival. Jews on the "Aryan" side of Warsaw] (Warsaw: Wydawn. "Neriton," 2004); Barbara Engelking, *"Szanowny panie gistapo". Donosy do władz niemieckich w Warszawie i okolicach w latach 1940–1941* ["Dear Mr Gistapo". Denunciations to the German authorities in Warsaw and the surrounding area in the years 1940–1941] (Warsaw: Wydawnictwo IFiS PAN, 2003); Andrzej Krzysztof Kunert et al., *"Żegota"—Rada Pomocy Żydom, 1942–1945* ["Żegota"—Council to Aid Jews 1942–1945] (Warsaw: Rada Ochrony Pamięci Walk i Męczeństwa, 2002); Aleksandra Namysło, ed., *"Kto w takich czasach Żydów przechowuje? . . ." Polacy niosący pomoc ludności żydowskiej w okresie okupacji niemieckiej* [Who would hide Jews at the times like that? ... Poles providing help to the Jewish population under the German occupation] (Warsaw: Instytut Pamięci Narodowej—Komisja Ścigania Zbrodni Przeciwko Narodowi Polskiemu, 2009); Barbara Engelking, Jacek Leociak, and Dariusz Libionka, eds., *Prowincja noc. Życie i zagłada Żydów w dystrykcie warszawskim* [Night in the province. The life and mass murder of the Jews in the Warsaw district] (Warsaw: Wydawnictwo IFiS PAN, 2007); Barbara Engelking and Dariusz Libionka, *Żydzi w powstańczej Warszawie* [Jews in Warsaw during the 1944 Uprising] (Warsaw: Stowarzyszenie Centrum Badań nad Zagładą Żydów, 2009); Jan Grabowski, *Hunt for the Jews: Betrayal and Murder in German-Occupied Poland* (Bloomington: Indiana University Press, 2013); Barbara Engelking and Jacek Leociak, *The Warsaw Ghetto: A Guide to the Perished City* (New Haven, CT: Yale University Press, 2009).

This new direction can be defined as "integrative national historiography." There may be some articulation incompatibility here, inasmuch as integrative history must take account of broader dimensions and not focus only on the national narrative. To gain an insight into this particular direction, we can examine what two of the most important students of the fate of Polish Jewry in the Holocaust have written about the goals of Holocaust studies in their country. This is how Dariusz Stola defines the post-1989 watershed in Polish historiography of the Holocaust and its goals:

> It means an effort to integrate the history of Polish Jews into Poland's history, including integration of the Holocaust—as the Jewish catastrophe—into the Polish narrative of Poland's past. Through examination of the Polish reactions to the Holocaust and the consequences the Holocaust had, and has had for the Poles, comes the integration into the narratives of the Poles' past as well.

And, he continues: "Polish historiography had a tendency to blur these differences [between the Jewish and Polish fates during the occupation] and the unique feature of the Holocaust."[27]

Another example can be found in Jacek Leociak's introduction to a collection of articles about Jews in the small towns of the Warsaw district during the German occupation. He defined the goals of Holocaust studies in Poland as follows:

> [Cultivating] one's ability to see oneself through the eyes of the others is one of the foundations of group psychotherapy. And indeed, in a certain sense of effort to reconstruct the image of the Poles as recorded in Jewish testimonies from the Holocaust can also play a therapeutic role. What do we learn about ourselves from texts written in the face of extreme threat? ... All of these texts ... impose upon us Poles a painful but simultaneously genuinely therapeutic task. We are not free from sin. Our world is not ideal. Together with good things that we have done there are also bad things, very bad things. We must accept the fact, taking pride in the glorious pages of our history without ignoring the stain we bear. Then we will stop seeing enemies around us lying in wait for us and mocking us and seeking only to harm us, to humiliate us, and to revile us ... We shall

---

27 Stola, "New Research on the Holocaust," 270.

cease rebuffing attacks and constantly defending ourselves from incessant threats. We shall become a mature community.[28]

These statements provoked a bitter debate after they were criticized by David Engel, who argued that it is not the job of historians to write a history aiming at the "self-rectification" of their nation because historical writing must have universal meaning.[29] But this is not necessarily the most important point. What is important is that in Poland, as in Israel, the Holocaust continues to be an event with an absolutely contemporary meaning. Holocaust studies have continued to be linked to the desire to "understand ourselves"; that is, the desire to achieve a more correct and more accurate understanding of national history. In Israel, the memory of an annihilated people is frequently expressed in evasive and apologetic treatments of the harsh injustices that the country is wreaking today.[30] In Poland, there is an aspiration to "understand ourselves" vis-à-vis the unique tragedy that struck our neighbors and kinfolk of Jewish descent and determine our own part and place in that tragedy.

---

28 Jacek Leociak, "Wizerunek Polaków w zapisach Żydów z dystryktu waszawskiego" [The image of the Pole in Jewish accounts in the Warsaw district] in *Prowincja noc*, 440–441, quoted in David Engel, "Scholarship on the Margins: A New Anthology about Jews in the Warsaw District under the Nazi Occupation," *Yad Vashem Studies* 37, no. 1 (2009): 186.
29 Engel, "Scholarship on the Margins," 186–87.
30 Much has been written about the place of the Holocaust in the consolidation of Israeli identity and its ramifications on how the use of force by Israel and the Palestinians is perceived. The instrumentalization of the Holocaust has implications for almost every area of Israeli life, including the education system, public discourse, and the IDF. See, for example, Ilan Gur-Ze'ev, "Defending the Enemy Within: Exploring the Link between Holocaust Education and the Arab/Israeli Conflict," *Religious Education: The Official Journal of the Religious Education Association* 95, no. 4 (2000): 373–401; Daniel Bar-Tal, "Why Does Fear Override Hope in Societies Engulfed by Intractable Conflict, as It Does in the Israeli Society?" *Political Psychology* 22, no. 3 (2001): 601–27; Johanna R. Vollhardt, "The Role of Victim Beliefs in the Israeli–Palestinian Conflict: Risk or Potential for Peace?" *Peace and Conflict* 15 (2009): 135–39; Hava Shechter and Gavriel Salomon, "Does Vicarious Experience of Suffering Affect Empathy for an Adversary? The Effects of Israelis' Visits to Auschwitz on Their Empathy for Palestinians," *Journal of Peace Education* 2, no. 2 (2005): 125–38; Gerald Cromer, "Amalek as Other, Other as Amalek: Interpreting a Violent Biblical Narrative," *Qualitative Sociology* 24, no. 2 (2001): 191–202; Moshe Zuckermann, "The Shoah on Trial: Aspects of the Holocaust in Israeli Political Culture," in *Across the Wall: Narratives of Israeli-Palestinian History*, ed. Ilan Pappé and Jamil Hilal (New York: I. B. Tauris, 2010), 75–86.

III

I would argue that in order to achieve a true integrative history of Polish Jewry during the Holocaust, we need to pursue new directions that are free of the millstones that currently weigh down those working in this area, both in Israel and in Poland. Now that an entire generation has passed since the political changes in Poland that enabled the revolution in the study of the history of its Jews, a different theoretical and methodological approach is in order, one that would write a *single unified history* of Poland during the war and occupation. This would be a history of Poland as a whole—of Poles, Ukrainians, Jews, Germans, Lithuanians—not one that compares their different fates or, perish the thought, defines a hierarchy of victims, but one that seeks to understand the similarities and differences in what happened to the various ethnic and national groups that lived in the country and presents a history that is both multinational and supranational, based on a common spatial notion of Poland during the war years.

Poland during the war was a genocidal space in which several forms of genocide, ethnic cleansing, and other mass violence were all taking place simultaneously. The broader perspective can make a major contribution to the study of the policy that made the massacres and other violence possible. The perspective of political and social geography permits us to weave together the variables of territory, politics, identity, and power—elements that are key ingredients of genocide and mass violence and relate directly to the space in which it takes place. The spatial analysis illustrates the dynamics of the political forces in a broad context and the emergence of the genocidal project at various levels and stages of its implementation. Understanding the spatial component makes it possible to understand the genocide beyond the context of the particular state or national group that is marked as its victim.[31]

It was Friedrich Ratzel, in his well-known 1901 article on Lebensraum, who created the theoretical basis for the link he detected between the competition for space and a nation's ability to survive. Hence the "living space" can easily become the arena for genocide. This idea is much more than a purely geographic theory with no political ramifications. Ratzel's Spatial Darwinism had implications, which scholars have been discussing for many years, for the genocide in southwest Africa in 1904–1908 and the genocidal space that the

---

31 Shannon O'Lear and Stephen L. Egbert, "Introduction: Geographies of Genocide," *Space and Polity* 13, no. 1 (2009): 2.

Nazis created in Poland and Eastern Europe.[32] But Ratzel's theory also helps us understand occupied Poland as a "pariah landscape." As defined by social geographer Douglas Jackson, a pariah landscape is a geographical zone, whose size is not necessarily important, in which various patterns of exclusion, discrimination, dispossession, deportation, and other forms of extreme violence unfold. The patterns of violence employed against them are not necessarily identical for all who live there, but all of them are the persecuted inhabitants of that space and victims of the same exclusionary policy.[33]

There are countless examples of national, ethnic, religious, or social groups who were not accepted by the majority or the regime, who were segregated physically, discriminated against, and, in extreme cases, became the targets of mass violence and genocide. Those who were unacceptable or social pariahs were spatially isolated from society, whether by deportation to a colony, concentration in a reserve, camp, or ghetto, or other means. These spaces can be designated "extinct landscapes." The most extreme examples are the Nazi death and concentration camps and the Soviet gulags, along with other camps to which pariahs were sent to perish, in one way or another. These landscapes may have some characteristics in common, but others are unique to each. They are not necessarily geographic or territorial, but may also be social. However, many pariah landscapes do have a clear territorial dimension.[34]

The most important recent attempt to address the spatial aspect of genocide is that by Timothy Snyder in his controversial *Bloodlands*.[35] Without going into the various claims made by critics of the book,[36] the spatial examination of the patterns of genocidal violence that he proposes constitutes a new and important direction in the study of the mass murder that took place in Eastern Europe during the war. Indeed, the lack of a discussion of

---

32 Friedrich Ratzel, *Der Lebensraum: Eine biogeographische Studie* [Lebensraum: A biogeographic study] (Darmstadt: Wissenschaftliche Buchgesellschaft, 1966). See also Sarah K. Danielsson, "Creating Genocidal Space: Geographers and the Discourse of Annihilation, 1880–1933," *Space and Polity* 13, no. 1 (2009): 63.

33 W. A. Douglas Jackson, *The Shaping of Our World: A Human and Cultural Geography* (New York: Wiley, 1985), 309.

34 Ibid., 310.

35 Timothy Snyder, *Bloodlands, Europe between Hitler and Stalin* (New York: Basic Books, 2010).

36 See, for example, review forum, "Timothy Snyder, *Bloodlands: Europe between Hitler and Stalin*," *Journal of Genocide Research* 13, no. 3 (2011): 313–52; "Comment écrire l'histoire de l'Europe des massacres?" [How to write the history of the Europe of massacres?], *Le Débat, histoire, politique, société* 172, no. 5 (2012): 152–92.

the internal, inter-ethnic violence and the almost exclusive focus on regime violence blurs one of the most important features of the "extinct landscape" of Poland, Ukraine, and other parts of Eastern Europe during those years. Attention to the internal violence that took place in these areas, with its murderous aspect—Poles murdering Jews, Ukrainians killing Poles, and vice versa—reveals that there were also patterns of violence and murder within the "extinct landscape," in the internal ecological systems of the societies and groups that, although all under the control of the genocidal regime, still found a way to engage in intergroup bloodshed. But the integration of the murder of Jews with other acts of violence—internal and external—anchors the Jewish genocide in a complex system of murderous spatial conflicts that are shaped by the nature of the space in which they take place.

It would be appropriate to follow this direction when writing the history of Poland under occupation, too. Occupied Poland—the *Generalgouvernement*, the *Wartheland*, the eastern districts annexed by the Soviet Union—should be studied as a single extinct landscape in which various and changing patterns of exclusion existed from 1939 to 1945, and with an awareness that the events of those years continued to have implications until 1947. In these regions, restriction, persecution, and murderous violence were wrought both by murderous regimes and by internal forces (some of them organized, others unorganized groups without a formal membership), and the outcome was the creation of pariah landscapes for those they thought should be excluded. It is difficult to ignore the reciprocal influences among these forces. The Polish violence against the Jews cannot be explained in isolation from the Nazis' murderous polices, nor the Ukrainian attitude toward the Poles without the Ukrainian participation in the murder of the Jews in 1941 and 1942 and the Soviet persecution of the Polish population in the annexed districts between 1939 and 1941. And of course, there were also political, economic, and social elements that existed in this multi-violence space.[37]

The Lublin district provides a good example of the latent possibilities of an integrative spatial history. Under the Nisko Plan, it was to serve as a closed reservation for Jews; as a result in 1940, thousands of Jews were deported there from Austria and the Protectorate. Later, the Jews were locked up in ghettos, Jews and Poles were employed in forced labor camps, and, after 1941, camps were established for Soviet prisoners of war.

---

37 Dariusz Stola, "A Spatial Turn in Explaining Mass Murder," *Journal of Modern European History* 10, no. 3 (2012): 303–4.

The Majdanek camp began operating in October 1941; in the spring of 1942, extermination facilities were built there for Jews, in which hundreds of thousands were killed. Late 1942 saw the start of violent ethnic cleansing of Poles from the Zamość region. Poles and Ukrainians were murdered there in 1943, when interethnic conflict broke out between them. Finally, in 1947, thousands of Ukrainians were deported from the region and forcibly resettled elsewhere as part of Operation Vistula (Akcja Wisła).

Western Poland, which was annexed to Germany 1939, was another space of multinational genocide. Consider the Warthegau, where a first wave of bloody violence against Poles spread after the German invasion in 1939, continued with the ethnic cleansing of Jews and Poles in 1940, the establishment of ghettos for the Jews who remained there, the establishment of labor camps for Poles and Jews, the deportation there of Jews and Roma from the Altreich, and the construction of a mass-murder facility where Jews and Roma were killed.[38] After the war, thousands of Germans were expelled from the region during the general ethnic cleansing of Germans from the western regions attached to the new Poland.

IV

The Holocaust is an event of geographical significance that took place in a specific physical space, specific time, and specific landscape. Because it was so intimately bound up with spatial processes—concentration, deportation, resettlement, spatial dispersion, and the designation of specific places as extermination sites—its spatial aspects must be studied and analyzed. The destruction of the national infrastructure in so many countries, the unprecedented dimensions of plunder and theft of property, the forced migration and deportation of millions of human beings, and the innumerable sites where people were murdered—these are only some of the geographic aspects involved in the implementation of the Nazi genocide. Particular geographical or local elements of the Holocaust have been addressed by several scholars, mainly those engaged in regional studies, along with scholars who study the formation and influence of Nazi policy on the environment.[39] But the abundance of research and knowledge about the Holocaust has yet to be expressed in a study of social

---

38 Catherine Epstein, *Model Nazi: Arthur Greisler and the Occupation of Western Poland* (New York: Oxford University Press, 2010).
39 Tim Cole, *Holocaust City: The Making of a Jewish Ghetto* (New York: Routledge, 2003).

geography and an attempt to fathom the relationship between the Nazi policy of extermination and its broader spatial and social context. Paradoxically, we know very little about how Nazi policy influenced the space in which the ghettos and camps were established, the places where deportation took place and murders were carried out, and the multiethnic and multinational social fabric of its residents.[40] But a spatial approach to Holocaust studies enables us to do more than simply release the Holocaust from the shackles of national history. It is also important because it facilitates a better understanding of the social aspects of genocide, inasmuch as a genocidal space creates patterns of human interactions that have universal aspects. Thus, it would also foster a better and more complex understanding of the relations between Jews and non-Jews in the years of the Nazi regime in various places in Europe.

---

40 Waitman Beorn et al., "Geographies of the Holocaust," *The Geographical Review* 99, no. 4 (2009): 563.

The Postwar Period

Violence against Jews in Poland, 1944–47: The State of Research and its Presentation

GRZEGORZ BERENDT

For the general populace in Poland the expulsion of the German occupying forces marked the end of an unprecedented period of persecution. However, it did not mean liberation and a return to a state of security. In the years 1944 to 1947 within the new borders of Poland, at least 30,000 people suffered violent deaths as a result of politically motivated killings or criminally motivated murders. The victims included soldiers fighting for the pro-independence underground, functionaries and supporters of the new regime,[1] and those whom we

---

1 According to official publications dated before 1990 the balance sheet of irreversible losses in the years 1944–48 is as follows: officers of the State Security Service and Civic Militia, soldiers of the Internal Security Corps, Border Protection Troops and Polish Army, and members of the Civic Militia Volunteer Reserve—approx. 12,000; civilians associated with the communist regime—approx. 8000; Soviet soldiers—approx. 1,000; soldiers of the anti-communist, pro-independence underground—approx. 8,000; see Henryk Dominiczak, Ryszard Halaba, and Tadeusz Walichnowski, *Z dziejów politycznych Polski 1944–1984*, [On the political history of Poland 1944–1984] (Warsaw: Książka i Wiedza, 1984), 171–72; Ryszard Halaba, ed., *Polegli w walce o władzę ludową. Materiały i zestawienia statystyczne* [Those who fell for people's power. Materials and statistical evaluations] (Warsaw: Książka i Wiedza, 1970), 7–72; Kazimierz Chociszewski, ed., *Księga pamięci poległych funkcjonariuszy SB, MO, ORMO* [Memorial book of fallen functionaries of the Security Service (SB), Civic Militia (MO), Volunteer Reserve of Civic Militia (ORMO)] (Warsaw: Komitet Obchodów 25-lecia Milicji Obywatelskiej i Służby Bezpieczeństwa, 1971). Today, it is estimated that the

can call the country's ordinary citizens. The figures cited do not include soldiers fighting against the German forces until May 1945. Under these conditions, the end of the German occupation soon turned out to provide no guarantee of a peaceful life or security for the Jews.

To date, the state of anomie in which the Polish populace functioned for months on end from 1944 to 1947 has been most fully described by Marcin Zaremba, who in 2012 introduced the very useful concept of the Great Fear.[2] With regard to the situation of the Jews, the most comprehensive study was produced four years earlier by Jan Tomasz Gross.[3] Today anyone who wishes to understand the situation in which the Jews found themselves in this period should first consult Zaremba's work and only then that of Jan Tomasz Gross.

Within the scope of the "final solution to the Jewish question," the German Nazi state organized the murder of some three million Polish citizens. It was such an efficient operation that on the territories controlled by the Third Reich at most only 2 percent of Polish Jews survived. Consequently, the few survivors were all the more in need of security. As we know, it was not granted to them. Some became a target for aggression for the very same reasons as the victims of robbery, homicide, and murder of members of other ethnic groups. However, for Jews there were very often specific reasons behind the antipathy, hatred, or active hostility shown toward them.

Homegrown criminals, who had been actively involved in the machinery of the Holocaust and were often its material beneficiaries, aimed to obliterate Jews who had witnessed their deeds. Others accused Jewish survivors of collaborating with the Soviets and with native communists in opposition to Polish independence. The strangest manifestation of hostility to Jews

---

number of people killed in fighting and repression alone was as many as 50,000, though it is important to remember that this figure also includes soldiers in the Polish underground who were killed in the Eastern Borderlands following the reinvasion of the Red Army; see Marek J. Chodakiewicz, *Po Zagładzie. Stosunki polsko-żydowskie 1944–1947* (Warsaw: Instytut Pamięci Narodowej. Komisja Ścigania Zbrodni Przeciwko Narodowi Polskiemu, 2008), 36. This was originally published in English as *After the Holocaust: Polish-Jewish Conflict in the Wake of World War II* (Boulder, CO: East European Monographs, 2003).

2 Marcin Zaremba, *Wielka trwoga. Polska 1944–1947* [The great fear. Poland 1944–1947] (Kraków: Wydawnictwo Znak: Instytut Studiów Politycznych Polskiej Akademii Nauk, 2012).

3 Jan Tomasz Gross, *Strach. Antysemityzm w Polsce tuż po wojnie. Historia moralnej zapaści* (Kraków: Znak, 2008)—originally published in a somewhat different form in English as *Fear: Anti-Semitism in Poland after Auschwitz: An Essay in Historical Interpretation* (New York: Random House, 2006).

revived accusations of ritual murder. A transformed version of this "black legend," whose proponents emerged in more than a dozen large cities, not to mention smaller places, was the most extreme manifestation of aggressive anti-Semitism to have cast its shadow on postwar Polish–Jewish relations. Its victims' only "crime"—as during the German occupation—was the fact that they were born Jewish. Not surprisingly, it is the crimes that were clearly prompted by racism that have occupied and continue to occupy the attention of commentators.

The conditions for conducting historical research in Poland before 1989 meant that the earliest studies on the real reasons for pogroms and other displays of anti-Jewish violence were described mostly in books published outside Poland, perhaps with one exception—an essay written in 1983 by Józef Orlicki, a former employee of the communist security apparatus in Western Pomerania who had spent many years working on "Zionist issues."[4]

Foreign publications took a different approach. The first to write at length about such violence were journalists visiting Poland in the first few years after the war.[5] Then, in the 1950s and 1960s, one could find remarks about this question in memory-books published by emigrants from the destroyed Jewish communities of Poland. In his memoir published in 1959, Jonas Turkow detailed events from the first year after the German occupation ended.[6] So too did Salomon Strauss-Marko[7] and Yitzhak Zuckerman,[8] a few years later. Their information came from the press and accounts of Polish citizens. The fact that these first books were published in Yiddish limited their range of influence.

---

4 Józef Orlicki, *Szkice z dziejów stosunków polsko-żydowskich 1918–1949* [Sketches on the history of Polish-Jewish relations 1918–1949] (Szczecin: Krajowa Agencja Wydawnicza, 1983).

5 For example, Ch. Szoszkes, *Poyln—1946 (Eyndrukn fun a rayze)* [Poland—1946 (Impressions of a journey)] (Buenos Aires: Tsentral-farband fun Poylishe Yidn in Argentine, 1946); Sz. L. Sznajderman, *Tsvishn shrek un hofenung (A rayze iber dem nayem Poyln)* [Between terror and hope (A journey in the New Poland)] (Buenos Aires: Tsentral-farband fun Poylishe Yidn in Argentina, 1947); P. Nowik, *Oyrope tsvishn milkhome un sholem* [Europe between war and peace], (New York: Ikkuf Farlag, 1948); M. Tsanin, *Iber shtayn un shtok. A rayze iber hundert khoyrev-gevorene kehilot in Poyln* [Over stone and branch. A journey to a hundred destroyed Jewish communities in Poland] (Tel Aviv: Letste nayes, 1952).

6 Jonas Turkow, *Nokh der bafrayung (Zikhroynes)* [After the liberation (Memoirs)] (Buenos Aires: Tsentral farband fun Poylishe Yidn in Argentine, 1959).

7 Salomon Strauss-Marko, *Di geshikhte fun yidishn yishuv in nokhmiklhomdikn Poyln* [The history of the Jewish community in postwar Poland] (Tel Aviv: Aroysgegebn fun meḥaber, 1987).

8 Yitzhak Zuckerman ("Antek"), *A Surplus of Memory: Chronicle of the Warsaw Ghetto Uprising* (Berkeley: University of California Press, 1993).

The information in them came from the press and from the testimony of local inhabitants.

Scholars who subsequently analyzed postwar events include Lucjan Dobroszycki,[9] Michał (Mosze) Chęciński,[10] and Marian Muszkat.[11] Israel Gutman explored the issue in his short history of Jews in Poland after 1944, as did other historians from Israel and the United States.

A major contribution to understanding the circumstances of aggression toward Jews in postwar Poland is found in David Engel's article, "Patterns of Anti-Jewish Violence in Poland 1944–1946" (1998).[12] Engel essentially produced the first academic statistical analysis of incidences of murders committed in that period whose victims were Jews. Similarly, and writing in Polish in more recent years, Marek J. Chodakiewicz explored the same topic,[13] but also referenced territories that belonged to Poland before September 1, 1939. Probably the best-known work on this issue is, as alluded to above, Jan Tomasz Gross's *Fear*, published in English in 2006 and in Polish in 2008.[14]

In Poland itself, Alina Cała, in a brief work published in 1992, was one of the first to write about the antipathy shown to Jews after the war.[15] Evidence of this antipathy still remained in the minds of the twenty-seven witnesses whom she interviewed several decades after the war. The tragedy of the Kielce pogrom was also touched on in Krystyna Kersten's monograph, *Narodziny systemu władzy* (The birth of a system of power).[16]

---

9 Lucjan Dobroszycki, "Restoring Jewish Life in Post-war Poland," *Soviet-Jewish Affairs*, 3 (1973): 58–72; "Re-emergence and Decline of a Community: The Numerical Size of the Jewish Population in Poland, 1944–1947," *YIVO Annual* 21 (1993).

10 Michał Chęciński, *Poland. Communism–Nationalism–Anti-Semitism* (New York: Karz-Cohl Publishers, 1982).

11 Marian Muszkat, *Philo-Semitic and Anti-Jewish Attitudes in Post-Holocaust Poland* (Lewiston, NY: Edwin Mellen Press, 1992).

12 David Engel, "Patterns of Anti-Jewish Violence in Poland 1944–1946," *Yad Vashem Studies* 26 (1998): 43–85.

13 Marek J. Chodakiewicz, *Żydzi i Polacy 1918–1955. Współistnienie—Zagłada—Komunizm* [Jews and Poles 1918–1955. Co-existence—Genocide—Communism] (Warsaw: Fronda, 2000); Marek J. Chodakiewicz, ed., *Ejszyszki, kulisy zajść w Ejszyszkach. Epilog stosunków polsko-żydowskich na Kresach, 1944–45. Wspomnienia-dokumenty* [Eyshishok, the background of the violence in Eyshishok. An epilogue to Polish-Jewish relations in the Eastern Borderlands, 1944–1945] (Warsaw: Fronda, 2002); Chodakiewicz, *Po Zagładzie*.

14 See footnote 3.

15 Alina Cała, *Wizerunek Żyda w polskiej kulturze ludowej* (Warsaw: Wydawnictwa Uniwersytetu Warszawskiego, 1992), English edition: *The Image of the Jew in Polish Folk Culture* (Jerusalem: Magnes Press, 1995).

16 Krystyna Kersten, *Narodziny systemu władzy. Polska 1943–1948* [The birth of a system of power. Poland, 1943–1948] (Paris: Libella, 1986).

Four incidences of mass or organized aggression toward Jews are covered in detailed monographs. Bożena Szaynok was the first to write at length on the Kielce pogrom of July 4, 1946.[17] Her findings were supplemented by other publications,[18] including two volumes of analyses and materials published by the Institute of National Remembrance.[19] At about the same time, though providing less thorough research, Krystyna Kersten also explored the causes and consequences of the Kielce pogrom,[20] a massacre that for the past quarter century has received particular attention. This is understandable, considering that forty-two Jewish victims were killed within the city of Kielce and about thirty more were murdered in the surrounding area. Scholars have mentioned the significance of the criminal behavior of soldiers and civic militia functionaries, the criminal and hostile behavior of some of the civilian population of Kielce, the incomprehensible passivity of local communist security service agents and political decision makers, and also the far-reaching consequences of the panic that overcame the Jewish community when they realized that once again they were unsafe, even in a relatively large city, and that those who should have been defending them were among the aggressors.

A few years after the scholarship on the Kielce pogrom was published, two other mass actions against Jews finally acquired their own researchers and analysts: the incidents that took place in June and August 1945, in Rzeszów and Kraków, respectively. Anna Cichopek wrote about the pogrom in Krakow,[21] and Krzysztof Kaczmarski produced a study on the earlier incident in Rzeszów.[22]

---

17 Bożena Szaynok, *Pogrom Żydów w Kielcach 4 lipca 1946* [The pogrom of Jews in Kielce on July 4, 1946] (Warsaw: Bellona, 1992).

18 Tadeusz Wiącek, *Zabić Żyda. Kulisy i tajemnice pogrom kieleckiego 1946* [Kill the Jew. The background and secrets of the Kielce pogrom] (Kielce: Wydawnictwo DCF, 1992); Stanisław Meducki and Zenon Wrona, eds., *Antyżydowskie wydarzenia kieleckie 4 lipca 1946 roku. Dokumenty i materiały* [The anti-Semitic events in Kielce on July 4, 1946. Documents and materials] (Kielce: Urząd Miasta Kielce, 1992); and *Kielce—July 4, 1946. Background, Context and Events* (Toronto: The Polish Educational Foundation in North America, 1996).

19 Łukasz Kamiński and Jan Żaryn, eds., *Wokół pogromu kieleckiego* [On the Kielce pogrom] (Warsaw: Instytut Pamięci Narodowej, Komisja Ścigania Zbrodni przeciwko Narodowi Polskiemu, 2006), Leszek Bukowski, Andrzej Jankowski, and Jan Żaryn, eds., *Wokół pogromu kieleckiego* [On the Kielce pogrom], vol. 2 (Warsaw: Instytut Pamięci Narodowej, Komisja Ścigania Zbrodni przeciwko Narodowi Polskiemu, 2008).

20 Her most detailed work is *Polacy, Żydzi, komunizm. Anatomia półprawd 1939–1968* [Poles, Jews, communism. The anatomy of half-truths 1939–1968] (Warsaw: Niezależna Oficyna Wydawnicza, 1992).

21 Anna Cichopek, *Pogrom Żydów w Krakowie 11 sierpnia 1945 r.* [The pogrom of Jews in Kraków, August 11, 1945] (Warsaw: Żydowski Instytut Historyczny, 2000).

22 Krzysztof Kaczmarski, *Pogrom, którego nie było. Rzeszów, 11–12 czerwca 1945 r. Fakty—hipotezy—dokumenty* [The pogrom which didn't take place. Rzeszów, June 11–12, 1945. Facts, hypothesis, documents] (Rzeszów: Instytut Pamięci Narodowej, Komisja Ścigania Zbrodni przeciwko Narodowi Polskiemu, Oddział w Rzeszowie, 2008).

A selection of sources on displays of aggression was published in a collection on postwar Jewish life in Poland by Alina Cała and Helena Datner.[23] The topic has also been discussed by Natalia Aleksiun[24] and August Grabski.[25]

In 2011, Andrzej Żbikowski compiled a countrywide-scale work on the consequences of aggression by identifying causes and pretexts, phases, and numbers of victims.[26] A year later Alina Cała published a comprehensive book, covering several centuries, on the causes and manifestations of antipathy toward Jews on Polish territory. By necessity, in this work she devoted relatively little space to the years 1944–1947;[27] however, she described the same issue far more extensively in 2014, in a publication about the "Special Commissions" set up by the Central Committee of Jews in Poland.[28] Incidents of postwar aggression toward Jews were also discussed in studies published in the past few years by Joanna Tokarska-Bakir[29] and Jolanta Żyndul.[30]

---

23 Alina Cała and Helena Datner-Śpiewak, eds., *Dzieje Żydów w Polsce 1944–1968. Teksty źródłowe* [The history of Jews in Poland, 1944–1968. Sources] (Warsaw: Żydowski Instytut Historyczny, 1997).

24 Natalia Aleksiun, *Dokąd dalej? Ruch syjonistyczny w Polsce (1944–1950)* [Where to proceed? The Zionist movement in Poland, 1944–1950] (Warsaw: Centrum Badania i Nauczania Dziejów Żydów w Polsce im. Mordechaja Anielewicza, 2002).

25 August Grabski, *Żydowski ruch kombatancki w Polsce w latach 1944–1949* [The Jewish combatant movement in Poland in the years 1944–1949] (Warsaw: Trio, 2002); *Centralny Komitet Żydów w Polsce (1944–1950). Historia polityczna* [The Central Committee of Jews in Poland, 1944–1950. A political history] (Warsaw: Żydowski Instytut Historyczny im. Emanuela Ringelbluma, 2015).

26 Andrzej Żbikowski, "Morderstwa popełniane na Żydach w pierwszych latach po wojnie" [Murders of Jews in the first years after the war] in *Następstwa zagłady Żydów. Polska 1944–2010*, ed. Feliks Tych and Monika Adamczyk-Garbowska (Lublin: Wydawnictwo Uniwersytet Marii Curie-Skłodowskiej and Żydowski Instytut Historyczny im. Emanuela Ringelbluma, 2011). English version, *Jewish Presence in Absence: Aftermath of the Holocaust in Poland, 1945–2010* (Jerusalem: Yad Vashem, International Institute for Holocaust Research, 2012).

27 Alina Cała, *Żyd—wróg odwieczny? Antysemitizm w Polsce i jego źródła* [The Jew—an eternal enemy? Anti-Semitism in Poland and its origins] (Warsaw: Wydawnictwo Nisza, 2012).

28 Alina Cała, *Ochrona bezpieczeństwa fizycznego Żydów w Polsce powojennej. Komisje specjalne przy centralnym Komitecie Żydów w Polsce* [The physical protection of Jews in postwar Poland. The Special Commissions of the Central Committee of Jews in Poland] (Warsaw: Żydowski Instytut Historyczny im. Emanuela Ringelbluma, 2014).

29 Joanna Tokarska-Bakir, *Legendy o krwi. Antropologia przesądu* [The legends of blood. The anthropology of a prejudice] (Warsaw: Wydawnictwo WAB, 2008); *Okrzyki pogromowe. Szkice z antropologii historycznej Polski lat 1939–1946* [Pogrom shouts. Sketches of the anthropological history of Poland in the years 1939–1946] (Wołowiec: Wydawnictwo "Czarne," 2012).

30 Jolanta Żyndul, *Kłamstwo krwi. Legenda mordu rytualnego na ziemiach polskich w XIX i XX wieku* [The falsehood of blood. The myth of ritual murder on the Polish lands in the nineteenth and twentieth centuries] (Warsaw: Wydawnictwo Cyklady, 2011).

Research on regional incidents includes a highly significant, if not definitive, work by Adam Kopciowski on the Lublin region.[31] Recently, Mariusz Bechta wrote in detail about the attack by partisans on Parczew on February 5, 1946;[32] his essay demonstrates how this particular attack fits the definition of both a pogrom and an act of revenge, aimed at people and institutions belonging to the regime, but in which all local Jews were treated as the enemy regardless of their individual responsibility for the way the communists were exercising power in the town and the surrounding area.

In alphabetical order, the Polish scholars Mariusz Bechta, Alina Cała, Anna Cichopek, Krzysztof Kaczmarski, Adam Kopciowski, Bożena Szaynok, Joanna Tokarska-Bakir, and Andrzej Żbikowski have published detailed source analyses that describe in context postwar incidences of aggression toward Jews. Other scholars of note have within the scope of their research recorded facts relevant to the killing of Jews in various locations in Poland after July 1944. These include Maciej Korkuć,[33] who wrote about the circumstances in which more than a dozen Jews were killed outside Krościenko in May 1946, and Dariusz Libionka, author of a text on the circumstances under which Chaim Hirszman was killed in Lublin in March 1946.

Research conducted over the past three decades has the forms, and to some extent the scale, of patently anti-Semitic behavior. However, analyses have faced obstacles in establishing the true circumstances under which most of the murdered Jews were killed between July 1944 and the beginning of 1947. Without such information, we cannot establish how many Jews were killed because of their ethnicity and how many died for the same reasons as the thousands of other inhabitants of Poland who were killed in this period.

It has been essential for historians and other specialists since 2000 to gain access to the files of the state security service, the civic militia, the civil and military prosecution service, the courts, and the Polish People's Republic. Since the files of local administration services and political organizations became accessible, the political and social context can now be recreated. The files of

---

31 Adam Kopciowski, "Zajścia antyżydowskie na Lubelszczyźnie w pierwszych latach po drugiej wojnie światowej" [Anti-Semitic violence in the Lublin area in the first years after the Second World War], *Zagłada Żydów. Studia i Materiały* 3 (2007): 178–207.
32 Mariusz Bechta, *Pogrom czy odwet? Akcja Zbrojna Zrzeszenia "Wolność i Niezawisłość" w Parczewie 5 lutego 1946 r.* [Pogrom or revenge? The armed action of the Wolność i Niezawisłość organization in Parczew on February 5, 1946] (Poznań: Zysk i S-ka Wydawnictwo, 2014).
33 Maciej Korkuć, "Horror podmalowany" (A spruced-up horror), *Tygodnik Powszechny* no. 9 (2008).

the Soviet special services then operating within Poland are still inaccessible, but they may ultimately also cast light on other incidents that none of the aforementioned scholars has yet researched.

If we compare statistics under the category of Jewish deaths as a result of aggression aimed at Jews in 1944–1947 with cases known to us, we can conclude that the figures provided by David Engel are most strongly based on sources. He has presented statistical records of incidents of the murder of Jews mentioned in the press, in documents of the Central Committee of Jews in Poland, and in documents issued by the state civil administration. I should stress that although seventeen years have passed since Engel's text was published, the absolute majority of incidents have not been subjected to historical analysis based on research of archival material. Certain figures in the sources have not yet been fully confirmed in the incomplete materials known to us. These include, for instance, the figure of 353 Jews who were murdered in 1945, or the approximately 200 persons apparently killed in armed attacks on trains.

So far, we lack an analytical record of all known cases of aggression against Jews that resulted in death. Alina Cała has gone furthest, in her book from 2014, in citing the largest number of source quotations with descriptions of specific killings.

Only when a complete record based on source materials has been produced will we be able to cite a more accurate minimum number of victims. We shall never know the full figure, but we can already maintain that the existing information citing 1,500–2,000 or even 3,000 fatalities does not result from full research of accurate sources. I cannot say how the authors reached these figures because they have not presented their methods for establishing them. An initial list of recorded instances of killings provides us with confirmation that between 1944 and 1947 about four hundred Jews were killed within the new borders of Poland, for a variety of reasons. Additionally, a study about people regarded as builders of the new regime from 1944 to 1948 cites forty-six people with Jewish names who were killed;[34] recent sources indicate that at least two other persons included in this publication were Jews as well, although at the time of their death they had Polish surnames.[35] These examples imply that there may be more cases of this kind. If we compare the

---

34 Halaba, *Polegli w walce*, 73–564.
35 They were Wanda Brzozowska (real name Dora Goldkorn), see Halaba, *Polegli w walce*, 101; *Folks-Sztyme* no. 3 (January 1947): 6; and Lieutenant Henryk Pszenica, see Halaba, *Polegli w walce*, 534; *Dos Naye Lebn* no. 28 (1946): 9.

circumstances of the deaths of Jews who had no connection with the communist regime with the deaths of those who were its functionaries, we can see that representatives of the former category were often attacked and killed in groups, whereas most so-called "supporters of people's power" died alongside their political comrades of other ethnicities, which leads us to conclude that they died for political rather than racial reasons, or as the victims of common banditry.

Regardless of how researchers ultimately establish the minimum number of Jews killed, we should note that in many of the cases known to us from descriptions, some of the potential victims only escaped death because their attackers ran away, or thought they were dead when they were only badly wounded. These victims clearly owed their lives to luck, rather than to the mercy or sympathy of the aggressors. This means that the number of fatalities resulting from known cases of attacks may be even greater.

In view of the state of research, I believe that the curators of the postwar gallery at the Museum of the History of Polish Jews were right in their decision not to include estimates for the number of victims of postwar aggression.

The descriptions to be found in the postwar gallery of the deaths of Jews in places such as Bolesławiec, Irena, Parczew, and Sokoły are very brief. However, these and other incidents were highly significant, because they were reported by the various political strands of the Jewish press. These press reports undoubtedly contributed to the intensification of a sense of alienation and threat among survivors who were aware that antipathy or hostility were present in many places, and that their personal negative experiences were not isolated incidents but part of a wider trend.

In time, some of the descriptions and content presented by the museum's multimedia displays and exhibits will have to be changed in accordance with new research findings. This is inevitable. A typical example is the attack by partisans on Parczew on February 5, 1946. We can already modify the description, as we now know that the Jewish victims were killed because they had contributed to the establishment of the local communist apparatus, and died because they were at their official posts when the attack took place. Had these positions been held by people of a different ethnicity, they would certainly have been killed, as were thousands of Polish citizens who "died in the struggle for people's power" throughout the country, starting in 1944.

The exhibition's display on postwar aggression toward Jews clearly presents the absurdity of some of the accusations aimed at them, and the destructive intensity of the anti-Jewish mood that prevailed within parts of Polish society. Without this section of the exhibition it is impossible to understand why 150,000 Jews saw no future for themselves in Poland and hurriedly left it, and why those who remained never forgot the events that came to be symbolized by the Kielce pogrom of July 4, 1946.

Translated from Polish by Antonia Lloyd-Jones

The Jews and the "Disavowed Soldiers"

AUGUST GRABSKI

The attention paid in recent years to "disavowed soldiers" (*żołnierze wyklęci*) in Polish historical education has aroused very diverse reactions. On the one hand, the cult of these members of the underground who continued after the Nazi defeat to fight the new communist-dominated government and the Red Army which assisted it has been actively supported not only by the most important institutions in the state, including the president, the prime minister and the speaker of the Sejm (parliament), but also by the main state institution responsible for the investigation of the recent past, the Institute of National Remembrance (Instytut Pamięci Narodowej—IPN), which commenced operation in 2000. On the other, the rehabilitation and promotion of these "disavowed soldiers" has been opposed by some veteran circles, by some of the political parties, and by organizations representing some of the national minorities in Poland.

The rehabilitation of armed opposition to the communist regime was a natural consequence of the political changes in 1989. Since anti-communist groups were now given state legitimation, organizations that had fought against the communist order were subjected to reevaluation by state institutions. Yet the journey from the gradual rehabilitation of the "disavowed soldiers" to their active promotion by the state was a long one, lasting a dozen years. Even the term "disavowed soldier" is a relatively recent coinage. It was first used in 1993 as the title of an exhibition organized by the far-right Republican League at the University of Warsaw, which later became the basis for an album edited by Grzegorz Wąsowski and Leszek Żebrowski.[1] It was then popularized by Jerzy

---

[1] Grzegorz Wąsowski and Leszek Żebrowski, eds., *Żołnierze wyklęci. Antykomunistyczne podziemie zbrojne po 1944 roku* [The disavowed soldiers. The military anti-communist underground after 1944] (Warsaw: Rytm, 1996).

Ślaski, who published a book with that title in 1996.[2] Significantly, the term "disavowed [or rejected] soldiers" was not questioned by liberal historians in either public or academic discourse, in spite of its apologetic character. At the same time, the pejorative communist description "reactionary bands," in use until 1989, completely disappeared.[3]

While intensified efforts to study and popularize the armed anti-communist opposition were already observable in the 1990s, its actions were not yet a major subject of debate. The most important historical debates in the 1990s were, above all, about People's Poland: over the legacy of the Polish People's Republic, the extent to which it was a sovereign state and whether it should be described as authoritarian or totalitarian.[4]

Nevertheless, those who had fought in the postwar underground could now claim veteran status, streets began to be named after their commanders, and some who had committed crimes against national minorities were legally or politically rehabilitated. For example, Mieczysław Pazderski (aka "Szary" [Grey]), a soldier of the Special Emergency Action Unit (*Pogotowie Akcji Specjalnej*; PAS) of the National Armed Forces (*Narodowe Siły Zbrojne*; NSZ), whose men murdered nearly two hundred Ukrainian inhabitants of the village of Wierzchowina in the Krasnystaw district in June 1945, was posthumously awarded two medals (the National Military Action Cross and the Partisan Cross) by President Lech Wałęsa in 1992.[5]

In 1995, the Warsaw District Military Court revoked the death sentence passed in 1949 against Romuald Rajs (aka "Bury" [Dun]), the commander of a Special Action Unit (Pogotowie Akcji Specjalnej—PAS) of the National Military Union (Narodowe Zjednoczenie Wojskowe—NZW) responsible for numerous crimes against Belarusians in the Białystok region. In particular, in

---

2   Jerzy Ślaski, *Żołnierze wyklęci* [The disavowed soldiers] (Warsaw: Rytm, 1996).
3   The term *cursed soldiers* (żołnierze przeklęci), though popularized by part of the left-wing press (*Trybuna, Przegląd*), has remained on the margins of public discourse and has not entered academic language at all.
4   Andrzej Friszke, "Spór o PRL w III Rzeczypospolitej (1989–2001)" [The dispute about the People's Republic of Poland in the III Republic (1989–2001], *Pamięć i Sprawiedliwość* 1/1 (2002): 9–28.
5   On this crime, see Mariusz Zajączkowski, "Spór o Wierzchowiny. Działalność oddziałów Akcji Specjalnej NSZ w powiatach Chełm, Hrubieszów, Krasnystaw i Lubartów na tle konfliktu polsko-ukraińskiego (sierpień 1944 r.—czerwiec 1945 r.)" [The dispute about Wierzchowina. The actions of the units of the Special Action Force of the NSZ in the districts of Chełm, Hrubieszów, Krasnystaw and Lubartów against the background of the Polish-Ukrainian conflict, August 1944–June 1945], *Pamięć i Sprawiedliwość* 1/9 (Memory and Justice, 2006): 266–301.

late January and early February 1946, the men under his command carried out the "pacification" of six Belarusian villages, murdering in a cruel manner eighty-seven randomly selected people and wounding dozens of others. The inhabitants of the village of Zaleszany were locked in a building and then burned alive. The court found that Rajs was "fighting for the independence of the Polish State," and that in giving orders that included the pacification of Belarusian villages he was forced by "a state of higher necessity . . . to undertake actions that were ethically ambiguous."[6]

Nevertheless, in 2005 the Institute of National Remembrance (*Instytut Pamięci Narodowej*; IPN), in its evaluation of the actions of "Bury" decided as follows:

> Without questioning the idea of the struggle for the independence of Poland conducted by organizations opposing the imposed [Communist] authority, among them the National Military Union, it must be stated categorically that the murder of [Belarusian] wagon-drivers and the pacification of [Belarusian] villages in January–February 1946 cannot be seen as part of the battle for an independent state, since they bear the marks of genocide. Quite the opposite: the actions carried out by "Bury" against the inhabitants of villages in Podlasie aided the Communist ruling apparatus, above all by diminishing the prestige of the underground organizations and providing propaganda arguments that these partisan units were merely bandits. Without doubt, it facilitated the implementation of the agreement between Poland and the Soviet Union on resettling people of Belarusian descent in the Soviet Union. It is true that this resettlement action realized the national slogan "Poland for the Poles," but at the time it worked to the advantage of the goals of the Polish and Soviet Communist State organs.
>
> The pacification actions carried out by "Bury" can in no sense be seen as having a positive effect on Polish–Belarusian relations or on how the battle of the Polish underground for the independence of Poland should be conducted. On the contrary, they often created implacable enemies and supporters of separatism in the Białystok region. Thus in no circumstances can these actions be justified.[7]

---

6 On this subject, see Eugeniusz Mironowicz, *Polityka narodowościowa PRL* [The nationalist policy of the People's Republic of Poland] (Białystok: Wyd. Białoruskiego Towarzystwa Historycznego, 2000), 45.

7 "Informacja o ustaleniach końcowych śledztwa S 28/02/Zi w sprawie pozbawienia życia 79 osób—mieszkańców powiatu Bielsk Podlaski w tym 30 osób tzw. furmanów w lesie koło

The stance of the IPN in this case, which concerned the crimes of this "disavowed soldier" against members of a national minority, was exceptional. However, while in the 1990s the topic of the "disavowed soldiers" remained outside the mainstream of historical politics in Poland, this situation changed at the beginning of the twenty-first century. Particularly active promoters of the cult of the "disavowed soldiers" proved to be the IPN itself and the group around President Lech Kaczyński (2005–10).[8]

HEROES FOR NEW TIMES

There can be no doubt that the intensified promotion of the "disavowed soldiers" was connected with the appearance in Polish politics of the ideological concept of a Fourth Republic, based on the radical decommunization of Polish society and the alteration of the mentality of Polish citizens. This was to be achieved, in part, by the creation of new heroes, the radical anti-communists. Thus, while the 1990s had brought about the full rehabilitation of the civilian anti-communist resistance, in the new century armed anti-communist resistance was to be not only rehabilitated but also made the object of a cult promoted by the state.

This program was bound to arouse controversy on the grounds that the "disavowed soldiers" represented a numerically small and politically extremist

---

Puchał Starych, dokonanych w okresie od dnia 29 stycznia 1946 r. do dnia 2 lutego 1946" [Information on the final determinations of investigation S 28/02/Zi in the matter of the homicide of 79 inhabitants of the Bielsk Podlaski district, among them 30 so-called wagon-drivers, in the forest near Puchały Stare, committed between 29 January 1946 to 2 February 1946], http://ipn.gov.pl/wydzial-prasowy/komunikaty/informacja-o-ustaleniach-koncowych-sledztwa-s-2802zi-w-sprawie-pozbawienia-zyc, accessed November 23, 2016.

8 The earliest anticipation of the promotion of the "disavowed soldiers" by the right in the Sejm was the Resolution of the Sejm of the Republic of Poland adopted on March 14, 2001, honoring the fallen, murdered, and persecuted members of the organization Freedom and Independence (*Wolność i Niezawisłość*; *WiN*). The resolution included the statement "that the organization Freedom and Independence, continuing the tradition of armed struggle of the Home Army (*Armia Krajowa*; AK), served the Fatherland well." Of 357 deputies present, 239 voted for the resolution, 10 against, and 108 abstained. Longin Pastusiak spoke for the Democratic Left Alliance (*Sojusz Lewicy Demokratycznej*; *SLD*), which opposed the resolution. (Uchwała Sejmu Rzeczypospolitej Polskiej z dnia 14 marca 2001 r. w sprawie hołdu poległym, pomordowanym i prześladowanym członkom organizacji "Wolność i Niezawisłość," M.P. 2001 nr 10 poz. 157) [Resolution of the Sejm of the Polish Republic, 14 March 2001, concerning the question of honouring the fallen, murdered and persecuted members of the organization, "Freedom and Independence," M.P. 2001 no. 10, item 157].

grouping within the anti-communist opposition, which had been condemned at the time even in the press of the mass anti-communist Polish People's Party (*Polskie Stronnictwo Ludowe*; PSL). The estimated number of "disavowed soldiers" fighting as partisans in 1945 was barely 13,000–17,000, while more than 330,000 soldiers were serving at the same time in the ranks of the Polish People's Army (*Ludowe Wojsko Polskie*; LWP).[9] Nor was the behavior of this group typical of the great majority of the more than 300,000 soldiers of the Polish Underground State (*Polskie Państwo Podziemne*; PPP), who emerged from the underground and became active en masse in the new Poland even before the underground state was dissolved in August 1945.

As we have mentioned, President Lech Kaczyński proved to be a great promoter of the cult of the "disavowed soldiers." On August 13, 2006, he participated, along with Andrzej Przewoźnik, the secretary-general of the Council for the Protection of the Memory of the Struggle and Martyrdom of the Polish Nation, in the unveiling of a monument to Józef Kuraś (aka "Ogień" [Fire]) in Zakopane. The participation of the president was disquieting given that "Ogień" had committed numerous crimes against Jews who had survived the Holocaust (estimates of the numbers killed range from a dozen to more than thirty).[10] He decided to take part in the ceremony even though he knew that it was opposed by representatives of both the Jewish community and the Slovak minority (against whom "Ogień" also committed numerous crimes)—and even by the Nowy Targ branch of the World Union of Soldiers of the Home Army (*Armia Krajowa*; AK), which had prevented the erection of a monument to "Ogień" in their city, calling him "bandit."[11]

---

9 Of course, the armed underground was also assisted by rural and urban civilian groups. In response to the amnesty of February 22, 1947, a total of 76,574 people came forward, including members of underground organizations and partisan units as well as deserters from the Polish Army, the Citizens' Militia (*Milicja Obywatelska*; MO), the Internal Security Corps (*Korpus Bezpieczeństwa Wewnętrznego*; KBW) and the Security Offices (*Urzędy Bezpieczeństwa*; UB). (*Atlas polskiego podziemia niepodległościowego 1944–1956* [Atlas of the Polish independence underground, 1944–1956], ed. Rafał Wnuk et al. (Warsaw–Lublin: Instytut Pamięci Narodowej—Komisja Ścigania Zbrodni przeciwko Narodowi Polskiemu, 2007), XXXII).

10 Notable among recent publications on the subject of "Ogień" is Bolesław Dereń's apologetic work, *Józef Kuraś "Ogień." Partyzant Podhala* [Józef Kuraś "Ogień." A partisan of Podhale] (Kraków: "Secesja," 2000) and Maciej Korkuć's *Józef Kuraś "Ogień". Podhalańska wojna 1939–1945* [Józef Kuraś "Fire." The war in Podhale 1939–1945] (Kraków: Instytut Pamięci Narodowej, Wydawnictwo Attyka, 2012).

11 Voices opposing the rehabilitation of "Ogień" were described, for example, by Leszek Konarski, "'Ogień' był bandytą" ["Ogień" was a bandit], *Przegląd* 9 (2012): 20–24.

In February 2010, President Kaczyński proposed a law establishing a National Day of Remembrance for the Disavowed Soldiers,[12] which was passed by a large majority in the Sejm on February 3, 2011, after the tragic death of the president in April 2010. Of the 417 deputies present, 406 voted for the law and only eight against it, with three abstaining. Voting against were five deputies of the Civic Platform (*Platforma Obywatelska*; PO), two independents and, astonishingly, only one, Artur Ostrowski, from the Democratic Left Alliance (*Sojusz Lewicy Demokratycznej*; SLD).[13] However, in subsequent years, deputies of the left and center-left boycotted events commemorating the "disavowed soldiers," as evidence surfaced of numerous ordinary crimes committed by them, even against children.[14] Paweł Dybicz wrote in the left wing weekly *Przegląd* (Review):

> When on March 1st, the National Day of Remembrance for the Disavowed Soldiers, ceremonies were being observed; when from all sides, praise was heard for the "men of the forest" [*sic*]; when the president of the Polish Republic [Bronisław Komorowski] once again was handing out medals and orders to "the greatest of patriots, the staunchest of heroes": somehow no one suggested that it was worth commemorating their victims as well, and honoring them at least with a minute of silence. In the years 1944–1948, regardless of whether we call that period a civil war or something else, the "disavowed" killed more than 5,000 civilians, including 187 children fourteen years old or younger. But one does not speak of that, because for the Right, these people can be dismissed as Communist stooges and informers for the UB [Urząd Bezpieczeństwa—the Office for Security].

---

12 March 1, the date of the National Day of Remembrance for the Disavowed Soldiers, marks the anniversary of the execution of seven members of the IV Main Board of WiN, along with Lt. Col. Łukasz Ciepliński, shot in the Rakowicka St. prison in Warsaw by functionaries of the UB.

13 After "Artur Ostrowski," http://www.sejm.gov.pl/sejm7.nsf/posel.xsp?id=277, accessed November 23, 2016.

14 For example, on March 1, 2012, when the Sejm observed a minute of silence in memory of the "disavowed soldiers," the SLD deputies waited until the ceremony was over before entering the hall. During the ceremony, the speaker of the Sejm, Ewa Kopacz, said among other things that "[t]he manliness, patriotic posture and adherence to the highest values of the disavowed soldiers deserves our admiration and respect." The SLD's protest was supported by some of the deputies of the Palikot Movement ("SLD nie chciało uczcić żołnierzy wyklętych" [The SLD did not want to honour the disavowed soldiers], *Wprost*, March 2, 2012, available online at: http://www.wprost.pl/ar/308755/SLD-nie-chcialo-uczcic-zolnierzy-wykletych/, accessed November 23, 2016).

The uncritical glorification of the "disavowed soldiers," without taking into account the whole historical context and the realities of those times, is nothing more than a repetition in reverse of the slogans and propaganda of the Stalinist period. Today, the "disavowed," as viewed through the prism of the historical politics conducted by the IPN apparatus, by right-wing publicists and politicians, appear as defenseless angels dying at the hands of Communist murderers. Meanwhile, one must regard the "disavowed" not only as a collective, but also as individuals, since only then can we see their true face. It is true that very many became victims of repression and torture at the hands of the UB and the NKVD; yet one must also remember that the "disavowed" themselves often became criminals, no less cruel than those who persecuted their colleagues. No one should question those facts, since witnesses to those events are still alive, while the archives contain documents, though recently, by strange coincidence, they have often disappeared.[15]

REJECTING THE MEMORY OF SURVIVORS OF THE SHOAH

The establishment of the National Day of Remembrance for the Disavowed Soldiers was completely at odds with the postwar experiences of Polish Jews and declarations by the leaders of their community, which in the postwar political conflict wholly supported the new authorities.[16] The Central Committee of Jews in Poland (*Centralny Komitet Żydów w Polsce*; CKŻP), as well as other Jewish organizations, repeatedly condemned the armed underground and the crimes committed by it, particularly against Jews.

These crimes were furthermore treated not as something new but as a continuation of crimes committed by the AK and the NSZ during the German occupation.[17] It is worth stressing that fact, since crimes against Jews committed by the structures of the Polish underground state remain to this day for the great majority of Poles a taboo subject, as was well demonstrated by the many

---

15 Paweł Dybicz, "'Wyklęci' mało święci" [The "Disavowed" are hardly saints], *Przegląd* 10 (2014).
16 On this subject, see, for example, August Grabski, *Centralny Komitet Żydow w Polsce (1944–1950), Historia polityczna* [The Central Committee of Jews in Poland 1944–1950, a political history] (Warsaw: Żydowski Instytut Historyczny im. Emanuela Ringelbluma, 2015).
17 The historians Israel Gutman and Shmuel Krakowski stated that they knew of 120 instances of Jews being murdered by Polish partisans of the Home Army and the National Armed Forces (*Narodowe Siły Zbrojne*; NSZ), describing twenty-nine of them in their book, *Unequal Victims: Poles and Jews during World War Two* (New York: Holocaust Library, 1986), 120–34.

outraged voices in the Polish media after the airing in 2013 of the German television series *Unsere Mütter, unsere Väter* (Our Mothers, Our Fathers), even though its portrayal of anti-Semitism among AK partisans was marginal and relatively mild.[18] Those truths turned out to be absolutely unacceptable to the Polish public yet again in 2015, when Jan T. Gross claimed in *Die Welt* that during the war Poles killed more Jews than they did Germans.[19]

The CKŻP saw the crimes of the "disavowed soldiers" as one of the main reasons for the postwar emigration of Polish Jews. In a memorandum dated February 1946, from the CKŻP to the Anglo-American Committee of Inquiry Regarding the Problems of European Jewry and Palestine, which investigated, among other things, the situation of Holocaust survivors, we read:

> In 1945, 353 Jews were murdered. These acts are inspired and carried out by reactionary underground groups which are in constant communication with the reactionary General [Władysław] Anders in Italy and with the

---

18 Juliusz Braun, the president of the Polish State Television (TVP), wrote a special letter to the head of the German network ZDF, in which he stated that the depiction of AK soldiers in the series "has nothing to do with historical truth, and must therefore be condemned and rejected. In German-occupied Poland, the least form of help to the Jews was punishable by death. Despite that fact, many Poles decided to bring them such aid, and the AK was even obligated to do so by the authorities of the Polish Underground State. Whenever possible, the AK ruthlessly punished those who supported the Germans in realizing their criminal plan to exterminate the Jews, whereas in the series, an opposite, entirely false picture emerges" ("List prezesa TVP do ZDF ws. niemieckiego serialu 'Nasze matki, nasi ojcowie'", [Letter of the Director of TVP to the ZDF concerning the German serial, "Our mothers, our fathers"], *Polska Newsweek*, 27 March 2013. On line at: http://polska.newsweek.pl/list-prezesa-tvp-do-zdf-ws—niemieckiego-serialu—nasze-matki—nasi-ojcowie-,102906,1,1.html, accessed November 23, 2016).

19 Jan T. Gross, "Die Osteuropäer haben kein Schamgefühl" [East Europeans have no sense of shame], *Welt* Online, September 13, 2015. Marcin Wojciechowski, the spokesperson of the Foreign Affairs Ministry, described Gross's article as "historically untrue, harmful and insulting to Poland." ("Jest śledztwo w sprawie słów Jana T. Grossa. Zarzut: znieważenie narodu polskiego" [An investigation is taking place in relation to the words of Jan T. Gross. The accusation: insulting the Polish nation], *Gazeta Wyborcza*, October 15, 2015). Gross also said: "A reporter from *Rzeczpospolita* contacted me in connection with the [German] TV series, hoping that I would condemn the German media for portraying [some] Poles as perpetrators. I replied that since it was true, why should they not say so? I have also noted that since the Final Solution was highly organized and efficient, it is entirely possible that there were more direct Polish perpetrators than German ones. In Warsaw, for example, 300,000 Jews were killed at Treblinka, which was staffed by about 30 Germans, while I estimate that 3,600 Jews were betrayed or murdered 'on the Aryan side,' hounded by 3,000–4,000 Polish blackmailers and police agents."

remnants of the former Government-in-Exile in London. The same criminal hand that threatens the activists of the democratic parties, officers of the Polish Army, etc., also carries out an antisemitic campaign . . . The Polish government and the democratic parties combat antisemitism, rooted in the tsarist period and reinforced by Nazi Hitlerite propaganda. The decree concerning summary courts [of November 16, 1945] provides for the death penalty for terrorist activity motivated by hostility to a nationality, race or religion. Yet incidents of fascist anti-Jewish activity still occur.[20]

As a result of its unambiguous support for the Communist authorities, the Jewish press was extremely hostile to the anti-Communist underground and portrayed its methods in a similar fashion. I add the voice of one left-wing Zionist:

Currently, as the democratic government makes every effort to rebuild the country and eradicate the harmful habits of the past, the supporters of [Tomasz] Arciszewski [head of the rump government in exile in London] and Anders can find no place in the new reality. These "professional patriots" of the gun and the grenade cannot return to normal life, but go to the forest, blow up bridges and railway tracks, murder Jews, socialists, and peaceful citizens, deluding themselves with the hope of a renewed world conflagration, when their homeland will once again become a battleground and "liberation" will follow. Such is the fate of fascist patriotism in decline.[21]

It is highly significant that this assessment of the armed anti-Communist underground did not undergo any revision in the memoirs of Jewish activists published after they left Poland. The memoirs of Yitzhak ("Antek") Zuckerman and Stefan Grajek can serve as examples.[22]

---

20 *Biuletyn Żydowskiej Agencji Prasowej*, February 11, 1946.
21 Mordechaj Bentow, "Bankructwo iluzji" [The bankruptcy of illusions], *Mosty* 8, no. 3 (1946). Bentow served five terms as a member of the Knesset in Israel, and for about ten years as a minister in governments led by the social-democratic party Mapai.
22 Yitzhak Zuckerman ("Antek"), *A Surplus of Memory: Chronicle of the Warsaw Ghetto Uprising* (Berkeley: University of California Press, 1993); Stefan Grajek, *Po wojnie i co dalej* [After the war and what next] (Warsaw: Żydowski Instytut Historyczny, 2004).

THE ANTI-SEMITISM OF THE "DISAVOWED"

Although its statements and archives contain considerable information about anti-Semitic crimes committed by the anti-Communist underground, the CKŻP did not make a comprehensive list of these. What we know today we owe above all to research conducted in the 1990s and the early twenty-first century by David Engel,[23] Marek J. Chodakiewicz,[24] Andrzej Żbikowski,[25] Adam Kopciowski,[26] Julian Kwiek,[27] and other historians.[28] The most recent important study of postwar anti-Semitic violence is a monograph by Alina Cała, published in 2014 dealing with the Special Commission of the CKŻP.[29]

Before turning to the statistics of such crimes, let us examine the anti-Semitic propaganda produced by the "disavowed" that led to the violence. Marek Jan Chodakiewicz, an expert on the anti-communist underground, admits that the underground "had a somewhat antipathetic attitude towards the Jews, but its antipathy expressed itself mainly in anti-Semitism of the Christian-conservative kind," which advocated "expelling Jews from the country and isolating those who remain."[30] This position was in line with the political programs of the main political parties of the Polish right during the Holocaust, the National Party and the (Christian democratic) Labour Party.

---

23 David Engel, "Patterns of Anti-Jewish Violence in Poland 1944–1946," *Yad Vashem Studies* 26 (1998): 43–85.
24 Marek J. Chodakiewicz, *After the Holocaust: Polish–Jewish Relations in the Wake of World War II* (Boulder, CO: East European Monographs, 2003).
25 Andrzej Żbikowski, "The Post-War Wave of Pogroms and Killings," in *Jewish Presence in Absence: The Aftermath of the Holocaust in Poland, 1944–2010*, ed. Feliks Tych and Monika Adamczyk-Garbowska (Jerusalem: Yad Vashem, 2014), 67–94.
26 Adam Kopciowski, "Zajścia antyżydowskie na Lubelszczyźnie w pierwszych latach po drugiej wojnie światowej" [Anti-Jewish violence in the Lublin area in the first years after the Second World War], *Zagłada Żydów. Studia i Materiały* 3 (2007): 178–207.
27 Julian Kwiek, "Zabójstwa ludności żydowskiej w Krakowskiem w latach 1945–1947: fakty i mity" [The murder of Jews in the Kraków area in the years 1945–1947], *Kwartalnik Historii Żydów* 248, (2013): 679–95.
28 For example, A. Bańkowska, A. Jarzębowska, and M. Siek, "Morderstwa Żydów w latach 1944–1946 na terenie Polski. Na podstawie zbioru 301. Relacje z Zagłady w Archiwum ŻIH" [The murder of Jews in Poland in the years 1944–1946. On the basis of collection 301. Accounts on the Holocaust from the Archive of ŻIH], *Kwartalnik Historii Żydów* 231, (2009): 356–67.
29 Alina Cała, *Ochrona bezpieczeństwa fizycznego Żydów w Polsce powojennej. Komisje Specjalne przy Centralnym Komitecie Żydów w Polsce* [The defense of the physical safety of Jews in post-war Poland. The Special Commissions of the Central Committee of the Jews in Poland] (Warsaw : Żydowski Instytut Historyczny im. Emanuela Ringelbluma, 2014).
30 Chodakiewicz, *After the Holocaust*, 53.

It is clear that anti-Semitism was a constant feature of the propaganda of the anti-communist opposition. According to Rafal Wnuk, among the publications of the Home Army (AK), the Delegation of the Armed Forces and the group Freedom and Independence (WiN)—Jews were portrayed in a negative light in ("only") 10 percent of newspapers and ("as many as") 40 percent of leaflets. Wnuk identified three images in the perception of Jews in the underground and in the anti-Semitic part of Polish society: the "Communist Jew," the "Alien Jew," and the "Jewish usurer." At the same time, however, he claimed that the verbal anti-Semitism of the "independentists" (*niepodległościowcy*) was reflected only to a small extent in military actions directed against Jews.[31]

How, then, did WiN represent the Jews in its propaganda? According to a proclamation issued in September 1945 by the commander of the Lublin district of the AK-WiN:

> Finally, thanks to the communist work of the Jews, whom imperialist Russia has hired for its expansionist purposes, tens of thousands of the most creative Polish men and women were arrested and deported during the period of the PKWN.[32]
>
> Since then, Poland has groaned under the heavy pillory of the Jews, flogged mercilessly in advance by the orders of the Jewish PKWN. Foreign opinion is deceived with the vision of a sovereign democratic Poland, while many thousands of the most valuable Poles fill the prisons or live in exile.
>
> And where are the sacred principles of democracy? Where is freedom of speech and the press, and respect for property? The falsification and deception is clear, but while we Poles have for some time been powerless against Russia, whose mission is to absorb us, we as a Nation have no right to feed in our womb the declared parasite and traitor. By doing so, we commit an error toward our neighboring nations and ourselves that our own children and our Fatherland will never forgive. For that reason,

---

31 R. Wnuk, *Lubelski Okręg AK 1944–1947* [The Lublin District of the AK 1944–1947] (Warsaw: Volumen, 2000), 199–219.

32 The Polish Committee of National Liberation (Polski Komitet Wyzwolenia Narodowego; PKWN), was a provisional Communist government of Poland officially proclaimed on July 22, 1944. It exercised control over Polish territory retaken from Nazis and was fully supported by the Soviet Union. At the end of December 1944, the PKWN renamed itself as the Provisional Government of the Republic of Poland.

therefore, I order a just battle of the Pole against this venomous Jewish tribe.

We sell nothing to the Jews and buy nothing from them.

Remember this slogan, Citizens! Remember the wrongs done to us by the Jews, since only in this way will we remove the traitor and parasite from our Soil. I warn you that every commercial transaction with a Jew will be severely punished, and in the case of repeated offenses, even with the burning of your property.[33]

Similarly, a leaflet distributed by WiN in the Lublin region before the referendum of June 1946 asked rhetorically:

Poles!!! Do you want the continued occupation of Poland? Do you want Soviet armies within the borders of the Polish State? Do you want Soviet Russia to take our food, our wealth, creating hunger and high prices at home? Do you want the Polish intelligentsia to be replaced by Jews? Do you want the Polish worker to be the slave of the Soviet–Communist–Jewish authorities?[34]

This does not mean that we cannot also find in the WiN documents strong disavowals of anti-Semitism, on behalf of Polish society as well as those who support it. Whether they are credible or not is another matter:

No right-minded person supported the brutal Hitlerite system of exterminating the Jews, and no one thinks of denying the defenders of the Warsaw ghetto their place in the Polish National Pantheon. We bow our heads to the heroes who fell in the battle against the Germans. But if the "democratic" officials present at the ceremony [in honor of the heroes of the Warsaw ghetto uprising] regard themselves as the only Poles who are not blinded and duped, and the survivors of the Hitlerite pogrom against the Jews as stalwarts in the battle against reaction, and embolden each

---

33 After Mariusz Bechta, *Pogrom czy odwet? Akcja zbrojna Zrzeszenia "Wolność i Niezawisłość" w Parczewie 5 lutego 1946 r.* [Pogrom or revenge? The armed action of the *Wolność i Niezawisłość* union in Parczew on 5 February 1946] (Poznań: Zysk i S-ka Wydawnictwo, 2015), 253.

34 Cited after Alina Cała, *Żyd—wróg odwieczny? Antysemityzm w Polsce i jego źródła* [The Jew—an eternal enemy? Anti-Semitism in Poland and its sources] (Warsaw: Wydawnictwo Nisza, 2012), 464.

other to a life and death struggle [with reaction]—then a righteous Pole must involuntarily call this "raison d'etat" the most monstrous betrayal and inhuman wrong against those heroes who fell for *Poland*, but *not a Jewish-Communist one* [emphasis in original]. Calumnies are hurled at the Poles: that they helped Hitler exterminate the Jews, that they supported and to this day support the greatest cruelty in history. This is yet another instance of the assault on our nation exploited all too forcefully by the "paiok-pisateli" [Russ.; writers for profit], in order to numb completely the vigilance and self-defense of society. The crime of murdering defenseless Jews is one thing, to which the conscience of the Polish nation has never acquiesced. [Our conscience] is clear. But self-defense against a flood of traitors, spies, and agitators of Soviet origin, who have taken over *security and political education* [emphasis in original] is something else. Such creatures defile even the Polish uniform, perverting soldierly Polish souls according to the Russian model through so-called political and civic education. A Polish uniform, a Polish name, and agitation according to the Judaeo-communist formula!!![35]

Generally, the lower the level of the conspiratorial cell, the more often anti-Semitic strains appear in its publications. Yet we find anti-Semitic accents even in the "Memorandum to the UN Security Council" drawn up by the central administration of WiN in 1946, and intended for Western readers. A scurrilous pamphlet openly alleging that the Jews aimed to seize power in postwar Poland (referring to an apocryphal speech by Jakub Berman that supposedly encouraged his fellow Jews to do so) is added as an appendix to this document.[36]

On the one hand, the authors of this memorandum describe Jewish Communists as one of the main agents of the "destruction of the Polish nation"; on the other, they deny that anti-Semitism is widespread in Poland:

> After the entry of the Red Army into Poland, Jews-communists, putting themselves entirely at the service of the NKVD as experts on the situation and the terrain, were, along with a few communist Poles, the group

---

35   *Zrzeszenie "Wolność i Niezawisłość" w dokumentach* [The *Wolność i Niezawisłość* union in documents], ed. Józefa Huchlowa et al., vol. II, lipiec 1946–styczeń 1947 (Wrocław: Zarząd Główny WiN, 1997), 192.

36   The memorandum was supported by other anti-Communist groups concentrated in the Joint Committee of the Organizations of Underground Poland (Komitet Porozumiewawczy Organizacji Polski Podziemnej; KPOPP).

that played the most important role part in mass arrests, executions, and deportations, especially of members of the Polish independence movement, through their activity as spies and informers. Jewish communists, along with the afore-mentioned Polish communists, were the first to occupy administrative posts, taking the place of the Gestapo in Poland, in the despised Security Offices, the Internal Security Corps and the like. While torturing arrested Poles by the above mentioned cruelest of methods, Jewish communists exhibited and continue to exhibit the most sadistic cruelty. Jews-communists, taking control of the political and economic life of Poland from the top, most faithfully serve the current Soviet-communist agencies in Poland in the work of destroying the political and economic independence of Poland.

These facts can easily be verified, and the positions of the Jews checked, by examining the makeup of the personnel staffing all the leading state, economic and military organs, where they occupy privileged positions. For that reason, misleading world opinion and harming the Polish nation by publicizing its alleged antisemitism is deliberately substituting the effect for the cause.

On the subject of manifestations of anti-Semitism in Poland, the authors of the memorandum write:

> It must be stressed emphatically that contrary to the lying Soviet-communist propaganda, mainly directed by precisely the Jewish communists, antisemitism on racial grounds is not a general phenomenon in Poland. The hatred of a certain part of Polish society toward the Jews has arisen against the background of the hostile, though concealed, activity of the Jews during the present Soviet occupation.[37]

After reading the WiN texts concerning Jews, it is no wonder that many of the best-known commanders of partisan units were strongly anti-Semitic. Major Hieronim Dutkowski (aka "Zapora" [Barrier]), a member of WiN active in the Lublin region, declared that his soldiers "fight for Poland, so that in Poland there would be no jews [sic] and soviets [sic]." Capt. Zdzisław Broński (aka "Uskok" [Escarpment]), also active in WiN in the Lublin region, even left an

---

37 *Memoriał Zrzeszenia Wolność i Niezawisłość do Rady Bezpieczeństwa Organizacji Narodów Zjednoczonych* [Memorial of the *Wolność i Niezawisłość* union to the Security Council of the United Nations], ed. Wojciech Frazik and Tomasz Łabuszewski (Warsaw: Instytut Pamięci Narodowej, 2015), 42–44.

anti-Semitic poem entitled "Slavery," in which he describes the "Jewish scourge" which compels obeisance to the "Bolsheviks." Józef Zadzierski (aka "Wołyniak" [Volhynian])—of the National Military Organization (*Narodowa Organizacja Wojskowa*; NOW), which was even more radically hostile to Jews than WiN—was active in the Rzeszów region and was responsible for the deaths of not only hundreds of Ukrainians, but also at least a few Jews.[38]

Among the radical anti-Semites active in the Łódź voivodeship were Stanisław Sojczyński ("Warszyc," of the Special Emergency Action Unit of the National Military Union [PAS-NZW]) and Eugeniusz Kolski (aka "Groźny" [Dangerous]), of the Directorate for the Struggle against Lawlessness [Kierownictwo do Walki z Bezprawiem]).[39] This list could easily be expanded.

A PORTRAIT OF THE CRIMES

Despite the efforts of researchers, described above, to analyze the interactions between Jews and "disavowed," the picture of anti-Semitic crimes by the anti-communist underground is still rather fragmentary. We know neither the exact number of victims of anti-Semitic crimes in the years 1944–47, nor the exact number of crimes committed by the "disavowed soldiers." We can accept as an estimate that the minimum number of Jews killed in Poland after its liberation from Nazi occupation was between 650 and 750.[40] These figures should be seen against the background of the continuing so-called "limited civil war" in Poland, in which 25,000–50,000 people were killed.[41] In the light of current research, it seems that only a minority of postwar anti-Semitic crimes were committed by the underground: thus, according to Chodakiewicz, 132 Jews died at the hands of the underground, against 371–474 killed in other circumstances.[42]

Jews were killed for various reasons. According Joanna Tokarska-Bakir, the sources of postwar violence against the Jews were the feeling of being

---

38 Chodakiewicz, *After the Holocaust*, 58–59, 137.
39 For example, J. Wróbel, "W cieniu Holocaustu. Odrodzenie społeczności żydowskiej w Łódzkiem po II wojnie światowej" [In the shadow of the Holocaust. The revival of Jewish life in the Łódź region after the Second World War], *Biuletyn IPN* 11 (2005): 32–35.
40 Żbikowski, "The Post-War Wave of Pogroms," 94.
41 I adopt the expression "limited civil war" after Ryszard Nazarewicz. The war was supposedly "limited" mainly to partisan activity, in only a part of the Polish state. See: Ryszard Nazarewicz, *Armii Ludowej dylematy i dramaty* [Dilemmas and dramas of the People's Army] (Warsaw: Oficyna Drukarska, 1998), 290. The number of fatalities in the postwar political conflict is still debatable. Cited estimate after Chodakiewicz, *After the Holocaust*, 25.
42 Chodakiewicz, *After the Holocaust*, 147.

threatened by Communism; opposition to the social advancement of Jews that took place in the People's Poland; fear of a "Jewish plot" in the form of a "masonic conspiracy" or a "world Jewish government"; demographic panic evoked by the repatriation of Jews from the USSR and fear that they might demand the return of property taken over by Poles; fear of the supposed threat to Poland and Polishness created by the growing number of mixed marriages and increased Jewish influence; and, finally, the ritual murder myth.[43]

Jews were rarely the main target of attacks by the underground. As a rule, they were killed when they fell into the hands of "disavowed soldiers" or during attacks on other targets. Exceptional in that respect was the attack on Parczew carried out on February 5, 1946, by the local WiN commander, Leon Taraszkiewicz (aka "Jastrząb" [Hawk]). Before the attack, "Jastrząb" openly declared that the main target of the attack was to "drive out" the Jews and return local trade to the hands of Polish merchants. In their action against a Jewish community numbering about two hundred, the WiN soldiers could count on the general participation of the local Polish population, with the result that Jewish property was stolen or destroyed (an apologist for WiN called this the "repair of organizational finances").[44] Three Jewish members of the city defense guard (Abraham Zysman, Dawid Tempy, and Mendel Turbiner) were killed, along with a Polish militia man (Wacław Rydzewski). Soon after, the frightened Jews began leaving Parczew en masse, and the local Jewish community ceased to exist.

The Parczew pogrom was meant to return Jews to the traditional, subordinate role that they had occupied in the Second Polish Republic. As Mariusz Bechta from the IPN wrote about the event:

> It is worth noting that this type of activity was in a certain sense the continuation of identical preventative actions during the Bolshevik invasion of Poland in 1920. From this perspective, the action by the WiN forces in the Włodawa region in February 1946 was part of a long-standing political conflict, with roots in the Second Republic, which played out between the institutions of the independent State and pro-Soviet activities inspired by the Kremlin in the Polish countryside.[45]

---

43   Paper by Joanna Tokarska-Bakir, "The Pogrom as an Act of Social Control. Springfield 1908—Poland 1945–46," given at the conference "Pogroms: Collective Anti-Jewish Violence in the Polish Lands in the 19th and 20th Centuries," Warsaw, June 10, 2015. The conference was organized by the Historical Institute of the University of Warsaw and the Museum of the History of the Polish Jews.
44   Bechta, *Pogrom czy odwet*, 261.
45   Ibid., 21.

In Bechta's eyes, equality of rights for the Jewish minority in the People's Poland represented galling "privilege," while their "society was an integral part of the institutionalized Communist system of rule," despite the fact that most Jews were not Communists. In Parczew before the pogrom, in his opinion, "the Poles perceived the self-importance and arrogance of the armed Jews as a problem that they could not handle by applying methods adequate to their feeling of oppression . . . Help could come only from outside. Hence, the citizens of Parczew were left waiting for the armed underground to administer a firm reprimand to the Jews who lorded over them."[46] The local WiN organization meted out "justice" on February 5, 1946

It is worth noting Bechta's use of the term *Poles* as by definition an anti-leftist category, standing in opposition to the world of moral evil created by the "native Communists" (Bechta thereby avoids speaking of "Polish Communists"), "Sovietized Poles," "Jewish veterans strutting about at every step," "collaborationist authority," and "gradual degeneration in the Communist system."[47] This portrayal by apologists for the "disavowed soldiers" is clearly at odds with the rapidly developing membership base of the Polish Workers' Party (*Polska Partia Robotnicza*; PPR) and its allies. According to the actual (not the falsified) outcome of the 1946 referendum, the communists at that point had the support of more than a quarter of Polish society—a considerable proportion, given that neither the Second Republic after 1926, nor much of the underground (especially the part associated with the national-democratic movement—Endecja), could reasonably be characterized as liberal-democratic either.[48]

It is this Manichean falsification, which refused to accept the accession of a significant part of society to the PPR camp, that underlies the aggressive rhetoric by which a small extremist group tried to lay claim to the values of independence and the traditions of past national uprisings. According to this rhetoric, robbery and looting (as in Parczew), crimes not only against state functionaries (which might be justified by the logic of civil war) but also against ordinary sympathizers of left-wing parties, and against members of national minorities treated as Communist sympathizers, were all completely justified.

---

46 Ibid., 212, 241, 306.
47 Ibid., 21, 27, 28, 178, 191.
48 On this subject, see, for example, Czesław Osękowski, *Referendum 30 czerwca 1946 roku w Polsce*, [The referendum of 30 June 1946 in Poland] (Warsaw: Wydawnictwo Sejmowe, 2000).

Praising Bechta's work, Sławomir Cenckiewicz of the IPN wrote: "the recovery of Parczew from the hands of the Communists by partisans of the WiN organization at the beginning of 1946 will be for me a symbol of the Polish uprising against the authority imposed by Moscow."[49] One is tempted to ask whether, if Polish uprisings are difficult to distinguish from anti-Semitic pogroms, all of them are worth supporting?

Of the armed organizations that killed Jews, the most important was WiN, which claimed to be the continuation of the AK, largely because its numbers were greater than those of armed formations originating in the Endecja. Among commanders, however, it was the unaffiliated, independent Józef Kuraś (aka "Ogień" [Fire]) who killed the largest number of Jews. Beyond doubt, the number of Jews killed is correlated with fluctuations in the level of underground activity; hence, the largest number of crimes were committed in the spring of 1945, with a marked increase again in the spring of 1946.[50]

Apologists for the "disavowed soldiers" tend to treat anti-Semitic crimes as politically motivated responses to the participation of Poles of Jewish descent and of Jews in the structures of the new authority. Yet from the research of Marek J. Chodakiewicz, we learn that among Jews killed by the so-called independentists, the clear majority cannot be connected with the Communist apparatus (as functionaries or secret informers).[51] Adam Kopciowski's research on the Lublin region yields similar results. According to Kopciowski, about 80 percent of all murders of Jews in the region (94 of 118 cases) were motivated by robbery or were anti-Semitic, and were not political in character.[52]

Research on the subject of the "disavowed soldiers" evokes clashes between extremely varied ideological options and various (often contradictory) sensitivities, which makes open discussion difficult. An example is the discussion of the attack on Leżajsk by Józef Zadzierski on February 18–19, 1945, in which probably fourteen people were killed, among them Jews, including women

---

49 Back cover of Bechta.
50 Chodakiewicz, *After the Holocaust*, 208–12.
51 In a sample of 132 Jews killed by the so-called independentists, the great majority (seventy-nine) cannot be clearly associated with the security apparatus. According to Chodakiewicz, twenty-five were "civilian bystanders," while fifty-four were of "undetermined affiliation" (147).
52 Kopciowski adds: "It should also be pointed out that the 118 victims certainly do not represent all the murders committed against Jews in that region. For many reasons, it is impossible to establish the factual state of affairs." (Kopciowski, "Zajścia antyżydowskie na Lubelszczyźnie," 205, 206).

and children.⁵³ In describing these events, Chodakiewicz claims that Israeli historians (Israel Gutman and Shmuel Krakowski), in their condemnation fail to take "into account the anti-Soviet causes of the attack." For Chodakiewicz, then, the most important thing was the struggle against Communism, while for the Israeli historians, it was the safety of the Jews, especially women and children. It is very difficult to imagine that either side in this kind of discussion could make concessions on such matters of principle.⁵⁴

CONCLUSION

Although it should be possible to ascertain more accurately the precise number of Jews killed by the "disavowed soldiers," it is unlikely that this will have any effect on their growing cult, which cult is, above all, part of the historical politics of the Polish state, implemented by a number of state and local government institutions. Realistic questioning of this cult in the context of the historical politics of the Polish state would be possible only if politics were pluralist and could accommodate different narratives, whereas the activity of the IPN—the main instrument of the historical politics of the Polish state—is manifestly dominated by one ideological option—the nationalistic-conservative right. This means in practice that work critical of, for example, the Home Army, the Roman Catholic Church, or the Solidarity trade union movement will not be supported within the framework of the IPN.

Thus, even if we learn more about the crimes of individual units of the "disavowed soldiers," they will still be the subject of apologetics because they fought against the Communist authorities. This situation is analogous to the failure of protests against the unveiling of a monument to Roman Dmowski

---

53 According to David Engel, almost three times as many Jewish as Polish women (among supporters of the communist regime) were killed, what constitutes almost 20 percent of female victims among the killed Jews and "similarly, the proportion of children under age seventeen among the Jewish victims was almost twice as great as among the Polish victims—4.3 percent as opposed to 2.5 percent", 43–85.

54 Generally, Chodakiewicz trivializes the number of Jews killed in Poland in 1944–47, contrasting "400–700" Jewish victims with 5,794–13,443 Poles denounced, arrested or killed "as a result of the activities of the Jews." He does not explain anywhere in his calculations why, when a given group of UB functionaries included Poles, Jews, and others, and he cannot show that Jews constituted the majority of the group; he classifies all victims of the group as victims of Jews and not as victims of Poles (Chodakiewicz, *After the Holocaust* 137, 212–14).

in the immediate vicinity of the Cabinet Office in 2006. Protests against the erection of this monument by a segment of public opinion—in which figures with moral authority like Marek Edelman and Professor Maria Janion participated—were ignored by the state authorities, since Dmowski's anti-Semitism was considered less significant than other aspects of his political activity. It can be expected that, in coming years, protests against further memorialization of the "disavowed soldiers" will meet a similar fate.

Translated from Polish by Gunnar Paulsson

In or Out? Identities and Images of Poland among Polish Jews in the Postwar Years

AUDREY KICHELEWSKI

The postwar gallery of the museum offers the visitor a series of doors, some wide open, others only half-open. In order to illustrate the survivors' dilemma between choosing to stay or to go in the aftermath of the war, doors open toward displaced persons' camps or toward what would become the Jewish State in Palestine. During the Stalinist period, doors are almost totally closed, barely opened to let us see the very few who managed to flee the country and voice their criticism against the regime, such as Józef Światło. The same doors open much more widely in 1956, showing double movement: some Polish Jews were freed from the USSR and came to Poland—most of whom then moved further west—and some Jews in Poland fled the country, fearing for their children or fearing being victimized for their own presumed Stalinist past. In 1968, the doors are open wide, as Jews are chased away under a hideous campaign of hatred. This particular emigration is visualized by the reconstitution of the northern Warsaw railway station—Warszawa Gdańska. This permanent in-and-out movement probably best illustrates the situation of Polish Jews in the postwar period—and even today. While the postwar gallery considers this dimension of history, I will show that this perspective is crucial and that it has not been fully acknowledged until recent research stressed its points.

Indeed, while Polish Jewish emigration did, of course, not start with the aftermath of the Holocaust but has long been an important phenomenon, with complex and fruitful links between Polish Jews in and outside the moving borders of Poland (especially for those who left between the end of the nineteenth century and the 1930s), I argue that it is crucial to examine the relationship between the small and ever decreasing Jewish minority who survived the Holocaust and remained in Poland, and the Polish Jewish diaspora, now clearly living primarily outside Poland. With the destruction of 90 percent of Polish Jewry during the Second World War, the topic of emigration is essential to grasp if we are to understand the major turning point within the history of the Jewish presence in Poland as well as the rifts in the ways surviving Polish Jews self-identified, no matter where they survived. We need to explore how Jews survived while emigrating from Poland during the war—in the USSR, elsewhere in Europe, and even abroad. My point is to show the relevance of the images, speeches, and attitudes about Poland of those—the majority— who were no longer living within the shifting borders of the country after 1945. This population was very diverse and included Polish Jews in displaced persons' camps—as shown in the postwar gallery, reflecting the current better state of knowledge about the issue.[1] Less explored in the museum, although increasingly considered in recent historiography, Polish Jewry saw successive waves of emigration from 1945 until at least 1968,[2] to various countries in

---

1   See, for example, Ruth Gay, *Safe Among the Germans: Liberated Jews after World War II* (New Haven, CT: Yale University Press, 2002); Angelika Königseder and Juliane Wetzel, *Waiting for Hope: Jewish Displaced Persons in Post-World War II Germany* (Evanston, IL: Northwestern University Press, 2001); Zeev W. Mankowitz, *Life Between Memory and Hope: The Survivors of the Holocaust in Occupied Germany* (Cambridge: Cambridge University Press, 2002); Françoise Ouzan, "Rebuilding Jewish Identities in Displaced Persons Camps in Germany, 1945–1957," *Bulletin du Centre de recherche français à Jérusalem* 14 (2004): 98–111.

2   To quote but a few titles among the copious bibliography of the subject: Julian Ilicki, "Changing Identity among Younger Polish Jews in Sweden after 1968," *Polin* 4 (1990): 269–80; Elżbieta Kossewska, *Ona jeszcze mówi po polsku, ale śmieje się po hebrajsku. Partyjna prasa polskojęzyczna i integracja kulturowa polskich Żydów w Izraelu (1948–1970)* [She still speaks Polish but laughs in Hebrew. The Polish-language party press and the cultural integration of Polish Jews in Israel, 1948–1970] (Warsaw: Wydawnictwo Uniwersytetu Warszawskiego, 2015); Marcin Starnawski, "Historically Conscious Cosmopolitans: Jewish Identity and the '68 Generation of Polish Jews in Exile," *East European Jewish Affairs* 32, no. 2 (2002): 1–24; Teresa Torańska, *Jesteśmy* [We are here] (Warsaw: Wydawnictwo Świat Książki, 2008); Ewa Węgrzyn, "Emigracja ludności żydowskiej z Polski do Izraela w latach 1956–1959. Przyczyny, przebieg wyjazdu, proces adaptacji w nowej ojczyźnie" [The emigration of Jews from Poland to Israel in the years 1956–1959. The causes, the departure, and the process of adaptation in a new homeland], *Prace Historyczne* 137 (2010): 137–51; Joanna Wiszniewicz, "Przed i po szoku: budowanie nowej tożsamości przez młodych emigrantów marcowych w Ameryce" [Before and after the shock: young March '68 emigrants building a new identity in America], in *Społeczność żydowska w PRL przed kampanią antysemicką lat 1967–1968 i po niej* [Jewish community in the Polish People's Republic

Europe (including Germany, Austria, France, the United Kingdom, Sweden, and Denmark) as well as to Israel and North America. At the same time, the stories of Polish Jews who remained in the USSR remain unexplored.[3]

Because of the scale and significance of postwar Polish Jewish emigration, it is important that the Museum of the History of the Polish Jews does not only reflect the fact that Polish Jews existed abroad, but also points out that their points of view and attitudes influenced their daily lives and identifications, at both an individual and a collective level.

At present, I cannot cite strong results of any finished study, as analyses are just beginning, yet I can present the directions of research—my own and of colleagues undertaken in the past few years, especially in France. I shall mainly concentrate on issues from the post-1968 period, aiming thus to understand better the relationship that crystallized between those who stayed and those who had already left or who left at that point.

VARIOUS AND CHANGING REPRESENTATIONS OF POLAND AMONG POLISH JEWISH EMIGRANTS

I shall first examine representations of Poland among those who left, at various stages of their migration. The contrast between those who left and those who stayed appeared very early after the Second World War. Of course, this dichotomy may have already existed, but it acquired a new context after 1945. As Stanislaw Krajewski recalls in his chapter on the postwar period in the catalogue of the museum's permanent exhibition, writings directed to Polish Jews living in displaced persons' camps early on insisted that the link was irrevocably

---

before the antisemitic campaign of 1967–1968 and after it] (Warsaw: Instytut Pamięci Narodowej—Komisja Ścigania Zbrodni przeciwko Narodowi Polskiemu, 2009), 208–17; Joanna Wiszniewicz, *Życie przecięte. Opowieści pokolenia Marca* [A life severed. Stories of the March '68 generation] (Wołowiec: Wydawnictwo Czarne, 2008).

3 Except for data on the Polish Jewish population within the USSR during the war and on their repatriation to Poland in 1945–46 and 1956–57, there is hardly any work devoted specifically to the Polish Jewish population that remained in Soviet Ukraine or elsewhere in the USSR. See Joseph Litvak, "Jewish Refugees from Poland in the USSR," in *Bitter Legacy: Confronting the Holocaust in the USSR*, ed. Zvi Gitelman (Bloomington: University of Indiana Press, 1997); on the history of Jewish life in Soviet Lwów (Lviv) as a case study, see Katrin Boeckh, "Fallstudie: Lemberg in Galizien. Jüdisches Gemeindeleben in der Ukraine zwischen 1945–1953" [A case study: Lviv in Galicia. Jewish communal life in Ukraine between 1945 and 1953], *Glaube in der 2. Welt* 4 (2002): 20–24.

broken with the homeland and native country: "*We* didn't betray Poland, it is Poland which betrayed us!"[4]

But was the link indeed irrevocably broken? The answer to this question is not simple. While a comprehensive overall study of representations of Poland among Polish Jewish emigrants scattered around the world after 1945 has not been written, several hypotheses and conclusions have been drawn from case studies in two countries. In an international conference which I organized in 2011 in Warsaw, researchers presenting reflections on images of Poland that emigrants took with them in their moves either to France or to Israel[5] concluded that those representations were not at all uniform but varied greatly according to several parameters, starting obviously with an individual's personal trajectory. The character of the country of immigration is also crucial. In this respect, France and Israel were quite different in their ways of perceiving Poland as a whole. Another major factor is the time of emigration. The successive emigration waves of 1946, 1956, or 1968 did not have the same impact on the emigrants' perception of Poland, nor did the same sociocultural population leave at each period. Lastly, the images forged by the emigrants depended greatly on their personal situations when they left: age, profession, level of integration within Polish society, and so on.

Another finding of this conference concerned the nature of the images of Poland created by the emigrants. These evolved and changed as time went by. Nostalgia for the country could eventually win over bitterness, especially when it became easier to go back to Poland after 1989.[6]

Yet a general pattern could be identified, of course with many exceptions. According to this pattern, limiting my analysis to the French situation, since I am currently studying Polish Jewish emigration to France, it appears that the earlier the emigration occurred (1945–50) the less the contact remained with the country—whether with its language or with visual memories of Poland.

---

4 "To nie my zdradziliśmy Polskę, lecz Polska nas zdradziła!"—quoted in Stanisław Krajewski, "Powojnie, od 1944 do dziś" [The postwar period, from 1944 to today], in *Polin. 1000 lat historii Żydów polskich*, ed. Barbara Kirshenblatt-Gimblett and Antony Polonsky (Warsaw: Museum of the History of the Polish Jews, 2014), 365.

5 Proceedings of this conference can be found online, published by the Bulletin du Centre de recherche français à Jérusalem 22 (2011): http://bcrfj.revues.org/6451.

6 See, for example, in this same source (http://bcrfj.revues.org/6451), the two papers presented by Eik Dödtmann, "Between Aversion and Nostalgia: Immigration and Integration of Polish Jews from 1968 in Israel—An Interview Analysis and Documentation Film," and Kamila Dąbrowska, "Relocating Significance of Materialized Memories among Postwar Jewish Immigrants from Poland."

At best, those representations faded away as time went by and respondents could barely talk about their home country, but more often, the images they took with them *and* that they continued to preserve were in general quite negative. By contrast, those who left in 1956 and even more, in 1968, whose identity or personal self had been formed mostly or almost completely during the period of the People's Republic of Poland, have another relationship with Poland. They are more sensitive to the country, exhibit a kind of love-hate relationship, or, at least, have maintained some kind of link, even if this link is based on total and enduring rejection.

Of course, the details of this pattern need to be made more specific; additional interviews need to be conducted. Within my research project, based on the study of Polish Jewish *émigrés* in France, based on interviews as well as the study of *landsmanshaftn* as places of socialization in postwar France until the 1970s, I question the concept of being in exile (*exilé*) for its relevance to Polish Jewish emigration to France after 1968. The definition of exile is here understood, following the French sociologist Stephane Dufoix[7]—who studied Hungarian, Czech, and Polish exiles in postwar France—as having a political dimension; exile is the place from where the political struggle is fought against the regime. Do Polish Jewish post-1968 émigrés follow a similar pattern, still maintaining a (political) link to Poland, or does their Jewish identity set them apart from the rest of the Polish intelligentsia living in Paris? Many questions remain unanswered—especially ones dealing with Jewish identity, which for most of them emerged only *during* and *after* emigration, and which at some point—especially in the 1970s and during the period of Solidarity—could have resulted in conflicts within the political struggle led by their non-Jewish fellow citizens in emigration.[8]

MEASURING THE IMPACTS OF POLAND'S IMAGES

The second major point to examine is the role played by the images of Poland among émigrés, not only in the country of immigration, but also in turn reverberating in Poland itself. There are multiple aspects of relevance in questioning

---

7 Stéphane Dufoix, *Politiques d'exil, Hongrois, Polonais, Tchécoslovaques en France après 1945* [The politics of exile, Hungarians, Poles, Czechoslovaks in France after 1945] (Paris: Presses universitaires de France, 2002).

8 See my paper presentation entitled "Les juifs polonais, des exilés comme les autres?" at the international conference *L'influence et le poids des exilés d'Europe centrale en France (1945–1989)* (Paris, Sorbonne, December 10–11, 2015).

successive waves of Polish Jewish emigrants about the representations they retain about their home country.

First, the images of Poland and of Polish–Jewish relations among emigrants are subject to change with time and can even be passed to descendants. The same could be argued with regard to the way memory is conveyed to the second or the third generation of Polish Jewish emigrants—for which another distinct study would also allow us to understand better the process of transmission.[9] Yet even when focusing solely on the first generation, the one that directly experienced life in Poland and emigration, the representations they forged before and after they left the country can vary with time and can be influenced by the recent history of Poland. To be more precise, the public debate that has been going on for the past three decades about Poland's role and Poles' attitudes toward their Jewish neighbors during the Second World War may have fundamentally reshaped the émigrés' perceptions of Poland and of Polish–Jewish relations. I will cite just one example. One of my masters' students is currently studying images of Poland as voiced in video testimonies of Polish Jewish Holocaust survivors living in France after the war, gathered both by the USC Shoah Visual History Foundation (1994) and the French Memorial de la Shoah (2005), hence respectively before *and* after the year 2000.[10] This year is considered to be a turning point because of the publication of Jan T. Gross's *Neighbors*, a book bringing into the public sphere the murders in Jedwabne, creating a major debate in Poland and beyond.[11] The student noticed that those who testified for both collections altered their observations about Poland: in

---

9 On the second and third generation of Polish Jews in Poland, see Katka Reszke, *Return of the Jew: Identity Narratives of the Third Post-Holocaust Generation of Jews in Poland* (Boston: Academic Studies Press, 2013) and Irena Wiszniewska, *My Żydzi z Polski* [We Jews from Poland] (Warsaw: Wydawnictwo Czarna Owca, 2014). On the second and third generation of French Jewish descendants of Holocaust survivors, not necessarily conveying representations of Poland, see Denise Epstein, *Le traumatisme en héritage: conversations avec des fils et filles de survivants de la Shoah* [Inherited trauma: Conversations with the sons and daughters of survivors of the Shoah] (Paris: La cause des livres, 2005); Hélène Oppenheim-Gluckman and Daniel Oppenheim, *Héritiers de l'exil et de la Shoah: entretiens avec des petits enfants de Juifs venus de Pologne en France* [Inheritors of exile and the Shoah: Interviews with the grandchildren of Jews coming from Poland in France] (Toulouse: Érès, 2006).

10 Tess Gagnage, "La Pologne et les Polonais pendant la Seconde Guerre mondiale et sous l'occupation nazie: la parole du témoin" [Poland and the Poles during the Second World War and under the Nazi occupation: The word of the witness] (MA thesis, ENS-Lyon, 2015).

11 On the book and the debates, see Joanna Beata Michlic and Antony Polonsky, eds., *The Neighbors Respond: The Controversy Over the Jedwabne Massacre in Poland* (Princeton, NJ: Princeton University Press, 2004).

the second testimony, they talked much more about Poland's attitude toward Jews and in a slightly more negative way. This change of attitude, she claims, clearly reflects the recent debates, adding new layers of memories of Poland. However, this shift in representations also revealed that the questions asked to the survivor were not the same decades later, and much more emphasis than before was made to encourage the interviewee to touch on memories about Poles' attitudes during the war.

This leads us to a second reason why it is valuable to study representations of Poland among Polish Jewish émigrés. It is clear that these images in turn reverberated and were echoed far beyond the sole sphere of the émigrés themselves and their families. They affected the whole Jewish street in France in which, since the immediate postwar years, only a small minority of Jews had actually come from Poland.[12] Only one Jewish person in France out of seven now is of Polish background—most French Jews are of Eastern European, Alsatian, or North African origin. However, regardless of where they come from, Jews in France have more or less the same image of Poland. This image is broadly speaking that of a country that was hostile to Jews for ages, if not genetically anti-Semitic. As French sociologist Michel Wieviorka noted in the epilogue of his 1984 study on Poles, Jews, and the Solidarity movement, French Jews had very precise expectations about how Polish–Jewish relations had to be told:

> Tell us about the *shtetl*, recreate the Yiddish culture—show us what the Nazi barbarism has destroyed . . . and mention that the Poles were not uninvolved in this destruction . . . This is what an informed and educated audience demands, flattered by the reference to roots and a lost—or rather assassinated—identity.[13]

---

12 For figures on Polish Jews in France before and after the Second World War, see Didier Epelbaum, *Les enfants de papier. Les juifs immigrés de Pologne en France jusqu'en 1940* [Paper children. Jewish immigrants from Poland in France until 1940] (Paris: B. Grasset, 2002) and Mônica Raisa-Schpun, "L'immigration juive dans la France de l'après-guerre, 1945–1950" [Jewish immigration in post-war France, 1945–1950], in *Terre d'exil, terre d'asile. Migrations juives en France aux XIXe et XXe siècles* [Land of exile, land of asylum. Jewish migrations to France in the nineteenth and the twentieth centuries], ed. Colette Zytnicki (Paris: Eclat, 2010), 115–31.

13 "Parlez-nous du shtetl, recréez la culture yiddish—montrez nous ce que la barbarie nazie a détruit . . . et laissez entendre que les Polonais n'ont pas été étrangers à cette destruction. . . . Voilà ce que demande un public pourtant averti et cultivé, que flatte la référence aux racines et à l'identité perdue, ou plutôt assassinée," quoted in Michel Wieviorka, *Les Juifs, la Pologne et Solidarność* [The Jews, Poland and solidarity] (Paris, 1984), 194.

These images, not only this very negative one, but also some that are more nuanced, seem to have dominated from at least the 1980s—although a more comprehensive study would be needed to trace the factors behind the prevailing negative image of Poland within the Jewish street in France since 1945.

Yet, to be sure, many aspects of this negative image have echoed far beyond the Jewish milieux, reaching the French intelligentsia and the public sphere. One example can be quoted here. In her dissertation dedicated to relationships between French and Polish intellectuals between 1966 and 1983, Lidwine Warchol, although not initially concentrating on the Polish Jewish environment in France, wrote a chapter on how the "Jewish question" in Poland during those years reverberated within the public debate in France.[14] The "Jewish question" was a source of argument and deep division, and can be explained mostly from the French political context. To put it briefly, the electoral alliance between socialists and communists between 1972 and 1977 prevented the former from supporting Polish dissidents as strongly as they would have liked, while they had to endorse communist propaganda that stressed anti-Semitic aspects of the Polish dissident movement, and especially Solidarity, in order to delegitimize it. On the other hand, this study explores the major role played by Polish intermediaries who diffused information about what was going on in Poland, not only in 1968, but also afterward, giving details about Polish dissent in the 1970s—the KOR [Komitet Obrony Robotników—Workers' Defense Committee] and Solidarity. The fact that some, if not most, of these informers were of Jewish descent or at least were perceived as Jewish by their counterparts (Adam Michnik, Krzysztof Pomian, Georges Mink, Bronisław Geremek, Bronisław Baczko) definitely played an important part in the fact that they were listened to when they presented the situation of Polish opposition to French intellectuals but also when they alluded to the anti-Semitic campaign in front of Jewish audiences at meetings. This situation in turn most certainly contributed to diffusing and reinforcing the image of an anti-Semitic Poland, among the French Jewish community but also far beyond.

---

14 Lidwine Warchol, "Les relations entre intellectuels français et intellectuels polonais de 1966 à 1983" [The Relations between French and Polish intellectuals from 1966 to 1983] (PhD diss., Sorbonne University, Paris, 2014). On the image of Solidarity within the French press, see Karolina Pietras, "L'image de Solidarność dans la presse française et allemande dans les années 1980" [The Image of Solidarity in the French and German Press in the 1980s] (PhD diss., Sorbonne University, Paris, 2011).

This image of a country suffused with anti-Semitism was revealed after 1968 first by two famous articles in the leading French journal *Les temps modernes*, which were published under pressure from the journalist Claude Lanzmann, then a writer for the journal edited by Jean-Paul Sartre—Lanzmann would become chief editor after Simone de Beauvoir's death in 1986.[15] This interest in Poland and the political focus and prism through which he got access to information on this country probably played in important part in generating his most famous film, *Shoah*, prepared over the decade after 1973 and finally released in 1985. This documentary film decisively shaped French public opinion on Poland and its relations to Jews, in a very negative way.[16] It is hence important to trace back the intellectual context of the making of this film.

Third and last, the images of Poland constructed abroad and circulating in various circles, as they were imported by emigrants and reshaped in their welcoming country, are also interesting inasmuch as they help us to understand the reactions they provoked in Poland itself—among the Polish government and officials on the one hand, among the intellectuals and dissidents on the other, and eventually, of course, on the Jews living in Poland—whether they were within the Jewish community, or, more often, outside it.[17]

Already in 1945, a dialogue, or, at least, echoes, could be heard between the acts and words of the Polish authorities on the one hand, and what Polish Jews wanted and said outside of Poland. For instance, during the first years of the Polish People's Republic, Polish authorities did not exercise much control over Jewish emigration, or at least they provided only ambivalent official declarations. In July 1945, the government stated that it "would not hamper

---

15 Those two articles were the anonymous "Pologne: un printemps sinistre" [Poland: A sinister spring], *Les Temps Modernes* 265 (July 1968): 111–24 and Claude Eriale, "Claude Eriale, Pologne: l'antisémitisme comme instrument politique," [Claude Eriale, Poland: Anti-Semitism as a political tool], *Les Temps Modernes* 271 (January 1969): 1271–89.
16 On the film and its reception in France, see Michel Deguy, ed., *Au sujet de Shoah, le film de Claude Lanzmann* [On *Shoah*, the film of Claude Lanzmann] (Paris: Belin Editions, 1990).
17 A lengthy historiography now exists on the issue of relationships between Polish Jews in the Diaspora and in Poland itself. One good case study is Grzegorz Berendt, "Starania organizacji działających w Polsce o przystąpienie do Światowego Kongresu Żydowskiego (1945–1961)" [The efforts made by organizations in Poland to join the World Jewish Congress], in *Studia z historii Żydów w Polsce po roku 1945 roku* [Studies in the history of Jews in Poland after 1945], ed. Grzegorz Berendt, August Grabski, and Albert Stankowski (Warsaw: Żydowski Instytut Historyczny, 2000), 9–66.

the emigration of citizens of Jewish nationality,"[18] but in December of the same year, the prime minister stated that this emigration should be regulated and that illegal emigration should be combated.[19] However, Polish authorities took no real action against the illegal activities of Bricha, the main illegal emigration organization acting in Poland to enable eighty thousand Polish Jews to leave the country between 1944 and 1947.[20] The aim was to give the impression to the outside world that Poland was a country that provided freedom for its Jewish minority. Such was also the case advocated in 1956, when the ban on Jewish emigration was officially lifted on "humanitarian" grounds—allowing families to be reunited. In 1968 and in the following years, Polish authorities would very often state that they were only reacting to positions held by Polish Jews in emigration. This, of course, started with the blunt propaganda of the spring campaign—for instance when Gomułka in his First of May discourse talked about "a hideous anti-Polish campaign led by Zionists."[21] Polish officials systematically raised the specter of "anti-Polishness" in order to delegitimize any statement, thought, book, or critique about Polish Jewish emigration. Many examples could be cited, starting with the 1965 campaign against Jerzy Kosiński's novel, *The Painted Bird*, which was read literally as a depiction of an intrinsically anti-Semitic Polish peasantry. Orders were given for this campaign against Kosiński after his book received quite positive initial reviews.[22] Similarly, it was clearly with the aim of reaching Jews abroad that the Polish government focused on the anti-Semitic statements of some leaders of Solidarity in 1980.

---

18 Archives of Polish Minister of Foreign Affairs, Biuro Konsularne, vol. 20, folder 4.
19 *Robotnik* 365, December 30, 1945.
20 On the issue of Polish-Jewish illegal emigration in the immediate postwar period, see Natalia Aleksiun-Mądrzak, "Nielegalna emigracja Żydów z Polski w latach 1944–1949" [The illegal emigration of Jews from Poland in the years 1944–1949], parts 1–3, *Biuletyn Żydowskiego Instytutu Historycznego*, nos. 2–4 (1996): 67–70, 34–49, 36–48 respectively. On its international aspects, see Audrey Kichelewski, "Les Juifs comme enjeu et outil de la politique extérieure polonaise, 1944–1949" [The Jews as an issue and as tool in Polish foreign policy, 1944–1949], *Bulletin de l'Institut Pierre Renouvin: Religion et relations internationales* 22 (Autumn 2005): 73–92.
21 Quoted from Michał Głowiński, *Pismak 1863 i inne szkice o różnych brzydkich rzeczach* [The Scribbler of 1863 and other sketches on all sorts of unpleasant matters] (Warsaw: Open, 1995), 67.
22 Monika Adamczyk-Garbowska, "The Return of the Troublesome Bird: Jerzy Kosiński and Polish–Jewish Relations," *Polin* 12 (1999): 284–94.

Jerzy Urban, then the government's spokesperson, even called in leaders of the main Jewish organization, the Towarzystwo Społeczno-Kulturalne Żydów (TSKŻ—The Social-Cultural Association of Jews in Poland), to make them listen to Marian Jurczyk's anti-Semitic statements, assuring that these leaders would pass the information abroad among the Polish Jewish diaspora.[23]

Even more interesting is the study of how the reactions of the Polish Jewish diaspora in turn influenced the attitude of Polish Jews remaining in the country, as well as that of a growing number of non-Jews dedicating themselves to the study of Polish Jewish past and culture. A "Jewish revival" can be observed in Poland as early as the middle of the 1970s, with intensification in the 1980s—shown only *en passant* in the last small room of the exhibition, with mention of the Jewish Flying University and the first beginnings of the restoration of Jewish sites. This "revival" also needs to be considered in relationship to the resumption of links with the Polish Jewish diaspora—more frequent trips from foreign visitors, with some important turning points such as the 1978 and, even more so, the 1983 commemorations of the Warsaw Ghetto Uprising, the subsequent exchange of scholars that led to the Oxford conference of 1984, and the creation of the journal *Polin*. For instance, the book *Remnants: The Last Jews of Poland* by Małgorzata Niezabitowska and Tomasz Tomaszewski, which was first published in New York in 1986—and only in 1993 in Polish—is a good example of how images from abroad could shape "answers" and actions in Poland. This book of photographs, which was initially an exhibition, demonstrates this very well.[24] In the 1990s, the presence of international Jewish institutions such as the Lauder Foundation only strengthened the "Jewish revival" trend already present since the 1980s, and more consciously helped to rediscover or strengthen the Jewish roots of growing numbers of Polish citizens. Eventually, identities inevitably reshaped themselves according to and in response to those who left. Men such as

---

23 TSKŻ Archives, Protocols of Meeting of Central Bureau of the TSKŻ, December 2, 1981, non-paginated.

24 On this exhibition and its historiographical significance, see Kamila Posert, "Wystawa 'Żydzi Polscy' (1989–1990) a rola sztuki w przywracaniu zbiorowej pamięci" [Polish Jews exhibition (1989–1990) and the role of art in the re-establishing of collective memory], http://www.sztetl.org.pl/pl/cms/wiedza/1971,wystawa-zydzi-polscy-1989-1990-a-rola-sztuki-w-przywracaniu-zbiorowej-pamieci/#_ednref26.

Bronisław Geremek[25] or Adam Michnik[26] would agree in several interviews given after 1989 that the Jewish part of their identity built itself more specifically *because* they remained in Poland.

Resonances that can be observed between Jews who left and Jews who stayed gradually developed into dialogue, still tinged with silences and sometimes misunderstandings, but nevertheless always present and ongoing. As the sociological study by Katka Reszke, *The Return of the Jew,* has shown, a certain number of young Poles advocate their Jewishness, especially when questioned by foreign Jews:

> As a Polish Jew, I didn't feel recognized or respected enough by American institutions and of course not by Israeli institutions... it was as if we were second-rate Jews (Bożena).[27]

Those foreign Jews, who are often of Polish Jewish background, tend to voice over-simplified opinions about this young generation of Polish Jews. Claire Ann Rosenson already identified these opinions in the late 1990s. They can be summed up as follows: no Jewish culture remained in Poland after the Holocaust; being Jewish in Poland means coping with what is believed to be an intrinsically anti-Semitic country; and surviving as a Jew in Poland was not possible; therefore, those who stayed cannot be "real" Jews.[28] In turn, Reszke's young interviewees replied by showing the extent to which they have shaped their own identity in reaction to those clichés:

> I want to show them [American and Israeli Jews] that we exist and that we are human beings and that we have a lot to say about our struggle with dis-

---

25 See, for example, the long interview given to the journalist Jacek Żakowski, Maria Braunstein, ed., *Rok 1989—Bronisław Geremek opowiada, Jacek Żakowski pyta* [The year 1989—Bronisław Geremek recounts, Jacek Żakowski enquires] (Warsaw, 1990), in which Geremek mentioned a "Jewish consciousness" he had in him, writing on page 106: "Nie znaczy to jednak, że tej świadomości żydowskiej w sobie nie noszę. Noszę ją, ona pojawia się wtedy, gdy wyłania się kwestia antysemityzmu, gdy staję wonec szowinizmu czy wręcz rasizmu" [This doesn't mean, however, that I don't have a Jewish consciousness. I do have it, and it reveals itself whenever the issue of anti-Semitism raises itself, when I find myself confronted with chauvinism or, indeed, racism].
26 Adam Michnik, "O czym nie lubią pamiętać Polacy i Żydzi" [What Jews and Poles don't like to remember], *Tygodnik Powszechny* 29 (July 16, 1995).
27 Reszke, *The Return of the Jew,* 121.
28 Claire Ann Rosenson, "Jewish Identity Construction in Contemporary Poland: Dialogue between Generations," *East European Jewish Affairs* 26 (1996): 67–79.

continuity of Polish Jewish community and about our disconnectedness from the entire Jewish world.[29]

In conclusion, it is important to keep in mind that present-day Jewish life in Poland in part built itself through a long and complex dialogue with the Polish Jewish diaspora that still needs to be delved into more deeply, described, and analyzed in its historical depth, in order to understand not only the last decades of the history of Jewish presence in Poland, which it is the aim of this museum to show, but also the present debates still going on in Poland and within the Jewish world each time the issue of Poland is raised.

---

29 Reszke, *The Return of the Jew*, 122.

Index

A

Abramovich, Roman, 161
Adamczyk-Garbowska, Monika, 69
Adler, Cyrus, 316
Agudas Yisroel, xxxv
aguna, 304–305
Aleksiun, Natalia, 70, 447
Alexander, King of Poland, 215
Alexander II, Tsar, 18
Altman, Ilya, 152
Akcja Wisła (Operation Vistula), 440
Ambrosewicz-Jacobs, Jolanta, xlii, 134
American Jewish Committee, xv
Anders Army, 411
Anielewicz, Mordecai, lvi, 24
anti-Jewish violence, xiii, xlv, xlvi–xlvii, xlviii, xxi, xxii, xxxvi, 4, 23–24, 46, 55, 57–58, 187, 217, 285–291, 445. *See also* Pogroms
in Poland 1944–47, 444–451
    postwar aggression toward Jews and victims, 447–451
    Rzeszów incident, 446
    statistics of Jewish deaths, 449–451
    understanding of circumstances of aggression, 445
anti-Semitism, xiii, xl, xlvi, xxxviii, 14, 17–19, 25, 28, 43, 46–47, 53, 56–58, 65, 68, 73–75, 91, 108–109, 112–114, 174, 286–287, 337, 378, 384, 395, 420, 444, 459, 461–466, 480
anti-Zionist campaign of 1968, xiv, xlvii
Appenszlak, Jakób, 384
Arczyński, Marek, 406
armed anti-communist opposition, 453–456
Armia Krajowa (Home Army, AK), 456, 459n18, 462
Asch, Sholem, lii
Assaf, David, 66, xxvii, xxx
Assmann, Aleida, 177
assumptions in exhibit selection for POLIN Museum, 40–41
    account of Jewish Stalinists, 55–56
    continuous narration, 45–46
    history of Polish Jews, 53–54
    issue of assimilation, 50–51
    issues specific to postwar period, 42–44
    Jewish communists, 52–53
    Jewish emigration from Poland, 45–46
    Jewish identities, 49–52
    Jewish life and Jewish presence in Poland, 52–53
    Jewish story in Polish context, 46–48
    Jews of Poland, 41–42
    Jews who lived in Poland, 44–45
    lives of average Jews, 48–49, 53
    nonjudgmental attitude of presentation, 54–55
    photo albums, 48
    photographs, 43–44
    postwar anti-Jewish feeling and activities, 57–58
    relations of Jews to communism, 55–57
    of Shoah, 43
    Solidarność (Solidarity) movement, 46–47
Auerbach, Karen, 67
Augustus II, 241
Auschwitz, 32, 37, 389
Auschwitz Jewish Center, liv
    Auschwitz museum, 143–146
        bifocal historical narrative and identity, 144, 144n12
        kinds of narrative available at, 144–145
        monument in Birkenau, 143, 143n11
        multiethnic visiting and multidimensional programming at, 145–146
        survivors' accounts, 144
        as a symbol of Polish victimhood, 143, 145
Avraham Dov of Ovruch, Rabbi, 96

B

Baal Shem Tov (Israel b. Eliezer), xxii, xxv–xxvii, xxxi, 94, 101
Bacon, Gershon, xxxviii, 67
    The Jews in Poland and Russia (with Gershon D. Hundert), 61
Bais Yaakov movement, 357, 365
    innovations adopted, 359–360

Bais Yaakov schools, 94, 360
Bais Yaakov teachers, 360
Balcerak, Wiesław, 406
Balfour Declaration, 22
Bartal, Israel, 66, 259
Bartoszewski, Władysław, 130, 406
Salo W. Baron, 60
   The Jewish Community, 60
   Social and Religious History of the Jews: Poland-Lithuania, 1500–1650, 63
Bartov, Omer, xlii
Basok, Ido, 66
Batory, King Stefan, 236
Bauer, Ela, 66
Bauer, Yehuda, 428–429
Bechta, Mariusz, 448, 467–469
Becker, Rafał, 383
Begin, Menachem, 24
Beilis, Mendel, 154
Beilis-Legis, Shlomo, lii
Beit Ha-Sofer (The Writers House), 96
Belarusians, xiv
Ben Gurion, David, 15
Benedict XIV, Pope, xxi, 80, 193, 196
Berendt, Grzegorz, 422
Berger, Lili, lii
Bergman, Eleonora, lv, 69
Berman, Adolf, xlix, 48
Bezpartyjny Blok Współpracy z Rządem (Nonpartisan Bloc for Cooperation with the Government, BBWR), 334
Bieniarzówna, Janina, 249, 251
Bikont, Anna, 415
Bilewicz, Michał, 170
Bilu, Yoram, 302
Birkenthal, Dov Ber of of Bolechów, 209
   The Memoirs of Ber of Bolechów, 60
Biuletyn Żydowskiego Instytutu Historycznego (BŻIH), 69–70
Black Death, xxi
Blatman, Daniel, xlii, 66
Blau, Moshe Isaac, 102
Blaustein, Otto, 340
Blavatnik, Len, 161
Bloch, Jan, 16
Blumental, Nachman, 399
Bnos movement, 359
Bobowa, 26
Boder, David, 44
Bogucka, Maria, 233
Bolesław, Duke, 81
Bolshevik revolution, 22
Błoński, Jan, xxxix–xli, 137, 399, 404, 416, 430

Borejsza, Jerzy, l
Boroda, Rabbi Alexander, 158
Bové, Osip, 151
Broński, Capt. Zdzisław, 465
Browning, Christopher, 400
Brubaker, Roger, 285, 366
Brześć, xvii, 223, 317
Buchen, Tim, 292
Budny, Szymon, 6

C

Cała, Alina, 69, 445, 447–449, 461
Cenckiewicz, Sławomir, 469
Centralny Komitet Żydów w Polsce (Central Committee of Jews in Poland, CKŻP), xlviii–xlix, 48, 458
Center for Historical Research of the Polish Academy of Sciences, Berlin, 5
Center for Holocaust Studies of the Jagiellonian University, 179
Center for Jewish Culture, liv
Center for the Future of Museums, 171, 181
Central Organization for the Care of Orphans (CENTOS), 28
Centrum Badań nad Zagładą Żydów (Polish Center for Holocaust Research), xlii, 178, 405, 409
Chaim, Nathan, 250
Chęciński, Michał (Mosze), 445
Chodakiewicz, Marek Jan, 409–410, 412, 445, 461, 466, 469–470, 470n54
Chofetz Chayim (Rabbi Yisroel Hacohen), 361-362
Chojnowski, Andrzej, 69
Christianity, xix
Christian nobility-Jewish relations, xx, xxii, 184–197
   1670 Act of the Sejm, 193
   anti-Jewish canons, xix–xx, 185, 187–188, 194
   anti-Jewish church regulations, 192–193
   charters issued to Jewish communities, 186–187
   conversion of Jews, 188n12
   in eighteenth century, 185
   exhibit on, 9–10
   fear of demographic expansion of Jewry, 185–186
   practice of employing Jews as manorial clerks, 190–191
   prohibition on employment of Christian servants by Jews, 188–190, 205
   restrictions on construction of new synagogues, 186–187

Index | 487

social interactions between clergy and
    Jews, 210–211
support for Jewish settlements, 195–196
tenancy agreements, 190–192
traditional view, 185
use of Jews for economic reasons, 189,
    196–197
Chrostowski, Waldemar Fr., xl
Chwilka, 339–340, 350
Cichopek, Anna, 446, 448
Cichy, Michał, xl, 404
Clement XI, Pope, 196
Clement XIII, Pope, xxi, 195
Clement XIV, Pope, xxi
collective memory, 120, 129, 178, 280, 283,
    386–387, 397, 423
communism, xiii–xv, xli, xlv–xlvi, l–liii, 43, 46,
    53, 55–57, 113, 130, 140n2, 388–391,
    399, 467, 470
Connorton, Paul, 79
    How Societies Remember, 79
Conrad, John, 137
Council for the Protection of the Memory of
    the Struggle, 456
Council of Four Lands, 3, 82, 255, 256, 257, 259
Ćwik, Władysław, 243
CYSHO, Yiddish secular schools, 27
Cygielman, Shmuel Artur, 65
Cylkow, Rabbi Izaak, 15, 17
Czacki, Tadeusz, 253
Czapski, Walenty Antoni, 191–192
Czechowic, Marcin, 6
Czekanowski, Jan, 377
Czerniaków, Adam, 31, 35
Czortkower, Salomon, 381
Czyżewski, Krzysztof, 132

D

Daniłowicz, Jan, 241
Datner, Helena, 43, 69, 447
Datner, Szymon, 43, 406
Davies, Norman, xxxvi, 69
Dawidowicz, Lucy, 21
Dąbrowska, Maria, 57
Dąmbski, Jan Paweł, 187
De Iudeis constitution, 222–223
Departments of Jewish history, xiii
Diaspora Jewish communities, 324
Dilthey, Wilhelm, 131
Dinur, Ben-Zion, xxx, 95, 424
disavowed soldiers (*żołnierze wyklęci*),
    452–455
    anti-Semitism of, 461–466
    crimes committed by, 466–470
    events commemorating, 457
    glorification of, 455–458, 455n8
    National Day of Remembrance for,
        457–458
    term, 452–453
Długosz, Elżbieta, 101
Długosz, Jan, 204–205
Dmowski, Roman, xxx, 108–109, 116
Dobroszycki, Lucjan, 445
    *Image before My Eyes: A Photographic
        History of Jewish Life in Poland,
        1864–1939* (with Barbara
        Kirshenblatt-Gimblett), 63
Doktór, Jan, xxiv, 69
Dov Baer, Magid of Międzyrzecz, xxvii, 96,
    98–99
Dubnow, Simon, xxvi, xxx, 95, 183
    History of the Jews in Russia and Poland, 60
Duneier, Mitchel, 78
Dutkowski, Hieronim, 465
Dybicz, Paweł, 457
Dynner, Glenn, xxix, 67
Dzienniczek, 339–340, 354
    attitude to mothers expressed in, 345
    on gender equality, 347
    ideology of, 349–350
    principle of publishing its readers' works,
        354
    readers of, 344, 349–350
    religious significance, 348
    writing on Eretz Israel, 348–349, 353

E

Early Modern galleries, 1
    conceptions of history popular in
        Poland, 6
    concept of "Polishness," 2
    "Corridor of Fire," 4, 4n5
    Dance of Death exhibit, 6
    Jewish Polishness, expression of, 7–8
    Jewish vision of the shtetl, 8–9
    major audiences, 2
    Miasteczko, 3–4
    Moshe Isserles, exhibit on, 3, 6
    narrative language of, 1–2
    Paradisus Judaeorum gallery, 3, 6
    Polish-Lithuanian Jewry, construction
        of, 3–4
    Roman Catholic Church-Jewish
        relations, exhibit on, 9–10

synagogue roof exhibit, 10–11, 132
tavern dialogues between Jews and non-
	Jews, 8–9
use of facades, 8
views of Polish Jewish history, 5
Eastern European Jewish history, xxx, 104,
	307–308
economic history of the Jews
	activities in retail trade, 240
	activity of Jewish minters and bankers,
		234–235
	agriculture, 243–244
	case of smuggling, 241–242
	commercial activities, 235–236
	crafts, 242–243
	debts of the Jewish communities and,
		250–251
	economic ties between Jews and
		magnates, 239–241
	in eighteenth century, 240–241
	entrepreneurial nature, 235n16
	industry and manufacturing, 245–246
	during mid-seventeenth century, 238
	names listed in customs records,
		246–249
	participation in foreign markets, 250
	production and sale of liquor, 238–239
	research, 231–233, 246–251
	trade privileges given to Jews, 236
	vs Christian merchants, 237
Edelman, Marek, 130, 471
education on the Holocaust, 173
	comparativist attitudes toward the
		Holocaust, 175–176
	in context of teaching, 172–174
	definition of, 172
	ethnic Poles' collective group memory of
		Holocaust, 176
	experimental education and
		experimental teaching, 175, 181
	"Holocaust" as a term, 176
	Poles' multiple attitudes toward Jews,
		179
	programs and projects, 173
	role of musuems in, 179–182
	in textbooks, 177–178
	theoretical, methodological, and
		logistical problems, 180
	transmission of memory, 174–175
Eger, Akiva ("the Younger") b. Moses Guens,
	xxxiii
Eisenbach, Artur, xxvii–xxviii

Eišiškės (Ejszyszki), 126
Elbaum, Yaakov, 66
Eliezer, Elijah ben, xxxi
Endecja Party, 116
Engel, David, 45, 67, 71, 397, 413, 436, 445,
	461, 470n53
Engelking, Barbara, 21, 125, 400, 416,
	419–420
Etkes, Immanuel, 66
Ettinger, Shmuel, 66, 95, 183n2
extinct landscape, 439

F
Federation of Jewish Communities of Russia
	(FJCR), 158
Fejgin, Anatol, 1
Fijałkowski, Paweł, 69
Final Solution of the Jewish Question, 388,
	395
Fishman, David, 67
Flesch, Rabbi Moshe, 358
Florian, Hieronim, 191
Fram, Edward, 67
Franczak, Artur, 181
Frank, Jacob, xxii, xxiv, 9, 262–263
	as Archbishop of Lwów, 265–267
	conversations with the Paulines,
		270–271
	denunciation of church authorities and
		arrest of, 267–271
	exile in Brno, 271–275
	incidents in Lanckoroń and, 262–265
	Kamieniec Debate in 1757, 265–267
	stay in fortress of Jasna Góra, 268–20
Frankel, Jonathan, 17
Frankism, xxiv, 261n1
	after Frank's death, 275–279
	Porges's memoirs, 276–278
French historiography of the Vichy period,
	425–426
Frenk, Ezriel Nathan, 60
	Burghers and Jews in Poland, 60
Friedberg, Ḥayim Betsalel, 200
Friedlaender, Rabbi Israel, 316
Friedländer, Saul, 400
Friedman, Philip, 399
Friedrich, Klaus-Peter, 414
Fuks, Marian, 69

G
Galas, Michał, 69
Gal-Ed, 61

Galicia Jewish Museum, 146–148
  awards and recognition, 148
  photos of ruined synagogues or ruined Jewish cemeteries, 147–148
  post-Holocaust narrative, 146
  sections or themes, 147
  "Traces of Memory," 146, 146n15
Gancwajch, Abraham, 127
Ganganelli, Cardinal Lorenzo, *see* Clement XIV, Pope
Garage Center for Contemporary Culture, 159
Garncarska-Kedari, Bina, 64
Gawron, Edyta, 69
Gdynia, 26
Gebert, Konstanty, liv, 55
Gebirtig, Mordkhe, 22
Gefter, Mikhail, 152
Gelber, Natan M., 276
Genizat Herson, 96
genocidal space, 437–440
genocide studies, 391–392
Gens, Jacob, 125
Gerber, Alla, 152
Geremek, Bronisław, 47, 49, 483
Gierowski, Józef Andrzej, 69
Glagolev, Aleksey, 154
Gmiterek, Henryk, 233
Golczewski, Frank, 69
Gold, Artur, 26
Goldberg, Jacob, 65, 70, 199, 233, 238, 241, 259
Goldhagen, Daniel Jonah, 113
Gomułka, Władysław, xlvii, 56
Good Order Commission, 229–230
Górecki, Henryk, 154
Gorin, Rabbi Boruch, 158
Gottlieb, Maurycy, 17, 142
Głowiński, Michał, 177
Grabowski, Jan, 21, 178, 400, 415, 417–418, 420
Grabski, August, 447
Grabski, Władysław, 23
Grajek, Stefan, 460
Great Northern War, 184
Green, Arthur, xxx
Green, David, 14, 16
Gregory XIII, 196
Gries, Zev, 66
Grinberg, Daniel, 69
Gross, Jan T., xlviii, 21, 403, 405, 416, 434, 443, 445
  Neighbors (*Sąsiedzi*), xli, 399–400, 415, 433, 477
Gross, Zehavit, 181
Grotius, Hugo, xxi
Grünbaum, Itzhak, 291
Grynberg, Henryk, lii
Gąsiorowski, Stefan, 69
Guesnet, François, 70
Guldon, Zenon, 69, 253
Guttmacher, Rabbi Elijah, 297–298, 302–306, 309
Gwoździec synagogue, 10, 76, 132–133

H

Halbersztadt, Jerzy, 57, 105
Halpern, Israel, 66
Handelsman, Marceli, 108
Handshouse Studio, 11
Harrington, James, 83
Harshav, Benjamin, 130
Hasidism, xiv, xxiv–xxvii, xxx–xxxiii, 73
  being a Hasid, 94
  Chabad, 97
  curatorial perspective, 103
  Czas chasydów (Time of the Hasidim) exhibition, 101
  early, 94–95
  first exhibition, 96–97
  In the Footsteps of the Besht exhibition, 101–102
  Gerer Hasidism, 105
  importance of books and manuscripts in, 98–100
  late, 94–95
  mature period of, 95
  in a museum setting, 93–104
  opponents of, 100
  opposition to, xxxiii
  period of emergence, 95
  in Poland, 99
  portraying in exhibition, 96–98
  tzaddikim, 100
  A World Apart Next Door: Glimpses into the Life of Hasidic Jews exhibition, 101–103
Haskalah (Jewish Enlightenment), xiv
Haynt, 15, 25
Hebrew University, xiv
Heller, Binem, lii
Heller, Celia, 63
  On the Edge of Destruction, 63
Hertz, Zygmunt, 59
Herz, Feyvel, 250
Heschel, Rabbi Avraham Yehoshua of Apt (Opatów), 96
Heyde, Jürgen, xviii, 70

Higier, Henryk, 381, 383
Hilberg, Raul, 124, 393–394, 393n17, 404
Himka, John Paul, 288
Hirsch, Samson Raphael, 359, 361
Hisdai, Yaakov, 66
Holocaust, xi, xliv, xxxv, 106, 402, 440–441.
 See also Shoah, Education on the
 Holocaust, and Holocaust historiography
  witnesses (bystanders), 404
  Polish, 409
Holocaust Gallery, 131, 136, 171–173, 177, 179
  aesthetics and ethics of representation, 38–39
  anti-Jewish sentiment in Poland, 113–115
  "Aryan Side," 31, 34
  assumptions relating to exhibition, 29–30
  audience, 33
  authorial concept in, 33
  bystanders' perspective, 35–36
  curatorial challenges, 32–33
  death camps (Auschwitz II-Birkenau and Treblinka II), 32, 37
  division of information, 33–34
  exhibition space, 30–32
  exhibit on Umschlagplatz, 30, 34–35
  experiencing the exhibit, 39
  history of Poland under German occupation, 112–113
  issue of perspectives, 35–37
  location, 30
  memory of the war, 117–118
  meta-rule of, 38
  photographs displayed, 37–38
  postwar gallery, 32
  presentation of Polish Jews, 111–112
  problematics of the Core Exhibition, 115–116
  September campaign, 30–31
  Shoah Corridor, 32, 37
  Third Reich attack on Soviet Union, 31–32
  topography of, 34–35
  Ukrainian and Polish view of the Jews, 117–118
  victims' perspective, 35
  Warsaw Ghetto, 30–31
Holocaust historiography, 386–387, 403
  categorization of protagonists, 393–397
  contribution of new methodologies, 397–398
  and genocide studies, 391–392
  political developments in Europe and impact on research, 388–391
  research, 399–401

Holocaust Museum, Washington, 173
Holzer, Jerzy, 69, 105–106
Horn, Maurycy, 69, 243, 252
Horodetsky, Shmuel, xxx, 95
Horowitz, Donald, 289
Höss, Rudolf, 37
Huberman, Haya, 300
Hubka, Thomas, 10
Hundert, Gershon D., 67, 74, 106, 209, 247, 254, 336
 The Jews in Poland and Russia (with Gershon Bacon), 61
 The Jews in a Polish Private Town, 67
 The YIVO Encyclopedia of Jews in Eastern Europe, 42, 45, 74–76
Hurwic, Józef, 48
Hurwic, Sara, 45, 48–49

I

Ickowicz, Gdal, 191
Ickowicz, Szmujło, 191
Innocent IV, Pope, 81
Insler, Abraham, 384
Instytut Pamięci Narodowej (Institute of National Remembrance, IPN), 405, 452, 454–455
integrative national historiography, 435
International Association of Holocaust Organizations, 152
International Auschwitz Council, 144
International Summer Schools for the Study of the Holocaust, 179
Interwar gallery
 American and Israeli Jewish visitors, perspectives of, 106–107
 Bude (the Shack), 25
 Café Ziemiańska, 107
 challenges in Jewish life, 24
 childhood, family life, and education, 27
 Chinese wall, 106
 critique of, 105–110
 culture gallery, 24–26
 daily life and growing up, 26
 exhibits on courtyards with children's games and songs, 107
 Holocaust survivors, 20
 interwar Polish Jewry, 21–23
 Jewish adolescents, 27–28
 Jewish schools, 27, 107
 Jewish towns, 26–27
 Jewish Writers' Club, also known as Bude (the Shack), 25

parts (politics, culture, daily life, and growing up), 22
Polish Jewish life, 21, 107
Polish pogroms and acts of violence against Jews, 23–24, 109–110
Polish visitors, perspectives of, 106
"The Jewish Street," 21–22, 24, 107, 109
transitional gallery, 22
Vilna exhibit, 25, 107
youth movements, 27–28
interwar Polish Jewry
citizenship, 336
gap between generations, 332–333
gender disunity, 335–337
intra-religious disunity, 334–335
phenomena of unity and disunity, 331–332
religious-secular disunity, 333–334
represented in *POLIN* museum, *see* Interwar gallery
rifts and splits, 336
women's movements and youth movements, 335
Isaac of Troki, 6
Israeli Holocaust historiography, 423–425
about Holocaust in Poland, 429–436
challenges, 426–427
concept of uniqueness, 428–429, 432–433
Nazi genocide in Eastern Europe, 427
Israeli national identity, 423
Isserles, Rabbi Moshe, 3, 6
Izraelita, 15

J

Jaakow Josef of Połonne, xxvi, xxvii, 102
Jaeger Report, 126
Jagiełło, Eugeniusz, 287
Jagodzińska, Agnieszka, 69
Jakimyszyn, Anna, 69
Janiszewski, Tomasz, 376
Jasiewicz, Krzysztof, 411–412
Jasińska-Kania, Aleksandra, 170
Jeleński, Jan, 91, 286
Jewish Community Center (JCC), 148
Jewish education. *See also under* Jewish history in Poland, CYSHO, Tarbut
Jewish girls' Torah study, 299, 357–358. *See also* Bais Yaakov movement
Jewish school networks, l, liv
Jewish emigration from Poland, 45–46, 459, 472–474
images of Poland among émigrés, 476–484
representations of Poland, 474–476
Jewish health in Poland, 375–383. *See also* Obshchestvo Zdravookhraneniia Evreev, Towarzystwo Ochrony Zdrowia Ludności Żydowskiej w Polsce
assessment of health status, 380–381
impact of racial factors, 380–381
of Jews in the Polish army, 377–378
parameters of Jewish body, 382
Jewish identity, transformations in, liii, 432. *See also* Jewish Polishness
academic perspective, 85–86
in economic terms, 86–87
emancipation and, 87–88
in intellectual climate, 86
national identity, 281
nationalism, in context of, 86, 90
nineteenth century, 85
processes of modernization and, 88–90
Polish Jewish modern identity, 284
rural and agrarian reforms, 87
Jewish immigration to Poland, 5
Jewish labor movement, 17
Jewish Museum and Tolerance Center (JMTC), 158–168
Joseph Isaac Schneerson's library, 165
Jewish-non-Jewish relations, 198–199
accusations of desecration of Host, 204–205
anti-Jewish legislation of 1538 and incidents, 198, 211–218
business partnerships, 202
conflicts between burghers and Jews, 207–209, 223
guidelines for coexistence of Jews and Christians, 203–204
neighborhood contacts, 202
norms for encounters with non-Jews, 201–202
perceptions and attitudes, 199–207
practices/encounters in everyday life and business dealings, 207–211
prohibition on employment of Christian servants by Jews, 188–190, 205
restraints in sexual relations, 202
social interactions between clergy and Jews, 210–211
Jewish Polishness, 367, 369–375, 384
in multilingual environment, 369–375
Jewish Publication Society of America (JPS), 316
Jewish tourism to Poland
advantages and disadvantages of present-day approach, 146–147

Auschwitz museum, 143–146
foreign Jews, perspectives of, 140, 140n1
Galicia Jewish Museum, 146–148
history of Polish Jews, visitor perspective, 140
POLIN Museum, 141–142
temporary exhibition in Kraków, 142
Jewish women's lives, 297–299. *See also under* Jewish education
barriers to girls' religious education, 299
divorce and female status, 303–307, 305n37
Guttmacher petitions and, 297–298
matchmaking procedures, 299–303
modes of female empowerment, 299
working women and economic-based agency, 307–311
Jewry law, 82
Jews, xii
accusations against, xxi
Ashkenazi, 6, 66, 75, 158
assimilated, 17, 30–31, 43–46, 49–51, 53–54, 63, 74, 117, 125, 137, 181, 284, 336, 408
expulsion of, xxi
fair-haired, 381–382
harassment against, xxi
violence against, *see* Anti-Jewish violence
in France, 475–480
in interwar Poland, xxxv. *See also* Interwar Polish Jewry
in Poland, *see* Jewish history in Poland
under Nazi rule, xiii
religious and spiritual life, xxii
Jezierski, Jacek, 253
John Paul II, Pope, 42
Johnpoll, Bernard, 62
The Politics of Futility: The General Jewish Workers' Bund of Poland, 1917–1943, 62
Joint Jewish Distribution Committee, xlviii
Judaism, xxvi, xxxiii, 3, 46, 50, 56, 71, 85, 101, 157, 187–188, 190, 197, 206
Judeophobia, 290
Judt, Tony, 426
Jurczyk, Marian, 47

K
Kac, Daniel, lii
Kaczmarski, Krzysztof, 446, 448
Kaczyński, Jarosław, xliii
Kaczyński, Lech, 456

Kąkolewski, Igor, 5
Kalik, Judith, 66, 70
Scepter of Judah: Jewish Autonomy in the Eighteenth-Century Crown Poland, 255
Kamiński, Aleksander, 406
Kapralski, Sławomir, 178
Karczewska, Agnieszka, 350
Karetti, Józef, 189
Karpeles, Gustav, 321
Karski, Jan, 406
Kassow, Samuel, 67, 106, 367, 403
Katz, Jacob, 66, 75
Kaźmierczyk, Adam, xxii, 69, 233, 257, 259
Kazovsky, Hillel/Grigori, 165, 168
Kershaw, Ian, 400
Kersten, Krystyna, 445–446
keyver-oves, 107
Khmelnytsky, Bohdan, xviii
uprising, xxi, 132, 184
Kichelewski, Audrey, xlviii
Kieniewicz, Stefan, xi–xii, xxviii
Kirshenblatt-Gimblett, Barbara, 11, 21, 40, 52, 57, 74, 78–79, 85, 106, 111, 130, 139, 141
Image before My Eyes: A Photographic History of Jewish Life in Poland, 1864–1939 (with Lucjan Dobroszycki), 63
Kitowicz, Jędrzej, 209
kitvei kiyyumeihen, 82
Kizwalter, Tomasz, xxix, xxvii
Kleinmann, Yvonne, 70
Klub Inteligencji Katolickiej (Club of the Catholic Intelligentsia), liii
Kobielski, Franciszek Antoni, 191, 193, 196
Kołakowski, Leszek, 132
Kolski, Eugeniusz, 466
Komisja Historyczna (Historical Commission), xlix
Komitet Obrony Robotników (Workers' Defense Committee, KOR), 53, 479
Komitet Organizacyjny Żydowskich Zrzeszeń Religijnych (Organizational Committee of Jewish Religious Associations), xlviii–xlix
Kongregacja Wyznania Mojżeszowego (Jewish Religious Congregation), xlix
Koniecpolski, Stanisław, 186
Koordynacja, xlviii
Kopciowski, Adam, 448, 461, 469
Korczak, Janusz, 339
educational achievements, 343–344

Korkuć, Maciej, 448
Korzec, Paweł, xxxv
Koszarska-Szulc, Justyna, 40
Kosiński, Jerzy, 48 1
    The Painted Bird, 481
Kovner, Abba, 24
Kowalik, Piotr, 119
Krajewska, Monika, 44
Krajewski, Stanisław, liv, xlv, 130, 474
krajoznawstwo movement (*landkentenish* movement), 26, 336
Kraków, xvii, xxi, 13, 82, 212, 215, 220, 222, 225, 250, 339, 359, 400
    Jewish trade, xviii
Krall, Hanna, lii
Kramsztyk, Stanisław, 30–31
Kranz, Tomasz, 173, 180
Kraushar, Aleksander, 15, 18
Krawczyk, Piotr, 181
Kronenberg, Leopold, 16
Kruk, Herman, 125
Krupa, Bartłomiej, 403
Krzemiński, Ireneusz, 170
Kucia, Marek, 180n22
Kula, Marcin, 170
Kula, Witold, 59
Kunert, Andrzej Krzysztof, 408
Kuraś, Józef, 456
Kurek-Lesik, Ewa, 407
Kwiek, Julian, 461

L

Lahdelma, Ilmari, liv
Laitin, David D., 285
Landau, Henan, 250
Landau, Moshe, xxxv, 64
Landau-Czajka, Anna, xxxvii
landkentenish movement (*krajoznawstwo* movement), 26, 336
Lane, Arthur Bliss, l
Lanzmann, Claude, 404, 480
    Shoah (film), 480
Lateran Councils, xix
Lauder-Morasha School, liv
Lazar, Rabbi Berel, 158
Lechtman, Wera, 132
Leociak, Jacek, xliv, 125, 131, 435
Leśmian, Bolesław, xxxvii
Lestchinsky, Jacob, xxxv
Leszczyński, Anatol, 243, 246
Levin, Shmarye, 16
Levine, Hillel, 67

Levy, Hanno, 55
Lewin, Gershon, 383
Lewin, Sabina, 65
Lewin, Zofia, 406
Liberman, Haim, 98
Libionka, Dariusz, xlii, xliv, 407, 418, 448
Liebes, Esther, 101
Liflyand, Leonid, 155
Lithuania, xii. *See also* Poland-Lithuania
Lithuanian perspectives on the Holocaust, 120–122
    experience of Holocaust Gallery, 124–129
    issue of native participation in genocide, 127
    Jewish-Polish-Lithuanian interaction, 122–124
Litvak invasion, 286
Łódź, xlv, 14–17
    textiles, 16–17
Londinski, Helen, 300
Louis IX, King of France, 83
Lubavitch library, 97
Lublin, xxi, 24, 32, 181, 218–223, 225–227, 243, 258, 334, 359, 429, 439, 448, 462–463, 469
    Lublin Jewish community, 219
Lubomirska, Teresa, 191–192
Ludowe Wojsko Polskie (Polish People's Army, LWP), 456
Lwów (Lviv), xvii, xxi, 13, 109, 220, 263, 338, 381

M

Mach, Zdzisław, 170
Małecki, Jan M., xviii, 232, 248–249
Magdeburg law, 207
Magid of Międzyrzecz, *see* Dov Baer
Mahlamäki, Rainer, liv
Mahler, Raphael, xxxv, 95, 243
    Jews in Poland between the Two World-Wars: A Socio-Economic History on a Statistical Basis, 62
Maimon, Salomon, 209
Majdanek camp, 440
Maklev, Uri, 102
Manger, Itsik, lii
Małopolski Institute of Culture, 182
Marcus, Joseph, xxxv, 23, 65, 337
    Polish poverty and Jewish overpopulation, xxxvi
Markiel, Tadeusz, xlii
Markowski, Artur, 291–292

Martyrdom of the Polish Nation, 456
Marx, Karl, 13–14
   Communist Manifesto, 13–14
Marzyński, Marian, 44, 50
maskilim, 100
Mały Przegląd, 339–355
   articles on Palestine, 351–352
   attitude to mothers expressed in, 345
   challenging the authority of adults, 353
   feature of articles in, 351–352
   on gender equality and nondiscrimination, 346–347
   linking *Dzienniczek* with, 342
   principle of publishing its readers' works, 354
   readers of, 344
   religious significance, 348
   writing on Poland, 351, 353
Mazurke, Madzia, 342–343
Medem Sanatorium, 28
Melnikov, Konstantin, 158
Meltzer, Emanuel, xxxv, 64
Mendelsohn, Ezra, xxxiv, xxxvi–xxxvii, 23, 67, 72, 130
Michałowska-Mycielska, Anna, 69, 233
Michman, Dan, xlii, 424–425
Michnik, Adam, 132, 483
Miczyński, Sebastian, 205–206
Minc, Hilary, 1
Mintz, Binyamin, 96
mitnagdim, 100
Modelski, Krzysztof, 251
Moment, 15
Morgensztern, Janina, 233
Moscow, Jewish museums in
   Jewish Museum and Tolerance Center (JMTC), 158–168
   memorial to the Great Patriotic War (Museum of Jewish Heritage and Holocaust at Poklonnaia Gora), 150–154
      exhibition displays, 154–155
      Holocaust-themed *Free to Cry*, 154
   Museum of Jewish History in Russia (MJHR), 155–158
      Ashkenazi Jewry, 158
      Jewish history in Russia, 157–158
      main departments, 157
      preservation of historical memory and Jewish culture and tradition, 157
      synagogue, 153–154
Moscow Dixi Film Association, 154
Moscow Jewish Community Center, 158
Moses, Dirk, 427
Muchawsky-Schnapper, Ester, 102
municipal authorities and Jewish communal bodies, agreements between, 221–222
   in cases of conflicts and disputes, 230
   between Christians and Jews, 222
   context of process of, 228
   eternal or forever binding, 227
   Good Order Commission as mediator, 229–230
   Lwów agreements, 222
   open-ended or signed, 227
   penalty clause, 227
   on privileges, 228, 230
   in Przemyśl, 228
   for purchasing properties from Christians, 225
   resolutions of the *Sejm*, 224
   restrictions on trading activity, 236
   signed in Brześć, 223
   signed with guilds, 225–226
   terms of, 226
   time period, 227
   in vibrant urban centers, 222, 225
   wording of, 229
municipal customs books, 249
Museum Path, 3–4
Museums and Society 2034, 171
Museum Voice, 2–3, 10
Musiał, Adam, 181
Musiał, Stanisław, Fr., xxxix
Muszkat, Marian, 445
Muszyńska, Jadwiga, 208

N

Nachman of Bratslav, Rabbi, 96, 101
Nahman ben Samuel, 263
Nacht-Samborski, Artur, 49
Nadav, Mordechai, 65, 244, 256
Nalewajko-Kulikow, Joanna, 69
Namysło, Aleksandra, 407
narrative museum, 2–3
National Military Organization (Narodowa Organizacja Wojskowa; NOW), 466
National Armed Forces (Narodowe Siły Zbrojne; NSZ), 409, 453
National Military Union (Narodowe Zjednoczenie Wojskowe, NZW), 453
Nasz Przegląd, 25
Natanson, Ludwik, 17

Nathan, Jacob, 250
Nathans, Benjamin, 161
National Polish-American Jewish-American Council (NPAJAC), xv
Netzer, Shlomo, xxxv, 64
Newerly, Igor, 342
Nicholas I, Tsar, 317
Niedenthal, Chris, 132
Niezabitowska, Małgorzata, 482
   Remnants: The Last Jews of Poland (with Tomasz Tomaszewski), 482
Nineteenth-century gallery
   anti-Semitism, portrayal of, 18–19
   Jewish acculturation and integration, 17–18
   Jewish nationalisms, 18
   Partitions of Poland, 13
   planning of the gallery, 14
   problems in presentation, 13
   railway station, 17
   theme of industrialization and modernization, 16–17
   Tłomackie synagogue model, 17
Nisko Plan, 439
Nizio Design International of Warsaw, 1
No'am Elimelekh, 99
Nolte, Ernst, 113
Nowak, Zenon H., 248
Nowakowska, Irena, *see* Hurwic, Sara
Nowy Korczyn, 190

O

Obshchestvo Zdravookhraneniia Evreev (Society for the Protection of Jewish Health, OSE), 379
Ojrzyński, Wiktor, 246
Oleszak, Agnieszka, 358
Olitski, Leib, lii
Olkusz, xxi
Organization for Child and Orphan Care, *see* Central Organization for the Care of Orphans
Organizaciia Ukrains'kyh Natsionalistiv (Organization of Ukrainian Nationalists, OUN), 117
Orlicki, Józef, 444
Orthodox Jews, 43
Osmecki, Kazimierz Iranek, 407
Ossowski, Stanisław, 59
Oyneg Shabes group (the Ringelblum Archive), 29, 31

P

Paczkowski, Andrzej, xlv
Pale of Settlement, 16, 154, 286–287, 291–293, 319
Paulsson, Gunnar, xliii
   Secret City: The Hidden Jews of Warsaw 1940-1945, 408
Pawlak, Judyta, 40
Paxton, Robert, 425–426
Pazderski, Mieczysław, 453
Peretz, Y. L., 18, 26, 282
Petelwicz, Jakub, 416
Petersburski, Jerzy, 26
Petrusewicz, Marta, 132
Pikulski, Gaudenty, 267
Pinkas Ha-Kehillot, 60
Pinkas of Medinat Lita, 61
Pinsker, Lev, 18
Piłsudski, Józef, xiii, xxxviii, 24, 117
Platforma Obywatelska (Civic Platform, PO), 457
Płock, xxi, 109, 306
Podraza, Antoni, 238
Pogotowie Akcji Specjalnej (Special Emergency Action Unit, PAS), 453
pogroms, 285–289
   as acts of violence, 289–290. *See also* Anti-Jewish violence
   Jedwabne pogrom, 404-5
   in Grodno province, 292–293
   impact of Jewish political groups, 293–294
   in Lithuania, 290–291
   Kielce pogrom, 46, 57, 59, 136–137, 404, 445–446, 451
   Kishinev pogrom, 116, 290
   Kraków pogrom, 446
   Lwów pogrom, 23
   Mińsk pogrom, 23
   Parczew pogrom, 467–468
   Przytyk pogrom, 23, 108
Poland, xii, 325–326, 399. *See also* Polish-Lithuanian Commonwealth
   anti-Semitism in, 15
   citizenship to Jews, 23
   exodus of Jews from, xlvii. *See also* Jewish emigration from Poland
   as a genocidal space, 437–440
   issue of economic anti-Semitism, 23
   Jewish communities in, xvii
   Jewish population in, 14–15, 200
   Jewish presence after 1989, 137

Polish Jewish diaspora, xiii, 42, 63,
   141, 143, 348, 350, 424, 473,
   482, 484
Polish-Jewish relations, xiii, xv, 23, 35, 65,
   71, 81–82, 211–212
preservation of Jewish heritage in, lv–lvi
Solidarity movement, xiv
Poles
   awareness of Polish Jewish past, xiv–xv
   rescuers of Jews, xlii–xliv
   under Nazi occupation, xii
   Solidarity movement and, xiv
*Polin: A Journal of Polish-Jewish Studies
   (Polin: Studies in Polish Jewry)*, xv
POLIN Museum of the History of Polish
   Jews, lv, xi, xlv, xvi, xxvii, 70–71, 74, 85,
   130, 134, 149, 158, 171, 176, 182, 282,
   313, 450. *See also* Assumptions in exhibit
   selection for POLIN Museum, and
   Hasidism in a museum setting.
   Postwar gallery, 134–138
   Early Modern galleries, *see separate entry*
   history of Polish Jews, visitor perspective,
      140
   Holocaust gallery, *see separate entry*
   Interwar gallery, *see separate entry*
   Jewish Town gallery, 3–4
   Kirshenblatt-Gimblett's role at, 139n1
   newspapers as part of exhibition, 25
   Nineteenth-century gallery,
      see separate entry
   Paradisus Judaeorum gallery, 3, 7, 80
   planning for, 130–133
   Postwar gallery, 131
   Warsaw Ghetto fighters, glorification of,
      132, 136
Polish-American Congress (PAC), xv
Polish-American Jewish-American Task
   Force, xv
Polish history
   nation-building process after 1918, 375
   thirteenth- and fourteenth-century
      Polish urbanization, 82
   Polish People's Republic, 453
Polish-Jewish historiography, 429–436
   archival collections, 62
   articulation between the Jewish and
      Polish institutions, 73
   bibliographical appendixes, 61
   bibliographies and bibliographical essays,
      61–62
   books on Polish Jewish history, xvi
   classic works of historiography, 60
   collective image of Jews, 288

collective memories, 283
deconstructionist approach to historical
   research, 418–419
discussion, xxvii
existentialist approach to historical
   research, 419–420
Hasidism, 66, 73
Haskalah, 66
impact of modernities on Polish Jewish
   life, 282–284
integrative history, 435, 437
of interwar Polish Jewry, xxxiv–xxxv
Jewish culture, 66
Jewish-inspired Westernizing process, 282
Jewish politics in Poland during interwar
   years, 64–65
Jewish studies worldwide, 69
Jewish treatment of non-Jews, 75
Land of Israel studies, 66
modern Jewish identities, 284
new cadre of scholars of 1970s, 64–71
non-Jew scholars, 68–70
objective conflicts of interests between
   Jews and Poles, 71
"objectivist" and "subjectivist" terms, 71
periodization, 72
of Polish anti-Semitism, 75–76
Polish-Jewish relations, 71
Polish Jews' connection to Judaism, 71
posthumous integration of the Jews into
   Polish history, lv–lvi
reestablishment of Polish Jewry in the
   postwar period, 65
relationship between Polish Jewry and
   German court Jews, 72
scholars specializing in Jewish studies, 69
of Shoah, 75–76
social relations between Jews and
   Christians, 72
struggles of Jews for rights during
   interwar period, 73
Weinryb and Baron's narratives, 63–64
Polish-Jewish history, xv, lii, 43, 115, 232, 280.
   See also Jews in interwar Poland
anti-Jewish attitudes, xl, xvii–xviii, xxii
canon law against Jews, xix–xx
encyclopedia of Jewish communities,
   60–61
gender in Jewish life, xxxiii–xxxiv
inferior position of Jews, xix
interwar period, xxxv–xxxvii
Jewish acculturation, xxxviii, lii. *See also*
   Jewish Polishness, interwar Polish
   Jewry

UNESCO Chair for Holocaust Education at the Jagiellonian Museum, 172
Union of Jewish Religious Communities, 47
Ury, Scott, 15, 70
Urynowicz, Marcin, xliii, 407
Ustinov, Sergei, 155–156

V
Vayter, A., 109
Vekselberg, Victor, 160–161
Vilna, 25, 107
Vilnius Ghetto Theater, 125
Vishniac, Roman, 63
    Polish Jews: A Pictorial Record, 63

W
Warsaw, 13, 400, xii
Warsaw-centrism, 16
Warsaw Ghetto, liii, lv–lvi, xiv, xliii, 30–31, 34–36, 38, 105, 124, 419
    uprising, liii, lvi, xiv, 36, 419, 463
Wasilewski, Zygmunt, 384
Wassercug, Moshe, 201
Wawelberg, Hipolit, 17
Weeks, Theodore, 69, 286
Węgrzynek, Hanna, xviii, 69
Weinberg, Shayke, 106
Weinreich, Max, 21
Weinryb, Bernard Dov, 63
    The Jews of Poland: A Social and Economic History of the Jewish Community in Poland from 1100 to 1800, 63
    Neueste Wirtschaftsgeschichte der Juden in Russland und Polen, 60
Wengeroff, Pauline, 313
    cultural positioning, 317–318
    depiction of Haskalah, 317
    on Germany and German language, 320
    historical consciousness, 314
    idealization of *Ostjuden*, 323
    Jewish ethnicity, 318–319
    as a Jewish nationalist, 322
    language used, 319–320
    Memoirs of a Grandmother, 313–316, 321–322
    on Russification, 321
    terminology about Jewish and European culture, 318
    transformation of Jewish society, 314
    writing, 314–316

Westerners, 67, 73
Western historiography, 67
Wielkopolska, xxxiii
Wierzbicki, Marek, 412
Wijaczka, Jacek, xix
Wiśniowiecki, Michał Korybut, 219
Władysław IV, King of Poland, 236
Wnuk, Rafal, 462
Wodziński, Marcin, xxvii, xxx, 16, 69–70, 72, 83, 106, 244
Wojdowski, Bohdan, lii
Wolność i Niezawisłość (Freedom and Independence, WiN), 462–465, 467
Woyna-Okołów, Jerzy, 249
Wróbel, Piotr, 69
Wroński, Stanisław, 406
Wąsowski, Grzegorz, 452
Wulman, Leon, 380
Wygodzki, Stanisław, lii, 132
Wynot, Edward, 69
Wyrozumska, Bożena, 222
Wyżycki, Mikołaj Ignacy, 190, 195

Y
Yaacov Yisrael of Krzemieniec, Rabbi, 201
Yad Vashem, xiv, 60, 424
Yad Vashem Memorial Institute, xliii
Yitzhak Alfassi, 96
Yosef ha-Kohen, 79
YIVO (Yiddish Scientific Institute), 25

Z
Zadzierski, Józef, 466, 469
Zak, Avrom, 16
Zakrzewski, Franciszek, 40
Zalman, Eliyahu ben Shlomo, 104
Zambrowski, Roman, l, lii
Zaremba, Marcin, 443
Zaremska, Hanna, 69, 78–79, 81, 222
Żaryn, Jan, 407, 409
Żbikowski, Andrzej, 447–448, 461, xlii, xlv–xlvi
zbratanie, 15
Żebrowski, Leszek, 452
Żebrowski, Rafał, 69
Żegota, 125, 406–408
Zevi, Shabbatai, xxii, 263
Zhukova, Daria, 159
Ziębińska-Witek, Anna, 38
Zienkowicz, Michał, 191

Śląski, Jerzy, 452–453
Śleszkowski, Sebastian, 206
Slonik, Binyamin, 203
Smetona, Antanas, 124
Smolar, Hersz, 48
Smólski, Władysław, 407
Snyder, Timothy, 390, 421
    Bloodlands, 438
Sobieski, King Jan III, 184, 218-219
Sojczyński, Stanisław, 466
Solidarność (Solidarity) movement, xiv, 46–47
Sołtyk, Kajetan, xxi, 192
Sommerstein, Emil, xlix, 48
Słonimski, Antoni, xxxvii, 132
Soviet Union, xv, xlv, xlvii, li, 23, 31, 44, 96, 333, 388, 390, 439, 462n32
Sojusz Lewicy Demokratycznej (Democratic Left Alliance, SLD), 457
spatial Darwinism, 437
Śpiewak, Paweł, lv
Srulówna, 295–297
Staliūnas, Darius, xxix
Stalinism, xi
Stalinization, 46–47
Stampfer, Shaul, xxxi, 67
Stefaniak, Anna, 170
Steffen, Katrin, xxxvii, 70
Stein, Edith, 131
Stein, Leopold, 275
Steinlauf, Michael, xxxvii, 67
Stern, Abraham, xxxii
Stevick, Doyle, 181
Stojanowski, Karol, 377–378
Stola, Dariusz, 130, 413, 431, 435
Stow, Kenneth, xxii
Stowarzyszenie Dzieci Holokaustu (Association of Children of the Holocaust), liv
Strauss, Hermann, 380
Strauss-Marko, Salomon, 444
Stroop, General Jürgen, 36
Strumiłowa, Kamionka, 228
Stryjkowski, Julian, lii
Studia Judaica, 70
Studies on Polish Jewry (ed. Joshua Fishman), 62
Sułek, Antoni, 170, 176
Sužiedėlis, Saulius, xlii
Słupecki, Jerzy, xxi
Światło, Józef, 56
Świętochowski, Aleksander, 18–19
Szaniawski, Felicjan Konstantyn, 253
Szapiro, Paweł, 414
Szarota, Tomasz, 414

Szaynok, Bożena, 69, 446, 448
Szkliar, Moshe, lii
szlachta, 216–217
Szuchta, Robert, 180

T

Tanikowski, Artur, 40
Tarbut, Hebrew Zionist Schools, 27
Tatz, Colin, 392
Tautinio darbo apsaugos batalionas (National Labor Security, TDA), 128
Taylor, A. J. P., 113
Tazbir, Janusz, 199
Teller, Adam, xviii, 66, 70, 79
Teter, Magdalena, 70, 200, 206
Thon, Ozjasz, 21
Tokarska-Bakir, Joanna, 418, 448, 466
Tollet, Daniel, 67
Tłomackie 13, 25–26
Tomaszewski, Jerzy, 23, 69, 130
Tomaszewski, Tomasz, 482
    Remnants: The Last Jews of Poland (with Małgorzata Niezabitowska), 482
Topolski, Jerzy, 239
Towarzystwo Ochrony Zdrowia Ludności Żydowskiej w Polsce (Society for Safeguarding the Health of the Jewish Population, TOZ), 28, 336, 379
Towarzystwo Społeczno-Kulturalne Żydów (Social-Cultural Association of Jews in Poland, TSKŻ), 1, 482
Treaty of Riga, 366
Treaty of Versailles, 366
Treblinka II, 32, 37
trial of Trent, 1475, 204
Trojański, Piotr, 180
Trunk, Isaiah, xxxv, 399
Turkow, Jonas, 444
Turowicz, Jerzy, xli
Tuwim, Julian, xxxvii, 24, 137
Tych, Feliks, lv, xlvi, 130
tzaddikim, xxx, 98, 100, 297

U

Ukraine, xvii, xxxiii, 4n5, 70, 116–118, 126, 128, 146n15, 152, 239, 244, 291, 293, 389, 439
Ukrainian-Jewish conflict, 291
Ukrainians, xiv
Ukrains'ke natsional'no-demokratychne ob'ednannia (Ukrainian National Democratic Alliance, UNDO) party, 117
Underhill, Karen, 69

Radziwiłł, Prince Michał Kazimierz, 190
Rajs, Romuald, 453–454
Rakovsky, Puah, 16
Ralph Appelbaum Associates, 160
Rapoport-Albert, Ada, xxx
Ratzel, Friedrich, 437–438
Ravich, Melekh, 21
Rączy, Elżbieta, 407
Realgymnasium, 25
Reimanowa, Ruta, 350
Reiner, Elhanan, 66
Reinhardt, Aktion, 32
Reitmanowa, Runa, 338
religious life of Polish Jewry, xxii–xxiii, 38, 74, 157
    Besht's teaching and practice, xxvi–xxvii
    development of Hasidism, xxiv–xxvii, xxx–xxxiii
    influence of Kabbalah, xxiii
    kavanot (mystical devotions), xxiii
    messianic movement, xxiv
    shtibl and *shtiblekh*, establishment of, xxxi–xxxii
Reszke, Katka, 483
Riddell, Bréon George, 154
Righteous Among the Nations, 154
Ringelblum, Emanuel, 21, 31, 35, 108
Rogers, Carl, liii
Roman Catholic Church, xiii, xix, 4n5, 5, 9, 20, 24, 108, 184, 186–187, 197, 203, 211, 213, 267
Roman Jews, 79
    acculturation, 80
    diet, 80
    language of, 79
Ronald S. Lauder Foundation, liv
Ropp of Vilna, Bishop Edward von der, 288
Rosenson, Claire Ann, 483
Rosman, Moshe, xi, xvi, 67, 79, 141–142, 200, 233, 251, 336, 432
    How Jewish Is Jewish History, 41
Rostworowski, Karol Hubert, 385
Rubin, Hadasah, lii
Rupniewski, Stefan, 185–186, 193
Rybarski, Roman, 232, 237, 252
Rydzewski, Wacław, 467

S
Sabras, 66, 73
Salmon-Mack, Tamar, 66
Samsonowska, Krystyna, 407
Sarnowski, Stanisław, 189
Sasson, Havi Ben, 403

Scharf, Rafael, xxxix–xl
Schenirer, Sarah, 356–358
    association with biblical Sarah, 364
    Bleter fun mayn lebn, 358
    influence of Hasidism, 359
    personal life, 365
    setting up of Bais Yaakov schools, 360
    speaking of girls' formal Torah study, 363
    vision of religious education for Jewish girls, 358–359
    writings, 362n6
Schiper, Ignacy, 237
Schudrich, Michael, liii
Schulz, Bruno, xxxvii
Schwarz, Fred, liv
Scott-Irvine, Garry, 154
Scripta Judaica Cracoviensia, 70
Second World War, xii
Seidman, Naomi, xxxviii
Sejm constitution of 1775, 195
Sejm of 1534, 215–216
Sejm of Kraków, 1532, 213–214
Sejm of Piotrków, 1538, 211–218
Sejm of Radom, 1505, 213
Sendler, Irena, xliii
Shahar, Yishai, 66
Shapiro, Robert M., 67
Shivhei Ha-Besht: In Praise of the Ba'al Shem Tov, 61, 99
Shlomi, Hannah, 65
Shmeruk, Chone, xiv, 25, 66
Shneur Zalman b. Barukh of Lady (Liady), xxvi, xxxi, xxxiii, 97
Shoah, 32, 37, 43, 399–400. *See also* Holocaust
Sholem Aleichem, 14
    "Tevye the Dairyman," 14
Shore, Marci, 70
Shtif, Nokhem, 25
Shukhov, Vladimir, 158
Shulhan Arukh, 94
Siła-Nowicki, Władysław, 54
Sieniawska, Elżbieta, 189
Sienkiewicz, Henryk, 89, 116
Sierakowski, Wacław Hieronim, 192–193
Silesians, xiv
Singer, Bernard, 108, 295
Singer, Isaac Bashevis, lii
Sirkes, Yoel, 202
Sixtus IV, Pope, 80
Skarbek, Jan, 185, 189
Skibińska, Alina, xlii, 416, 418
Skimborowicz, Hipolit, 268

Index | 497

Jewish commerce, xviii–xix, 82
Jewish craftsmanship, 242–243
Jewish doctors, 378–379
Jewish education, 356–357, 356n1
Jewish newspapers, 25
Jewish poll tax assessment, 260
   Hebrew documents on, 259
   mechanism behind fluctuations of, 256–257
   poll tax assessed for Ordynacja Zamojska and Wołyń, 257–258
   reasons for tax reduction, 257
   rotation schedule, 255
   systematic and sporadic records of, 259–260
   tax potential, 255
Jewish women, xxxiii–xxxiv
Jews in the Polish security apparatus, li
limitations on rights of Jews, xix–xx
memories, xiii
monuments, lv–lvi
Polish-Jewish relations, xi, xl–xlii, 198.
   See also separate entry
postwar Jewish history, lii–liii
postwar Poland, xxxix
primary sources, 60–61
relations between Jews and local Catholic hierarchy, xx, xxii
religious landscape of Polish Jewry, xxii–xxiii
research on, xv–xvi
revival of Jewish life, lii–liv, xlviii–xlix
during Second World War, xxxix
subject of Jewish integration, xxviii
undermining of noble hegemon (*szlachta*), xxix
Polish-Jewish relations, xi, xiii, xl–xlii, 23, 35, 65, 71, 81–82, 198, 211–212, 404, 406, 430, 444, 477–478
   attempts to contextualize, 421–422
   blackmailing of Jews, 415–418
   exploitation of Jews by Poles, 408
   Jews' hostile attitude toward the Poles, 411–413
   Poles' hostile attitude toward the Jews, 409–411
   Poles supportive of Jews, 409
   reactions of the Polish Underground, 413–415
   during Second World War, 403
   under Soviet occupation, 412–413
Polish-Jewish society, formation of, 83–84
Polish-Jewish survivors, xiii
Polish Jews, liv, xlviii–xlix, xv, xxii, xxxviii, 3, 10, 20–24, 27–28, 40, 44, 47–48, 53–55, 64, 71, 80–81, 89, 103, 111, 135, 137–138, 140, 142, 147, 176, 181, 233, 236, 244–246, 263, 265, 324, 326–327, 330, 336–337, 352, 367, 370, 403, 406, 411, 414, 417, 422, 429–430, 432, 434, 443, 458–459
Polish-Lithuanian Commonwealth, xii, xvi–xviii, xxi–xxii, xxxi–xxxiii, 3–4, 9, 63, 87–90, 116, 183, 196, 199–200, 203, 205–207, 209, 229, 250, 281, 284, 286.
   see also Jewish-non-Jewish relations
   Jews in, xvii
Polish Military Intelligence Service, lii
Polish national identity, 431
Polonsky, Antony, 42, 67, 74–76, 130, 430
   The Jews in Poland and Russia, 74
Polska Partia Robotnicza (Polish Workers' Party, PPR), xlix, 468
Polska Zjenoczona Partia Robotnicza (Polish United Workers' Party, PZPR), xlvii
Polski Komitet Wyzwolenia Narodowego (Polish Committee of National Liberation, PKWN), 55, 421
Polskie Państwo Podziemne (Polish Underground State, PPP), 456
Polskie Stronnictwo Ludowe (Polish People's Party, PSL), 456
Polskie Towarzystwo Studiów Żydowskich (Polish Association for Jewish Studies), lv
Porges, Leopold, 277
Porges, Moses, 275–276, 278
Portheim, Max von, 276
Potel, Jean-Yves, 404
Potocki, Michał, 191
Poznań, lv, xvii, xxi, 13, 202, 208, 220, 251
Poznański, Israel, 17
Poznański, Samuel, 15
Prekerowa, Teresa, xliii, 407
Prokop-Janiec, Eugenia, 69
Przewoźnik, Andrzej, 456
Puławski, Adam, 413
public health, 368. *See also* Jewish health in Poland

R

Rada Pomocy Żydom (Council to Aid Jews), *see* Żegota
Radkiewicz, Stanisław, li
Radziwiłł, Anna, 191
Radziwiłł, Leon Michał, 253

Zinberg, Israel, 60
   History of Jewish Literature, 60
Zimmerer, Jürgen, 427
Zionism, 18, 24, 90, 117
Żuchowski, Stefan, 190
Zuckerman, Yitzhak, 444, 460
Związek Partyzantów Żydowskich (Union of Jewish Partisans), xlviii
Związek Religijny Wyznania Mojżeszowego (Religious Union of the Jewish Faith), xlix
Zwolakowa, Maria, 406
Żydowska Ogólnopolska Organizacja Młodzieżowa (All-Poland Jewish Youth Organization), liv,
Żydowski Instytut Historyczny (Jewish Historical Institute), xii, lv, 69, 399
Żydowski Uniwersytet Latający (Jewish Flying University, ŻUL), liii
Żydowskie Towarzystwo Kultury (Jewish Art and Cultural Society, ŻTK), l
Zygmunt, King of Poland, 212, 214, 217, 236
Żyndul, Jolanta, 69

www.ingramcontent.com/pod-product-compliance
Lightning Source LLC
Chambersburg PA
CBHW071353300426
44114CB00016B/2040